MOSCOW WORKERS
AND THE
1917 REVOLUTION

Studies of
the Russian Institute
Columbia University

MOSCOW WORKERS AND THE 1917 REVOLUTION

by Diane Koenker

PRINCETON UNIVERSITY PRESS

The Russian Institute of Columbia University sponsors
the *Studies of the Russian Institute* in the belief that
their publication contributes to scholarly research and
public understanding. In this way the Institute,
while not necessarily endorsing their conclusions,
is pleased to make available the results of
some of the research conducted under its auspices.
A list of the *Studies of the Russian Institute*
appears at the back of the book.

Publication of this book was assisted by a grant
from the Publications Program of the National
Endowment for the Humanities

This book has been composed in Linotron Caledonia

Clothbound editions of Princeton University Press books
are printed on acid-free paper, and binding materials are
chosen for strength and durability

Printed in the United States of America by Princeton
University Press, Princeton, New Jersey

For ROGER

Contents

List of Tables

List of Illustrations

List of Figures

List of Appendices

Acknowledgments

THIS book could not have been completed without the support of many colleagues, friends, and institutions. The Horace Rackham School of Graduate Studies of the University of Michigan, the International Research and Exchanges Board, and the Fulbright-Hays dissertation fellowship program all helped to finance the preparation of my doctoral dissertation, which served as the foundation for the present work. A grant from the joint Soviet studies program of the American Council of Learned Societies and the Social Science Research Council, a Temple University summer faculty fellowship, and released time from the Temple history department provided essential support for subsequent research and writing. A senior fellowship at the Russian Institute of Columbia University offered a convivial and stimulating base for the final stage of my work on this book.

Much of the research was carried out at the libraries of the University of Michigan, Hoover Institution, University of Illinois, Columbia University, and Princeton University, and at the Library of Congress and the New York Public Library. Essential research was also done in Moscow at the Lenin Library, the Social Sciences Library of the Academy of Science, and the State Public Historical Library, and in Leningrad at the Library of the Academy of Science. I am grateful to the staffs of all these libraries for their kind assistance. Some additional research was carried out in the foreigners' reading room of the State Archival Administration in Moscow.

I have been fortunate along the way to receive advice, criticism, and encouragement from a number of generous friends and colleagues. Tsuyoshi Hasegawa, Jeffrey Brooks, David Longley, and David Ransel offered helpful suggestions at various stages of this project. Laura Engelstein carefully read much of the manuscript and supplied valuable comparisons from her own work on Moscow in 1905. Lewis Siegelbaum has read parts of the manuscript and provided stimulating comments.

At the Russian Institute, Mark David Mandel's parallel work on Petrograd workers in 1917 afforded many hours of stimulating discussion. Ziva Galili y Garcia and Alexander Erlich at the Russian Institute were also very kind in offering comments and contributions based on their own knowledge of 1917. I owe a special debt to Leopold Haimson and Ronald Suny for their careful readings of my doctoral dissertation and for their suggestions for expansion and revision. Their comments in a variety of ways encouraged me to make the important conceptual leaps that transformed a doctoral thesis into the present book. Finally, Roderick McGrew and Moshe Lewin read the final manuscript and offered valuable advice.

I am especially grateful to my academic adviser in the Soviet Union, P. V. Volobuev, for his interest in this project and for all the assistance he was able to render me in Moscow. His superb knowledge of the Russian Revolution and his suggestions and comments have enriched the present work. Also in the Soviet Union, A. Ia. Grunt shared with me his expert knowledge of the revolution in Moscow.

From the beginning of my study of Moscow workers at the University of Michigan to the present moment, William G. Rosenberg has provided immeasurable assistance, counsel, advice, sympathy, and support. Both as an adviser and as a friend, he has cheerfully given the many drafts of this work thorough and incisive readings; he has managed to offer criticism and encouragement in just the right proportions and at just the right moments to make the long process of research and writing both stimulating and rewarding. Whatever errors remain in this book are mine alone, but Bill Rosenberg deserves much of the credit for this work's having become a book at all.

This project has been part of my life for many years; from its beginning it has been part of the life of my husband, and lately, that of our daughter. We are hardly unique in this respect; after all, work is work and family is family, and most people manage somehow to combine them both. Authors are more fortunate than most because they can say publicly how much their families' support has meant to them and their work. In my own case, I began the final draft of this book while I was awaiting the birth of my first child, and more than one friend drew the parallel between producing a child and producing a book. The parallel soon vanished; the birth of our daughter Hannah proceeded naturally and easily, but somehow the book did not grow unless I worked at it. Now that I have completed the manuscript, still another difference is clear: although the book is out of my hands and on its own, Hannah remains with me still, and I can enjoy caring for her and watching her grow for many years to come.

One parallel between Hannah and this book remains, and that is the active participation in the progress of both by my husband Roger. He has shared with me his own expertise in economics and statistics and has furnished important assistance for some of the statistical analyses in the book, but more fundamentally, he has taught me to think statistically. He has provided critical readings of the manuscript at crucial points in my work. And he has given me the support and encouragement that I probably did not always deserve but certainly always needed. To him the book is dedicated.

Note on Dates and Transliteration

ALL dates unless otherwise indicated refer to the Old Style (Julian) calendar in use in Russia until February 1918.

The system of transliteration used here is a modified version of the Library of Congress system, with diacritical marks omitted. In the case of certain well-known names such as Kerensky or Trotsky, the more familiar English form has been retained.

Abbreviations

CPO	Committee of Public Organizations
GAMO	Gosudarstvennyi arkhiv moskovskoi oblasti
Izv. MSRD	*Izvestiia Moskovskogo soveta rabochikh deputatov*
S-D	Social-Democratic party
Sots.-Dem.	*Sotsial-Demokrat*
SR	Socialist Revolutionary party
SSD	Soviet of Soldiers' Deputies
Stat. ezhegodnik	*Statisticheskii ezhegodnik goroda Moskvy i moskovskoi gubernii*
SWD	Soviet of Workers' Deputies
TsGAOR	Tsentral'nyi gosudarstvennyi arkhiv oktiabr'skoi revoliutsii
TsSU	Tsentral'noe statisticheskoe upravlenie

MOSCOW WORKERS
AND THE
1917 REVOLUTION

Introduction

THE epic-heroic aspects of the Russian Revolution have long commanded world attention. Lenin's triumphant arrival at the Finland Station and his single-minded struggle to Leninize the Bolshevik party, Kerensky's desperate escape across the Finnish border in October to rally the anti-Bolshevik forces, and the tragic fate of the Imperial family in their last refuge in remote Ekaterinburg have all captured the imagination of writers, scholars, and the reading public the world around.

Whereas the appeal of the great leaders and great events of 1917 continues to generate excellent history,[1] the world remains in relative ignorance of the unheroic side of the Russian Revolution, of the ordinary men and women whose participation was essential to the revolution's outcome and whose lives in turn were profoundly affected by the momentous events of 1917. It is indeed surprising that given the tremendous interest in the Russian Revolution for so many years, historians have paid so little attention to the social underpinnings of the revolution, to the process by which peasants, workers, townspeople, and soldiers and sailors became involved in the revolution. It is especially surprising that the role of the workers, in whose name the 1917 revolution was mounted, has received such scant attention.

Furthermore, the revolutionary capital Petrograd has always been a natural focus of historical interest, but the revolution could hardly have occurred as it did without the participation of inhabitants of the entire Russian Empire. Nonetheless, the revolution outside Petrograd has received, with some recent important exceptions, only passing mention.[2]

This study takes as its subject the doubly neglected area of the workers of Moscow in 1917. In exploring the role of Moscow workers in the revolution and the impact of the revolution on the workers, I intend the study to serve a multiple purpose. First and most important is an ex-

[1] For example, William G. Rosenberg, *Liberals in the Russian Revolution*, and Alexander Rabinowitch, *Prelude to Revolution* and *The Bolsheviks Come to Power*. Such recent biographies as Stephen F. Cohen's *Bukharin and the Bolshevik Revolution* and Robert C. Tucker's *Stalin As Revolutionary* continue in the exemplary tradition of Bertram Wolfe's *Three Who Made a Revolution* and Isaac Deutscher's book on Trotsky, *The Prophet Armed, 1879-1921*.

[2] Ronald G. Suny's *The Baku Commune, 1917-1918* is an important exception to the Petrograd emphasis. Other works on 1917 elsewhere include Andrew Ezergailis's *The 1917 Revolution in Latvia* and Roger Pethybridge's *The Spread of the Russian Revolution*.

amination of the unheroic underside of the revolution in order to learn how such a perspective modifies the conclusions drawn about 1917 by more conventional approaches. Secondly, this study can begin to fill the gap in historical understanding about what happened in 1917 beyond the city barriers of Petrograd, about the revolution in particular places as shaped by particular circumstances. Finally, this study illustrates the importance of the questions and techniques of social history, or "history from below," in such a way that it can serve as a point of comparison for students of social phenomena in other places at other times.

The last point is important because it is really no accident that historians have so long neglected the social framework of political phenomena. Only in the last few decades has the apparent failure of the explanatory power of ideology led historians away from the history of ideas toward the history of society.[3] Scholars ask new questions of old material, not for the sake of something new to do, but because the old questions no longer help people to comprehend their world. The exclusive focus on individuals, on heroes and villains, is not unique to the history of the Russian Revolution. Recent events in Iran, and before that in Vietnam, indicate that students of contemporary society remain intrigued with individual leaders and tend to see the world through their eyes. In the process, the social complexities that actually shape events are ignored.

The study of Russian history has of course begun to change. In recent years, Western historians in particular have begun to investigate the social background of the workers' revolution, particularly the social and economic changes affecting the working class which have contributed to the way in which the events of 1917 unfolded. The work of Reginald Zelnik, Ezra Mendelsohn, Robert E. Johnson, Allan Wildman, and, especially, Leopold Haimson has enriched our understanding of the preconditions and processes of social change before the revolution and has stimulated further investigation into this important period.[4] Soviet historians have generally chosen to work within the strict confines of a Marxist-Leninist interpretation of history, which interpretation argues for the inevitability of great events like 1917. Nevertheless, within these limits, there have been some recent valuable contributions to the social history of twentieth-

---

[3] See E. J. Hobsbawn, "From Social History to the History of Society," pp. 20-45.

[4] Reginald E. Zelnik, *Labor and Society in Tsarist Russia* and "Russian Bebels"; Ezra Mendelsohn, *Class Struggle in the Pale*; Robert E. Johnson, *Peasant and Proletarian*; Allan K. Wildman, *The Making of a Workers' Revolution*; Leopold H. Haimson, "The Problem of Social Stability in Urban Russia, 1905-1917." Further research along these lines is currently being undertaken by Victoria E. Bonnell, "Radical Politics and Organized Labor in Pre-Revolutionary Moscow, 1905-1914" and "The Politics of Labor in Pre-Revolutionary Russia"; Rose Glickman, "The Russian Factory Woman, 1880-1914" and Laura Engelstein, "Moscow in the 1905 Revolution."

century Russia, particularly from L. M. Ivanov, Iu. I. Kir'ianov, and V. Iu. Krupianskaia.[5]

Until quite recently, however, social historians have sidestepped the 1917 revolution itself. Attempts to study the revolution as it affected workers are frequently based on the perceptions of leaders about what was happening to workers rather than on the workers' own attitudes and perceptions.[6] Part of the problem has been the nature of the sources; published documents generated by those at the top have been more easily accessible than records from participating workers and peasants. But broad new work by Marc Ferro and John Keep, and more specific studies by Alexander Rabinowitch, Ronald Suny, Allan Wildman, and others have indicated that the history of 1917 can indeed be fruitfully explored from a point beneath the very top stratum of participants, that is, from the perspective of participants other than political and intellectual leaders.[7]

Soviet historians do not suffer from the same inaccessibility of sources as do Western scholars, and literally hundreds of volumes on the Great October Socialist Revolution have been published in the Soviet Union; a good many of these have concentrated on the working class. But with few exceptions, Soviet histories of the revolution, whatever the specific topic, tend to deal with the two themes of mass allegiance to the Bolsheviks and the unswerving path to Great October. Within these strictures, the works of P. V. Volobuev, G. A. Trukan, A. Ia. Grunt, V. Ia. Selitskii, A. M. Lisetskii, Z. V. Stepanov, and G. L. Sobolev have enriched our own understanding of the complex processes of 1917.[8] In the future, one hopes Soviet scholars will follow these examples and continue to mine the rich archival material available to them on workers and political processes in 1917.[9]

[5] L. M. Ivanov, "O soslovno-klassovoi strukture gorodov kapitalisticheskoi Rossii" and "Preemstvennost' fabrichno-zavodskogo truda i formirovanie proletariata v Rossii"; Iu. I. Kir'ianov, "Ob oblike rabochego klassa Rossii," *Rabochie Iuga Rossii*, and *Zhiznennyi uroven' rabochikh Rossii*, Moscow, 1979; V. Iu. Krupianskaia, "Evoliutsiia semeino-bytovogo uklada rabochikh."

[6] This is particularly true of Paul Avrich, "Russian Factory Committees in 1917"; Pethybridge, *Spread of the Russian Revolution*; and Frederick I. Kaplan, *Bolshevik Ideology and the Ethics of Soviet Labor*.

[7] Marc Ferro, *La Révolution de 1917*, vols. 1 and 2; John H. L. Keep, *The Russian Revolution*; Rabinowitch, *Bolsheviks Come to Power*; Suny, *Baku Commune*; Norman Saul, *Sailors in Revolt*; Allan K. Wildman, *The End of the Russian Imperial Army*, Princeton, 1980; Graeme J. Gill, *Peasants and Government in the Russian Revolution*, London, 1979.

[8] P. V. Volobuev, *Proletariat i burzhuaziia v Rossii v 1917 g.*; G. A. Trukan, *Oktiabr' v tsentral'noi Rossii*; A. Ia. Grunt, *Moskva 1917-i*; V. Ia. Selitskii, *Massy v bor'be za rabochii kontrol'*, A. M. Lisetskii, *Bol'sheviki vo glave massovykh stachek*; Z. V. Stepanov, *Rabochie Petrograda v period podgotovki i provedeniia oktiabr'skogo vooruzhennogo vosstaniia*; G. L. Sobolev, *Revoliutsionnoe soznanie rabochikh i soldat Petrograda v 1917 g.*

[9] Such work has lately met with disfavor. See I. I. Mints, "Velikii oktiabr'—povorotnyi

On balance, however, the general view of the Russian Revolution remains largely untouched by the new trends in historical scholarship. The
standard classroom texts are still William H. Chamberlin's two-volume
history published in 1935 and Leon Trotsky's polemical but highly read-
able *History of the Russian Revolution*. With respect to the workers' role
in the revolution, Harrison E. Salisbury's recent popular study of 1917
offers the familiar view of the working classes as "dark masses." Accord-
ingly, the crucial period between March and October, when the "dark
masses" came to the fore, receives short shrift from Mr. Salisbury; this
eight-month period is also omitted from the standard abridged edition of
Trotsky's history. Serious scholars have long realized that these so-called
dark masses appear so only because the bright light of the intellectuals
who gazed down at them obscured the masses' own innate illumination,
but the myth persists.[10] The consequence of this view is an image among
Western historians of these masses as irrational, easily swayed, and prey
to the machinations of political leaders. They are acted upon, they do not
act.[11] In most Soviet literature, although the workers are not so dark, they
are still treated as an undifferentiated mass; this mass is idealized as
marching triumphantly toward an ever-growing proletarian consciousness. Neither view does justice to the diversities, the antagonisms, and
the range of experience among workers in Russia in 1917.

One reason for the persistence of this dark-masses view has been the
method used to study the revolution. Looking from above, historians rely
on memoir literature, the product primarily of intellectuals. Workers'
memoirs and other documents concerned with their role in 1917 have
been published in abundance in the Soviet Union first in the 1920s and
again after 1956, but by and large this material has been used impres-
sionistically rather than systematically.[12] It is in this area, the uses to
which these materials are put, that the methods employed by social his-

punkt v istorii chelovechestva," p. 10; and the more pointed discussion in "Postanovlenie
biuro otdeleniia istorii AN SSSR," *Voprosy istorii*, 1972, no. 8, pp. 141-145. For Western
commentaries on this discussion, see D. A. Longley, "Some Historiographical Problems of
Bolshevik Party History," and John H. L. Keep, " 'The Great October Socialist Revolution.' " For a longer perspective on Soviet historiographical conflicts, see Nancy W. Heer,
Politics and History in the Soviet Union.

[10] William Henry Chamberlin, *The Russian Revolution*; Leon Trotsky, *History of the
Russian Revolution*, trans. by Max Eastman, abridged version edited by F. W. Dupee,
Garden City, 1959; Harrison E. Salisbury, *Black Night, White Snow.* Salisbury's view
derives from that of the contemporary intellectuals whose memoirs he uses for his book.
Cf. John Reed, *Ten Days That Shook the World*, for an idealistic view of the dark masses.

[11] This is to some extent true of John Keep's otherwise admirable study of the social
history of 1917.

[12] Keep and Ferro are the two most prominent examples. Much Soviet work on the
subject also falls into this category.

torians, examining history from below, can help to focus the scholar's view.

In the present study, I have chosen to look at the working class of Moscow in order to gather all the available evidence on the revolutionary experience of one important group of revolutionary participants in one important locality. I have combed the contemporary newspapers and journals, the workers' own memoirs, published documents, and statistical materials in order to accumulate knowledge about the everyday political, social, and economic activities of workers in 1917. In the course of this book, I shall reassemble this mass of detail in a way designed to demonstrate that what happened in Moscow in 1917 between March and October was far more complex, significant, and worthy of understanding than is generally recognized.

The city of Moscow was a natural choice for this study for a number of reasons. It was the economic center of Russia's largest industrial region; its economy was diversified, and its workers represented a wide range of occupations and social origins. Moscow was not a "typical" Russian industrial city, for Russia was too recently industrialized to have developed uniform industrial towns, but the city possessed many features representative of the Russian urban economy: important textile and metal industries, a large artisan class, and a politically active entrepreneurial class.[13] Another attraction of Moscow was the wealth of both pre- and postrevolutionary materials on the city, its economy, and its working class.

I have chosen to limit the scope of the study to the months from March to October 1917, that is, the eight months between the fall of the tsarist regime and the assumption of power by the Soviets. These eight months were rich in political activity and represent a crucial period in the revolutionary experience of the working class. But in choosing October 25 as the end point of this study, I do not mean to imply that the onset of Soviet power somehow resolved all the problems created during the preceding eight months. It will become clear that 1917 was really only the beginning of the social revolution. Nonetheless, with the political change of October came a reduction in the information reported in local newspapers, a major source for this study, and so October 25 provides both a logical and a convenient stopping point. I shall, however, look beyond the October revolution in a final chapter in order to suggest some implications of the trends established prior to October and to indicate possibilities for further research.

Before proceeding further, it is important here to say a few words about the use of the term *working class*. The "workers" under consideration

---

[13] On Moscow's industrial class, see V. Ia. Laverychev, *Po tu storonu barrikad*; P. A. Buryshkin, *Moskva kupecheskaia*; Alfred J. Rieber, "The Moscow Entrepreneurial Group."

will be defined more fully in Chapter One, but the word "class" is more problematic. The term is generally defined in an economic context. The Granat encyclopedia in 1913, for example, described class as "that group, the members of which are united, not by juridical, but by economic characteristics."[14] In this sense, the working class comprises those individuals who shared the common characteristic of working for wages, whether their passports labeled them "peasants," "artisans," or "townspeople" (*meshchane*). The Marxist definition, which was of particular importance in Russia, goes further. Class is determined first of all, but only in part, by economic factors, by a person's relationship to the means of production. Workers, as wage earners, do not own these means and have only their labor power to sell. But for Marx, class becomes important solely in struggle, only as workers engage in a common battle with another class, a battle based on common class interest.[15] Marx in fact suggests two stages in the rise of a working class. Economic conditions create workers, a mass with a common plight and common interests. This is the working class in itself, a class as opposed to the class of capitalists. This working class, however, is not a class for itself, it cannot by its economic position alone defend its class interests. Only as workers struggle against capital as an institution do they become conscious of their identity and of the inevitability of political conflict with the owners of the means of production. At this point workers reach the "politically significant stage" of their development.[16] The development of this class consciousness, the emergence of the working class for itself, becomes an integral part of the historical process. As E. P. Thompson has so influentially argued, class is an evolutionary concept. It is not a category or structure, but "something which in fact happens (and can be shown to have happened) in human relationships."[17]

This evolutionary definition of class is well justified by the experience of Moscow workers in 1917. But this study must begin with the first stage of the rise of the working class, and as a starting point, I shall be using the term *working class* primarily in a descriptive sense to refer to all individuals labeled as workers. A common struggle emerged in 1917, but I wish to stress first of all the diversity within the class. In this emphasis, I am following current usage among social historians who reserve the term *labor history* for the study of the labor movement, of organized

[14] *Entsiklopedicheskii slovar'*, 7th ed., vol. 24, pp. 290-291.

[15] Karl Marx and Friedrich Engels, *The German Ideology*, ed. C. J. Arthur, New York, 1947, p. 82.

[16] Karl Marx, *The Poverty of Philosophy*, New York, 1963, p. 173. See also Ralf Dahrendorf's reconstruction of the unfinished chapter on class in volume 3 of Marx's *Capital* in Dahrendorf's *Class and Class Conflict in Industrial Society*, especially p. 14.

[17] E. P. Thompson, *The Making of the English Working Class*, p. 9.

labor, and who employ the term *working-class history* to denote the study of the whole experience of workers. Implicit in this distinction is the assumption that all aspects of the experience of those who work, including everyday life as well as organized activity, are related to one another and can help to explain particular political or economic phenomena. This assumption lies at the heart of the present study.

Because of the peculiarities of Russian social and economic development, it would be a mistake, however, to ignore completely the notion of class as an analytical concept even from the very beginning. For English workers in the throes of the Industrial Revolution, to return to Thompson, class "happened"; it was not a category imposed from outside by theoreticians, politicians, or historians. Consciousness of class identity in fact was first acquired by the English middle class to distinguish itself from the aristocracy and to give a sense of coherence to what previously had been known as the "middling classes," "trading classes," or "manufacturing classes."[18] Consciousness of class in Russia did not evolve in the same way. Indeed, there were scarcely candidates enough for an English type of middle class. But class had already become an accepted component of political and social analysis in the Western world before Russia began its drive toward economic development. Therefore, class in Russia could not just happen; Russian society was too conscious of the Western European and English models for this to occur.[19]

Thus almost before there were substantial numbers of workers to form a working class, Russian society anticipated the eventual existence of this class. Marx's influential *Das Kapital* had appeared in Russia well before the industrial boom of the 1890s, and his analysis was widely accepted.[20] For these reasons, therefore, the development of the consciousness of class in Russia proceeded according to the same kind of "laws of combined development" which Trotsky and others ascribe to the revolutionary process. At the same time as there emerged a working class defined simply by its relationship to work, these workers were conscious a priori of being a class with common interests in opposition to other classes. Marx took his class model largely from English experience, but in Russia the model itself helped to shape workers' experience.

A brief example can illustrate the peculiarity of the telescoped Russian

[18] See Asa Briggs, "The Language of 'Class' in Early Nineteenth-Century England"; see also T. H. Marshall, *Citizenship and Social Class*, and G.D.H. Cole, *Studies in Class Structure*.

[19] The article "Class" in the authoritative Brokgauz-Efron encyclopedia of 1895, for instance, discusses the example of conflicts of interest in constitutional systems between industrial and landowning "classes" but then adds that Russia did not yet conform to this system; estates (*sosloviia*) were still more important than classes (vol. 15, pp. 323-324).

[20] See Arthur P. Mendel, *Dilemmas of Progress in Tsarist Russia*; Wildman, *Making of a Workers' Revolution*; and Richard Pipes, *Struve: Liberal on the Left*, Cambridge, 1970.

case. The general pattern of labor organization in the West began with elite artisan groups uniting to protect their small group interests; only gradually did individual trades begin to perceive that their interests corresponded to other trades in the same situation and that they had interests in common as a class. In Moscow, the first group of workers to organize was the printers, a typically elite artisan occupation. True to Western form, the goals of the first printers' organization in 1903 and of its successors centered on protecting and promoting the interests of the particular group. But at the same time, in obeisance to the widely accepted class theory of society, these organized printers declared that their union was not a closed craft union, but an industrial union embracing all workers in the printing industry.[21]

Consciousness of class among Russian workers was therefore part of the package of ideas and values that workers acquired upon their entry into the industrial world. On the other hand, I have indicated above and shall emphasize throughout this study the important diversities within this working class. This diversity helped to produce varying interpretations of class by workers and their allies and varying patterns of class consciousness. For example, the position of the peasantry in one's class view of the world was by no means clearly spelled out by Marx and depended upon the particular experiences of workers. Class consciousness in particular was shaped by several factors. It was encouraged by prevailing social theory, especially by Marxism. But class consciousness was also shaped by the concrete experience of Russian working-class life. Let me stress here one element of this experience, that of the spatial relationships among classes. Workers, such as artisans or printers, who had occasion to enter into regular contact with their employers or with middle-class intellectuals developed a sense of class separateness and identity different from that of workers in large plants, such as metalworkers or textile workers, whose only exposure to the middle class was vicarious and theoretical. Therefore, although the general notion of class permeated the workers' experience before and during 1917, I shall refrain from using the term *class* analytically as a single construct in order to emphasize the diversity within the working class of Moscow. Yet during 1917 in Moscow, class awareness was also growing, and an important theme in the pages to follow will be the process by which the diverse Moscow working class developed a sense of itself as one single class, a sense that became translated by October into widespread support for the program of the Bolshevik party.

In conclusion, I would like to add a few words about the organization

[21] V. V. Sher, *Istoriia professional'nogo dvizheniia rabochikh pechatnogo dela v Moskve*, p. 190.

of this book. In order to stress the multiform character of the working-class experience in 1917, I have departed from a traditional narrative structure. Chapters One and Two explore the economic and social background of Moscow workers in order to establish and explain working-class diversity and to examine the factors that influenced workers' activities in 1917. Chapter Three offers a brief narrative overview of the 1917 revolution in Moscow, which overview will provide the chronological framework for the discussion to follow. Chapters Four through Eight then probe more deeply into various interrelated aspects of workers' involvement in the revolution: organizational experience, partisan political behavior, political attitudes as expressed in resolutions and cash contributions, and labor-management conflict as demonstrated in strike activity. Chapter Nine returns to the narrative of 1917 with an examination of the October revolution and its aftermath in Moscow.

ONE. *Moscow 1917*

THE IMAGE OF THE CITY

AN aerial photo of Moscow taken toward the start of the twentieth century shows a sea of low red-brick and yellow-stucco buildings, dotted by the onion-shaped domes of hundreds of churches. The ancient fortress of the Kremlin dominates the city center, the citadel's red-brick walls surrounding the tall Ivan bell tower and cathedrals. Southwesterly along the river arise the massive golden dome of the Cathedral of the Resurrection, and beyond, the red bell tower of Novo-Devich'e monastery. The low profile of the city is broken by red factory smokestacks that stand side by side with the gold and green and blue church cupolas; a few new five- and six-story buildings tower over the squares of the central city.[1] In general, by the turn of the century Moscow was spreading outward, not upward, sprawling across the northern bend of the Moscow River and reaching, by 1917, far along the river's tributaries, over drained marshlands, into the fields that once belonged to the wealthy monasteries and the nobility.

The city of Moscow in 1917 was defined, approximately, as the area within the limits of the Okruzhnaia, or circular railroad, which ringed the city, shuttling freight from one rail depot to another.[2] Such an economic definition was quite fitting for the city that once had symbolized Russia's spiritual life but which was now the secular capital of native Russian industry and trade.

The city had grown in concentric circles (see map); the original town was the Kremlin on the north bank of the Moscow River. Later, outside the Kremlin's gates and along the great Red Square, a settlement of tradesmen and artisans developed. Ultimately, this quarter was surrounded by its own wall and became known as the Kitai-gorod, after the Tatar word for fortress. The walls were important to the city's survival, for these were the days of perpetual Tatar raids into the territory of the Grand Princes of Muscovy. On the eastern and southern frontiers of the city was a line of fortress-monasteries to provide further protection from the Tatar threat.

At the end of the sixteenth century, the growing city was bounded by

---

[1] A panoramic photograph in color of Moscow ca. 1890 can be seen in *Istoriia Moskvy*, vol. 5, 1955, opposite p. 12. A black-and-white panorama of Zamoskvorech'e, across the river to the south, is printed in *Oktiabr' v Zamoskvorech'e*, opposite p. 6.

[2] This railroad was also the boundary set by the Provisional Government for elections to the city duma in June (*Trud*, 20 June 1917).

a new wall, whitewashed; the new area became known, appropriately, as the White City. Later, the Tatar danger long past, the wall was replaced by a ring of boulevards lined with trees and parks. Beyond this ring, during the reign of the first Romanov tsar, an earthen wall was constructed which completely circled the city on both banks of the river. In time, the growing population expanded beyond this barrier, and the rampart became a new boulevard garden ring, the Sadovoe kol'tso. By the nineteenth century, the Sadovoe had become the unofficial boundary of the censused (*tsenzovaia*) or privileged Moscow.

In subsequent decades, the city continued to grow, absorbing nearby villages. Factories were built in the shadows of the old fortress-monasteries. By 1900, Moscow extended as far as, and in places farther than,

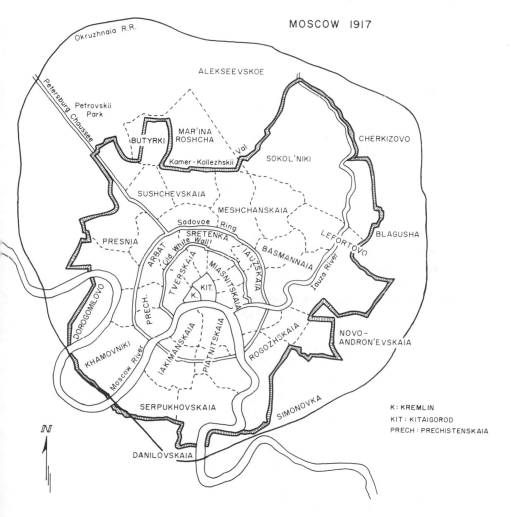

the Kamer-Kollezhskii val, another earthern rampart built earlier as a customs barrier.[3] And by 1917, the city encompassed not only the area inside the old boundary but also the suburbs of Blagusha and Simonovka to the east, Cherkizovo and Bogorodsk to the northeast, Alekseevskoe, Mar'ina roshcha, and Butyrki to the north.[4]

Most, but not all, of the workers of Moscow lived within official city limits, but the problem of defining a "Moscow worker" remains somewhat complicated. Official citizenship was to some extent voluntary. An inhabitant of a marginal suburb could choose whether or not to consider himself a city resident; city election officials in 1917 stipulated that those in the outskirts who wished to vote in municipal elections could attach themselves to an adjacent urban precinct.[5] Participation in the Moscow city workers' soviet in 1917 was likewise voluntary; the municipal metal-rolling plant, located about seven miles from the city, sent its deputies to the Moscow Soviet, but the workers of Tushino, only a mile farther away, formed their own soviet. For the purposes of this study, it is both reflective of the period and convenient to take as a formal definition the one adopted by the city Soviet in 1917: Moscow workers were those who sent deputies to the Moscow Soviet.

Boundary vagaries aside, there was an important distinction between the city of Moscow, which is the subject of this study, and other territorial entities that also went by the name "Moscow." The city was located in the center of Moscow province (*guberniia*), which included, in addition to the capital, several large manufacturing towns and numerous small settlements, both agricultural and industrial. This province was divided into thirteen districts, or *uezdy*. Moscow district (*uezd*) surrounded the city of the same name; as the city expanded, the size of the uezd gradually diminished. Besides these general administrative divisions, the name Moscow was also occasionally given to the entire Central Industrial Region, an area of manufacturing activity defined by the Factory Inspectorate to include the provinces of Moscow, Iaroslav, Kaluga, Kostroma, Nizhnyi-Novgorod, Riazan, Tula, Tver, and Vladimir. The Bolshevik party included these provinces and three more in an organizational district called Moskovskaia Oblast, the Moscow Region, which became the power base for the radical faction led by Nikolai Bukharin in 1917. In cultural life, Moscow had come to stand for a set of relationships implying ethnic Russianness and native economic endeavor, with Slavophile overtones.[6]

---

[3] This brief sketch of the growth of Moscow is taken primarily from Karl Baedeker, *Russia, A Handbook for Travellers*; and *Moscou et ses environs*.

[4] Today there is a new ring which defines the city—the circular highway, beyond which a Muscovite may not reside and still maintain his right to live in the capital.

[5] *Vpered*, 27 May 1917.

[6] Factory Inspectorate divisions may be found in E. E. Kruze, *Polozhenie rabochego*

Thus, the name Moscow, when it appears in the sources and literature, can designate any one of these several administrative, political, or cultural units. In the present study, then, Moscow signifies only the city proper.

For administrative purposes, the city was divided into sixteen police districts (*chasti*), which corresponded roughly to the earlier historical divisions of the city (see map). Thus the old Kitai-gorod was now simply Gorodskaia; the ancient settlement of cotton weavers retained its name, Khamovniki, although it had lately become the home of fashionable suburban estates such as that of Leo Tolstoy. Each of these districts was further subdivided into two, three, or four police precincts (*uchastki*), to make fifty-one in all in 1917. The average population of a precinct was about forty thousand inhabitants; the size of inner-city precincts (within the Sadovoe on the north side of the river) was much smaller than that of the fast-growing outlying ones.[7] The precincts were the basis for the municipal statistical data collections that provide much of the information about patterns of urban life in Moscow. They were also the electoral units in the June 1917 election and will be used to examine voting patterns of workers in Chapter Five.

In 1917, eleven larger units—*raions*—emerged to function side by side with the administrative precincts. These raions, which had been used by socialist party organizations before 1917, were sanctioned by the Moscow Soviet to serve as local centers of working-class activity; they corresponded, generally, to existing industrial and working-class neighborhoods. The limits of these raions were by no means so strictly defined as those of the police precincts. Workers who were situated in an inactive district might send deputies to a local soviet in a neighboring raion; and the political parties' raion organizations did not always embrace the same workers that were constituents of that raion's soviet. There were eight of these raions in March 1917; during the course of the year some of them consolidated and others, which emerged first as sub-raions, separated completely. Thus, there were eleven active raion centers by October: ten corresponded to geographical divisions and the eleventh united all of the workers employed on the railroads anywhere in Moscow. As the tempo of events quickened in 1917, these raions competed with central organs as focuses of working-class activity, and it is therefore important to keep in mind the distinctive characteristics of these various neighborhoods.

The city's center was its economic hub and was also the center of

---

klassa Rossii v 1900-1914 gg., p. 48; L. S. Gaponenko, *Rabochii klass Rossii v 1917 g.*, p. 109n, uses the broader party definition; see also Cohen, *Bukharin and the Bolshevik Revolution.* The cultural definition of Moscow has most recently been employed by Rieber, "Moscow Entrepreneurial Group," no. 1, p. 2.

[7] *Statisticheskii ezhegodnik goroda Moskvy i moskovskoi gubernii*, p. 12. (Hereafter *Stat. ezhegodnik.*)

traditional Moscow. Here were located the Moscow Exchange (the central institution of the native Russian textile industry) and the wholesale and retail centers represented by the Upper and Lower Trading Rows. Also in this Gorodskoi precinct were numerous religious institutions. Four monasteries as well as many cathedrals and chapels were located inside the old Kitai-gorod walls.[8]

In among the banks, wholesale houses, and churches lived the numerous small tradesmen and artisans who constituted the bulk of the population of the center. The composition of this district in 1917 had probably changed little from that reported in the 1897 all-Russian census, the only year for which occupational data by precinct is available. One-third of the precinct's residents were artisans employed chiefly in the clothing trades, and one-fourth each were in trade and in service.[9] There were only a few factories here, accounting for fewer than eight hundred workers.[10] The area was a male stronghold; few children were born, and with the exception of apprentices, few lived in the old city center.[11]

Close beyond the walls of the Kitai-gorod, in what used to be called the White City, modern Moscow was emerging. Here in the Tverskaia and Miasnitskaia districts were the city's cultural centers: the university, conservatory, library, and theaters. Well-to-do Muscovites shopped along fashionable lanes and partied in the stylish new Metropol' and Natsional hotels. In general, this first ring of the city housed the comfortable houses and flats of Moscow's ruling classes, of government officials, merchants, and intellectuals; but there were also residential pockets with quite distinct personalities. For example, university and conservatory professors were clustered on the Nikitskaia street, near their institutions.[12] At the other extreme, the third Miasnitskii precinct, located at the far eastern edge of this ring, was probably the most down-and-out quarter of Moscow. The Khitrovo market in this precinct was the center of the city's demimonde, "the most horrible ulcer of the whole city."[13] It was surrounded by cheap lodging houses, taverns, alehouses, and brothels. The death rate in this one precinct was twice the city average; the illegitimacy rate

[8] Baedeker; G. G. Antipin, *Zariad'e*; P. A. Buryshkin, *Moskva kupecheskaia.*

[9] *Pervaia vseobshchaia perepis' naseleniia Rossiiskoi Imperii, 1897 g.*, vol. 24, tetrad' 2, table 21.

[10] *Spisok fabrik i zavodov goroda Moskvy i moskovskoi gubernii.* (Hereafter *Spisok fabrik.*)

[11] *Stat. ezhegodnik*, p. 12; *Ezhemesiachnyi statisticheskii biulleten' g. Moskvy*, 1915, no. 7. The birthrate is calculated for 1912 based on the census of that year reported in *Trudy statisticheskogo otdela moskovskoi gorodskoi upravy*, vyp. 1, *Glavneishiia predvaritel'nyiia dannyia perepisi goroda Moskvy 6 marta 1912 g.* (Hereafter *Trudy stat. otdela MGU.*)

[12] *Istoriia Moskvy*, vol. 5, p. 20.

[13] *Sovremennoe khoziaistvo goroda Moskvy*, p. 175 (from a report of an 1898 investigating commission).

was also twice that of the rest of the city.[14] Thousands of job seekers passed through the market every year, many falling prey to its "life of drunkenness, debauchery, and crime."[15] Despite an ambitious municipal program to build scattered dormitories for this transient population (especially after a cholera epidemic swept through the district in 1910),[16] the quarter remained a problem even in 1917; the Moscow Soviet sanctioned a raid into the Khitrovo market in July, which raid yielded three hundred military deserters and a number of forged Soviet mandates.[17]

In the belt between the boulevards and the Sadovoe were located Moscow's finest residential neighborhoods. Along tree-lined streets in Prechistenskaia and the Arbat lived many of the city's distinguished citizens: nobility, officials, industrialists. These were the only two districts in the city in which women far outnumbered the men in the population, a fact explained by the large numbers of domestic servants employed in the great mansions in the quarter.[18] What industry there was in this area of gardens, parks, and ponds, apart from the printshops and binderies that catered to the area's affluent population, was clustered in the far eastern section on the banks of the Iauza River.

The population of these central precincts grew relatively slowly in the years before and during the war. While the population of the city as a whole grew by 24 percent between 1912 and 1917, the center—between the Sadovoe and the river—grew by only 18 percent.[19] There were so few workers here that in 1917 the entire area comprised only one soviet raion, known as Gorodskoi. The leading industry in this raion was printing. Over half (55 percent) of all printers in the city were employed here in shops averaging sixty workers each. Although residential data is less accessible than industrial location, it is probable that many printers lived in or very near this privileged central core as well.[20]

[14] In 1913 and 1914 almost one-half of the births in the third Miasnitskii precinct were illegitimate. The death rate is calculated for 1916 from *Ezhemesiachnyi statisticheskii biulleten'*, 1916, nos. 1-12; the illegitimacy rate, in ibid., 1914, no. 11, table 1. Although the Imperial Foundling Hospital was located in this precinct, its births were recorded separately, so the precinct's high illegitimacy rate is not explained by the illegitimate infants registered at the hospital.

[15] *Sovremennoe khoziaistvo g. Moskvy*, p. 175.

[16] Ibid., pp. 175-196.

[17] *Izvestiia Moskovskogo soveta rabochikh deputatov*, 4 August 1917. Hereafter *Izv. MSRD*.

[18] One-third of all women in the Prechistenka and Arbat districts were domestic servants, compared to 22 percent for the city as a whole (*Pervaia vseobshchaia perepis'*, table 21).

[19] *Stat. ezhegodnik*, pp. 12, 14.

[20] Data on industrial composition of these districts is derived from the author's file of Moscow factories, which is described in Appendix A. On residential location of workers, see the discussion in Chapter Two.

1. Semirural outskirts of Moscow in Rogozhskii. Secret meetings would frequently be held in suburban areas such as these.

The major industrial districts of Moscow were located south and east of the city center. Although fashionable homes had of late been built in the quarter immediately across the river from the Kremlin, they stood side by side with massive red-brick factories, all within sight of the Kremlin. Here in Zamoskvorech'e—the name means "across the Moscow River"—were some of the city's largest defense plants, including the stalwart revolutionary bastions of Bromlei, Mikhelson, and the Gustav List plants. Zamoskvorech'e, the first suburban area to be settled, was more densely populated than other outlying sections, especially in its two inner districts of Piatnitskaia and Iakimanskaia. In the precincts of both these districts closest to the river (see map), the density of population was twice that of Zamoskvorech'e as a whole.[21] Once known as the Tatar quarter of Moscow, this area was now the neighborhood of the Tretiakov art gallery and the industrialists' mansions as well as factories and workers' barracks. Beyond the southern rim of the Sadovoe, industrial enterprises encroached on the fields once belonging to the nearby monasteries. A string of factories lined the Shabalovka, which led past the Donskoi monastery, and an entire industrial suburb grew up around the Danilovskii monastery farther to the east. By 1917, the city limits were pushed even past Danilovka, along the road to the town of Serpukhov. Workers in the old

[21] The density in the first Iakimanskii and first Piatnitskii precincts was nine and a half square *sazhen'* per person, as opposed to nineteen for the entire Zamoskvorech'e (*Trudy stat. otdela MGU*). One sazhen' equals seven feet.

villages of Nizhnye kotly and Khavskaia sloboda, while legally still in Moscow uezd, participated with the Danilovka workers in their own sub-raion soviet.

To the east of the center were the districts of Basmannaia, Lefortovo, and Rogozhskaia. Lefortovo was once the site of the German suburb of Moscow, and the religious center of the Old Believers was (and is) in Rogozhskaia, but in 1917 the eastern quarter was almost purely working class. Many factories had sprung up along the Iauza River, which curved away to the northeast. Preobrazhenskoe, where young Peter I was said to have built the first Russian fleet, was now an area of factories, taverns, and low wooden buildings that housed workers, their families, and an occasional cow or pig. This was an area dominated by small textile factories. Farther to the east was the new industrial suburb of Blagusha; here newly evacuated factories from Poland and the Baltic provinces were built alongside local plants. The eastern quarter was a sprawling region expanding east to Blagusha, southeast to the village of Khokhlovo in the Novo-Andronevskaia area, and south to the Simonovskaia suburb, just across the river from Danilovka. Here, along the river, the government had financed several gigantic war plants. In this southern half of the Rogozhskaia raion, in sharp contrast to Lefortovo, metal and machine-building plants shaped the character of the neighborhood.

Most of the rail traffic to Moscow terminated in this eastern quarter, and it was the site of the large Kursk and Kazan railway workshops, employing hundreds of repair workers. Beyond the city limits, in Perovo, was another large railway yard whose workers frequently participated in the life of the city. Closer to the Sadovoe, near Taganskaia square, were clustered small enterprises in which artisans engaged in a variety of industrial activity. The residents of these quarters were almost exclusively workers; there were so many that the region was divided into four, sometimes five, soviet raions. Its class composition can further be attested to by the advice of the Baedeker guidebook for 1914: "A visit to the E. quarter of the city offers little interest."[22]

Before 1917, much of the city's recent growth had been spurred by the annexation of several artisans' settlements north of the city which became the communities of Butyrki, Mar'ina roshcha, Alekseevskoe, Sokol'niki, and Petrovskii park. These areas were poorly built up, with few services. In 1917, Butyrki contained numerous alehouses but not one secondary school.[23] The adjacent Mar'ina roshcha, the Maria Wood, remained the center of gold and silver work in Moscow. Formerly, it had been a favorite recreation spot for Muscovites, but by 1917 it had been built over with the gridlike pattern of streets which was common to many of the city's

[22] Baedeker, p. 312.   [23] *V oktiabr'skie dni*, p. 4.

newer industrial districts. The northern districts closer to the Sadovoe—four Meshchanskii precincts and three in Sushchevskii—were also settled by working people; both districts, like the eastern quarter, had large numbers of railway workers and because of the evacuation of the western provinces, an increasing number of non-Russian workers—Letts, Poles, and Lithuanians—as well. About 12 percent of the population in the northernmost precincts—Butyrki, Sushchevskii, Mar'ina roshcha, Bogorodskoe, Alekseevskoe—were non-Russian refugees.[24] Three raion soviets were active here: Butyrki, Sushchevsko-Mar'inskii, and the Sokol'niki raion encompassing the workers around Sokol'niki park and in the fourth Meshchanskii precinct.

The least densely populated quarter of Moscow was the western edge, the districts of Khamovniki and Presnia. Khamovniki, which extended southwestward from Prechistenskii, was known as the medical suburb because of its large number of university and philanthropically endowed hospitals and clinics. Across the Moscow River to the west, Khamovniki included the Briansk railroad station and yards and the village of Dorogomilovo, a haphazardly built-up area inhabited by artisans, railway workers, carters, and other nonindustrial workers. The three precincts of the Presnia district were closer in character to those of the northern periphery, featuring low wooden houses whose residents would often keep gardens and livestock (42 percent of the outermost precinct was, in fact, classified as agricultural),[25] small workshops, and scattered large factories. Very few well-to-do homes, except those of the factory owners themselves, were located here; in 1905, the workers of isolated "Red Presnia" had joined the Moscow rising, and the district was the last barricaded enclave to fall to tsarist troops in December of that year.

The peripheral districts all had in common a slight majority of men in the population and a relatively high birth rate (32 to 35 births per thousand residents, compared to the progressively lower rates—24, 19, and 16—as one moved deeper into the inner city). Families on the outskirts tended to be larger, more extended: the farther away from the center, the greater was the share in the population of children and old people.[26] But despite the fact that buildings were scattered, residents within these dwellings were crowded—the average density was about nine persons per apartment in 1912.[27] City services were minimal; the tram system extended to only a few of the outlying districts and sanitation was poor. Partly for this last reason, but also because of the high birth rate here (infants had the highest

[24] *Ezhemesiachnyi statisticheskii biulleten'*, 1916, no. 1, Appendix 2.
[25] *Trudy stat. otdela MGU*, p. 12.
[26] *Stat. ezhegodnik*, p. 12.
[27] *Trudy stat. otdela MGU*, p. 31.

rate of mortality in all areas of the city), the mortality rate in these districts generally was high.[28]

The image of early twentieth-century Moscow was one of relative social heterogeneity. True, workers tended to be clustered on the city outskirts, but there was no sizable enclave of industrial workers in Moscow similar to the Vyborg district of Petrograd, which provided so many of the radical cadres in 1917. Within neighborhoods, there was a considerable mixture of social classes: printers and artisans rubbed elbows with the center-city bourgeoisie, and even in the most purely working-class eastern districts, industrial workers shared their communities with artisans and shop-keepers on the one hand and symbols of the privileged world—gentry estates, monasteries, academies—on the other. This lack of strong spatial segregation accounts in part for Moscow workers' less hostile attitude toward the ruling classes. The sense of "them" and "us" was not so intense as in highly segregated working-class communities such as Vyborg in Petrograd and the Central Industrial Region's factory towns of Ivanovo-Voznesensk and Orekhovo-Zuev. Thus the physical image of the city provides one element in understanding the workers' revolutionary ex-perience to be discussed below.

THE ECONOMY

The city was known as "calico Moscow" for the dominant role that textiles played in its economic and public life. The textile industry was the only major Russian industry to be financed by native capital, and Moscow was the center of the great textile barons: the families of Naidenov, Morozov, Tretiakov, and Riabushinskii.[29] Such families made their fortunes in textile production, later invested in banks and other branches of industry, and were the city's leading public figures. The actual production of textiles, however, took place largely beyond the Moscow city limits in scattered industrial villages in the outlying reaches of the province, in towns such as Bogorodsk, Kolomna, Serpukhov, Orekhovo-Zuev, and in neighboring provinces such as Vladimir and Kostroma. Of all the textile workers in Moscow province in 1917, only one-fifth of them actually worked in fac-tories within the city.[30] Nonetheless, this one-fifth accounted for 35 per-cent of the city's work force;[31] before the war the textile industry, led by

[28] *Ezhemesiachnyi statisticheskii biulleten'*, 1916, nos. 1-12.
[29] *Istoriia Moskvy*, vol. 5, p. 213; Buryshkin, pp. 59-209.
[30] *Stat. ezhegodnik*, p. 171.
[31] The actual total of textile workers in Moscow is open to question. The figure 35 percent was originally argued by A. Ia. Grunt, *Pobeda oktiabr'skoi revoliutsii v Moskve*, but was challenged by F. L. Kurlat in his article, "Nekotorye voprosy istorii oktiabr'skoi revoliutsii

cotton production, was the largest sector in Moscow's factory economy in terms of numbers of workers and just behind food production in terms of the value of output[32] (see Table 1-1).

The second most important industry in Moscow's economy was metalwork and machine building, including steel rolling, manufacture of motors and farm machinery, and mass production of metal dishes, buttons, cable, and wire. Metalworkers accounted for 26 percent of the city's factory work force, but Petrograd, rather than Moscow, was the center of the Russian metal industry. Petrograd accounted for 37 percent of the country's total metalworkers, Moscow only 9 percent.[33]

The third-largest industry in terms of the size of the work force, and tha largest in terms of value of output, was food processing; from Moscow factories came candy, pastries, preserves, tinned meat, sausages, tobacco, tea, coffee, vodka, and beer. Confections from the Abrikosov, Einem, and Kade factories were known throughout Russia and recommended to travelers from abroad.[34] Moscow merchants, led by the Popov, Karavan, and Botkin firms, controlled practically the entire tea trade of the empire.[35]

Although textile- and metal-production industries, known for large-scale factories, accounted for over half of the city's factory labor force, the dominant characteristic of the city's industrial economy was in fact the small scale of its enterprises. Less than half of the city's industrial workers (46 percent) were employed in factories at all; the rest were employed in small artisan workshops. Half the factory labor force worked in plants employing fewer than 51 workers, but since a very few large

---

v Moskve," pp. 31-43. Kurlat argues that Grunt had ignored important metal plants in his calculations and that metalists composed the largest sector of the work force. This argument, however, is convincingly quashed by Grunt in "V podderzhku predlozhenii I. F. Gindina i L. E. Shepeleva." Grunt demonstrates that certain of Kurlat's figures were taken out of context, and in general he exposes Kurlat's careless use of statistical and archival material. Grunt reasserts his original finding in "Moskovskii proletariat v 1917 g." This controversy over which sector was the largest is more than a debate over statistics, for the composition of Moscow's industrial work force is an important factor in the interpretation of Moscow's role in the 1917 revolution. Kurlat's line of argument is that metalists, generally a much more revolutionary group of workers, dominated the economic and political scene and that Moscow was an important stronghold of radical activity. Grunt, in the works cited here and elsewhere, argues that the political situation in Moscow was much more complex, that during 1917 neither Moscow's Bolsheviks nor its workers had a clear vision of the city's revolutionary destiny.

[32] *Fabrichno-zavodskaia promyshlennost' goroda Moskvy i moskovskoi gubernii 1917-1927 gg.* p. 2.

[33] Grunt, "Moskovskii proletariat"; A. G. Rashin, *Formirovanie rabochego klassa Rossii,* pp. 75, 83, 85.

[34] Baedeker, p. 274.

[35] Seven-tenths of the tea sold in Russia was processed in Moscow tea-weighing enterprises (*Izv. MSRD,* 10 October 1917).

TABLE 1-1. *Moscow Work Force, 1912*

Factory Workers		165,184	Total
Textile	57,247		
Metal	25,542		
Clothing	4,164		
Chemical	4,504		
Food	18,340		
Printing	10,694		
Leather	2,285		
Wood	4,303		
Mineral	1,441		
Paper	4,013		
Construction	3,211		
Other: guards, drivers	16,155		
Day laborers	13,286		
Artisans (includes self-employed artisans)		252,784	Total
Tailors	49,353		
Boot makers	21,826		
Construction workers	19,388		
Metalworkers	22,465		
Textile workers	5,774		
Woodworkers	13,210		
Other	79,109		
Apprentices	41,659		
Transportation workers		29,189	Total
Tram and railroads			
Carters			
Service workers		135,836	Total
Domestic servants	99,074		
Waiters and cooks	14,170		
Yardkeepers, etc.	22,492		
Total workers in 1912		582,993	

SOURCE: *Statisticheskii ezhegodnik g. Moskvy i moskovskoi gubernii,* results of Moscow census of 1912, pp. 68-73.

factories accounted for the upper half of this size distribution, the average size of a factory was 202 workers.[36] Elsewhere in the Moscow industrial region, the average factory was much larger: 247 workers were employed in the average Moscow province factory and 482 in the neighboring textile center of Vladimir province. The scale of Petrograd industry also outstripped Moscow's: in 1917, the average Petrograd plant employed 389 workers.[37] On the other hand, the average factory in other cities in the

[36] Grunt, "Moskovskii proletariat," pp. 98-100. The few large factories were so big, however, that half of all factory workers were employed in plants larger than five hundred.

[37] Tsentral'noe statisticheskoe upravlenie (hereafter TsSU), *Trudy,* vol. 7, vyp. 1, p. 1, table 1; *Istoriia rabochikh Leningrada,* vol. 2, p. 12.

empire was smaller in size than Moscow's. In terms of scale, Moscow represented a bridge between the large plants characteristic of the concentrated industrial regions and the smaller plants typical of most urban industrial centers such as Kiev, Tiflis, Odessa, and Baku.

Nonfactory production workers included artisans, self-employed masters, hired workers in small shops or at home, and apprentices. The artisan trades were primarily tailoring and shoemaking, but the large group of nonfactory industrial workers—there were almost a hundred twenty-seven thousand of them in 1912—also included locksmiths, cabinetmakers, laundresses, stocking knitters, building workers, and some thirty other trades.[38]

Transport accounted for another important group of nonfactory workers. Ten railroad lines converged on the city, connecting Moscow with the seaports of Petrograd, Arkhangel, and Vladivostok, with Poland, Kiev, the Caucasus, and Siberia, and with the numerous factory settlements in the Central Industrial Region surrounding the city. Railroads and Moscow's location on the river-transport network made the old capital the center for the supply of raw and semifinished materials. American and Egyptian cotton was shipped from the southern port of Odessa and sent to Iaroslavl and Orekhovo-Zuev to be spun into yarn; the yarn came back to Moscow and went out again to the mill towns around Moscow and in Ivanovo-Voznesensk, where it was made into cloth to be once again stored and traded by Moscow merchants.[39]

In the expansion years after 1900, several new industries arose to compete for prominence with the traditional textiles, metals, and foodstuffs. The printing, electrical, and chemical industries expanded rapidly in the first decade of the twentieth century and contributed to an increasing diversification of the Moscow economy.[40] Whereas by 1914 metalworkers and machine workers accounted for over 40 percent of the St. Petersburg labor force, and the second-largest industry, textiles, accounted for only 17 percent, Moscow's industrial workers, despite the dominance of textiles, were more widely distributed among the industrial sectors (see Table 1-2). This difference was to be further accentuated by the effect of World War I on the Russian economy.

Both St. Petersburg, renamed Petrograd in 1914, and Moscow soon felt the effects of Russia's critical need for military production. The war effort demanded armaments, explosives, transport, and military clothing; fine foodstuffs and calico cloth became dispensable luxuries. Through the stimuli of profitable military contracts, generous government subsidies for conversion to war production, and a network of patriotic public or-

---

[38] *Stat. ezhegodnik*, p. 71.
[39] *Istoriia Moskvy*, vol. 5, pp. 47-48.
[40] Ibid., p. 35.

TABLE 1-2. *Relative Distribution of St. Petersburg and Moscow Workers in Industries, 1913-1914*

Industry	St. Petersburg, 1914	Moscow, 1913
Metal	41.5%	15.3%
Chemical	8.9	8.4
Textile	16.5	37.7
Food	9.4	15.3
Printing and paper	11.3	8.7
Clothing	4.2	7.8
Wood	2.1	—
Leather	—	2.1
Total workers	242,600	148,200

SOURCE: A. G. Rashin, *Formirovanie rabochego klassa Rossii*, pp. 83, 85. The figures for Moscow are not so precise as those employed elsewhere in this study, but they are useful here for comparative purposes.

ganizations dedicated to improving military supply, Russian industrialists transformed the face of the economy. By late 1916, nine-tenths of the Moscow labor force worked on defense orders. Textile production sharply declined, and metal production employed the largest share of the city's workers.[41]

Yet even as metal production came to dominate the war economy, the former differences between the two capital cities increased. In Petrograd, metal production expanded to employ over 60 percent of the labor force; textile, food, and printing industries all sharply declined. Moscow took up the slack. Only its textile output declined during the war, and the city's industrial labor force by 1917 was even more evenly distributed across the industries than it had been before the war, as Table 1-3 shows.

This industrial diversity helped to shape Moscow's response to the revolutionary events of 1917. Groups of industrial workers had different social and economic characteristics and expectations, and no one group of workers in Moscow could easily be expected to dominate the revolutionary scene the way the Petrograd metalists were to do in 1917. Because some knowledge of the structure of the work force in Moscow is crucial in understanding the dynamics of the revolution there, a consideration of the nature and composition of this labor force is now in order.

THE MOSCOW WORKING CLASS

The label "worker" (*rabochii*) embraces a wide range of Moscow wage earners, but they can all be grouped in three major categories: factory

[41] Ibid., p. 284; A. L. Sidorov, *Ekonomicheskoe polozhenie Rossii v gody pervoi mirovoi voiny*, p. 370.

TABLE 1-3. *Relative Distribution of Petrograd and Moscow Workers, 1917*

Industry	Petrograd	Moscow
Metal	61.3%	27.6%
Chemical	11.1	11.8
Textile	9.4	24.0
Food	4.0	11.1
Printing and paper	6.0	6.9
Clothing	3.8	13.0
Wood	1.4	—
Leather	—	2.1
Total workers	384,600	205,900

SOURCE: Rashin, *Formirovanie rabochego klassa Rossii*, pp. 83, 85.

workers, artisans, and those employed in transport and other services. White-collar employees (*sluzhashchie*) are not included in the working class considered here. Unlike the situation in Petrograd, Moscow employees generally formed their own associations, declining to join with factory workers or artisans. They had their own soviet in 1917 and did not participate in working-class institutions. An exception was the transport employees on both railroads and tramways, who collaborated with their blue-collar co-workers. Eventually the tram employees elected to distinguish themselves from clerical and sales workers and called themselves the "lower employees" (*nizshie* sluzhashchie). These employees considered themselves as part of the working class and will be so considered here.

Factory workers, who counted for something below half of the work force, were the largest category of wage laborers in 1917. But such workers often had in common only that they were employed in enterprises numbering at least sixteen people (or thirty if unmechanized) and were therefore eligible for supervision under the government's factory legislation. This Factory Inspectorate definition is of marginal utility at best, for different administrative divisions used different criteria, and on the smallest scale there is no important difference between a "factory worker" in a factory of sixteen and a "workshop worker" in a shop of fourteen.[42] This

[42] The census definition of a factory (tsenzovaia *fabrika*) is arbitrary but not, unfortunately, uniform. Most exclusive was the Factory Inspectorate; its domain was industrial enterprises with sixteen or more workers if mechanized, and thirty or more if not mechanized (S. I. Antonova, *Vliianie stolypinskoi agrarnoi reformy na izmeneniia v sostave rabochego klassa*, p. 147), but there are a number of smaller enterprises included in its 1916 list of Moscow factories (*Spisok fabrik*). The owners' association was more catholic in its definition; many plants are included in its list which are excluded from the Factory Inspectorate's (Sovet s"ezdov predstavitelei promyshlennosti i torgovlia, Peterburg, *Fabrichno-zavodskaia predpriiatiia Rossiiskoi Imperii* [hereafter Sovet s"ezdov]). Tea weighing, for example, was not

problem aside, however, characteristics of workers in factories varied greatly by industry, and to a lesser extent, within industries as well.

These characteristics will serve, in the ensuing discussion, to explain political and social behavior of the Moscow workers in 1917. Among the factors influencing a worker's "cast of mind" (*oblik*) and his or her propensity for types of political activity, I rely most heavily on those easily identified: sex, age, place of birth, wage level, and literacy. Male workers, because of the prevalent culture, tended to participate more in public life than women, who were taught to be submissive to the authority of men, the church, and the state. Young workers tended to participate more in public life because they were less burdened by family responsibilities, less discouraged by past political setbacks, and more willing to take risks with their futures.[43] The impact of urban life on the propensity for activism will be discussed more fully in the next chapter, but historical evidence shows that urban workers tend in general to be more prone to action than those with strong ties to the countryside. Workers with different wage levels will be interested in different goals: well-paid workers tend to be more concerned about noneconomic issues such as rights in the work place and their own positions in the society outside, whereas for poorly paid workers the basic need to earn a living occupies their time most. This issue too will be discussed more fully in the next chapter.

Wage levels also indicate a level of skill, which together with literacy affect a worker's oblik. Skilled workers have learned to make decisions on the job, can handle more responsibility, and are accustomed to acting independently.[44] Literate workers, or more properly those who make a habit of reading, tend to be more familiar with the world around them. They can combine the capacity for independent judgment with an ability to gain information, and so they are likely to be active in political and revolutionary affairs. By politically active I do not mean just yet to suggest politically radical, although many of these same factors will also influence the direction of a worker's political activity. Young workers tend to be more extremist than older workers for the same reason they are more active: they have less to lose by such radical behavior. The risk of a

---

considered to be an industrial activity by the Factory Inspectorate, but both owners and workers in such plants agreed it was. The Moscow provincial local government (*zemstvo*) statistical committee included as factories enterprises as small as five workers (Antonova, p. 145), and the city statistical administration probably used its own criteria for its censuses, criteria that have not been found.

[43] Diane Koenker, "Urban Families, Working-Class Youth Groups, and the 1917 Revolution in Moscow," offers a discussion of these attributes of young workers.

[44] The traits of skilled workers are discussed in a stimulating way for Petrograd workers by a sociologist, Mark David Mandel, "The Development of Revolutionary Consciousness among the Industrial Workers of Petrograd between February and November 1917," chap. 1.

twenty-year prison sentence seems less daunting to a twenty-year-old than to a forty-year-old.

There is another set of factors less easy to measure which supplements those mentioned above. The organizational history of a group of workers is important in providing experience from which to respond to current problems. Interaction among workers with different sets of characteristics affects how all will act; workers with low propensities for action—such as middle-aged women of low skill levels—may well become galvanized to action by the example and leadership of metalworkers in neighboring factories. Or workers whom one expects to be active might remain passive because they are isolated from others holding a similar view; they lack a critical mass necessary to act. For this reason, factory size becomes an important explanatory index of activity. As this study will show, large factories tended in 1917 to be more involved in political life on almost every level. Such factories themselves provided a critical mass for action; they facilitated organization and mutual support.

A final factor in explaining workers' political activity is the relationship of workers to the other members of society. Workers such as printers come into frequent contact with members of the intelligentsia and the educated middle class; their attitudes toward the rest of society are shaped by personal contact. Workers, such as metalists and textilists, in heavy industry have scarcely any direct contact with the rest of society other than their employers, with whom they are often in an adversary relationship. These segregated workers form their views of the rest of society in a more theoretical way, often, as was discussed in the introduction, on the basis of a theory of relentless class struggle. Such segregation was an important factor in determining the extreme radicalism of certain segments of the Petrograd work force.[45]

These are some of the factors that must be kept in mind as one considers first the variety of workers in Moscow and later the role played by these workers in the eight stormy months between February and October 1917.

Metalworkers were among the most skilled workers in Russia; most jobs in the industry required the application of knowledge and reasoning ability as much as physical force, particularly in the more sophisticated branches such as engine and instrument building. The level of literacy for an industry is a convenient correlative of the level of skills required, and for all of Russia in 1918, for example, the level of literacy of metalworkers was second only to that of printers; 84 percent of machine builders and 76 percent of all other metalists were able to read and write.[46] (See Table 1-4.) The most highly skilled workmen were concentrated in Petrograd, which had a larger share of machine-building plants than Moscow

[45] Ibid.   [46] Rashin, p. 601.

TABLE 1-4. *Russian Workers' Literacy Rates by Industry, 1918*

Industry	Men (Percent Literate)	Women (Percent Literate)
Printing	97	89
Metal	84	54
Wood	84	47
Chemical	79	55
Paper	78	53
Food	75	48
Mining	74	43
Textile	74	38
Leather	70	45

SOURCES: E. E. Kruze, *Polozhenie rabochego klassa Rossii*, p. 115; cf. Rashin, *Formirovanie rabochego klassa Rossii*, p. 601.

did; and the literacy rate of its male metalists in 1918 was 92 percent (70 percent for women).[47] But even in a 1908 study of Moscow province, the metalworkers' literacy rate was 90 percent; cotton workers in the same study had only a 44 percent literacy rate.[48] Based on the 1908 study, metalworkers tended also to be hereditary workers. Despite their official registration as peasants, 54 percent (compared to 43 percent of male textile workers) had fathers who were also workers, and almost none of the surveyed metalists left the plant to do agricultural work in the summer.[49] Metalists tended to be more urbanized than most workers; in 1912, 14 percent of the registered metal-factory workers had been born in Moscow, against only 9.5 percent for all factory workers.[50] Before the war and in 1918, Moscow metalists were primarily men; the more highly skilled the occupation, the higher the proportion of men. In 1918, for example, less than 1 percent of the toolworkers (*slesary*), the most common specialization, were women, but women made up 37.5 percent of miscellaneous semiskilled metalists.[51]

By 1917, almost all Moscow metalworkers worked on military orders in some way or another: munitions and armaments production, motor building, cable and barbed wire, wagon building and repair. Throughout Russia, 53 percent of metalworkers (of both sexes) received military exemptions in order to work on defense, compared to an average of 27 percent for all occupations.[52] Half of the Moscow metalists were engaged

[47] *Istoriia rabochikh Leningrada*, vol. 2, p. 16.

[48] The data are drawn from I. M. Koz'minykh-Lanin's massive survey of Moscow workers in 1908, reported in *Grammotnost' i zarabotki fabrichno-zavodskikh rabochikh moskovskoi gubernii.*

[49] Rashin, p. 541, from another valuable Koz'minykh-Lanin study, *Ukhod na polevye raboty fabrichno-zavodskikh rabochikh moskovskoi gubernii.*

[50] *Stat. ezhegodnik*, p. 69.   [51] *Ibid.*, p. 46.

[52] *Rossiia v mirovoi voine 1914-1918*, p. 101.

in "mechanical production": manufacture of machine parts, instruments, engines. The largest Moscow factories fell into this mechanical category: Dinamo, in Simonovka, with 2,200 workers; the Military Artillery plant, with 3,300; Bromlei Brothers in Zamoskvorech'e, with 2,000. Only 10 percent of Moscow metalists were engaged in the actual production of steel—two-thirds of them at one large plant near Rogozhskaia barrier, the French-owned Guzhon mill. Much of the raw metal for Moscow factories came from the new industrial areas in and around the Donbass in the south. The remaining 40 percent of Moscow metalists were scattered among new specialized branches of production—medical instruments, electrical parts, cable—and old artisan-derived trades—jewelry production (many of these workers were employed at intricate mechanical work in defense plants), blacksmithing, and the production of small metal items such as buttons, tableware, religious crosses.[53] The average plant size for Moscow metal factories was 196 workers; for machine-building plants, 216; and for rare-metal factories, 49 workers (see Table 1-5).

TABLE 1-5. *Average Factory Size of Moscow Industries*

Industry	Average Number of Workers Per Plant
Tram	1,564
Leather	288
Power and gas	271
Clothing	241
Textile	236
Chemical	226
Machine	216
Metal	196
Mineral	72
Printing	71
Wood	68
Paper	55
Rare metals	49
Animal byproducts	43

SOURCE: Author's factory file.

The size of the factory work force in the textile industry in Moscow seems to vary according to which statistics are used. The Factory Inspectorate included clothing production, laundry, and dyeing in its list of factories; later Soviet statisticians created a special category of clothing factories, combining workers from both the textile and the leather industries. In either case, the number of textile workers was large. The average factory employed 236 workers, but production in Moscow's textile industry was divided among small and extremely large factories: the range

[53] *Spisok fabrik.*

in factory size was from 5 workers to 6,000.[54] The industry did not require particularly sophisticated workers. Although one memoirist claims many of the factories were equipped with the "latest word" in textile technology,[55] this technology enabled operation by relatively simple tasks, and not much training was required of textile workers. Much of the industry was mechanized by 1917; even hand producers, however—primarily weavers and knitters—were only applying rudimentary skills passed on from generation to generation in peasant families. Literacy among textile workers in Russia was only slightly over 50 percent in 1918.[56] The industry was a major employer of village girls who had little opportunity for schooling, for it did not require much education to perform the mechanical tasks required of most textile workers. Women composed half the textile work force in 1912, 70 percent in 1918. They predominated, as in the metal industry, in the more menial occupations of weaving, carding, and knitting.[57]

The major employer of textile workers in Moscow city, as in Moscow province, was the cotton industry. About 25,000 were employed here in factories ranging from a tiny (10 workers) hand-spinning factory in Blagusha to the huge Prokhorov conglomerate at Trekhgornaia gate in Presnia (6,000 workers) and Zamoskvorech'e's Danilovskaia manufacture (5,400 workers). These latter were *manufaktury*, in which all processes of cotton production were combined: the *manufaktura* started with raw cotton and ultimately turned out finished, dyed, and printed cloth.

About 13,000 workers were employed in wool factories, spinning, weaving, finishing wool, and processing sheepskin. Another 10,000 were engaged in silk production, dominated by two giant factories: Zhiro in Khamovniki with 3,600 workers and Mussi in Lefortovo with 2,400. The remaining textile workers were scattered among linen production, ribbon weaving, embroidery, and knitting. Most of the factories in this last miscellaneous category were quite small, many were unmechanized, and almost all were located in the industrial neighborhoods of Lefortovo and Serpukhov.[58]

Within the textile industry, there was little difference among workers in terms of sex composition or literacy levels. Cotton workers in Russia, who were most highly concentrated in large factories, had been in the forefront of a wave of economic strikes during World War I, strikes that would resume in the Central Industrial Region in the summer of 1917.[59] But Moscow's cotton workers, less concentrated, less isolated, played no role in this movement either before or during 1917, as will be seen below.

[54] Author's factory file; *Spisok fabrik*.
[55] Buryshkin, p. 265.
[56] Rashin, p. 601.
[57] *Stat. ezhegodnik*, pp. 69-70.
[58] *Spisok fabrik*.
[59] Strike data are summarized in TsSU, *Trudy*, vol. 7, vyp. 2, tables 8-14.

Closely connected to the textile trades were workers in the "clothing and toiletry" industry, who numbered over 25,000 in 1917.[60] These included those tailors, boot makers, and such who were considered to be factory, not artisan workers.[61] Some were grouped in giant military supply factories: 6,700 at Mars, 9,300 at two branches of Postavshchik, others in small shops of 20 or 30. In both categories, however, the mode of production was similar: women predominated, operating nothing more complex than Singer sewing machines. In Russia, as elsewhere, males were dominant in the more highly skilled jobs of cutting and cap making.[62]

The chemical industry had only recently emerged as a major employer of Moscow workers. Most chemical plants, producing rubber, perfume, dyes, and pharmaceuticals, had been built since 1890. By 1917, many of these plants were engaged in the production of explosives, gas masks, and other military materials. Overall, chemical workers were not highly skilled, and most of them by 1918 were women. Only 28 percent of all chemical workers received military exemptions, partly because so much of the work was performed by women, who were of course draft exempt.[63] The rubber workers were an exception; here the workers were men, well paid, many of them natives of the industrially advanced western provinces. Two of Moscow's five rubber plants—Kauchuk and Provodnik—had been evacuated from Riga during the war.[64]

Chemical plants were big: N. A. Vtorov employed 6,500 workers in his riverside plant;[65] Bogatyr in Bogorodskoe, which produced rubber footwear, employed over 2,200. Perfume factories were also, on average, large: Brokar in Serpukhov employed 900 workers, about 75 percent of them women.[66]

Most of the food-industry workers were employed as *konditery*—literally, confectioners—but the output of such factories ranged from chocolate candy to jam to tinned meat for military use. Of konditery in 1912, slightly more than half were men, and a surprisingly large proportion of the women—35 percent—were Moscow natives.[67] Many of the Moscow-

---

[60] *Stat. ezhegodnik*, p. 171. (Identical information appears in *Fabrichno-zavodskaia promyshlennost' goroda Moskvy*.)

[61] The criteria for inclusion into the ranks of tsenzovye factories here are hopelessly muddled. Thus, the modish Maurice hat shop on Tverskaia street was classified as a factory, the equally posh English-owned Shanks tailor shop on Kuznetskii most was not.

[62] *Stat. ezhegodnik*, p. 47.   [63] *Rossiia v mirovoi voine*, p. 101.

[64] *Spisok fabrik.*

[65] This figure is the estimate reported by police in the archive, Tsentral'nyi gosudarstvennyi arkhiv oktiabr'skoi revoliutsii (hereafter TsGAOR), f. 63, op. 21, ed. khr. 69, l. 21. *Spisok fabrik* gives only 802.

[66] *Ezhemesiachnyi statisticheskii biulleten'*, 1916, no. 2, Appendix 2, Bol'nichnyia kassy goroda Moskvy.

[67] *Stat. ezhegodnik*, p. 69.

born women may have been married or related to skilled male workers; a large number of women workers at the Einem factory were wives or daughters of metalists at the nearby Bromlei plant.[68] Most konditery worked in large plants: there were several concerns with over a thousand workers—Einem, Abrikosov in Sokol'niki, and Siu in Presnia; the median plant size was large for Moscow—327 workers. Literacy among food workers was not particularly high; for all Russia in 1918, three-fourths of male food workers, but less than half the women, claimed to be able to read and write.[69]

Except for two large sugar refineries, the remaining food-producing enterprises were small: twenty-four sausage factories and countless artisan shops were clustered around the city slaughterhouses in Rogozhskii and Danilovka; most sausage makers worked in establishments of 26 workers or fewer.[70] The scope of the beverage industry is more difficult to assess since the Factory Inspectorate excluded tea packers from its list of factories. The tea packers' union, however, had 4,000 members in mid-1917.[71] In addition, there were 1,600 beverage workers in 1916 employed in plants processing mineral water, coffee, and beer (*kvas*) and in breweries like the one in Khamovniki managed by writer Ilya Ehrenburg's father.[72] Vodka distilleries had been converted to the production of explosives, and former vodka producers were classified as chemical workers.[73]

After konditery, the tobacco workers were the second largest segment of the food industry if workers in the cigarette-paper (*papirosy*) plants are included. The work—cigar rolling and cigarette stuffing—was not particularly complex, and the majority of tobacco workers, even in 1897, were women.[74] Increasing mechanization further simplified the work; one machine could make 65,000 papirosy in ten hours, replacing thirty workers. By 1917, 75 percent of Moscow's tobacco industry was mechanized, and 82 percent of its workers were women. Some of the men performed the same tasks as women, but many were skilled mechanics who tended the machinery; their wages were much higher, and they held themselves aloof from the mass of production workers, forming their own trade union in 1917.[75]

Workers in the printing trades were almost a group apart. Printshops were concentrated in central, nonindustrial Moscow; only one-fourth of

---

[68] *Slavnye traditsii*, p. 87.   [69] Rashin, p. 601.

[70] *Spisok fabrik.*

[71] *Moskovskie pishcheviki do ob"edineniia (1917-1921 gg.)*, p. 7.

[72] Ilya Ehrenburg, *People and Life*, p. 20, describes a visit to the brewery by his neighbor Leo Tolstoy.

[73] Sidorov, p. 387.

[74] *Pervaia vseobshchaia perepis'*, table 20.   [75] *Moskovskie pishcheviki*, p. 73.

all printshops, including the two giants, Sytin and Kushnerev, were located outside the Sadovoe. Most shops were small, employing fewer than thirty-four workers.[76] Unlike their skilled counterparts in the metal industry, printers were brought by the very nature of their work into frequent contact with intellectuals and the well-to-do. To some extent, they adopted the style and often the politics of their social superiors, traits that were to distinguish this trade from all others in 1917.[77]

Production in the industry had fallen off during the war years, but this decline turned around in 1917; the end of tsarist censorship saw the publication of at least ten new democratic daily newspapers and the printing of numerous other periodicals and pamphlets to be distributed throughout the liberated country. Printers in Russia had a literacy rate of 95 percent in 1918,[78] and those who could not read and write were probably employed as watchmen and janitors, rather than as compositors and pressmen. Most printers were men—84 percent in 1918.[79] Highest paid were the compositors, especially those who set type by machine; their wages were twice the average for the industry as a whole in 1907.[80] The industry was an attractive one for young city boys and correspondingly difficult to enter. One Moscow printer who began his career as an apprentice at the Kushnerev printshop in 1908 recalled that it was difficult to be hired without connections: "without friends, without a patron, it was impossible even to dream of getting a job anywhere."[81]

Two traditionally artisanal occupations that had lately been transformed into factory trades were those of leather work and woodworking. Factory production had enlarged the scale of production in these industries but had not changed the nature of the work. Leather factories in Moscow produced saddles, harnesses, boots, tarpaulins, and transmission belts, and even the largest factories—such as Dement and Postavshchik in Zamoskvorech'e—were organized by small shops rather than production lines.[82] Leather workers were of overwhelmingly rural origin—only 6 percent of those working in Moscow factories in 1912 were city-born; they were primarily males and had a low literacy level, 64 percent.[83] The leather industry was distinguished by the high concentration of workers within small areas of the city. Almost two-thirds of all of the 25,000 leather-factory workers were located in just three of the city's fifty-one precincts, 10,000 of these in the Zamoskvorech'e precinct unofficially known as

[76] *Spisok fabrik.*   [77] See Mandel, chap. 1.   [78] Rashin, p. 601.

[79] TsSU, *Trudy*, vol. 26, vyp. 1, *Vserossiiskaia promyshlennaia i professional'naia perepis' 1918 g.*, 1926, pp. 24-39.

[80] V. P. Orlov, *Poligrafîcheskaia promyshlennost' Moskvy*, p. 272.

[81] *Leninskii zakaz*, p. 100.

[82] *Na barrikadakh za vlast' sovetov*, pp. 86-99.

[83] *Stat. ezhegodnik*, pp. 68-74; for literacy, Rashin, p. 601.

Kozhevniki, or "leather workers."[84] The close proximity of many of the leather factories and the large scale of production were undoubtedly important factors in the cohesive strike waged by the leather workers' union in early autumn of 1917.

Woodworkers like other traditionally artisanal trades were rural (6 percent city-born), male (91 percent), and poorly educated (their literacy rate was 70 percent).[85] There were only 3,300 woodworkers employed in fifty-five Moscow factories in 1917. The largest of them was Benno-Rontaller's button factory in Lefortovo, which employed about 400 workers, slightly more than half of them women.[86] In furniture, parquet, and joiners' shops, men predominated; most factories were small, employing only 68 workers on the average.[87]

The remaining employers of Moscow factory workers—producers of animal byproducts, paper, and minerals—were equally small-scale. Animal-byproducts workers included soap makers, candle and glue makers, and brush makers. Business was slow in the war years; very few of the workers were entitled to military exemptions, and only one factory, Nevskii stearic, fulfilled any military orders at all.[88]

Paper workers were engaged primarily in the manufacture of wallpaper, cardboard boxes, and envelopes. None of these factories employed more than 150 workers, most had fewer than 38. About half the workers in 1918 were women; the literacy rate was 68 percent.[89]

The mineral industry included mirror workers, cement workers, and marble cutters. In addition, 6,600 brick workers were employed just outside the city limits; many of them were located in Troitsko-Golenishchaia volost' to the southwest on the site where Moscow University stands today. Of twenty mineral-working factories, only three employed more than 100 workers; Diutfua, producer of perfume bottles and light bulbs, employed 550 workers, Dmitriev's mirror factory employed 150, and V. F. Karnats, the "first Russian manufacturer of pencils,"[90] employed 121. Most of these workers were men, only 7 percent were Moscow-born, and two-thirds of them throughout Russia could read and write in 1918.[91]

It can be seen from the industry profiles above that different industries required different levels of skill; machine building and printing were more exacting industries and required skilled, educated, and experienced work-

---

[84] Author's factory file.

[85] *Stat. ezhegodnik*, pp. 68-74; Rashin, p. 601.

[86] *Ezhemesiachnyi statisticheskii biulleten'*, 1916, no. 2, Appendix.

[87] *Stat. ezhegodnik*, pp. 69-71; *Spisok fabrik*.

[88] *Spisok fabrik*; *Rossiia v mirovoi voine*; and *Spisok fabrichno-zavodskikh predpriiatii moskovskogo raiona, zaniatykh ispolneniem rabot na gosudarstvennuiu oboronu*.

[89] *Spisok fabrik*; *Stat. ezhegodnik*, p. 46; Rashin, p. 601.

[90] Sovet s"ezdov.

[91] *Spisok fabrik*; *Stat. ezhegodnik*, pp. 69-71; Rashin, p. 601.

ers (who were not in great abundance in wartime Russia). Industries such as woodworking and leather work required training but did not demand the same ability to read plans and make independent decisions. The most mechanized industries, such as textiles and chemicals, required little of their workers in terms of either education or experience. Thus it was that in these last two were women most commonly found, for unlike their male counterparts they were not taught a trade by their fathers nor did they spend much time in village or city schools. However, women were also concentrated in those labor fields related to sewing and cooking, which were traditionally women's work and for which they did receive some kind of at-home experience.

In the chapters to follow, these industries will serve as convenient sets of social and economic characteristics through which to describe the revolutionary activities of industrial workers. The assumption ought to be made that workers within each industry were relatively more homogeneous than those in different industries, but this assumption deserves some qualification. Even within one factory, disparities existed among workers performing different operations. At textile factories, for example,

2. Textile-printing machinery at the Giubner cloth manufacture. The Moscow textile industry was technologically advanced, obviating the need for large numbers of skilled workers.

totally unskilled women filled the mechanical and spinning sections, while experienced men supervised the machinery and performed the more exacting tasks of printing patterns on the cloth.[92] Metalworkers, although on average more skilled than those in other industries, included both highly trained craftsmen and unskilled laborers (many of them women) who fulfilled the routine functions of cartridge production and other forms of metal stamping. A similar split occurred in the chemical industry, where the rubber workers formed an elite stratum.

After factory workers, the most important group of Moscow workers was the artisanry, those workers employed in small workshops, most with fewer than four hired workers.[93] In Moscow, these small producers made up more than half the work force: of the 350,000 production workers reported in the 1912 census, 17 percent were self-employed craftsmen and 36 percent were hired artisans.[94]

The term *artisan* as used here does not have a direct equivalent in Russian, so this term is somewhat difficult to define. The closest Russian word, *remeslennik*, had a narrow legal definition in Tsarist Russia; it was applied to members of urban artisans' guilds that were themselves introduced into Russia in the eighteenth century. Artisanal workers were also called "workshop men" (*masterovye*), a more general term. An artisan workshop commonly was composed of the proprietor (*khoziain*), master craftsmen (*mastery*), occasionally journeymen (*podmastery*), and apprentices (*ucheniki*). (Such small production is occasionally referred to in the literature as *kustar* production, although kustar refers usually to rural artisan crafts.)[95]

Russian artisans, like factory workers, traced their origins to villages. In 1912, they were only slightly more "urbanized" than factory workers: 11 percent of hired workers and 16.6 percent of self-employed artisans were born in Moscow; the corresponding figure for factory workers was 9.5 percent.[96] Most artisanal recruits came from the surrounding uezds and provinces: Central Industrial Region peasants had a long tradition of combining agriculture with handicraft, for the soil was too poor to support the whole population exclusively by farming. Various towns had their traditional specialties, traditions continued by young boys sent to be

[92] M. K. Rozhkova, "Sostav rabochikh Trekhgornoi manufaktury nakanune imperialisticheskoi voiny."

[93] N. I. Vostrikov, *Bor'ba za massy*, p. 18, based on *Remeslenniki i remeslennoe upravlenie v Rossii.*

[94] *Stat. ezhegodnik*, p. 68.

[95] The zemstvo definition of kustar production was an enterprise in which "the owner of the enterprise or members of his family work at the same bench together with hired workers" (Antonova, p. 93). For urban artisans, see I. Belousov, *Ushedshaia Moskva*; and Zelnik, *Labor and Society*, chap. 1.

[96] *Stat. ezhegodnik*, pp. 68-74.

3. Shoemaker and apprentices in an artisanal workshop.

apprenticed in Moscow. Thus, in the 1870s, boys from Tver were apprenticed as boot makers, those from Riazan were sent to tailors and hat makers, and those from Vladimir province became woodworkers, carpenters, and joiners.[97]

The largest number of artisans worked in tailoring and boot making: about 20 percent of the artisan population were tailors (12,000 self-employed, 20,000 hired workers); 10 percent were boot makers. By 1912, certain of these artisan trades were more urban than others: 20 percent of tailors, hat makers, and certain metalworkers were Moscow natives, which proportion was roughly equivalent to the native population of merchants and professionals. On the other hand, leatherworkers, boot makers, and woodworkers were still overwhelmingly of rural origin; only about 5 to 6 percent of workers in these trades were Moscow-born.[98]

The population of artisans in 1917 was no smaller than in 1912, although

[97] Belousov, p. 14. [98] *Stat. ezhegodnik*, p. 68.

no precise figures are available. Much of the military-supply industry organized by public organizations was concentrated in small workshops; the intention was to provide employment for wives and dependents of soldiers.[99] About 30,000 workers were employed in these organizations' uniform-supply shops, producing linen, uniforms, and boots.[100] A number of workers were also employed on the "out-work" or "putting out" system, especially in clothing manufacture; materials were issued at central distribution points (*razdatochnye kontory*), prepared at home, and returned for payment. As many as 200,000 women—probably wives of factory workers or of absent soldiers—may have been involved in this type of production.[101]

Workers in the building trades accounted for 5 percent of the Moscow work force (factory and artisan) in 1912; virtually all of them were men. Some worked on repair crews—as house painters (*maliary*), carpenters, and pipe fitters—which were permanently attached to particular enterprises. The largest number of construction workers, 90 percent by one account, were seasonal migrants only.[102] They were recruited in the villages by local bosses for six-month terms, from April until October.[103] Teams of workers (*artels*) traveled to the city, each artel under the strict supervision of a boss who contracted with engineers at city building sites. The artel boss was responsible for the workers' food and shelter, and the workmen saw little or no money until the end of the contract period. Such organization of construction work tended to isolate the builders in their own village groups; individual builders had a hard time finding jobs since work crews were filled before reaching town.[104] An exception was the distinctively urban trade of water-pipe work, whose workers tended to be individually employed in large buildings in the city. Ten percent of these pipe fitters were Moscow natives in 1912, as opposed to only 1 or 2 percent for resident carpenters and painters. Pipe fitters received

[99] William Gleason, "The All-Russian Union of Towns and the All-Russian Union of Zemstvos in World War I," p. 88.

[100] *Sotsial-Demokrat*, 19 May 1917. (Hereafter *Sots.-Dem.*)

[101] *Moskovskii soiuz rabotnikh-portnykh v 1917 g.*, p. 9. The figure of 200,000 seems large, but it is plausible. There were in 1917 about 706,000 women of working age in Moscow; 91,000 of these were factory workers in 1918, so it is not inconceivable that 30 percent of the rest worked at home in this fashion (*Stat. ezhegodnik*, p. 46).

[102] T. V. Sapronov, ed., *Iubileinyi sbornik po istorii dvizheniia stroitel'nykh rabochikh Moskvy*, p. 219.

[103] The building season, as was true of most other work, was tied to the religious calendar: it ran from Easter until the holiday of the festival of the Virgin (Pokrov). The first pay day, after which contractors had to compete with vodka for the workers' time, was St. Peter's day, June 29. Likewise, for artisans the start of the night-work season, when work began to be done again by lamplight, was marked by the birthday of the Virgin, September 8. See Belousov, p. 46; Sapronov, *Iubileinyi sbornik*, p. 12.

[104] Sapronov, *Iubileinyi sbornik*, p. 12.

the highest wages and had been the first group of builders to organize a trade union after 1905.[105]

According to the engineers and architects who employed them, Russian builders, uneducated and wedded to rural habits, were abominable workers. A government study done in 1912 summarized the opinion of a St. Petersburg architect: "The workers are frightfully slow-witted and inexperienced; and in the ten years during which he [the architect] has been engaged in construction work, he has never observed any worker who has mastered his trade."[106] In the boom years before the war, however, there was great demand for builders, no matter how poorly skilled, and the war did not diminish this trend. Although private construction in Moscow had stopped, by 1917 there were a number of large-scale projects employing thousands of migrant builders: the new Kazan railway terminus, the AMO auto plant, and new freight warehouses. Construction of the Moscow branch of the evacuated Provodnik factory alone employed 5,000 workers.[107]

Transport of goods and people utilized another major segment of the labor pool. In 1918 the railways and trams employed 16,405 workers and local transport another 22,000.[108] Railroad workers were a special category. For line crews especially, but also for stationary workmen based in Moscow's freight yards and repair shops, the first allegiance was to the line rather than to the city near which they lived. This solidarity created special possibilities for the spread of political ideas, but the railroad workers' lack of local ties diminished their participation in Moscow affairs. Most localized were workers in the "traction service" (*sluzhba tiagi*); these were largely skilled metalists and mechanics based in big shops on the outskirts of Moscow. Gang workers (*sluzhba puti*) tended to be less-skilled track-layers and repairmen and lived scattered along the length of the rail lines.[109]

Most of the 22,000 workers in local transport were either drivers of horse-drawn wagons or freight handlers called *kriuchniki*, after the hooks they used to unload goods. These workers were primarily of rural origin; even of tram conductors in 1912, only 4 percent were Moscow-born. This surely changed by 1917, for the wartime labor shortage required the city to hire tram employees wherever they could find them. Women began to drive trams for the first time; others pressed into service were students, like the young Konstantin Paustovsky, who worked as a tram conductor

[105] *Stat. ezhegodnik*, p. 68; Sapronov, *Iubileinyi sbornik*, p. 10; Bonnell, "The Politics of Labor in Pre-Revolutionary Russia," p. 384.

[106] V. V. Groman, *Obzor stroitel'noi deiatel'nosti v Rossii*, p. 64.

[107] Sapronov, *Iubileinyi sbornik*, p. 243.

[108] *Stat. ezhegodnik*, pp. 47-48.

[109] P. F. Metel'kov, *Zheleznodorozhniki v revoliutsii*, pp. 26-32.

at the Miusskii terminal in the first months of the war.[110] Possibly because of the changing composition of this occupation, tram workers had become by early 1917 the leaders in the growing strike movement among Moscow workers. They initiated a large political strike in the fall of 1916, the first major political action among tram employees, and again sparked a wave of political strikes in February 1917, just two weeks before the fall of the autocracy.[111]

Domestic service accounted in 1912 for almost 100,000 wage workers, of whom 93 percent were women. About a quarter of these *domashnye prislugi* were employed as household kitchen help, the rest either as personal maids or valets or as all-purpose help in a one-servant household.[112] Domestics, too, were overwhelmingly rural-born; but unlike the other groups of workers surveyed here, they had little family life of their own in the city. The 1912 census lists separately the number of dependents for each group of the population; for domestic servants, dependents represented only 6 percent of the number of workers. Artisans' dependents, on the contrary, came to 73 percent of the number of workers; factory-worker dependents constituted 47 percent.[113] Domestic servants were not of a class that reproduced itself; replacements came rather from the villages.[114]

Besides personal servants, the category of service workers (*prislugi*) included coachmen in private service, porters or concierges (*shveitsary*), and yard keepers—the ubiquitous *dvorniki*, who swept snow from the streets, hauled trash, and served as part-time informers for the local police. All of these functions were served primarily by men.[115]

Other workers in service occupations in 1917 included waiters and cooks, primarily in taverns (*traktiry*), laundresses, and cleaning women. These latter two functions were filled mainly by women working part-time to supplement a husband's or father's factory income; such workers were inherently uncountable, and specific information on their social background is hard to find. The mother of a young Presnia woman activist, for instance, who cleaned and did laundry for students, was not likely to

[110] *Stat. ezhegodnik*, p. 68; Konstantin Paustovsky, *Story of a Life*, pp. 268-275.

[111] See below, Chapter Three.

[112] *Stat. ezhegodnik*, p. 73.

[113] Ibid., pp. 68-74.

[114] The low dependent rate is not due to the young age of servants; in 1897, the median age of female domestics was thirty-four years (calculated from *Pervaia vseobshchaia perepis'*). Much remains to be known about the position of domestic servants in Russia, but if such women had children, they were likely to be raised with relatives in the country or given up to the Imperial Foundling Hospital, which accepted legitimate as well as illegitimate children (David Ransel, "Abandonment and Fosterage of Unwanted Children").

[115] Based on 1918 data in *Stat. ezhegodnik*, p. 48.

be included in official statistics, except possibly as a female dependent of her worker husband.[116]

Moscow workers were largely male, rural rather than city-born, employed in workshops and small factories as well as in large plants. They were a disparate group. Different industries had their own particular characteristics; women were a minority in the labor force as a whole, but they predominated in such industries as textiles, chemicals, and tobacco processing. About 90 percent of all workers had been born outside Moscow, but city-born workers were a much larger component in trades such as printing and tailoring.

To understand the social underpinnings of the revolution in Moscow, one cannot just count the workers and place them in categories; however, the counting and the classifying do prepare the way for evaluating the response of various types of workers to revolutionary events. The next chapter will deal with the lives of these workers in Moscow and with the ways in which urban life affected the different categories of workers, for it is this process of urbanization as well as the social background which affected workers' responses and behavior in 1917.

[116] Anna Litveiko, "V semnadtsatom," *Iunost'*, p. 4.

TWO. *Life in the City*

THE Russian worker has long been characterized as a unique amalgam of rural peasant and urban worker, and the Russian labor movement has been interpreted in this light.[1] This stress on the Russian worker's recent rural past tends, however, to minimize the role of the urban environment in shaping working-class culture, in producing an articulate, autonomous labor movement. The workers who made the revolution in Moscow, Petrograd, and other Russian cities were responding not only to national political and work-related economic grievances but also to the special problems of urban working-class life, and responding with a set of values (oblik) shaped by their experience in the urban setting and by the everyday (*bytovoi*) aspects of their culture. In this chapter, I shall examine the urban sources of this working-class culture, sources of the values shared by Moscow workers in their revolutionary year of 1917.

URBAN LIFE: INTRODUCTION

Historically, the processes of urbanization and industrialization have complemented each other. Developing cities, as concentrations of economic and political power, offered a wider variety of economic opportunities for inhabitants of their regions than were available in sleepy backwater towns and hamlets. Population pressures and state policies favoring economic growth prompted peasants to leave the land and enter the expanding labor markets of the cities. Manufacturers took advantage of the coexistence of a growing labor supply with an established economic-communications network (roads, railways, wholesale merchants) and began to build factories in these cities, thereby creating more opportunities for economic expansion, which in turn lured more villagers away from the provinces—and so cities grew.

Moscow had been expanding at a steady rate since the emancipation of the serfs in 1861. The city increased its population by about 10 percent every five years, largely because of increased migration. In the prosperous years after 1905, the rate doubled. Moscow grew by 27 percent between 1905 and 1910 and continued to increase, growing by 21 percent between

[1] See, for example, Jerzy Gliksman, "The Russian Urban Worker"; Theodore H. Von Laue, "Russian Peasants in the Factory, 1892-1904" and "Russian Labor between Field and Factory, 1892-1903"; Reginald E. Zelnik, "The Peasant and the Factory"; Haimson, "Problem of Social Stability"; R. E. Johnson, *Peasant and Proletarian* and "Peasant Migration and the Russian Working Class"; Keep, *Russian Revolution.*

1910 and 1915.[2] What was the effect of such rapid growth on the residents of the city and on the newcomers who helped to swell the population? How might the 1917 revolution have been related to ineluctable pressures of urban growth? To begin to answer such questions, one must first sort out the processes by which the urban working class was formed, what working-class urban life was like, and the kinds of changes that affected Moscow workers in the period before 1917.

Much has been written about the relationship between urbanization and political action. Some scholars, for example, suggest that the effect of migration to an alien urban environment makes new settlers particularly prone to violence and radical activity.[3] Another common view is that industrialization invariably leads to the exploitation and impoverishment of workers, who thereby gain the incentive to rebel against their situation. I shall try to define some of these problems below and then examine aspects of working-class life in Moscow which can help to illuminate the varieties of political activity in which Moscow workers engaged during the revolutionary months of 1917.

The most fundamental of these problems is the degree of urbanization of Moscow workers; then the question arises of how that urbanization affected their lives. Regardless of occupation, most workers were of rural origin; they had been born and raised in peasant families. How were these peasants affected by the transition to the city? Scholars have noted the correlation of a rapid influx of migrants with mass upheaval and have concluded that there must be a causal relationship. The economist Mancur Olson writes, "The man who has been tempted away from his village, his manor, his tribe or his extended family, by the higher wage of a burgeoning urban industry may well be a disaffected gainer from economic growth. He has been, albeit voluntarily, uprooted and is not apt to acquire comparable social connections in the city. He is, therefore, prone to join destabilizing mass movements."[4]

Menshevik leaders in 1917 saw uprooted nonurban workers as the main source of radical Bolshevik support, a view that has continued to exercise a powerful influence on more recent scholarship.[5] Leopold Haimson, in his seminal article "The Problem of Social Stability in Urban Russia," argues that the rise in labor unrest in the years before the First World War was indeed fueled by "a vast mass of workers who combined with

---

[2] *Stat. ezhegodnik*, p. 88; *Istoriia Moskvy*, vol. 4, p. 226.

[3] Mancur Olson, "Rapid Economic Growth as a Destabilizing Force"; Kenneth Johnson, "Causal Factors in Latin American Political Instability"; Herbert Blumer, "Early Industrialization and the Laboring Class."

[4] Olson, "Rapid Economic Growth," p. 534.

[5] I. G. Tsereteli, *Vospominaniia o fevral'skoi revoliutsii*; Leo Lande, "The Mensheviks in 1917"; Haimson, "Problem of Social Stability"; Keep, *Russian Revolution*, p. 25.

their resentments about the painful and disorienting conditions of their new industrial experience a still fresh sense of grievance about the circumstances under which they had been compelled to leave the village."[6]

On the other hand, Soviet historians, following Marx, insist that it is a hereditary urbanized proletariat that will provide the foot soldiers for radical political movements, and it has been the task of these historians to prove the existence in Russia of such a proletariat.[7] Moscow workers, Bolshevik leaders feared in 1917, were still too closely tied to the land to be of much use in a revolutionary situation.[8] And recent Western scholarship of revolutionary movements elsewhere has indicated that it is the most urbanized segments of the urban population who tend to participate in destabilizing politics.[9]

Why the discrepancy? It is due, in part, to the ambiguity of terms like *destabilizing behavior*. Russian peasants, known for their *buntarstvo*, or the tendency to rise spontaneously against immediate local threats, were assumed to carry this tendency to city factories.[10] On the other hand, the so-called destabilizing behavior of an urbanized proletariat might take a different path, that of agitation, organization, or conspiracy. But the discrepancy is rooted as well in some false assumptions about urban society and about the process of urbanization. Olson, for example, assumes that urban migrants drift singly, aimlessly to the city, abandoning "social connections." In Russia, as elsewhere, this assumption was in fact false, as will be shown below. But if urban migrants were not "uprooted," neither were they full-fledged urbanites, and they might well be expected both to possess values and exhibit behavior different from that of their native Muscovite comrades.

Can one define an urban working-class culture that might have affected the way new and old residents responded to events around them? On the onc hand, urban life encouraged workers to act together: food-supply problems were solved by cooperative eating arrangements, and sick funds provided some insurance in case of illness or injury. The experience of working in large coordinated factories also encouraged the cooperative habit. On the other hand, the size of an urban work force encouraged diversity among workers; aristocracies of skilled workers arose, and some

[6] Haimson, "Problem of Social Stability," p. 636.

[7] Examples are Gaponenko, *Rabochii klass Rossii*, and Kruze, *Polozhenie rabochego klassa Rossii*.

[8] V. I. Lenin, "Krizis nazrel," in *Polnoe sobranie socheneniia*, vol. 34, p. 58. The article was written in September 1917.

[9] Joan Nelson, "The Urban Poor," pp. 393-412; Wayne Cornelius, "Urbanization as an Agent in Latin American Political Instability," pp. 833-857; E. J. Hobsbawm, "Peasants and Rural Migrants in Politics," pp. 45-65; Myron Weiner, "Urbanization and Political Protest," pp. 44-50; Jacques Rougerie, *Procès des Communards*.

[10] R. E. Johnson, *Peasant and Proletarian*, pp. 157-161.

of these workers perceived that they could help themselves more by cooperating only with their elite confreres than with the entire mass of city workers.[11]

Certainly cultural opportunities were greater for workers in cities than for rural residents. Urbanites were more likely to be exposed to the philanthropic educational efforts of the well-to-do urban classes. Urban workers were influenced by the presence of universities and of an active publishing industry. Where great concentrations of workers existed, as in a city, workers more easily found culturally minded comrades with whom to form reading circles and subscribe to publications. As a result of these opportunities, as one might expect, those who lived longest in cities might be the most likely to take advantage of the cultural and educational possibilities offered by the urban milieu. Furthermore, workers accustomed to reading could familiarize themselves with basic political ideas and might be prepared to play a more critical role in political activities in a time of revolution.

For all these reasons, one would expect to find that urbanized Moscow workers played the most important role in the revolutionary events of 1917 as well as before, and so it becomes important to identify as closely as possible the social characteristics of the urban working population. This will be the focus of the next two sections of this chapter.

A second characteristic of workers' experience, urban or otherwise, that shaped their responses to political events was past organizational experience. The existence of urban working-class institutions such as trade unions, cooperatives, and sick funds provided a base for action, a mechanism for disseminating information, a source of funds for political purposes. Even when formal organizations were moribund, as in Tsarist Russia, past participation—such as in outlawed trade unions or in the Moscow Soviet of 1905—could provide workers with remembered practical experience for future efforts. The problem here is to find the links between past and present: did the 1905 uprising linger in the memory of participants; were its lessons transmitted to new generations of urban workers? Were the trade unionists of 1917 in fact the same as those of earlier trade unions?

Finally, one must consider the impact of economic conditions on workers' lives and political activity. Under the rubric "standard of living," there are two factors that are relevant to a worker's world view and

---

[11] For Russian examples, see Sher, *Istoriia professional'nogo dvizheniia rabochikh pechatnogo dela v Moskve*, on the elite mutual aid society of printers and Iu. N. Netesin, "K voprosu sotsial'no-ekonomicheskikh korniakh i osobennostiakh 'rabochei aristokratii' v Rossii," for a study of the economic preconditions for such an aristocracy. A Western European case can be found in E. J. Hobsbawm, "The Labour Aristocracy in Nineteenth-Century Britain."

propensity to action. One is the absolute standard of living—the size of the margin between income and expenditure on necessities. The second is the relative standard of living—the change in a worker's standard of living over time. Theories of economic determinism usually suggest that it is impoverished workers who are prone to the most violent political action; the frustrations of economic exploitation and misery produce an angry proletariat, ready to participate in mass destabilizing movements.

A relative decline in a worker's standard of living might produce the most volatile reaction to economic conditions; this indeed is the element that has been most closely linked by historians with revolutionary behavior.[12] For example, the "declining artisan class" was a potent force in the political and social upheavals in France and Germany in 1830 and 1848.[13] Their perceived recent decline in economic status made these workers much more determined to recover their lost position than impoverished workers who had never known a better life for themselves or their ancestors. The early twentieth century in Russia was also a period of economic crisis and boom, followed by the ultimate crisis of the world war. The change in relative prosperity of different industries and the effects of inflation and selective supply shortages all tended to alter the standards of living of Russian workers.

On the other hand, workers with high incomes had different reasons for participating in political life. They had the greatest resources for carrying out sustained political activity and were likely to play a significant role in political actions. The direction of such well-paid workers' political activity depends on other factors. Those who felt comfortable within the existing framework, such as the printers in 1917, might direct their energies toward peaceful improvements. Those who were alienated from the existing framework, as were the printers in 1905 and the skilled metalists in 1917, might use their extra resources to work for greater, perhaps revolutionary, social change.

URBAN LIFE IN MOSCOW

Barely 10 percent of Moscow's working class in the census year 1912 had been born within the city of Moscow. The rest had migrated, as adults or children, from the nearby villages and provinces. Most newly arrived workers came from the immediately surrounding provinces; in 1902, for example, about one-quarter of the migrants to the city came from Moscow province, the remainder from other neighboring provinces in the central

---

[12] E. Labrousse, *Le Mouvement ouvrier et les théories sociales en France de 1815 à 1848*; Georges Duveau, *La Vie ouvrière en France sous le second empire*, pp. 385-386.

[13] Jean Bron, *Le Droit à l'existence du début du XIXe siècle à 1884*; P. H. Noyes, *Organization and Revolution*; Theodore S. Hamerow, *Restoration, Revolution, Reaction*.

region: Kaluga, Riazan, Tula, Smolensk, Vladimir, Tver, and Iaroslavl. These eight provinces supplied three-fourths of all Moscow's migrants and 95 percent of its factory workers in 1902.[14]

What happened when these peasants from neighboring provinces arrived in the city to find jobs? Were they thrown willy-nilly into the alienating life of the city, pounding the pavements in search of work, living from day to day in lodgings of dubious respectability? Of course, the Khitrovo market (see Chapter One) attracted a share of the transient population, but the evidence suggests that most migrants were in fact absorbed into communities of family and friends from home—*zemliaki.* These village ties, known as *zemliachestvo,* played a crucial role in easing the transition from village to city. The village community helped to find jobs and housing for the newcomer (frequently a migrant came only after a zemliak had reported a job opening); friends were ready-made since the urban community was just an extension of the village back home.

The evidence of the existence of these communities is fragmentary but nonetheless convincing.[15] Bernard Pares observed before the revolution, "These peasants would go to a given street in a given part of the town where there were already some of their own village, who like themselves continued to be peasants, and they would find their place in some given trade, as cabmen, carpenters, or kitchen gardeners."[16]

Robert E. Johnson, in his study of Moscow workers in the period 1880-1900, finds numerous indications of zemliak ties, particularly in residential patterns. Migrants from Kaluga province were especially concentrated in the Lefortovo district of the city, for example.[17] Seventeen percent of Kaluga natives lived there, although only 8 percent of the entire migrant population settled in Lefortovo in 1882. Other migrants clustered their

[14] Rashin, p. 418.

[15] On the whole, Soviet authors tend to ignore the role of these village ties in their otherwise admirable studies of the urbanization of workers. A. M. Pankratova, "Proletarizatsiia krest'ianstva i ee rol' v formirovanii promyshlennogo proletariata Rossii," p. 215, notes that workers at one factory under study appear to be from the same district but does not explore this phenomenon further. D. L. Kasitskaia and E. P. Popova, in "Polozhenie i byt rabochikh Prokhorovskoi Trekhgornoi manufaktury," report that migrant women continued to wear native costumes on holidays even five years after arriving in the city and attribute this to lack of money to buy proper urban dress when, in fact, the wearing of such costumes may well have been an effort to retain local, if transplanted, peasant customs. Soviet studies of the phenomenon of zemliachestvo itself confine themselves to treating the institutional manifestations of these village ties, especially concentrating on the formal organizations of zemliaki created in 1917 by the political parties. See A. S. Smirnov, "Zemliacheskie organizatsii rabochikh i soldat v 1917 g.," pp. 86-123, and V. A. Demidov, "Zemliacheskie organizatsii i ikh rol' v bor'be bol'shevistskoi partii za soiuz rabochego klassa s trudiashchim krest'ianstvom v period podgotovki oktiabria," pp. 79-108.

[16] Bernard Pares, *My Russian Memoirs,* p. 65.

[17] R. Johnson, *Peasant and Proletarian,* p. 70.

settlements in different parts of the city: 18 percent of migrants from Moskovskii uezd settled in Sushchevskaia; 20 percent of Bogorodsk uezd natives lived in Rogozhskaia. The pattern was even more pronounced for smaller groups of migrants. One-third of the two thousand Viatsk natives lived in Khamovniki; forty-one of the forty-five Tomsk migrants lived in the Prechistenskii district.[18]

There is no reason to believe that these patterns of zemliak settlement had changed by 1917. Three documents list striking workers at separate Moscow factories in 1916; all of them indicate this same cluster effect. At Zelig and Meier's rubber-weaving factory in Lefortovo, forty-five workers (of 399 at the factory) were reported by police as strikers; seventeen of them (38 percent, as opposed to 11 percent at Trekhgorka in 1917) were from Smolensk province. Furthermore, the seven of them from Sychevsk district of that province were all natives of the same volost (native village was not reported).[19] Strikers at two leather factories in the center of Moscow showed a similar pattern. At the Loginov factory (with 42 workers), nine of twenty-two strikers were natives of one uezd, Bronnitsy, at the eastern edge of Moscow province, and all these were from two volosts within the uezd. At the Gvozdev leather factory (with 58 workers), half of the twenty reported strikers were from Bronnitsy uezd, six of them from the same village. None of the Bronnitsy natives at Loginov's factory came from this village.[20]

This concentration could hardly have been coincidence, and Johnson suggests a number of reasons for such patterns: first, factory recruiters, most of them from big manufactures, traveled to the provinces to hire peasants, and their task was made much easier if they could hire a large number of workers from a small area. In some factories, workers arriving singly were hired only if they had someone to vouch for them and guarantee they would fulfill their contracts; an urban newcomer would most likely find such a guarantor from among his co-villagers.[21] Most important was the effect of informal contacts and information; a worker might hear of an opening at his factory and write home for a younger brother or cousin to come to fill it. A Moscow weaver born in Orel province, at age thirty, "moved to Moscow, where at first he worked as a street sweeper at the city duma, and then, with help of relatives [*rodnykh*], got work at Prokhorov's Trekhgornaia." Printing jobs were so scarce in the years after 1905 that a printer could only be hired if he had some contacts already

[18] *Perepis' Moskvy 1882 g.*, vyp. 2, 1885, pp. 74-75; R. Johnson, "The Nature of the Russian Working Class," p. 131.

[19] TsGAOR, f. 63, ed. khr. 25 T. 1/1916, ll. 40-42; M. K. Rozhkova, "Sostav rabochikh Trekhgornoi manufaktury v 1917 g.," 1931, no. 8.

[20] TsGAOR, f. 63, ed. khr. 25 T. 1ᵃ, ll. 51-53.

[21] R. Johnson, *Peasant and Proletarian*, pp. 72-74.

in a printshop. Such hiring of friends (*po znakomstve*) was the bane of the Moscow metalists' trade union in 1917; the union pleaded throughout the year for members to report openings to the union's labor exchange and not recruit friends off the street.[22]

What was the net effect of this pattern? At the very least, zemliachestvo helped to make the newcomer feel less lost in the city and provided a ready-made community that could provide jobs, aid in time of need, and social contact. Belonging to such a zemliak community may well have postponed a new migrant's entry into a more specifically urban working-class world.

On the other hand, the long history of migration between village and city may have mitigated the newcomer's sense of anomie. Whole villages did not simply send all their sons to work in the alien city; typically, in Moscow province, one or two family members would go off—either to a local factory or to the capital—work for a few years to earn extra money for the family, and then return to raise a family themselves.[23] Even if the working member of the family stayed in the city, his wife and children often remained in the country, with the father making frequent visits on weekends and holidays. As a result, there grew up generations of workers' children who were peasants by birth and by registration. When these children migrated to the city looking for work, they were therefore not entirely unfamiliar with city ways. In 1899, 94 percent of the workers at Tsindel's cotton mill in Moscow were peasants, but 56 percent of these workers had fathers who had also been factory workers.[24]

Other peasant-workers eased the transition from village to city by working first in local industry (especially those from Moscow province, which was highly industrialized) or as carters hauling goods to the city; later they might find permanent work in city factories or shops.[25] A joiner at Trekhgorka, born in Moscow province, studied at the school run by the factory where his widowed mother worked, was apprenticed in Moscow for three years, and worked in a small shop in a provincial town for almost ten years before finally settling permanently in the capital city. Women too entered the urban world by stages. The wife of a metalworker surveyed in 1924 reported she had been employed as a nursemaid from age seven to fifteen, then returned home. But restless, she soon was attracted by the lure of factory life and departed for Moscow, where she worked until her marriage. Another woman textilist began her working life as a nursemaid in Moscow at age thirteen; at seventeen she began as an apprentice at a rural textile factory, returning to Moscow finally with her

[22] E. O. Kabo, *Ocherki rabochego byta*, p. 55; *Leninskii zakaz*, p. 100; *Vpered*, 13 July 1917; *Sots.-Dem.*, 14 July 1917; *Izv. MSRD*, 28 July 1917, 4 August 1917.

[23] Antonova, chap. 2; B. N. Vasil'ev, "Sotsial'naia kharakteristika fabrichnykh rabochikh."

[24] Ivanov, "Preemstvennost' fabrichno-zavodskogo," p. 80.

[25] Ibid., p. 73.

husband. A third woman worker, a seamstress from age fifteen, spent her childhood commuting between Riazan province and Moscow with her father and mother, who were domestic servants.[26]

The class of peasant-workers was becoming increasingly urbanized by 1917 in Russia. There were many juridical "peasants" in Moscow who had never seen the village of their parents. Even in the 1870s, Ivan Belousov, son of an artisan, was "a peasant as were my father and grandfather, but, except for short periods of time, I never lived in the country."[27] As early as 1902, one-third of the peasants living in Moscow had lived in the city ten or more years.[28] The rapid industrialization of the succeeding years might have driven down this percentage, as peasants came to the city from villages, other towns, and other factories, but the absolute number of long-term residents probably continued to grow. At Prokhorovskaia Trekhgornaia, for example, which grew from 5,700 workers to 7,400 from 1905 to 1914, the proportion (as well as the number) of veteran workers increased from 28 percent in 1905 to 48 percent in 1914.[29]

One key indication of the degree of urbanization of peasant-workers was their relationship to the family property. By rights, from 1861 most members of the peasant class had some landed property, however meager, however unworkable. Even in 1917, most workers retained some connection with their village property. Only in extreme cases, and in occupations with seasonal unemployment such as construction, did workers themselves engage in agriculture, but the land could be worked by other family members or rented out for cash income. In 1918, one-fourth of all surveyed workers in Russia reported they owned land in 1917, ranging from 13 percent of printers to 35 percent of food workers.[30] In addition, since this survey was taken after the Soviet land decree, it is a safe guess that many landed workers had already left the factories and were not counted as workers, so the real proportion of some form of landholding among Moscow workers in 1917 was probably higher than 27 percent.[31]

The land owned by workers served as a piece of insurance, a place to go in case of strikes, layoffs, and other hard times, a way to feed family members more cheaply than in the city, a vacation spot for the frequent religious holidays that interrupted the factory calendar. The wife of a Moscow weaver, a hereditary worker herself, tenaciously held onto an allotment of land in her husband's village that was farmed by his relatives.

[26] Kabo, pp. 48, 65, 69.   [27] Belousov, p. 8.

[28] Ivanov, "O soslovno-klassovoi strukture," p. 339.

[29] Rozhkova, "Trekhgornoi manufaktury nakanune imperialisticheskoi voiny," p. 174. A veteran worker was defined as working in the same place for five or more years.

[30] TsSU, *Trudy*, vol. 26, vyp. 2, *Fabrichno-zavodskaia promyshlennost' v period 1913-1918 gg.*, 1926, pp. 120-121. These figures are for all of Russia; statistics presented by Ivanov ("Preemstvennost' fabrichno-zavodskogo," p. 134) indicate that Moscow oblast had a higher than average rate of landholding. This is as close as one can come to Moscow city.

[31] See Appendix A on statistical sources.

To keep it, she reported, she often visited there, bringing gifts from Moscow despite the expense.[32] Although most workers who owned land reported that family members were involved in farming (about two-thirds, regardless of industry), like the weaver's wife above, few workers themselves engaged in agriculture. By 1917, less than 2 percent of all industrial workers departed for farm work each summer.[33]

The transition to a full-time labor force was a product of three processes that occurred around the end of the nineteenth century. The mechanization of many factories required owners to employ a year-round labor force in order to make efficient use of the capital invested in machinery. This mechanization was partly responsible for the crisis of overproduction which in turn engendered the depression that was a second stimulus for a full-time work force: workers could not afford to leave their jobs for the summer because there were too many other unemployed workers who could be hired in their places. Finally, the Stolypin reforms of 1907 to 1914 encouraged peasant-workers to consolidate their land, sell it, and leave permanently for the city. Moscow province, which supplied about a quarter of its capital city's labor force, had the highest rate of land consolidation during the Stolypin period of any province in European Russia.[34]

Since land served as a bit of insurance for workers and provided some maintenance as well, why would even full-time workers relinquish their claims to property? For many peasants, especially young men, the city was so much more attractive a place to live that they wished to sever all ties with the village. Rural life was terribly dull, said one worker in 1924; there were nothing but "meowers and howlers."[35] Rural local government (*zemstvo*) officials in the late nineteenth century observed that young boys in rural Russia begged their parents to apprentice them in St. Petersburg,

> Once a boy has been trained in Peter he certainly won't fail to work outside the village. The great ease and high pay of a trade in the capital, the total ignorance of agricultural work on the part of all youths who have been to St. Petersburg, all the fascinations of life in the capital, and, finally, habit and the example of departing comrades—all this compels every inhabitant of Chukhloma and Soligalich to rise with the spring tide and ride the crest of the huge wave moving toward St. Petersburg, Moscow, and other centers.[36]

[32] Kabo, p. 56.

[33] TsSU, *Trudy*, vol. 26, vyp. 2, pp. 130-133. Koz'minykh-Lanin reports similarly low departure rates for Moscow province workers in 1908 in *Ukhod na polevye raboty*.

[34] Antonova, pp. 195, 53.

[35] Kabo, p. 30.

[36] Quoted in M. I. Tugan-Baranovsky, *The Russian Factory in the Nineteenth Century*, p. 410.

Other sources suggest that ownership—especially in poor agricultural areas—was simply a burden. Taxes and redemption payments were due regardless of whether or not the land was farmed; "the ideal of almost every factory worker living in the city," wrote an observer in 1901, "was the desire to enter the ranks of the landless, that is, to break with the land and not have to pay taxes or make payments in kind."[37] Peasants around Moscow especially, who were already assimilated into the production process, had little use for property owning. Eduard Dune, a Bolshevik worker who spoke at peasant meetings around the factory suburb of Tushino in 1917, observed that peasants were more interested in the question of wages than of land: "The village willingly listened to speeches against the war, for peace, but showed no interest at all in the redistribution of landlords' estates. . . . For Moscow-area peasants, land was a heavy burden, binding them to their miserable little plots and to their homes in the country."[38]

What was the effect of this land connection on the political lives of workers? Bolshevik agitators in Moscow in 1917 dismissed certain groups of workers as being "tied to the land" and of no use in the revolutionary struggle.[39] True enough, a single worker or working family with close ties to the village would have relatively little time to spend on political activity in the city, but if the land were truly a burden, it might be sensible for the encumbered worker to expend the effort to ease restrictions on selling his land. Situations among workers differed, depending on economic need, conditions in the village, and family life, but as will be seen later in this study, workers with rural connections were less inclined to engage in political activity than their city-born comrades.

Migrant or not, urban workers tended to reside close to fellow workers in the same factory. Proximity both on and off the job surely fostered close social relations among co-workers, facilitated the transmission of information and ideas, and quite possibly increased workers' propensity to act in a concerted manner.[40] Direct evidence apart from an 1882 census is scanty, but several sources confirm that workers tended to live near their places of work. An urban geographer has deduced from the records of St. Petersburg that the expense and limited availability of public transport, plus the time involved in walking great distances, obliged workers to live in close proximity to their factories.[41] Although Moscow tramlines

[37] Aleksei Smirnov, "Zemledelie i zemledelets tsentral'noi promyshlennoi gubernii," p. 177.

[38] Eduard Dune, "Zapiski krasnogvardeitsa," pp. 40, 68.

[39] *Oktiabr'skie dni v Sokol'nicheskom raione*, p. 33.

[40] See Michael P. Hanagan, "The Logic of Solidarity: Social Structure in La Chambon-Feugerolles," *Journal of Urban History*, vol. 3, 1977, pp. 409-426.

[41] James H. Bater, "The Journey to Work in St. Petersburg, 1860-1914," *Journal of Transport History*, n.s. 2, 1974, pp. 214-233.

extended into the factory districts by 1917 and some workers commuted long distances to work, this pattern was undoubtedly true for Moscow.[42] Almost all of the forty-five striking workers from the Zelig and Meier factory (above) lived within easy walking distance of the plant; twenty-five were clustered within two blocks of their place of work. A different source confirms this pattern. Of sixty-nine worker candidates for public office in 1917 whose addresses and places of work were known, fifty-five lived within a kilometer's walk of their factories, and only five lived farther than two kilometers away.[43]

In the case of artisans, many of them lived right in their workshops, sleeping on the benches at which they worked during the day.[44] Enlightened factory owners, among them Prokhorov, Tsindel, and Giubner, constructed housing for their workers, in which lived about one-third of the Moscow factory work force in 1907.[45] In many cases, these were barracks accommodating two hundred fifty to three hundred workers at a time. Workers on different shifts sometimes doubled up on the beds, which were often nothing more than a series of boards built across a room. The rows of beds occupied virtually the entire floor space. Workers in the young women's barracks at Trekhgorka had no place else to go during their free time, so they read, sewed, and gossiped on these beds. Prokhorov also provided barracks for married couples and for families with children; couples lived eight people to a room, a family with children shared with one other such family.[46] Calico curtains divided the living space of the occupants. But other factories were not even this generous; the Ferman factory in the suburb of Alekseevskoe forbade couples to live in its housing, and married workers had to seek more expensive private housing in the village.[47]

Most workers in fact lived in private housing, ranging from a shared cot (*koika*) in the corner of a room to an entire (if small) rural cottage. Subleasing was common—a family renting an entire apartment (usually defined as one or more rooms plus a kitchen)[48] would rent out rooms or

---

[42] *Sovremennoe khoziaistvo g. Moskvy* has a map of the tram lines opposite p. 416 (it is also an excellent street map of Moscow); Eduard Dune, for example, lived in Moscow and commuted daily by train, along with other co-workers, to his factory in Tushino.

[43] The strikers' addresses are given in TsGAOR, f. 63, ed. khr. 25 T1/1916, ll. 40-42. Factory addresses are given in *Spisok fabrik*. Candidates are listed in *Vpered*, 21 September 1917.

[44] Belousov, p. 43; Bater, p. 223.

[45] I. M. Koz'minykh-Lanin, *Vrachebnaia pomoshch' fabrichno-zavodskim rabochim g. Moskvy*, table 2a. Thirteen of the above worker duma candidates—19 percent—lived in factory housing.

[46] Kasitskaia and Popova, p. 178.

[47] *V oktiabr'skie dni Oktiabr'skogo raiona*, p. 21.

[48] *Usloviia byta rabochikh v dorevoliutsionnoi Rossii*, p. 116.

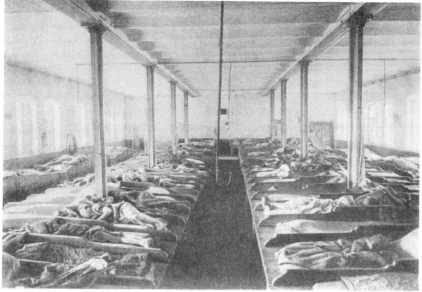

4. Men's dormitory at the Prokhorovskaia Trekhgornaia manufacture, early 1900s. Such facilities were provided by a small proportion of Moscow manufacturers.

corners of its single room to other lodgers, which brought in some extra income for the family. Much of the housing occupied by workers was probably similar to the apartment of a metal roller in E. O. Kabo's 1928 study. Since 1910, this worker had lived in a two-room flat located in a two-story wooden building with a total of eleven apartments housing eighty people. A common kitchen with an old Russian stove provided cooking facilities for the eighty people; the only source of water was a tap located on the street.[49]

Regardless of the type of housing, living space was small: the rooms shared by four couples at Trekhgorka measured thirteen feet square; rooms for families—which housed up to twelve people—were just twelve feet square.[50] The families in the Kabo study who lived in prerevolutionary housing lived in areas of from nine feet square to fifteen feet square. (Admittedly, there was a serious housing shortage in Moscow in the 1920s, but these dimensions are not appreciably smaller than those of the so-called model barracks at Trekhgorka.)

A worker's living arrangements determined how he or she could eat: single workers living in barracks generally ate in boarding (*kharchevye*) artels attached to the factory; families in barracks and workers living

[49] Kabo, pp. 38-39.   [50] Kasitskaia and Popova, p. 178.

privately either cooked their own meals or ate at inns or traktiry. Either way, the average worker spent about 50 percent of his income on food in the years before the revolution; this percentage went up to 70 percent in 1918.[51] The staple food, regardless of where one ate, was bread; workers consumed an average of two and a half pounds of it per person per day. Bread—primarily black bread (consumption of white bread tended to rise with income)—provided 55 percent of a worker's daily caloric intake.[52]

Boarding artels provided contemporary statisticians with much of the data used to calculate workers' eating habits.[53] Artels were usually organized by workshop, so that workers with similar incomes partook of the same fare. Members paid a daily amount—in 1913 ranging from nineteen kopecks per day for women to twenty-nine kopecks for skilled mechanics—which was deducted from monthly wages. At Trekhgorka, the meals consisted of a piece of black bread for breakfast (tea and sugar had to be purchased separately), cabbage soup with meat and kasha with oil for dinner (the main meal), and meatless soup and kasha for supper. These were occasionally supplemented by pickled cucumbers, herring, lamb, or potatoes. At the Giubner factory artels, the variety was somewhat greater; macaroni and vermicelli were sometimes substituted for bread. Tea in Russia, as in industrializing England, was a favorite beverage. Although it provided no nutritional value, it at least warmed the stomach, and in rural textile mills, workers spent up to 8 percent of their entire annual budget on tea.[54]

Although the quality and variety of artel food was poor, at least it was hot; artel boarders ate a hot meal at least six days a week, but their co-workers who cooked for themselves ate hot food only about three times each week. Families with non-wage-earning mothers, presumably those of longer-term urban workers, also more frequently ate meals that were both hot and more nutritional. The type of food consumed at home, however, was about the same as in artels: soup, kasha, potatoes, and on special days pastries, sausage, or fowl.[55] In either case, with such a large

[51] A. St., "Biudzhet moskovskogo rabochego," pp. 1-5; *Usloviia byta rabochikh*, p. 107.

[52] F. D. Markuzon, *Zarabotnaia plata fabrichno-zavodskikh rabochikh g. Moskvy v 1913-1920 gg.*, p. 30; N. A. Svavitskii, "Pitanie moskovskikh rabochikh vo vremia voiny"; Roger Koenker, "Was Bread Giffen?"—all discuss the relationship between income and bread consumption.

[53] See Svavitskii; I. M. Koz'minykh-Lanin, *Artel'noe kharchevanie fabrichno-zavodskikh rabochikh moskovskoi gubernii* and *Artel'noe kharchevanie rabochikh odnoi shelkokrutil'noi fabriki v Moskve*.

[54] Kasitskaia and Popova, p. 181; Svavitskii, nos. 9-12, pp. 70-100. On tea, see Thompson, *Making of the English Working Class*, p. 318.

[55] *Usloviia byta rabochikh*, pp. 110, 113; M. Davydovich, "Khoziaistvennoe znachenie zhenshchiny v rabochei sem'e"; Krupianskaia, "Evoliutsiia semeino-bytovogo uklada rabochikh," p. 280.

part of their income already going to buy food, workers were especially vulnerable to the rapid rise in food costs which occurred in 1917.

Such crowded conditions and harried lives were mitigated in part by increased incomes; well-paid workers could afford greater privacy and more stable family lives. Workers at the lower end of the wage scale were more likely to live communally and if they married at all, to keep their families away from the city. Scarce urban housing was a major reason why the number of married male peasants in Moscow in 1897 was more than twice as great as the number of resident married female peasants.[56] Even in 1918, only 74 percent of married workers lived with their entire families, although only 10 percent of workers lived completely alone.[57] In separated families, younger children tended to live in the country with relatives until the children were of school or apprenticeship age. Trekhgorka worker Morozin was born at the Tsindel factory where both parents had worked from age twelve, but he was immediately sent to the country to live until he was six years old.[58]

Urban workers married later than rural workers or peasants. A study of rural workers in the Urals around 1900 suggests most women there married between ages eighteen and twenty; any woman over twenty was considered too old for a regular marriage and had to find a widower to marry if she could.[59] In Moscow in 1914, however, the median age of marriage was well above twenty years old: half of the women getting married that year were 22.6 years or older; the median age of marriage for men was 25.9.[60]

One effect of the late marriage pattern was to prolong the period of youth when young men and women had no family responsibilities. This stage of delayed maturity was especially pronounced for those urban workers who did not have the village connections either to provide a spouse or to shelter one if the young family could not survive together

[56] *Pervaia vseobshchaia perepis'*, p. 59. A much fuller discussion of family life in Moscow can be had from R. Johnson, *Peasant and Proletarian.*

[57] TsSU, *Trudy*, vol. 26, vyp. 2, pp. 106-111. The figures pertain to workers of all parts of Russia and in all industries. Shoemakers and chemical workers were relatively more separated from their families, woodworkers relatively less so (despite the fact that very few woodworkers were native-born city dwellers in Moscow).

[58] R. Johnson, "Nature," p. 115; V. I. Romashova, "Obrazovanie postoiannykh kadrov rabochikh v poreformennoi promyshlennosti Moskvy," p. 155.

[59] See *Pervaia vseobshchaia perepis'*, vol. 24, on marriage rates by age for Moscow province peasants. On Urals workers, see V. Iu. Krupianskaia and N. S. Polishchuk, *Kul'tura i byt rabochikh gornozavodskogo urala*, p. 74.

[60] *Ezhemesiachnyi statisticheskii biulleten'*, 1915, no. 7, p. 29. In Western Europe, the age of marriage in the nineteenth century was much later—twenty-five and twenty-six for women in England and France. See Peter Laslett, "Age at Menarche in Europe since the Eighteenth Century," and Pierre Goubert, "Historical Demography and the Reinterpretation of Early Modern French History."

in the city. This prolonged period of independence for urban youth was yet another reason why urban workers became more involved in revolutionary political activities.[61]

Additionally, historical demographers point out that when women marry late, family sizes tend to be small—to delay marriage reduces a woman's number of childbearing years.[62] And indeed, the number of children born to urban workers was smaller than for noncity workers. In Moscow in 1897, only 38 percent of working-class families had three or more children; in the Urals mining towns, where women married before they were twenty, 60 percent of the families had three or more children. And in agricultural Ruzskii uezd, almost half of the families had three or more children.[63]

Family size was determined not only by birth rates but by mortality rates as well. One Soviet scholar estimates that between fifty-nine and sixty-four children of every hundred died before the age of ten in worker families.[64] The infant mortality rate—deaths in the first year of life—was appalling: fifty-one children out of one hundred died before their first birthday. (A rate of twenty-seven infant deaths per hundred is considered to be high.)[65] For Moscow, as was noted in Chapter One, birth and death rates were highest in the outlying working-class districts of the city, and much of the mortality rate was accounted for by children's deaths. In the summer, one-half of all deaths were of children under the age of one year.[66]

The statistics paint a grim picture of working-class life in the early twentieth century, one which is reinforced by personal accounts of family life of urban workers. Expenditures usually exceeded income; workers lived by borrowing; there was little food to go around. There was no room indoors for children to play, so they roamed the corridors or the courtyards of their dwellings. In many worker families, both husband and wife were employed at factories, and supervision of the children was entrusted to neighbors. "Kitchen mothers" received a ruble or two a month to look after the neighbors' children; some families hired nannies (*n'ianki*) in exchange for room and board, and sometimes for a small salary besides. The family of P. P. Starostin, for example, who lived in a shared twelve-by-twelve-foot room in the Trekhgorka barracks, hired a young relative to live in and look after its five children.[67]

[61] See Koenker, "Urban Families."

[62] E. A. Wrigley, *Population and History*, p. 19.

[63] *Pervaia vseobshchaia perepis'*, tetrad' 2; Krupianskaia, p. 275; *Pervaia vseobshchaia perepis'*, tetrad' 1, table 2.

[64] Krupianskaia, p. 275.

[65] I. Veger, in *Izv. MSRD*, 24 May 1917; Wrigley, p. 20.

[66] *Ezhemesiachnyi statisticheskii biulleten'*, 1912-1916.

[67] *Usloviia byta rabochikh*, pp. 55-58, 135; Davydovich, p. 123; Kasitskaia and Popova, p. 180.

The longer a family lived in such circumstances, the more one could expect a rebellion against them. But environment alone was not enough to produce a successful rebellion. Workers needed to learn to marshal their forces, to calculate what should be done, but these needs required a clear understanding of the nature of things to be changed. Acquiring this understanding, as part of the workers' striving for knowledge and self-improvement, was a unique and integral element of urban life.

Consequently, working-class children who were reared in Moscow benefited from a special feature of urban life which potentially outweighed the negative aspects of the urban environment. The greater access to education in the city not only provided a degree of economic mobility for the working class but also injected an intellectual element into working-class culture which helped to distinguish the truly urban worker from the recently migrated factory hand.

Rural children were served by three-year zemstvo and church schools, which taught the bare rudiments of literacy, but the city of Moscow provided more extensive educational opportunities. In 1910, the city required four years of schooling for all urban children, boys and girls. By 1912, municipal schools enrolled some fifty-six thousand students, about 62 percent of the city population of the school-attending age of eight to eleven.[68] Moscow's system of postprimary education also distinguished the city schools from those in the country, and indeed in other cities as well. Early in the twentieth century, Russian schools had begun to offer a supplemental two-year course for graduates of primary school: Moscow, in addition, offered vocational training, which in 1910 attracted about 20 percent of primary school finishers. For boys there were commercial, tailoring, and several mechanical and woodworking schools. All of these schools also devoted some time to general education subjects: language, arithmetic, and science. For girls, twelve municipal handicraft schools taught sewing and a smattering of design, along with general subjects. The length of a course in these schools was four to five years.[69]

A primary school education was not only an added benefit of urban life, but a prerequisite for many jobs in the city; apprentices in the gold and silver trades were required to be literate, for example,[70] and the vocational schools would accept only primary school finishers. This requirement especially was a strong impetus for equal education for boys and girls; in the Moscow province villages, for example, only 30 percent of the pupils were girls, but in Moscow, girls were almost half of the primary school population—47 percent.[71] Judging by the workers surveyed in 1924, one

[68] *Stat. ezhegodnik*, p. 15; *Sovremennoe khoziaistvo g. Moskvy*, p. 34.

[69] *Sovremennoe khoziaistvo g. Moskvy*, pp. 79, 85-91.

[70] N. Mamontov, "Dvizhenie rabochikh po obrabotke blagorodnykh metallov v Moskve," p. 183.

[71] *Pervyi obshchezemskii s"ezd po narodnomu obrazovaniiu 1911 g.*, p. 247.

could conclude that general education for girls did not have a high priority but vocational training did. The son of a textile worker was preparing to study literature at the university, but the daughter was allowed to attend primary school only because her sewing classes required literacy. The father's attitude was, "Young girls, what's the use of them? They go and get married and that's that." Indeed, of the fourteen worker families in Kabo's study (all of whom reached school age before 1917), the average husband had had three years of schooling, the average wife had had none.[72]

The aim of the school system was to impart the essentials of literacy, and a third-grade education was considered to be sufficient preparation for working life. This was minimal enough, but it was a great improvement over pre-reform Russia. Basic literacy was therefore more widespread among younger age groups. Koz'minykh-Lanin's study of literacy among Moscow province factory workers shows that the percentage of literate workers fell from a high of 82 percent for workers aged twelve to fifteen (93 percent of males in this group) to 27 percent for workers sixty years and older.[73]

In 1917, furthermore, there were discrepancies in the literacy levels of workers in different industries: Table 2-1 shows (regretably only for Russia, as a whole, not for Moscow alone) literacy rates with median ages by industry. The impact of the literacy requirement for girls' sewing schools can be seen in the high literacy rate for female clothing workers— 65 percent is well above average. Note too that the median age of these workers is relatively low. Conversely, for men, the oldest (in terms of workers' median age) trade, rare metals, has the lowest literacy rate (this despite the requirement of literacy for apprentices).

Even though three years of school provided only rudimentary literacy, and statistical sources do not really define the category "literate" (*grammotnyi*), the result of the educational system was that most male workers in Moscow had at least a third-grade education and possessed some tools with which to continue to learn if they chose.[74] In fact, young urban workers sought to distinguish themselves from the mass of workers by adopting the style of the intellectuals. Such young workers dressed like students on their days off, and these workers furnished their rooms with writing desks, books, and portraits of famous authors.[75]

Reading circles were extremely popular among young radical workers

[72] Kabo, p. 58.

[73] Koz'minykh-Lanin, *Grammotnost' i zarabotki*, p. 6.

[74] No literacy data for Moscow workers are available. The literacy rate for male Muscovites in 1912 was 81 percent; it was 81 percent in a working-class district, Butyrki, and 88 percent in upper-class Prechistenskii. For women, the literacy rate was 57 percent (52 in Butyrki, 68 in Prechistenskii). *Ezhemesiachnyi statisticheskii biulleten'*, 1915, no. 10, pp. 27-30.

[75] Krupianskaia, p. 283.

TABLE 2-1. *Literacy and Median Age by Industry*
(FOR RUSSIAN WORKERS)

	Men		Women	
Industry	Percent Literate	Median Age	Percent Literate	Median Age
Mineral	67	31.1	53	20.1
Rare metals	53	40.5	37	39.0
Metal	73	33.4	48	25.9
Machine	72	33.5	51	25.4
Wood	66	33.8	40	18.5
Chemical	68	35.9	49	23.7
Food	77	33.2	45	23.8
Animal byproducts	79	36.9	54	22.1
Leather	61	33.9	41	24.2
Cotton	61	34.9	31	28.0
Wool	59	35.5	33	25.9
Silk	64	37.7	34	28.1
Clothing	73	29.8	65	23.2
Paper	70	34.4	50	25.7
Printing	91	30.1	83	23.6
Power and water	75	36.1	46	31.6
Total	68	33.4	38	25.9

SOURCE: TsSU, *Trudy*, vol. 26, vyp. 2, table 6.

in the years before the revolution, and some workers availed themselves of evening classes offered at the Prechistenskie school and other centers. The municipal government also provided free public libraries located throughout the city. Such institutions offered aspiring worker-intellectuals the tools they needed for further development. These workers were a small minority of the city's working population, but they were a significant social group. The total enrollment in the Prechistenskie courses in 1911 was only seventeen hundred, but these students were primarily young urban men and women who furnished recruits for informal and illegal study circles, trade unions, and political parties.[76] The entree of this group of potential revolutionary leaders into the activist milieu was facilitated by the urban workers' quest for learning and the ability of the city to provide these opportunities.

The Prechistenskaia library, open to nonstudents, attracted a substantial number of workers. In 1910, it recorded over nineteen thousand readers, about one-third of them workers and artisans. Over one-half of all readers were between the ages of eighteen and twenty-five.[77] On the other hand, municipal authorities complained that the city's public libraries drew

[76] *Sovremennoe khoziaistvo g. Moskvy*, p. 77; M. Dergachev, "Iz proshlogo (1915-1917 gg.)," in *Nashe rozhdenie*, ed. A. Atsarkin and A. Zverev, pp. 19-28.

[77] *Prechistenskie rabochie kursy*, p. 100.

mainly school children and students and that the number of working-class readers had declined since 1905.[78] Clearly not all workers were possessed with the thirst for learning, but for those young urban workers most eager for knowledge, possibilities did exist.

Differences among the worker clientele at the Prechistenskaia library and elsewhere in working-class quarters are apparent from the kind of reading matter selected. At Prechistenskaia, belles lettres (especially Leo Tolstoy, Turgenev, Dostoevski) and natural science appealed most to working-class readers.[79] In municipal libraries, especially those in working-class districts, most of the readers preferred nonserious literature; workers here selected stories of bandits and adventure more often than natural philosophy, and newspapers and popular magazines more than novels and treatises.[80]

Kabo questioned the workers in her study about their newspaper-reading habits before the revolution: most commonly cited were *Moskovskii listok*, a "boulevard" newspaper that featured serialized adventure stories, and *Russkoe slovo*, a more serious liberal paper. In 1917, working-class readers turned away from *Russkoe slovo* in favor of the new socialist press, which better appealed to their interests, but even in 1917, the number of working-class readers of the socialist press was not large. A report from the local soviet in Khamovniki raion complained that the language of so-called worker newspapers was too difficult for workers to comprehend.[81] *Moskovskii listok* also received some abuse in workers' letters to socialist papers, but other boulevard newspapers—*Gazeta-kopeika* and *Trudovaia kopeika*—enjoyed continued popularity.[82]

Reading these newspapers, *lubok* novels (small illustrated booklets of serialized popular fiction), and magazines was one form of recreational activity for workers, but there was in fact little leisure time. When the majority of workers left work, they turned to two far more popular preoccupations: alcohol for men and religion for women.

Over 90 percent of married male textile workers consumed alcoholic beverages, according to a St. Petersburg study done in 1908;[83] they spent

[78] *Sovremennoe khoziaistvo g. Moskvy*, p. 100.

[79] *Prechistenskie kursy*, pp. 99-100, 106.

[80] *Sovremennoe khoziaistvo g. Moskvy*, p. 100; I am grateful to Jeffrey Brooks for the information on some of these points. See his "Readers and Reading at the End of the Tsarist Era."

[81] *Sots.-Dem.*, 17 March 1917; *Vpered*, 16 March 1917.

[82] *Gazeta-kopeika* was the more sensational of the two: it was featuring a serial on Rasputin at the time of the February revolution, and it continued throughout the year to focus on murders, suicides, and other *skandaly*. It did, however, feature a "town meeting" column beginning on March 24, to which workers were invited to contribute their ideas about the eight-hour working day.

[83] *Usloviia byta rabochikh*, p. 52.

ten to thirty rubles a year, primarily on vodka. (Family men spent 3 to 5 percent of their income on alcohol, single men up to 10 percent; but since family incomes in general were larger, the amount spent was actually about the same.)[84]

Even though one of the first acts of the tsarist government upon the outbreak of war in 1914 was to ban the sale of alcohol, this prohibition did not seriously affect the Russian worker's favorite pastime. In Tushino, near Moscow, there was so much vodka available by 1916 that it was no longer profitable for peasants to make home brew; and before the February revolution, not an evening or a Sunday passed without vodka or beer.[85] In south Russia, an observer noted in 1916, "drunkenness and card games serve as the constant recreation of workers in their leisure time, especially on pay day, which never goes by without fighting, and frequently even killings."[86] In 1917, the Petrograd Soviet saw the need to publish an appeal against drunkenness, reprinted in the Moscow Menshevik party's *Vpered*: "Drunks have appeared on the streets, in railway carriages, in factories, in barracks. Vodka is seen in cities and villages, in the rear and at the front." The message was, stop drinking and save the revolution.[87]

Outsiders and organized workers saw this chronic drunkenness as the workers' escape from their intolerable working conditions and treated alcoholism as an evil to be shunned by class-conscious workers. Along with factory safety, alcoholism was a major concern of legal trade unions before the war. On summer outings of workers from the Prechistenskii school, participants pledged to abstain from alcoholic consumption on penalty of losing the privilege to join future outings. People's Houses, established by Moscow public groups before and during the war, were designed in part to keep working-class youths from spending their free time in drinking, stealing, and other debauches.[88]

Women workers were of less concern to the moralists, for their usual

[84] This pattern continued after the revolution: one woman in Kabo's study spent forty-five rubles a year—6 percent of her income—on spirits and one ruble on cultural items, such as books and schooling (Kabo, p. 50).

[85] Dune, pp. 17, 29.

[86] Quoted in Kir'ianov, *Rabochie Iuga Rossii*, p. 104.

[87] *Vpered*, 18 May 1917. And while most recollections of 1917 focus on party building and the great events of October, one woman worker at the Military Artillery plant remembered how her husband spent the revolution: getting drunk and arguing at factory meetings (M. K. Filipenko, "Moia zhizn'," p. 18). An office worker in a military plant (probably Sanitarnaia tekhnika in Presnia) recalled a similar scene on the eve of the October revolution: "Many of those present were drunk and argued violently among themselves about the political situation. Others, who were working while drunk, endangered the expensive instruments and machinery" (Jan M. Yarkovsky, *It Happened in Moscow*, p. 193).

[88] Sher, pp. 456-457; *Prechistenskie kursy*, p. 267; *Izvestiia Moskovskoi gorodskoi dumy*, 1917, no. 2, p. 51.

form of escapism—religion—was passive; it did not hinder their ability to work, and it posed no social dangers. Consequently, government and employers encouraged religious practice within the factory and without. In Russian villages, with the onset of industrialization women rather than men most ardently supported the church, and this continued to be true of workers in the city. Men tolerated religious customs, for they were an integral part of social life,[89] but it was the women who attended church and carried on religious traditions.[90] For one woman worker at Trekhgorka, the mother of eight, religion was all she knew outside the factory and her family.[91] At the Abrikosov confection plant in Sokol'niki, where most of the workers were women, M. T. Andreeva, having paid a ten-ruble bribe to be hired in the first place, was soon fired for refusing to cross herself. Work there began and ended with prayers, an icon hung over the factory gate, and workers took subscriptions to buy oil for the icon lamps in each workshop. As late as 1922, when the plant's new manager ordered the icons removed, the workers protested.[92]

In general, there was little time for recreation. Young people, whose workday was regulated by law, had more opportunity, and they took advantage of what recreation was available. The Preobrazhenskii People's House reading room, established to serve all the working population of the Bogorodsk-Cherkizovo area, was inundated with readers between ages fifteen and twenty; within the club were story-telling circles, choral-singing groups, drama and balalaika circles. Evening schools, such as Prechistenskii, and cultural clubs also offered similar kinds of recreation. The Trekhgornaia textile factory boasted a factory orchestra and a dramatic circle (which had occasionally enjoyed the attendance of Leo Tolstoy).[93]

In many factories that employed men and women, the two sexes were

[89] Sula Benet, ed., *The Village of Viriatino*, p. 127. "Social religion" included the customs of matchmaking and marriage ceremonies. See G. V. Zhirnova, "Russkii gorodskoi svadebnyi obriad kontsa XIX-nachala XX v."

[90] Krupianskaia, p. 286. Religious holidays were closely entwined with the work year. Contracts and work schedules, as discussed in Chapter One, were based on the religious calendar. In 1918, the new labor contract signed by the Moscow union of tailors (one of the more urbanized occupations) included twenty-five religious holidays and three secular ones (International Workers' Day, the anniversary of Bloody Sunday, and the anniversary of the October revolution [Gosudarstvennyi arkhiv moskovskoi oblasti (hereafter GAMO), f. 633, op. 1, d. 6, l. 3]). In some factories, well into the twentieth century women still observed the old peasant religious customs, such as the holiday of Semik, the Thursday before Trinity Sunday. On this day, the women would decorate their mechanical looms with branches and green saplings (Krupianskaia, p. 286).

[91] I. Kor, ed., *Kak my zhili pri tsare i kak zhivem teper'*, p. 8.

[92] *Moskovskie pishcheviki*, pp. 63-64.

[93] *Izvestiia Moskovskoi gorodskoi dumy*, 1917, no. 2; *Prechistenskie kursy*; G. A. Arutiunov, *Rabochie dvizhenie v Rossii v period novogo revoliutsionnogo pod'ema 1910-1914 gg.*, pp. 101-103, 254-257; *Materialy k istorii Prokhorovskoi Trekhgornoi manufaktury*, p. 410; Krupianskaia, p. 288.

kept separate within the factory, so young people had to meet one another away from work. Clubs, evening schools, and illegal circles provided some opportunity to get together; another favorite activity was to stroll in the outskirts of the city. Favorite spots for strolling and courting were the amusement park beyond the Trekhgornaia barrier in Presnia and the Annenhof palace grounds in Lefortovo.[94] In 1917, it appeared that one reason for the popularity of the socialist parties' youth groups was not so much compatible ideology as the chance to meet people of the opposite sex. Anna Litveiko, a young worker and organizer of the Presnia Bolshevik youth group, was chagrined to discover that what motivated her co-workers to join was the news that the girls could meet young men from other factories at the group's meetings.[95] In summertime, excursions to suburban spots were popular; before the revolution, conspiratorial groups used such outings as covers for their underground meetings, but the excursions continued in 1917. Trade unions, political parties, and youth clubs all organized weekly outings to rustic spots such as the Izmailovskii menagerie and the Sparrow Hills.[96]

The urban environment posed special problems for the growing working class of Moscow. Crowded housing restricted normal family life; the high cost of housing and food and the predominance of working wives made ordinary housekeeping difficult; the pressure of work limited social and recreational possibilities. But these harsher aspects of the environment were mitigated by the special opportunities available in the city, especially cultural and educational activities. The longer a worker's experience in the city, the more likely he or she could learn about these opportunities and take advantage of them.[97]

The general urban environment was not alone in shaping the culture of the working class. Work experience was also a central element in the formation of workers' attitudes toward their own lives and toward the milieu in which they lived.

FACTORY LIFE IN MOSCOW

Factory life for most Russian workers began from about the age of sixteen (child labor under sixteen had been prohibited since 1882) and continued

[94] Krupianskaia, p. 283n.   [95] Litveiko, p. 7.

[96] The socialist press in 1917—*Sotsial-Demokrat, Vpered, Trud, Zemlia i volia, Proletarii, Izvestiia MSRD*—regularly published news of activities such as these.

[97] Examples of this process can be found in the memoirs of Prechistenskie students. V. N. Gruzdev was a house painter at the Einem confections factory when a colleague who spent his evenings reading instead of drinking told Gruzdev about the courses (*Prechistenskie kursy*, p. 255). P. P. Nikitina lived near Moscow all her life and attended illegal mass meetings in the woods near her home in 1905. Seven years later she enrolled in the courses in response to a newspaper announcement (pp. 263-264).

until age or infirmity forced retirement.[98] Apprenticeship in artisan shops began at about age twelve, or as soon as most youths had completed the three-year municipal or village schools. Apprentices "studied" for three to five years, although the quality of instruction was not uniform. In some shops, the main duties of apprentices consisted of running errands for the journeymen, fetching food, and delivering goods.[99] The contracted term completed, apprentices were entitled to be journeymen; after three years in this intermediate status, and having reached age twenty-one, the journeyman could become his own master.[100]

Some factories, especially the printing and metal industries that required technical expertise, also took on apprentices, but more commonly a new worker was hired as a common laborer (*chernorabochii*), and was expected to acquire skills as best he or she could. New workers learned from their parents or from relatives and co-workers; P. Sleptsova, who entered Prokhorov's Trekhgorka at age sixteen, paid a cousin three rubles a month to teach her the work in the weaving section[101] (yet another function of zemliachestvo). P. Vorob'ev ruefully remembered the success of his on-the-job training: at age seventeen, he had found work as an assistant toolworker (slesar) at the Morits Palm works in Presnia. After six months, by mid-1917, he thought he knew the trade and moved up to the Tilmans plant, where the wages were higher. "I had become used to toolmaking—I knew how to mark, to file, to cut metal. . . . The foreman, when we weren't arguing [about politics], and the senior workers in the shop often told me that I worked no worse than any true slesar." But Vorob'ev was skilled only in relation to his co-workers at Morits Palm and was a failure at the more precision-oriented Tilmans plant. In the end, the Tilmans foreman allowed him to stay on as an apprentice, but at a lower wage than he had received at Palm.[102]

Trade schools were rare. The city's eighteen technical schools in 1911 trained 1,336 girls and 686 boys, but they could not accommodate all who wished to learn.[103] Some factories—Trekhgorka and Tsindel among them—provided schools for children of their workers, but these were generally reserved for the sons of highly skilled workmen and foremen.[104]

Russia had of course embarked upon industrialization relatively recently, and in the rush to modernize, industrialists were compelled to recruit great numbers of workers with no prior experience with factory

[98] Rashin, p. 275; V. Ia. Laverychev, *Tsarizm i rabochii vopros*, p. 60; R. Johnson, "Nature," pp. 77-90.

[99] Belousov, p. 17; N. V. Strelkov, *Avtobiograficheskii ocherk bol'shevika-podpol'shchika*, p. 7.

[100] *Remeslenniki i remeslennoe upravlenie v Rossii*, pp. 8-10.

[101] See Rashin, p. 610, on the inheritability of trades; and Kor, p. 29.

[102] *Moskva v trekh revoliutsii*, pp. 303-314.

[103] *Sovremennoe khoziaistvo g. Moskvy*, pp. 87-90.   [104] Krupianskaia, p. 279.

life. Not only were these new proletarians without the specific skills required for modern factory jobs but they also lacked the sense of discipline and time important for rational factory operation.[105] One indicator of this situation was the low productivity of Russian factories. In the nineteenth-century cotton industry, for example, 16.6 Russian workers were needed for every thousand spindles, compared to 3 workers per thousand spindles in England.[106] Bernard Pares cites the observations of a foreign engineer about Russian labor: "Everywhere in Russia, in factories as in offices, but little work is gotten through in the day. Factory hands smoke cigarettes whilst at their business. To knock off one and a half hours from the working day would make but little difference to them." To which Pares adds a footnote, "I have heard the same story from officials, employees of the Zemstvo, and businessmen, and I have often seen how true it is."[107]

Perhaps lax work habits were the workers' revenge for long hours and meager pay; if they could not have time for leisure after work hours, they would have it on the job. But the owners sought to maximize the return on their investments. To exact a higher rate of production and to enforce time discipline, managers employed two devices: wages were paid on a piecework rather than on an hourly basis and fines were imposed for all kinds of infractions of rules, such as late arrival, drunkenness, or work stoppages of any kind.[108] The limits of these fines were controlled by the factory inspectors, and the money collected was supposed to be used for the welfare of the workers, but abuses could and did occur. For example, the Dvina uniform workshop's factory committee in 1917 demanded the right to go through fine books back to 1912 and to force the directors to return improperly assessed fines.[109]

The institution of piecework reduced the need for constant supervision to ensure that workers were really working. At the Provodnik rubber plant, the manner of payment was set by agreement between foreman and worker; but if the worker chose to work for a daily wage, he was so hounded by the foreman that he soon preferred the old piece rate.[110] Other enterprises used the "task" (*urok*) system, which set a specific number of pieces to be turned out in a given period. If the task was not completed, a large fine was assessed.[111]

A worker's income came primarily from wages, which were paid more or less according to skill and experience and were subject to the constraints

[105] See E. P. Thompson, "Time, Work-Discipline, and Industrial Capitalism," 1967, no. 38.

[106] Tugan-Baranovsky, p. 306.

[107] Bernard Pares, *Russia between Reform and Revolution*, p. 415.

[108] Ibid., p. 397.   [109] *Moskovskii soiuz rabochikh-portnykh*, p. 27.

[110] Dune, p. 7.   [111] *Moskovskii soiuz rabochikh-portnykh*, p. 27.

of supply and demand. Master hand-loom weavers were not in great demand after the introduction of power looms, for example, and could not command the same wage as a master mechanic whose skills were still needed. Among occupations and social groups, there were great differences in wage levels. Married workers with families tended to have higher incomes than single workers; low-paid workers could not afford to raise families in the first place.[112]

Compensation came as well in the forms of housing and credit at the company store. Factories that did not provide dormitories for their workers sometimes paid those living privately a monthly housing supplement. Factory owners also sponsored cooperative shops on their premises, which supplied workers' needs somewhat more cheaply and conveniently than the open market.[113]

Wages for men were uniformly higher than for women, regardless of occupation. In no industry did women earn more than three-fourths of what men earned in 1914 (and the difference increased even more during the war).[114] In 1917, striking workers occasionally demanded equal pay for equal work, but even then it was common to find a sex-linked pay differential in the workers' own demands. Although women as a class were less skilled than men and therefore concentrated in industries that required little training, such as textiles or tobacco, their low wage was not simply a measure of their productivity.[115] Most women, whether single or married, worked to supplement family earnings, and were willing, apparently, to work even for miserable wages. And Russian industrialists were not loathe to exploit this willingness.

There was no legislated protection for women laborers in Russia before the revolution; only in August 1917 did the Provisional Government prohibit night work for women as well as children factory workers (and this prohibition did not affect the thousands of seamstresses who worked at home).[116] Young women were subject to the whims of their foremen, as in the case of a section at Provodnik where the foreman hired only beautiful young girls and allegedly did what he liked with them.[117] Working mothers were poorly provided for: women might lose their jobs if they stopped working to bear and care for children. Poor pre- and postnatal care was one cause of the alarmingly high infant mortality rate discussed

[112] *Usloviia byta rabochikh*, p. 30.

[113] Kir'ianov, *Rabochie Iuga Rossii*, p. 69; R. Johnson, *Peasant and Proletarian*, pp. 87-90.

[114] S. G. Strumilin, *Zarabotnaia plata i proizvoditel'nosti truda v russkoi promyshennosti*, pp. 70-71.

[115] On women workers in Russia in general, see Glickman, "The Russian Factory Woman."

[116] *Vrachebnaia zhizn'*, 15-22 October 1917.

[117] Dune, p. 8. The foreman was eventually fired.

above.[118] Trekhgorka was one of the very few factories to provide any kind of nursery facilities for working mothers.[119]

The biggest plants provided medical facilities for all workers, although observers considered medical care to be inadequate and safety precautions nonexistent.[120] Ten Moscow factories in 1907 had their own hospitals with beds for from two to sixty-six patients, and 274 others had at least medical personnel available. But for the majority of workers in small factories and artisan workshops, there was no readily available medical aid.[121] Generally, health conditions were very poor. Lung disease was a hazard in all occupations, but especially in poorly ventilated textile factories, where the air was hot, arid, and dusty. Of a thousand slesars in machine-building factories in Moscow, according to a study covering the years from 1911 to 1915, sixty-five suffered from lung disease. For slesars in textile factories, the rate was four times as great.[122]

Accidental injuries and burns were another hazard: slesars in textile factories suffered 440 injuries per thousand workers; the rate for male cotton spinners was 232 per thousand workers. In general, men were more prone to such accidents (but not to burns) than women, suggesting that in the textile industry, at least, men performed the more dangerous functions.[123]

Such hazardous work conditions in Russian factories added one more element to the growing list of workers' grievances which were to fuel the labor movement in the early years of the twentieth century. Wages, hours, all manner of conditions within the work place provided labor organizers with concrete goals with which to attract workers to the idea of organization. The rise of industrial labor and its inevitable abuses was thus accompanied by a rise in the labor movement, expressed both in workers' organizations and in the less-organized strike movement, both growing out of work-centered grievances. The experience of this prerevolutionary labor movement provided workers with the framework to build legal

---

[118] *Vrachebnaia zhizn'*, 15-22 October 1917.

[119] *Materialy k istorii Prokhorovskoi Trekhgornoi manufaktury*, p. 407.

[120] *Vrachebnaia zhizn'*, 15 August 1917.

[121] Koz'minykh-Lanin, *Vrachebnaia pomoshch' fabrichno-zavodskikh*.

[122] S. M. Bogoslovskii, *Boleznost' fabrichno-zavodskikh rabochikh moskovskoi gubernii*. Tuberculosis affected a small share of the working population, according to this study; it was more common among family members than among workers themselves, which itself is a clue to conditions in barracks and lodgings.

[123] Ibid. This difference between the sexes can be seen in another study of the incidence of death in various industries for the period from 1913 to 1916. Overall, eight of a thousand male workers died, and only five of every thousand women workers died during this three-year period. The tobacco industry was the most lethal: its male death rate was sixteen per thousand (V. Zaitsev, "Zabolevaemost' i smertnost' rabochikh v Rossii v 1913-1916 gg." The figures are for overall death rates, not just job-related fatalities).

institutions in 1917, but just as important, the history and the dynamics of the earlier labor movement shaped workers' conceptions about economic and organizational questions, about their role in the society and the political process. It is therefore important to understand just how this pre-1917 labor movement developed in Moscow, to realize to what extent the political and social issues and structures of 1917 emerged from the past experience of Moscow workers.

THE LABOR MOVEMENT IN MOSCOW BEFORE 1917

For the purposes of this study, the labor movement can be considered in two parts. Labor organizations, such as trade unions, cooperatives, mutual-aid societies, and workers' socialist parties constituted one element—although a very limited one in terms of numbers of participants. More widespread but less organized was the movement of strikes, both political and economic, by which can be charted the waves of protest which peaked with the overthrow of the autocracy in 1917. These two elements, although distinct, of course interacted with each other. Trade unions, illegal political parties, and other groups provided the leadership for otherwise inarticulate striking workers; their press provided information that gave workers in isolated locales explanations for their grievances and examples for them to follow. And the grievances expressed by striking workers provided the organizations with signals about what was important to the mass of Russian workers whom they hoped to organize.

Labor organizations were the leading edge of the movement. Their participants included members of the radical intelligentsia and "advanced workers"—generally skilled, educated urban workers who had gained some familiarity with the history of the European labor movement and with the basic ideas of socialism and political organization. Such workers were the products of the nineteenth-century *kruzhki*, educational and political circles of workers, often led by *intelligenty*, which dated back in Moscow at least as far as the 1870s. Out of such beginnings grew illegal political parties, uniting in 1898 as the Russian Social-Democratic Workers' Party, and semilegal, nonpolitical institutions such as mutual-aid societies, whose members collectively provided benefits for one another in cases of death, injury, sickness, or conscription.[124]

Among the first of these in Moscow was the Typographers' Support Fund (Vspomogatel'naia kassa tipografov), founded in 1869. Because so few workers, even in the well-paying printing industry, could afford this

[124] On the origins of the organized labor movement see Zelnik, *Labor and Society in Tsarist Russia*; Richard Pipes, *Social Democracy and the St. Petersburg Labor Movement 1885-1897*; Wildman, *Making of a Workers' Revolution*. On the early labor movement in Moscow, see R. Johnson, *Peasant and Proletarian*, chap. 6; and Sher.

form of insurance, the fund's membership remained small. Less than 4 percent of Moscow's printers joined during the fund's forty-year history to 1909, and the well-to-do members who controlled the organization were concerned primarily about conserving their treasury, therefore minimizing any risk to their capital. It was not the kind of organization that sprang to the defense of fellow workers outside its privileged circle.[125]

Other workers, however, perceived greater benefits to be had in wider worker organizations. This was a particular lesson of conflicts between workers and employers: workers could be more successful if they organized. In the early twentieth century, a Moscow security police official, Sergei Zubatov, recognized this drive toward organization and also the dangers that the drive presented if allowed to merge with the political goals of the underground revolutionary parties. Zubatov's solution was to assist workers in organizing for economic purposes in order to divert their attention from broader changes and to allow the state to aid workers in their conflicts with capital. Despite opposition both from within government and from business circles, Zubatov managed to sponsor unions of textile workers, confectioners, woodworkers, tobacco and perfume workers, and printers in Moscow before 1905. But industrialists succeeded in 1902 in curbing the Zubatov unions' collective-bargaining powers, and the unions were soon reduced to police-sanctioned social clubs. Activist workers in Moscow soon turned to new trade unions, which although illegal addressed workers' real needs; these unions provided the organization necessary for economic improvements or self-defense, and as the 1905 crisis matured, for political discussion.[126]

The trade union, *professional'nyi soiuz*, which in Western Europe had evolved from craft guilds to industrial unions only over painful decades, emerged on the Russian labor scene in a matter of a few years. The first union of Moscow printers, the Union of Moscow Printers for the Struggle for Improving the Conditions of Labor, emerged in the aftermath of a successful citywide printers' strike in 1903, aided by sympathetic Social-Democratic intelligenty.[127] This interplay of workers and intellectuals was characteristic of the formative period of the Moscow labor movement. But such underground unions were of necessity much constrained in their activities, and with the exception of the now-declining Zubatov unions, only a handful of Moscow workers before 1905—several hundred printers—engaged in organized labor activity.

The 1905 revolution changed all this. The immediate response of labor to the crisis of authority was a tumult of strike activity. In Moscow,

[125] Sher, pp. 78-91.
[126] Jeremiah Schneiderman, *Sergei Zubatov and Revolutionary Marxism*; Sher, pp. 128-135.
[127] Sher, pp. 112-125.

industrywide groups of ribbon weavers, furniture makers, and printers met in August and September to coordinate strike activity, and it was from these nuclei that the first generation of trade unions was spawned.[128] In the aftermath of the October Manifesto, which legalized labor organizations, over fifty trade unions were formed in Moscow, ranging from the printers, with four thousand members, to tiny craft unions with very specialized memberships, such as the union of workers in gold-thread production.[129]

Union development continued in the two years after 1905; over forty thousand Moscow workers joined unions during this period.[130] But with society appeased, the government began to reduce sanctioned labor activity. Unions were legal but were required by a law of March 1906 to operate within strictly defined limits. Union leaders were watched by police and frequently arrested for political activities not strictly connected with union business. This precarious situation was not conducive to further union development. Within the confines of the law, however, unions published regular journals (with the participation of sympathetic intellectuals), coordinated economic demands, provided (through a Central Bureau of Moscow Trade Unions) a canteen for unemployed workers, and some unions began to operate placement bureaus. Strikes themselves were outside the law, and so the ultimate recourse of collective bargaining was denied to organized labor.[131]

The performance of the unions was uneven, of course. Some never progressed beyond the registration stage—several names on a charter was their beginning and end. Others held a few meetings, and when tangible improvements did not immediately materialize, members lost interest and the organizations fell apart. As the political climate worsened, unions were able to offer less and less to their constituents, and of the sixty unions that existed in Moscow in March 1907, only fourteen remained by January 1908.[132] Not until 1917 would trade unions attract the numbers of adherents they had had in the ebullient months after 1905.

With the decline of the trade unions after 1907, labor activists separated into two groups. One element concentrated its energies on economic work: cooperatives and workers' insurance funds. The second focused its attention on cultural work (clubs and circles) as a way to prepare a new generation of worker activists in anticipation of an improvement in the

---

[128] Ibid., pp. 161-181; Engelstein, "Moscow in the 1905 Revolution"; Bonnell, "Politics of Labor."

[129] Engelstein, chap. 6. See also Solomon M. Schwartz, *The Russian Revolution of 1905*, p. 142; Iu. Milonov, ed., *Moskovskoe professional'noe dvizhenie v gody pervoi revoliutsii*; and Bonnell, "Politics of Labor."

[130] Bonnell, "Politics of Labor," Appendix 3; Sher, p. 402.

[131] Sher, pp. 248-256.

[132] Engelstein, chap. 6; Bonnell, "Politics of Labor," p. 162.

political climate. Factory cooperatives had existed in Russia since the 1860s, formed as a way to avoid the abuses of company-owned stores, but they received renewed attention after 1907. By 1912, in Moscow, there were 153 worker cooperatives, united under the Moscow Union of Consumer Societies.[133] These cooperatives, some attached to specific factories and others independently attracting members from a given neighborhood, supplied their members with foodstuffs, clothing, and other necessities. The biggest ones even took over the function of producer as well as supplier: the Iamskoe Consumer Society in Butyrki acquired its own bakery,[134] and the umbrella organization, the Moscow Union, owned the Triumf confection factory in Basmannyi. The extent of actual working-class participation in the cooperatives, however, is not clear. Paid employees—those who managed the shops—tended to be intellectuals, and in the dependent factory cooperatives, the factory owners who furnished the basic capital retained some measure of control.[135]

Of far broader impact on the lives of the mass of Moscow workers was the insurance movement, which culminated in the establishment in 1912 of a network of sick funds (*bol'nichnye kassy*). An alternative to the labor movement's preferred state insurance scheme, the funds were financed strictly from workers' and employers' contributions. These funds were organized very much like cooperatives: employers contributed 40 percent of the upkeep and retained a large measure of overall control, but the funds were administered by an elected group of workers and employees.

Decisions about investing the fund and payment schedules for benefits were made by the entire membership at general meetings, meetings at which the members could and did discuss problems other than those purely related to insurance matters.[136] The Simonovskii sick fund, for instance, passed a highly political resolution in 1915 under the pretense of trying to deal with the influx of refugees. The resolution called for an eight-hour workday, a labor exchange, unemployment insurance, and

[133] R. Johnson, *Peasant and Proletarian*, pp. 86-90; P. Garvi, *Rabochaia kooperatsiia v pervye gody russkoi revoliutsii.*

[134] *Trudovaia kopeika*, 22 February 1917.

[135] One such *intelligent*, Ian Grunt, describes his experiences at the Petrovsko-Razumovskii cooperative in "Stranitsy proshlogo." After the revolution in 1917, the cooperatives, like trade unions, greatly expanded their activity; dependent co-ops struggled to become independent of their factory administrations, and local co-ops, such as "Our Shop" in Dorogomilovo, trebled their memberships in a few months. By midsummer, a purely working-class cooperative association—the Central Workers' Cooperative—was created to rival the intellectuals' Union of Consumer Societies. The Moscow Central Workers' Cooperative charged the union with being a "petty-bourgeois" (*obyvatel'*) organization, but the union replied in its defense that 80 percent of its members were workers (*Golos rabochei kooperatsii*, 9 July 1917).

[136] Zh. Z. Falkova, "Strakhovanie rabochikh nakanune i v gody pervoi mirovoi voiny," p. 353.

other job-related demands, but it also demanded freedom of assembly and universal suffrage for municipal elections.[137] Both the Bolshevik and Menshevik parties published legal organs for the movement; they featured articles on the political situation and general labor problems, as well as reports of sick-fund activity in individual factories. By January 1916, there were eighty-nine individual factory funds in Moscow, five district funds, six industrial funds (the one for the confectioners had almost 14,000 members, the single largest sick fund in Moscow), and seven "central" funds with no specific constituency. In all, 144,200 workers, or 77 percent of the Moscow workers supervised by the Factory Inspectorate, were insured by membership in a sick fund.[138] The sick funds thus were easily the largest mass working-class organizations prior to 1917.

The second alternative for former trade unionists, cultural work, affected a much smaller segment of the working population. Educational work had always been an important focus of the Russian labor movement, beginning with Sunday schools in the 1860s and the intelligentsia-led circles of the 1870s. Now, in the post-1905 era, cultural and educational institutions were legalized, and workers emerged from the underground. People's Houses and clubs, whose activities of legal necessity excluded politics, attracted young urban male workers and revolutionary intellectuals who sought to use these clubs to spread surreptitiously their political ideas.[139] The official activities of these organizations included reading, singing, and dramatic circles, social events, and field trips to historical sites.

Despite the ban on political activity (enforced by the omnipresent infiltration of the security police), these institutions served the function of bringing people together to talk about social problems and soon about politics. A Prechistenskie student recalled, "Young people became acquainted with one another at the school, and there soon began among us illegal political work."[140] A dramatic circle at the Dinamo machine factory in Moscow excluded political discussion, recalled one member, but attracted the same set of workers who belonged to illegal trade unions. The circle's repertory included revolutionary poetry. Another dramatic group attached to the Lefortovo metalworkers' union, Unity, boasted fifty members; they performed weekly, often touring the surrounding factory towns to raise money for the union.[141]

[137] I. Menitskii, *Russkoe rabochee dvizhenie i sotsial-demokraticheskoe podpol'e Moskvy v voennykh godakh*, vol. 2, *Konets 1915 g.*, p. 143.

[138] *Ezhemesiachnyi statisticheskii biulleten'*, 1916, no. 2.

[139] I. D. Levin, "Rabochie kluby v Peterburge," p. 101; Arutiunov, pp. 101-103.

[140] *Prechistenskie kursy*, p. 196. The student was A. V. Shestakov, who later became a noted Soviet historian.

[141] *Dinamo: 25 let revoliutsionnoi bor'by*, pp. 46, 63; Sh. N. Ibragimov, "O Lefortovskom raione," p. 161.

By 1914, there was a significant network of such cultural organizations in Moscow. In addition to several evening schools, there was a women's club sponsored by Bolshevik intellectuals, People's Houses such as the one at Preobrazhenskoe, and even four specifically working-class clubs whose names described their official focus: "Intelligent Leisure" (Razumnyi otdykh), "Education," "Enlightenment," "Progress."[142] Almost all of these groups combined culture with a strong flavoring of political discussion, and it is no surprise that many of the workers who emerged as leaders in 1917 had participated in such organizations.

The list of labor organizations by 1914 included sick funds, cooperatives, workers' clubs and schools, as well as illegal trade unions and political party cells. The common feature of all these organizations was that the active members were very few compared to the number of workers in Moscow, and indeed to the number of participants in the strike movement. The activists, as in the trade unions, were most frequently long-time urban workers, many employed in skilled artisan trades.[143] Intellectuals played a major role in their direction, although their interests were not always the same as the workers'.[144] Organizations such as these served as the progenitor of 1917's organizations in two important ways—in personnel and in structure. Despite the debilitating effects of police repression, some participants of the pre-February organizations returned to active life in Moscow after the fall of tsarism. And even though such leadership would actually be a scarce commodity in the massive push to organize in 1917, the prerevolutionary experience provided valuable organizational lessons for the groups to come. The general meeting (police willing) as the source of an organization's legitimacy, the alternative delegates' meetings to decide policy, the election of permanent executive boards and separate auditing committees—these were features of early trade unions, sick funds, cooperatives, and evening schools' student councils that would be repeated in 1917.[145] The multiple concerns of economic improvement, political pressure, cultural work, and social activities also carried over from these early institutions. So even if the active membership in the early Moscow labor organizations was pitifully small compared to the unorganized mass of workers, this early movement did provide some measure of continuity, a base on which to build.

[142] Arutiunov, pp. 254-255.

[143] Bonnell, "Politics of Labor," p. 230.

[144] Sher, p. 145.

[145] P. P. Nikitina described the function of the Prechistenskie school's elected council of students: "In the Delegates' Soviet we learned how to conduct organized meetings and assemblies, how to solve problems in an organized way. There were always on the Soviet a significant group of politically prepared workers, from whom we studied organizational methods and habits. Many of them occupied responsible positions after October" (*Prechistenskie kursy*, p. 270).

The second element of the labor movement, the strike movement after 1900, can be seen as an indicator of growing labor unrest, directed first toward local work conditions and eventually toward the governmental system under which these conditions were permitted to evolve. Three great strike waves characterize this period, all accompanying "revolutionary situations" in 1905-1907, 1912-1914, and finally in 1916-1917, culminating in the February revolution itself. In all three of these waves, according to government sources, political strikers outnumbered economic strikers. For example, whereas 92 percent of all strikers in the period 1895-1904 made economic demands, 64 percent of strikers in the 1905-1907 wave struck for political reasons. Again in 1912-1914, following the massacre by government troops of striking workers in the Lena goldfields, 72 percent of all strikers were political.[146] Political strikes had become a favorite tool of revolutionary parties to commemorate important events and thus to raise the political awareness of workers whose strike impulse was a familiar response to grievances on and off the job. Thus political strikes clustered around the January 9 anniversary of Bloody Sunday, on May 1, or International Workers' Day, and after 1912 on the anniversary of the Lena shootings. They were also provoked by specific occasions: by the prorogation of the State Duma in July 1906, by subsequent duma elections, and in 1914, by the declaration of war on Russia by Rumania.[147] Such strikes were not necessarily the results of agitation and careful preparation; they may also have represented deep feelings of anger and discontent which could most safely and immediately be expressed by walking off the job. Thus during the entire period 1905-1916, 9.5 million Russian workers, an annual average of 65 percent of the work force, went on strike. Political strikes accounted for 62 percent of this total.[148]

The situation in Moscow corresponded to the Russian pattern but with certain variations due to the industrial peculiarities of the region. In scope, the strike movement in Moscow province was much smaller than in industrially advanced St. Petersburg. During the period 1895-1916, government statisticians recorded 17.6 strikes for every Petrograd worker, but only 3.5 for each Moscow province worker.[149] Much of this difference can be explained by the different industrial composition of the two capitals. The dominant industry in St. Petersburg was metalworking, and metalists were by far the most active strikers: for every hundred Russian metalworkers, an average of fifty-six struck each year between 1895 and 1916. The corresponding figure for textile workers, predominant in Moscow province, was twenty-five per hundred, and for food workers, another

---

[146] K. N. Iakovleva, "Zabastovochnoe dvizhenie v Rossii za 1895-1917 gg.," p. 8.

[147] Ibid., pp. 12-14.　　　　　　　　　　[148] Ibid., pp. 5-6, 8.

[149] Ibid., p. 17.

big Moscow industry, only seven of one hundred workers struck each year.[150] These industrial differences can be explained in part by low wages and high numbers of women in less strike-prone industries, but the net result was that Moscow was, by and large, a backwater of the strike movement.

Taken by itself, however, important developments were occurring in the Moscow strike movement during this period. Although 1905 remained the province's peak year in terms of strikers, Moscow shared in the resurgence of strike activity in the 1912-1914 period. Fully 38 percent of the work force struck during 1912, another 36 percent in 1914.[151] And more important, Moscow was becoming more involved in political strikes. According to police reports, 92,000 workers struck to protest the Lena shootings in April 1912; 60,000 responded to the call in November to protest the sentencing of mutinous Black Sea sailors. The next year, 50,000 Moscow workers struck on May 1 (April 18 Old Style). The year before, prior to the Lena strikes, there had been no May Day strikes in Moscow. And in 1914, when the strike movement in Petrograd threatened on the eve of the world war to engulf the old regime, 92,000 Moscow workers again joined the July wave of political strikes.[152]

Of special interest in the Moscow strike movement is the composition of the strikers. In the years of the immediate prewar upsurge, metalworking provided the greatest number of strikers and the industry with the greatest participation rate. In 1914, for example, 96,000 Moscow province metalists struck, a colossal 178 percent of the metalist labor force. Second in terms of participation were workers in paper and printing, where 99 percent of the work force went on strike. This proportion corresponds to the situation in St. Petersburg, where metalists and printers also led the strike movement.[153] Despite the fact that strikes were generally unorganized, it was still the industries with the greatest number of skilled, well-paid, literate, and urban workers which led the strike movement. This phenomenon serves to emphasize the relationship between the small organizational movement and the mass strike movement on the eve of the war and the revolution. However small, labor organizations and political parties helped to catalyze the larger movement of strikes with their press, agitation, and leaders. The first mass strike in Moscow, for example, had been in the printing industry in 1903. The strike led to the formation of the first printers' trade union, it will be recalled, and set a standard for strikes and organization to come. Throughout the bleak years of repression between the 1905 and 1917 revolutions,

---

[150] Ibid., p. 24.   [151] Ibid., table 3, p. 63.

[152] Arutiunov, pp. 128, 147, 188, 273, 375; cf. Haimson, "Problem of Social Stability," 1965, no. 1.

[153] TsSU, *Trudy*, vol. 7, vyp. 2, table 8, pp. 140-141.

it was the printers who remained organized and who, with the metalists, led the strike movement.

Of equal significance is the overwhelming proportion of political strikes by printers in the final prewar years. In Russia overall in 1914, for example, 82 percent of metalists but 90 percent of printers struck for political reasons. In 1915, when war pressures and patriotism sharply reduced the overall share of political strikers to 28 percent (from 74 percent in 1914), three-quarters of the striking printers had political motives, but only 56 percent of striking metalists did.[154] This militant behavior of the printers will seem all the more remarkable when one examines the moderate role played by this group after the fall of tsarism. It illustrates just how radically the February revolution changed the context of Russian political life.

THE IMPACT OF THE WAR ON THE WORKING CLASS

Russia's mobilization for war in July 1914 sent shock waves throughout the country. Industrial production had to be rechanneled to serve the military effort, and manpower had to be found to fill the ranks of the gigantic tsarist army. Some 5 million men were mobilized in the first six months of the war; by 1917, 15 million had been called up, including 4 million city dwellers.[155] The standard Soviet interpretation of the impact of the war is that the drafted male factory workers were replaced by unskilled women, youths (*podrostki*), and children (*maloletki*), and also by petty shopkeepers seeking to avoid military service by landing positions in draft-exempt jobs. This exodus of skilled and experienced male workers, argue Soviet historians, is to blame for the lack of firm class consciousness that characterized the early months of the revolution in Moscow and elsewhere.[156] In order to present a general overview, the previous discussion of the composition of Moscow's work force has purposely ignored the shifts that occurred in the labor force between 1914 and 1917. But now the point has come to examine what, in fact, was the effect of the mobilization and the war economy on the nature of Moscow's industrial work force.

There is, unfortunately, no direct information on who was drafted and who took the places vacated by mobilized workers. Some authors assert as many as 40 percent of all workers were drafted,[157] but more thorough analysis shows that the number is probably much lower. A careful study by Soviet scholars Leiberov and Shkaratan concludes that only 17 percent

[154] Ibid., table 13.
[155] Michael T. Florinsky, *The End of the Russian Empire*, p. 34; Gaponenko, p. 75.
[156] I. I. Mints, *Istoriia velikogo oktiabria*, vol. 1, 1967, p. 667.
[157] Gaponenko, p. 75.

of the Petrograd labor force was actually called up during the war years,[158] and following their lead, one can make a comparable calculation for Moscow. According to the 1897 census, 67 percent of male industrial workers were between the ages of seventeen and thirty-nine (the draftable age interval in 1914).[159] Although 1897 is the last year before 1914 for which age by occupation is available, the proportion of workers in that age group probably did not change much since the share of that age group in the entire male population between 1897 and 1912 changed scarcely at all.[160] In 1912, which is as close as one can come to 1914, there were about 243,300 male industrial workers of all ages in Moscow; assuming that the proportion of seventeen- to thirty-nine-year-olds was the same as in 1897, that calculation would result in 163,000 workers of draftable age in 1912, or 40 percent of the entire work force, male and female. However, not all eligible workers were drafted; exemptions were granted for important defense workers, for illness, for family need. In the Moscow Industrial Region, 40 percent of eligible workers were in fact deferred from military service because of work in defense plants.[161] (No information is available on medical or family exemptions in Moscow. Leiberov and Shkaratan calculate, however, that 9 percent of the first group of recruits in Petrograd were dismissed on medical grounds.) Thus, only 60 percent of the eligible 163,000 workers were actually drafted, or 97,300. If 9 percent of these were subsequently found to be unfit, the final number of drafted Moscow workers would be 88,500, or 27 percent of the total industrial work force. While not so high as other estimates, the removal of over one-quarter of the labor force certainly suggests a significant upheaval.

Not all branches of industry were equally affected: 53 percent of draft-age metalists were draft exempt, but only 37 percent of eligible textilists were exempt. However, because the textile industry as a whole employed so many more women than did the metal industry, only 18 percent of all textilists left for the army, as opposed to 28 percent of all metalists.[162] Manuscript evidence for one Moscow metal plant, Guzhon, corroborates this rough estimate of mobilized metalists: during the war, 1,100 of its 4,000 workers—28 percent—were drafted.[163]

Despite the mobilization of one-quarter of its labor force, Moscow's industrial army continued to grow during the war years as military orders

[158] I. P. Leiberov and O. I. Shkaratan, "K voprosu o sostave petrogradskikh promyshlennykh rabochikh v 1917 g."
[159] *Pervaia vseobshchaia perepis'.*
[160] Ibid.; and *Stat. ezhegodnik*, p. 15.
[161] Leiberov and Shkaratan, p. 52n.
[162] The calculations follow the same pattern as above.
[163] Gaponenko, p. 76. The same source, however, indicates that 37 percent of workers at an unnamed Moscow textile factory were mobilized.

poured into its factories. Table 2-2 indicates the increase in factory labor during these years for the city of Moscow.[164] As discussed in Chapter One, certain branches of industry expanded during the war, while output and workers at others sharply declined. Thus, the number of metalworkers increased from 24,800 in 1914 to 56,900 in 1917, and textilists declined from 55,400 to 49,400.[165] The total number of metalworkers in this period more than doubled, yet one-fourth of the original number was sent to the army. The mobilization of 28 percent of these workers in 1914 would mean a loss of 6,940 metalists, and in addition, another 32,200 workers had entered the metal industry by 1917. Where did all these workers come from?

TABLE 2-2. *Increase in Moscow Factory Labor Force, 1913-1917*

Year	Workers
1913	148,212
1914	153,223
1915	173,323
1916	196,980
1917	205,919

SOURCE: *Fabrichno-zavodskaia promyshlennost' g. Moskvy*, p. 1.

Some of them were unskilled women and youths. The share of women in the metal industry in the Moscow Industrial Region in 1914 was just 12 percent; by 1917 this had risen to 24 percent. Children under twelve years old and youths twelve to sixteen had been less than 1 percent of the metalist labor force in 1914 but were 13 percent in 1917.[166] Others, to be sure, were draft-evading members of the middle class; although when a commission in 1917 got down to the task of verifying exemptions, relatively few workers were found to be unlawfully deferred.[167]

Some of the increase in the metal-industry work force came from evacuated plants from the western provinces: 5,740 workers were associated with the evacuated metal plants recorded by the Factory Inspectorate, and many more of the 42,000 adult male refugees surely found work in

[164] An identical table can be found in *Stat. ezhegodnik*, p. 171. Note the discrepancy between the figure of 148,000 factory workers in 1913 and the number of 165,184 given by the 1912 census (see Chapter One). There is no unified set of statistics concerning the labor force, but presumably these are at least internally consistent and give an indication of the direction of change in the labor force, if not the exact magnitude.

[165] *Fabrichno-zavodskaia promyshlennost' g. Moskvy*, p. 1.

[166] E. Mindlin, "Izmeneniia chisla, sostava i oplaty truda rabochikh moskovskogo okruga za 1911-1916 gg.," p. 50.

[167] *Soldat-Grazhdanin* and *Trudovaia kopeika* printed only partial results of the commission's work, so this statement cannot be absolutely certain.

other Moscow metal plants.[168] In addition, some mobilized workers' military duties turned out to be factory work; the workshop of heavy seige artillery (Mastiazhart) in Lefortovo employed over 3,000 soldiers evacuated from the artillery shops of the western fortresses.[169] Prisoners of war were also pressed into factory work, 4,100 of them in munitions factories alone in the Moscow region.[170] Finally, military authorities eventually realized that skilled workers were of better use in factories than in trenches, and so some, at least, of the 7,000 drafted Moscow metalists soon came marching home again.[171]

What then was the ultimate change in the composition of Moscow metalists? Scholars would like to know more about the social background of those who were drafted and those who replaced them, but one can guess that it was the experienced but unessential chernorabochie males who were the first to go. The metalists who remained were probably polarized into a group of highly skilled specialists, bolstered by evacuees from the west, and a group of unskilled female and adolescent workers. If it was the specialized metalworkers who were leaders of the labor movement before 1917, as appears to have been the case, then their ranks were probably the least affected by the disruption of mobilization.

This pattern of polarization in metalists' labor forces probably held true for other industries as well, but since the information is no better for them than for metalists, it would be inexpedient to hypothesize further. But there does exist fairly specific information on the change caused by the war in one Moscow textile factory, Trekhgorka, so one can look to see if the effects were the same there.

Overall in Russia, the share of men in the textile industry fell from 42 percent in 1914 to 32 percent in February of 1916.[172] At Trekhgorka, the share of men fell only from 60 to 56 percent of the work force, but the total number of workers fell from approximately 7,400 to 5,700, largely at the expense of male workers. The number of men of draft age fell by one-half: there were 3,348 of them in 1914 and 1,627 in 1917.[173] Positions formerly held by men went to women during the war: the dye preparation, chemical laboratory, and mechanical sections had employed only men in

[168] *Spisok fabrik; Ezhemesiachnyi statisticheskii biulleten'*, 1916, no. 2.

[169] *Velikaia oktiabr'skaia sotsialisticheskaia revoliutsiia*, vol. 1, *Sbornik vospominaniia uchastnikov*, pp. 454-463. (Hereafter *Velikaia oktiabr'skaia sotsialisticheskaia revoliutsiia* [*vospominaniia*].)

[170] *Rossiia v mirovoi voine*, p. 85.   [171] Florinsky, p. 34.

[172] Tsentral'noi Voenno-promyshlennyi komitet, otdel po obezpecheniiu promyshlennykh predpriiatii rabochim sostavom, *Materialy k uchetu rabochago sostava i rabochago rynka*, vol. 1, p. 34. According to sick-fund data, however, the change for Moscow was smaller—from 49 percent in 1912 to 46 percent in 1916 (*Stat. ezhegodnik*, pp. 68-70; *Ezhemesiachnyi statisticheskii biulleten'*, 1916, no. 2).

[173] Rozhkova, "Trekhgornoi manufaktury v 1917 g."

1913; by 1917, the share of women in these sections averaged 20 percent. The mechanical section, which employed the skilled workmen who kept the machinery running, was crucial to the running of any textile mill, and one would expect these workmen to receive deferments to stay and work in the factory. In fact, by 1917, only 15 percent of the workers in this section at Trekhgorka had worked there since before the war. But Trekhgorka's mechanics were notoriously underpaid, and this turnover in mechanical personnel did not necessarily signify that these skilled workers were drafted—only that they could have taken their skills to other factories that offered both deferments and higher wages.[174] The engravers (*gravery*) were another highly skilled group of workers at Trekhgorka, but this skill was specific to the textile trade, and engravers could not change jobs as readily as metalworkers. Here, the workers remained exclusively male, 78 percent of whom had worked at the factory since before the war. (To be sure, the total number of engravers fell, so in fact only one-half of the engravers in 1914 were still working there in 1917.)[175]

The net effect of the wartime mobilization in the textile industry was less severe than in the metal industry because textile plants had fewer draft-eligible workers. But the evidence of Trekhgorka shows a definite shift toward younger and female labor, a shift that was surely replicated in other plants. All things being equal, one would expect that these new workers would have less experience in the work force and less of a tradition that might stimulate political activity in the future.

This hypothesis is supported by an examination of the overall shift in the Moscow male and female populations between 1912 and 1917. For example, of 133,000 males aged fifteen to nineteen residing in the city in 1917, almost half had not lived there five years earlier when the ten- to fourteen-year-old age group included only 68,000 males. Although not all of the newcomers were workers, this comparison does suggest that a correspondingly large share of workers in this age group was not of urban background. On the other side of the coin, there was a net loss of almost 20 percent in the fifteen- to nineteen-year-old age group of males of 1912, young men who were ages twenty to twenty-four in 1917. Those young men who had spent their adolescence in the city were no longer in residence, replaced by even younger men of nonurban origins. The pattern repeats itself with respect to women; the biggest net increases came in the young-adult age group. Over 100,000 more women of the prime

[174] Rozhkova, "Trekhgornoi manufaktury nakanune imperialisticheskoi voiny," p. 174. Indirect confirmation of the mobility of skilled males comes from M. Romanov, "Rabochii sostav i ego dvizhenie v promyshlennykh predpriiatiiakh g. Moskvy v period voiny," who shows that men changed sick funds (i.e. factories) more frequently during the war than women did.

[175] Rozhkova, "Trekhgornoi manufaktury v 1917 g."

working ages of fifteen to twenty-four lived in Moscow than there were eleven- to twenty-year-olds five years before.[176]

These figures do not describe only the working population, of course, and not all new workers were necessarily of rural stock. Some of the newly hired women may have been ex-workers themselves, soldiers' wives or widows who had stopped working in order to raise families but who went back to work when their men left home. And some of the youths were probably brought up within factory barracks, learning their skills at factory schools; these workers would be more attuned to urban and factory ways than the peasant youth freshly arrived to "boil in the factory cauldron."[177] So within these younger age groups as well, one would expect to find a polarization between the newly employed city youths and women and the large numbers of outsiders who must also have found work in the expanding war economy.

The demands of the Russian war machine necessitated some major shifts in industrial production: metalists, chemical workers, leather workers, and tailors were needed to produce munitions and equipment for the army; the textile, wood, food, and mineral industries, which were not as important, declined.[178] The combined effect of the mobilization of the army and the mobilization of a defense industry resulted inevitably in a severe labor shortage, felt most sharply in specialized defense factories. A labor survey in 1916 reported: "There are on the market no workers in leather production—saddlers, harness makers, and bootmakers, no spinners or weavers. In addition, no specialists such as solderers, stampers, copper workers, tinsmiths, and also experienced rollers, pattern makers and turners can be found at the present time for any amount of money."[179] The local voluntary labor exchange turned out to be a clearinghouse for unskilled laborers; any skilled worker could easily find work without bothering to register with the exchange.[180]

When the demand for a commodity exceeds its supply, the price generally rises, and wages for the most highly skilled workers in Russia did indeed rise during the war years. Although available data on workers' wages are inconsistent, incomplete, and further confused by the inflation of the wartime period, it is possible to make a rough calculation of the impact of the war on the real wage levels—the standard of living—of workers in different industries in Moscow.

The historical debate about the change in the standard of living—regardless of the specific group of workers—centers on the relationship

[176] *Stat. ezhegodnik*, p. 15.   [177] Romanov, p. 7.
[178] *Fabrichno-zavodskaia promyshlennost' g. Moskvy*, p. 2.
[179] Tsentral'no Voenno-promyshlennyi komitet, *Materialy k uchetu rabochago sostava i rabochago rynka*, pp. 55, 58.
[180] Ibid., p. 58.

between the money (nominal) wage paid to the laborer and the price of
the goods he must buy with that wage. Thus, for the period between the
revolution of 1905 and the outbreak of war in Russia, K. A. Pazhitnov
shows that nominal wages rose by 29 percent and the price of bread by
19 percent, so that the real wage—the worker's purchasing power—increased during the period. But using a more detailed survey of the movement of prices, A. I. Utkin shows a decline in the real wage; not only did
prices rise faster than wages, he says, but other costs, such as fines,
increased as well. He also contends that the increasing share of bread in
the workingman's diet is further proof that the standard of living was
declining over these years.[181]

The vitality of the debate over the eighteenth- and nineteenth-century
English laborer's standard of living is clear warning that this issue cannot
be conclusively settled for Russia in the twentieth century.[182] Clear
"proof" that real wages rose or fell in a given period can always be offset
by arguments about "quality of life"; crowded, filthy housing vitiates
apparent rises in real wages, whereas improved health services and street
lighting may offset a fall in the real wage.[183] In the end, the important
aspect of the standard of living is how its change affects the worker himself;
does he perceive himself better or worse off, and how does this perception
affect his behavior? But these perceptions cannot easily be observed, and
the quantitative estimate of changes in real wages can at least provide a
gross indication of the direction of the changes in the standard of living
during the war—were workers in Moscow very much worse off or much
better off, and indeed, did all workers share the same experience?

The change in nominal wages for Moscow, which F. Mindlin examines
in a 1919 article, indicates a phenomenal rise in workers' wage levels.[184]
The machine workers' annual wage rose from 469 rubles in 1913 to 1,062
in 1916 and to 2,382 in 1917, so one might conclude, with Mindlin, that
the machinists' lives were growing better and better. On the other hand,
when the 1917 ruble is expressed in terms of its prewar value, the picture
is quite different. From 469 rubles in 1913, machinists' wages rose only
to 516 rubles in 1916 and went down to the equivalent of 308 prewar
rubles in 1918.[185] But these official figures reflect a discount rate for the
ruble which was uniform across Russia, and this study is interested pri-

---

[181] K. A. Pazhitnov, *Polozhenie rabochego klassa v Rossii*, vol. 3, pp. 47-49; A. I. Utkin,
"Ekonomicheskoe polozhenie moskovskikh rabochikh posle pervoi russkoi revoliutsii," pp.
41-53.

[182] On the English debate, a summary of the long discussion is in R. M. Hartwell, "The
Standard of Living during the Industrial Revolution."

[183] See, on quality of life for French workers, Jean Fourastié, *Machinisme et bien-être*.

[184] E. Mindlin, "Rabochee vremia i zarabotnaia plata na predpriiatiiakh moskovskoi oblasti
za 1914-1918 gg."

[185] TsSU, *Trudy*, vol. 26, table 15, pp. 156-161.

marily in the specific conditions for Moscow. To determine the change, if any, in real wages for Moscow workers during the war, then, one needs to use the information of the USSR's Central Statistical Administration (TsSU) for nominal wages, but these wages should be weighted by a price index based on the Moscow market prices of the goods that workers consumed.

Information collected about food consumption (see Table 2-3) in six

TABLE 2-3. *Daily Food Consumption of Moscow Textile Workers* (IN FUNTS)

Meat	.64
Fat	.13
Potatoes	.60
Groats	.30
Bread	2.56
Sugar	.16
Salt	.06

SOURCE: N. A. Svavitskii, "Pitanie moskovskikh rabochikh vo vremia voiny," *Vestnik statistiki*, 1920, nos. 9-12, pp. 70-100.
NOTE: 1 funt = 0.41 kilograms; 1 pound = 0.45 kilograms.

large textile factory boarding artels (four from Trekhgorka, two from Giubner), produces a "market basket" of food consumed by the average worker in 1913-1914. Now, using prices for these goods reported in the monthly statistical bulletin of the city of Moscow, one can calculate the cost of this market basket for each year between 1913 and 1917 (see Table 2-4). (This

TABLE 2-4. *Cost of a Worker's Market Basket, 1913-1917*

Year	Daily Cost (Kopecks)	Change (1913 = 100)
1913	24.23	100
1914	26.53	109
1915	31.70	131
1916	49.47	204
1917 (January)	87.51	361

basket does not represent the entire range of goods purchased by workers but serves as a proxy to measure the effect of inflation. Since food expenditures constituted 50 to 70 percent of a working-class family's budget, changes in the cost of food can be assumed to be representative of changes in the cost of living generally.)[186] Setting the cost of this basket of goods in 1913-1914 equal to one hundred, one can calculate how much prices rose and then compare that rise to the increase in workers' wages. This

[186] Kabo; *Usloviia byta rabochikh*; A. St.

procedure requires two simplifications that deserve some explanation. First, it assumes that the contents of the market basket remained constant during this period, when in fact, as relative prices changed, workers changed their eating habits: a 1916-1917 market basket contained only half the amount of meat and one-third the amount of potatoes (whose price on the Moscow market had soared) of the 1913-1914 basket.[187] Secondly, this is an average market basket for all Moscow workers, based on a very limited number of textile workers. The cost of the basket for workers who consumed more meat and less bread in 1913 would have risen more than for those workers who lived on bread and little else.

Table 2-5 shows the result of these calculations for thirteen industries for which there is information about wages. The first two columns represent the change in wages from 1913 to 1916 and the relationship between

TABLE 2-5. *Change in Real Wages of Moscow Workers, 1913-1916*

Industry	1916 Wage (1913 = 100)	1916 Wage ÷ 1916 Prices	1917 Wage (1913 = 100)	1917 Wage ÷ 1917 Prices
Mineral	186	.91	523	1.49
Rare metals		(included under metalists)		
Metal	232	1.14	537	1.49
Wood	164	.80	274	.76
Chemical	217	1.06	664	1.84
Food	205	1.00	659	1.83
Animal byproducts	166	.81	498	1.38
Leather	247	1.21	1,072	2.97
Textile	210	1.03	703	1.95
Clothing	198	.97	877	2.43
Paper	204	1.00	577	1.59
Printing	165	.81	431	1.19
Power and water	183	.90	387	1.07
Construction	277	1.36	354	.98

SOURCES: Wages from TsSU, *Trudy*, vol. 26, vyp. 2, table 15; price index derived from Svavitskii, "Pitanie moskovskikh rabochikh vo vremia voiny," and *Ezhemesiachnyi statisticheskii biulleten'*; construction workers' wages from *Ezhemesiachnyi statisticheskii biulleten.'*

NOTE: The 1916 change in prices, with 1913 price equaling 100, was 204; the 1917 change (January only) was 361.

the change in wages and the change in prices. If the change in wages was greater than the change in prices (that is, if the real wage increased), the value in the second column would be greater than one. As the second column shows, industries were divided about equally between gainers and losers. Leather workers, metalists, builders—who were in great demand for defense work—received wages high enough to offset the in-

[187] Svavitskii.

creasing cost of living; woodworkers and tailors, whose ranks were swollen by the women entering the labor force, did not.[188]

The results for 1916 differ quite a bit from those given by the Central Statistical Administration's "prewar rubles," which show real wages uniformly declining, regardless of industry. Pazhitnov's study indicates a uniform rise in real wages, at least until the middle of 1917.[189] But my results conform to the expectation that workers in industries with growing production did not fare so badly, in terms of wages, during the war. Under the hypothesis that a decline in wages stimulates revolutionary activity, it would be appropriate to look to see what role those industries with declining wages played in the revolutionary movement of 1917.

Changes in real wages can tell only part of the story of the impact of the war on Moscow workers. They say nothing about the declining quality of food on the market, the long hours waiting at bakeries only to find there is no bread to be had, the loss of wages due to shutdowns in production because of lack of fuel or raw materials. The shortages in food and other necessities did not become serious until the autumn of 1916, with the first sign of a meat shortage. By February 1917, bread was to be rationed at one pound per person per day. The prices of cabbage and potatoes more than doubled between September 1916 and February 1917; the cost of charcoal almost tripled. Prices were only part of the problem. The peasants, many of whom were in the army, were unable to produce the grain required for military and urban needs; the rationing of bread in Moscow was a response to short supply, not to high price. In January 1917, the city received only one-half of its normal daily requirement of flour. Furthermore, the increase in the number of women in the work force meant there were fewer nonworking family members to cook and to shop. Workers who did not board in artels were faced with problems like that reported at the tea factory Karavan in early February 1917. To wait in the bread line in the morning meant being late for work, so

---

[188] The second set of columns shows the 1917 level of wages and the difference between the change in wage and change in prices. This suggests great gains for the workers in 1917, but the information is simply not reliable. Sometimes the negotiated wage increases were never paid, and strikes and long-term layoffs significantly lowered the level of take-home pay; in any case, the wage increases reported here are an average for the entire year, while the price reflects the level for January only. There is no systematic information for prices after January, but available information indicates they rose fastest of all in 1917 (Pazhitnov, p. 54). The price of bread jumped from 2.50 rubles per pood (one pood equals thirty-six pounds) in January 1917 to 4.80 by July, to 80 rubles by January 1918 (Markuzon, p. 44). Furthermore, the introduction of rationing, beginning with meat in October 1916 and bread in March 1917, renders prices irrelevant (S. A. Pervushin, "Dvizhenie vol'nykh tsen v gody revoliutsii [1917-1921]"). One must measure the cost of living in 1917 in terms of time spent standing in line, black market prices, and the cost of fetching one's own food supplies from the countryside.

[189] Pazhitnov, p. 54.

workers waited instead during the noon dinner hour. By that time, what bread there was (this was before rationing went into effect) was gone.[190] Access to food as much as its cost was to be a major concern of workers in the coming months.

Family life during the war years was disrupted as husbands and sons went off to war, and wives and children entered the factories. The Moscow birthrate declined by almost one-third from 1913 to 1917; despite the explosion in the number of Muscovites of marriageable age, marriages in 1916 were down to one-fourth their prewar level (but rose again in 1917).[191] Until the fuel and materials shortages of 1916, factories kept their workers on long hours, nine hours a day plus frequent overtime to fill military orders. (Refusal to work overtime was a cause for dismissal and loss of a worker's draft deferment.) Consequently, there was little time for social activity. No information is available for Moscow, but in southern Russia during the war, many Sunday schools and worker clubs were forced to close because of declining participation.[192]

In fact, especially during the first two years of the war, there was little activity of any kind. There was, at first, a great mobilization of will for the war effort. Reforms, such as expanding the sick funds, were postponed for the duration of the war. Workers willingly worked overtime to defeat the German enemy. When large numbers of women and children fell ill at Trekhgorka, the rumor spread that German agents had poisoned the water system, and a purge of German foremen was carried out.[193] The metalists at Dinamo cooperated in an anti-German pogrom, driving out workers and employees with German surnames.[194] But workers also labored under the threat of being sent to the front if they did not remain quiet; the 40 percent of draft-eligible workers who were deferred were kept under close watch by police to guard against activity that could harm the military cause. Indeed, elsewhere in Russia, half the workers in a factory would be packed off to the army for striking for higher wages.[195]

But news of the government's disastrous conduct of the war filtered down to the working classes of Moscow, and those who cared knew how badly Russia was managing to fight the German enemy. The boulevard press printed gossip about Rasputin and the "German Empress" Alexandra. In the tram depots, the talk turned early to the state of the war: "We talked about how there was no visible end to the war, about Rasputin,

[190] *Russkoe slovo*, 23 and 8 February, 10 January 1917.

[191] *Stat. ezhegodnik*, p. 88.

[192] Kir'ianov, *Rabochie Iuga Rossii*, pp. 59, 101.

[193] Menitskii, vol. 1, p. 263.

[194] V. Fokin, "Moi vospominaniia o partiinoi rabote za 1915-1917 gg.," in *Put' k oktiabriu*, vol. 3, 1923, p. 131.

[195] Kir'ianov, *Rabochie Iuga Rossii*, p. 241.

how the autocracy was thoroughly rotten, and that its end was soon approaching."[196]

Despite the threat of mobilization, strikes both for wages and in protest of the political situation began to increase. The average monthly number of striking workers in Russian defense plants grew from 7,000 in the last half of 1914 to 16,000 in 1915 and to 82,000 in 1916.[197]

In Moscow province, the level of strike activity in 1915 was about the same as the year before, with 40 percent of all workers striking during the year. A major contributor to this total was the normally quiescent cotton workers, of whom 67 percent struck in 1915 entirely for wage-related demands. Nonetheless, a good half of all metalists and nearly the same proportion of printers walked off their jobs; the printers especially were motivated by political demands.[198] Tram workers in Moscow city began to participate in the movement toward the end of 1915; they initiated a strike in September to protest the dissolution of the Duma and in the course of several days were joined by 11,000 more workers in the city, including 7,600 metalists (but no printers).[199] The thirty-two plants involved in this September strike were distributed throughout the city's industrial districts, but within each district the striking factories were closely clustered, suggesting that word-of-mouth was a prime cause of the strike's spread. Police could find no evidence of any prior coordination of the strike, but informal communication among workers was surely facilitated by the existing network of labor organizations, including both illegal trade unions and legal "public" organizations.

Bolshevik party activities had been completely stymied by police repression as group after group emerged, printed a leaflet or two, and disappeared into the Butyrki prison.[200] But despite government efforts to keep the labor movement quiet during the war, its policies in fact aided the spread of antigovernment sentiment. Worker agitators in Petrograd were too valuable as workers to be sent to the front, so their strikes were broken by sending them to other parts of the country. A contingent of Social-Democratic metalists from Petrograd's Putilov works thus came to Dinamo in Moscow in mid-1915, and while the local Social-Democratic group at first mistrusted the Putilovtsy and refused to cooperate with them (to the point that the two groups led separate but equal strikes), the newcomers played an important role in educating the Dinamo workers.[201]

[196] *Moskva v trekh revoliutsii*, p. 168.
[197] *Rossiia v mirovoi voine*, pp. 86-87.
[198] TsSU, *Trudy*, vol. 7, vyp. 2, table 13.
[199] "Rabochee dvizhenie v Moskve v 1914-1917 gg.," pp. 476-477.
[200] Ibid.; Menitskii, vols. 1-2.
[201] *Dinamo: 25 let*, p. 64.

The severe shortage of skilled metalists especially made it possible for labor agitators to move easily from factory to factory to spread political propaganda and to discredit the government's war effort. This mobility can to some degree explain how metalists were so extraordinarily active in political strikes such as that of September 1915; they were far more likely than other types of workers to have established ties with workers in other factories. Then too, despite the dormant state of most prewar worker organizations, there still existed a few mechanisms for worker cooperation and discussion: sick funds, elections to the Workers' Group of the War Industry Committee, and "sanitary trusteeships" created in 1915 to deal with health problems in the Moscow suburbs.[202] Trade unions still existed, some even by police-sanctioned charter, but the most active ones tended to be small neighborhood unions.[203] The citywide heirs of the 1905-1907 unions were mostly defunct.

The year 1916 was crucial in the conduct of the war, both at the front and in the rear. The army, undersupplied and undermanned, took great losses in a summer offensive; their suppliers, the workers, were facing growing shortages both of raw materials with which to manufacture armaments and of food with which to keep going themselves. The amount of metal produced by one worker fell from 11.8 funts per hour in 1915 to 9.1 in 1916, and to 3.5 in 1917.[204] Price controls were imposed on necessities like salt and bread, followed by the imposition of rationing of these and other products.

The strike movement in 1916 increased in intensity. Nationwide summaries give 134,000 strikers for Moscow province in 1916 (down somewhat from 1915), with especially intense waves in April, May, and November.[205] Police reports made available from Soviet archives indicate a different pattern. The month of June saw the highest number of strikers in the city of Moscow—17,700 (compared to 13,000 reported for the entire province by a different source). Over three-fourths of these June strikes were political, protesting the conviction of the Social-Democratic duma deputies, with metalists and printers once more leading the way. Overall for Moscow city, police figures report 59,000 strikers in 1916, about equally distributed between political and economic strikes. (May 1, which fell on a Sunday, was not observed as such but was followed immediately by a wave of economic strikes among metalists.) Almost 34,000 of the strikers in 1916 were metalists, encompassing 41 percent of that industry's labor

[202] See S. V. Tiutiukin, *Voina, mir, revoliutsiia*; G. G. Kasarov, "Bor'ba moskovskogo proletariata protiv 'Rabochei gruppy' moskovskogo oblastnogo voenno-promyshlennogo komiteta," pp. 34-45; Menitskii, vol. 2, pp. 185, 120.

[203] Ibragimov.

[204] *Trud*, 24 June 1917.

[205] TsSU, *Trudy*, vol. 7, vyp. 2, table 14.

force. Second in intensity once again were the printers, whose 4,600 strikers represented 34 percent of the workers in that industry.[206]

The entire economic and political situation seemed only to be growing worse by the beginning of the new year of 1917. It was an unusually cold winter in Moscow; the temperature in December and January rarely rose above fourteen degrees Farenheit and by the end of January was frequently as low as eighteen to twenty degrees below zero.[207] Fuel for heating and for production was in short supply, and several large factories were forced to close down during this cold spell. Bread rationing was announced for March 1, as soon as the ration cards could be printed; but in the meantime, lines were long and bread not always available. Disorders in food lines and in factories were becoming epidemic in Moscow. In Petrograd, even farther away from the source of bread, the disorders were much more serious; and by late February, strikes and food-supply unrest were daily involving greater numbers of hungry and angry workers. The capital city by the end of February was in the throes of a spontaneous general strike. In these circumstances, the government lost its authority to deal with the situation; the old regime was swept away by the mass unrest, a movement that quickly spread to the streets of Moscow.

Moscow's Workers on the Eve of Revolution: Summary

Working-class urban life performed a double function in workers' participation in the 1917 revolution. On the one hand, the various aspects of urban life discussed above and in Chapter One describe the group of actors who will take center stage in the following part of this study; they describe the values that workers carried with them into the revolutionary epoch of 1917: a sense of community, self-improvement, a cautious departure from tradition, and a receptivity to new experiences. The urban workers' special relationship to the land and to village social ties, their living arrangements in the city, their family lives, especially in contrast to other social groups in the city, provided a milieu in which urban culture was formed and developed. This milieu was characterized by expanded educational possibilities, political contacts with students, intellectuals, and like-minded workers, by recreational opportunities provided by social groups, clubs, unions, and the very concentration of many workers in one city. All these combined to give urban working-class culture a special role in influencing the model Russian "half-peasant, half-proletarian." The

---

[206] These documents were provided from TsGAOR in Moscow, fondy 63 and 102 (reports of the security police). I cannot tell how complete they were, but they provide much more information than the introductory article to "Rabochee dvizhenie v Moskve v 1914-1917 gg.," ostensibly based on the same archival material.

[207] *Ezhemesiachnyi statisticheskii biulleten'*, 1916, no. 12; 1917, no. 1.

urban element in this model does make a difference, and when one considers the activities of Moscow workers in the events of 1917, this difference will become more readily apparent.

And if the urban environment shaped the general outlook of these Moscow workers by encouraging new forms of association and activity and by fostering a sense of personal mobility, the same environment provided workers with concrete examples of their unacceptable position within the society. Crowded housing, inadequate food supply, and the pressures these conditions placed on normal family life became an important source of working-class discontent. Abuses within the work place—long hours, precarious wages, authoritarian discipline, unhealthy work conditions, and above all, the lack of a legitimate means to negotiate improvements in these conditions—created potentially explosive sources of conflict between the working class and privileged society. Finally, it was the urban environment that fostered the means through which to change these unacceptable conditions; labor organizations from their inception flourished most readily in Russian cities, and Moscow workers over the years had developed a repository of organizational experience which would aid them in their political endeavors in 1917.

Some questions remain. How isolated were these urban workers? How much contact did even the most urbanized workers have with the rest of society? Even though urban workers adopted many of the outward trappings of the bourgeoisie (dress, marital customs, cultural interests), there is little evidence that even the most urbanized workers wished to join the ranks of the middle class. Those middle-class individuals with whom workers came in contact were likely to be socialist-minded intellectuals, such as school teachers and cultural group sponsors, or else employers, whose interests workers assumed were antithetical to their own. Worker-students shared their classrooms with many members of the lower-middle class—clerks and shop assistants particularly—but the memoirs of such workers indicate very little community of interest and often outright hostility between these two groups. The workers studied for the sake of knowledge and joined illegal political study groups to advance the interests of their community. The other students were contemptuously characterized as being interested only in personal economic and social mobility.[208] Even printers, who came into daily contact with the bourgeois world, shared this general ethos of class separateness and solidarity; their early trade unions were always industrial, not craft-specific. The bourgeoisie may not have appeared so monstrous to them as to urban workers with less regular contact, but printers shared the same strong sense of class identity. Thus urban working-class culture, although

---

[208] *Prechistenskie kursy*, p. 210; A. Atsarkin and A. Zverev, eds., *Nashe rozhdenie*, p. 25.

shared at the time by a relative minority of Moscow workers, had assumed a distinctive form, characterized by self-improvement, sobriety, collegiality, and pride in class identity.[209]

The war of course effected some changes in the general picture of urban working-class life and culture. New categories of workers, relatively untouched by the urbanization of the past ten years, entered the labor market. Pressures of the war economy worsened the conditions under which workers lived and worked. Government policy curbed such traditional outlets for discontent as legal organization and alcoholic consumption, and dissatisfaction and unrest began to rise in Moscow, even with the wartime reduction of veteran urban cadres. The underlying unrest was quite great enough so that when the news came of mounting disorders in Petrograd in late February 1917, Moscow workers readily dropped their tools and defied the police to flock to the municipal duma building in the center of the city. The old bastion of authority became the focus of revolutionary expectations.

[209] Cf. Wildman, *Making of a Workers' Revolution*; R. Johnson, *Peasant and Proletarian*, p. 108; Sher.

THREE. *Moscow in the 1917 Revolution*

Old Moscow has paled before the younger capital, like a dowager clad in purple before a new empress.

ALEXANDER PUSHKIN[1]

THE city of Moscow, the historic capital of the Russian Empire, had long been second to St. Petersburg in political status and in the revolutionary movement. In 1917, Petrograd again set the pace, and Moscow, from the February days to the Soviet seizure of power in October, lagged behind. February street demonstrations occurred in Moscow only after the news arrived that the old regime in Petrograd had collapsed. Angry demonstrations in June in the capital, when workers and soldiers demanded radical solutions to the problems of war and political power, were echoed in Moscow only by hastily organized neighborhood rallies. The July days, which provoked armed confrontations in Petrograd between revolutionary soldiers and workers and defenders of the Provisional Government, brought forth in Moscow a small procession of unarmed Bolsheviks, taunted by larger crowds of local citizens. And whereas the seizure of power in Petrograd was essentially accomplished within twenty-four hours, the same conquest was achieved in Moscow only after prolonged and bloody street skirmishing, a conflict brought on in large measure because of the reluctance of either the Bolsheviks or the defenders of the Provisional Government to take the swift measures that had brought success in the first capital.

A large part of Moscow's tendency to lag behind Petrograd in 1917 can be ascribed to the social composition of the city. Moscow's work force was far less dominated by the metalworkers who made up the revolutionary cadres in Petrograd. Moscow's workers were more dispersed geographically and distributed more widely in small factories and workshops. Middling classes of society—shopkeepers, office workers, businessmen, and professionals—dominated the city's social life to a greater extent than in Petrograd, where the court and bureaucracy had been paramount. As a result, class friction was not so highly developed, and nonpartisanship and social unity at all levels characterized the early stages of the revolution to a far greater extent than in Petrograd.

[1] From "The Bronze Horseman," in *The Heritage of Russian Verse*, ed. Dimitri Obolensky, Bloomington, Ind., 1976, p. 113.

Moreover, Moscow's distance from the center of power also helped to moderate the city's response to crises in the center. Intricacies of high politics did not seem so urgent in Moscow; the force of strong personalities was diminished by the transmission of their speeches through the printed page. Moscow was Russia's trade center, and nongovernmental figures such as the great textile barons and liberal leaders like Riabushinskii affected local life as much as the maneuvers of politicians in the Provisional Government and the Soviet's All-Russian Central Executive Committee.

Finally, the character of revolutionary leadership for all parties in Moscow differed from that in Petrograd. The latter capital was the center of political power, and naturally, leading politicians gravitated to that center, leaving Moscow and other regional centers with second-level activists or people whose local ties were more important to them than being in the center of revolutionary activity. So political leadership in Moscow was marked by restraint and moderation, not only among socialist parties but among nonsocialists as well.[2]

Moscow's leadership of revolutionary events did not therefore compare to Petrograd's, but Russia's second capital nonetheless encountered similar problems, issues, and choices to those faced elsewhere and was forced to respond to them. The course of the 1917 revolution in Moscow was based on the same interplay of local and national politics and economics experienced in revolutionary Petrograd. In its own special way, therefore, Moscow had to come to terms with the basic problems of the revolutionary era; and if high politics did not matter so much, then basic questions of economic survival and local public order took on added importance. This special character will become apparent in this chapter, which will present an overview of the politics and economics of the revolutionary period from February to October 1917.

THE FEBRUARY REVOLUTION IN MOSCOW

The end of tsarism came as no great surprise to the second capital. Moscow's economy had been badly damaged by the pressures of war; by January, the problem of supply had become critical. Swollen with refugees from the war-torn western provinces, with wounded soldiers and evacuated workers, Moscow could not mobilize enough food to feed its inhabitants or fuel to run its factories. Food supply had been adequate until March of 1916 when a sudden crisis arose in the supply of meat. Next sugar almost disappeared, and its rationing was ordered from mid-August

[2] Boris Dvinov, *Moskovskii sovet rabochikh deputatov, 1917-1922*, p. 3, gives this as a reason for Moscow's moderation. See also Rosenberg, *Liberals in the Russian Revolution*, and Oliver H. Radkey, *The Agrarian Foes of Bolshevism*, for intercity differences in the Kadet and Socialist Revolutionary parties.

1916. By December, there was not even enough of the most basic commodity, black bread, and its rationing was ordered for February.[3] The particularly hard winter had depleted fuel supplies. In January 1917, directors of the huge Danilovskaia textile manufacture in Zamoskvorech'e announced that their calico and spinning sections would have to close for lack of fuel, sending over five thousand workers onto the streets.[4] Partial shutdowns occurred at other plants, and at important military plants such as Dinamo and Guzhon, operations continued at only half the normal rate.[5]

For the Moscow population, the villain was neither the winter nor the German invader; the widespread feeling in the city, as in Petrograd, was that the government was inept. On January 12, striking workers at the Gustav List machine plant opposite the Kremlin explained their action in a resolution intercepted by security police (*okhrana*). They cited the role of the government in creating the food-supply crisis, in refusing to permit the Congress of Zemstvos and Towns to meet, and in arresting the workers' representatives to the War Industry Committee. "Following from the above," they wrote, "we have come to the conclusion that such a regime [*vlast'*] is incapable of governing the country. And we therefore protest with a one-day strike."[6]

Led by machine workers such as these, the strike movement in Moscow gained momentum in January and February. According to police, one-third of the work force, 120,000 workers went out on strike during these months, compared to 59,000 reported by the same sources for all of 1916. Most of these striking workers made no explicit demands, and both they and the police knew that the target was not factory management but the government. Only 12,000 of these workers struck for purely plant-related economic reasons. Of the remaining strikers who declared their grievances, most cited the lack of bread—one immediate way to express outrage over the visible deterioration of government competence. The dates of the major strikes suggest the degree of the politicization of the strike movement: on January 9, the anniversary of Bloody Sunday, 31,780 workers struck. On January 12, in protest over the delay of the convocation of the State Duma, 18,180 workers struck, demanding bread. On February 13 and 14, in solidarity with the assembling State Duma, 16,000 workers walked out on strike.[7]

---

[3] "Prodovol'stvennoe polozhenie v Moskve v marte-iiune 1917 g."; *God raboty moskov-skogo gorodskogo prodovol'stvennogo komiteta* (hereafter *God raboty MGPK*). See also reports in local newspapers: *Russkoe slovo* is particularly informative on food supply.

[4] TsGAOR, f. 63 (Delo okhrana), ed. khr. 25, T. I, l. 8, police pristav report.

[5] TsGAOR, f. 63, op. 37, ed. khr. 214, l. 86, police pristav report; ibid., f. D.O. (102), ed. khr. 341, ch. 47B/1917, l. 15ob., Report of the Moscow Workers' Group on the situation of workers with respect to the fuel shortage.

[6] TsGAOR, f. 63, op. 21, ed. khr. 72, l. 40.

[7] Ibid., f. D.O., ed. khr. 307A/1917, l. 39.

Three groups of workers stood out in these political strikes. In the three above strikes alone, 45 percent of all Moscow metalists participated, 32 percent of all tram workers, and 16 percent of all printers. The southern industrial districts of Simonovka and Zamoskvorech'e, with their high concentrations of metalists, led the movement. (Almost all of the January 12 strikers worked in the Zamoskvorech'e district.) Despite the strict supervision by the police and the swift suppression of political agitators, word of mouth and the proximity of so many restive factory workers were sufficient to produce a sizable, if unstructured, demonstration of political protest.[8]

The police, if not the monarchy, realized the seriousness of this threat to the regime's stability as the Moscow okhrana gravely reported after the February strikes:

The state of extreme agitation of the working mass and in social circles, the aggravation of the bread shortage in Moscow, and the activities of revolutionary circles could create, under a new onslaught of strikes and demonstrations, a much more serious threat to official order and to public security.[9]

Their fears, of course, turned out to be justified.

News of similar disorders that had begun in Petrograd on February 23 was suppressed by local officials in Moscow until February 27.[10] But on the afternoon of the twenty-seventh, rumors of the collapse of tsarist authority spread throughout Moscow factories, and workers began to leave their benches, some going home, others gravitating to the city center to seek more news. On the next day, the twenty-eighth, the city was in the throes of a burgeoning general strike. Workers sacked police precinct houses, seized weapons, and arrested gendarmes. Prisoners were liberated. Before finally succumbing to the revolutionary tide, the disintegrating okhrana apparatus reported that 22,600 workers had left their jobs on their own accord or were called out by neighboring factories. Crowds of workers and citizens from all corners of Moscow gathered once again in the center, at the city duma building, to celebrate their joy at the dawn of a new order and to participate in its creation.[11]

---

[8] Ibid., ff. 63, D.O.

[9] Ibid., f. D.O., ed. khr. 307A/1917, l. 40.

[10] I. V. Gorshkov, *Moi vospominaniia o fevral'skoi i oktiabr'skoi revoliutsii 1917 g. v Rogozhsko-Simonovskom raione*, p. 13; E. N. Burdzhalov, *Vtoraia russkaia revoliutsiia*, p. 10.

[11] TsGAOR, f. 63, ed. khr. 37, d. 214, ll. 139-217; *Moskva v trekh revoliutsiiakh*, pp. 172-175; *Na barrikadakh za vlast' sovetov*, p. 102; *Slavnye traditsii*, p. 8; Nikolai Morozov, *Sem' dnei revoliutsii; Izv. MSRD*, 3 March 1917; A. N. Voznesenskii, *Moskva v 1917 g.*, pp. 1-6; *Dinamo: 25 let*, pp. 81-82, 77-78; Dvinov, *Moskovskii sovet*, pp. 3, 7-8; *Moskovskie bol'sheviki v ogne revoliutsionnykh boev*, pp. 19-21, 185; M. Popov, "Moskovskie pechatniki v dni fevral'skoi revoliutsii," pp. 13-14; *Velikaia oktiabr'skaia sotsialisticheskaia revoliutsiia*

5. Revolutionary crowd at the City Duma building, February 1917. The walls of Kitai-gorod, the inner city, can be seen at right.

The revolution was nearly bloodless. "There was no shooting in the streets, no barricades," recalled the Kadet businessman P. A. Buryshkin. "The old regime in Moscow in truth fell all by itself, and no one defended it or even tried to."[12] At the Iauza bridge, the southeast approach to the city center, a large crowd of workers was blocked by a police detachment (the small Moscow garrison remained neutral during these days). "Give us the road!" a metalist named Illarion Astakhov was reported to have cried. The assistant police superintendent replied with gunfire, and Astakhov was killed. The crowd surged on the police, threw the offending officer into the river, and continued on to the center. Astakhov became Moscow's first 1917 revolutionary martyr, and one of only three or four victims of the February revolution.[13]

The revolutionary disorders of February 28 gathered momentum on March 1. Military units declared their support for the revolution, and

---

(*vospominaniia*), vol. 1, p. 458; *Za vlast' sovetov*, p. 85; *Ot fevralia k oktiabriu*, pp. 235-238; S. Rigosik, "Pervye komsomol'tsy," pp. 119-120; N. Rozanov, "Revoliutsionnaia rabota"; *Krasnaia Presnia v 1905-1917 gg.*, pp. 441-443.

[12] Buryshkin, p. 319.

[13] *Dinamo: 25 let*, p. 97; Gorshkov, pp. 13-14; *Ot fevralia k oktiabriu*, pp. 237, 241; *Za vlast' sovetov*, p. 93; Burdzhalov, *Vtoraia russkaia revoliutsiia*, p. 27. Burdzhalov reports another worker was also killed in the skirmishing at the Iauza bridge (p. 27n) but does not give his source.

6. First appearance of newspapers after the fall of the old regime, probably March 2 or 3, 1917.

police were powerless to carry out the order to prevent crowds from converging on the center. By March 2, it was all over. Eyewitnesses recall the holiday atmosphere of that glorious morning of the revolution; red banners and armbands abounded; factory managers joined their workers in revolutionary greetings.[14] Inside the city duma, representatives of labor and society met feverishly to establish foundations for a new civil power; outside, the joyous general strike continued. On March 3, fire broke out in the headquarters of the Moscow okhrana, probably set by the okhrana agents themselves. A large crowd prevented firefighters from fighting the blaze as others piled the archives of the hated security police onto a bonfire.[15]

On March 4, with major newspapers finally on the streets once again, the city learned of the tsar's abdication for himself and his son. And on Sunday, March 5, the reborn Moscow Soviet of Workers' Deputies voted, after heated debate, that the revolution was secure enough now for the workers of Moscow to return to their factories, to continue with the

[14] Dune, pp. 22-24; Yarkovsky, p. 87; Morozov, p. 7; Voznesenskii, *Moskva v 1917 g.,* pp. 10-11. The plant manager at the Tsindel textile and armaments factory provided an automobile to transport workers' deputies to the first meeting of the Soviet (*Dinamo: 25 let,* p. 82).

[15] Morozov, p. 10; Voznesenskii, *Moskva v 1917 g.,* pp. 2-16.

business of organizing political parties, trade unions, and factory committees, and to prepare for the coming Constituent Assembly that would democratically decide the future of Russia.[16] The new order was under way.

FROM MARCH TO JULY: THE ERA OF GOOD FEELING

"Workers of Russia, Unite!"

In Petrograd, a provisional committee of the State Duma emerged from the rumor-filled halls of power to form a government that could tide the country over until a permanent and legitimate system could be organized. But in fact effective power at this time lay with another body, the Soviet of Workers' and Soldiers' Deputies, which represented the cadres of the revolutionary movement and without whose sanction the Provisional Government could not function. The Petrograd Soviet, partly for ideological reasons, declined to participate in the actual exercise of state power; by definition, this was a bourgeois revolution, and power should be held by a bourgeois government. The leaders of the Soviet, veteran revolutionary socialists (and excluding some of the most experienced veterans, who were still abroad or in exile), saw their role as keeping the new rulers honest; any attempt by the Provisional Government to renege on the general achievements of the revolution would summon the active opposition of the "forces of democracy." The Soviet issued its famous Order Number One to the troops of Petrograd, commanding them not to obey directives from this new government unless countersigned by the Soviet. By this act the Soviet intended to forestall any attempt to transfer revolutionary troops from the capital. With its veto power understood, the Soviet then passed a resolution of conditional support for the new regime: "We suppose that insofar as the new government fulfills its promises and effectively combats the old regime, the democratic forces must give it their full support."[17] With the exception of Alexander Kerensky, who appointed himself the "hostage of democracy" and joined the government as minister of justice, none of the Soviet leaders would participate in the cabinet but kept in touch with the new power by means of a contact commission. This was the system which became known as dual power.

The devolution of power in Moscow paralleled the situation in Petrograd, although only control of the city was at stake, not the ship of state. Under the old regime, state authority was delegated to a governor-general who reported directly to the government in the capital. A duma, or

---

[16] Morozov, p. 14; *Izv. MSRD*, 8 March 1917; Burdzhalov, *Vtoraia russkaia revoliutsiia*, pp. 72-73.

[17] Quoted in Marcel Liebman, *The Russian Revolution*, p. 118.

council, elected on a very narrow franchise, had exercised control over some aspects of city life, such as education and public welfare. A sizable city bureaucracy (*uprava*) had administered these activities in behalf of both the State Duma and the local duma.

With the fall of the old regime, the tsar's representative found that his mandate to govern had disappeared, and the old privileged, or tsenzovaia, duma had lost its legitimacy. Into this local power vacuum on the evening of February 27 stepped the Moscow version of the Provisional Government, the Committee of Public Organizations (CPO). The Committee saw itself and was widely regarded as a representative of all the people of Moscow: the hundred and fifty people attending the constituent meeting included representatives of the old city uprava, the War Industry Committee, political parties, workers' professional organizations, sick funds, and cooperatives. This meeting created a smaller executive committee of fifteen members, five representatives each from three so-called curiae: the tsenzovaia (representing the old city duma), the "democratic," and the workers.[18]

From its formation until the convocation of a democratically elected city duma, the Committee of Public Organizations governed Moscow. Public order was administered through a network of committees for militia, food supply, finance, local duma, labor problems, legal affairs, and others as the need arose. Additionally, the CPO sent representatives to the new military government of Moscow, the provisional council of the Moscow garrison. And when the Provisional Government appointed a new representative to replace the old *gradonachal'nik*, the CPO flexed its political muscle by insisting that its choice replace the government's nominee; thus the Kadet Nikolai Kishkin became the chief administrative officer for the city.[19]

If the Committee of Public Organizations came to exercise administrative power in Moscow, the real tribune of the working population, as in Petrograd, was the Soviet of Workers' Deputies, which emerged simultaneously with the CPO and from the same source, the February 27 meeting of local political activists. It was this body, dubbing itself the "provisional revolutionary committee," which issued an appeal the next morning to the people of Moscow asking them to follow the example of Petrograd, to go to the barracks and bring the soldiers over to the revolution, and to organize meetings in factories.[20]

[18] *Russkoe slovo*, 2 March 1917; *Utro Rossii*, 2 March 1917. The workers' representatives on the committee's executive committee included L. M. Khinchuk and A. M. Nikitin (Mensheviks), I. I. Egorov (Unity Social-Democrat), V. V. Rudnev (Socialist Revolutionary), and S. S. Belorussov (Bolshevik). See also *Sbornik materialov moskovskogo komiteta obshchestvennykh organizatsii*.

[19] Grunt, *Moskva 1917-i*, pp. 54-55; Rosenberg, *Liberals*, pp. 59-61.

[20] *Utro Rossii*, 2 March 1917.

The new soviet was the natural heir to the soviet that had formed in Moscow to direct the strikes of 1905; despite longstanding differences on other issues, the idea of a soviet was supported by all Moscow socialists, from the defensist Menshevik Cheregorodtsev to the Bolshevik cooperative activist V. P. Nogin.[21] On February 28, as crowds converged on the duma, the call to form a soviet spread. A tram conductor who was there recalled hearing the words, "Comrades from the districts, send up your representatives! Allow them to pass up to the duma." Inside, a group of about twenty intellectuals received the representatives and urged them to return to their districts to organize elections.[22]

The first meeting of the Moscow Soviet took place at noon on March 1 in the presence of fifty-two delegates (thirty-three from factories, the rest from other organizations such as cooperatives, sick funds, and trade unions). After reports on the current situation and the election of an executive committee of forty-four (of the total fifty-two!), the meeting adjourned until seven o'clock that evening when a larger assembly could be expected.

Over six hundred delegates arrived for the evening meeting. They elected as chairman the Menshevik lawyer A. M. Nikitin, who had won fame as a defender of the victims of the Lena shootings five years before. Nikitin, however, resigned the next day to become the city's commissar of militia, an appointment itself symbolizing the close ties at the time between the workers and the bourgeois supporters of the CPO. To the Soviet chairmanship was elected another Menshevik, L. M. Khinchuk, who remained in his post until the Bolshevik party won a majority in the Soviet in September. On this first day of its reincarnation, the Soviet cautiously consolidated its influence, sending representatives to the military soviet and to the Committee of Public Organizations, calling on workers to resume essential services, but warning that the revolution was still not secured.[23]

[21] According to Nogin, the two factions met first separately, the Workers' Group under Cheregorodtsev and a meeting of fifty to sixty activists from workers' cooperatives; the idea of a central soviet and of going to the duma came independently to both. Opponents of the scheme feared a central organ would be too quickly crushed and favored alternatively organizing district centers, but they were soon overruled by events (V. P. Nogin, "Sredi moskovskikh bol'shevikov," *God bor'by*, Moscow, 1927, pp. 8-9).

[22] One of the intellectuals present, Boris Dvinov, recalled that this early group included the future soviet leaders G. A. Kipen, L. M. Khinchuk, Boris Kibrik (Mensheviks), Gendel'man (SR), and L. Galperin (Unity). Cheregorodtsev was at the time meeting with the nascent Committee of Public Organizations; the only Bolshevik to join the meeting was a trade unionist, Katan'ian (Dvinov, *Moskovskii sovet*, pp. 9-10). It would appear that the Bolshevik group had not yet come around to the idea of a central workers' soviet, a fact alluded to by both Nogin and another underground party worker, V. A. Obukh (in *Moskovskie bol'sheviki v ogne revoliutsionnykh boev*, p. 73).

[23] *Biulleten' Soveta rabochikh deputatov*, 1 March 1917; *Organizatsiia i stroitel'stvo sovetov rabochikh deputatov v 1917 g.*, pp. 13-15.

The Soviet and CPO worked closely together in the next few days. On March 2, the first regular issue of the Soviet's organ, *Izvestiia*, appeared under the joint editorship of Bolshevik I. I. Skvortsov-Stepanov and Menshevik Boris Kibrik. To demonstrate its common social and political interests with the working class, the CPO quickly allocated fifty thousand rubles (presumably from the city treasury) for *Izvestiia*'s support.[24] The Soviet, reassured by Nikitin's appointment to a position in charge of public order and the CPO's recognition that Soviet representatives would serve as watchdogs in all local precincts, voted to end the general revolutionary strike as of Monday, March 6.[25] By the time the city had returned to some semblance of normal operation, the pattern of peaceful and amicable cooperation had been established. The Committee of Public Organizations represented the state and its ruling bourgeois class; the Soviet would defend the interests of the workers by mobilizing the working class to defend itself. This was the agenda the Soviet set for itself in the very first days of the February revolution.

The Soviet of Workers' Deputies remained the most important tribune for the wishes of the Moscow working class, although at critical times the Soviet was superseded by other bodies more in tune with the current mood. The rank and file of the body, confirmed later in the spring after official publication of electoral rules, reflected this working-class base. Of a total of 625 deputies, 80 percent were workers, 16 percent were employees, sluzhashchie; the remaining 4 percent—26 in all—were employed in intellectual occupations. Most of the deputies were elected from either individual large factories or clusters of smaller ones; the rules allowed 1 deputy for every five hundred workers up to a total of 3. Factories with fewer than four hundred workers were to combine and choose a common representative. Together, the factory-chosen deputies represented 469,000 workers.[26] Additional deputies represented trade unions, railroads, sick funds, cooperatives, and political parties; their constituencies in most cases overlapped with those of factory representatives.

---

[24] *Russkoe slovo*, 7 March 1917; I. I. Skvortsov-Stepanov, "Pered oktiabrem," pp. 218-229.

[25] *Izvestiia komiteta obshchestvennykh organizatsii*, 2 March 1917.

[26] The analysis of Soviet membership is reported in *Izv. MSRD*, 17 June 1917, and also in E. N. Ignatov, *Moskovskii sovet rabochikh deputatov v 1917 g.*, pp. 446-450. A list of individual deputies was published serially in *Izv. MSRD* beginning with the June 1 issue, giving names and affiliation. The 469,000 workers represented far exceeds the reported size of Moscow's industrial work force; the figure includes non-Moscow factories technically ineligible to send representatives to the city Soviet but whose mandates were apparently never effectively challenged. See *Izv. MSRD*, 9 April 1917. Grunt (*Moskva 1917-i*) has found an archival list of Soviet deputies which provides in addition to name and affiliation the numbers of electors for each deputy, but the original source for the more detailed analysis of Soviet composition summarized in *Izvestiia* and in Ignatov has not been located.

The Soviet, however, was not a mirror-image of the Moscow work force. Even though the Soviet mandate commission established that representation be proportional to factory size, the distribution of deputies by occupation did not correspond to that of the working population as a whole. Metalworkers accounted for 230 deputies, or 46 percent of the workers in the Soviet; textilists, who counted for one-quarter of the working population, supplied only 12 percent of working-class deputies. Metalworkers, unlike workers in most other occupations, were widely employed in non-metal-working plants since all mechanized factories required at least a few skilled machinists. Thus many of the metalist deputies may have come from factories in other industries. This distortion was common in revolutionary institutions and contributed to occasional breaches between the "masses" and their representatives, as will be seen.

A large percentage of deputies had been active in the revolutionary movement prior to 1917. Over half of those who were members of political parties (362 of the 625) had joined their parties no later than 1905. One-quarter of the deputies (157) had been arrested at least once for political activities under tsarism. The workers chosen by their peers for the Soviet, in short, tended to be experienced activists; this experience was one reason they were trusted by their electors to be representatives. And it also explains why so many nonmetal plants sent metalist deputies to the Soviet: metalworkers had had the most experience in the pre-1917 revolutionary movement. (Printers, also active before 1917, did not send many deputies to the Soviet. This is probably due to the fact that, unlike metal workers, printers were employed exclusively in printshops; there were few opportunities for a printer to represent a factory of another type.)

The 625 Soviet deputies constituted the legitimate decision-making tribune of the working class, but the policies of the Soviet throughout 1917 were in fact determined first of all by a seventy-five-person executive committee, which in turn was guided by the real nerve center of the Soviet, a seven-person presidium. Elections to the executive committee were organized to give each major party equal weight, so the Bolsheviks, Mensheviks, and Socialist Revolutionaries each had about twenty of its members on the committee. The executive committee was far less proletarian than the Soviet at large; only slightly more than half (thirty-nine) of its members were workers by profession (although slightly more—forty-five—represented either factories or trade unions). Twenty-eight committee members were professionals, including lawyers, statisticians, physicians, and civil servants. Of the thirty-nine workers, twenty-nine were metalists, further confirming the important reserve of experience acquired by this group in the years before 1917.

Executive committee members, to a much greater degree than the rank and file, were political veterans: thirty-five of seventy-five had joined a party before 1905, another fifteen during 1905. (The statistical reports do not indicate which parties, if any, could claim a larger share of the long-time activists.) In contrast to the general body of deputies, of whom 25 percent had been arrested for political activities before 1917, only 25 percent of the executive committee *had not* been arrested during the tsarist years. Their crimes were also more serious: the median prison sentence for rank-and-file "politicals" was 4.2 months; for those on the executive committee the median was 1.33 years. Again, these committee members were chosen by the Soviet to lead them, and their greater experience was clearly an important factor in their perceived ability to lead.

The presidium of the Soviet consisted of seven party representatives. L. M. Khinchuk and A. M. Nikitin, two of the most popular individuals in the Soviet, represented the Mensheviks. Khinchuk, a veteran of the cooperative movement, was a tireless worker, respected by Right and Left alike for his fairness and moderation.[27] The two Socialist Revolutionaries, D. S. Rozenblium and V. V. Rudnev, represented the right wing of their party, and only the lawyer Rozenblium was very active. Rudnev, a veteran of 1905, had become a patriotic socialist during the war and by 1917 was ideologically closer to the Kadet party than to his populist forerunners.[28] Like Nikitin, he was called to higher responsibilities; when he was elected as the new chairman of the city duma in June, Rudnev ceased to be an active participant in Soviet affairs. I. I. Egorov, a veteran cooperativist, represented the United Social-Democratic (Ob"edinenie) faction and continued to work in the Soviet until the October revolution. Filling out the presidium were two long-time Bolsheviks, V. P. Nogin and P. G. Smidovich. Both were once workers (although Smidovich was born to an aristocratic family); they had since become professional revolutionaries. Nogin, in addition to his Moscow duties, was a member of his party's Central Committee, and it was he who replaced Khinchuk as chairman of the Soviet in September.

Since the main business of the Soviet was acknowledged by all participants to be organization and consolidation, Soviet leaders studiously ignored the thorny issues that would soon divide the socialist parties—such as the war, the economy, and dual power itself. In this focus on procedure rather than substance, the Menshevik leadership held sway, but the Bolsheviks on the executive committee concurred in the approach. It was hard to believe that power had been won so easily, and all socialists felt that only a great show of unity could preserve the gains won so far against the expected counterattack by partisans of the old regime.

[27] A. I. Verkhovskii, *Na trudnom perevale*, p. 260; Skvortsov-Stepanov, p. 231.
[28] Oliver H. Radkey, *The Sickle under the Hammer*, p. 40.

The Soviet leadership did not realize how very strong it was. Mensheviks held steadfastly to the view throughout 1917 that its constituency, the working class, was still a minority of the Russian people, that they must take no actions to alienate themselves from the rest of the *narod*, particularly the conservative peasantry. Addressing a plenum of the Soviet on March 7, Chairman Khinchuk alluded to earlier reports of tumultuous organizational activity in Moscow working-class districts, which indicated the "surprising influence" of the Soviet.[29] Unconvinced of the firmness of their authority, the Soviet leaders directed their activities toward consolidating support within the working class, not to extending its influence beyond. Although the Soviet accepted the CPO's aid for its newspapers, it refused to petition the Provisional Government for funds for its general upkeep. The Soviet was a working-class organization and should remain unsullied by contact with the state.[30] Leaders of both Social-Democratic parties opposed a merger with the Soviet of Soldiers' Deputies on the grounds that the workers' soviet must keep itself pure.[31] Later, when pressed by the Soviet rank and file to assume more direction to save the failing economy, Boris Kibrik argued that to become involved in such regulation would deflect workers from their primary task of class struggle and would weaken the process of consolidation of the working class as a class.[32]

Its "surprising influence" soon forced the Soviet to take action on one pressing matter after another, but in its existence under Menshevik leadership, the Soviet never abandoned its quest for unity and consolidation or for compromise with the other elements of society. To understand this slow and painstakingly cautious approach to revolutionary leadership, one must not underestimate the feeling that, from the perspective of the events of March, the possibility of a more radical revolution seemed extremely remote. The leaders of the revolution expected that the Constituent Assembly would soon become the real authority in the land. The process begun in February was expected to be long and arduous, and proper institutions had to be constructed in order to carry society through the coming era of transformation. This need is why the early actions of the Moscow Soviet were all procedural; watchdog commissions were created in the fields of labor, militia, food supply, fuel, local organization, and cultural activities. In the new order, the soviets and other working-class institutions would defend the interests of the workers in a pluralistic society. No one in February would have predicted that they would have only a few months to make this new society work before more dramatic solutions would be forced upon them. There was no implicit deadline

[29] *Izv. MSRD*, 8 March 1917.   [30] Ibid., 21 March 1917.
[31] Ibid., 12 April 1917.   [32] Ibid., 14 June 1917.

hanging over the heads of the leaders of Soviet. If one remembers this fact, it is not so difficult to understand the lack of urgency for leaders of the revolution, even if the democratic revolution was, from today's perspective, terribly insecure. And however justified, it was the lack of any feeling of great urgency and the need above all for revolutionary unity which characterized this first period of the revolution, not only for workers and their representatives but for all elements in society as well.

Events quickly overtook the institution builders in the Soviet, however, and the next eight months saw a constant battle at all levels of society between the conflicting needs to continue the process of organization and to respond to the immediate problems of the day. The course of the revolution in Moscow was in large part determined by these immediate problems, summoned often by crises in Petrograd but also by local conditions and events.

The first serious challenge to revolutionary unity came on the question of the eight-hour working day. For the Socialist International, "eight hours to work, eight hours to sleep, eight hours to recreate" was a specific demand of the labor movement.

In few places had this goal been attained, but Russian workers felt that having helped to overthrow the old regime, they were now entitled to reap some of the benefits of their new power. First on the agenda was the eight-hour working day.

But how was it to be achieved? Presumably, work hours were negotiated between workers and factory management, but the demand was more than a job-related issue. Besides, the government had intervened in labor-management relations for years. But which government should make this decision—local, central, or the Soviet? The fact of the war also presented problems; workers already labored overtime to turn out munitions and supplies for the army and still failed to keep up with the demand. What would become of this effort if the workday were shortened to eight hours? Despite the many complexities of the issue, revolutionary workers in Moscow and in Petrograd expected satisfaction. Many indicated they would end their revolutionary general strike only if the eight-hour workday was made the rule.[33]

For action on this issue, Moscow workers turned to their own Soviet of Workers' Deputies. At first the Soviet tried only to mediate between workers and employers as befit a purely class organ; the presidium, besieged with appeals from local factories, referred all demands to a conflict commission.[34] Meanwhile, workers in the factories were solving the issue in their own way, by instituting the shortened workday by themselves,

[33] Mandel, "Development of Revolutionary Consciousness," p. 172. See also below, Chapter Six.

[34] March 11 meeting of the Soviet presidium, *Izv. MSRD*, 14 March 1917.

iavochnym poriadkom. Such an unstructured movement threatened the revolutionary solidarity the Soviet leaders cherished, but pressure mounted from below for some sort of solution.[35] On March 18, the Soviet gathered to hear the views of local delegates and to decide on a course of action.

In many factories, it turned out, the eight-hour workday was implemented with or without the cooperation of factory management. The other factories, reported delegates, had refrained from following suit only in the expectation that the Soviet would act. These workers saw the Soviet as the logical instrument to carry out this demand; only a few deputies shared the views of the majority of the executive committee that something as drastic as shortening the workday could be done only on an all-Russian scale, by an all-Russian government.[36]

The legitimacy of the Soviet in the eyes of its constituents was on the line. The delegate from the Presnia district reported, "One-third of our factories already have the eight-hour working day; the remainder have been restrained with difficulty by members of the Soviet until the question is resolved by the Soviet." In Sokol'niki, the mood was militant and expectant. "The least hesitation from the side of the Soviet of Workers' Deputies in introducing the eight-hour workday will create tremendous problems and difficulties." And from Khamovniki: "a negative decision by the Soviet will not be obeyed, which will dreadfully undermine the authority of the Soviet. . . . To delay is dangerous."[37] It is significant that the districts most insistent on an immediate implementation of the eight-hour workday were those which had hardly participated in the prerevolutionary strike wave. The veteran revolutionary districts of Zamoskvorech'e and Simonovka, with their large contingents of metalworkers, reported that workers favored the shorter workday and awaited its interim introduction by the Soviet, but these districts acknowledged that the issue must finally be settled by the central government.

The Bolshevik Nogin spoke most forcefully for a uniform, organized solution to the question. For one city to declare the shortened workday, as had already occurred by agreement between Petrograd workers and a factory owners' association there, would leave others in the backwash of the revolution. Only a decree by the Provisional Government would be a legitimate solution to the problem, one which would not alienate the working class from its revolutionary allies in the army and the countryside.

Fellow Bolshevik M. P. Vladimirov also spoke of organization but to

[35] March 14 meeting of the Soviet of Workers' Deputies executive committee, ibid., 15 March 1917.

[36] The debate on the issue was reported in ibid., 19 March 1917.

[37] Ibid.

a different end: a Soviet decree for the eight-hour workday was far better than the continued movement of independent actions, and only such a Soviet decree would preserve the body's authority as the workers' tribune. At last a compromise was reached; the Soviet voted, nearly unanimously, to "demand the Provisional Government decree an eight-hour workday for all of Russia," and in the meantime, to sanction the eight-hour working day for all Moscow workers with overtime permitted by mutual agreement and with no reduction in pay.[38]

The first crisis had passed, but it augured the problems that would continue to plague the revolutionary leadership in Moscow: the conflict between procedure and substance, the problem of restraining the rank and file when it did not understand the disorganizing aspects of immediate demands. The isolation feared from this decision by moderates like Nogin soon became evident. The bourgeois press emphasized the selfishness of an eight-hour working day for workers when soldiers and peasants continued to toil with no reduction in hours.

Public reaction seemed to turn against the workers and their soviet on this issue. Khinchuk told the executive committee on March 29 that soldiers were hostile toward the Soviet because of the eight-hour day, and he proposed creating a commission of soldiers and workers to explain the reasons for and implications of the decree.[39] Letters from workers to a newspaper forum on the eight-hour workday stressed that rested workers were now more productive than before, but a peasant wrote bitterly that he too would like eight hours to sleep and eight hours to study, but "this is no time for discussion: the Germans are knocking at the gates of Russia."[40] Such reactions placed the working class on the defensive and confirmed for the leadership the danger of isolation and the need for even greater organizing work among the working class.[41]

The sense of working-class isolation and the need for greater unity was also a factor in the attitude toward the war taken by Moscow workers and their soviet. The entire issue was so volatile that all revolutionary leaders had shunned it at first, hoping to smooth over the bitter divisions among socialist parties and factions. Government propaganda had stressed from the outset of the war that the German army was the aggressive warmonger, and that Russia, like the other allies, fought only to defend itself, plucky Belgium, and brave Serbia. But many in the international socialist movement, after initial support for the war, joined the growing trend begun at Zimmerwald in Switzerland to pressure all governments into ending the fighting on a basis of no territorial annexations and self-determination

---

[38] Ibid.
[39] Ibid., 31 March 1917.
[40] *Gazeta-kopeika*, 29 March, 8 April 1917.
[41] Dvinov's reaction was that the decree was like a gift from heaven for the bourgeoisie, driving a wedge between the hitherto united soldiers and workers (*Moskovskii sovet*, p. 16).

for all nations. The Russian socialists were badly split on the issue. Bolsheviks lined up against the war, although not all shared Lenin's Left Zimmerwald position that the war should be transformed into a revolutionary civil war and that the best outcome for the Russian Revolution would be a Russian military defeat. Mensheviks divided into opponents of the war, who called themselves Internationalists, and defenders, who rallied around the War Industry Committees, hoping to organize a workers' revolution under the legal guise of the effort for greater war production. The Socialist Revolutionaries also divided along patriotic-internationalist lines.[42]

During the February days, workers carrying hand-lettered banners with the Leninist slogan "Down with the war!" had been arrested by others in the revolutionary crowd. Soldiers who supported the revolution reacted negatively to defeatist slogans. So on March 6, when meeting to plan a grandiose demonstration to celebrate the victory of the revolution, the Soviet presidium voted that the war not be raised as an issue.[43] But the question was too pressing to postpone, however great the need for socialist unity, and a joint plenum of the workers' and soldiers' soviets met immediately after the big March 12 demonstration to air the opinions of the revolutionary mass.

The mood of the workers who spoke tended to be defensist: the war was benefiting only the capitalists, they acknowledged, but fighting could not be terminated unilaterally, "disgracefully." Much of the discussion focused on the role of the German people and their army. Until they too overthrew their militarist government, Russia would have to defend its newly won freedoms. Soldiers tended to be more hostile toward the German enemy and were bitter about the working class's reluctance to support a successful prosecution of the war. All this talk about extending our hand to our German brothers was rubbish, declared one soldier. "I would ask you, comrades, to extend your hand to your work bench, to give us ammunition, and then we'll give a present to the German junkers. Only then will we receive the liberated hand of the German proletariat in return."[44]

The meeting produced no final resolution but seemed to confirm the wide gulf of opinion on the war; it again indicated the need to preserve democratic unity. The Moscow Soviet did not take a position on the war until March 25, after the Petrograd Soviet had arrived at its own decision (but before the policy-setting All-Russian Conference [Soveshchanie] of Soviets). Then, at a regional conference of soviets, with representatives from as far away as Voronezh, Smolensk, and Nizhegorod provinces, the

[42] Boris Dvinov, *Pervaia mirovaia voina i rossiiskaia sotsial demokratiia*; Radkey, *Agrarian Foes*, pp. 96-112.
[43] *Izv. MSRD*, 8 March 1917.

combined soviets adopted the Petrograd Soviet's resolution: the war was begun from acquisitive motives, and it was now up to the people of each country to take steps to end it. Toward that end, the Provisional Government ought to declare immediate peace terms, renouncing annexationist goals. Until then, it was in Russia's interests and those of the international working class to continue to fight to defend their new freedom.[45] This was the doctrine of revolutionary defensism which won the support of a wide spectrum of revolutionary parties, workers, and soldiers.

The Petrograd Soviet applied pressure on the Provisional Government to express publicly its agreement with the Soviet's views, and on March 27, the government issued a declaration that "the objective of free Russia is not domination over other peoples, nor depriving them of their national possessions, but the establishment of a stable peace based on national self-determination."[46]

The influence of the democratic mass, exerted through the Soviet pole of dual power, appeared to be working. Consequently, when the Provisional Government turned to the democracy for material support for its policy, soliciting Soviet endorsement of a new Liberty Loan to ease the government's critical financial situation, the Soviets in Petrograd and Moscow gave their cautious approval. The question, however, was not clear-cut. Speaking for the executive committee at an April 11 session of the Moscow Soviet, Menshevik D. V. Kuzovkov acknowledged that support for the loan was like voting for war credits, the act that in 1914 had tolled the death knell for the Second Socialist International. The difference now was that the army was defending the revolution. In refusing to support the loan, the Soviet might alienate the army, leaving democracy with no real force to oppose the Provisional Government if that should become necessary. Support for the Liberty Loan again boiled down to the overwhelming need for unity. More objectionable were the conditions of the loan; money borrowed from Russian capitalists would be repaid with revenue garnered through unjust indirect taxes on the poorest strata of the population. Therefore, the Soviet proposed to support the loan, but only under strict conditions: the Provisional Government ought to renounce all annexationist goals and support the self-determination of nations. The loan ought only to be a temporary expedient, and the Soviet's support rested on the expectation of passage of a new property-based progressive income tax.[47] With these conditions, the Soviet voted to endorse the loan on April 15 by a margin of 242 to 127. The Bolshevik party,

[44] Ibid., 21 March 1917.
[45] Ibid., 28 March 1917. See also the discussion in Tsereteli, pp. 45-73, and N. N. Sukhanov, *The Russian Revolution 1917*, vol. 1.
[46] Sukhanov, vol. 1, p. 249.
[47] *Izv. MSRD*, 13 April 1917.

arguing that the lack of funds would persuade the government to seek a speedier peace settlement, opposed the loan.[48]

Three days later, the conditions attached to the Soviet's support for the Liberty Loan were defied by the publication of a note from the Provisional Government's foreign minister, Kadet Pavel Miliukov. Clarifying Russia's war aims for the benefit of its allies, Miliukov issued a statement on April 18 that Russia would continue to prosecute the war until its victorious conclusion, would fulfill its obligations to its allies, and shared with its allies the confidence that the peace settlement would "obtain those guarantees and sanctions which are necessary for the avoidance of new sanguinary clashes in the future."[49] With not a word about renunciation of annexations or of the self-determination of nations, the note was a slap in the face to those in the Soviet who hoped to use their authority to force an internationalist settlement of the war.[50]

Petrograd workers and soldiers responded angrily to the note's publication. On April 20, thousands of soldiers demonstrated outside the seat of the Provisional Government; they bore banners reading "Down with Miliukov!" "Down with annexationist policies!" "Down with the Provisional Government!"[51] The soldiers were joined the next day by workers from the industrial outskirts of Petrograd, some of whose banners called for the transfer of power to the Petrograd Soviet. But on this day, antigovernment demonstrators were met by Kadet-led counterdemonstrators in support of the government. Shots rang out, and the spector of civil war was raised. Leaders of the Soviet and Provisional Government met hastily to resolve the crisis, to restore order, and to "save the revolution."

Soviet leaders were in a quandary over the next few days. Should they now abandon their position as outsiders, form a coalition government with members of the opposing capitalist class, and use their presence within the cabinet to preserve the democratic goals of the revolution? Or would their entry into a government of capitalists suggest to workers that the socialist camp possessed greater power than in fact was true, which could only falsely raise expectations and result ultimately in a loss of Soviet authority in the eyes of its constituents? Most Soviet leaders at first concluded that a coalition strategy was wrong, but the existing cabinet put pressure on the socialists to enter a coalition and to abandon the Soviet's claim to independent authority. After two weeks of political crisis, the Soviet agreed to send six representatives to the Provisional Govern-

[48] Ibid., 21 April 1917.

[49] Quoted in Chamberlin, *Russian Revolution*, vol. 1, p. 444.

[50] See Rosenberg, *Liberals*, pp. 104-106; Rex Wade, *The Russian Search for Peace, February-October 1917*.

[51] Rabinowitch, *Prelude to Revolution*, p. 43.

ment, although under specified programmatic conditions. Power would be shared now by the representatives of democracy, but Soviet leaders insisted they remain a minority within the cabinet.[52]

In Moscow, far from the scene of the decisions that provoked the April demonstrations and formation of the coalition, the crisis passed with less tension. On April 18, the city had observed the holiday of International Workers' Day (May 1 on the New Style [Gregorian] calendar used in the West) in a spirit of great unanimity and comradeship. Despite cold weather and gray skies, over half a million people marched through the streets, carrying banners proclaiming "Long live the International!" "Peace and brotherhood of all nations!" "Workers of the world, unite!" "Long live the Constituent Assembly!"[53] When news came to Moscow on April 21 of the Miliukov note and the previous day's demonstrations in the capital, workers in some factories left their benches, and carrying slogans such as "Down with Miliukov!" and "Down with the Provisional Government!" converged on the Soviet headquarters in Skobelev square. But the demonstrators were few; perhaps two thousand workers assembled at the Soviet to be told by Soviet officials that the crisis in Petrograd was over and the Petrograd Soviet was in command.[54]

As in the pre-February days, workers from Zamoskvorech'e factories led the movement toward the center. The Moscow telephone factory was reported to have gone first to the local militia commissariat to seize weapons (although the factory's Soviet deputy denied this). Perhaps it seemed to them like February all over again: the revolution was in danger! Moscow was indeed agitated on that day, with rallies and meetings of supporters as well as opponents of the Provisional Government, but the Soviet appealed for order and discipline, and the city's workers obeyed. The Moscow telephone factory promised it would not disregard the Soviet again; another Zamoskvorech'e metal factory that had demonstrated also voted to obey the Soviet's ban on all but organized demonstrations.[55] The next day, a plenum of the combined workers' and soldiers' soviets voted to continue "active supervision" over the Provisional Government—dual power—and to be ready to act if called upon. Only an organized proletariat could exert meaningful pressure on an uncooperative bourgeois govern-

---

[52] Rosenberg, *Liberals*, pp. 108-109; Tsereteli, pp. 94-106, 135; Ziva Galili y Garcia, "The Menshevik Revolutionary Defensists and the Workers in the Russian Revolution of 1917."

[53] *Russkoe slovo*, 20 April 1917; *Izv. MSRD*, 20 April 1917; Ignatov, *Moskovskii sovet*, p. 126.

[54] *Izv. MSRD*, 22 April 1917.

[55] *Trud*, 22 April 1917; *Russkie vedomosti*, 26 April 1917; *Vpered*, 27 April 1917; Voznesenskii, *Moskva v 1917 g.*, pp. 45-47; Ignatov, *Moskovskii sovet*, pp. 135-136; Grunt, *Moskva 1917-i*, pp. 137-139.

7. May Day demonstration at the City Duma building, April 1917. Note the mixture of soldiers and civilians.

ment, voted the majority; the Bolshevik resolution suggesting that the soviets assume full power themselves received a scant seventy-four votes at this session.[56]

Thus the formation of the coalition government two weeks later appeared to Muscovites as a fait accompli. Bolsheviks and Mensheviks alike opposed the coalition, and the Moscow Menshevik organization formally declared against entry of socialists into the government on April 28. But once their Petrograd counterparts had decided to enter the Provisional Government, Moscow's socialist leaders accepted the decision and devoted their attention to consolidating local positions.[57]

[56] *Izv. MSRD*, 23 April 1917.
[57] Galili y Garcia, p. 63; L. M. Khinchuk, "Avtobiografiia," *Entsiklopedicheskii slovar' (Granata)*, 7th ed., vol. 41, p. 205.

Organization and democratic unity continued to be the hallmarks of Soviet activity as the weeks wore on. The city was now preparing for the election of a new municipal duma on June 25, which would replace the Committee of Public Organizations as the official government of Moscow. There was no suggestion of dual power or of boycotting bourgeois government at the local level; all socialist parties actively prepared to use this democratic occasion to proselytize for their positions and together to win control of city administration for the socialist parties of the Soviet.

Once again, events in Petrograd intervened. Growing manifestations of an antirevolutionary backlash and preparations for a new military offensive convinced part of the Petrograd garrison to demonstrate its protest on June 10, a display endorsed by the Bolshevik party. Soviet leaders in Petrograd feared this new breach in revolutionary unity and managed to dissuade the Bolsheviks from the demonstration, scheduling instead a peaceful demonstration for June 18 to coincide with the opening of the All-Russian Congress (S"ezd) of Soviets in the capital. In Moscow, rumors surfaced that an antigovernment demonstration was also planned—rumors the local Bolshevik organization emphatically denied. The joint executive committees of the workers' and soldiers' soviets met to consider the new crisis on June 10. The Socialist Revolutionary Rudnev expressed the familiar refrain: separate actions by individual parties will destroy revolutionary unity. If the counterrevolution does become real, the Soviet would call out the workers and soldiers simultaneously and in an organized way to defend the revolution.

Bolshevik representatives grumbled that since they were not planning a demonstration, there should be no resolution condemning them for it, but a resolution calling for restraint in light of the Petrograd events received the sanction of a majority of the executive committees.[58] The approved Soviet June 18 demonstration coincided with the official commencement of the municipal election campaign in Moscow; further, all the Moscow Soviet's leaders were in Petrograd for the All-Russian Congress. For lack therefore of adequate time or means to prepare a citywide demonstration, the Soviet called for separate processions and rallies in each working-class district.[59] The Socialist Revolutionary newspaper *Trud* accused the Bolshevik party of using the rallies to advance its partisan program,[60] but with the duma election only a week away, such activity was construed as democratic politicking and not a dangerous breach in revolutionary unity.

The Socialist Revolutionaries turned out to have little cause for complaint. In the elections on June 25, the Socialist Revolutionary (SR) party

---

[58] *Izv. MSRD*, 11 June 1917.
[60] *Trud*, 20 June 1917.

[59] Ibid., 16 June 1917.

won 58 percent of the vote, the Bolsheviks and Mensheviks evenly split another 23 percent. The socialists had won a commanding majority in the new city government, a tribute to the tactics of revolutionary unity and organized political work. (The election and its results are examined in detail in Chapter Five.) This victory of the Soviet's socialist parties marked the high tide of the period of peaceful and constructive revolutionary development. Hostility among socialist parties in Moscow had not reached the levels already attained in Petrograd; workers' and capitalists' participation in the duma electoral process affirmed their willingness to cooperate in matters of local government. But events elsewhere were developing to shatter this spirit of cooperation. Class tensions exploded in Petrograd on July 3 in an armed uprising by workers and soldiers against the government; in Moscow, trouble was also brewing beneath the surface of revolutionary good feelings in the form of a growing economic crisis that by June had quite overshadowed the problems of power and foreign policy as the prime concern of the Soviet and local government.

Revolutionary Unity and the Problem of Provisions

The demand for bread had propelled Moscow's factory workers onto the streets in January and February 1917, and the problem of food continued to dominate the city's concerns through all the political crises of the first four months of the revolution. Feeding the city was of paramount concern for both the Moscow Soviet and the Committee of Public Organizations; nowhere was the success of the Soviet's policy of revolutionary unity more tested than by this question.

The old regime had planned to institute a bread-rationing system to begin on March 1, 1917. Under this plan, each Muscovite would be entitled to buy one funt (about one pound) of bread per day; workers would receive their rations at their places of work to avoid lines at bakeries. City officials anticipated requiring in this way 35 railway carloads of grain a day; since Moscow was then receiving 46 carloads daily, a reserve could be accumulated for the leaner days expected ahead.[61] But with the outbreak of the revolution, the supply of bread had plummeted. In February, 1,234 carloads of grain had arrived in Moscow; in March this number fell to 868, and by April only 679 carloads were received. On March 28, the Moscow Soviet learned the city had only a six-day reserve of flour, and April and May were always the most critical months for such supplies.[62]

The shortage was grounded both in the disruption by the war of the traditional grain market and in the changing terms of trade between village and city. Before the war, Russia had been a grain-exporting nation, but with the mobilization of millions of peasants and their livestock, produc-

[61] *Russkoe slovo*, 23 February 1917.   [62] *Izv. MSRD*, 31 March 1917.

tion fell and the number of nonproducing consumers increased. Still, since most of Russia's grain now remained within the country's borders, the total supply should have been enough to meet the basic needs of the population. The serious problem was that grain producers were now reluctant to send their grain to the city. Prices were rising all the time, so by waiting even a little while, a peasant could increase his income. Besides, there was nothing to buy. With most of Russia's industrial capacity devoted to military production, the commodities that peasants wanted—cloth, tools, foodstuffs and vodka—could not be purchased.[63]

The city of Moscow responded to these problems after February 1917 by appealing to the central government to take firm measures to regulate the distribution of grain and by undertaking its own campaign to pry more grain out of the countryside. The Moscow food-supply committee, a quasi-governmental organization composed of representatives of the Soviet and of public organizations, sent its agents increasingly farther afield to persuade the grain-producing districts of Russia to send supplies to Moscow.[64] An all-Russian food-supply conference was to convene in Moscow on May 21 in order to coordinate these activities for all cities; meanwhile, the city's bread norm was reduced on April 17 to three-quarters of a funt of bread per person per day.[65]

The Moscow Soviet sent its own agents to ensure that the city's workers would be fed, and a Soviet official attributed a huge increase in the grain supply for May—200 percent more than had been received in April—to the enormous prestige of the Moscow Soviet throughout central Russia.[66] The food-supply committee's explanation for the increase is more realistic: the price paid for this grain in May was almost half again as high as the price in April, and it was this fact that convinced the peasants to supply the cities.[67] Furthermore, the May bonanza was only 4 percent over the city's normal requirements; the shortage persisted and with higher prices to boot.

The increase in the cost of bread in this period was a major factor in the overall rise of the average worker's cost of living. What happened to prices and wages in the war months prior to the February revolution has already been seen: everything increased, but for about half the occupations, wages rose faster than the cost of food. The lack of good information on wages in the post-February period makes an analogous determination for March through October extremely difficult, but even an approximation

[63] E. E. Iashnov, *Dostatochno-li khleba v Rossii?*
[64] *God raboty MGPK*, pp. 41-42; *Izv. MSRD*, 2 May 1917.
[65] *Sots.-Dem.*, 18 April 1917.
[66] *Izv. MSRD*, 13 May 1917, reports the Soviet sent representatives to Orel, Tambov, Khar'kov, and Penza provinces. See also Ignatov, *Moskovskii sovet*, p. 210.
[67] *God raboty MGPK*, p. 43.

of the change in the standard of living can convey the magnitude of the crisis facing Moscow's population in the spring of 1917.

Based on the "market basket" of foodstuffs calculated for 1916-1917 consumption patterns (which already reflected an adjustment from 1913 to growing shortages), the cost of living changed for Moscow workers in the first six months of 1917, with January as the base month. (Look at Table 3-1.) In the first two months of the revolution, prices remained stable, but costs rose by 21 percent in May, reflecting the jump in the price of bread; the increase in June was substantial as well.[68]

Meanwhile, wage levels fluctuated in both directions but did not increase significantly.[69] (Look at Table 3-2.) Tables 3-1 and 3-2 indicate an

TABLE 3-1. *Change in Cost of Living in Moscow, January-June 1917*

Month	Price Index	Percent Increase
January	100	—
February	102	2
March	102	—
April	103	1
May	125	21
June	142	14

SOURCE: V. Ia—ii,"Tseny na produkty i zarabotnaia plata moskovskogo rabochego."

[68] Calculations made by Gosplan and the Central Statistical Administration, presumably using the same price data but a different method of weighting, yield somewhat different index numbers, but theirs too show a sharp rise in prices from April to May; they find a 25 percent increase, compared to my calculation of 21 percent. See Z. S. Katsenelenbaum, *Uchenie o den'gakh i kredite*, vol. 1, p. 410; M. P. Kokhn, p. 160. The prices that all these indices are based on are not themselves completely reliable. Given rationing and the existence of a black market, one cannot expect official prices to correspond too closely to real market prices (see Pervushin).

[69] The movement of wages is difficult to assess. First of all, there were wide fluctuations among occupations, in part because of varying levels of skill but also because some groups of workers organized to raise wages earlier than others. Second, there are no sources of compiled monthly wages. However, some indication of the movement of wages can be gleaned from the wage demands made by workers before and during strikes, from random reporting of current wages, and from the going rates for workers finding employment through the Soviet's labor exchange. Even these data are hardly comparable: in addition to allowing for industrial and occupational differences, some reported wages include food, housing, and clothing. Allowing for these discrepancies as best I could, Table 3-2 represents a straight average of wages received or demanded across industries and for the separate category of unskilled labor. For the unskilled workers especially there were too few observations for these numbers to be truly convincing, but notice that on all three scales, the wage in May has fallen. The decline may not have been significant: none of the wage observations shows that wages at a given factory were actually lowered during this period, and those workers reporting their wages in May might have tended to be lower paid, which is why they were making a case for raising their wages. But it certainly does not look as if wages were rising very much, and this is the very same time at which the cost of living had taken its biggest jump yet!

TABLE 3-2. *Change in Daily Wage in Rubles for Moscow Workers, January-June 1917*

Month	Average for All Industries		Unskilled Workers
	Received	Demanded	
January-February	3.00	—	2.10
March	2.10	4.60	—
April	3.10	5.50	4.60
May	2.50	5.00	4.00
June	4.80	6.00	0.75

SOURCES: Labor exchange reports in *Izv. MSRD*, 14 May, 28 June, 5, 15, and 22 July, 6 August, 21 September 1917, and from scattered reports culled from other Moscow newspapers and from the documentary sources cited in the Bibliography. The reports for the period March–October represent 235 separate observations of wage levels.

economic crisis in May of alarming proportions. Indeed, as will be seen below and in Chapter Eight, it was at this time that the Soviet began to be concerned with the "economic crisis" and that the strike movement in Moscow reached a greater number of factories than in any other month.

The economic crisis reflected in the falling wage and rising cost of food gnawed at the euphoria created by the fall of the old regime and underscored the multiplying crises on issues like the war and dual power. The old problems of transport and supply were not yet solved. The Provisional Government could not meet its expenditures with current revenues any more than the tsarist regime could. By April, the war alone was costing 54 million rubles a day.[70] The Liberty Loan was one attempt to balance the books, but the printing press was not forgotten. By May the government was printing new notes as fast as its equipment would allow;[71] prices, quite naturally, soared. Meanwhile, productivity plummeted as factories could not secure the materials and fuel they needed for production.

Pressed by these worsening conditions, the Moscow Soviet began in May to consider what could be done to protect its constituents from economic disaster. Predictably, the solutions seemed to lie in a more organized approach to the national economy, in planning and regulation, and in a united cooperative attack on the problems of the economy. On June 13, after a week of organized local discussion of the economic situation, the Soviet met again to debate the economic issue. Speaking for the majority, veteran trade unionist P. N. Kolokol'nikov (now the assistant minister of labor in the Provisional Government) spoke of the need to maximize production and to optimize distribution by means of a series of giant government trusts. A coal monopoly would be implemented soon,

[70] Tereshchenko's speech to the Moscow Soviet, reported in *Izv. MSRD*, 17 April 1917.
[71] P. V. Volobuev, *Ekonomicheskaia politika vremennogo pravitel'stva*, pp. 353-357.

followed by a monopoly on beet sugar. Controls such as these would allow the government to restrain the anarchic tendencies of the free market and curb the appetite of speculating middlemen. Profits would be taxed on a sliding scale, so that no class would benefit unduly from the current troubles.

The minority Bolshevik report was given by Nikolai Bukharin. To him, the war was the chief cause of the economic crisis, which could only be solved by ending the war. Further, only a government of Soviets could take the necessary steps to restore economic health to the country by ending the war, nationalizing land, repudiating government debts, and syndicalizing the main branches of industry.

Bukharin's proposal to give regulatory control to trade unions and factory committees touched a raw nerve on the Menshevik benches. Kolokol'nikov warned "these organs will approach these issues from a local and small-group point of view, and not from a statewide viewpoint." The Unityist Egorov echoed these thoughts. "For now, I see that the task of trade unions is confined to struggle with the bourgeoisie, and not to join with it in regulatory functions and supervision of production."[72]

In the end, despite reports from many district soviets that their meetings had endorsed the Bolshevik position, the plenum voted 262 to 182 for the executive committee majority line: economic catastrophe was inevitable without "immediate, conscious [read: organized], totally planned state intervention" in the economic and social affairs of the country. The Provisional Government should create an economic council to prepare a plan for supply and distribution; private enterprise should be strictly controlled and profits limited; some branches of industry should be monopolized; banks should be supervised to end speculation; the issuance of paper money should be stopped. It was the Provisional Government who should act; the Soviet was able only to express the will of the working people.[73]

Ultimately, Bukharin, who doubted that the Provisional Government would ever adopt the plan of its assistant labor minister Kolokol'nikov, turned out to be correct.[74] The pressure of the organized working class in Moscow was not felt very keenly in Petrograd.

FROM THE JULY DAYS TO THE MOSCOW STATE CONFERENCE

The Collapse of the Strategy of Unity

The June 25 elections in Moscow were followed by a momentary relaxation in the climate of political conflict. For one thing, a new democratic gov-

[72] *Izv. MSRD*, supplement to no. 109, stenogram of June 13 plenum.
[73] Ibid., 14 June 1917.   [74] Ibid. See also Volobuev, *Ekonomicheskaia politika*.

ernment of Moscow could now be organized; the Committee of Public Organizations, which by June had assumed many government functions, transferred its power to the new duma, which was to meet for the first time on July 7. Also, many workers were leaving the city for agricultural work in the villages, either because of temporary or long-term layoffs, normal slack periods (especially in the artisan trades), or because living conditions in the city had become so unbearable.[75] Thus many in the city were taken quite unaware by the street fighting that erupted in Petrograd on July 3 and 4, when enraged soldiers and workers demanded that the soviets take power.

The events leading up the July days in Petrograd were largely specific to that city, and they reflected a much greater degree of class polarization and hostility than existed in Moscow. The tension in Petrograd which had begun with the aborted June 10 demonstration was exacerbated by the start of a new military campaign on the southwest front, the first offensive action under the Provisional Government. Petrograd troops were ordered to leave for the front and they refused.[76] Meanwhile, the industrial work force of Petrograd was also threatened with removal, as government officials considered evacuating the city's industry to ease the burden on supply. Seen together with stalled wage negotiations, cutbacks in production, the flight of capital abroad, and the growing claims from the State Duma that it and not some upcoming Constituent Assembly was the legitimate state power, the threatened "unloading" (*razgruzka*) of Petrograd convinced many of the city's workers that an attack on the revolution itself was under way.[77]

The July demonstrations in Petrograd lasted two anguished days. Machine gun units took up positions along Nevsky prospect and at railway stations to defend the rising against incoming troops. The workers' section of the Petrograd Soviet had earlier passed the Bolshevik resolution for soviet power, and angry crowds of workers and soldiers now demanded that the Menshevik and SR leaders act on this resolution. At one point, a crowd threatened to arrest the SR Minister of Agriculture, Chernov, who was saved only by the intervention of Leon Trotsky. The Bolshevik Central Committee was somewhat embarrassed by the turn of events; the soldiers had been encouraged by the more radical Bolshevik military organization, and the Central Committee members did not feel the situation was ripe for a violent seizure of power. The second day of the demonstration, July 4, brought sniper shooting and panic in the streets.

---

[75] It is hard to measure the impact of this exodus. The only real indication that it occurred is that workers' organizations urged their members to postpone their departure from the city until after the duma election. Tallies of eligible voters in June and September indicate a slight increase in the total number, so these departures were in any case not long-term.

[76] Rabinowitch, *Prelude*, p. 149.   [77] Mandel, pp. 272-288.

The Provisional Government, with the acquiescence of its socialist ministers, called for troops to return to the city to put down the rising. The minister of justice issued a report that the Bolshevik party had sparked the rising on orders from the German General Staff, and with this rumor spreading rapidly through the city, the demonstrators retreated. On the next day, the Bolshevik Central Committee called for an end to the demonstration, and the Provisional Government gave orders for the arrest of Bolshevik leaders and seizure of its newspaper, *Pravda*.[78]

The crisis was over, and although the conditions that provoked it were not, the memory of defeat in these two days in July contributed to a sharp decline in working-class activism in Petrograd. For radical Petrograd workers, to demand "power to the soviets" now meant more than expressing an opinion. Even if the Petrograd Soviet could be convinced to accept power, workers felt that organized resistance by the bourgeoisie would compel an armed struggle.[79] At the same time, the forces of the Right used this defeat to strengthen their own attacks on the legitimacy of the revolution and the soviets. The Provisional Government, meanwhile, was unable to offer any leadership at all in this critical time. The Kadet ministers had resigned on the eve of the crisis over the issue of Ukrainian autonomy, and a new coalition was not patched together for another three weeks, while the deep social divisions reflected in the July days continued to widen.[80]

None of these problems were felt quite so strongly in Moscow. The recently appointed district military commander, A. I. Verkhovskii, was sympathetic to the Soviet and managed to restore some semblance of discipline to the garrison, which was not in any case tapped for immediate transfer to the front.[81] The slogan "power to the soviets" for Moscow was more abstract than in Petrograd: after all, local power had just been won by an elected majority of socialists. And although the economic situation in Moscow was grave, the capitalists and the right wing of the Provisional Government were not yet seen as the chief villains. Nonetheless, when the Moscow Committee of the Bolshevik party learned of the demonstrations in Petrograd, they voted reluctantly to join their comrades and called for workers to march to the center to demand soviet power. The march was scheduled for six o'clock on the evening of July 4.

The Moscow Soviet leaders meanwhile feared such a demonstration would provoke counterrevolutionary violence, and the executive committee voted to ban all demonstrations for three days, until tension abated. Bolsheviks and their supporters were now faced with a dilemma: to flaunt the authority of the Soviet in demonstrating their wish for that body to

[78] Rabinowitch, *Prelude*, p. 218.   [79] Mandel, chap. 4.

[80] See Rosenberg, *Liberals*, chap. 6.

[81] Verkhovskii, *Na trudnom perevale*, pp. 261-278.

take power, or to call off the demonstration and risk loss of revolutionary face. Many would-be participants, once informed of the Soviet's decision, abandoned their plans to march and settled for short meetings in their neighborhoods.[82] The Moscow Committee, which was dominated by older, more conservative party members, would have acceded to the Soviet decision, but they realized that very young party members were determined to continue with the demonstration. Rather than let the public think that the party was nothing more than a crowd of unruly adolescents, the Moscow Committee reluctantly disobeyed the Soviet's decision and ordered the demonstration to proceed.[83]

By all accounts, the demonstration was a pathetic affair. Columns of demonstrators were harassed on their way to the city center by groups of "drunken hooligans."[84] By ten o'clock that evening, only a few hundred marchers had actually reached Skobelev square in front of Soviet headquarters, and these were outnumbered by a hostile crowd who jeered and insulted the small band of Bolsheviks. After some brave speeches, the demonstrators moved off—retreated, actually—to Bolshevik party headquarters nearby, to tend their wounds and assess the damage the July days had done to their party.[85]

The July demonstration reinforced Soviet leaders' belief that the working class was isolated and could not effectively take power. The crowds in the street who jeered and stoned the Bolsheviks were never really identified; participants later described them as bourgeoisie, Black Hundreds, hooligans, "scum" from the Khitrovo market. But they sufficiently frightened the Soviet that the ban on outdoor public meetings was continued indefinitely, and the Soviet began a campaign to restore a socialist united front by agitating against the rumors now branding the Bolsheviks as German spies.[86]

Meanwhile, the crisis of power in Petrograd continued. The Petrograd Soviet was attempting to help form a new government, and the Moscow revolutionary leadership awaited further developments. On July 8, the Soviet's All-Russian Central Executive Committee had issued a program of goals for a new coalition: strengthening of external and internal order

---

[82] *Izv. MSRD*, 5 July 1917.

[83] Skvortsov-Stepanov, p. 234; Atsarkin and Zverev, eds., *Nashe rozhdenie*, p. 207.

[84] Voznesenskii, *Moskva v 1917 g.*, pp. 66-67; *Desiat' let*, p. 73.

[85] *Desiat' let*, pp. 72-73; Ignatov, *Moskovskii sovet*, p. 267; *Ot fevralia k oktiabriu (v Moskve)*, pp. 52-53; *Moskovskie bol'sheviki v ogne*, p. 139; *Velikaia oktiabr'skaia sotsialisticheskaia revoliutsiia (vospominaniia)*, pp. 465-466; Dvinov, *Moskovskii sovet*, pp. 24-25; *Dinamo: 25 let*, p. 83; *Oktiabr' v Zamoskvorech'e*, p. 134; *Izv. MSRD*, 5 July 1917; *Put' k oktiabriu*, vol. 1, p. 192; *Ot fevralia k oktiabriu*, p. 229. See also E. Levi, "Moskovskaia organizatsiia bol'shevikov v iiule 1917 g.," pp. 123-151, and *Ocherki istorii moskovskoi organizatsii KPSS*, pp. 249-252.

[86] Executive committee meeting of July 10, in *Izv. MSRD*, 14 July 1917.

linked with strong measures to prevent a return of the old regime, declaration of a democratic republic, more active land and labor policies, and state regulation of the economy.[87] The conditions seemed promising to the Moscow Soviet's Menshevik-SR majority, and it endorsed the new coalition, once again conditional on the July 8 program's being fulfilled.

The Bolsheviks, meanwhile, retreated to the factories to rebuild their bases of support after the July fiasco. In the corridors of higher power, signs appeared that the opponents of the revolution now felt strong enough to prepare a counterattack. The death penalty, restored at the front, was now proposed for the rear as well. The hated tsarist ministers Shturmer and Gurko were released from prison.[88] Rumors of an imminent military coup abounded, fostered by the public posturings of Kerensky and his new military commander Kornilov about the restoration of "iron discipline."[89] To lend some semblance of legitimacy, the Provisional Government now conceived of a State Conference of all the country's "vital forces." The conference was scheduled for Moscow, the home of the loyal bourgeoisie and far removed from the menacing revolutionary crowds of Petrograd. It would begin on August 12.

The "vital forces" of the country were meant to include representatives of the Soviets as well as members of the government and the old privileged classes. In the Moscow Soviet executive committee, Menshevik and SR leaders decided to participate, although with some misgivings about what the conference could accomplish.[90] The Soviet plenum reached the same conclusion. A compromise resolution proposed by the Mensheviks pledged participation but called on the Soviet to mobilize the masses through meetings and resolutions to thwart a potential counterrevolution.[91]

This question arose, however: were meetings and resolutions enough to forestall the counterrevolution? The Bolshevik party and many others in Moscow felt the answer was no, and they prepared for more demonstrative action. Assessing the mood of the working population of Moscow on August 8, the Moscow Committee of the Bolshevik party considered and then abandoned the idea of a mass demonstration in the city center to meet the opening of the conference. Still remembering the July fighting, party activists feared "we would not be safe from counterrevolutionaries, who might clash with our demonstrators; bloodshed is not desirable."[92] The workers of Moscow, however, could impress their revolutionary

---

[87] Ibid., 9 July 1917.

[88] Stenogram of Soviet plenum of August 1, in ibid., supplement to no. 153.

[89] Verkhovskii, *Na trudnom perevale*, pp. 303-304; Rabinowitch, *Bolsheviks Come to Power*, pp. 99 ff.

[90] *Izv. MSRD*, 11 August 1917.   [91] Ibid.

[92] *Revoliutsionnoe dvizhenie v Rossii v avguste 1917 g.*, p. 384.

unity on the conference delegates in another way—by declaring a one-day general strike in protest over the gathered worthies of the counter-revolution.

From the beginning, the Bolsheviks doubted that the Moscow Soviet executive committee would support such an overt action, so they decided to appeal to the trade union movement to endorse the protest and lend greater legitimacy to the strike call than the party alone could provide.[93] The coordinating trade union council, the Central Bureau of Trade Unions, had convened on August 7 to consider the strike. It was a purely informational session; there would be no vote, and reports were solicited about the mood of the rank-and-file trade unionists. These reports indicated that "the proletariat expresses sharp indignation with the activity of the ever-more-insolent counterrevolution and with the Provisional Government's toleration of this behavior."[94] The assembled trade unionists decided to canvass their constituents and meet again on August 9.

Representatives of the Central Bureau, plus delegates from forty-one trade unions, parties, and the Moscow Soviet, attended this meeting; and after heated debate about the propriety of the trade unions' becoming involved in political actions, voted that representatives of revolutionary democracy should attend the State Conference in order to declare their disapproval. They would then walk out, and the Russian proletariat would protest the conference with mass meetings and a one-day strike.[95] This message was sent to the next day's meeting of the Soviet executive committee, who rejected the strike. A final decision, however, had to come from the joint general session of the Soviets of Workers' and Soldiers' Deputies, set for August 11.

Emphasizing its role as a militant but nonpartisan labor organization, the Central Bureau of Trade Unions presented its position. "This decision [to strike] is not partisan, it is not a decision of bolsheviks, mensheviks, or SRs, but a decision of the proletariat." Reports from local deputies indicated that they favored a strike, but wished to have the Soviet's approval.

The delegate from the Blagusha-Lefortovo district soviet declared, "The workers of our district irrespective of parties stand for a strike." Of thirteen districts, six spoke in favor of the strike, three more spoke against the conference without having decided whether to strike, three favored a strike if the Soviet approved. Only one district supported outright the

[93] E. N. Ignatov, "Mobilizatsiia kontr-revoliutsionnykh sil k moskovskomu gosudarstven-nomu soveshchaniiu i vseobshchaia zabastovka moskovskikh rabochikh," pp. 55-64.

[94] Ibid., p. 57.

[95] *Revoliutsionnoe dvizhenie v Rossii v avguste,* pp. 386-387. Keep, *Russian Revolution,* argues that the Central Bureau of Trade Unions opposed the strike, but his sources do not support his contention (p. 99).

executive committee's proposal of conditional participation in the conference.[96] Yet when a vote was taken on an amendment to delete a strike ban from the executive committee's resolution, proponents of the strike narrowly lost, 312 to 284. Thereupon the entire executive committee resolution was adopted by a vote of 364 to 304.[97]

Unfortunately, further analysis of this vote cannot be found in the published accounts of this meeting. Why, given the clear groundswell of support for a strike, did the strike vote lose at the general meeting? Menshevik and SR party discipline and the great prestige of the executive committee as an institution may have been factors, but it should also be pointed out that this was a joint meeting of the workers' and soldiers' soviets. The impact of the attitude of the garrison on the votes taken in these joint soviet meetings are never considered by Soviet students of the Moscow revolution, yet theoretically, the soldiers and workers each could send 625 deputies to these meetings.[98] What one does not know is the relative weight of each of these groups in the 600 or so deputies who attended the August 11 meeting. In any case, the only soldiers' deputy to participate in the strike debate endorsed the executive committee's position, and the soldiers' soviet in general was far more amenable to its Socialist Revolutionary leadership throughout 1917. The soldiers present might well have provided the margin for defeat of the strike.

It is certainly possible that if a vote had been taken in the workers' soviet alone, a majority might have voted for the one-day strike. The majority of district soviets favored a strike, although for some only if the central Soviet approved. The majority of trade unions endorsed the strike. But the Soviet said no. The Moscow proletariat was faced with a serious duality of authority: whom were they to obey? On the day of the opening of the conference, most of Moscow's workers left their jobs in open or reluctant defiance of the Soviet resolution. The contemporary socialist press reported that 400,000 workers had struck, although this number took in many striking factories well beyond the city limits.[99]

Whatever the actual number of protesters, it was clear to all that Moscow on August 12 was in the midst of a general political strike unlike any

[96] *Soldat-Grazhdanin*, 12 August 1917. It is curious that only the newspaper of the soldiers' soviet published a complete account of the debate on the strike, perhaps in order to explain to soldiers why the strike proceeded in spite of the Soviet ban.

[97] *Izv. MSRD*, 12 August 1917.

[98] Neither the recent work by Grunt nor that by I. P. Zubekhin and M. S. Koloditskii, "Moskovskii sovet rabochikh deputatov nakanune oktiabria," considers this problem.

[99] Based on the list of striking factories published in *Izv. MSRD, Trud*, and *Sots.-Dem.*, I have counted at least 116,000 Moscow city workers who participated in the strike. Another 17,000 workers passed resolutions condemning the conference, but whether or not they struck is unknown. These figures do not include nonfactory workers who struck, such as waiters, cooks, drozhky drivers, and other service personnel.

since February. Nikolai Sukhanov, the Petrograd Menshevik-Internationalist who had arrived that morning to attend the conference, described his impressions:

> The trams in Moscow had stopped, and there were almost no *drozhky* drivers either. There was a strike, not a general one, but very impressive and sufficient to manifest the will of the masses. A number of factories and works were on strike, as was every municipal undertaking except those satisfying the daily needs of the population. Restaurants, waiters, and even half the drozhky drivers were on strike. This whole working-class army was following the Bolsheviks *against its own Soviet!* Toward evening, the demonstration would become still more perceptible: Moscow was to be submerged in darkness since the gas works was also on strike.[100]

In spite of the decision not to demonstrate, crowds of young workers gathered outside the doors of the Bolshoi theater to watch the arriving participants. In what must have been a satisfying turnabout from the Bolsheviks' July-days experience, whistles and hisses now greeted Miliukov and the Black Hundreds leader Purishkevich, although Tsereteli, representing the Central Executive Committee of Soviets, drew applause.[101] There was no question about the targets of the strike and demonstration: the stoppage of the tramway system obliged the delegates to walk from the railroad terminals to Theater Square; the first- and second-class restaurants, catering to more expensive tastes, were closed. "We just had to tighten our belts," recalled the Moscow military chief Verkhovskii.[102]

The dynamics of the strike recalled those of the political strikes of the February days. Because of the conflicting pulls of the Soviet ban and trade union sanction, the strikers were not unanimous; the Soviet's newspaper conceded that a majority of workers had gone out, but not all.[103] As in February, militant protesters managed to rally their more reluctant neighbors. In Lefortovo, the Socialist Revolutionary newspaper *Trud* reported that although most workers showed up at their factories as usual, they were soon convinced to leave, and the whole district shut down. (Their factories in any case were probably the first place most workers learned of the final decision on the strike call.) At the big Guzhon steel plant in Rogozhskii, one department after another shut down until the entire plant had stopped. Workers at the Duks metal plant in Butyrki

---

[100] Sukhanov, vol. 2, p. 494.

[101] Anna Litveiko, "V semnadtsatom," describes the scene at the Bolshoi theater on this day; see also Verkhovskii, *Na trudnom perevale*, p. 304.

[102] Verkhovskii, *Na trudnom perevale*, p. 303.

[103] *Izv. MSRD*, 13 August 1917.

were narrowly divided on whether to defy the Soviet ban; by a vote of 731 to 716 the strike supporters won and insisted the entire plant submit to the will of the majority.[104]

The one-day strike had serious implications for the future of the revolution. The authority of the Soviet was severely damaged by its inability to respond to the demands of its constituents, a fact noted with concern by newspapers of both the Right and the Left.[105] The front of revolutionary unity so carefully nurtured by the Menshevik leadership of the Soviet was now shattered, a breach the counterrevolution could not fail to notice.

What is most stunning about Moscow's response to the State Conference is the comparison with events just five weeks earlier during the July days. Then Moscow's workers and socialists were cautious, trusting in the patience and restraint of the Soviet. The counterrevolutionary threat did not seem to warrant a display of force. In August, the balance of strength seemed to have shifted because for workers, passing resolutions and trusting in revolutionary-democratic unity was no longer sufficient. By striking to protest the State Conference, Moscow's workers had placed themselves in the forefront of the revolution.

On the other side of the barricades, the strike reinforced the Right's perceptions of the growing intransigence of so-called democracy.[106] Kornilov's plans for a military coup consequently gathered force. Polarization along class lines, which in Petrograd had contributed to the July crisis, was now a major aspect of Moscow social life as well. Even Bolshevik party leaders now seemed wary of the whirlwind they had helped summon up and hastened to restrain militant workers, especially from Zamoskvorech'e, who threatened more active forms of protests than the strike. Amidst rumors that a military force was accompanying General Kornilov to Moscow, all soviet parties hurried to put on a belated united front and called for a halt to the demonstration they thought they had unleashed. An extraordinary declaration signed by the Soviets of Workers', Soldiers', and Peasants' Deputies, the Moscow Menshevik organization, the Moscow Committees of the Bolshevik and Socialist Revolutionary parties, the United Organization of the Social-Democratic Workers' Party (Ob"edinenie), and the Central Bureau of Trade Unions, insisted that none of these groups had called for any demonstration and that workers should not under any circumstances participate in one.[107] An emergency revolutionary Committee of Six, with two representatives from each major party,

---

[104] *Trud*, 13 August 1917.

[105] *Utro Rossii*, 13 August 1917; *Vpered*, 23 August 1917; *Izv. MSRD*, 20 and 22 August 1917.

[106] For the reaction to the Moscow Conference in other industrial areas, see the discussion in Lisetskii, *Bol'sheviki vo glave massovykh stachek*, pp. 80-85.

[107] *Vpered*, 13 August 1917, carries the joint appeal to avoid demonstrations.

issued an urgent appeal for calm and unity in the face of the impending coup attempt. They were only two weeks premature.[108]

The Deterioration of Economic Conditions

A basic factor in Moscow's increased involvement in revolutionary protest was the ever-worsening economic situation. Food supply remained critical, and shortages were exacerbated by the continued upward spiral of prices of all necessities. And to add to these troubles, the local and national bourgeoisie began to take a harder line against workers' economic demands, preferring often to shut down production entirely rather than yield either profit margins or managerial prerogatives.

The influx of grain to Moscow had reached its peak in May, and reserves thereafter steadily diminished. Each report by the Soviet's provisions expert, M. E. Shefler (a Bolshevik) was grimmer than the last. On July 1, Shefler announced that grain reserves existed for the period until August 15.[109] The 2,000 carloads of grain that had arrived in May had dropped to 1,052 in June. Only 883 carloads arrived during July; in July 1916, Moscow had received almost 2,200.[110] On August 1, therefore, the Soviet again heard bad news: supplies were available only until August 9. One thousand cars were said to be en route, but their arrival time was uncertain. Meat, eggs, and oil were all scarce. The ministry of food supply had established consumption quotas for non-grain-producing districts, but it was unlikely that Moscow would receive its entire August allotment of 1,400 carloads.[111] By the month's end, only 785 cars had in fact reached the city.[112]

The August 1 meeting of the Soviet unanimously resolved to ask both for a monopoly on all manufactured goods in order to trade for grain and for the Provisional Government to increase the supply of food coming into the city.[113] But the Provisional Government had been flooded with such resolutions from the beginning of the revolution and had given little indication of action. The mood of the session was impatient. We talk and talk about monopolies and controls, declared deputy Bushurin, but nothing is done. "We already hear from every corner that under Tsar Nicholas things were better—then we received two funts of bread, and now one and a half and even less." Another delegate proposed a solution:

> Beyond Simonovka district is a warehouse with a huge reserve of food products. We submitted a petition, we stated that in Simonovka there are several thousand pounds of tobacco, but our petition went

---

[108] Grunt, *Moskva 1917-i*, p. 203.
[109] *Izv. MSRD*, 2 July 1917.
[110] *God raboty MGPK*.
[111] *Izv. MSRD*, 2 August 1917.
[112] *God raboty MGPK*.
[113] *Izv. MSRD*, 2 August 1917.

unanswered. If we had power, then we could act. If we had power, we could find hundreds of thousands of pounds of food products.[114]

The Provisional Government's response was to consider raising the price of grain to encourage rural holders to sell.[115] This rumor was enough to slow any further shipment until the price was allowed to rise to meet expectations; on August 19, Moscow's daily bread ration was reduced to one-half funt per person. Disorders at food shops began to mount. Crowds would gather at empty bakeries, then attack the local militia station, demanding food. Such incidents increased in frequency and intensity with the approach of autumn.[116]

The cost of living continued to increase after June; the rise was now a steady 10 to 12 percent a month[117] (see Table 3-3). In all probability, real costs for workers did not rise quite this fast since the market basket was based on the daily consumption of two and one-half funts of bread, whose cost rose especially rapidly during this time. But by late August, the bread ration was only one-half funt per person per day.

TABLE 3-3. *Change in Cost of Living, June-October 1917*

Month	Price Index	Percent Increase
June	142	14
July	159	12
August	175	10
September	196	12
October	217	11

NOTE: Cost of living is based on a 1916/17 market basket; January = 100.

As far as can be determined, average wages tended to rise during this period but not nearly so rapidly as rising costs. Continuing the rough estimate used above, Table 3-4 shows the progression of wages from June on.

Temporary or long-term unemployment resulting from supply and fuel shortages drove down the wage level. The city government announced on July 7 that Moscow's fuel reserves were nearly zero and appealed to the Provisional Government for help. Tram movement was curtailed because of the energy shortage. The textile industry's six-week layoff, ex-

[114] Joint Soviet plenum of August 1, reported in *Izv. MSRD*, supplement to no. 153.

[115] Volobuev, *Ekonomicheskaia politika*, p. 438; *Izv. MSRD*, supplement to no. 181, stenogram of August 26 plenum.

[116] *Gazeta-kopeika*, 11 August 1917; *Zemlia i volia*, 9 August 1917; *Russkoe slovo*, throughout July, August, and early September 1917.

[117] The indices reported in Katsenelenbaum and in Kokhn give a significant decline in prices for August but an inordinate rise for July, neither of which conforms to the trend shown here. I suspect their indices are at fault.

TABLE 3-4. *Change in Daily Wage in Rubles, June-October 1917*

Month	Received	Demanded
June	4.80	6.00
July	4.30	6.70
August	5.30	7.00
September	6.10	6.40
October	5.10	9.50

pected to end on August 17, continued, and there were reports that many workers were not receiving the two-thirds of their salary for this time which had been promised.[118] By late August, the situation had deteriorated so much that there was again talk of an "unloading" of Moscow as well as Petrograd;[119] the city could simply not supply all its citizens.

The Moscow Soviet appealed again and again to the Provisional Government to ease the crisis. But in the view shared by N. V. Nekrasov, the Kadet minister of finance, the workers themselves were partly responsible for the trouble. Workers made wage demands, and their employers simply turned to the government for more loans to pay their workers. (One wonders where the surplus came from to pay idle textile workers at two-thirds the normal rate.) And recently, Nekrasov continued, "it has become a common occurrence that it is not the enterprise's owner, not the plant administration, who requests the loan, but representatives of the workers." The workers should understand, he concluded, that they must increase their productivity to deserve higher pay.[120]

Indeed, continuing a trend begun early in the war, productivity had fallen since the start of 1917. In late July, a survey of Moscow plants working on military orders indicated declines in productivity of from 33 to 75 percent.[121] Throughout the year, factories had been closing for various reasons: unsettled strikes, fuel and raw-material shortages, lack of orders. Output inevitably declined. But who was to blame? Industrialists pointed to the eight-hour workday, to the wasted hours of political discussion and factory meetings which further eroded productivity.[122] The city of Moscow announced in late September it would have to close its large armaments plant. Because of low production and "abnormally high wages," the plant was losing 250,000 rubles a day.[123]

[118] *Russkoe slovo*, 7 July 1917; *Izv. MSRD*, 28 June, 23 August 1917.

[119] *Izv. MSRD*, 25 August 1917; *Delo naroda*, 26 August 1917.

[120] *Ekonomicheskoe polozhenie Rossii nakanune velikoi oktiabr'skoi sotsialisticheskoi revoliutsii*, vol. 2, 1957, p. 415.

[121] Ibid., vol. 1, p. 148.

[122] Workers at the Dinamo plant denied such charges, claiming they spent time in discussion only because of the assaults made by the management on their standard of living (*Izv. MSRD*, 4 July 1917).

[123] *Russkoe slovo*, 30 September 1917.

At the August 3 session of a conference of the Trade and Industrial Society, P. P. Riabushinskii pointed the finger at the Soviets, who were unable to convince their constituents of the primacy of productivity in exchange for pay raises. And he added, in the notorious phrase that was quickly perceived as a threat to working-class involvement in the revolution: "It will take the bony hand of hunger and national destitution to grasp at the throat of these false friends of the people, these members of various committees and soviets, before they will come to their senses."[124]

Workers, individually and through their soviets and trade unions, were not willing to accept complete responsibility for the state of affairs. After all, they had read and heard about the soaring war profits of their employers while they themselves were struggling just to keep pace with inflation.[125] Increasingly, individual employers and then capitalists as a class were seen as encouraging the fall in output and living standards, especially after Riabushinskii's August speech. The rhetoric of class so fundamental to the rise of Russian labor organization now offered a logical explanation for the economic events of the spring and summer: this was not just a revolution against the old order, it was class war.

From March onward, complaints from workers about their employers' tactics regularly appeared in the Moscow socialist press. When workers at the Provodnik rubber-tire plant were laid off, allegedly for lack of fuel, they protested that not only was there plenty of fuel but also that the plant had been producing rubber toys instead of the tires for which the government had contracted.[126] At the Russkii vodomerov copper-pipe factory, 140 of its 200 workers were sacked before Easter because of the lack of orders, copper, and fuel. Here the factory committee investigated and located reserves the plant administration had hidden, proving, said the workers, that the decline of production was due not to the eight-hour workday but to the speculative hoarding by factory owners.[127]

By summer, the word "sabotage" appeared more frequently in these

---

[124] *Ekonomicheskoe polozhenie*, vol. 2, p. 201.

[125] *Sots.-Dem.*, 13 June 1917. For a discussion of the complexity of estimating the profit levels of Russian firms during the war, see Theodore Cohen, "Wartime Profits of Russian Industry, 1914-1916," pp. 217-238. For the period under study, at least, Cohen finds evidence indeed of enormous profits; his sources, the reports issued by the ministry of finance, were also available at the time, and socialist economists probably drew on them to make similar deductions. See Volobuev, *Ekonomicheskaia politika*, pp. 279-286. I am grateful to Lewis Siegelbaum for calling my attention to the Cohen article.

[126] *Izv. MSRD*, 25 March 1917; *Delo naroda*, 25 March 1917; *Trudovaia kopeika*, 24 March 1917. The workers here more than protested through the press; they arrested five plant engineers and turned them over to the local militia commissariat.

[127] *Trudovaia kopeika*, 16 April 1917; *Izv. MSRD*, 14 April 1917.

complaints.[128] At one military plant, the owner tried to appropriate the plant's kerosene supply for his personal use.[129] Such major enterprises as the Guzhon steel mill and Riabushinskii's own AMO automobile plant were under constant threat of permanent shutdown. Guzhon complained that low productivity and high wages had made his plant unprofitable. But after workers pressured the state to sequester the plant, productivity increased dramatically.[130] The AMO plant, heavily subsidized by the state, had not yet produced a finished automobile. When finally ordered closed because some imported equipment never arrived, workers themselves continued production. The government responded with a scheme to use the facilities for repairing automobiles, but the plant was to be staffed with soldiers; the workers were all to be fired.[131] The cosy relationship of the Riabushinskiis of Moscow to the government became clearer each time such a move was reported.

THE BREAKDOWN OF THE FEBRUARY REVOLUTION, AUGUST TO OCTOBER

The Bolsheviks Conquer the Moscow Working Class

The contrasting scene within the Bolshoi theater and outside in the streets during the Moscow Conference symbolized the accelerating social polarization of this time. Despite an outward show of national unity, as when the Soviet leader Tsereteli embraced the Trade-Industrialist Aleksandr Bublikov in front of the conference, the Soviet as a local institution was already in danger of losing the support of its followers. Likewise, the State Conference had failed to prop up the faltering authority of the Provisional Government. Elements on the Right now began to prepare for a military putsch to establish once and for all the source of state power; the Left continued warily on the defensive, but the working-class mood in the two capitals was now openly hostile to the ruling coalition.

Social strata in the middle—moderate intellectuals, artists, and bureaucrats who had helped to staff the myriad of public organizations spawned by the February revolution—now seemed in Moscow to with-

---

[128] The word was repeated constantly in the debates at the all-city conference of factory committees held on July 23. Reports of the conference can be found in *Vpered*, 25 July 1917; *Soldat-Grazhdanin*, 25, 26, 27, and 28 July 1917; *Trud*, 25 July 1917; *Izv. MSRD*, 25, 26, 27, and 28 July, 6 August 1917.

[129] *Vpered*, 11 August 1917.

[130] *Russkoe slovo*, 15 July 1917.

[131] *Izv. MSRD*, 31 August 1917. See also S. V. Voronkova, "Stroitel'stvo avtomobil'nykh zavodov v Rossii v gody pervoi mirovoi voiny."

draw from active politics; they turned to their private lives and waited and hoped for a strong leader, a Napoleon-figure to break the deadlock of power.[132] This dissatisfaction spread from the salons to the streets; pogrom activity, touched off by food shortages, began to rise. House-holders in Moscow could no longer rely on public authorities to maintain order; to guard against robberies, they created neighborhood vigilante groups, which at the sound of an alarm would rush into the street to apprehend miscreants.[133]

Nor did the breakdown of order affect only middle-class property own-ers. On August 9, members of the Moscow Soviet's executive committee requested permission to carry weapons, a right denied since the July days. Committee members feared to return to their homes in the city's outskirts after late-night meetings without some form of protection against the dangerous elements lurking there.[134] In the weeks before the October insurrection, workers in suburban Bogorodsk found public safety had completely broken down and themselves organized the defense of the population from growing "lawlessness and hooliganism."[135]

Within working-class circles, the prestige of the Soviet had fallen very low with its unpopular decision on the Moscow Conference strike. Half-hearted preparations were begun on August 21 to observe the half-year anniversary of the Russian Revolution August 27, but the mood in the Soviet was not celebratory.[136] The chief point of discussion was whether finally to lift the six-week-old ban on outdoor meetings. Bolsheviks in the Soviet had demanded the right to agitate in the barracks; the coming district duma elections slated for September 24 also mandated reconsid-eration of the ban.

Noting the army's collapse at Riga and the obvious weakness of the Provisional Government, the Mensheviks and SRs in the Soviet feared open meetings would just encourage conflicts between working-class par-ties. Unity remained their theme. The Bolshevik speakers urged action; a simple appeal to unity was baseless, "to sing celebratory songs when we have come to a ration of a half-funt of bread is impossible," declared the Bolshevik trade unionist Ignatov.[137] Bolshevik party proposals to turn the August 27 observance into a day of agitation were narrowly defeated; the party did manage, however, to defeat the executive committee's pro-posal to take public collections for the use of the Central Executive Com-mittee of Soviets. The majority at the meeting agreed that workers would be likely to rebel against giving money for such a cause. This is how low

[132] Voznesenskii, *Moskva v 1917 g.*, pp. 70-72.　　　[133] Ibid., pp. 58, 146.

[134] *Izv. MSRD*, 10 August 1917.　　　[135] *Desiat' let*, p. 108.

[136] Ignatov, *Moskovskii sovet*, p. 314.

[137] Stenogram of August 25 joint SWD-SSD plenum, in *Izv. MSRD*, supplement to no. 175.

the Soviet's prestige had fallen on the very eve of the Kornilov mutiny.

The Kornilov rebellion was a pivotal episode not so much for what happened in Moscow as for its demarcation of the end of hopes for a compromise solution to the problems raised by the revolution. The main thrust of the rebel general's attack was revolutionary Petrograd, the seat of power, where the Right hoped for a Bolshevik uprising they could conclusively suppress. Moscow was strategically significant only as a transit point for Ataman Kaledin's cossacks coming from the south. Moreover, the Moscow military commander Verkhovskii was a firm supporter of the coalition government and he had made his loyalty clear in a warning to Kornilov: any attempted coup in Moscow would be opposed by the 15,000 seasoned troops under his command and 400,000 workers led by the Soviet.[138] But as long as the outcome of Kornilov's attempt was in doubt, Moscow's workers prepared to resist. The major soviet parties agreed on August 28 to form an "organ of revolutionary action" to fight the counterrevolution (although the Bolsheviks entered only "for technical reasons," to coordinate the resistance).[139] A clamor arose from the working-class neighborhoods for arms for self-defense. The creation of a Soviet-sponsored "Red Guard," hitherto confined to small units of workers for protection of individual factories, became the issue of the day. Despite the low level of Soviet prestige, Moscow's workers immediately rallied in the emergency to the one institution that represented them all and them alone.

The Kornilov rebellion itself, opposed by most supporters of the Provisional Government as well as soviet partisans, was soon crushed, and the crisis in Moscow never materialized. But the distrustful mood in the city toward the government now hardened into hostility. The Bolshevik party had been warning against the counterrevolutionary character of the government for months; the Soviet's Menshevik-SR leaders had insisted they were quite prepared to fight if the counterrevolution arose. As recently as August 18, the Menshevik Kibrik had declared, in defense of the politics of unity, "There are not now the objective conditions for a dictatorship [of Kornilov or Kerensky] and there cannot be. Our organization is too strong."[140] As reports reached Moscow of the complicity of some members of the Kadet party in the coup attempt, even the Mensheviks now lost faith in the possibility of a coalition with the party of the bourgeoisie.

The Soviet executive committee discussed the changed political situation on September 1. Nobody favored a continuation of the old coalition; Mensheviks and SRs spoke for a general democratic government com-

[138] Verkhovskii, *Na trudnom perevale*, p. 309; Grunt, *Moskva 1917-i*, pp. 206-209.
[139] *Izv. MSRD*, 30 August 1917.   [140] Ibid., 19 August 1917.

posed of representatives from soviets, cooperatives, and city and zemstvo organizations. It was an attempt to reach out to the middle of Russian society which they saw as dividing the working class from the now-discredited ruling bourgeoisie. The Bolsheviks countered, however, that it was precisely this kind of ineffectual coalition which had allowed Kornilov and friends to attempt their coup. The soviets should not fear to take a position of leadership.[141] And on September 5, at the first Soviet plenum after Kornilov's defeat, the Bolsheviks proposed a resolution calling for a government that would decree a democratic republic, nullify secret treaties, abolish the sale of land until the Constituent Assembly, and establish a statewide system of workers' supervision over the economy. In an historic vote, the Bolshevik resolution was adopted by a margin of 355 to 254, the first time the party had won a majority.[142] There can be no question that the Kornilov mutiny finally convinced the deputies that the Menshevik-SR majority's compromise tactics were futile.

The Bolshevik triumph in the Soviet set off a flurry of activity unparalleled in Moscow since March. On September 19 the Soviet elected a new executive committee to correspond to the new political alignment of the Soviet plenum. The Bolshevik list received 246 votes, compared to 125 for the Mensheviks, 65 for SRs, and 26 for the United Social-Democrats. V. P. Nogin replaced Khinchuk as chairman.[143] The Soviet had already approved the formation of a Red Guard to defend the city; now commissions and committees were reorganized to conform to the new disposition of party support. The impression conveyed by the Bolshevik-led Soviet, after months of lethargy under the old leadership, was one of great energy and construction.

At the same time, a campaign was under way for district duma elections. Immediately after the revolution, functions formerly executed by police and city administration were taken over by local committees of citizens' groups; these functioned loosely as local arms of the Committee of Public Organizations. With the election of an official city duma, it was decided to regularize the status of these local administrative units, of which there were over fifty. Elections to seventeen new district dumas were finally scheduled for September 24. The Bolshevik party, on a platform of energetic activity in local affairs about which working-class daily lives were most concerned, carried out a strong campaign. Indeed, when one reads the accounts of party activity in the Bolshevik organ *Sotsial-Demokrat* during the month of September, one would never suspect that Lenin was at that time rallying the party around his plan for a soviet seizure of power. Local Bolsheviks were out to prove their fitness to rule by showing

---

[141] Ibid., 2 September 1917.

[142] Ibid., 6 September 1917.

[143] Ibid., 20 September 1917.

that workers could administer their local affairs. On the wave of their capture of the Soviet majority, the Bolsheviks scored an astounding victory in the local duma elections as well. The election will be considered at greater length in Chapter Five; suffice it to say here that on September 24, albeit in relatively light voting, the Bolsheviks received 52 percent of the total vote cast, winning an outright majority in eleven of the seventeen districts.

The picture of local dynamism contrasted sharply with the situation in Petrograd and the country at large. In mid-September, Kerensky had called a Democratic Conference, his latest attempt to prop up the sagging authority of the Provisional Government. The conference, comprised of representatives of soviets, peasant organizations, and cooperatives, urged the expedition of the Constituent Assembly, which had been repeatedly postponed for one reason or another, and for the interim, agreed to a coalition government. But on the very next vote, the conference adopted an amendment to exclude the Kadet party from such a coalition. The amended resolution for a coalition government was then soundly defeated. The conference adjourned with no success, leaving behind it a Preparliament to advise the Provisional Government until the Constituent Assembly could meet.

The Preparliament, or Council of the Republic, was boycotted by the Bolsheviks, now clearly the most important voice of the working class, while the Kadets transformed it into a miniature duma, with all its procedures, commissions, and attendant inability to respond to rapidly changing conditions.[144] On September 25, Kerensky assembled his last coalition; despite the manifest sentiment of the Democratic Conference against the Kadet party, the new cabinet included four Kadet ministers, including the key minister of foreign affairs.

Meanwhile, a second All-Russian Congress of Soviets was scheduled to begin on October 20. Perhaps this body would assume the leadership of the revolution after so many months of the current Soviet Central Executive Committee's refusing to do so. In the aftermath of the Moscow district duma elections, Bukharin expressed the Bolshevik party view in the Moscow Soviet: "The proletariat grows stronger, organizes itself, is achieving political maturity, in sharp contradiction to the bourgeoisie."[145] But the Menshevik-SR minority still recoiled from the concept of working-class power and urged cooperation with a broad base of democratic society. With the Constituent Assembly elections now scheduled for November 12 in Moscow, perhaps a final solution to the question of interim power would be unnecessary.

[144] See Rosenberg, *Liberals*, p. 255.
[145] *Izv. MSRD*, 29 September 1917.

If the rebirth of the Soviet as a leader of working-class activity and the new beginnings of the district dumas recalled the optimistic days of March, there were three crucial differences in the September-October period. The bourgeoisie, through the Kadet party, had disqualified itself as an acceptable partner in furthering the revolution. The army, routed by the Germans at Riga, was totally devoid of the will to fight what now seemed more than ever to be a meaningless war. The new war minister, Verkhovskii, argued as much to the Preparliament on October 20; he was forced to resign for his pains.[146] Most fundamentally, and of far greater immediate impact, the economy seemed to be disastrously out of control. Elections, changes in party influence, debates in the Democratic Conference and Preparliament, and the Constituent Assembly all became secondary to the growing threat of Moscow's economic collapse.

Economic Conditions toward October: The "Bony Hand of Hunger"

Food supply continued as a critical issue for Moscow's population in the last months under the Provisional Government. From a peak of 2,019 carloads of grain shipped to Moscow in May, receipts had fallen to 883 carloads in July, and 785 in August.[147] As has been seen, the bread ration in Moscow dropped to one-half funt per person on August 19. In a last attempt to increase the grain supply, the Provisional Government finally acceded to pressure from grain suppliers and on August 27 permitted the base price for grain to double. Although reneging on the old so-called fixed price encouraged some peasants to wait even longer for a new higher price, the result once again for Moscow was to pry loose some withheld reserves. The September inflow of grain jumped to 1,284 carloads, and the ration was increased to three-quarters funt on September 15.[148]

If one can believe that the Moscow press reported all food disorders that occurred, it would appear that such disturbances diminished after the increase in the ration. Only one disorder attracted press attention: an angry crowd refused to believe that its bakery had already sold all its bread, forcibly searched the premises, but indeed found no bread. The bakery owner, claiming he had baked the same amount of bread that day as always, blamed the shortage on the recent appearance of counterfeit ration cards and promised bread for the next day, and the crowd dispersed.[149] But the daily reports of similar incidents, so common before September 15, now ceased. Perhaps three-fourths of a funt was the psychological minimum the population could tolerate; anything below summoned spontaneous resistance. It was ominous, then, that when October

---

[146] Rosenberg, *Liberals*, p. 258.
[147] *God raboty MGPK.*
[148] *Izv. MSRD*, 12 September 1917; see Volobuev, *Ekonomicheskaia politika*, p. 438.
[149] *Trudovaia kopeika*, 24 September 1917.

grain shipments again fell to eight hundred carloads, the city food-supply committee ordered the ration cut back to one-half funt—effective October 24.[150]

Meanwhile, as they had been since April, representatives of the working class in the Soviet were still wrestling with the broader implications of the collapse of trade and industry. The gravity of the crisis was made clear in a session of the Soviet plenum on August 26. D. V. Kuzovkov, the Menshevik financial specialist, pinned the blame for the crisis on the Provisional Government's practice of deflating the currency with its constant issue of paper money. Already government presses printed 55 million rubles' worth of notes daily; a second press had been opened in July, and government officials were negotiating in Western Europe to add to its capacity to produce the paper notes.[151] "The highest wage, depreciating, is quickly transformed to a starvation wage, and workers have to lead a continual struggle to raise it," reported Kuzovkov. This struggle leads to conflicts, conflicts to strikes, strikes to lockouts—all of these lower productivity, and output falls, furthering the decline of the ruble.[152] The Soviet had repeatedly demanded firmer measures from the Provisional Government: limits on profits, more power to food-supply committees, and a campaign against those opposing the government's grain monopoly. But the government was under heavy pressure from its bourgeois constituents to preserve free trade in food supply, to limit the powers of food-supply committees, to recognize the right of free enterprise to maximize profits. Between these two forces, the government had done nothing. Kuzovkov described his effort to gain the support of the government.

> I was sent by the Executive Committee to Petersburg in order to support our position. I spoke with the director of the finance commission, who at the time was Shingarev, and I saw that we were standing before a deaf wall, off of which bounced all our requests, all our demands. I came to Petrograd a Menshevik but have returned from there practically a Bolshevik.[153]

The connection between economic collapse and governmental inaction was described somewhat more graphically by the deputy from a Zamoskvorech'e metal plant. He understood Kuzovkov's near-conversion; in his plant, workers made demands on May 3 and received nothing. All their requests remained "voices crying in the wilderness." The workers saw how their rights were curtailed daily, how the death penalty was reintroduced first at the front, then in the rear. Now, he said, we notice

[150] *Sots.-Dem.*, 24 October 1917.
[151] Volobuev, *Ekonomicheskaia politika*, p. 357.
[152] Stenogram of joint Soviet plenum, August 26, in *Izv. MSRD*, supplement to no. 181.
[153] Ibid., p. 3.

that the street kiosks are full of fruit—but no bread. "Everything for the bourgeoisie, nothing for the worker."[154] Clearly Kornilov, who was just then making his move on Petrograd, was not the only factor in shifting the balance of support in the Soviet to the Bolshevik party.

Boris Kibrik, who was still a Menshevik, tried to convince the August 26 assembly that the government was not entirely at fault. Local organs were not doing all they could to solve the supply problem. He cited the case of his own neighborhood, where bread queues had become endemic. A local capitalist hired a horse and cart and distributed bread from the bakeries to small shops; the queues were eliminated. The capitalist may believe in "war to the victorious end," said Kibrik, but he knew how to solve problems. If the Soviet could not deal with food supply on a local scale, how could they hope to govern the country? Here in a nutshell was the Menshevik philosophy in 1917; up to their elbows in practical work themselves, they were under no illusions that a transfer of power alone could effect the miracles the Bolshevik party promised. But when Kibrik rhetorically queried, would there be bread within three days after the Provisional Government was replaced, a voice from the assembly cried, "There would!"[155]

The problems of food supply were but one aspect of the complex economic situation by autumn. Because of the shortage of transport and the labor conflicts in the coal-producing Donbass, the supply of fuel in Moscow was once again as critically low as it had been on the eve of the February revolution. A new wave of factory closings was announced, which threatened to add to the growing unemployment in Moscow.[156] The metalworkers' union published figures on workers seeking and receiving jobs through its labor exchange from July to mid-October (see Table 3-5). In July, almost 75 percent of male job seekers found new employment; this number dropped to 47 percent in August, rose to 66 percent in September, but plummeted to 38 percent in the first two weeks of October. (Women, whose average skill level did not compare to men's, fared even more poorly.) What was worse, the absolute number of unplaced metalists rose each month, from 128 at the end of July to over 800 on October 14. And metalworkers were easily the most highly sought-after workers in this period of skilled-labor shortage. The unemployment picture must surely have been even grimmer in less-specialized industries. The tailors' union reported 400 members seeking work, despite the fact that the army would absolutely require more warm clothing for the coming winter.[157] Now, in September, "self-demobilizing" soldiers

154 Ibid., p. 10.
155 Ibid., p. 11.
156 P. V. Volobuev, *Proletariat i burzhuaziia*, pp. 314-320.
157 *Soldat-Grazhdanin*, 20 September 1917.

TABLE 3-5. *Unemployment among Moscow Metalists,*
July-October 1917

Month	Percent Unemployed Finding Work		Total Without Work	
	Men	Women	Men	Women
July	79.9	41.9	85	43
August	47.1	12.5	422	236
September	66.0	11.4	498	450
October 1-14	37.8	6.6	596	230

SOURCE: *Moskovskii metallist*, 1917, throughout.

were swelling the ranks of the unemployed, competing with veteran workers for the diminishing supply of jobs.[158]

Here too, as with food supply, workers saw the government as the villain. When conflicts arose over wages, the government encouraged mediation, negotiation, and restraint. Since wage increases were immediately canceled by inflation, workers increasingly demanded more control over access to jobs; the right to approve the hiring and firing of workers by factory committees or trade unions became a key issue in several major strikes in Moscow in this period (see Chapter Eight). And yet Menshevik Labor Minister Skobelev opposed workers' input into the hiring process.[159]

The strike movement, although not so widespread now as in the peak months of May and July, became more bitter. The entire leather industry had been on strike since August 11; the chief issue was the workers' right to control hiring. A nationwide railroad strike, threatening the total breakdown of supply, was scheduled for September 20. The union of municipal employees, after months of fruitless negotiations with its democratic employer, had begun to prepare for a total shutdown of city services, beginning gradually with trams and munitions shops on October 15 and moving up to hospitals and bakeries by October 21 if their demands were not met. Textile workers in Moscow province went on strike on October 21, with the city textilists threatening daily to join them.[160]

Riabushinskii's "bony hand of hunger" speech, Kornilov, the Provi-

[158] More precise data on unemployment or factory closings cannot be found. Surely eight hundred unemployed metalists in a work force of fifty thousand is not "massive unemployment." The joblessness situation in Moscow may not have been so severe as in Petrograd or elsewhere, but the trends reported here indicated worse was to come, and concerned delegates to the Soviet and in factories may well have been reacting to the expectation of further crisis.

[159] Skobelev's refusal to back the workers on this issue was a source of disillusionment with Menshevik policies in an analogous situation in Baku in August. See Suny, *Baku Commune*, p. 127.

[160] See below, Chapter Seven; Trukan, *Oktiabr' v tsentral'noi Rossii*, pp. 210-217; *Izv. MSRD*, 24 October 1917; *Trud*, 13 October 1917.

sional Government's inability to alleviate shortages, and now these intractable strikes all served to convince the representatives of Moscow's working population that economics and politics could not be treated as separate departments. No longer could the Mensheviks plausibly declare that the workers' participation in government regulation was a usurpation of the job properly reserved for the bourgeoisie. The question of political power was inextricably bound up with the direction of the economy. The majority in the Moscow Soviet now felt that, at least until the Constituent Assembly, only a government of soviets could honestly deal with these problems and save the victories of the revolution from complete annihilation.

For the leaders of the Bolshevik party in Moscow, the only question remaining was how to obtain this government. Expanding the current strike wave to a general strike (and through this means, seizing power) was rejected. A general strike was too difficult to control.[161] Finally, the Bolsheviks decided simply to act as though the Soviet were in fact the government. On October 19, the Soviet declared by decree that all strikes were now settled in favor of the workers, and any capitalist who refused to obey would be arrested. To back up this order, the Soviet called on its fighting arm, the newly chartered Red Guard.[162]

Also on October 19 in Kaluga, eighty miles to the south of Moscow, a unit of cossacks under Provisional Government orders raided the local soviet and placed its members under arrest. Lenin had not yet emerged from hiding, the Bolshevik Central Committee in Petrograd had not yet begun the insurrection that would place state power in the hands of the soviets; but in central Russia, as elsewhere, the daggers of class warfare were already drawn. When the Petrograd Bolsheviks did seize control of the government on October 25, Moscow attempted to follow suit; and after ten days of bloody street fighting, Moscow too passed under soviet control.

I shall return to these days in the conclusion of this book. But now that the main lines of the development of the revolution in Moscow have been reviewed, a return to the workers is in order; and by considering their role and activities during this period, one can more fully understand the complex process that underlay the seizure of soviet power in Russia in October 1917.

[161] Grunt, *Moskva 1917-i*, p. 257; *Moskovskii sovet professional'nykh soiuzov*, pp. 101-111.
[162] *Izv. MSRD*, 20 October 1917.

FOUR. *Organizing the Revolution:*
THE EVOLUTION OF WORKING-CLASS
INSTITUTIONS

REGARDLESS of political hue, the key word for all participants in the February revolution was *organization.* The outcome of events was still very much in doubt; and if a Constituent Assembly was widely conceded to be the only legitimate architect of a new regime, the immediate task was to preserve and protect the revolution until such an assembly could take place. The old institutions, whether Imperial State Council or local police, were bankrupt. Something had to replace them until a permanent and workable new system could be constructed. And some way had to be found to institutionalize, to channel, to mobilize permanently the massive revolutionary energy that had swept the old regime from power.

There were few blueprints for revolutionary institutions in February 1917. Some organizations arose to fill immediate needs as did the militia, which replaced the disarmed gendarmerie. Some arose because they had mobilized workers in Russia's revolutionary past, as was the case with the soviets. And some arose, as the factory committees and trade unions did, from existing but moribund institutions such as councils of elders (*sovety starost*) and both legal and illegal professional societies. The impulse to form revolutionary organizations came from two directions and often simultaneously. From above, as this study has shown, party and public leaders urged the formation of such working-class institutions as soviets and unions. From below, workers spontaneously created organizations in order to take advantage of the gains of the revolution—freedom to participate fully in public life, to organize, and to bargain with employers as equals.

In this chapter, I shall explore the process of institution building in 1917, focusing on three institutions that represented the entire working class: factory committees, soviets, and trade unions.[1] While each of the

---

[1] Other institutions, formed from subgroups of the working class, also deserve study for what they can tell us about the process of revolutionary mobilization, but space and source limitations preclude such study here. These institutions include the cooperatives, the militia and Red Guard, the youth groups, and the cultural and social institutions such as schools, clubs, and special interest groups forming outside the aegis of the three umbrella institutions considered here. The political party as an institution also deserves study, but here one is hampered by the abundance of sources, often tendentious, on the Bolshevik party and the lack of sources on the Menshevik and Socialist Revolutionary parties. Some studies of the above institutions include V. V. Kabanov, *Oktiabr'skaia revoliutsiia i kooperatsiia*; Rex A.

three enjoyed its own sphere of competence, the activities of all three overlapped in many areas. Consequently, the competition among working-class institutions such as these to serve the needs of the workers (just like the rivalry between the Provisional Government and the quasi-governmental Petrograd Soviet) was an important part of the revolutionary experience in 1917, one which is often ignored as a source of friction in the history of the revolution. If the preceding overview of the revolutionary months of 1917 has suggested a linear progression toward an inevitable October, the examination here and in later chapters will help to modify the impression of the 1917 revolution as a one-dimensional process. The interaction between workers and their institutions, and among the institutions themselves, produced conflicts within the working class which affected the shape of the revolution and perhaps also its outcome. Menshevik leaders in the Moscow Soviet, so concerned about unity, for example, were in fact responding to these very real problems of organizational experience.

This study will not concern itself here with the leaders of the working class and what they thought about the problems of organization. For too long these institutions have been studied only through the prism of their leadership. The process of institution building will be examined from the perspective of the participants, particularly from the roots of the revolution in Moscow. This chapter will therefore be concerned with the way in which workers translated their revolutionary enthusiasm into new kinds of permanent organizations, with their expected (and the actual) achievements of these institutions, with sources of leadership, and with the relationship between leaders and led. I shall also attempt to explore the problem of "revolutionary consciousness": who were more "conscious," the workers who took to the streets to achieve maximalist goals (the seizure of political power) or those who worked diligently within permanent organizations to achieve the same end? The issue here is the old problem of the relationship between spontaneity and discipline—as well as the meaning of consciousness. Just how complex these concepts are will become more readily apparent when the processes of institution building within the Moscow working class are examined in more detail in the pages to come.

ORGANIZATIONAL EMERGENCE

Until the Soviet officially asked for all work to resume on March 6, Moscow seemed to be one continuous round of meetings. Workers took the op-

Wade, "Spontaneity in the Formation of the Workers' Militia and Red Guards, 1917"; Tsuyoshi Hasegawa, "The Formation of the Militia in the February Revolution," pp. 303-322; Koenker, "Urban Families"; *Prechistenskie kursy*.

portunity at these meetings to express their expectations of the revolution (see Chapter Six), but they were also building new democratic institutions. At many of these first meetings, workers elected Soviet deputies according to the instructions handed down from the center and chose factory committees to deal with purely local matters. By March 3, when the Soviet issued a call for the formation of factory committees, local delegates reported thirty factories in their districts had already formed such committees.[2]

Factory committees formed most quickly in the biggest plants, whose general meetings soon proved incapable of handling day-to-day affairs. In the first two weeks of March, newspapers reported the formation of committees in twenty-nine factories (seven of which were machine-building plants). These plants employed an average of 1,670 workers, compared to the average of 920 for all plants with known factory committees (and 202 for all Moscow factories). Usually the committees were elected by shop (*tsekh*), especially at so-called universal factories like the Postavshchik military supply plant, which employed workers from several different trades.[3] And in at least one factory, there were two separate workers' committees: at Prokhorovskaia Trekhgornaia, there were both a formally named factory committee and a "factory soviet" composed of the enterprise's thirteen deputies to the Moscow Soviet. These continued to meet, sometimes separately and sometimes together, until new Soviet rules reduced the factory's delegation to five.[4]

It is difficult to tell if the factory committees were formed by local initiative or if they were organized by outsiders. Very little firsthand reporting of the actual formation of factory committees exists, but the occasional report that describes their organization mentions the presence of outside speakers who proposed various resolutions on political themes. At the Faberzhe factory, for example, five hundred workers heard a report of a representative of the Bolshevik city committee, discussed the war, and then organized a factory committee that would send its representatives to the local Bolshevik raion committee.[5] It is more than likely that the decision to form the committee was made at the suggestion of the Bolshevik speaker. Soviet deputies from the Rogozhskii district reported on March 3 that they had elected a commission of nine who would organize factory committees where none yet existed.[6] On the same day, the Soviet's new Section for the Organization of Raion Committees called for workers to form "raion committees"—both factory committees and also local committees of factory representatives—for the purpose of establishing order

[2] *Izv. MSRD*, 4 March 1917.   [3] *Vpered*, 5 May 1917.
[4] S. G. Al'tman, "Bol'shevizatsiia raionnykh sovetov Moskvy i ikh deiatel'nost' v marte-oktiabre 1917 g.," p. 58.
[5] *Sots.-Dem.*, 5 March 1917.   [6] *Izv. MSRD*, 5 March 1917.

in the localities.[7] It would seem, then, that the suggestion of factory committees came from above, but in any case local factories quickly responded to the suggestion. Comprehensive data on the creation of these committees do not exist, but local newspaper reports indicate that 167 factories (representing 153,000 workers) formed factory committees in 1917; no cases were reported in which factories did not organize committees.

The functions of factory committees, and indeed of the Soviet, were not yet clear in the first two weeks of the revolution. Their major purpose seemed to be simply to propagate working-class organizations further. The next step after committee formation was to create commissions and assign responsibilities. On March 2, the Dobrovo-Nabgolts factory committee organized commissions on food supply, culture and enlightenment, finance, and military units.[8] At the half-finished AMO automobile plant, I. V. Gorshkov found himself appointed to create a factory library, subscribe to newspapers, and collect dues. (He was also the factory committee chairman and one of AMO's Soviet deputies, and he later became commissar of the Simonovskii district militia.)[9]

From the earliest moments of its existence, the Moscow Soviet was also concerned about establishing strong local working-class organizations. Eight raions, corresponding to major working-class districts, were established on March 3; and Soviet deputies from these areas were urged to organize raion soviets, the more effectively to organize local factories. Members of local soviets were often the area's central Soviet deputies or members of area factory committees or both, and it was not infrequent that the scarcity of qualified workers, such as AMO's Gorshkov, meant that the same individuals assumed several responsible posts.[10]

The emphasis on local organization also helped to take advantage of existing working-class organizations. There had been strong localist tendencies throughout Moscow's revolutionary history—in December 1905, the Presnia district held out alone after the Moscow uprising of that month,[11] and subsequent organizations also tended to be formed by district. A wartime metalist union, Unity (Edinenie), was confined to workers in the Lefortovo district, and the existence of locally based cooperatives—such as in Preobrazhenskoe in the northeast and Simonovka in the southeast—also helped develop regional cohesiveness. This study has already

[7] Ibid., 3 March 1917; *Vechernii kur'er*, 4 March 1917.

[8] *Letopis' geroicheskikh dnei*, p. 19.

[9] I. V. Gorshkov, *Moi vospominaniia o fevral'skoi i oktiabr'skoi revoliutsii 1917 g. v Rogozhsko-Simonovskom raione*, passim.

[10] Dune, p. 28; Al'tman, p. 79.

[11] Laura Engelstein stresses the importance of neighborhoods in mobilization in 1905 in "Moscow in the 1905 Revolution."

shown how proximity helped to spread strikes in the immediate pre-February period, when Zamoskvorech'e factories dominated the movement. Underground party organizations were also decentralized, largely out of the need for secrecy, and it was the eight Social-Democratic party raions that formed the basis for the local soviet districts in 1917.[12]

In fact, it was sometimes difficult to distinguish between local party committees, called *raionnye komitety*, and the first local soviets, also called raionnye komitety. For example, the concerns of a Social-Democratic raion committee meeting in Rogozhskii on March 4 were similar to those of nonparty soviets elsewhere: organizing local committees and meetings, and discussing the Constituent Assembly.[13]

The activities of the local soviets in the first days varied with the nature of the districts they represented. The Simonovskii raion was an isolated area, almost exclusively working class, with an established cooperative society and club, "Enlightenment," and a sick fund with 4,500 members.[14] With this strong experience in local government, workers in the Simonovskii soviet played an active role in establishing revolutionary order in the district. Cooperating closely with the local committee of public organizations, in a spirit of interclass unity typical of the early stage of the revolution, the soviet took major responsibility in creating a local militia and in dealing with matters of food supply.[15]

Conditions in the central Gorodskoi district were quite different from those in Simonovskii and prompted a different response from the local soviet there. Where Simonovka was dominated by a few huge plants, most workers in the Gorodskoi district did not work in factories at all. The only way to organize the thousands of tailors, shoemakers, domestic servants, cooks, waiters, and other artisans living in the center was through trade unions; and while other soviets were instructing workers to elect factory committees, the Gorodskoi raion soviet was organizing meetings of workers by trade. By March 14, the soviet had organized over twenty meetings of plumbers, hospital workers, theatrical workers, barbers, boot makers, dyers, domestic servants, maintenance workers, and four kinds of hat makers.[16]

The earliest unions to form were not those representing the largest segments of the work force, such as metalists and textilists, but those that

[12] *Izv. MSRD*, 5 March 1917. The emphasis on decentralization was carried even further by the acting city government, the Committee of Public Organizations. Raion dumas and their administrative arms, upravy, were formed haphazardly, combining two or three old police precincts, or sometimes on the basis of the sanitary trusteeships created during the war to aid refugees. Workers played important roles in some of these dumas, particularly in the eastern part of the city. See Gorshkov, pp. 17-18.

[13] *Sots.-Dem.*, 8 March 1917. [14] *Utro Rossii*, 22 February 1917.

[15] Gorshkov, pp. 6-13. [16] *Izv. MSRD*, 17 March 1917.

were based on artisan trades or else industries with a small number of factories, such as confectioners. These were the unions that had been most active in the years betweeen 1905 and 1917, and though their activities had been on a small scale, a foundation existed for further organizational work. Even though the tailors' union leaders had all been arrested by January 9, 1917, and the number of union members was small, the union quickly expanded after February: "workers left work by the shopful and went to enroll in the union; after a week the union had grown from 150 members to tens of thousands of members."[17] Of the eleven other unions that formed in the first two weeks of March, all but one represented artisans and service workers; and a few of these had established the rudiments of organization before the February revolution: bakers, purse makers, and cooks. Only the confectioners' union represented factory workers, and this was a union that had never gone out of existence. Its board of directors (*pravlenie*) had met weekly during January and February 1917, and after the revolution simply convened its regular meeting on March 3, this time to lay plans for the legal expansion of the union's activities.[18]

The early history of the confectioners' union illustrates a major problem in determining the level of organization of trade unions in Moscow. It was frequently the case that unions existed in name only or were represented by a very few—sometimes one or two—individuals who called themselves leaders of a given trade union. The confectioners had a board of directors which met on March 3, but the union's first general membership meeting was not scheduled until March 19, and a union charter was not adopted until June 17.[19] Thus union organization took place on two levels. At the top level, individuals proclaimed themselves as union representatives and undertook organizational work on behalf of the union. These individuals tended to be veterans of the labor movement, often professional organizers and not workers at all. And because the Bolsheviks had been the dominant party in the 1912 to 1914 union period, these individuals also tended to be Bolsheviks. At this level, union representatives organized a Central Bureau of Trade Unions and set about promoting the same kinds of general organizational work performed by the Moscow Soviet. Thus the Central Bureau, which came to rival the Soviet as a focus of working-class power in August, was in no sense a representative body of trade unions. It began, really, as a coterie of comrades from the prerevolutionary underground movement, organized, says one

[17] O. Burachenko, "Dumy i vospominaniia."

[18] *Trudovaia kopeika*, January-February 1917; *Izv. MSRD*, 5 March 1917.

[19] *Sots.-Dem.*, 17 March, 17 June 1917. Actually, it is not even clear that the March 19 meeting took place. The only record of it—as for most union meetings in 1917—was a notice that it was scheduled to be held.

participant, to counter the Menshevik-SR dominated Soviet with a Bolshevik working-class center.[20] But once this partisan body existed, it became a natural focus of all trade union activity. Likewise, the early organizers of individual unions were simply self-selected, not chosen by their constituents, so their existence did not imply that there was a union of which they were the leaders.

It did not take such experienced activists long to take the first steps toward defining their organizations, but at the lower level, that of mass participation, unions developed rather more slowly. The typical pattern of union formation involved a process of several stages. First, a meeting had to be organized for all members of a trade interested in forming a union. At this meeting, a "provisional board of directors" or "organizing commission" would be chosen which would prepare for another meeting at which the union could be formally constituted. With proper publicity and organizational work, a second meeting would attract a larger crowd, a permanent set of leaders could be elected, and the union could officially open its activities.[21] It was easy enough for workers to form factory committees, for these committees represented existing bodies—the factories. But for workers to perceive that they had interests in common with other members of their industry whom they did not know was an abstraction that seemed to require additional experience and education;[22] thus it was that the unions who were first to form were those that existed previously and who had leaders to rekindle organizational energy.

Organizational Development

One consequence of the explosion of organizational activity in the early days of the revolution in Moscow was that the relationship of these organizations to one another was poorly defined. No organization had a monopoly on any area of working-class activity. Factory committees, soviets, and trade unions were all involved in labor conflicts and in negotiations for improved economic conditions. All three institutions assumed responsibility for the management of local life—from establishing social clubs to securing control over food supply or even production. And all three institutions were involved in representing the policy views of their constituents. This lack of delineation of responsibility was apparent from the creation of the Central Bureau of Trade Unions to rival and not complement the Soviet. Throughout the year, factory committees and

[20] T. Sapronov, *Iz istorii rabochego dvizheniia*, p. 124.

[21] Such was the case of the union of lower city employees, which united workers in municipal bakeries, warehouses, tram parks and other city-owned enterprises (*Sots.-Dem.*, 15 March 1917).

[22] K. Polevoi, in *Vpered*, 15 March 1917.

local soviets performed similar functions; in several districts the two held regular joint meetings. Factory committees were sometimes acknowledged to be subordinate units of trade unions or soviets, but at other times they acted as coequal representatives of the working class.

Such overlapping of functions of different institutions could and did lead to problems. One was a shortage of leadership, which resulted in poorly qualified people assuming responsible posts—like the factory committee secretaries who could not read or write.[23] Eventually, workers became disillusioned with poor performance and either replaced these leaders or turned to different institutions entirely—such as the Bolshevik party. Thus while the large number of working-class organizations meant that all workers might be reached by one or another working-class institution, the organizations also may have spread themselves too thin by this effort and disillusioned many workers with their poor performance. These problems can be examined in greater depth by looking at the different functions served by the major working-class institutions.

A primary task of all these organizations was to represent the workers' economic interests, which ranged from higher wages to the many aspects of workers' control. At the local level, these economic interests of the workers often came into conflict with the interests of employers, and workers were often motivated to organize in order to deal with such conflicts at almost every level of working-class life. The factory committees, as the organization closest to factory workers, were frequently in the center of labor-management conflicts. Indeed, the chief issues raised at the first meeting of seamstresses at a military-supply warehouse were the economic needs of the workers and how to deal with them. The meeting elected a factory committee to formulate and present demands to the military administration.[24] Unless the demands led to strikes, this kind of activity was seldom reported in the press, but evidence that economic negotiations were a significant part of the normal functions of factory committees is found in the protocols of the Prokhorovskaia factory committee, which were published in full in 1931. At its third meeting on March 13, the committee agreed to press for eight separate workers' demands, including payment of holiday bonuses to all workers (not just those of favored sections), for bath water to be available at all times for the various shifts, and for workers to be given money for housing during periods when the factory was not operating.[25] Later meetings were con-

[23] At the Einem candy factory, for example, all those nominated for the position of committee secretary declined because of poor literacy (*Oktiabr' v Zamoskvorech'e*, p. 120).

[24] *Vpered*, 11 March 1917.

[25] "Protokoly fabrichno-zavodskogo komiteta Prokhorovskoi Trekhgornoi manufaktury," no. 8, p. 106. This factory was not typical of Moscow enterprises; the owner, Prokhorov, was notorious among Moscow industrialists for his paternalistic attitude toward his workers. (See Buryshkin, pp. 143-146.)

cerned with Easter bonuses, inflation adjustments, and nurses' conditions in the factory hospitals.

When economic issues did lead to strikes, it was frequently the factory committee that directed the action. Specific information on strike leadership is available for only about half of all strikes reported in individual factories, but of these 93 strikes, 21 were led explicitly by factory committees and an additional 8 by factory-level strike committees. In addition, it is reasonable to assume that when negotiations took place prior to the strike ("the workers of factory X made these demands . . ."), it was probably the factory committee that coordinated the local-level negotiations that occurred in 50 of the 215 strikes in individual factories.[26]

Probably the broadest economic function of factory committees, because it encompassed most of the others, was that of *kontrol'*. Much has been written about the theoretical problems of worker control of industry,[27] and the term was frequently heard in revolutionary rhetoric; but what was the meaning of worker control within the factory? The word *kontrol'* in Russian connotes "checking" rather than the usual English sense of "regulation." Simply stated, the workers did not trust the management and wanted to supervise factory operations, just as the Petrograd Soviet wanted to supervise, not replace, the Provisional Government. In practice, this control could mean anything from auditing the company's books or sending a worker delegation to measure actual fuel reserves against what the managers claimed to have on hand, to sending a team to the countryside to secure fuel or food for the factory's workers.[28]

Whatever the specific area, worker control at the factory level appeared

---

[26] The figures on strikes are based on data discussed in Chapter Eight.

[27] For example, see Selitskii, *Massy v bor'be za rabochii kontrol'*; P. V. Volobuev, "Leninskaia ideia rabochego kontrolia i dvizhenie za rabochii kontrol' v marte-oktiabre 1917 g."; T. A. Ignatenko, *Sovetskaia istoriografiia rabochego kontrolia i natsionalizatsii promyshlennosti v SSSR, 1917-1967 gg.*; Paul H. Avrich, "The Bolshevik Revolution and Workers' Control in Russian Industry," pp. 47-63; Keep, *Russian Revolution*; William G. Rosenberg, "Workers and Workers' Control in the Russian Revolution."

[28] The most recent Soviet study of workers' control in 1917, by V. I. Selitskii, lists seven areas of concern:
  1. production-technical control—use of fuel, materials, upkeep of equipment
  2. financial-commercial control—regulation of profits, cash on hand, orders
  3. protection of enterprise—supervision of incoming materials and outgoing goods, fire prevention
  4. personnel control—hiring and dismissal of workers and employees
  5. labor-conditions control—length of work day, internal discipline
  6. consumption-goods control—factory stores, dining room, clothing
  7. worker management—result of departure of administration
Selitskii has compiled over 1,500 cases of workers' control in Russia between March and June; of the seven areas, control over labor conditions, personnel, and production accounted for the great majority of cases of kontrol'. Actual worker self-management was noted in only 36 cases altogether, and in only 3 cases (of 151) for Moscow (pp. 193-195, 200).

to be a largely ad hoc, spontaneous way for workers to defend their economic existence. Workers did not appear to be interested in controlling factories for a more just distribution of goods and profits, but instead they simply wanted to keep the factory running so they could earn a living. For example, at the big Dinamo defense plant, the administration claimed it had no cash to run the plant; a workers' committee investigated and found out that the administration was telling the truth; only then did the factory committee vote to have the plant sequestered by the state and operated by a joint committee of workers and employers.[29] Factory committees responded most quickly to explicit threats; they became particularly active in their control functions in the face of an imminent shutdown. After Prokhorov announced the shutdown of his Trekhgornaia factory for lack of fuel, the factory committee's control commission discovered reserves to last one more month, and the committee demanded work at the factory continue.[30]

Even when workers' committees took over the management of factories, their motive was not typically greater gains for the workers. At the small Gulavi metal factory, the factory committee took control in May, pending the Soviet's appointment of an administrative commission, because the owner was a German.[31] Later on, when the bourgeoisie loomed as a more serious enemy than the Germans, factory seizures were still viewed as a temporary measure to force the owner to meet demands.[32]

While the factory committees looked out for workers' economic interests at the local level, the soviets and trade unions were also very much involved in economic matters. In fact, the trade unions' explicit purpose was to represent workers' economic interests; but since unions were the slowest of the worker organizations to form, the soviets also became involved in economic matters. Among its many sections and commissions, the Moscow Soviet organized a labor section (*otdel truda*) whose function was to help settle conflicts in factories.[33] This was followed by the formation in early April of a provisional body under the labor section, the Commission for Assistance to Trade Union Organization. The activists in the Soviet's body were old Menshevik unionists and those in the Central Bureau of Trade Unions were Bolsheviks, but the real issue between them was the ineffectiveness of the Central Bureau at coordinating trade

[29] *Istoriia zavoda "Dinamo,"* p. 166; *Revoliutsionnoe dvizhenie v Rossii v iiule 1917 g.,* p. 349.

[30] "Protokoly fabrichnogo-zavodskogo komiteta," no. 8, p. 100.

[31] *Revoliutsionnoe dvizhenie v Rossii v mae-iiune 1917 g.,* p. 284.

[32] Such was the case at the Benno-Rontaller and Ganzen factories (see below, Chapter Eight) (*Russkie vedomosti*, 15 October 1917; *Sots.-Dem.*, 30 September 1917). The same defensive motives for take-overs applied to Petrograd workers (see Mandel).

[33] Zubekhin and Koloditskii list all of the sections and commissions of the Soviet. The labor section was formed on March 22 (*Izv. MSRD*, 24 March 1917).

unions. As an organ of the Soviet, the Commission for Assistance could draw on both the Soviet's prestige and finances to carry out its activities; the Central Bureau ultimately accepted the role the Soviet could play in these affairs but insisted that the Bureau, as historically more correct (that is, it had first arisen after the 1905 revolution), should preserve its separate existence. Thus, the two bodies agreed to combine their executive secretariats but to remain juridically separate.[34] The leader of the Soviet's commission, the Menshevik printer Chistov, told the Soviet's executive committee that his commission would indeed dissolve as soon as the Central Bureau could function on its own.

Later, the Soviet sponsored a Central Arbitration Board (Primiritel'naia kamera), a joint labor-management board intended to arbitrate disputes. (Trade unions, and even some factories, also organized their own arbitration boards.)

The district soviets were even more closely involved in the economic problems of the workers they represented. These soviets also formed conflict commissions; and since they were closer to the site of labor disputes, they were more readily available to mediate. Thus, the chairman of the Zamoskvorech'e district soviet was able to claim, "The raion soviet enjoys great popularity. In our district there have been up to twenty strikes, and everywhere that our raion soviet conflict commission intervenes, the strikes are settled in the workers' favor."[35]

Veterans of the Presnia district soviet remembered that they were constantly called upon to settle local conflicts that arose over the related issues of the eight-hour working day and wage increases. But their jurisdiction was confined primarily to smaller factories where workers presumably did not have either the organization or the force of numbers to confront their employers alone.[36]

Most other local soviets had at least the mechanism for dealing with labor disputes—either labor or conflict commissions were part of raion soviets' permanent apparatus—but their effectiveness was not reported. In general, the performance of local soviets as defenders of working-class economic interests appeared to be uneven. The Butyrki and Lefortovo raion soviets, rather than factory committees or trade unions, announced the boycotts of two striking factories.[37] But the local soviet in the Simo-

---

[34] *Izv. MSRD*, 20 April 1917—April 16 meeting of the executive committee; *Moskovskii sovet professional'nykh soiuzov*, p. 13—meeting of April 7; E. N. Ignatov, "Iz istorii moskovskogo tsentral'nogo biuro professional'nykh soiuzov," pp. 121-122.

[35] Al'tman, p. 118, from the archive of the Moscow Soviet (no date). But a report of that district's conflict commission on May 11 indicated the opposite—the commission was ineffective and received no cooperation from area factory committees (*Vpered*, 13 May 1917).

[36] *Oktiabr' na krasnoi Presne*, 1922, p. 9; *Trud*, 30 March 1917.

[37] *Sots.-Dem.*, 6 May 1917 (Moskovskii Shtampoval'nyi plant); *Izv. MSRD*, 7 May 1917 (G. K. Kuz'min factory).

novka district was not so successful. Here the failure of the conflict commission to negotiate successful outcomes resulted in a loss of prestige for that institution, and local factory committees assumed the burden of dealing with conflicts.[38]

Although trade unions were further removed than local soviets from the needs of individual factories, they were in principle the institution best suited to work for the improvement of workers' economic positions. In unity was strength, union organizers continually argued; the employers had already long since united, so workers must also unite to counter the power of the employers.[39] It took time, however, for a union to build its membership and its economic clout, and meanwhile workers demanded immediate improvement. Quite naturally, then, they turned first to factory committees and to soviets. But unions gradually improved their capacity to lead the economic struggle. Taking strike leadership as an index of organizational activity, one can roughly chart the rise of union participation in the economic lives of Moscow workers (see Table 4-1).

TABLE 4-1. *Strikes with Reported Trade Union Leadership*

Month	Strikes	Trade Union-led	Percent Union-led
March	23	3	13.0
April	39	9	23.1
May	61	16	26.2
June	45	13	28.9
July	31	14	45.2
August	21	7	33.3
September	28	15	53.6
October	21	9	42.9

Since over half of all strike reports indicated nothing about leadership, the size of the percentage is not reliable; the statistics presented here are almost surely underestimated. What is significant, however, is the change in known union participation: there is a clear jump in union involvement between June and July, and union activity in the second four months was consistently higher than in the first four.[40]

Unions also tended to be most active in economic affairs among artisanal workers; only in strikes among rare metalists and tailors were unions

[38] *Izv. MSRD*, 8 June 1917.

[39] This line of argument was offered by the woodworkers' union (*Sots.-Dem.*, 30 May 1917) and the textilists (GAMO, f. 627, op. 2, d. 14, 1. 1, instructions to textile factory committees).

[40] Corresponding factory committee leadership of strikes declined over the period. They were known to lead 10 percent of strikes from March to June and 5 percent from July to October. (See Appendix A for sources.)

reported to be involved in over half of the cases. Unions, as already mentioned, organized earliest in the artisan trades. The greater involvement of unions in artisan strikes was due to the same factors that promoted their organizational successes: past history of organization and the dispersed location of artisanal workers, who realized that singly they could wield no economic power at all. Unions of artisans tended also to be smaller, and the leaders were in closer reach of the rank and file; whereas in industries with large factories, union representatives were often too distant to play an active role in economic conflicts.

The advantage the unions had over local committees and soviets in the economic sphere was their permanence as an institution, which gave them the ability to plan. Instead of responding piecemeal to economic conflicts as they occurred, unions sought to investigate local conditions on an industrywide scale and then to negotiate for economic improvements on the basis of detailed evidence of the existing situation.

Such deliberative methods could be employed only by the largest unions, for they required a rather large structure to carry out the investigations. And it took time and money to build up this structure. The textile union created a commission to investigate wages in early May; a month later the union chose a negotiating team, armed presumably with the results of the wage commission's work.[41] The metalists began to investigate wages at the same time, also for the purpose of negotiations, and in July the union distributed a detailed questionnaire for the purpose of keeping track of the economic situation in all metal plants.[42]

This kind of elaborate apparatus contributed to the labor-organization bureaucratization described somewhat critically by some scholars of the Russian labor movement.[43] The growing reliance on commissions and subcommissions to solve various problems necessarily delayed those solutions and placed the unions that used commissions at a relative disadvantage in dealing with a rapidly deteriorating economic situation. But the bureaucratic structures themselves were created of necessity. For example, the Soviet's labor section was continually barraged by requests from individual factories to investigate conflicts with management. D. S.

---

[41] *Izv. MSRD*, 7 May 1917; *Sots.-Dem.*, 2 June 1917. The commission was scheduled to report to a union delegates' meeting on May 21 (*Izv. MSRD*, 19 May 1917), but no account of that meeting was subsequently published.

[42] *Sots.-Dem.*, 5 May 1917; *Izv. MSRD*, 21 July 1917. The questions included whether the management belonged to the employers' association, whether it had actually implemented negotiated agreements, and whether the plant had had a vacation. The metalists' journal reported one-third of these questionnaires were returned and outlined some results (*Moskovskii metallist*, no. 4, 16 October 1917). I have found no reference that indicates if the originals of the questionnaires still exist.

[43] See Marc Ferro, "La Naissance du système bureaucratique en U.R.S.S.," and Keep, *Russian Revolution*, pts. 2 and 4.

Rozenblium described how the Soviet's response was limited by the "handicraft" (kustar) means at its disposal when mass production methods were required:

> A worker comes to us and says: our factory is closing because there are no materials. Now we have to take one comrade from the Soviet of Workers' Deputies, one from the Soviet of Soldiers' Deputies, find an automobile, and go investigate. But this is a kustar approach. In the first place, we cannot investigate the whole situation, we cannot examine all the stores, we cannot review all the books, we cannot contact the Special Conference on Fuel, and this means, we cannot verify whether the proprietor's declaration is correct.[44]

All soviet and union officials were sorely overburdened with such tasks, and the creation of commissions and committees was the only way rationally to utilize the scarce commodity of leadership. The example above comes from the central Soviet's experience, but trade unions also faced this problem.

Labor exchanges were another aspect of the unions' attempt to institutionalize economic life. These exchanges had a threefold purpose: to help union members cope with the growing problem of unemployment, to enhance thereby the status of the union, and to keep track of the supply of and demand for labor.[45] The first union exchange to open was that of the metalists on June 5; factory committees were asked to report vacancies to the union, and unemployed metalists could come to the union and be placed according to their position in the queue. The drawback to the system was that most hiring, in 1917 as before, was done through personal connections. Factory committees would simply not report openings and then hire friends, or else they would announce the vacancies and hire their friends anyway. This practice is illustrated by the large discrepancies in the union's reported statistics; for example, for the week of July 3-8, there were thirty-nine openings for toolmakers (slesary) and assistant slesary and sixty-eight applicants, but only twenty-five were actually placed.[46] The extra places may have gone begging because of the lack of qualified applicants, but they may also have been filled po znakomstve, by personal acquaintance. "How strongly rooted in factory life is the domestic habit of hiring workers by personal acquaintance, through the

[44] *Izv. MSRD*, 14 April 1917: Soviet plenum of April 11.

[45] Between March and October at least nine Moscow unions opened exchanges, but here, as elsewhere, the Soviet had preceded the unions. A Central Labor Exchange, with representatives from all unions, was created under the Soviet as early as May 14; its patrons, however, were primarily seasonal workers in the building trades (*Izv. MSRD*, 14 May 1917, and throughout the year).

[46] *Izv. MSRD*, 9 July 1917.

foreman," lamented the metalworkers' union journal.[47] The plea for orderly registration through the union was a constant theme in metalworkers' union communications.[48] No other unions' exchanges were so well publicized, but then other unions were smaller than the metallists' and had less need of the press to disseminate information on employment. The textilists, bakers, builders, and tailors all had functioning labor exchanges.[49] Those of the domestic servants, porters, and chauffeurs functioned weakly, if at all.[50]

It can be seen from the above discussion that in the area of economic concerns, there was no clear delineation of functions among factory committees, soviets, and trade unions. All three functioned as mediators in disputes between labor and management; all three functioned to regulate unemployment—the factory committees by demanding the power to approve who was hired or fired in a given plant, the other two by operating their own labor exchanges. The same imprecision in the allocation of responsibilities was true for a second area of organizational activity, which can be called "administration of daily life." Under this rubric are included the more routine aspects of workers' activity, such as regulating disputes among workers, preserving public order, and providing for both food supply and the workers' cultural and educational needs.

Factory committees, where they existed, were the workers' first line of attack in their efforts to gain control over their everyday lives. The single most striking aspect of the protocols of the Prokhorovka factory committee is the concern with day-to-day problems of local order, and the chief source of problems appeared to be pilferage and petty theft. Having successfully deprived the factory administration of its right to search its workers, the committee now had the responsibility of preventing its constituents from helping themselves to factory goods. At the committee's second meeting on March 10, a majority voted to fire two workers for the theft of cloth. On other occasions the punishment was loss of military deferments; the lucky ones were merely ostracized.[51] The emphasis was on the workers' ability to regulate their own lives; theft was handled within the factory—when one worker was brought before an outside tribunal, the committee recommended that there was not enough evidence to prove his guilt.[52] But pilferage increased despite all the com-

[47] *Moskovskii metallist*, no. 5, 15 November 1917.

[48] *Vpered*, 13 July 1917; *Izv. MSRD*, 25 July, 1 and 18 August, and 1, 5, and 22 September 1917; *Moskovskii metallist*, no. 1, 12-25 August 1917 and no. 3, 1-15 October 1917.

[49] *Sots.-Dem.*, 26 August 1917; *Trud*, 23 September, 20 July 1917; *Moskovskii soiuz rabochikh-portnykh*, p. 19.

[50] *Vpered*, 1 August, 30 July 1917; *Trud*, 2 September 1917.

[51] "Protokoly fabrichno-zavodskogo komiteta," no. 8, p. 108.

[52] Ibid., p. 112.

mittee's efforts and by September it reluctantly permitted the factory administration to resume its right to search workers coming off the job.

The Prokhorovka factory committee had additional problems because workers there not only worked together, but most lived together as well. Theft was common in the dormitories. Fights among workers were frequent, and in extreme cases the factory committee reassigned the combatants to different workshops so their antagonism would not jeopardize the work of others.[53] Complaints arose over trash in the dormitories, improper use of washbasins, whether smoking should be allowed and in which part of the dormitories; in short, the factory committee dealt not only with work-related problems, but with all the petty details of communal life.

The response of the factory committee at Prokhorovka to growing theft was to press the administration repeatedly to supply watchmen for the dormitories. Elsewhere, factory committees took on this police function themselves. With the routing of the old police and their slow replacement by citizens' militia (comprised largely of students and invalided soldiers),[54] public order had suffered. In Simonovka, even the people's militia committed crimes, and the streets there were not safe to walk at night.[55] The boulevard press was full of stories of armed bandits and of robbing and looting in the underpopulated quarters of Moscow.[56] As seen above, not even the members of the Soviet's executive committee were immune from the prevailing lawlessness. In the face of growing crime, individual factories began to form squads (*druzhiny*) for self-protection.[57] At first these units supplemented the local militia and especially watched for fire, which in Moscow was always a threat to workers' livelihoods. During strikes, the factory or strike committee would deploy the druzhina to prevent the owner from bringing in strikebreakers or improperly removing his goods. (Eventually some of these factory guards evolved into Red Guard units; but even during the October fighting, most Red Guard units were posted at their factories to guard against forays by counterrevolutionary forces into the working-class suburbs.)[58] According to available figures, armed units of factory guards (whether called militia, druzhina, or Red Guards) were known to have existed in sixty-nine factories in 1917,

---

[53] Ibid., p. 142.

[54] *V oktiabr'skie dni Oktiabr'skogo raiona*, pp. 57-65.

[55] Gorshkov, p. 21.

[56] See especially *Gazeta-kopeika* throughout the year.

[57] *Slavnye traditsii*, p. 88; *Dinamo: 25 let*, p. 82; G. A. Tsypkin, *Krasnaia gvardiia v bor'be za vlast' sovetov*.

[58] The Varshavskii armature plant reported to the Soviet on June 8 that it had assumed control over factory fire protection (GAMO, f. 66, op. 13, d. 3, 1. 1); *God bor'by*, p. 105.

but most were organized late in the year; only eleven units were reported from before the July days.[59]

Perhaps the most basic function carried out by the organizations in 1917 was the supply of foodstuffs. In much of working-class Moscow even before the revolution, distribution of food was conducted at the factory level. Boarding artels were organized at factories (especially in those where large numbers of workers lived in factory dormitories, such as Prokhorovka); many factories also provided company or cooperative stores that furnished food, clothing, and other necessities. And when the growing bread shortage required new regulatory measures, the government not only instituted rationing but also arranged for bread to be issued at workers' places of employment to reduce waiting time.[60]

With many food-supply functions already located in the factory, it was an easy step for factory committees to acquire authority over the food distribution process. Locally, factory committees assumed control or management of factory dining rooms and factory shops.[61] M. I. Loiko's specific responsibility on the local committee of the Zolotorozh tramway park was to supervise the park canteen.[62] Prokhorovka's factory committee elected two commissions to deal with food—one to deal with supply itself, the other to supervise the distribution of bread coupons.[63] Factory committees sent their representatives to assorted food-supply bodies, such as the Zamoskvorech'e cooperative food-supply soviet,[64] but they also tried to solve the supply crisis in their own separate ways. The Gnom and Ron factory committee in thinly settled Blagusha requisitioned one hundred sacks of potatoes from the municipal stores for workers to plant during their free time.[65] If they could not grow their own food, workers sent

[59] On Red Guards in Moscow, see below, Chapter Nine, and also Tsypkin, *Krasnaia gvardiia*; Tsypkin's study is based on archival records, including an analysis of individual Red Guards based on their later pension applications. See also Tsypkin, "Ankety krasnogvardeitsev kak istoricheskii istochnik"; Al'tman, p. 223; and for a less satisfactory study, T. A. Logunova, *Moskovskaia krasnaia gvardiia v 1917 g.*

[60] *Russkoe slovo*, 23 February 1917.

[61] L. I. Balashova, "Rabochii kontrol' nad raspredeleniiam v period podgotovki sotsialisticheskoi revoliutsii," pp. 47-58, discusses this aspect of workers' control in Moscow using a wide range of archival sources.

[62] *Slovo starykh bol'shevikov*, p. 235. This also occurred at the *Russkoe slovo* printshop (*Pechatnik*, no. 1, 11 June 1917).

[63] "Protokoly fabrichno-zavodskogo komiteta," no. 8. Factory committee control over coupons was an enticing source of graft for the committee at the Gofman spinning factory in Khamovniki. Here the committee charged extra for the coupons they were given free by the local soviet. When a worker protested this corruption, a factory committee member threatened the dissenter with a revolver and hints about the Moscow river (*Proletarii*, 31 May 1917).

[64] *Golos rabochei kooperatsii*, 21 May 1917.　　　　[65] *Vpered*, 23 May 1917.

teams to other provinces to procure supplies—an elevator-building plant sent a delegate to Tula to purchase a carload of potatoes, and workers at several other metal factories sent representatives on trips paid for by the factory administration to secure needed food supplies.[66]

Finally, in the midst of attempting to secure for their constituents the physical means of subsistence, factory committees also took on the function of providing for their cultural needs, for workers' lives outside the limits of the factory workday. At every level of working-class organization, in fact, the indispensability of cultural institutions was taken for granted. What was more in doubt, given all their other functions, was the ability of workers' organizations to provide for such activities. A contemporary pamphlet described the new horizons for social life created by the eight-hour workday: sports, books, local government, music and drama circles, and excursions were now within reach of every factory worker.[67] For their part, factory committees organized cultural commissions to supply some of these activities: libraries and clubs were common cultural centers at the local level.[68] At Provodnik in Tushino, the administration financed the remodeling of a barracks building into a worker's club "Third International." Inside the club, spirits were prohibited and workers donated their books to start a library.[69] In Khamovniki, a tavern was converted to a club for the textilists at the Giubner factory.[70] Yet overall, the published record, at least, of factory committees' cultural activities was unimpressive. A memoir by four leather workers enumerated the accomplishments of their factory committee: having won an eight-hour working day, new work rules, and control over hiring and firing, the next requirement was cultural and educational work, but the committee had too little strength left.[71] The cultural commission of Prokhorovka's factory committee announced ambitious plans on March 21 to organize a club, a kindergarten, and a lecture series, but with the exception of two lectures (one on anarchism) in May, no further mention was made of these activities either in the committee protocols, in the press, or in memoirs. On July 4, the committee as a whole discussed the need for a library, but clearly nothing had been done in the interim.[72]

Factory workers whose own cultural commissions were inactive did not lose all possibilities for a cultural life, for the trade unions and district soviets (as well as political parties, dumas, and many public organizations)

[66] Balashova, p. 57.   [67] I. Sukhodeev, *Svobodnye chasy rabochego*.

[68] See *Oktiabr' v Zamoskvorech'e*, p. 120.

[69] Dune, p. 29.

[70] *Oktiabr' v Khamovnikakh 1917 g.*, p. 130.

[71] *Na barrikadakh za vlast' sovetov*, p. 93.

[72] "Protokoly fabrichno-zavodskogo komiteta," no. 8, pp. 109, 146. The first seven-member commission was replaced on May 5 with a new two-person commission.

also assumed responsibility for cultural and educational work, as well as other aspects of the management of daily life.

The responsibilities of district soviets in the area of local administration, like those of factory committees, evolved to meet local needs. In most areas of Moscow, police functions were assumed by local dumas, organized in the old police precincts. But where these dumas were weak, as they were in factory neighborhoods, the district soviet took on the job of enforcing public order. Thus in Simonovka it was the soviet's representative who commanded the militia; and when the municipal government finally sent its own nominee to take charge of the district, the early militia organized by the soviet was retained.[73] Elsewhere, there was close cooperation between raion dumas and raion soviets, which in any case furnished a certain number of representatives to the duma boards.[74]

Patrolling the streets against bandits was one function of local militias (and a highly dangerous one—the Simonovka militia commissar missed the first days of the October revolution because he had fallen off his horse chasing a bandit, and a student militiaman in Butyrki was killed foiling a robbery attempt).[75] But local soviets also fulfilled a more universal, less glamorous police function and one shared by factory committees: the mediation of domestic quarrels. Participants in the Presnia raion soviet recalled that they were often visited by women seeking refuge from their sometimes-violent husbands.[76]

Insofar as drink was a leading contributor to local disorder, public and private, raion soviets also attempted to regulate the flow of alcohol. Drinking had been the bane of worker-intellectuals since the very beginnings of the labor movement, and the campaign against alcohol during the war was one of the few areas legally open for working-class activism. Now, local soviets formed temperance commissions to educate workers about the evils of alcoholic spirits. During the October fighting in Moscow, these soviets (now dominated by Bolsheviks and subordinate to the orders of the Military Revolutionary Committee) organized the defense of liquor warehouses and confiscated liquor reserves to prevent drunkenness from interfering with the defense of the revolution.[77]

More than anything else, however, raion soviets were involved, along with factory committees, in the struggle to provide food supplies to working-class districts. Food distribution was poorly organized in Moscow; every representative body declared its intent to deal with the problem, but it was often the raion soviets on whom the responsibility of supplying

---

[73] Gorshkov, p. 7.

[74] On the raion dumas see L. I. Arapova, "Bol'shevizatsiia munitsipal'nykh organov (raion-nykh dum) Moskvy nakanune velikoi oktiabr'skoi sotsialisticheskoi revoliutsii," pp. 135-151.

[75] Gorshkov, p. 26; *V oktiabr'skie dni Oktiabr'skogo raiona*, pp. 57-65.

[76] *Oktiabr' na krasnoi Presne*, 1922, p. 9.   [77] Al'tman, pp. 65, 245.

foodstuffs ultimately fell. In their very first announcements, the raion soviets of Zamoskvorech'e, Khamovniki, Sokol'niki, and Presnia declared their existence and their intention to deal with the problem of bread.[78] The Zamoskvorech'e soviet, in particular, elected a district supply commission, issued its own ration cards, and arrogated the power to arrest speculators. Here and in Rogozhskii, the soviets worked closely with independent workers' cooperatives in coordinating food distribution. In Khamovniki, the soviet also helped distribute ration cards while Bolsheviks in the soviet minority complained that the soviet spent too much time on "narrow, everyday matters," such as food supply, and not enough on politics. Elsewhere, the Butyrki soviet instituted control over bakeries to make certain that all available flour was properly utilized.[79]

A final area of responsibility assumed by local soviets was the promotion of workers' intellectual life. The goal of the soviets' cultural-enlightenment commissions was as much to instruct workers about their rights and duties in free Russia as to provide recreational outlets. It was culture and education, argued soviet representatives, that could set the workers on the road toward autonomy, could prepare them to take part in the political life of the country.[80] The central Soviet formed a cultural section, which helped to organize demonstrations, May Day concerts, and fund-raising theatrical performances. Serge Koussevitzky, later for many years the conductor of the Boston Symphony, volunteered the services of his orchestra for a benefit performance commemorating International Workers' Day.[81] There was an artists' group that worked on restoring the frescoes in the Uspenskii cathedral in the Kremlin. On September 10, the Soviet inaugurated its own theater with an opera series program that featured a new opera by S. I. Taneev. (The avant-garde work enthralled critics but was not especially well received by the workers in the audience.)[82]

Opportunities for raising the level of working-class culture were more favorable at the local level, where soviets were in closer contact with those they served. Many district soviets had cultural commissions, and in seven districts these created or planned worker or socialist clubs. On April 5, the executive committee of the Zamoskvorech'e soviet was directed to look for suitable premises for cultural activities; on August 10, the soviet was able to report it had opened a reading room and buffet for

[78] *Vpered*, 18 March 1917; *Sots.-Dem.*, 12 March 1917; *Izv. MSRD*, 16 March 1917; *Sots.-Dem.*, 11 March 1917.

[79] Al'tman, p. 117; *Golos rabochei kooperatsii*, 21 May 1917; *Sots.-Dem.*, 17 and 31 March 1917; Balashova, p. 55.

[80] *Izv. MSRD*, 11 July, 17 May 1917.

[81] *Izv. MSRD*, 1 April 1917: executive committee meeting of March 30.

[82] GAMO, f. 66, op. 12, d. 266, ll. 1-6, report on the activities of the artistic-enlightenment section, August 1; *Izv. MSRD*, 13 and 27 September 1917.

its workers.[83] Other clubs also planned lectures, discussions, musical evenings, and scientific and artistic excursions. In Presnia, the soviet ceremoniously opened its club on May 28; flowers decorated the stage, an
orchestra played military music, and speeches were given about the "great
leaders of the past": Marx, Chernyshevskii and Mikhailovskii. Afterward,
a group of the local intelligentsia sang songs, and the evening was only
slightly marred by partisan friction between orators from the SR and
Bolshevik parties.[84]

These clubs had deep revolutionary roots in the circles of the underground revolutionary movement. Indeed, there was not much difference
between the activities of circles centered in People's Houses before the
revolution and those of the new socialist clubs created afterwards. In the
Alekseev-Rostokinsk soviet, workers simply voted to rename the local
People's House a workers' socialist club.[85] (The soviets and individual
factories were not the only institutions to sponsor clubs; district party
organizations also initiated clubs, both to provide cultural outlets and to
furnish a base for propaganda. Youth clubs came to play an important role
in mobilizing the energies of Moscow's working-class young people for
revolutionary goals.)[86]

Once again, however, as with the factory committees' cultural projects,
the soviets' plans were perhaps too ambitious for the times. It is difficult
to determine how active these clubs were; memoirs dwell more on party
club activities than on those of the nonpartisan soviets. But in Blagusha-
Lefortovo at least, where the soviet allocated five hundred rubles for a
club and buffet, a Bolshevik organizer admitted that life was too turbulent
for the culture and enlightenment commission to be very effective.[87] The
central Soviet's cultural group confessed in September, "We have here
many beginnings, we expend no little zeal, but the lack of organizational
and informational qualities leads to incorrect distribution and unproduc-
tive wastes of strength, leads to mistakes and failures."[88]

The trade unions, lacking the natural constituency afforded to factory
committees and local soviets by contact with the local districts, played
an even smaller role in workers' daily lives, although they too prepared
ambitious projects for culture and enlightenment. Apart from their function as mediators and coordinators of economic disputes, trade unions
had little impact on local worker concerns such as public order, internal
conflicts, and (with the exception of bakers) food supply. Indeed, the
problems of starting brand-new unions meant that union organizers had

[83] *Trud*, 7 April 1917; *Izv. MSRD*, 10 August 1917.   [84] *Trud*, 6 June 1917.
[85] *Trudovaia kopeika*, 9 February 1917; Al'tman, p. 119.
[86] See Koenker, "Urban Families."
[87] *Trud*, 15 June 1917; *God bor'by*, p. 199.
[88] *Izv. MSRD*, 13 September 1917.

first to worry about their own daily lives—for example, the Central Bureau of Trade Unions devoted many sessions to the problem of finding permanent office space for itself.[89] The problem was exacerbated by the fact that all the individual Moscow unions were looking for permanent space as well.

Trade unions did, however, recognize a responsibility for promoting working-class culture; this was a traditional function of Western trade unions,[90] and social and cultural activities had been a major aspect of the prerevolutionary legal unions and professional societies. At least eleven unions formed cultural commissions, and many others reported cultural activities during the March-October period. Significantly, the most active unions were those that had prior organizational histories, and most were also unions of craftsmen rather than factory workers; construction workers, bakers, tea packers, municipal employees, brick makers, confectioners, leather workers, house painters, printers, tailors, plumbers, and gold and silver workers all organized cultural commissions. Of course, the existence of a cultural apparatus did not guarantee that it would function, and unions admitted that education and propaganda work had to take second place to the economic struggle. The builders' union acknowledged in August that it was too busy settling conflicts and bargaining for a minimum wage to do much cultural work.[91] The printers' union directors, despite the existence of a library and reading room, were also too busy preparing for wage talks to spend time on cultural activities.[92]

The plans of the cultural-educational commissions were simply more ambitious than existing conditions permitted. It was a typical feature of working-class organizations to try to compress all the lessons and achievements of the European labor movement into the brief span of 1917, as though when the Constituent Assembly convened, Russia would have a fully matured (that is, Europeanized) labor movement, combining all the best features of Western trade unions.

Each cultural commission (an important-sounding name for what might be no more than a few overworked literate workers) tried to plan for libraries and reading rooms as a minimum: the bakers' library by September boasted seven hundred books, the leather workers owned a thou-

---

[89] See, for example, the July 25 report in *Moskovskii sovet professional'nykh soizov*, p. 51. On August 21, a five-man office-finding commission was named to find a place for permanent quarters (p. 73), and on December 1, the still-homeless Central Bureau elected a different fifteen-man commission to locate offices (p. 135).

[90] See Carl E. Schorske, *German Social Democracy, 1905-1917*, and Guenther Roth, *The Social Democrats in Imperial Germany*.

[91] *Vpered*, 5 August 1917. This admission was made despite the fact that the union had a cultural commission even before the revolution, which commission had met most recently on January 5, 1917 (*Trudovaia kopeika*, 5 January 1917).

[92] *Vpered*. 1 August 1917.

sand, and the Butyrki section of the metalist union, by September, had accumulated four hundred books.[93] Lectures and discussions were other avenues of cultural work, and during the summer, unions tried to organize Sunday excursions to various noteworthy spots around Moscow.[94] The bakers announced plans in September for literacy classes plus courses and lectures on social science themes; the tea packers' union also planned lectures, an orchestra and choir, concerts, excursions, and the ultimate in union educational work—its own journal.[95] And certainly a start was made along these lines; the Lefortovo section of the leather workers' union boasted in October it had opened its club "Proletarii," the first trade union club in Moscow.[96] But such instances appear to be exceptions; unions' intentions were to promote a flowering of working-class culture, but in 1917 they simply did not have the resources for organization, economic struggle, and on top of that, culture and education.

A third area of institutional activity will be discussed in another context in Chapter Six: the role of these organizations in representing the political views of their constituents. In addition to their practical duties, however well they were performed, all working-class organizations also engaged in publicizing their own political opinions on issues of the day.

Factory committees, of course, were often the conduit of resolutions passed at factory meetings and generated political resolutions themselves (see Chapter Six). In addition, citywide factory committee conferences met twice in 1917 and issued resolutions on issues specific to their own activities, such as strikes and the rights of factory committees. At the end of the first conference, on July 27, the Bolsheviks proposed a discussion on the "current moment"; the Mensheviks and SRs responded that the work of the conference was over and then departed, whereupon the Bolshevik rump proceeded to pass their party's resolutions. Thus the Moscow factory committee conference was on record as opposing the death penalty, the State Duma, and secret treaties and as favoring soviet power.[97]

[93] *Izv. MSRD*, 26 September 1917; *Golos kozhevnika*, nos. 2-3, 7 October 1917; *Moskovskii metallist*, no. 2, 1-16 September 1917.

[94] The printers' union published a list of suitable recreational and educational destinations, which included monasteries, historical monuments (the site of Tsar Alexis Mikhailovich's palace at Kolomenskoe), and aristocrats' estates. A copy of this list was found in the archive of the tailors' union, so presumably it was shared by other trade unions, but most of the excursions reported in the press in 1917 were directed toward closer and less exotic destinations: Izmailovskii park and menagerie (close to the factory district of Lefortovo), and the Sparrow Hills, southwest of Zamoskvorech'e (GAMO, f. 633, op. 1, d. 12, 1. 6, tailors' union cultural-enlightenment section).

[95] *Izv. MSRD*, 26 and 2 September 1917. The tea packers' journal never materialized.

[96] *Sots.-Dem.*, 18 October 1917.

[97] *Izv. MSRD*, 29 July 1917. Of 682 voting delegates at the conference, 191 remained to vote on the political resolutions.

District soviets in particular, as local units of a clearly political institution, regularly debated "the current moment," and their resolutions were published or sent to the Soviet. The fourteen district soviets published 110 resolutions, the bulk of them coming in August (as was the case for individual factories, which also issued the greatest number of resolutions in that month). The most frequent demands expressed in these resolutions were for power to the soviets and for soviet control over production (the Bolshevik resolution on the economic crisis). By midsummer, the district soviets had become an important strategic objective for the Bolshevik party; in comparison with the central Soviet, local delegates were more easily replaced to suit the changing local temper, and the party pointed to these resolutions passed in district soviets as the true barometer of the workers' mood. The support of district soviets for the Bolshevik resolution on the economy—passed by eight out of eleven in May and June—is taken by Soviet scholars to prove the extent of the grass roots' support for the Bolshevik party since the local units voted contrary to the resolution passed in the central Soviet.[98] But this analysis ignores the overwhelming victory of the SRs at the polls during this same period; what the district soviets' resolutions on the economy really prove is that political issues were not at this time neatly wrapped in partisan packages, a point which will be elaborated in Chapter Five.

Despite the supposedly economic nature of trade union concerns, the unions also took positions on political issues. In the case of the Moscow State Conference, after all, it was the decision of the Central Bureau of Trade Unions, meeting with representatives of the directing boards of forty-one unions, which approved the protest strike and convinced workers they were not violating revolutionary discipline by their action. On the Moscow State Conference and other issues, individual unions passed ninety-four resolutions, peaking in June and August-September. As with those from district soviets, trade unions also called most often for soviet control over production and power to revolutionary democracy. (Metalists', leather workers', and municipal employees' unions were most active in making political resolutions.)[99]

As for their role in the partisan political process, trade unions were not politicized to the same extent as district soviets. It is difficult to determine the party composition of unions, or even of their leadership, since the unions were formally constituted to be outside of parties. The fact that the umbrella organization for trade unions, the Central Bureau, was led by Bolsheviks had nothing really to do with the party affiliation—or non-affiliation—of individual unions, as was pointed out above. The Central

[98] Al'tman, pp. 133-134.

[99] The sources of raion soviet and trade union resolutions are the same as those for individual factories. See Chapter Six, note 4.

Bureau was created expressly to counter the Menshevik-SR mood of the nascent Soviet (a tactic that finally paid off on August 12) and was not chosen by union boards, which were created much later. Only in exceptional cases, such as the union of tailors, were unions led by Bolsheviks, veterans of the prerevolutionary union movement in a period when the semilegal unions attracted the more revolutionary activists of the Bolshevik party.[100]

As new unions formed and sent their representatives to the Central Bureau, that body lost some of its partisan character but not its Bolshevik leaders. As far as can be determined, of eighteen who served in the secretariat of the Central Bureau between March and October, nine were Bolsheviks, five were Mensheviks, and one was SR; the rest remain unknown.[101] The significance of such party affiliation should not be overestimated; in Moscow generally, party differences were played down, and there were divisions within as well as between parties. Not all Bolsheviks were hard-core Leninists. On September 4, in the wake of the Kornilov attempt at counterrevolution, the Central Bureau met to reconsider the issue of the political neutrality of trade unions, a position held dear by Mensheviks. Most Bolsheviks did indeed argue that the trade unions must assume the vanguard position if the Soviet refused, and the party cited the political role of the Central Bureau during the Moscow Conference strike. But a Bolshevik tailor, F. D. Denisov, dissented, saying that the Central Bureau's usurpation of the Soviet's power in August was an exception and should not be tried again.[102]

Overall in 1917, trade union activists tended to be Mensheviks or moderate Bolsheviks in party affiliation. For them, the February revolution meant new opportunities for trade union activity, but they assumed and believed such activity would take place within a bourgeois political and social system for some time to come. Therefore, the union activists (*professionalisty*) saw their primary task to be that of strengthening the economic position of the working class within the larger nonproletarian society.[103] This position contrasts sharply with the place of trade unions in the 1912 to 1914 revolutionary upsurge. Trade unions then were illegal, and they functioned as leading revolutionary political organizations rather than as one of many weapons for economic struggle. Consequently the prewar unions attracted some of the most politically radical activists,

[100] On prewar trade union activity in Moscow, see Bonnell, "Politics of Labor."

[101] *Moskovskii sovet professional'nykh soiuzov.*

[102] Ibid., pp. 80-83.

[103] See the discussion on "tasks of the trade unions" at the June All-Russian Conference of Trade Unions (*Tret'ia vserossiiskaia konferentsiia professional'nykh soiuzov*, pp. 76-148). The leading exponent of this view was the conference's Muscovite Menshevik chairman, V. M. Grinevich.

including many Bolsheviks. In 1917, however, the political and agitational functions of trade unions were taken over by soviets, factory committees, and the legalized parties themselves; radical activists naturally left the trade unions for these more suitable arenas for revolutionary work, and the trade unions fell into the hands of more moderate elements of the revolutionary movement.[104]

It can be seen from the foregoing discussion that the three major working-class institutions—factory committees, soviets, and trade unions—created to fill current local needs and not in accordance with any kind of predetermined organizational design, tended to perform similar kinds of functions. All three assumed competence in economic matters, daily administration, and political affairs. As the three institutions developed over the summer of 1917, attempts were made to define the areas of competence in some cases, and in others, institutions gradually merged and sometimes lost their separate identities.

A major problem was the place of the factory committee in the revolutionary scheme of things. The committee was the representative institution closest to the workers themselves; but in order to exert their maximum influence, committees had to become part of the larger structure of working-class organizations. Given the existence of both soviets and trade unions, it seemed sensible for the factory committees to exist as local units of one or both of these bodies, and indeed union and soviet representatives advocated this relationship. But members of the factory committees resisted losing their autonomy and instead sought to consolidate their influence by forming an umbrella organization of factory committees. Petrograd was the first city to hold a conference of factory committees; the first was held on March 13, and another was held in late May. At this time the Petrograd factory committees asserted their independence from the more moderate trade unions, and the factory com-

---

[104] The career of the Bolshevik professionalist T. V. Sapronov illustrates this point. Sapronov was an active figure in the underground unions before the revolution and wrote extensive memoirs about this period of his revolutionary activity. But Sapronov's memoirs are silent about his work in 1917. He represented the builders' union in the Central Bureau of Trade Unions, the records show, and continued to sit on the directing board of the builders' union. But he also represented a suburban factory in the Moscow Soviet, stood as a Bolshevik candidate for the Moscow uezd zemstvo in August, and agitated for the Bolshevik party in the districts surrounding his factory in Tushino. After the revolution, Sapronov joined the Left Opposition and perhaps his reticence to recall 1917 reflected the political necessities of the 1920s, but it is clear that in 1917 he was no longer the exclusive professionalist he had been in the underground years before the revolution. (Sapronov, *Iz istorii rabochego dvizheniia* and *Iubileinyi sbornik po istorii dvizheniia stroitel'nykh rabochikh Moskvy; Moskovskii sovet professional'nykh soiuzov; Izv. MSRD*, 5 May 1917; *Sots.-Dem.*, 22 August 1917; Dune [Sapronov first introduced the young Dune to Bolshevik ideas while painting the Dunes' Tushino residence]. See also Victoria Bonnell's introduction to a reprint of Sapronov's *Iz istorii rabochego dvizheniia*, Newtonville, 1976.)

mittees here continued to function as an alternative center for organized Petrograd workers.[105]

In Moscow, a conference of factory committees was called for July 23, preceded by several preliminary conferences of factory committee representatives in individual districts. In part, these conferences were called in response to the Provisional Government's law of April 23 severely limiting the rights of factory committees, rights that had already been arrogated in many Moscow factories.[106] Obviously, this issue lay within the factory committee's natural sphere of competence. But the conferences also tried to resolve the question of factory committee responsibilities in relationship to other organizations as well as to their employers. Was the factory committee an autonomous body, the Soviet's local representative, or a cog in the trade union machinery? The All-Russian Conference of Trade Unions, held in Petrograd in late June, had resolved that factory committees should play a role subordinate to the trade unions.[107] At the local preliminary conference in the Basmannyi district, factory committee representatives voted that their committees should be "closely connected" with both trade unions and soviets.[108] In Rogozhskii, a preliminary conference was more specific: the factory committees were to lead the economic struggle at the local level, organize workers in trade unions, and carry out the decisions of the Soviet of Workers' Deputies concerning the economic and political situation of the working class. More precisely, the conference decided that the trade unions should have primary responsibility for economic problems of the given trade, but in more general economic situations, both the Soviet and trade unions should direct the working-class response. But it was the Soviet, the meeting resolved, which was the supreme director of the workers' economic and political struggle in all general questions, and the creation of another central organization to manage workers' economic concerns (the Central Bureau of Trade Unions?) was a needless waste of energy.[109] Preliminary conferences in other districts produced even vaguer decisions on factory relations or published only resolutions on general political themes, such as soviet power and control over the economy.

The all-city conference, with 682 voting delegates, only briefly men-

---

[105] S. Schwartz, *Fabrichno-zavodskie komitety i profsoiuzy v pervye gody revoliutsii*, p. 9.

[106] The law set forth the mechanics of electing factory committees and defined their duties: to represent the workers to the administration with respect to wages, workday, rules of discipline; to deal with internal worker matters; to represent workers to the government; and to promote cultural affairs. The committees were to have no authority in the areas of firing and hiring or control over production (*Vestnik Vremennogo pravitel'stva*, 25 April 1917).

[107] *Tret'ia vserossiiskaia konferentsiia professional'nykh soiuzov*, p. 453.

[108] *Izv. MSRD*, 14 July 1917; *Sots.-Dem.*, 11 July 1917.

[109] *Izv. MSRD*, 9 July 1917.

tioned obedience to the soviet in its resolution and adopted a position very close to the one advocated by the All-Russian Trade Union Conference: factory committees were the local arms of trade unions, trade unions should supervise elections to factory committees, and all factory committee members should be trade union members as well.[110]

So much for theory. In practice, the relationships were much less rigid. The Sushchevsko-Mar'inskii soviet on May 5 had already determined that local economic conflicts (over wages) should be referred to the appropriate trade union but that so-called political conflicts (over firing of administrative personnel, work stoppage) should be handled by the labor section of the district soviet.[111] Furthermore, at the local level, most members of district and central soviets were also members of factory committees, a fact that may have accounted for the low level of attendance at the July 9 meeting of the Sushchevsko-Mar'inskii soviet. That soviet's executive committee published a notice threatening to list publicly the names of deputies who failed to attend meetings; but in fact on that same day, July 9, over one hundred local representatives attended that district's preliminary factory committee conference. Assuming most soviet deputies were at the factory committee conference, they must have considered the conference more urgent than the soviet.[112]

Eventually many factory committees and district soviets merged. Between April and August, all the district soviets had begun to hold occasional meetings with factory committees. Many such joint meetings went on record with political resolutions, especially in the aftermath of the Kornilov mutiny; possibly they were organized with the express purpose of providing a mass forum for issues like economic control and the formation of the Red Guard. The resolutions of these joint meetings could certainly be considered more authoritative than those passed by the few active members left in the soviet, but whether the mergers were initiated from below, from beleaguered soviet executive committees, by factory committees, or possibly by political parties cannot be determined from the evidence at hand.

The classic example of the transient legitimacy of working-class insti-

---

[110] *Trud*, 25 July 1917. Good accounts of the all-city conference can be found in *Soldat-Grazhdanin*, 25 and 26 July 1917; *Vpered*, 25 July 1917; *Izv. MSRD*, 25-28 July, 6 August 1917.

[111] A. E. Smirnov, "Bor'ba za rabochii kontrol' nad proizvodstvom i sovety v period dvoevlastiia," p. 29.

[112] *Izv. MSRD*, 22, 8, and 18 July 1917. In fairness to the Sushchevskii soviet, it is not exactly certain that the soviet was supposed to meet separately from the factory committee conference. The next regular meeting of the soviet was afterward reported as a general meeting of factory representatives (*Sots.-Dem.*, 2 August 1917). It is possible that the Sushchevsko-Mar'inskii "soviet" consisted of whoever showed up at meetings, a fact that itself is further evidence of the lack of clear distinctions among working-class institutions.

tutions was of course the Moscow State Conference on August 12. The Central Bureau of Trade Unions, which had reluctantly had to accept the support of the Moscow Soviet in April, now rallied the directing boards of forty-one unions to defy that same Soviet and call for the strike to protest the conference. But there were also plans, initiated by the Menshevik-dominated Sushchevsko-Mar'inskii soviet, to have a citywide council of all district soviet executive committees meet to call for the strike.[113]

The lesson of the Moscow State Conference strike was painful for the leaders of the Moscow Soviet. Like the Provisional Government in the earliest days of the revolution, the Soviet enjoyed legitimacy among the workers only as long as it acted in accordance with the workers' mood. If it did not, the workers' institutional loyalty could easily be transferred to any one of a number of equally representative working-class institutions.

ORGANIZATIONAL MALAISE

From the evidence offered by the contemporary press and presented above, Moscow by mid-1917 appeared to be in the full flower of organization. Over sixty trade unions were functioning, including all together, at their respective peaks, over 474,000 workers.[114] Local arms of the soviet network had penetrated into every working-class district; and inside factories, workers were becoming increasingly involved in the process of consolidating the revolution, an involvement indicated by their increasing control over factory functions, and were participating widely in political contributions to the electoral process.

At the same time as all this activity was taking place, however, working-

---

[113] Al'tman, p. 212, citing the archive of the Zamoskvorech'e soviet, and E. N. Ignatov, "Mobilizatsiia kontr-revoliutsionnykh." Ignatov gives a very candid account of how the Bolsheviks manipulated these various institutions to produce the strike call. At the meeting of the Central Bureau and union boards, for example, only Bolshevik orators were allowed to speak.

[114] A list of trade unions and their peak membership is given in Appendix C. Approximate membership totals are known for forty-one of the sixty-three existing unions, but the unions whose totals are not known were generally those of smaller industries or trades: the union of carters had probably the largest potential membership, but other unions with unknown size were the furriers (whose membership may be included in the 36,000 tailors), brush makers, cemetery workers, jewelry makers and watchmakers (the latter two groups may be counted as gold and silver workers since there was some merging and separation of these craft unions in 1917). It can be assumed that union membership was inflated in some cases; the 111,000 textile union members and the 40,000 glassworkers included a large share of non-Moscow workers. A. Ia. Grunt ("V podderzhku predlozhenii I. F. Gindina i L. E. Shepeleva") cites archival material for metalists indicating that union members sometimes allowed their membership to lapse and then rejoined, giving the impression, if all new members are counted, of a larger membership than actually existed.

class leaders and outside observers alike noticed an alarming decline in workers' interest in their own organizations. After the July 15 meeting of the Simonovskii consumer society (already the second time the meeting was called), an observer lamented that only 70 of the 3,800 members attended: "I was also told that workers have almost completely stopped attending the Cooperative Soviet, have lost interest in the district dumas, and that such absenteeism (abstention) is observed in all areas of political life."[115] On July 30, *Vpered* scolded members of the Central Arbitration Board for their "indifferent relationship" to their duties: a two-month backlog had piled up because there frequently was no quorum at the twice-weekly meetings.[116]

It appears from reports like these that working-class organizational activity reached its nadir in the period between mid-July and early September. What is especially puzzling about this phenomenon is that it coincided with a decisive shift toward partisan support for the Bolshevik party's program. Indeed, the Moscow Conference protest strike, which stunned labor leaders with its magnitude, occurred in the very middle of this period of apparent indifference. The question is, what was the nature of this "organizational malaise" of Moscow workers? Was it a real downturn in the level of working-class mobilization, or was it a superficial decline in interest while workers turned to other more immediate tasks? How much of the so-called apathy can be attributed to differences between workers' and organizers' perceptions of what it meant to be organized and "conscious"? And finally, was this apathy noted across all segments of the working class, or did it characterize only a certain segment of Moscow workers?

The evidence leaves no doubt that in certain areas of working-class life, workers were no longer responding to their institutions. Reports of worker indifference had begun as early as late March when inactivity could still be attributed to workers' lack of experience with organizations. Thus, the bakers' union directors complained on May 2 and again on June 1 that members were not involved in union activity, that there were only "paper members." Even when members came to meetings, they often left early, before all the business was concluded.[117] The union of bakers was one of the oldest of Moscow unions, with a long revolutionary past, so it is surprising that their members were so slow to participate in union activity. Even more surprising is that a special meeting of veteran bakers' unionists had to be postponed; such a postponement often signified in other cases that not enough people had shown up to conduct a proper meeting.[118]

---

[115] *Golos rabochei kooperatsii*, 29 July 1917.

[116] *Vpered*, 30 July 1917.

[117] *Sots.-Dem.*, 2 May 1917; *Proletarii*, 3 June 1917.

[118] *Izv. MSRD*, 14 June 1917; much of the information about meetings that never occurred

But reports of apathy in the early months of the revolution—before the July days, in fact—were few compared to the marked concern about worker indifference that began to surface from mid-July onward. For example, the Sokol'niki district soviet could not manage to hold a meeting. On July 17, it was scheduled to meet for the fourth time to try to reelect its executive committee because even the majority of its leaders had resigned for one reason or another. After three successive meetings without reaching a quorum, the soviet announced that however few attended the fourth one, the meeting would be considered legal.[119]

No report of that meeting was published, but on July 31 the Sokol'niki soviet again failed to attract a quorum. Its executive committee issued the following statement:

Comrades! At the same time that the newspapers daily bring us news about new encroachments on the conquests of the revolution, of the working class, at the same time as the counterrevolution raises its head ever higher, what do we see among ourselves? Do we close our ranks tighter in defense of the revolution? Do we form new ranks in order to defend our conquests? No, we see none of this!

What are the reasons? Weariness? The revolution dearly cost those who rotted and perished in prisons and at hard labor. It has come to us comparatively more easily, but for that reason it is incumbent upon us to strengthen and consolidate our gains.

An ineradicable disgrace will lie upon us for every inch we concede of the conquests of the revolution. We will be stigmatized by the episode, our descendants will turn from us with scorn! What shall we say in our defense? Not really that having received the eight-hour work day and increased wages, we stood aside. . . . We would be ashamed to say it, we will not say it!!!

Before it is too late, to work! Pay your dues to your political organizations—the Moscow Soviet of Workers' Deputies and Raion Soviets! Punctually attend their meetings! Demand reports from your elected representatives! If they do not attend meetings, replace them, for they are not worthy to be representatives of the proletariat![120]

From the concern of the Sokol'niki soviet and others, it appears that the indifference and the negligence of July and August were new phe-

---

is buried in the announcements sections on the back pages of Moscow newspapers. Sometimes a notice would announce the rescheduling of a previous meeting and explain why the first meeting was not held; when a reason was given, it was almost always because of low attendance. It is a fairly safe assumption that these second tries (*vtorichnye sobraniia*) resulted from unsuccessful first tries, even if a specific reason was not given.

[119] *Vpered*, 15 July 1917; *Izv. MSRD*, 16 July 1917.
[120] *Vpered*, 4 August 1917; *Izv. MSRD*, 4 August 1917.

nomena, not simply failures of organizations to get started at all. Organizers of the metalist union branch for the Gorodskoi, Presnia, and Khamovniki districts pointed out that a general meeting, rescheduled once for lack of a quorum, again failed to attract sufficient numbers on July 30, and they lamented that their comrades were "abandoning" their "native organizations."[121] The Iamskoe consumer cooperative, whose members worked in Butyrki factories, held a general meeting on August 20, but only 150 of 6,000 members came. So instead of the prepared agenda, those attending discussed how to attract more interest: "The orators noted in their speeches the fall in interest of workers at the present time in meetings in general, both at the factories and elsewhere. . . ."[122] The Butyrki section of the metalworkers' union began energetically, its leaders reported in September, but with summer, plus the rise of conflicts and "general apathy," their work slackened. After a few lectures and delegates' meetings, attendance declined, even in the local soviets. Indeed, at a metalworkers' delegate meeting in that district on the twenty-fifth of August, only 31 delegates of 126 showed up, and of these, one representative behaved rudely and tried to disrupt the meeting.[123]

A look both at the frequency of reported incidents of worker apathy and at the overall level of meetings during 1917 confirms that workers' interest in their organizations declined beginning in July. Of seventy-one complaints about apathy that year, forty-two were made between July 15 and August 30.[124] The number of scheduled trade union and soviet meetings also fell rather markedly after July, as Table 4-2 shows.[125]

Clearly there was a decline in organized activity, and this decline was widespread. Reports of indifference were carried through all sectors of the working class; and even at the same time as the stormy debate over the Moscow Conference protest, interest in organizations was low. On August 3, only 200 of 10,000 Rogozhskii metalists attended a meeting. On August 5, it was reported that not even the chemical workers' union directors attended meetings. On August 9, the Sushchevsko-Gruzinskii area leather workers were criticized for their poor attitude towards meetings. On August 10, just under 60 members of the Gorodskoi district

---

[121] *Sots.-Dem.*, 4 August 1917.

[122] *Golos rabochei kooperatsii*, 27 August 1917.

[123] *Moskovskii metallist*, no. 2, 1-16 September 1917, p. 20; *Sots.-Dem.*, 2 September 1917.

[124] "Complaints about apathy" ranged from the reports cited above and the observation that workers were not paying union dues to a decline in attendance at meetings (indicated by total votes cast on resolutions). This is not meant to be a precise measure.

[125] Reports of future meetings were compiled for each organization from the announcements (*izveshchenie*) sections of Moscow papers. There is no way to be sure how many of these meetings were actually held since they seldom produced follow-up reports of their activities.

TABLE 4-2. *Frequency of Scheduled Union and Soviet Meetings*

Month	Number of Union Meetings	Number of Local Soviet Meetings
March	57	7
April	102	17
May	133	48
June	136	18
July	135	43
August	95	27
September	88	24
October	79	21

soviet voted on the Moscow Conference strike; a little over 300 would vote on an anti-Kornilov resolution later in the month. The metalists could not hold an official meeting during August because only about 200 of their 700 delegates showed up.[126] Nor was this indifference confined to industrial unions. The plumbers' union, another artisan union with a long organizational past, attracted only 150 of their 2,200 members to a meeting on August 30. Moreover, several arrived at the meeting drunk and insulted the speakers; by the meeting's end only 30 members remained. "Do workers value alcohol more than solidarity?" appealed the reporter.[127] There is only indirect evidence that this spirit of indifference had penetrated the factory committees by this time, but on July 31 the Prokhorovka factory committee resolved: "Members of the Factory Committee, appearing to be drunk and causing rows, ought to be excluded."[128]

In trying to explain this phenomenon of late-summer apathy, two problems require further exploration. First, what were the factors that produced the notable decline in workers' interest in their institutions, and second, how can this decline be reconciled with indications of growing support of the Bolshevik party and with increasingly hostile relations between labor and management, reflected in the political climate and in the strike movement?[129] For the evidence suggests that in July and August, while workers appeared to lose interest in their class institutions, there was a simultaneous rise in workers' awareness of class antagonisms.

The possible reasons for the rise in apathy range from the simply mechanistic to the psychological; on the mechanistic level, probably a good number of Moscow workers were away from the city during this

[126] *Trud*, 6 August 1917; *Izv. MSRD*, 8 and 9 August 1917; *Letopis' geroicheskikh dnei*, p. 299; *Sots.-Dem.*, 1 and 2 September 1917; *Izv. MSRD*, 23 and 26 August, 1 September 1917.

[127] *Sots.-Dem.*, 30 August 1917.

[128] "Protokoly fabrichno-zavodskogo komiteta," no. 8, p. 157.

[129] See below, Chapters Six and Eight.

period, either because their plants were closed or else because they were enjoying the two-week vacations they had won during the year. The workers in Moscow's largest textile plants had all been temporarily discharged between early July and mid-August, and their absence may have contributed to the decline in attendance at the meetings. However, none of the five Moscow textile manufactures that closed during the period was located in a district that reported worker indifference; and in the hardest-hit district, Sokol'niki, only 10 percent of its factory workers were textilists.[130] That there was not a permanent exodus from the city is indicated by the increase in eligible voters between June and September (see Chapter Five), but this fact does not preclude the possibility that workers were taking off for short periods during July and August to renew contact with their villages. However, those who lamented workers' apathy did not point to workers' absence from the city as a factor; and this apathy was reflected not just in absenteeism, but also in rude behavior during, and early departures from, meetings.

If one reviews the early history of the revolutionary labor movement in Moscow, the 1917 summer doldrums do not appear to be so unusual. Of course, the political and economic situations differed, but even in 1905 the strike movement had trailed off during the summer only to pick up again in September and October.[131] In 1912, the year that labor activity began to increase, July and August saw a definite downturn in strike activity, which resumed in force again in October.[132] The beginning of war in August 1914 affected that year's late summer decline in activism, but the strike movement of July had already begun to wane even before mobilization was announced.[133] In 1916 in Moscow, strike activity had peaked in June and declined to zero in September, picking up again only in November.[134] In all these cases, of course, as with Moscow in 1917, other factors could have affected labor deactivism, but one should not be too hasty in dismissing the traditional rhythm of the work year as one factor even in revolutionary behavior. Five major religious holidays fell between the period from July 20 to September 8, and Moscow workers traditionally returned to the countryside to celebrate such holidays. And if the resumption of worker activity in late September and October in Moscow coincided with the aftermath of the Kornilov mutiny and the Bolshevik victories in the Soviet and at the polls, it also coincided with

---

[130] The Zamoskvorech'e soviet, representing a district with 18 percent textile workers in the district and three of the biggest textile plants, did show a decline in total votes on resolutions between 13 July and 18 August, but the three plants were already closed before July 13.

[131] See Engelstein, chap. 4.

[132] Arutiunov, p. 197.

[133] Haimson, "Problem of Social Stability," 1964, no. 4, p. 641.

[134] TsGAOR, fonds 63 and 102 (see Chapter Two).

the traditional intensification of the artisan work year, which began on September 8.[135]

On the other hand, it cannot be denied that the economic situation helped reinforce tradition in dampening workers' interest in organizational activities. Inflation was depriving workers of whatever gains they had won earlier in the year; even trade unions were forced to increase dues beginning in August to keep themselves afloat. The food shortage, after a respite, was once again becoming critical. Workers who were worried about whether they would receive their next day's food ration would conceivably pay less attention to factory or trade union meetings; they were too demoralized to look beyond private troubles. Even the cooperatives organized to fight the food shortage were also reporting lack of interest. The Moscow Central Workers' Cooperative, created in mid-June, had grown from 122 to 44,400 members by July 25; but a delegates' meeting on August 20 represented only 40,000 of its 71,000 members.[136]

The overall Russian political situation, I would argue, was a less important factor in the Moscow organizational malaise. Mark David Mandel has described similar symptoms of apathy among Petrograd workers right up to the October insurrection itself. But he suggests that this apathy was a reaction provoked by the demoralizing defeat of the July days. The most advanced workers realized that past peaceful forms of organization could not effectively combat the growing arrogance of the counterrevolution and that, if one were to judge by July, the working class was as yet too weak to take on the class enemy in military combat. Given this impasse, one can find it understandable that participation in soviets and trade unions to gain or defend piecemeal improvements seemed futile and irrelevant.[137] But Moscow's working class had not directly experienced the crushing blow of the July days. They were less sensitive to the all-or-nothing risks of confronting the bourgeoisie; they did not feel so isolated as the workers of Petrograd. The response to the State Conference seems ample proof of Moscow workers' insensitivity to the political climate that discouraged their comrades in Petrograd.

A more important factor in the decline of worker interest in organizations was the weakness of the organizations themselves. It will be recalled that different organizations frequently performed the same functions, a duplication wasteful both of leadership and of members' resources. Certainly there was a shortage of able working-class leaders, as contemporary anecdotes attest. The story of the treasurer of the Lefortovo metal-

---

[135] See Belousov, p. 46. On work rhythm in general, E. P. Thompson has written a stimulating article, "Time, Work-Discipline, and Industrial Capitalism," although he shirks the issue of annual rhythms.

[136] *Trud*, 6 August 1917; *Sots.-Dem.*, 30 August 1917.

[137] Mandel, pp. 363-458.

ists' union is illustrative. This official, a smith named Kapochkin, was an old union worker, and in fact was fired from his job early in 1917 because of his union activities. Because he had been a union member before the revolution and other unionists assumed he was therefore trustworthy, Kapochkin became treasurer of the Lefortovo union branch even though he was barely literate. Irregularities soon appeared in the membership records, but the auditing commission could not be convened right away because one member was on vacation and another had joined a different trade union. Meanwhile, Kapochkin began to come to meetings drunk, and an audit eventually revealed he had gambled away almost two thousand rubles of union money, the equivalent of a year's wages.[138] In another case, the chairman-treasurer of the union of smiths, which was about to merge with the metalworkers' union, disappeared with four hundred rubles from the union treasury.[139]

Surely most working-class leaders meant well, but they were painfully short on administrative experience. Extreme sensitivity to criticism was one result of this inexperience. Personality disputes dominated the second Moscow Oblast conference of glassworkers in early October, and finally two feuding members of the union bureau resigned—one because he felt himself inadequate to the job, the other because he had been censured for the quarrel. At this point, the man who was the driving force behind the union, who had himself been accused of responsibility for the union's disorganization, also offered to resign because of the criticism.[140] The ex-chairman of the ribbon workers' union, T. N. Fomin, recounted a similar tale; the meeting that elected him chairman authorized three officers to draw upon the union's bank account—the chairman, the treasurer, and a member of the directing board. The secretary, feeling unjustly slighted, demanded to be included, but Fomin refused, saying they did not know the man well enough. The secretary railed, demanded a change in the union's bylaws; and Fomin, because he could not command obedience, felt compelled to resign. Subsequently, the secretary claimed Fomin had insulted him; the meeting agreed, and Fomin was excluded from the union for three months.[141]

A writer in the soldiers' newspaper noted this growing problem: more and more often workers' committees were being reelected with such swiftness as to leave no trace of the old one. This usually occurred "after the committee has taken some decision not to the liking of this or that

---

[138] *Moskovskii metallist*, no. 2, 1-16 September 1917, pp. 17-19.

[139] *Vpered*, 15 June 1917; *Sots.-Dem.*, 16 June 1917; *Izv. MSRD*, 15 June 1917.

[140] *Moskovskii oblast'noi s"ezd rabochikh-stekol'no-farforovago proizvodstva, 2-i, 1917, protokol*, pp. 33-36. The chairman, Gopius, was an anarchist.

[141] *Vpered*, 17 October 1917.

group of workers, sometimes even of this or that individual worker"; the practice "creates an unhealthy situation and weakens authority."[142]

The result of unstable leadership was to alienate the followers. The factory committee at Levenson's printshop apparently had some trouble with its constituents and could not draw workers to its meetings. Even when the committee bolted the door at meetings to keep everybody in, the workers managed to find a way out.[143] Conflicts arose between trade unions and factory committees over these problems, with the result that factory committees withdrew from union activities.[144] In Simonovka, the able leaders all went to the center, leaving nobody qualified to organize local soviet affairs; and this was why Simonovka factory committees called a conference to replace the soviet. Rather than reform the nonfunctioning institution, the pattern was to create a new structure alongside.[145]

It would be extremely interesting to pursue further the problems of leadership. Who were the union, soviet, and factory leaders; and how many of the veterans of the prerevolutionary labor movement continued their activities in 1917? Evidence is at best sketchy, and what is available indicates a surprising lack of continuity. For example, of fifty-four members of the Prokhorovka factory council in 1905, only seven were active in 1917 and only two of these to any great extent.[146] It is true that the changes caused by the war affected Prokhorovka quite strongly, but the lack of continuity was apparently true between 1905 and the revolutionary upswing of 1912 to 1914 as well.[147] As for the identity of leaders in 1917, a cursory look at the evidence suggests that overlap between union leaders and factory representatives varied by union. In three unions in the chemical industry, for example, the directors were not found to hold any known position in the individual factories in the industry.[148] This lack of a relationship could well be due to a lack of data but might also represent a

---

[142] M. Kapitsa in *Soldat-Grazhdanin*, 13 October 1917.

[143] *Pechatnik*, no. 6, 28 October 1917. The report left the exact nature of the trouble "for another time."

[144] The Central Bureau of Trade Unions reported in June of hostility between the textile union and textile factory committees (*Moskovskii sovet professional'nykh soiuzov*, p. 37).

[145] *Izv. MSRD*, 7 May 1917. A more general report indicating similar disaffection appeared in the bourgeois *Utro Rossii*, 7 June 1917.

[146] Information on Prokhorovka's activists in 1905 comes from D. V. Antoshkin, *Fabrika na barrikadakh;* and *Moskovskoe vooruzhennoe vosstanie po dannym obvinitel'nykh aktov i sudebnykh protokolov;* and for 1917 from "Protokoly fabrichno-zavodskogo komiteta," nos. 8 and 9.

[147] Bonnell, "Politics of Labor," p. 251.

[148] The directing boards for the perfume workers and chemical workers are listed in *Moskovskii sovet professional'nykh soiuzov.* Information on individuals active in these and other organizations has been assembled in a file of activist-workers which contains about five thousand names.

basic mistrust between factories and unions. This mistrust could, in fact, explain the chemical factory workers' intense involvement in political affairs at the factory level (see Chapters Five through Seven) and the desultory record of their unions.[149]

On the other hand, the leaders of the metalists' and printers' unions were more frequently involved in other activities as well, especially the printers; many, although not most, of the members of these unions' directing boards were also reported to be active in factory committees, in the soviet and its commissions, and in political parties. But these two groups of workers were exceptionally active before 1917; it is likely that the mass of Moscow's organized workers corresponded more closely to the chemical workers' model, where lack of continuity among institutions was the rule.

Thus, a very plausible cause of worker apathy toward their organizations was the ineffectiveness of the institutions themselves, with a major factor being the inexperience of those suddenly thrust into positions of leadership and responsibility. Their mistakes certainly contributed to the disaffection of the rank and file. But there might well be another, more political reason for workers' loss of interest in their institutions, and this is their disillusionment with the inherently gradualist goals of permanent institutions. Working-class institutions were created to provide a framework for further consolidation of the revolution and by their nature could respond ideally more forcefully, but almost always less quickly, to the needs of the moment. For the chairman of the Moscow city employees' union, the principle of Soviet authority was more important than momentary opposition to the Moscow Conference; and despite his personal views, he opposed any protest strike against the Soviet's will. When the membership of the union disobeyed the directives of both the Soviet and the union and struck, the chairman felt compelled to resign.[150]

Perhaps working-class institutions were basically out of tune with their constituents. While the institutions advocated gradualism, the rank and file demanded more concrete results at whatever cost. The leaders of the institutions, through whom almost all of the reports of apathy were filtered, interpreted this reaction as indifference (*khalatnost'*, the "purely Russian disease"),[151] indiscipline, or lack of consciousness. One is confronted here with the vexing problem of consciousness. To participants (and historians), "consciousness" meant at some times holding back and at others going forward.[152] Thus, on one scale, consciousness was equated

[149] For a bleak report on the progress of the chemical workers' union by August, see *Izv. MSRD*, 8 August 1917.

[150] *Rabochaia zhizn'*, no. 4, 21 August 1917.

[151] *Moskovskii metallist*, no. 3, 1-15 October 1917.

[152] This problem is raised in a provocative article by Chris Goodey, "Factory Committees and the Dictatorship of the Proletariat."

with respect for organization, for procedures. This was the view espoused by Menshevik leaders in the Soviet when they opposed separate actions that would violate revolutionary unity. As shall be discussed in Chapter Eight, this conscious worker was one who made rational calculations about chances of success or failure of a strike and proceeded to act on these calculations. Such a conscious worker would tend to appreciate the importance of organization, of solidarity. In this sense, the behavior of Moscow workers in late summer definitely appeared to lack consciousness.

On another scale, however, consciousness was equated with the appreciation that the class struggle was tied up with the political struggle, that what was needed was to fight the counterrevolution and to seize power in the exclusive name of the revolutionary masses. It was this kind of consciousness which the Bolshevik party appealed to, which produced the strike against the Moscow Conference, and which may have appeared to the labor organizers to have dulled workers' interest in incremental change through institution building. It was also this kind of consciousness which the Kornilov rebellion in late August helped to strengthen.

Unfortunately, the sources fail at this point. There is no piece of evidence, no later recollection that suggests that any given worker walked out of a trade union or soviet meeting because he realized he should really be at the barricades. But this view does much to explain the apparent dichotomy between the summer malaise and the crescendo toward October which followed the Moscow Conference and Kornilov mutiny. By October in fact, the Bolsheviks were faced with "runaway consciousness": striking workers were so aroused that they were seizing their factories before the party planned to seize state power, thus jeopardizing the more general political solution. The "conscious worker" in October was again expected to hold back.

A final explanation of the workers' response to their institutions lies in their origins in the Russian countryside. According to populist ideology, the Russian peasant possessed the capability for spontaneous acts of anarchic outrage.[153] In this view, the peasants who came to the city brought their anarchism with them, which in its passive form was characterized by alcoholism, indifference, and apathy toward organization. Only at times of direct threats—the Moscow Conference or the Kornilov mutiny— would the peasant-workers rise to protest. The process of urbanization, as was discussed in Chapter Two, tended to transform this kind of worker into one who was aware of politics and of the need for organization and solidarity; yet the pattern of late-summer doldrums followed by a period of intense activity in Moscow in late 1917 seems to conform to the model of peasant behavior: passivity, then outraged violence. But if this were truly the case, one would expect those in the more urbanized groups—

---

[153] See Haimson, "Social Stability," and Mandel, chap. 1.

artisans, metalists, and printers—to be less apathetic than those in the more rural occupations like food workers, chemical workers, textilists. In fact, no such distinctions can be made. Nonetheless, one reason that metalists were so frequently chastised for their poor organizational habits was the combination in that profession of both skilled urbanized machinists and less-trained, recently arrived peasants; the skilled metalists at the top were more acutely sensitive to the deficiencies of their peasant co-workers than leaders less differentiated from the rank and file might have been.

Perhaps in the end, Moscow workers—peasant or proletarian—were not in fact apathetic, but simply transferred their activity to other institutions, particularly to the Bolshevik party. To be sure, there was a marked rise in partisan political activity after the July days. Workers began to form Red Guard units in July and August. The district soviet in Blagusha-Lefortovo attributed part of its weakness to the departure of Bolsheviks from its commissions; the Bolsheviks said the first task of the soviet should be to organize the workers, but they themselves could not help out because they had too much party work to do.[154] The announcements column in the Bolshevik press began to bulge at this time with notices of party meetings, but a closer look indicates most of these were for the newly forming youth groups sponsored by the party. The regular party organs did not noticeably pick up the slack left by failing soviets and unions.

Furthermore, if party activity also slackened during this period because of the economic situation and ordinary summer doldrums, no political party was likely to trumpet this fact.[155] Apathy toward working-class institutions could be blamed on low constituent consciousness, but apathy toward parties had to be seen in part as the fault of the parties themselves. For this reason, one may never know the whole story behind the organizational malaise of late summer. In any case, the Bolsheviks did not attract so many votes in September as their socialist opponents had won in June, and the Red Guard did not number more than six thousand members prior to the actual October fighting.[156] Those who continued their political activism into the autumn of 1917 were fewer than the masses who had participated in the revolution in the spring. Perhaps because the masses had taken themselves out of the ranks of the activists, they did not exert the kind of restraint on the political extremists that they had earlier.

[154] *Proletarii*, 15 June 1917.

[155] The published correspondence of the Bolshevik secretariat in 1917 suggests the party considered lack of worker response primarily a technical problem. Give us more organizers, more literature, was the common plea; once workers heard the message, the party activists seemed confident they could receive their support (*Perepiska sekretariata TsK RSDRP(b) s mestnymi partiinymi organizatsiiami*, p. 146).

[156] Tsypkin, *Krasnaia gvardiia*.

Whatever the explanations—and all of those advanced above have some validity—the institutional malaise of late summer was a definite fact of revolutionary life in Moscow. All of these factors—the weakness of institutional structures, the problems inherent in gradualism during times of rapid change, and the social habits of urban workers—must be considered along with political and economic factors in any analysis of the working class in the revolution.

TOWARD OCTOBER: WORKERS AND THEIR INSTITUTIONS

The rise of working-class interest in political and institutional life after the Kornilov episode is far more widely discussed than its decline in late summer, and the details need not be presented here.[157] There were some startling reversals in trade union activity; following a notice from the woodworkers' directing board critical of members' indifference, two thousand workers turned out for a meeting on October 1, the highest attendance since April. The Butyrki metalists' union reported in September that activity was again on the rise.[158] But the activity of the autumn was of a fundamentally different sort than that of the first euphoric days of the February revolution. There seemed no longer to be any widespread interest in preserving and consolidating the victories of February, for these now appeared to be disappearing with the growing polarization of political forces.

It is possible that this growing polarization, which will be documented in later chapters of this study, was itself a consequence of the apparent apathy among workers during the late summer. One can imagine that industrialists and other supporters of the Right may have felt so encouraged by the constant laments in the working-class press about the demobilization of the working class that they considered the time was especially ripe to intensify the campaign to win back the concessions they had made in the heady days of spring. But this campaign, epitomized in the Moscow Conference and the Kornilov mutiny, served further to convince workers of the futility of the tactics of compromise with the bourgeoisie. If the Right interpreted workers' apathy to mean they would not fight back, it proved to be a misinterpretation.

The focus on class polarization, however, masks another phenomenon that characterized working-class institutional life, a phenomenon that may have had far graver long-term implications than the intensifying class

---

[157] See, among others, A. Ia. Grunt, "Istoricheskie zametki o 'Moskovskom oktiabre,' " "Mogla li Moskva 'nachat' '?" and *Pobeda oktiabr'skoi revoliutsii v Moskve*; Trukan; Volobuev, *Proletariat i burzhuaziia*; Gaponenko, *Rabochii klass Rossii*; R. V. Daniels, *Red October*.

[158] *Izv. MSRD*, 4 October 1917; *Moskovskii metallist*, no. 2, 1-16 September 1917.

struggle. The roots of this other phenomenon lay in the same factors that produced the late-summer organizational apathy but can be traced throughout the history of revolutionary organization. I refer to a growing manifestation of what can be called the atomization of working-class institutional life. Elements of this atomization were apparent from the outset of the February revolution in the functional competition of soviets, trade unions, and factory committees. With no real differences in their areas of competence, none of these three could ever develop a compelling rationale for its validity in the revolutionary scheme of things. Trade unionist M. Marshev tacitly admitted the problem by noting its absence in the October days: union activists (*professionalisty*) and soviet workers had abandoned their hostilities to work together to wage the class struggle.[159] Political parties also contributed to this atomization in certain areas; parties as well as unions and soviets sponsored the social clubs that served as independent centers of working-class mobilization.

This observation is not intended to disparage the workers of Moscow. Duplication and competition among institutions was created in part by workers' natural tendency to adhere to local institutions rather than co-operate with the larger network around them. Thus, in large factories, factory committees provided workers with sufficient power over their daily lives, and they were reluctant to contribute time and money to trade unions or soviets that seemed to them superfluous. For a metalworker in a medium-sized plant, it may have appeared that membership in a union was inconsequential for the union's success; but his presence on his plant's factory committee seemed to have more impact, so he devoted what time he had to local, rather than industrywide affairs. This phenomenon is not limited to Moscow in 1917, of course; all trade unions, for example, are confronted with the problem of "free riders"; if an organization is sufficiently large, the contribution of any one member is marginal, and that member derives the benefits of membership whether he is active or not. Thus there is little incentive for that member to become involved. In small groups, each member is aware he will derive benefits only if he and all other members are active.[160]

Divisions along institutional lines were thus inevitable from the outset of the revolution. But the experience of 1917, the failure of these institutions to deliver all that they promised, encouraged further atomization on other lines as well. Regional divisions had always been important in working-class life; by early autumn, district allegiances if anything had become stronger. The rise in the authority of the district soviets vis-à-vis the center was due in part to the irresolution of the central Soviet but

---

[159] M. Marshev, *Moskovskie profsoiuzy v oktiabr'skie dni*, p. 64.
[160] These ideas are discussed in Mancur Olson, Jr., *The Logic of Collective Action*.

also reflected a preference for separatism, for local self-reliance. The localist trend can also be seen in union life; as big unions (such as those of the metal, textile, and leather workers) developed, they began to form sections by occupation, nationality, and geographical district. Decentralization, of course, can be viewed as a positive step toward making an institution more responsive to its large constituency. But in the context of the other institutional developments seen here, it can also be viewed as a concession to growing separatism within the working class.

There were many signs of this separatism. In mid-August, a new union announced its formation: "the union of metalworkers in small and medium-sized enterprises of Moscow."[161] This was a direct contravention of the principles of industrywide unity. The box makers at the Pelka cartridge plant, having followed the industrial principle of union organization and joined the metalists' union, decided in October to affiliate with the woodworkers' union instead.[162] The printers' union, the oldest in Moscow and the contributor of many experienced activists to the Soviet, unofficially withdrew from the activities of the Central Bureau of Trade Unions; none of its representatives attended meetings of the bureau after April 12.[163] Their tacit boycott may have been due to partisan differences between the Bolsheviks who dominated the Central Bureau and the Mensheviks in the printers' union, but this rationale too illustrates that partisan competition was another divisive element in working-class life.

Finally, this study has already shown how individual factories assumed food-supply functions that could have been handled by representative institutions, as with the delegates from the elevator-building plant who themselves foraged the countryside for food. Workers in an armaments factory cooperative refused to conform to the cooperative movement's dictum to open their ranks to local workers at other factories because they feared they would not then have enough food for themselves.[164]

Despite the Moscow Soviet's yearlong campaign for revolutionary unity, working-class institutional unity was still problematic by October. Whether this was due to inexperience, disillusionment with the inevitable failures

---

[161] *Izv. MSRD*, 12 August 1917.

[162] *Moskovskii metallist*, no. 4, 16 October 1917, p. 18.

[163] *Moskovskii sovet professional'nykh soiuzov*, throughout. (Not all protocols of the meetings listed participants by trade unions, so the printers may actually have come to some later meetings. But their known attendance record is by far the most dismal of any active union.)

[164] *Golos rabochei kooperatsii*, 9 July 1917. I have omitted mention here of the cooperative movement as an institution, but here too was the same kind of duality present elsewhere between the old established Moscow Union of Consumer Societies and the new Moscow Central Workers' Cooperative.

of institutions to respond quickly to current problems, or with the demoralizing growth of counterrevolutionary pressures, the Moscow working class was indeed fissured along regional, occupational, institutional,
party, and even individual factory lines.

By October, only a few institutions still remained capable of bridging
these fissures. One was the government, the traditional locus of authority
which under the Romanov tsars had united the Russian people for over
four hundred years. The Kadet party had rested its hopes on the belief
that the state in and of itself could continue to furnish the same kind of
political cement without the aid of a monarch, but as has already been
seen and will be seen further, the Provisional Government had not proven
capable of rallying the disparate elements of the empire.

Another candidate institution was the soviet, which represented all
workers through their factories, trade unions, districts, and other institutions. But the soviets had so far proven unwilling to utilize their great
potential as the unifier of the increasingly separate elements of the working class.

Finally, by October, there was the Bolshevik party, whose members
worked in factories, in trade unions, and in local soviets, whose organization consisted of local units in all the working-class districts as well as
a responsive central committee. No other socialist party was so effective
in representing its working-class constituency.

The next chapter will look at the limited extent of partisan influence
throughout 1917; the unifying potential of the Bolshevik party alone may
not have been sufficient to rally the fragmented workers of Moscow to
abandon their localism and join the fight to overcome the forces of counterrevolution in October. But when the Bolshevik party allied with the
institution of the soviet by calling for the transfer of power to the soviets,
here indeed was powerful mastic to bond, for at least one crucial historical
moment, the increasingly atomized working class. As other elements of
the revolutionary process in Moscow are explored, many reasons for the
success of the October revolution will be uncovered, but one must not
forget that divisions among workers also characterized the revolutionary
experience in 1917.

FIVE. *Political Parties and the Working Class:*
THE EVOLUTION OF PARTY CONSCIOUSNESS

Kto eto bol'shevik? Bol'shoi chelovek?

MOSCOW TEXTILE WORKER[1]

DURING much of the period between February and October, political partisanship, or affiliation with political parties, was a minor aspect of Moscow workers' revolutionary experience. The three major socialist parties quickly emerged from the revolutionary underground and began to make their views known at the end of February, but the general spirit of revolutionary unity in Moscow diminished factional strife and encouraged instead an attitude of interparty cooperation. It was only in retrospect that the Bolshevization of the masses became an important historical problem in Moscow. The Soviet, trade unions, and factory committees all announced they would operate without regard to party factions; political affiliation was to be a private affair between workers and their chosen parties.

Of course, as party differences became more defined, political affiliation increasingly became an indicator of broader political attitudes. The party more than any other institution became the conduit of political ideas. But it was not until the June 25 municipal elections in Moscow that workers were really forced to choose among the parties in order to express their opinions. Thereafter, reactions to political crises such as the July days, the Moscow Conference, and the Kornilov mutiny became increasingly hardened around party lines. And yet, as was seen in the Moscow workers' reaction to the Moscow Conference strike, it was not loyalty to the Bolsheviks as a party that compelled workers to follow the Bolshevik party line but rather that this particular party best expressed the attitudes of the workers at that time. Even in October, when the Bolsheviks prepared to seize power in the name of the Soviets, it was not at all clear that the majority of those in favor of soviet power were in favor of Bolshevik rule only, even if the Bolsheviks alone of all parties advocated this transfer of power.

This chapter will deal with the development of party consciousness

---

[1] "What is a bolshevik? A large person?" *Staraia i novaia Danilovka*, p. 147.

(partiinost') among Moscow workers.[2] In explaining consciousness here, I intend to include more information than mere statistics showing active party membership (for which the archival records are denied to most non-Soviet scholars); I also intend to look at a more passive measure of party mood, that is, attitudes favoring one party or another. Whatever the actual number of party members was in 1917, they never constituted the largest share of the working class. The role of political parties themselves in influencing partiinost' cannot be ignored, of course, for parties competed for support through their ideologies, organizational ability, and sensitivity to popular demands. However, the emphasis here will be on the response of workers to party agitation and on the interaction between workers and parties, rather than on the political parties, their structures, or their programs.

PARTIES AND WORKERS IN THE EARLY STAGES OF THE REVOLUTION

Among dozens of political parties with working-class constituencies, only three competed seriously for working-class support: the Socialist Revolutionaries, heirs to the old populist tradition, and the two wings of the Social-Democratic parties, Bolshevik and Menshevik.[3] There existed also

---

[2] The term *partiinost'* has come to denote partisanship in the one-party context: the degree of adherence to the Communist, or in retrospect, Bolshevik party line (see, for example, Harold R. Swayze, *Political Control of Literature in the USSR, 1946-1959*). Soviet historians, however, also continue to use the term in its broader sense, for example, P. V. Volobuev: "There is great interest in the question of the partiinost' of the working class, that is, about the workers' membership in political parties" ("Proletariat—gegemon sotsialisticheskoi revoliutsii," p. 57).

[3] Many of the minor working-class parties appealed to workers of non-Russian origin and were often aligned politically with one of the major socialist parties. Allied with the Mensheviks on the June city duma ballot were the Bund, a Jewish workers' party, a Latvian Social-Democratic party, and another Latvian party called "Utro" ("Rits" in Latvian). (It will be recalled that many of the evacuated factories relocated in Moscow had come from Riga.) (On Latvian politics in 1917 see Ezergailis, *1917 Revolution in Latvia*). In the Bolshevik camp were the Moscow Group of the Social-Democratic Party of the Kingdom of Poland and Lithuania (Rosa Luxemburg's party), another Latvian Social-Democratic party, and the Polish Socialist *Levitsa* party. A number of other parties did not participate in municipal elections but were represented in the Soviet of Workers' Deputies. These included several Jewish workers' parties: the social-democratic *Poalei tsion*, a Zionist workers' party, the Jewish Socialist Labor party (SERP), and the Socialist Territorialists (S.S.), also a Zionist group. The SERP and S.S. groups merged in May to form the United Jewish Socialist Workers' party, but none of the Jewish parties was ever a major force in Moscow politics (see Zvi Y. Gitelman, *Jewish Nationality and Soviet Politics*, pp. 71-73). Several anarchist groups were also active in Moscow: one "anarcho-individualist" and three syndicalists were members of the Moscow Soviet in June (Ignatov, *Moskovskii sovet*, p. 448), and, as shall be seen, the anarchists had some influence in selected factories and districts of Moscow

a strong movement for the union of the two S-D factions, but the effect of this tendency was to create still a third Social-Democratic party, the United Social-Democrats (Ob"edinitel'nye), complete with its own organ, *Proletarii*.[4]

Political parties in early 1917 were just one aspect of the working-class revolutionary experience, and most revolutionary leaders, in fact, took care to separate partisanship from the business of the revolution. Trade unions, for example, were supposed to be strictly nonpartisan; their function was to orchestrate working-class economic life. Even though founded by Bolsheviks, the Moscow Central Bureau of Trade Unions meeting March 3, 1917, formally resolved that unions were to be nonparty institutions devoted to the common class struggle.[5] As has already been seen, in August, when this group overrode the decision of the Moscow Soviet and called for a strike to protest the assembled State Conference, there was a concern that the Central Bureau, which professed to be a nonparty body, should be taking a partisan political stand.[6]

The Soviet itself was also constituted on a nonparty basis. Elections to the Soviet were conducted without regard to political affiliation: "Party membership did not play any kind of role," recalled a Bolshevik party member.[7] When in mid-March groups of party members began to caucus informally, the announcement by the chairman that the Soviet would continue to operate "without factions" (*nefraktsionno*) received loud applause.[8] To further divorce the Soviet from the specter of partisanship,

(Paul Avrich, *The Russian Anarchists*; Anatolii Gorelik, *Anarkhisty v rossiiskoi revoliutsii*). Finally, other nonworker parties also vied for working-class support. The supraclass Constitutional Democrats, or Kadets, were led by landlords, industrialists, intellectuals, and professionals such as lawyers and doctors but claimed to be able to represent all Russians, regardless of class; they had no representatives in the Moscow Soviet (Rosenberg, *Liberals*). The Popular Socialists and Trudoviki were also primarily professional in composition but did have one member each in the Soviet. Edinstvo, or Unity (not to be confused with the United S-Ds), a splinter group led by the founder of Russian Social-Democracy, G. V. Plekhanov, also had a representative in the Soviet but found no widespread support among any workers. There were certainly other parties and political factions in Moscow in 1917, many probably as ephemeral as the Christian Socialist Workers' party, whose socialism consisted of free minimal land grants to peasants (*Russkie vedomosti*, 23 June 1917).

[4] The Unity group shared the Bolsheviks' strong sense of internationalism on the war issue, but as their name implied, they shared the regular Menshevik organization's devotion to compromise in the name of working-class unity. Never a mass party, the group wielded more influence in Soviet circles than numbers alone might have suggested; but when one of its most influential leaders, Galperin, defected for a time to the Bolsheviks in July, the Unity faction lost much of its influence on Moscow political life. (See D. Kin, "Bor'ba protiv ob"edinitel'nogo udara"; Lande, "The Mensheviks in 1917"; Grunt, *Moskva 1917-i*.)

[5] *Moskovskii sovet professional'nykh soiuzov*, p. 9.

[6] *Vpered*, 23 August 1917.

[7] *Ot fevralia k oktiabriu (v Moskve)*, p. 12.

[8] Ignatov, *Moskovskii sovet*, p. 36.

its executive committee drafted special rules prohibiting parties from recruiting members in the presence of Soviet orators.[9] The editor of the Soviet's organ, *Izvestiia*, was the Bolshevik I. I. Skvortsov-Stepanov, chosen for his journalistic ability, not for his political beliefs.[10] There was strong support for a merger of the two wings of Social-Democracy; some local organizations did not bother to differentiate between Menshevism and Bolshevism, especially in the working-class stronghold of Lefortovo.[11] And even Bolshevik party activists seriously considered uniting with the Mensheviks now that they had all emerged from the long years underground.[12]

This lack of sharp party differentiation early in 1917 can be attributed to at least three factors that are not necessarily mutually exclusive. First was the pluralistic political atmosphere: the political parties were no longer alone in competing to be agents of the revolution as they had been before February. As Bolshevik member V. P. Nogin observed, in 1905 the parties competed equally with the Soviet for sole authority over the revolution; but in 1917 the Soviet was clearly the institution commanding working-class allegiance, and political parties had become subordinate, if independent, elements.[13] The same was true of trade unions; like the Soviet, they now had a legitimate existence of their own and legitimate tasks to perform, which the political parties could not. The role of parties was thus transformed with the coming of the February revolution.

Second, factional strife was seen to be disruptive of the functioning of the new revolutionary institutions; this is why the Soviet leaders and trade union activists tried to ignore party distinctions. Ignatov described this early atmosphere: "At the start, the work of the Soviet proceeded quite amicably and agreeably. If there were any disagreements, they were not of a factional character."[14] The Soviet executive committee criticized the practice of replacing deputies "for political, personal, or other motives" because it was bad for the continuity of the institution.[15]

Perhaps the most important factor in the diminution of partisan struggle after February was the extremely low level of partisan awareness among the workers in Moscow, which lack of awareness was itself fueled by the

[9] *Izv. MSRD*, 8 April 1917.

[10] Skvortsov-Stepanov, in *Slovo starykh bol'shevikov*, p. 213; L. Khinchuk, "Iz vospominanii o fevral'skoi revoliutsii v Moskve," pp. 178-186; N. Angarskii, *Moskovskii sovet v dvukh revoliutsii*, p. 15.

[11] Al'tman, p. 45.

[12] *Za vlast' sovetov*, p. 18; Al'tman, p. 44; *Sed'maia (aprel'skaia) vserossiiskaia konferentsiia RSDRP (bol'shevikov)*, p. 152; *Krasnaia Presnia v 1905-1917 gg.*, p. 417; see also Ignatov, *Moskovskii sovet*, p. 36.

[13] *Sed'maia (aprel'skaia) vserossiiskaia konferentsiia*, p. 129.

[14] E. Ignatov, "Moskovskii sovet ot fevral'skikh do oktiabr'skikh dnei," p. 60.

[15] *Izv. MSRD*, 30 May 1917.

relatively few differences in party programs at this time. The textile worker quoted at the beginning of the chapter provides but one of many examples. Party organization had touched only an elite stratum of the Moscow working class before 1917; underground parties had developed contacts primarily with illegal trade unions, and these were composed largely of skilled artisanal workers.[16] The mass of workers knew little about either trade unions or parties. This then was the dilemma of the worker Filippova: "The SR spoke well, the Menshevik spoke well, the Bolsheviks spoke well, but who of them is right we don't know."[17] A twenty-year-old apprentice turner at the Sokol'niki workshops, who ultimately joined the Bolshevik party (as did most of the published memoirists), explained his late decision to join by the fact that he did not consider it proper to join a party until he had understood the fundamentals of them all.[18] The Bolsheviks seemed especially prone to mistaken identity; another woman thought the party name meant "well-to-do-person," and scolded a young Bolshevik who was soliciting her vote: "Aren't you ashamed, Vasilii Mikhailovich, to join such a party of rich men?"[19] The Soviet's oblast bureau received the following letter:

> Comrades, members of the Soviet of soldiers', workers', and peasants' deputies . . . enroll us in which ever party will tie us to Bolsheviks and Mensheviks. . . . We have here mensheviks and bolsheviks, and we don't know which to follow.[20]

Not only were many workers ignorant of parties, they did not always want to learn about their differences. Outside organizers who came to Giubner's textile plant had to assure the workers they were not invited by the local Bolsheviks because the "backward workers" there did not like arguments between parties.[21]

The low level of partisan awareness manifested itself in the early organizational stages of the revolution. There is much confusion in the historical literature about the relative strength of the various parties in this period. The Bolsheviks boasted 250 members in the first Soviet (of 625 deputies), according to one account (although the first party caucus

---

[16] See Bonnell, "Politics of Labor," on trade unions before 1914.

[17] Quoted in M. Karpova, "Moskovskaia rabotnitsa v oktiabr'skoi vosstanii," p. 30.

[18] *Desiat' let*, p. 90.

[19] P. V. Vasil'ev, "Vospominaniia o 1917 g.," p. 115.

[20] Quoted in Al'tman, p. 44. This situation was true even in Petrograd, the citadel of the revolution. A recent study cites several recollections of the lack of party awareness, such as the following: "When we carried out the revolution, we paid little attention to partiinost'. That this is a Bolshevik, SR, or Menshevik—it didn't matter. What was important was strengthening the revolutionary struggle for the working class" (quoted from archival sources in Kh. M. Astrakhan, *Bol'sheviki i ikh politicheskie protivniki v 1917 g.*, p. 73).

[21] *Khamovniki v oktiabre 1917 g.*, p. 17.

attracted only 13 members).[22] But the secret of the Bolsheviks' early success, whatever its extent, lay more in the popularity of the party's members as individuals than as representatives of a particular party line, and this was undoubtedly true for other parties as well. The large textile factory Prokhorovskaia Trekhgornaia elected 9 Bolsheviks to its 13-person Soviet delegation.[23] A less active Bolshevik at the same factory recalled, however, that of 12 Soviet deputies, 6 eventually joined the Bolshevik party.[24] These contradictory recollections of party politics are quite typical and themselves constitute evidence of the relative unimportance of party distinctions. But even if the first figure is correct, by June the party sentiment at Prokhorovka had swung sharply toward the Socialist Revolutionaries, who in the city duma elections there received three thousand votes to about a hundred and fifty each for Bolsheviks and Mensheviks.[25] The point is rather that party sentiment did not "swing." Unformed in March, the party mood at Prokhorovka coalesced around the SRs by election time. One of the Bolsheviks originally elected to the Soviet recalled that workers did not vote by party but elected those they knew best, and the one-time chairman of the Prokhorovka factory committee also recalled that workers there voted for the person, not the party.[26] Nor was Prokhorovka alone in electing representatives by personality. At the Northern Railway workshops, the assembled workers "purely accidentally" elected an SR and an "Internationalist [*sic*]" to the Soviet.[27]

Thus, any claims for Bolshevik party superiority in March rest on extremely shaky foundations. If Bolsheviks appeared to dominate at Prokhorovka, or the SRs at Abrikosov's confections plant or at the Sokol'niki workshops, such party labels had little meaning. The Sokol'niki workshops were dominated by SRs almost up to the October revolution, yet six of their first ten Soviet delegates were Bolsheviks.[28] Workers at Prokhorovka, which also sent at least six Bolsheviks to the first Soviet, later developed such a hatred for the party that the mere mention "Bolshevik" was enough to produce shouts of "down with the speaker."[29]

The evidence suggests that the vast majority of workers in Moscow was

---

[22] A. V. Lukashev, "Bor'ba bol'shevikov za revoliutsionnuiu politiku moskovskogo soveta rabochikh deputatov v period dvoevlastii"; Al'tman, p. 51; Ignatov, *Moskovskii sovet*, p. 38.

[23] *Ot fevralia k oktiabriu (v Moskve)*, p. 227.   [24] Ibid., p. 223.

[25] "Sobranie rabochikh Trekhgornoi manufaktury-aktivnykh uchastnikov revoliutsii 1917 g.," p. 283.

[26] Ibid., p. 281; *Ot fevralia k oktiabriu (v Moskve)*, p. 227; *Oktiabr' na krasnoi Presne*, 1922, p. 8.

[27] *Desiat' let*, p. 94. Again, in Petrograd there occurred similar reactions: electors "were not interested in the political views of their deputies" (Astrakhan, p. 74).

[28] *Moskovskie pishcheviki*, pp. 63-68; *Oktiabr'skie dni v Sokol'nicheskom raione*, pp. 11, 32.

[29] "Sobranie rabochikh Trekhgornoi manufaktury," p. 281.

extremely naive with respect to political parties, and it was on this mass that political agitators went to work. Deputies were elected, in the main, without regard to party; parties won support because workers respected their representatives, rarely because workers grasped and approved of party ideals. All the workers in the joiners' shop at the Northern Railway workshops joined the Socialist Revolutionaries because their shop leader was an SR.[30] Or, take the SRs at Prokhorovka:

> The SRs played chiefly on the fact that the majority of members of their party were old workers who participated in the revolution of 1905. On this basis they told us the SRs were the true and the best revolutionaries, serving the interests of the laboring people, and as for the Bolsheviks, the SRs constantly cried, the Bolsheviks played no role whatsoever in the revolution of 1905.[31]

Elsewhere, workers turned to the Menshevik party because its members had been the leaders of prerevolutionary legal organizations such as trade unions, cooperatives, and sick funds.[32] The quality of party orators more than their messages often influenced workers' party attitudes; the Socialist Revolutionary Maistrakh had such influence in the Khamovniki district that the local tramway workers once drove him home in a special tram wagon.[33] The Bolsheviks were especially successful in recruiting members through nonparty but Bolshevik-influenced youth groups: members joined the party because their friends from the youth groups turned out to be Bolsheviks; they did not join the groups because of prior Bolshevik sympathies.[34]

It is clear that party affiliations were formed for a variety of reasons, not all of them having to do with the parties' political programs. However, most accounts agree that as party identities gradually sorted themselves out, the SRs became the most influential party among workers until sometime during the summer. Surely their appeal was grounded on more than talented speakers and venerated old revolutionaries. The SRs stood for the peasant, for land, and this simple fact could be grasped even by the most illiterate of workers. While the young would-be Bolshevik Anna Litveiko was struggling to understand the Marxist Erfurt program,[35] workers at nearby Prokhorovka did not care much for revolutionary theory, but they did respond to the populists' traditional promise of "land and freedom."[36] A worker at the International Harvester plant in provincial Liubertsy described how the SRs recruited members:

---

[30] *Desiat' let*, p. 94.   [31] Vasil'ev, "Vospominaniia o 1917 g.," p. 115.

[32] Dune, p. 33.   [33] *Khamovniki v oktiabre 1917 g.*, p. 19.

[34] *Krasnaia Presnia v 1905-1917 gg.*, p. 455.   [35] Litveiko, pp. 3-18.

[36] "Sobranie rabochikh Trekhgornoi manufaktury," p. 281; N. P. Gorozhankina, "Partiinaia organizatsiia Trekhgornoi manufaktury," p. 166.

"Are you a peasant?" asked the organizer.
"Yes, a peasant."
"Do you want land?"
"I do."
"Well, then, we admit you to our party."
"But what if I am attracted more to the Bolsheviks?"
"Then join—but you won't receive any land."[37]

Because of their reputation as the party who promised land, the SRs must have been especially attractive to workers of peasant origin, the half-peasant, half-proletarians who constituted a large portion of Moscow's work force. This is certainly how Bolsheviks in retrospect justified their lack of success in attracting members.[38] And evidence on party preferences in 1917 also indicates that the Socialist Revolutionaries had a strong attraction for the peasant-workers who formed such a large share of the work force in Moscow. From the compiled memoirs of participants in the Moscow revolution, from newspaper reports, and from the party affiliations of elected representatives, it is possible to ascribe a "dominant party mood" to those factories employing a total of 112,700 workers in March and April.[39] Always remembering how tenuous party affiliations were in those early days, can one find a relationship between SR supporters and rural origin? The overall breakdown of party support is shown in Table 5-1.

TABLE 5-1. *Party Mood in March 1917*

Party	Workers So Inclined	Percent
Socialist Revolutionary	33,400	30
Menshevik	29,400	26
Bolshevik	22,700	20
United Social-Democrat	9,200	8
None dominant	16,900	15

[37] *Ot fevralia k oktiabriu (v Moskve)*, p. 258.

[38] *Krasnaia Presnia v 1905-1917 gg.*, p. 417; and most recently among Soviet historians, Astrakhan, p. 234.

[39] The attribution of "party mood" was conceived of as a way to systematize the valuable but random notations of party influence which appear throughout the sources described above. Each time a factory was identified in a source with a particular party or set of parties, this information was noted on the factory's master card (see Appendix A). Information about party mood was recorded for three periods: March-April, June-July, and September-October. At the same time, the information was rated according to the reliability of the source. In the class of highest reliability were estimates from party documents and trustworthy memoirs. In the second class, the most numerous, were less reliable memoirs (those that were contradictory or mildly implausible on other topics), party affiliation of elected deputies, and reports from partisan newspapers. In the least reliable class were party mood descriptions of doubtful validity (such as the report of the existence of a specific party's cell

Table 5-2 shows each industry, listed in order of rural-born workers, along with its share of workers supporting the SRs (and the dominant party for that industry, if not the SRs). The table suggests that there may be some relationship between the share of peasants in an industry and its support for the peasant-oriented SR party, but it is not very meaningful in a statistical sense.[40] Given the nature of the data available and the level of political acumen discussed above, however, these results at least suggest that peasant-workers more than urban-born workers might have favored the SRs. Further confirmation is furnished by the fact that the

TABLE 5-2. *Relationship between Peasant-Workers and Socialist Revolutionary Support*

Industry	Percent Rural-born[a]	March-April Percent Leaning Toward SRs	March-April (Dominant Mood)[b]
Textile	96	9.1	Menshevik—15%
Tram	96	55.7	SR
Leather	94	0.4	None dominant—28%
Wood	94	0	Menshevik—3%
Mineral	93	0	None reported
Rare metals	91	9.7	SR
Food	89	6.9	Menshevik—10%
Metal	86[c]	24.1	SR
Chemical	86	1.6	United S-Ds—25%
Machine	86[c]	17.8	SR
Paper	85	0	None
Clothing	83	0	Bolshevik—19%
Printing	73	0	United S-Ds—5%

a. From the 1912 census, reported in *Stat. ezhegodnik*, pp. 68-74.

b. The percentages are based on share of workers with known party mood of all workers in the industry. On average, about one-third of workers reported a party mood, but for some industries—printing, wood, and rare metals—the total of workers with known mood is as low as 5 percent.

c. The 1912 census does not differentiate between metalists and machinists; but according to 1918 census material, machinists were less rural and so have been ranked third among metalists, chemical workers, and machinists. (See note 40.)

within a factory, which report says little about the majority mood), but which are included for what they were worth. It turned out that the overall distribution of affiliation among parties was about the same for all three classes of reliability, so the distinctions have been dropped from all discussions here. For obvious lack of more specific information, the number of workers in the entire factory is used for the number of party supporters. This absolute figure is surely inflated, but by allowing for different-sized factories, one can use it to make a comparison among parties and industries.

[40] Using Spearman's rank correlation technique gives $r = .385$. However, $Z = 1.334$, so one can only be about 80 percent confident of the validity of this relationship. (See Appendix E on the statistical procedures used in this chapter.)

machine workers, who were less connected with the village than ordinary metalworkers, demonstrated correspondingly less support for the SRs.[41]

Party consciousness in March and April was hardly well developed, as has been demonstrated. This was due in part to the low level of political awareness on the part of the workers, but it also was due to the low level of organization on the part of political parties themselves. Workers were unaware of differences in party programs because the parties themselves were unsure of what their goals ought to be. The history of the Socialist Revolutionary party in 1917 was one of continual disagreement,[42] and recent research has demonstrated that neither were the Bolsheviks united on party policy until well after Lenin's return from exile in April.[43]

Political parties relied on experience to forge their identities, and coherent programs were developed partially in response to unfolding events. The pressure of the war issue, the Miliukov note, and the resulting entry of the socialists into the Provisional Government all forced parties to formulate responses; these responses grew into programs. As the parties became more organized, they were better able to convey their messages to their constituents among the working class, and workers began to learn what each party stood for. Thus the Bolsheviks, the unpatriotic antiwar party, became unwelcome at Prokhorovka, while other factories recalled their Soviet deputies for voting for the Liberty Loan. By late May, differences among Moscow parties were sharp enough for the Bolshevik Skvortsov-Stepanov to have to be replaced as editor of the Soviet's official *Izvestiia*. A Bolshevik editor could not now be expected to carry out an editorial policy conforming to the views of the Soviet's SR-Menshevik majority bloc.[44]

THE JUNE MUNICIPAL DUMA ELECTIONS: FIRST TEST OF PARTY CONSCIOUSNESS

The development of party consciousness among Moscow workers reached its first climax with the June 25 elections to the city duma. Soviet deputies could be elected as party candidates or not; trade unions still insisted that party differences were irrelevant to their functions,[45] but in the municipal elections, the party was the sole instrument of political choice. Each party

[41] In 1918, for all Russia, 30 percent of metalworkers claimed to have owned land in 1917, and only 24 percent of machine workers did (TsSU, *Trudy*, vol. 26, table 26).

[42] Radkey, *Agrarian Foes of Bolshevism*.

[43] E. N. Burdzhalov, "O taktike bol'shevikov v marte-aprele 1917 g."; *Ocherki istorii moskovskoi organizatsii KPSS*, chap. 6; D. A. Longley, "The Divisions in the Bolshevik Party in March 1917."

[44] *Slovo starykh bol'shevikov*, p. 213; Khinchuk, pp. 178-186; Angarskii, *Moskovskii sovet v dvukh revoliutsii*, p. 15.

[45] Gorshkov; *Moskovskii sovet professional'nykh soiuzov*, pp. 39-40.

prepared a list of two hundred candidates for the new duma, and voters had to choose one list or another; they could not vote separately for individuals. The elections consequently provided all parties with an opportunity to clarify their programs and measure the response from the population. In the process, the level of partisan consciousness could not help but be raised.

The immediate issues at stake were the problems of running the municipal government, which included supervision of housing, food supply, and a growing number of municipally owned industrial enterprises. Seven parties assembled slates of candidates and prepared platforms. The three major socialist parties—SR, Menshevik, and Bolshevik-Internationalist bloc—were all endorsed by the Moscow Soviet and competed for the working-class vote. (There had been discussion before the election of combining two or more of these parties for electoral purposes, as was being done elsewhere in Russia, but in the end, the three chose to remain separate.)[46]

On local issues, the three socialist parties were in substantial agreement. Education, cultural institutions, medical care and insurance, taxes, municipal control over utilities and some enterprises, the extension of city services to working-class settlements beyond the city limits, democratization of municipal institutions, an eight-hour workday, and a minimum wage were common to all three parties' programs.[47] With so few differences, the electoral campaign instead stressed national issues on which parties did have significant disagreements. The SRs stressed their land program above all. All parties advocated social ownership of the land, but the SRs' program of abolishing the right to buy and sell land was the most extreme. The party used this program to attract both peasants and urban workers; peasants would receive land, of course, but this land program would also aid urban workers by siphoning off from the labor market the excess workers who were serving only to depress wages.[48] The SRs and Mensheviks also stood, implicitly, for the policies of the Provisional Government in which they participated, but the fact of their participation was not, in this pre-July period, a major issue.

The Bolsheviks stressed their internationalism, and prefaced their program of local reforms with a list of general political statements: "The working class and urban poor cannot enjoy the gains of revolution while

[46] A. N. Ul'ianov, *Pervye demokraticheskie vybory v moskovskuiu gorodskuiu dumu*, p. 11; Ignatov, *Moskovskii sovet*, p. 167; William G. Rosenberg, "The Russian Municipal Duma Elections of 1917," p. 138; A. Ia. Grunt, "Munitsipal'naia kampaniia v Moskve letom 1917 g.," p. 118; *Moskva 1917-i*, pp. 152-163.

[47] A summary of all the parties' programs is printed in Ul'ianov; see also Rosenberg, "Russian Municipal Duma Elections."

[48] *Trud*, 24 June 1917.

the war continues."[49] The Bolshevik-Internationalists, therefore, were against the war and war profits, against the antirevolutionary bourgeois government, and against the Liberty Loan and the Black Hundreds' State Duma. They were for a quick end to the war, limited profits, workers' control, a single structure of power organized around soviets, and a progressive income tax.[50]

Each party's slate of 200 candidates listed names, occupations, and public posts held by the candidates. Representatives from the working class itself were relatively few: 92 of the Bolshevik candidates can be identified as workers, as opposed to 65 Menshevik worker candidates, and only 45 from the SR party.[51] Lawyers, academics, municipal employees, and other intellectual professions dominated the lists of the moderate socialist parties; nonworker Bolsheviks were generally listed only by their public position, such as "Soviet deputy," so their occupational composition is less clear.

The working-class element in these lists gives a preliminary clue to the structure of the different parties and forecasts their appeal in this election and those to come. It is significant that the Bolsheviks nominated the largest number of workers. The distribution of candidates by occupation and political experience is also suggestive. From all available sources, I have assembled biographical information for each of 420 working-class candidates who ran in 1917 for municipal office, 208 in June and 261 in September.[52] (Some candidates of course participated in both elections.) The information is uneven: the Mensheviks, for example, listed the ages of all their September candidates, while ages of some Bolsheviks could be discovered only through Soviet-period biographical publications. The SR party tended to stress the public offices held by its candidates; the Bolsheviks seemed to emphasize working-class organizational experience, but many of their candidates may also have had other kinds of experience not reported. The selective descriptions of candidate qualifications were themselves no doubt part of the campaign process. Bolsheviks wished to identify with the working class; the other two parties may have wished to avoid an exclusive tie to workers and to appeal to other segments of society.

In all parties, metalworkers and machine workers dominated the work-

---

[49] Ul'ianov, p. 22.   [50] *Sots.-Dem.*, 14 June 1917.

[51] Ul'ianov, p. 16, reports fifty-six Bolsheviks, thirty-four Mensheviks, and forty-four SRs were workers by occupation. My figures are from a file of duma candidates known from the candidate lists and other sources to be workers.

[52] June lists of candidates were printed in *Proletarii*, 15, 16, and 17 June 1917; *Vpered*, 13, 14, 15, and 16 June 1917; *Russkoe slovo*, 14 June 1917; *Sots.-Dem.*, 14, 15, 17, 20, and 23 June 1917; September candidate lists for the Menshevik and Bolshevik parties were printed in *Vpered*, 21 September 1917, and *Sots.-Dem.*, 24 September 1917.

ing-class contingent: 54 percent of Bolshevik worker candidates in June, 54 percent of SRs, and 38 percent of the Mensheviks came from metal or machine-building plants. (The Mensheviks offered the highest proportion of the more highly skilled machine builders—16 percent compared to the Bolsheviks' and SRs' 14 percent.) Among other Bolshevik candidates, only railway workers, who represented 11 percent of the total, appeared in great numbers. Printers accounted for 14 percent of the Menshevik worker candidates, 12 percent of the SRs, and only 5 percent of the Bolsheviks. Most striking is the diversity of the Menshevik worker candidates, who reflected the Moscow labor force much more clearly than either the SR or Bolshevik lists. In addition to the metalworkers and printers, 10 percent of the Menshevik worker candidates were textile workers (the SRs put up none!) and 10 percent were leather workers. If one assumes these worker candidates to be representative of the party's working-class membership at large, a clear pattern emerges. The moderation of Menshevik politics vis-à-vis those of of the Bolsheviks may be explained by the same factors that promoted Petrograd's greater radicalism in comparison to Moscow's. The large share of metalists in both Petrograd and the Moscow Bolsheviks' duma list contributed to a world view characterized by an intense sense of class separateness. Such a sense was more difficult to preserve given the diversity of the Moscow work force itself and, as seen here, within the ranks of the more occupationally diverse Menshevik party.

Party differences also appear in the level of experience and ages of the candidates. The best indicator of experience is membership in the Moscow Soviet since this information comes from an independent and complete source, the list of Soviet deputies published in *Izvestiia*. Nearly half of the Menshevik and SR worker candidates in June belonged to the Soviet (49.2 percent and 48.6 percent); only one-third of the Bolsheviks could be found in the list of Soviet members.[53] Bolshevik candidates, on the other hand, appeared to be much more active in trade union leadership positions: 36 percent of them were known to hold a trade union office as compared to 22 percent of Mensheviks and 24 percent of SRs.[54] Finally, Mensheviks and SRs far outweighed the Bolsheviks in terms of experience in public organizations such as district dumas, the Committee of Public Organizations, and food-supply committees. Thirty percent of the Mensheviks and 24 percent of SR worker candidates held such positions,

[53] Bolsheviks appear to be better represented by local soviet members, but this may be due to their reporting: there is no independent list of members of district soviets as there is for the Moscow Soviet.

[54] The information here comes from various lists of trade union directing boards, printed in *Moskovskii sovet professional'nykh soiuzov* and in the newspapers, as well as what is provided in the lists and biographical collections.

compared to only 9 percent of Bolsheviks who did. Again, this difference may be due to the unevenness of the sources, but it corresponds to the broader differences between the parties. The Bolsheviks refused to participate in the bourgeois central government, unlike their Menshevik and SR colleagues. Whether this difference in experience at the local level was the result of the parties' differing attitudes toward class collaboration or possibly the cause of these attitudes cannot so easily be determined. I shall return to the problem of the nature of party differences later in this chapter. For now, let me suggest that the characteristics of party candidates discussed above demonstrate a close correlation with the actual results of the voting, as shall be seen below.

One final feature of the parties' candidates which unfortunately cannot be shown with great confidence is the age structure of the Menshevik and Bolshevik candidates. Only the Mensheviks systematically listed the ages of their nominees, so age information is available on 171 of them, but only on 37 Bolsheviks.[55] Table 5-3 gives a rough breakdown of their

TABLE 5-3. *Age Composition of Bolshevik and Menshevik Duma Candidates*
(IN PERCENTAGE OF CANDIDATES FROM EACH PARTY)

Age Group	Bolshevik	Menshevik
20-29	40	16
30-39	40	55
40 and over	20	29
Total	100	100

ages. Even this limited comparison indicates the youthful nature of Bolshevik candidates, who were chosen explicitly because they were among the most experienced members of their party.[56] These figures are corroborated by the age profile for all candidates in June, worker and nonworker alike. According to information supplied to the municipal election commission, 44 percent of Bolshevik candidates were in the age group twenty to thirty, only 19 percent of Mensheviks were.[57] This statistical picture corresponds to the frequently reported impressions of the relative youth of Bolshevik party followers.[58]

The published party programs and lists of candidates gave formal notice of the positions and personnel of the various parties, but to reach the voters—especially the workers—more direct methods than newspapers

[55] These include the entire sample for both the June and September elections: 163 Bolsheviks and 200 Mensheviks.

[56] Ul'ianov, p. 16.   [57] Ibid., p. 17.

[58] Dune, autobiographical supplement to MS.

were required. The campaign officially opened on June 18, one week before the election, and on that day, meetings and rallies were held all over Moscow. Some twenty trade unions held meetings that week, some specifically devoted to the elections, others on the intensifying economic situation, but surely the latter must have discussed the elections under the rubric of "current events." A meeting of municipal workers voted to endorse the Socialist Revolutionary ticket; a woodworkers' delegate meeting urged workers to vote for "party number five," the Bolshevik ticket.[59]

The campaign did not proceed entirely along peaceful lines. There was some hostility between the bourgeoisie and the working class; factory owners prepared to shut down their plants for annual summer leaves a few days early, a tactic interpreted as the bourgeoisie's desire to have workers out of town for the elections. The Soviet and trade unions firmly denounced this practice.[60] In more personal work relationships, jobs were tied to correct voting; a householder dismissed his stoker for declaring in favor of the SRs instead of the Kadets.[61] On the other side, some compositors refused to print an issue of the Kadets' election paper because of an anti-Bolshevik article.[62]

There was plenty of pranksterism in the election campaign, too. Skvortsov-Stepanov complained that Bolshevik election posters "were immediately glued over or simply torn down. On election day, while walking from Kalanchevskii square to the Soviet [a route which passed through lower-middle-class neighborhoods] I didn't find one intact Number Five poster—there remained only shreds." For their part, however, the Bolsheviks played the same game; a member of a Bolshevik youth organization recalled how his group helped the party by distributing leaflets and tearing down the placards of other parties—they even created a special tool just for this purpose.[63]

Election day itself brought surprisingly few disturbances. Representatives of the Moscow press were dispersed to some of the 270 polling places to capture the mood of the electorate, and they reported that voting went quietly and smoothly. Women turned out in large numbers, to the surprise of many, and were held responsible, by one reporter, for the general mood of seriousness and lack of excess. In working-class districts, the SRs appeared to predominate, especially among nonfactory workers; workers in factory districts were openly hostile to the Kadets, but there appeared no marked trend toward any of the three parties endorsed by the Soviet. "Every party has its districts where they predominate; for

---

[59] *Sots.-Dem.*, 14 and 13 June 1917.   [60] *Izv. MSRD*, 10 June 1917.

[61] *Sots.-Dem.*, 14 June 1917. The stoker replied indignantly that he was a peasant, not a bourgeois.

[62] Ul'ianov, p. 27.

[63] *Slovo starykh bol'shevikov*, p. 222; Rigosik, p. 123.

example, Prechistenka is the center of Kadetism, the workers in many factories vote as a whole for a given list."[64]

When the results were tabulated, however, it became clear that the Socialist Revolutionaries had won an overwhelming victory, winning 58 percent of all the votes in a seven-party field. The Kadets finished far behind, with 17 percent of the vote, and the two Social-Democratic tickets virtually tied for third place; the Mensheviks received slightly more votes—11.9 percent compared to the Bolsheviks' 11.7 percent. Table 5-4 gives a geographical distribution of the vote. The Kadets scored highest,

TABLE 5-4. *June Duma Election Results by Location*
(IN PERCENTAGE OF TOTAL VOTE)

	Kadets	SRs	Mensheviks	Bolsheviks	Total Vote
Center	29.5	55.4	7.8	3.8	43,825
Inner ring	31.9	50.1	9.7	4.8	76,811
Outer ring: north and west	16.1	60.8	12.4	9.2	241,549
Outer ring: south and east	12.7	57.0	13.0	15.5	249,122

SOURCES: A. N. Ul'ianov, *Pervye demokraticheskie vybory v moskovskuiu gorodskuiu dumu*; *Russkoe slovo*, 2 July 1917; *Izv. MSRD*, 27-29 June 1917. Complete returns by precinct are given in Appendix D.

as expected, in the residential inner ring of the city; the Bolsheviks and Mensheviks received their highest shares in the factory districts south and east, beyond the Sadovoe ring. But the Socialist Revolutionaries received a majority of the votes in every section of the city. Their best showing was in the north and west sections of the outer ring—working-class sections with few factories and large numbers of petty craftsmen, artisans, and transport workers.

A closer examination of the election results allows one to draw some conclusions about the working-class support for the three socialist parties. Election results were reported by police precinct, and one may compare the votes in the fifty precincts with corresponding demographic and occupational characteristics. The most important characteristics for this analysis are the working-class population of the precinct, represented by the number of workers in factories located in the precinct,[65] and the industries

---

[64] *Soldat-Grazhdanin*, 27 June 1917; *Russkoe slovo*, 27 June 1917. For other eyewitness accounts of election day, see *Russkie vedomosti*, 27 June 1917, and *Izv. MSRD*, 27 June 1917. The elections are seldom mentioned in the Soviet memoirs of the period, possibly because it was not a memorable episode in Bolshevik fortunes.

[65] This is at best an approximation: nonfactory workers were a significant element of the working population, but there is no way to identify these workers by precinct. Further, it

to which these factories belonged. Information about the sex ratio and level of literacy in each precinct can also help to describe the voters.[66]

First of all, the highest voter participation was registered in working-class districts. Overall, 63 percent of the eligible voters cast ballots in the election; but in precincts with large numbers of factory workers, turnout was much higher. In the south and east precincts of the outer ring, for example, where the number of factory workers sometimes exceeded the number of eligible voters (only adults twenty years and older could vote), 70 percent of the eligible voters participated in the election.[67] Further, precincts with large numbers of textile and chemical workers showed the greatest turnout, even after allowing for the high numbers of workers in those precincts.[68] (Briefly, "allowing for" the number of workers in a precinct means in this case that if there are two princincts with an equal number of factory workers, the one with a higher concentration of chemical or textile workers would have a higher rate of participation. See Appendix E for further explanation.) On the other hand, there was a negative relationship between concentrations of printers and participation. This is not to say that printers themselves actually voted less; all that can be said with certainty is that once one allows for the factory population of a precinct, it can be seen that participation was lower in precincts in which large numbers of printers worked.

Leaving aside individual industries, precincts with large numbers of women and high literacy levels were also marked by low voter turnout, again allowing for the working-class population. This is another way of saying that the central districts, with their high literacy rates, had low turnouts, but it also indicates that even in working-class districts, women

---

is assumed that factory workers lived near enough to their places of work to be in the same precinct as the factory. (Many polling places were located at factories and included as eligible voters all those factories' workers; see also Bater, pp. 214-233, and above, Chapter Two.) Information on the distribution of factories by precinct is recorded in the data-set on factories and comes primarily from *Spisok fabrik.*

[66] Information on sex-ratio is from *Stat. ezhegodnik,* p. 12, and on literacy from *Ezhe-mesiachnyi statisticheskii biulleten',* 1915, no. 10. Unfortunately, there is no available information on migrant status by precinct for any later than 1897. Electoral results by precinct are given in Appendix D.

[67] This finding contradicts Grunt, *Moskva 1917-i,* p. 181, who makes excuses for the low working-class turnout. In the residential inner ring, voter turnout averaged 53 percent, still higher than the prerevolutionary elections with a restricted franchise. (Thirty percent had voted in the most recent elections in 1912 and 1916 [Grunt, "Munitsipal'naia kampaniia," p. 122].) The lowest level of participation, 40 percent, was in the first Iauzskii precinct, adjacent to the notorious Khitrovo market (although the market's own precinct, third Miasnitskii, showed a 59 percent turnout). The highest level of participation occurred in the third Lefortovskii, where 39 percent of the population (of all ages) worked in factories.

[68] The procedure used to measure the effects of the different populations is multivariate regression by least squares. (See Appendix E on methods.)

had a negative effect on the level of voter participation. Even though observers particularly noted the numbers of women at the polls on June 25, their level of participation did not appear to equal that of men.

The Socialist Revolutionaries, as Appendix D shows, won a plurality of the vote in every precinct and received less than 50 percent in only ten of them—five in the center and five factory precincts in the east and south parts of the city. Clearly, they enjoyed a great deal of working-class support. A postelection analysis in *Izvestiia* calculated that 296,000 workers cast their ballots in the election; and even if the 152,000 votes for Mensheviks and Bolsheviks came exclusively from workers, the remaining 144,000 working-class voters must have supported the SRs. This means however, that only one-third of the SR vote came from workers. My own precinct analysis also suggests that the SRs were relatively less successful among workers than the other parties. There is a very strong correlation between the share of factory workers in a precinct and the level of the Bolshevik vote; no such correlation exists for the SRs. Furthermore, there is no such correlation between working-class population and Menshevik votes. This means that Bolshevik support was pretty much confined to areas of high working-class concentration, whereas SR and Menshevik support was not confined to particular areas of the city. This pattern of voting corresponds to the pattern of socialist candidate composition. The Bolsheviks relied most heavily on proletarian districts and on the highly proletarian metalists. Menshevik and SR voters and candidates were more diverse.

A factor of greater importance than working-class concentration in explaining the SR vote is the level of literacy in a precinct. Holding the share of workers (and women, who as a group were less literate) constant, there is a strong negative correlation between the SR vote and the level of literacy of a precinct. There was also an equally strong negative correlation between literacy and the Bolshevik vote, which relationship suggests the effectiveness of these two parties' simplistic appeals of "land" and "down with the war," respectively. This correlation suggests also that both parties appealed to the less-urbanized elements of the city population, for educational opportunities were much scarcer in the Russian countryside than in Moscow.

A look at the relationship between the industrial composition of precincts and the vote for various parties provides additional insight into the party allegiance of Moscow's workers. The Bolsheviks received their greatest share of the vote in precincts housing large numbers of textile workers and metalworkers,[69] allowing as always for the total number of workers

[69] Metalworkers and machine workers, except where noted, have been combined in this voting analysis in order to minimize the number of different industries, making the analysis as a whole more meaningful.

in the precinct. Metalworkers also supported the Menshevik party, and less significantly, the SRs. It is worthy of note that the textile workers, known for their close ties to the village, appeared to have a negative effect on the size of the SR vote; in precincts where the share of workers was the same, those with the larger number of textile workers tended to give less support to the Socialist Revolutionaries. This corresponds to the earlier finding that textilists' party mood favored the Mensheviks more than the SRs (see Table 5-1) and that most textile worker candidates represented the Menshevik party. Perhaps the stereotype of SR influence among textile workers is simply that, a stereotype, based on the much-studied Prokhorovskaia Trekhgornaia factory, and is not valid for other textile mills. The Danilovskaia textile complex, in the southeast corner of Zamoskvorech'e, was just as large as Prokhorovka, but the SRs reportedly had little influence there. In March, the factory committee was composed of two Bolsheviks, two Mensheviks, and three workers without party designation.[70] In June and September, Danilovskaia provided seven Menshevik duma candidates. The Givartovskaia lace factory and Giubner cotton factory in Khamovniki were two other large textile plants whose dominant mood favored the Menshevik party; memoirs of Bolshevik party workers there recall nothing about any SR influence.[71]

If textilists tended generally to vote for Mensheviks and Bolsheviks, the picture changes dramatically when one examines the effect of combinations of workers in the various districts. When large numbers of textilists and machine-building workers (not the less-skilled metalists) were located in the same precinct, one can observe a substantial increase in the Bolshevik vote which cannot be explained by the presence of the two groups individually. This effect, which statisticians call interaction, does not appear in any other party's vote or with any other industrial combinations. Thus, while Mensheviks enjoyed support from metalists (more so than from machine builders) and textilists, this support did not increase in districts with large numbers of both of these industries' workers. As stated earlier, machine builders led the pre-1917 revolutionary movement while the textile workers had been very inactive. It appears here that textile workers could be mobilized to support a radical party when in the proximity of the more stalwart machinists, but they were evidently not so inclined to follow more moderate metalists in voting for the Menshevik party.

[70] *Oktiabr' v Zamoskvorech'e*, p. 132.

[71] *Oktiabr' v Khamovnikakh 1917 g.*, pp. 6-7, discusses Menshevik influence at the Givartovskaia manufacture. The evidence of Menshevism at the Giubner factory was that its committee leaders were Mensheviks, and a number of Menshevik candidates for the city duma worked at Giubner. Angarskii notes, however, that Giubner's workers seemed to reject any kind of partisanship (p. 6).

Why did machine builders and textile workers together demonstrate so much more support for the Bolsheviks than either group did acting separately? One reason must surely be that where there were large numbers of machine workers and textilists, there were few other industries whose interests and viewpoints might have offset the Bolsheviks' and machine builders' appeal to class separateness and class antagonisms. Textile workers, especially where concentrated in large numbers, may have sensed this separation but could not articulate it without the aid of the more politically experienced machine-building workers. These results already allow for the degree of worker concentration in the electoral districts; this interaction effect suggests that one must be alert to the effect of combinations such as these on political behavior as well as to the influence of single factors such as industry, literacy, or place of birth.

Finally, the June election results indicate that printers as well as textile workers demonstrated a negative relationship to SR votes, but this is perhaps understandable because printers had fewer ties to the land than any other group of Moscow workers. Nonetheless, a surprisingly large number of SR duma candidates were printshop workers. What is more interesting, since the printers' union was strongly pro-Menshevik, is that there was no significant relationship between the number of printers in a precinct and the share of Menshevik votes. The relationships become more tenuous with the decreasing sizes of the industrial work forces in each precinct: metalists and textilists, together making up 50 percent of the factory work force, more clearly have a statistical effect on the voting results. The printers were concentrated in central city precincts, where they composed the vast majority of workers there. Once the total number of workers was allowed for, the additional effect of the printers on either SR, or Menshevik, or Bolshevik votes was very small.

There was no significant relationship between the vote for any one party and concentrations of workers from the other large industries: food, chemicals, railway, and clothing. So it appears, with the exception of the metalworkers, textile workers, and especially the machine builders and textilists together, that there was no strong relationship between particular industries and political parties. But the overall impact of working-class votes is unmistakable; they voted in much greater numbers than citizens in non-working-class precincts; they voted very rarely for the Constitutional Democrats; and they were, in effect, the sole supporters of the Bolshevik party. Even though most workers voted for non-Bolshevik parties, the June vote signaled that the Bolsheviks alone relied on no class but the working class. The other two socialist parties appeared to win substantial numbers of non-working-class votes. Therefore, although the size of the Bolshevik vote was small, its purely worker composition, epitomized by the interaction effect between machine builders and textile workers, was an omen for the future.

Special mention should be made here of the role of women in the election, for it was the first time that women, of whatever class, had been allowed to cast a vote in Moscow elections. They appeared in June 1917 to have a negative impact on voter turnout, but whether or not women did vote, the precincts in which they lived tended to support Kadets and Mensheviks and to oppose Bolsheviks and SRs. If one assumes that the Kadet votes did not come from working women, it appears that women workers supported the Menshevik party above all. The evidence, of course, is tenuous, but is reinforced by the nature of party mood in factories in both March-April and June-July. In both periods, factories in which women composed at least one-half of the work force were much more Menshevik-minded than factories known to employ less than 50 percent women.[72]

Why this strong showing of Menshevism among women? The Mensheviks, in general, seemed to appeal to advanced, knowledgeable workers (see below).[73] Evidence here and in Chapter Six, showing the proportionally low level of women's participation in the election and in political resolutions, suggests that women were less inclined than men to participate in politics. (Only forty of six hundred socialist party duma candidates were women; four of these were workers.) Therefore, the women who did express a political party preference were likely to be a special group, more attracted than the average worker to the cerebrally inclined Menshevik party. Or perhaps women's support for the Mensheviks was simply due to a process of elimination. Women workers

---

[72] The figures are presented below:

March Party Mood

	Menshevik	SR	Bolshevik	United	Total
Factories with work force less than half women	11,526	13,464	4,382	1,031	30,403
Factories with work force more than half women	12,578	4,850	2,088	478	18,994

June-July Party Mood

	Menshevik	SR	Bolshevik	United	Total
Factories with work force less than half women	13,008	9,563	1,458	1,713	25,742
Factories with work force more than half women	16,835	5,768	2,821	1,938	27,362

The Chi Squares are 3854.202 for March and 1829.73 for June-July.

It must be remembered that sex composition is known for factories employing only one-third of Moscow workers, and this correlation might well be considered accidental if not for the corroborating evidence of the election results. Both sets of results appear insignificant alone, but together they must be more than coincidental.

[73] Dune, p. 33.

tended to have a slightly more urban orientation than their male coun-terparts,[74] and probably many of the women who entered the labor force after 1914 were urbanized wives of mobilized workers. The peasant-ori-ented SRs had nothing to offer urban working women. For example, unlike the Mensheviks and Bolsheviks, the SRs had no program of nursery facilities in their municipal platform. Experienced women workers, those most likely to vote, were probably older than most, and these women may have felt more comfortable with the older and more moderate Men-shevik party.

THE INTENSIFICATION OF PARTY CONSCIOUSNESS FROM JULY TO SEPTEMBER

In comparison with the low level of party awareness in the early months of the revolution, the period from mid-June to mid-July witnessed a quantum jump in the identification of workers with political parties. One factor was of course the election itself, but this was followed almost im-mediately by the July days in Petrograd, which sharply accented the existing differences between the Bolshevik party and those in the coalition government who acted to put down the demonstrations.

Immediate working-class reaction in Moscow to the Bolshevik party as a result of the July days was mixed. The bourgeois press began a campaign to vilify the Bolsheviks as German spies; the Provisional Government ordered *Pravda* and other Bolshevik newspapers closed, although this order was never carried out in Moscow. These attacks provoked a strong reaction of protest from Moscow workers, evidenced by a flood of reso-lutions defending freedom of the press and protesting unfair harassment of Bolsheviks. The Soviet's policy of revolutionary unity now focused attention on the Bolsheviks as a party, both by condemning the party's unwillingness to submit to the Soviet majority and by defending party members as fellow workers from the venomous attacks of liberal and right-wing circles. Many observers noted that the shift of working-class political sentiment toward the Bolsheviks began after the July events. At the Mastiazhart artillery plant, the Bolshevik party cell grew from twenty to three hundred members at this time.[75] A number of Red Guard units (although not specifically affiliated with the Bolshevik party and often led by anarchists) also were organized in the aftermath of July as workers prepared to defend themselves against the kind of attacks now hurled at the party.

[74] In 1912, 11 percent of women factory workers in Moscow were Moscow-born, compared to 9 percent of males (*Stat. ezhegodnik*, pp. 69-70). And in 1918, for all Russia, 73 percent of women factory workers surveyed had no land at the time of the revolution, while only 65 percent of men had none (TsSU, *Trudy*, vol. 26).

[75] *Velikaia oktiabr'skaia sotsialisticheskaia revoliutsiia (vospominaniia)*, p. 467.

But others noticed a sharp decline in Bolshevik party support. In Presnia, especially at Prokhorovka, Bolsheviks were "beaten like Jews." The reaction was similarly severe on the Nikolaevskaia railroad; the party secretary there was prepared to burn his notes and membership receipts and go underground.[76] As the Moscow party leaders feared, their rising had isolated them from the broad working class.

My own compilation of party mood by factory for June-July confirms the decline of Bolshevik support in this period (although the time element is not specific enough to say that the fall was a direct result of the July uprising). Table 5-5 indicates the decline of pro-Bolshevik mood during

TABLE 5-5. *Party Mood in Factories, March-July 1917*

| | March-April | | June-July | |
	Workers	Percent	Workers	Percent
Menshevik	29,400	26	44,200	35
Socialist Revolutionary	33,400	30	41,800	33
Bolshevik	22,700	20	13,800	11
United Social-Democrat	9,200	8	10,300	8
Total with known mood	112,700	100	127,400	100

this period to the advantage, primarily, of the Mensheviks. The biggest decline in Bolshevik support seems to have been among railway workers (from 21 percent of all railway workers to 1 percent) and clothing workers (from 19 percent to 10 percent). But Bolshevik support probably increased among metalworkers and machine workers between March and July (mainly at the expense of the SRs); Mensheviks gained support among leather workers, textile workers, and clothing workers, and they continued to enjoy the strong support of chemical workers, food workers, and printers. The railway workers, whose only party preference was for Bolsheviks in March, were now equally strongly in favor of the SR party. Such a drastic shift in political support probably reflected more the lack of clear party commitment and the ease with which parties could manipulate the reported mood than a real political shift, although a number of

[76] *Krasnaia Presnia v 1905-1917 gg.*, p. 376; *Oktiabr'skie dni v Sokol'nicheskom raione*, p. 86. An anti-Bolshevik reaction was reported most frequently among railroad workers (*Desiat' let*, p. 106; *Oktiabr'skie dni v Sokol'nicheskom raione*, p. 86; *Oktiabr' v Zamoskvorech'e*, p. 147; Shelaev, "V masterskikh Moskovsko-Kazanskoi zhel. dorogi," p. 182), in Presnia, especially at Prokhorovka (*Ot fevralia k oktiabriu* [*v Moskve*], p. 229; *Za vlast' sovetov*, p. 29), and among armaments workers and tram workers (I. G. Batyshev, "O rabote sushchevsko-mar'inskoi raionnoi dumy v Moskve v 1917 g.," p. 185; *Velikaia oktiabr'skaia sotsialisticheskaia revoliutsiia* [*vospominaniia*], p. 480; *Ot fevralia k oktiabriu*, p. 230; *Desiat' let*, p. 118). An upswing in Bolshevik fortunes was noted in *Moskva v oktiabre 1917 g.*, p. 90; *Desiat' let*, p. 106; *Dinamo: 25 let*, pp. 106, 84; *Slavnye traditsii*, p. 84; *Khamovniki v oktiabre*, p. 19; *Oktiabr'skie dni v Sokol'nicheskom raione*, p. 47.

observers did report hostile reactions to Bolsheviks from railway workers in July. It was probably only the March party mood among railway workers that was "soft" for Bolshevism earlier.

It is important to note that the Mensheviks appeared to have greater worker support than the SRs, despite the Socialist Revolutionaries' big victory on June 25. This can be explained in part by pointing out that most of the able leaders of the "Menshevik-SR" Soviet bloc were Mensheviks.[77] If workers elected Menshevik representatives, they were considered to have Menshevik sympathies, although it was possible, given the low level of party commitment, that these same workers might have voted for the SR list in the duma elections.

In any case, the net effect of the duma elections and July uprising was to increase the party awareness of Moscow workers. Whether a Bolshevik was a German spy, as the bourgeois press railed, or the victim of unfair persecution, as the socialist press countered, it was less likely in July that a worker could wonder who exactly a Bolshevik was.

The party affiliations of Moscow workers continued to shift in the weeks between July and early September; but now the Bolsheviks steadily gained supporters while the Mensheviks and SRs steadily lost them. The United Social-Democratic movement, symbolizing the fading ideal of working-class unity, virtually disappeared. The party had run out of funds for its paper, *Proletarii*, in late June,[78] and its leaders began to defect to one or the other of the major S-D parties (although its Soviet fraction still voted together as late as August 11, and the party ran its own small slate of candidates in the September elections).

The exact timing of the change in party support is difficult to measure, but two events give some indication of the completion of Bolshevik ascendancy. On September 5, enough factories had replaced their Menshevik, SR, or nonparty Soviet deputies with Bolsheviks (or the deputies themselves had changed parties) for the Bolshevik party to pass its resolution for the first time in the Moscow Soviet. And on September 24, the city's second-ever set of democratic elections, this time to elect seventeen district dumas, produced a Bolshevik majority of 51 percent; the Kadets again finished second with 26 percent, while the SRs and Mensheviks finished far back with 14 and 4 percent, respectively, of the total vote. (Twelve other parties, including a "nonparty" party, divided the remaining 5 percent; the United S-D party won one-half of 1 percent.)

There were two significant aspects of the September elections: the first

[77] Radkey, *Agrarian Foes*, p. 168, discusses the balance between leaders and led of the SRs and Mensheviks.

[78] The last issue of *Proletarii* is dated 13 July; it reports the decision taken at a party meeting on 2 July to publish periodic leaflets instead of a newspaper until sufficient funds could be raised to start again.

was the clear polarization between the party of the Right, the Constitutional Democrats, and the party of the Left, the Bolsheviks. The parties of the center, the Mensheviks and SRs, which had both attracted the votes of workers and nonworkers alike in June, were now reduced to insignificance. At the same time, the active political base was shrinking. The total vote in September was 387,280, only 38 percent of the eligible voters.[79]

Part of the reason for the low voter turnout must have been procedural irregularities; apparently in June, all registered voters were automatically certified to vote, but this was not the case in September; and as early as August, the Soviet was mobilizing its forces to overcome the problem.[80] Even with this special effort, in at least one factory polling place the proper credentials were never issued, and voters there were not allowed to participate.[81] A second reason for the low voter turnout might have been the decline of the city's population because of food-supply difficulties, factory shutdowns, and the general economic depression. Moscow's population on February 1, 1917, was 2,017,173, and a rough census taken on September 17 showed an 8 percent decline to 1,849,816. However, the number of eligible voters appears to have risen slightly between May and September. The size of the electorate (adults over twenty years of age) in May was 990,614; according to the September census, there were 1,011,299 residents of twenty years or older, an increase of 3 percent.[82] If participation was down but the number of eligible voters up, voter apathy must have made an important contribution to the low turnout in September.

The existence of this apathy raises the question, was the Bolshevik victory due to the party's legitimate popularity, or did it "steal" the election by mobilizing its hard-core supporters from June while other parties did not bother? The total vote cast gives an answer: the total number of Bolshevik votes more than doubled between June and Sep-

---

[79] Students of American elections report that lower participation in local elections is a common phenomenon (William H. Flanigan, *Political Behavior of the American Electorate*). One reason for this, however, is the high cost of becoming informed about candidates for relatively minor posts (see Anthony Downs, *An Economic Theory of Democracy*), but this cost would be reduced considerably in places where voting is done strongly on the basis of the party, not the individual. In the Moscow elections, voters could choose only entire party lists; they could not cross over between parties.

[80] *Izv. MSRD*, 6 August 1917.

[81] *Letopis' geroicheskikh dnei*, p. 402.

[82] February census totals from *Stat. ezhegodnik*, p. 12. The number of voters varies according to source; these figures come from *Vpered*. Partial census results for September were reported in *Izv. MSRD*, 6 October 1917, and *Trudovaia kopeika*, 29 September 1917 (with some inconsistencies). The manuscript sources for this census, as well as any other compilation, appear to have been lost or destroyed, according to A. Ia. Grunt, who has made a thorough search for them ("Mogla li Moskva 'nachat' '?").

tember, the Kadets' total remained the same, and the totals for the center parties fell sharply. (The Bolsheviks' September total of 199,337 still compares unfavorably with the SRs' June vote of 355,237.)

A further look at the district breakdowns of the September vote, and a comparison with the June results in these areas, provides a better picture of the change in voters' party allegiance between the two elections.[83] Table 5-6 indicates that in each of the seventeen raion duma districts, the Kadet vote remained about the same, which similarity suggests that they were not any more popular in September than in June, especially in their middle-class stronghold of the third district—Prechistenskii-Arbat. The SRs lost votes everywhere; the biggest decline came in the Preobrazhenskii district, an area of recent industrial expansion. The smallest decline came in the Petrovskii district, which included a large and apparently loyal population of soldiers.[84] Since the SR vote loss outweighed the votes gained by Bolsheviks in the second election, it would appear that the June SR voters had become most apathetic by September. However, what votes the Bolsheviks gained appeared to be primarily at the expense of the SRs, not the Mensheviks. The Bolsheviks' biggest September increases, in fact, came in the districts where the Mensheviks had performed worst in June.[85] This observation indicates that substantial numbers of former Menshevik voters may also have dropped out of the electorate since they did not appear to go over to the Bolsheviks in September.

The composition of the September voters did not change so much as the parties' totals. The smaller number of election districts in September

[83] In most cases, the September duma districts were groups of whole precincts, and in the analysis to follow, the "June totals" for these duma districts are simple aggregates of the vote in the component precincts. In a few instances, parts of individual precincts were assigned to two different duma districts, and here the vote was simply divided equally. The same procedure was used for the demographic characteristics available by precinct. Assignment of individual factories can be more precise since knowing the factories' addresses makes it possible to locate the exact position of the factories with respect to duma district. The relationship of the seventeen duma districts to the fifty precincts is given in *Soldat-Grazhdanin*, 30 August 1917.

[84] See Grunt, "Mogla li Moskva 'nachat' '?'" on soldiers' votes.

[85] The percentage increase for the Bolsheviks in each of the seventeen districts from June to September and the total Menshevik vote in each of the seventeen districts in June were ranked, and the ranks correlated, producing a correlation coefficient $r = -.325$. The negative sign suggests that in districts in which Bolsheviks scored their biggest gains (not necessarily highest totals), the Mensheviks had received the fewest votes in June. Another way to determine at whose expense the Bolsheviks profited is to compare correlations between Bolshevik gains on the one hand, and Menshevik and SR losses (percentage decline in total votes in each district from June to September) on the other. The correlation between Bolshevik gains and SR losses is greater (.43) than that between Bolshevik gains and Menshevik losses (.21), again suggesting that Menshevik voters did not defect so much as drop out.

TABLE 5-6. Change in Party Votes, June–September 1917

Number	Duma District	Kadet		SR		Menshevik		Bolshevik		Total	
		June	Sept.	June	Sept.	June	Sept.	June	Sept.	June	Sept.
1.	Miasnits.-Iauza	12,185	11,547	25,014	4,435	2,990	910	2,440	8,109	44,086	25,904
2.	Gorodskoi	10,212	9,814	20,168	3,057	2,687	676	1,727	7,306	35,787	21,413
3.	Prechist.-Arbat	15,090	13,238	17,566	2,315	4,235	836	1,235	4,407	39,662	22,694
4.	Kaluzhskii	5,813	7,182	21,287	2,386	4,914	1,007	6,822	13,554	39,424	24,612
5.	Piatnitskii	7,255	6,782	29,060	4,231	5,370	1,482	8,367	24,334	50,796	38,503
6.	Simonovskii	2,660	2,254	19,431	2,287	2,664	0	2,498	9,979	28,921	15,748
7.	Rogozhskii	3,887	4,259	21,084	3,864	5,870		2,749	15,831	34,651	25,654
8.	Preobrazhenskii	3,620	2,774	22,743	2,130	5,756	995	7,676	14,055	40,010	21,255
9.	Sokol'niki	4,414	3,603	17,606	3,909	6,445	2,071	3,503	12,171	32,942	22,682
10.	Lefortovskii	7,722	6,772	26,100	4,639	5,794	972	9,216	20,759	53,680	33,995
11.	Alekseevskii	704	0	5,311	949	934	317	918	1,870	7,918	4,003
12.	Meshchanskii	6,750	9,183	21,921	3,886	4,504	1,252	3,024	10,803	36,810	25,804
13.	Sushchev.-Mar'in.	9,696	8,954	37,020	4,045	9,209	1,443	6,761	16,406	63,732	32,276
14.	Butyrskii	2,066	1,671	10,030	1,308	1,806	288	1,950	5,256	16,094	8,700
15.	Petrovskii	4,379	1,493	7,605	1,926	1,073	420	1,108	8,632	14,314	13,002
16.	Presnenskii	6,336	6,230	29,830	5,842	3,934	1,835	2,878	10,499	43,606	25,073
17.	Khamovniki	5,895	6,090	25,172	3,201	5,070	1,283	3,617	15,366	40,367	26,962
	Total	108,781	101,846	374,885	54,410	76,407	15,787	75,409	199,337	615,393	387,280

SOURCES for September election results: *Vpered*, 5 October 1917; *Russkoe slovo*, 28 September 1917.

makes it difficult to find significant relationships between votes and voter characteristics, but again, working-class districts tended to have the highest rates of participation, voting for Bolsheviks and against Kadets and Socialist Revolutionaries. It can be said with some certainty that the Kadets continued to appeal to female and literate voters in September, whereas the Bolsheviks did particularly poorly in districts with large numbers of these kinds of residents. Less expectedly, although working-class districts appeared to have higher participation, those districts with large numbers of metalists and textilists showed significantly lower voter turnout. Because of the small number of districts in the September election, it is not feasible to look for statistical interaction effects. But perhaps machine builders, who were now possibly most thoroughly disenchanted with the present system, influenced neighboring textilists also to abstain from voting.

If workers from the two largest industrial groups did not account for the greater working-class participation, who did? Chemical workers, who represented 7 percent of the work force, voted in large numbers. Even with the small number of districts used in this correlation and allowing for total working-class population, there is an extremely strong relationship between voter turnout and the presence in a district of chemical workers. Chemical workers and metalists also most strongly supported the Bolshevik party.

Finally, a new class of voters emerged in the September elections—refugees from the evacuated western provinces.[86] In June, these had little effect on the outcome of the vote except for a negative relationship to Kadet votes. However, in September, there was a strong positive relationship between both SR and Menshevik votes and the refugee population of a district. It is more difficult to determine the effect of the refugees—who at most constituted 16 percent of a district—on the party vote. Was it the refugees who voted for the two centrist parties? It is possible that the war issue was more important to these people on whose land the war was being fought—but would they vote for parties favoring a continuance of the war or for the party advocating its end? If the refugees tended to favor the antiwar Bolsheviks, perhaps the strong vote for Mensheviks and SRs was a reaction against the refugees by native voters of those districts.

Both the district duma election results and the situation in the Moscow Soviet indicate that by late September the Bolsheviks were the most popular working-class party. They had never been attractive to non-working-class voters, so not only were they supported by most of the workers, they were supported almost exclusively by workers. The parties with

[86] Data on refugee population by precinct is reported in *Ezhemesiachnyi statisticheskii biulleten'*, 1916, no. 10.

mixed worker and nonworker support virtually disappeared from the political scene. The remaining parties—Kadet and Bolshevik—represented the two opposing classes now facing each other over the bargaining table—and shortly in the streets. The polarization of Moscow's political life coincided with the increasing bitterness of the strike movement; economics and politics were becoming increasingly intertwined. The vast middle in Moscow may have dropped out of the political process because it had no role to play in this period of intensified class conflict.

Measurements of the party mood in the factories in September and October further confirm the Bolshevik conquest of workers' political sympathies (see Table 5-7). The Bolsheviks now received the support of 68 percent of the workers represented, the Mensheviks had the support of 16 percent of the workers with political sympathies, including 10 percent of all textile workers and 20 percent of all printers. The SRs in October had support from only 4 percent of the workers for whom party mood is known—chiefly from tram workers (the majority of whom were now Bolshevik sympathizers) and food workers.

TABLE 5-7. *Party Mood, September-October 1917*

Party	Number of Workers	Percent
Menshevik	15,300	16
Socialist Revolutionary	4,200	4
Bolshevik	66,100	68
None dominant	10,900	11
No partisan mood	800	1
Total	97,300	100

The concept of dominant party mood tends to obscure the partisan situation in the important leather industry. Throughout the year, in the majority of cases there was no dominant mood in leather plants; party organizations existed, but none could claim hegemony. In October 8,500 leather workers worked in factories where the mood was mixed and only 670 in pro-Bolshevik plants—there appeared to be no bandwagon rush to join the Bolsheviks in this particular industry. (In July, the number of mixed factories dropped, and the number of Menshevik-dominated factories rose. This might well have been attributable to the temporary low popularity of Bolsheviks, which allowed the Mensheviks to establish dominance.)

THE NATURE OF THE BOLSHEVIK ASCENDANCY

The fact of the Bolshevik party's conquest of the Moscow workers' party allegiance is clear enough from the evidence presented above, and it was a process that was occurring at that time in many cities and regions of the crumbling Russian Empire.[87] But some puzzling questions remain. How (and why) did the Bolsheviks, who lacked a political identity in March, become the leading working-class party by September? Was the change in political mood toward support for the Bolshevik party accompanied by an increased attachment to that party as the sole instrument of political activity?

To answer the first question, it is important to try to establish just when the Bolsheviks began to gain the support of Moscow's workers. Precise dating of collective party mood is risky at best, but there are some bench marks. The June and September elections, of course, define the extreme points of the transition. In between, there was a series of votes in the Moscow Soviet on major political issues by which one can chart the rise in Bolshevik support (see Table 5-8). Prior to August, the Bolsheviks regularly polled about one-third of the votes in partisan divisions. On July 4, the Soviet voted 442 to 242 to prohibit street demonstrations. On July 11 and 25, the Bolsheviks again gained about one-third of the votes (380 to 195 and 363 to 192) on resolutions of no confidence in the Provisional Government. Then on August 11 in the vote to delete the strike prohibition from the resolution on the Moscow Conference, the Bolsheviks (together with the United S-D group) won 284 votes for the strike to 312 opposed, or just under half the vote. This narrow defeat in the Soviet was, as already shown, offset by widespread support from local soviets and trade unions in favor of a strike. Also looked at earlier was the point that the strikers insisted their decision had little to do with parties, but rather with the issue of the counterrevolution. But the Soviet's failure to respond to working-class opinion on this issue paved the way for a wave of reelections of deputies; meanwhile, continued government ineptitude on economic questions convinced some remaining deputies, such as D. V. Kuzovkov, to transfer their allegiance. Thus on August 25 the Soviet Menshevik-SR leadership won only 50 percent of the vote to continue the ban on open street meetings, and their attempt to collect contributions for the Soviet's Central Executive Committee was actually defeated (although the newspaper account of the meeting did not specify the margin). Then came the Kornilov mutiny, and on September 5 the Bolsheviks finally won their first outright majority, 355 to 254.[88]

[87] See Rabinowitch, *Bolsheviks Come to Power*; Rosenberg, "Russian Municipal Duma Elections"; Suny, *Baku Commune*.

[88] Soviet historians have argued that the number of Bolshevik deputies in the Moscow Soviet was artificially low because of the Menshevik-engineered rules allowing a maximum of three deputies per factory. They argue that since the Bolsheviks did best in large factories, they were discriminated against by this rule. However, if every factory had been entitled to one deputy for every five hundred workers, if there had been no limit on the number from one factory, and if every additional deputy had been a Bolshevik supporter (a highly

TABLE 5-8. *Partisan Divisions in the Moscow Soviet, April-October 1917*

Date	Issue	Voting Body	Menshevik-SR	Percentage	Bolshevik	Percentage	Number of Abstentions	Total
April 15	Liberty Loan	SWD	242	63	127	33	16	385
April 22	Control over Provisional Government	SWD-SSD	"majority"	—	74	—	0	?
May 16	Support of Provisional Government	SWD-SSD	320	67	160	33	0	480
May 30	Stockholm Conference	SWD-SSD	420	69	188	31	0	608
June 6	Municipal workers' strike	SWD	(abstain)	—	137	—	—	?
June 13	National economy	SWD	262	59	182	41	0	444
June 27	Military offensive	SWD-SSD	391	61	232	36	15	638
July 4	Demonstration ban	SWD-SSD	442	64	242	35	6	690
July 11	Opposition to soviet power	SWD-SSD	380	64	211[a]	35	7	598
July 18	Military discipline	SWD-SSD	338	64	182	34	10	530
July 25	Support for July 8 program	SWD-SSD	363	63	192	33	25	580
August 11	Strike-ban amendment	SWD-SSD	312	52	284	48	0	596
August 11	Moscow Conference	SWD-SSD	364	54	304	46	0	668
August 25	End of ban on street meetings	SWD-SSD	335	50	322	48	19	676
August 25	Six-month anniversary of revolution	SWD-SSD	294	51	279	48	9	582
August 26	Food-supply question	SWD-SSD	185	52	170	48	0	355
September 5	Soviet power	SWD-SSD	254	42	355	58	0	609
September 19	Reelection of executive committee of SWD[b]	SWD	216	47	246	53	0	462
September 28	Current moment (Bolshevik resolution)	SWD-SSD	274	44	346	56	0	620
October 17	Constituent Assembly	SWD-SSD	297	44	384	56	0	681
October 17	Delegate selection to Second Congress[b]	SWD	120	34	231	66	0	351
October 19	End of strikes by decree	SWD-SSD	207	38	332	60	13	552
October 24	Red Guard charter	SWD-SSD	6	1	372	92	27	407
October 25	Creation of Military Revolutionary Committee	SWD-SSD	106	20	394	75	23	523
October 25	Opposition to seizure (Menshevik resolution)	SWD-SSD	113[c]	23	375	77	2	490

SOURCES: *Izv. MSRD;* cf. I. P. Zubekhin and M. S. Koleditskii, "Moskovskii sovet rabochikh deputatov nakanune oktiabria."

a. Total includes sixteen United S-D votes.

b. Votes taken strictly on party lines.

c. SRs abstain from voting on Menshevik resolution.

It is important not to confuse support of a Bolshevik position, such as the August 12 strike, with support for the party itself. Even some Menshevik workers were disappointed with their leaders' position on the Moscow Conference issue,[89] and the Bolsheviks' preferred tactic was a demonstration in central Moscow; but they did not believe they could win workers' support for this more extreme protest.[90] But in terms of growing identification between parties and policies, the August strike was an important watershed in terms of popular support for the Bolshevik party. The party certainly enhanced its authority with this event, just as the Soviet leaders diminished theirs with their opposition to the strike. With the Kornilov mutiny, working-class fears of a counterrevolution were realized, and it was immediately after the halting of that rebellion that the Bolsheviks won their first majority in the Soviet.

And yet despite the Soviet voting record, the tide must have begun to turn even before the August 12 strike. The July uprising in Petrograd attracted supporters to the party at the same time that it alienated or frightened others. One observer admitted a two-week period of Bolshevik doldrums after July 4, but then interest in the party began to revive.[91] It seems then that the partiinost' of Moscow's workers underwent its radical transformation during the period of mid-July to mid-August. What was going on at this time to produce such a change?

On July 12, the Provisional Government reintroduced the death penalty in military units for the "military and state treason, going over to the enemy, fleeing from the field of battle, unauthorized retreat during battle, and refusing to fight."[92] This action was seen by many as a betrayal by Kerensky of his earlier revolutionary principles, and the Bolshevik party in Moscow attempted to capitalize on this betrayal. Resolutions protesting the reintroduction of capital punishment were passed by 11,000 workers in July and 53,000 in August (see Chapter Six). On July 19, the Bolsheviks raised the issue at the city duma, probably in order to embarrass publicly their fellow socialists. Instead of condemning capital punishment, the SRs and Kadets voted to support the Provisional Government's decision, while

dubious proposition since the Bolsheviks did not do appreciably better in terms of party mood in large factories than other parties did), only sixty-eight additional Bolshevik votes would have been created; the party would thus have been allowed to capture the Soviet majority on August 11 and then by only eight votes including those of the United Social-Democrats. See S. Kukushkin, *Moskovskii sovet v 1917 g.*; Al'tman, p. 62; Lukashev, pp. 59-72.

[89] Ignatov, *Moskovskii sovet*, p. 301.

[90] *Revoliutsionnoe dvizhenie v Rossii v avguste 1917 g.*, pp. 379-385.

[91] *Ot fevralia k oktiabriu*, p. 229.

[92] *Velikaia oktiabr'skaia sotsialisticheskaia revoliutsiia. Khronika sobytii*, vol. 2, 1959, p. 562. The original announcement appeared in *Zhurnal zasedanii vremennogo pravitel'stva*, 12 July 1917.

the Mensheviks abstained because of "lack of sufficient information."[93] The SRs' stock among workers must surely have fallen with this vote. A tram worker recalled that the Mensheviks and SRs had won over the support of the Sokol'niki tram park after the July days but lost it all again when the death penalty was reintroduced.[94] And even though all parties voted in the Soviet on July 25 to demand repeal of the death penalty, the erosion of the Socialist Revolutionaries' revolutionary reputation had certainly begun.[95]

Another important factor in the erosion of Socialist Revolutionary support at this time was the impact of workers' return to their villages. One memoirist recalls that when factory workers went home for their summer leaves, they learned how badly off the villages still were and that no progress had been made toward redistributing land.[96] A large number of textile plants had closed for six or eight weeks, most until August 15; perhaps the workers returned to the city with a new awareness of the problems of the revolution and of the urgency of their solution.

But possibly the most important reason for the shift in party loyalty lay in the deteriorating economic situation. As conditions worsened, the coalition government appeared less and less capable or willing to deal with the crisis, as has been seen. The early high hopes of economic improvement had vanished by mid-summer, as one worker reported in the Prokhorovka plant.[97] The Bolshevik party had offered a consistent alternative to the coalition's economic policy: let the soviets assume power and they would run the economy in the interests of the workers, not the bourgeoisie. Whether this was a realizable solution was not the issue; the coalition of socialists and capitalists in the government had already demonstrated that its program had solved nothing.

In part, then, the Bolsheviks gained relative support simply through the process of elimination. Working-class memoirs tend unfortunately to slide over this crucial transition period in their recollections of the events of 1917; but Boris Dvinov, a Menshevik party worker who was hardly sympathetic to the Bolshevik cause, described the gradualness of the change in support. Moscow workers, he wrote, did not immediately transfer allegiance from the SRs or Mensheviks to the Bolsheviks; but once the parties of the coalition had discredited themselves, the Bolsheviks

[93] *Letopis' geroicheskikh dnei*, p. 269.   [94] *Desiat' let*, p. 116.

[95] *Izv. MSRD*, 26 July 1917: SWD-SSD plenum of July 25; *Ocherki istorii moskovskoi organizatsii KPSS*, p. 255. On the same day, a majority of the Soviet expressed its continued support of the coalition Provisional Government, which indicates that the Mensheviks and SRs, while winning the latter vote, did not have the discipline to enforce a uniform party line on the death-penalty issue.

[96] "Sobranie rabochikh Trekhgornoi manufaktury," p. 281, and in Gorozhankina, p. 165.

[97] Vasil'ev, p. 117; "Sobranie rabochikh Trekhgornoi manufaktury," p. 282.

were available to pick up the pieces. "I would say that the politics and tactics of the coalition Provisional Government were chasing—and finally completely chased—the Moscow worker to the Bolshevik party."[98] This was one contribution of the Soviet leaders' perpetual stress on unity and of their tripartisan effort to discredit those who attempted to discredit the Bolsheviks. They succeeded in making the party respectable. The anarchists too seemed to gain some support among factory workers in this period, for like the Bolsheviks, they were also untainted by the sins of power, but they did not seem to capitalize on this growing support.[99]

To some extent, the Bolshevik success can be explained by the failures of the other two socialist parties. Why were they so wrong and the Bolsheviks alone so right? Whatever happened, for example, to the SRs, who had so clearly won the mass support of Moscow's workers on June 25? Despite their great popularity among workers, the party's base of support appeared even in June to be shallow. The SRs had no real organization or plans to build upon their popularity, a failure that must be blamed in part on the political naiveté common to so many political actors in 1917. Having won its easy victory in June, the SR party perhaps assumed the mood of the electorate would not change and need not be cultivated. The SR party newspapers reported the least amount of factory news of any of the socialist papers; the lists of its political contributors contained the names of very few factories, although they did receive a larger sum from workers than did the Mensheviks (see below). The party's Moscow leadership tended to be right of center with respect to the party as a whole; and when the Left SRs formed their own faction in Petrograd, there was no one to lead the Moscow SRs who shared the Left position. Left-leaning Socialist Revolutionaries instead tended to gravitate to the Bolshevik party.[100]

What must have contributed to the SRs' easy victory in June was the general good will enjoyed by the party (influenced in no small part by the personal popularity of Kerensky) and the generally low level of partisan consciousness in the period leading to the June elections. To the ill-informed worker, the "Socialist Revolutionaries" might have seemed more qualified to lead the revolution than the "Russian Social-Democratic Workers' Party—Menshevik" or "Russian Social-Democratic Workers' Party—Internationalist." But the effect of the June election was to develop workers' awareness of parties, to encourage workers to think in terms of party and not personalities. In the process of rolling up their big margin of victory, the SRs were raising the level of party consciousness among workers. Ironically, once the party became the instrument of political

[98] Dvinov, *Moskovskii sovet*, p. 26.   [99] *Ot fevralia k oktiabriu*, p. 229.
[100] Radkey, *Sickle under the Hammer*, p. 52.

activity, the SRs' many weaknesses as an organized party prevented them from building upon or even keeping their early support.

The failure of the Menshevik party is more perplexing. Unlike the SRs, the Bolshevik and Menshevik wings of Social-Democracy both professed to follow Marxist principles, both claimed allegiance to the international labor movement. Why did they fare so differently in 1917? Far too little is known about the sources of support of the Menshevik party.[101] As the losers of the struggle for the revolution in Russia, Menshevik followers left few records of their experience in 1917; and the memoirs of the party leaders such as Tsereteli and Sukhanov focus on high politics rather than reasons for the precipitous decline in their working-class influence during 1917.

That the Menshevik party through July was very popular among Moscow workers has been mentioned above. In the early period, factories with 29,400 workers could be characterized by a dominant mood in favor of the Menshevik party. By July this figure had increased to 44,200. Much of the early support came from textile workers and metalists, who accounted together for 59 percent of the Menshevik supporters. In comparison with other parties, the Mensheviks were particularly strong among textile workers and food workers. The Mensheviks claimed the support of 26 percent of the Moscow workers who expressed a party mood in March and April, but 53 percent of the food workers and 39 percent of textilists. In July, it was textile workers and leather workers who most strongly backed the party, together furnishing 55 percent of its support. Within industries, the textilists, chemical workers, and printers were most strongly supportive—54, 45, and 84 percent respectively of these groups favored the Mensheviks, compared to the party's overall support by 35 percent of the work force. Also seen earlier was the observation that during the June elections, the Mensheviks received significant support in districts with large numbers of metalworkers. In terms of social and economic characteristics, these industries—textiles, chemicals, leather, food, printing, and metals—were quite diverse. Some were dominated by women, such as chemicals, food, and textiles; others by skilled men, such as metals and printing. Although these breakdowns by industry themselves do not say very much about the kind of individual who chose to support the Menshevik brand of Russian Marxism, they do suggest that the party had a broad appeal across a wide spectrum of the working class. Other sources offer a more penetrating look at the composition of the Menshevik party's support.

---

[101] Neither N. V. Ruban, *Oktiabr'skaia revoliutsiia i krakh men'shevizma*, Vostrikov, nor Astrakhan, who presumably have had access to the relevant archival materials, adequately deals with this problem.

The few accounts of 1917 which discuss Menshevik influence among workers suggest that the working-class party members tended above all to be older, skilled worker-intellectuals who were well versed, through years in underground study circles, in orthodox Marxist theory and who liked to use this theory in their everyday political activities.[102] Without access to Menshevik party records, one cannot conclusively confirm that this type of individual joined the party at the factory level, but one can learn something about the Mensheviks' working-class following from the candidates nominated by the party for election to the city and local dumas in June and September. Such an analysis is especially revealing when one compares the Menshevik nominees to those proposed by the Bolshevik party.

In terms of occupations, about half of the candidates of both parties were metalworkers, who as a group had long spearheaded the labor movement in Moscow as well as in St. Petersburg. The share of the more skilled machine-building workers to metalworkers was slightly higher among Mensheviks than among Bolsheviks. In the machine-building occupation one would expect to find the veteran worker-intellectuals whom the Mensheviks were said to attract; but even so, machine workers were also strong supporters of the Bolshevik party, as the election results attest. Both of these parties appealed to skilled workers and experienced revolutionaries, and one would have to probe more deeply into individual biographies to discover why, for example, the Duks machine-building-plant worker Timofei Ivanov became a Menshevik and his co-worker Ivan Grigor'ev joined the Bolshevik party. But if almost half of the Menshevik candidates were metalworkers, the others were more evenly divided among other occupations such as textiles, leather, and printing. It is likely that these individuals ranked among the more skilled workers in their factories, but nevertheless, as was suggested above, this diversity among Menshevik candidates put these workers in touch with a broader range of Moscow workers than the Bolshevik candidates. For example, the textile-worker-Mensheviks here, all men, were no doubt more highly skilled than the average textile worker; but having served their comrades on factory committees or as Soviet deputies, they knew the problems involved in mobilizing workers who did not yet share the level of political awareness attained by the Menshevik working-class leaders.

Menshevik and Bolshevik candidates differed much less with respect to the size of the factory they represented, which fact is somewhat surprising given the standard assumption of Soviet historians that equates Menshevism with petty-bourgeois-minded workers in small shops and factories.[103] Over half of both parties' candidates came from factories with

---

[102] Lande, p. 37; Dune.   [103] See note 88.

more than a thousand workers; only 3 of 165 candidates from both parties worked in factories with fewer than a hundred.[104] This lack of correlation between parties and factory size is borne out as well by examining the party mood for the three periods considered above. In March and June, both Social-Democratic parties did relatively better in smaller factories than the SRs. In the June-July period, for example, when the Bolsheviks appeared to be dominant in only 11 percent of the whole working population, they dominated in 29 percent of plants of under a hundred workers; the Mensheviks, with the overall support of 35 percent of the workers, dominated in 48 percent of plants of this size. The SRs, despite the support of 33 percent of the workers, could claim to be dominant in only 2 percent of these smallest factories. I shall indicate in the next two chapters that factory size indeed made a difference in the degree to which workers participated in political activity, but factory size did not appear to influence significantly the party character of this political activity, especially with respect to the Social-Democratic parties.

Other factors do distinguish the Menshevik from the Bolshevik candidates. The Mensheviks tended to be older than their Bolshevik counterparts: the median age of the 171 Mensheviks for whom ages are known was approximately 34.8 years. For 37 Bolsheviks, the median age was 30.7 years. All things being equal, older workers tended to be more moderate in their politics and to be less impatient with gradual processes, and moderation surely characterizes the Menshevik position in 1917. Mensheviks and Bolsheviks also tended to differ in their experience in working-class and public organizations, as Table 5-9 indicates. The Menshevik candidates lagged behind their Bolshevik counterparts here in terms of experience in working-class organizations, with the exception of the Moscow Soviet (for which membership data are most complete and therefore most reliable). The Bolsheviks' preponderance in trade union leadership comes as something of a surprise since trade unions in Moscow tended to be moderate and focus on incremental change (the Moscow Conference strike notwithstanding), a position characteristic of Menshevik politics in 1917. This relationship serves to illustrate once again that party label was not the be-all and end-all of political activity among Moscow

[104] The exact breakdown is:

Factory size	Bolshevik	Menshevik
1-100	1	2
101-500	20	24
501-1,000	9	10
1,001 plus	50	4

The Bolsheviks are represented by a slightly larger proportion of workers from big plants, but this relationship is not statistically significant, given the small sample size (Chi-Square = 1.742, degrees of freedom = 3).

TABLE 5-9. *Organizational Experience of Duma Candidates*
(IN PERCENTAGE OF CANDIDATES FROM EACH PARTY)

	June Candidates		September Candidates	
Organization	Menshevik	Bolshevik	Menshevik	Bolshevik
Moscow Soviet	45	34	32	37
Raion soviets	15	32	13	23
Soviet committees	26	29	22	27
Trade union leadership	23	36	11	30
Public organizations	28	9	19	10

NOTE: In September, the Bolsheviks listed only their first ten candidates for each of the seventeen districts; the Mensheviks listed as many as twenty-five. Since the Menshevik candidates farther down on the list tended to be younger and less experienced than those at the top (which was presumably also true of the Bolsheviks), this table was calculated using only those Mensheviks who were listed among the first ten candidates for each district.

workers; Menshevik and Bolshevik trade unionists were frequently closer on many issues than, say, a Bolshevik trade unionist and a Bolshevik activist from the radical oblast bureau.[105]

On the other hand, Menshevik candidates appear far more active in public organizations not confined to working-class membership: district dumas (before September), the Committee of Public Organizations, and other mixed groups such as food-supply committees and the War Industry Committee. This activity both reflects the prevailing Menshevik attitude about class collaboration and also influenced the development of this attitude toward continuing such collaboration. The Mensheviks believed the socio-economic conditions were not ripe for a socialist revolution and were willing to devote their energies to other organizations than those serving only the working class. Bolsheviks preferred to concentrate their energies on class institutions only, such as trade unions and local soviets. The effect of this choice was to isolate Bolshevik workers further from active cooperation with non-working-class elements of society, and the gulf between "them" and "us" became all the wider because of this lack of contact. The Mensheviks, more absorbed in the practical work of public administration, did not develop this same sense of separateness. Moreover, by devoting its human resources to these public organizations, the party had fewer workers to spare for organizing within the working class, in sharp contrast to the very active organization of the Bolshevik party.

These are perhaps sweeping generalizations to be based on the record of so few individuals, but the analysis corresponds to the broader outlines of behavior of these two groups of workers. As noted above, Bolshevik

[105] Marshev acknowledges this state of affairs in *Moskovskie profsoiuzy*, p. 64. See also the position taken by moderate Bolsheviks such as D. B. Riazanov and V. P. Miliutin at the All-Russian Conference of Trade Unions in June (*Tret'ia vserossiiskaia konferentsiia profsional'nykh soiuzov*).

activists in Blagusha-Lefortovo conceded, that they neglected their involvement in local affairs because of the press of party work.[106] This analysis of Menshevik party candidates' motivations also corresponds to the direction they received from the Menshevik leaders in the Moscow Soviet. Such workers, given their experience, responded positively to their leaders' analysis of February as a bourgeois revolution in which the workers' role was to strengthen its position as a class within the alien bourgeois society. The Mensheviks in the Soviet indeed spoke far more frequently than the Bolsheviks in terms of class rhetoric; the "class struggle" for them was the overriding issue for the proletariat, as it was in the West. But theirs was an abstract vision of class struggle, defined in terms of Western European experience rather than Russian reality. It was the struggle by a class very much in awe of its theoretical opponent, the petty-bourgeois peasantry. Menshevik worker-intellectuals no doubt knew what little regard Karl Marx had held for the Russian muzhik's revolutionary potential.

Both the Mensheviks and Bolsheviks can be called class conscious, especially in comparison to the mass of workers who were members of neither party. But the Bolshevik consciousness, grounded in more recent political experience in the Russian revolutionary movement, was the dichotomized consciousness of "them" and "us." The Menshevik brand of consciousness was more complex, based on abstract ideas and intellectual study of the Western labor movement. In appealing to workers whose own sense of class was based on experience rather than on theory, the Bolshevik consciousness surely held the edge.

This reasoning leads to the last explanation for the Bolshevik success among Moscow workers—their identification as a working-class party. For Moscow workers, the experience of 1917 had further defined for them their identity as a class. The Bolshevik activist Ignatov had observed that among workers, class loyalties had always been stronger than party loyalties; given a choice between voting for an SR lawyer and a non-SR worker, he found, an SR worker would choose his fellow worker over his fellow party member.[107] As seen already, the Bolsheviks in June, of the three socialist parties, offered the largest number of worker-candidates and drew their support almost exclusively from working-class areas. As the concept of "them" and "us" evolved during 1917 into "*kto kogo*" or "who will triumph over whom," the Bolshevik party surpassed its rivals as the party clearly felt to be most suited for leadership in this period of sharpened class conflict.

As in all political campaigns, success breeds more success, failure leads to more failure. The Bolsheviks in August were in the midst of a drive

---

[106] *Proletarii*, 15 June 1917. [107] Ignatov, *Moskovskii sovet*, p. 103.

to raise funds for their party press, and contributions rolled into the party coffers. The SRs' and Mensheviks' sources of support, on the other hand, had withered away, and as already noted, the United S-Ds could no longer afford to put out a newspaper. The Socialist Revolutionaries recorded having received 1,922 rubles in August (one-third of their total contributions until then), but they received nothing thereafter. Mensheviks collected 919 rubles in August, 250 in September, and nothing in October; during the same period, the Bolsheviks received over 37,000 rubles! The lack of funds made organization and agitation extremely difficult for the SRs and Mensheviks.[108]

Symptomatic of the problem (and also symbolic of the degree of party commitment even in September) was the sad plight of a Socialist Revolutionary organizer in artisanal Dorogomilovo. He was approached one day by a local carter, who said, "My wife sent me. She says it's time now for everyone to join a party." The carter took home a copy of the SR program and returned the next day to pay his membership dues. But when he saw the SRs did not even have a stamp to legitimize the receipt, he took back his money and said, "I'm going to find a party that will stamp their receipts."[109]

The rise in Bolshevik support at this time does not necessarily contradict the picture of working-class institutional apathy described in Chapter Four. Partisan support and organizational activity need not be measured on the same scale. The Bolshevik party itself did not appear to be any more active than usual during this period; the shift in party allegiance was of a passive, latent nature, manifested only later, after Kornilov and during the September elections.

It appears then that Bolshevik momentum began to build from early or mid-July and received its most resounding boost with the Kornilov mutiny, which proved to many workers (now back from the countryside) the validity of the Bolshevik version of the class basis of the revolution.[110] But this rise in popularity did not necessarily signify that the Bolsheviks by September had become the monolithic party that is so frequently suggested in Soviet historical literature. The Bolsheviks benefited from the increasing identification by workers of political issues with political parties; the era of the dominance of personalities was clearly over. (The once-popular SR orator Maistrakh was chased out of meetings at the Uvarov tram park after the Kornilov episode.)[111] But the Soviet as a

---

[108] Documents on Menshevik party finances in the town of Serpukhov illustrate this organizational collapse. The Mensheviks received 849 rubles in membership dues in June-July, 53 in August, 79 in September, and 9 in October. Nondues income dropped sharply in August and climbed but slowly until October (Vostrikov, p. 134).

[109] *Zemlia i volia*, 24 September 1917.

[110] Dune, p. 41.   [111] *Khamovniki v oktiabre*, p. 19.

workers' institution, although weakened, had not been supplanted by the Bolshevik party as a competing class institution.

The identification of a single party with the revolution was far from complete. There were still many workers like the woman who said the Bolsheviks in October were a party "about which I had no understanding at the time."[112] The low turnout in the September duma elections is another indication of the limited spread of party consciousness among workers. And it is possible that the "nonparty" designation (*bespartiinyi*) began to take on a new meaning; whereas earlier it meant simply not having chosen sides, perhaps now it was a refuge for ex-SRs or Mensheviks who did not yet want to join the Bolshevik party. In any case, to the once-SR-led factory committee at Abrikosov's candy factory in October were reelected only Bolsheviks and nonparty workers; at Mastiazhart in September it was the "nonparty" voters who gave the Bolsheviks their big margin.[113]

Consequently, there was still strong support for cooperation among parties—party ideology did not have greater influence than revolutionary ideology. Thus, during the Kornilov rebellion, leaders of all three parties thought it necessary to agitate in factories and barracks together, to show that the democratic parties were united against the counterrevolution.[114] In October, support for the soviet seizure of power was not the same as support for the Bolsheviks. The position of the Moscow metalworkers' leadership was, "We are for soviet power, but against power to one party," a position shared by a number of Bolshevik leaders.[115] The issues of the October seizure were quite different from those of the district duma elections; workers were not choosing among party lists but between governments, and the choice did not necessarily have to be made along party lines. This explains the sentiment of the slesar Grigor'ev at the Bromlei machine plant, who insisted in October that he was not a Bolshevik and would argue against them in debate. But once they said the workers should seize power from the capitalists, he was ready to take up his weapon.[116] The Bolsheviks' ultimate success as a party in Moscow lay in their ability to exploit this strong class hostility held by workers and to channel it along political lines.

[112] *Oktiabr' na krasnoi Presne*, 1927, p. 99
[113] *Moskovskie pishcheviki*, p. 67; Batyshev, p. 187.
[114] Grunt, "Mogla li Moskva 'nachat' '?" p. 7.
[115] B. Kozelev, "Oktiabr' i soiuzy," p. 17.
[116] *Slavnye traditsii*, p. 85.

SIX. *Dimensions of Political Attitudes:*
WORKERS' RESOLUTIONS

*Day and night, across the whole country, a continuous
disorderly meeting went on from February until autumn in 1917.*

KONSTANTIN PAUSTOVSKY[1]

FROM the fall of tsarism, the dominant form of revolutionary activity for
most Moscow workers was the rally (*miting*). Before and after work, and
during meal breaks, workers would gather in the courtyards of their
factories to exchange rumors, listen to reports from their own leaders or
to representatives from outside groups. During work hours, the meetings
often continued, shop by shop, around work benches or at the communal
samovar. During the first weeks of the revolution, some factories held
daily, even twice-daily meetings, and throughout the year such factory
meetings remained the workers' most frequent contact with the outside
world. "Never have I participated so much in meetings and rallies as in
unforgettable 1917," remembered one factory worker.[2] Outside of the
factories, too, the open spaces near the old city customs barriers, around
which many factories were clustered, became the sites of lively meetings,
with orators from the various political parties speaking to workers after
work and on Sundays.[3]

It was through these local meetings that workers heard the latest news
of the revolution; here representatives to the soviets, trade unions, factory
committees or negotiating teams reported to their constituents. Party
activists explained their programs (if they could be heard), and representatives from other working-class organizations—cooperatives, clubs,
and youth groups—came to recruit members.

The meeting served as the major source of information for most workers;
although the socialist newspapers were published for the benefit of these
workers, a newsprint shortage and the rudimentary level of literacy among
many workers probably meant that relatively few workers could learn
much directly from the press or from the how-to pamphlets published in

[1] *Story of a Life*, p. 481.

[2] *Slavnye traditsii*, p. 83; see also Shelaev, p. 181; *Moskva v trekh revoliutsiiakh*, p. 178;
Oktiabr' v Zamoskvorech'e, pp. 119, 131.

[3] E. D. Tumanov, "Vospominaniia," *Bor'ba klassov*, remembers "almost daily" meetings
at the Rogozhskaia barrier (now Ploshchad' Il' icha).

1917 to explain the mysteries of factory committees and cooperatives.[4] Moreover, the meetings, particularly those of establishments such as factories or trade unions, did not serve merely as one-way conduits of information from the center. Whether tacitly or explicitly, these meetings were recognized as the basic source of legitimacy of the hierarchy of working-class organizations. Through their meetings workers elected factory committees, soviet deputies, trade union delegates; they voted on strike demands and approved or disapproved of decisions made by their representatives. And it was through these meetings that workers could best make known their views about the revolution, their demands, their concerns, their reactions to events. In some cases, the sentiment of these meetings was not only conveyed to the responsible representatives but communicated to the press as well, to be shared with the reading public. In this way, the published resolutions of these assemblies of workers provide a very basic source of the attitudes, the concerns of the workers themselves.

These resolutions provide a means of measurement of working-class political attitudes and activity quite separate from organizations or parties. The concerns of workers on the shop floor were of course shaped by the same factors that influenced the behavior of parties and other working-class institutions, but the resolutions that came from these meetings are especially valuable because they did not necessarily emanate from these other institutions. By systematically looking at both the content of all workers' resolutions now available and how such resolutions indicated the varying levels and direction of working-class political activism, one is able to trace the process of the revolution from an entirely new vantage point. The results once again both confirm the sharp polarization of society as seen by the working class and also illustrate the enormous complexity of the issues facing workers in their response to this polarization.

Despite the extraordinary value of these resolutions in portraying working-class political attitudes, there are some very important reservations about using them to measure public opinion. Before one can examine the content of the resolutions, it is essential to explain their origins and some of their limitations. This chapter is based on an analysis of about a thousand resolutions voted at local meetings and published either in the Moscow press in 1917 or in more recent collections of archival materials published in the Soviet Union.[5] For each resolution, the meeting responsible was

---

[4] *Moskovskaia provintsiia v 1917 g.*, p. 12; *Ot fevralia k oktiabriu (v Moskve)*, p. 144.

[5] The reliability of the archival collections will be discussed below. Most of the resolutions included in them were taken from the archive of the Moscow Soviet, to which it appears resolutions from meetings were regularly sent. While many of these resolutions were also printed in the press, it is impossible to know just how many resolutions remain unpublished. The archive was closed to me and to most Western scholars, although Marc Ferro appears

identified and classified as either a general factory meeting or that of a small group within the factory; the date, source, other particulars of the meeting (attendance, presence of speakers, whether violence occurred), and finally the specific points in the resolution (up to a maximum of ten) were all recorded.[6] Since no attempt was made to group these points in the first stage of this process, the result was about four hundred separate issues, which were subsequently grouped into fifty-four categories.[7]

Historians must be somewhat wary of the degree of commitment implied in these statements of political opinion. Resolutions were essentially general affirmations of some current mood; there is scant evidence to indicate that resolution-passing meetings labored over the language or even the fine points of most of the resolutions reported in the press. Nor do published reports give much indication that there was any conflict involved in the voting.[8] However, given the prevailing climate of unity, workers may have wished to minimize internal conflicts once a decision was reached and so deliberately avoided mention of debates or discussion. If protocols of these meetings were available, the process by which these resolutions were passed might become clearer. But the very nature of the resolutions suggests that they must be considered with some caution; the

---

to have access to the Soviet's and similar archives ("The Russian Soldier in 1917: Undisciplined, Patriotic, and Revolutionary," "The Aspirations of Russian Society," and *La Révolution de 1917*). In any case, of the 1,051 resolutions used here, 110, or about 10 percent, are found only in post-1917-published collections. The remaining 90 percent were taken directly from newspapers or journals of the period. These and the published collections are listed in the Bibliography. Finally, two of the resolutions are taken from the archive of Moscow Oblast, GAMO, fond 2443 (zavod Dinamo), fond 633 (tailors' union, but the resolution is from a metal factory). Since these materials went through the same selection process as published collections (the archivist, not the reader, selected the material), they must be treated with the same degree of caution as resolutions from published collections.

[6] All of this information for individual factories was recorded in machine-readable form and then matched with the data on the corresponding factory in the master data-set of factories. See Appendix A for a more complete description of the data-sets. I owe special thanks to Marian Carter of the University of Illinois Social Science Quantitative Laboratory for her Herculean assistance in the regrouping of these resolutions.

[7] This grouping, while helping to uncover trends and patterns, can sometimes lead to errors of simplification. Take, for example, the issue of the eight-hour workday, which gave the Moscow Soviet so much difficulty in the first weeks of the revolution. The two points "Provisional Government should decree an eight-hour day" and "Soviet should declare an eight-hour day" were both grouped into the "eight-hour workday" category, and the distinction between appealing to the Provisional Government and to the Soviet, judged here to be less important than the issue of the eight-hour working day itself, is lost. The most frequent resolutions in all 1917, both before and after grouping, are listed in Appendices F and G.

[8] A rare reported example of conflict at one of these meetings occurred at the highly politicized Moscow telephone works (see below) in July, when a Menshevik speaker so displeased the assembled workers that he was bodily thrown out of the factory (*Sots.-Dem.*, 13 July 1917).

cost of passing a resolution on this or that topic was not great. To vote for the slogan of power to the soviets did not bind a worker to defend his position at the barricades or even to vote for a soviet deputy who would act on the slogan. Resolutions thus present the same problems for historians as public opinion polls do for the modern social scientist. By passing a resolution, workers were clearly sending a message but were not necessarily promising analogous action. Valuable as these resolutions are for indicating the kinds of messages workers wanted to convey, they should be accepted for what they were—the mood of a temporarily activated mass meeting, a formalization of debate or discussion on a variety of current problems.

Therefore, with the possible exception of the early weeks of the revolution, the resolutions passed by workers should not be compared with the *cahiers de doléances* of the French Revolution. Moscow workers were not asked to formulate lists of grievances and send them to the Soviet or government. As often as not, the subject of the resolution came from outside—a report by a delegate or an outside speaker. In the earliest days after the February revolution, for example, factory meetings were asked by Bolshevik speakers to endorse that party's *nakaz* to the Soviet—a list of basic principles which most socialists endorsed. Thus, the resolutions espousing these principles do not imply that the points in the nakaz were the most pressing problems on the workers' minds, just that they were on the Bolsheviks' minds, and the workers agreed to support them.

This malleability of the workers' response created fertile soil for political agitators to exploit the resolutions for propaganda value. Although the Bolsheviks' nakaz, for example, expressed ideas most parties supported and although most workers did not see much difference between socialist parties, by putting through their sponsored resolution, the Bolsheviks produced an illusion of partisan support. In general, it would seem the Bolsheviks exploited this device much more frequently than the other socialist parties,[9] and the press reported some blatant cases of the Bolsheviks' manipulation of the resolution process. The most frequent tactic seemed to be to continue voting for a Bolshevik-sponsored resolution until opponents went home in disgust, whereupon a meeting's rump would pass and publish the resolution.[10] It is also reasonable to assume

[9] The question of whether or not this was a conscious tactic of the Bolshevik party and was overlooked by other parties belongs to a study of political parties, which is not the subject here.

[10] Such a case occurred with the Simonovka raion soviet in a resolution on the economic situation in May and at the first all-city conference of factory committees in July (see above, Chapter Four). Complaints of such tactics seemed rarer at the individual factory level, but perhaps such abuses did not seem worthy of mention to the harried Menshevik and SR party workers eager to set the most important records straight first (*Izv. MSRD*, 2 June supplement). Bolshevik youth-group members boasted in retrospect that one of their func-

that beyond the maneuvering involved in passing a resolution, distortion for partisan purposes affected the publication of a resolution. Party newspapers presumably published resolutions that favored their party's policies and might ignore resolutions that did not correspond to the party's idea of workers' needs.

There are at least two further reasons why the sample of published resolutions does not correspond to the entire range of resolutions passed at the local level. First, a factory or workers' group required contact with the center in order to make its views known; probably it was the speakers at a meeting who wrote the report and sent the news of the resolution to the Soviet. Only the largest meetings could expect to have additional newspaper correspondents present. But what became of resolutions passed at meetings that had no contact with the outside? Of the sentiments expressed in these resolutions, there is no record, which is unfortunate since factories with little outside contact were thus less affected by what outsiders wanted the workers to discuss. If resolutions in these isolated places were passed and could be found, they might well be more characteristic of the *cahiers de doléances* than the resolutions presently available.[11]

A second source of bias is the selectivity of the newspapers. To begin, where did they find the material they published? Resolutions were primarily directed toward the Soviet, sent with representatives and kept with the Soviet's records. The newspapers might have obtained the resolutions either from the Soviet files, from the correspondents at the scene, or from party members at the factory; probably the press used all these methods, although the Soviet-press connection is purely speculative. But how did newspapers decide what to print? They might well have printed everything they could learn about workers' resolutions. If this was the case, the Bolshevik party was far and away the most successful digger for news—57 percent of the resolutions used here were published (not necessarily exclusively) in their organ, *Sotsial-Demokrat*. The *Izvestiia* of the Moscow Soviet printed only 22 percent of the resolutions included here;

---

tions in 1917 was to disrupt meetings when they could not win their points in more orderly fashion (Rigosik, p. 121). The SRs' newspaper *Trud* also complained generally about the Bolshevik practice of moving to adjourn a meeting not in their favor and then reopening it when their opponents had gone (20 June 1917).

[11] Judging from Soviet historiography, there are clearly many resolutions in the archive of the Moscow Soviet as yet unpublished. Possibly these merely reiterate the views of those resolutions already published; it is less likely that their contents contradict the prevailing attitudes presented here. Most likely, the untapped resolution reports are of marginal political significance, but they might reflect more on local and everyday problems. This would make them all the more enticing as a source for the student of the social history of the revolution.

the Mensheviks' *Vpered* and the two Socialist Revolutionary papers, *Trud* and *Zemlia i volia*, printed even less.[12]

Most likely, however, some selectivity was practiced, even by the nonparty Soviet organ, *Izvestiia*. Resolutions adopted by three factories in May protested the omission by that paper of an earlier resolution of no confidence in the Provisional Government; later one of the same factories published a protest in *Sotsial-Demokrat* that *Izvestiia* had distorted its resolution on worker control.[13] A comparison of other resolutions published in several newspapers indicates that not all newspapers published all resolutions: *Vpered* published an account of one antiwar resolution of the Blagusha-Lefortovo district soviet but omitted mention of a second resolution calling on the international proletariat to overthrow all governments; *Sotsial-Demokrat* carried both resolutions.[14] But was this a maliciously partisan distortion of the workers' will or simply laziness or ineptitude? Fortunately, such examples are few, and each paper had the opportunity to correct the errors of the others, so confidence in the resolutions as a source of workers' attitudes is somewhat restored.[15]

RESOLUTIONS AS AN INDICATOR OF POLITICAL MOBILIZATION

In spite of all these qualifications, the resolutions published by groups of Moscow workers in 1917 can still provide an important clue to the mood of the workers during the revolution. But they also serve to describe an important aspect of the process of revolutionary participation, and the first task is to establish whose mood was being expressed by these resolutions. Regardless of whatever message was conveyed by a resolution, the fact that a group of workers decided to express an opinion at all is significant. Even if one grants that to vote on some resolutions required little initiative on the part of the assembled workers (if complete resolutions were offered by outside speakers and accepted by acclamation), the involvement of these workers in this process made them a little more politically conscious and exposed them to the world beyond the factory; and voting was a signal that they did take some interest in political matters.

[12] This may be another factor in ultimate Bolshevik influence; workers liked to read about themselves (see Dune, p. 20) and could read more in *Sotsial-Demokrat*.

[13] *Sots.-Dem*, 23 May, 7 June 1917.

[14] *Vpered*, 1 July 1917; *Sots.-Dem.*, 29 June 1917.

[15] A more serious problem of distortion lies in the resolutions gathered from Soviet-period compilations. Since the compilers themselves claim their choices are "representative" rather than comprehensive, it can only be assumed that resolutions were chosen for inclusion because they represented the party's interpretation of the October revolution. Fortunately, such resolutions constitute only 10 percent of the total used here, and their value in extending the range of available opinion offsets the probable bias in their selection for publication.

The revolution involved more workers in politics than ever before, but there still remained many factories and shops where organizers never came, factories and shops whose workers never debated an issue, let alone sent a resolution to be published. As late as August 20, local organizers in the Khamovniki district lamented that only seven of eighty enterprises (representing 12,000 of 26,000 workers) were organized.[16] Therefore, it is useful to compare those factories that produced these political messages with those that did not.

The 840 resolutions in this sample (passed in individual factories in 1917) came from only 276—11 percent—of the 2,500 Moscow factories for which there is any record. But this 11 percent, which was most active in passing resolutions, tended to include the largest plants and in fact represented a majority—57 percent—of all the factory workers in Moscow. Only 5 percent of the plants with fewer than a hundred workers submitted resolutions, but 42 percent of plants larger than one hundred passed resolutions. Of the 50 Moscow factories with over a thousand workers, only 5 passed no resolutions in 1917. Large plants may only appear to be more involved in this political process because small factories were too insignificant for newspaper editors to bother publishing their resolutions. This bias in reporting is certainly true for strikes.[17] But the very small factories were frequently bypassed by organizers and agitators who were soliciting resolutions. With a limited number of agitators, a political party would certainly choose to concentrate its resources on plants with large numbers of workers (choosing, perhaps, to organize small plants through their trade unions). Small factories, moreover, had no Soviet representation of their own (the rule was one deputy for five hundred workers), so they had to rely mostly on the press and the occasional visits of their shared representatives for information on the political situation. But this does not mean that workers in small factories were inherently politically quiescent, only that their political support was probably not considered to be worth the effort it would take to mobilize.

Granted then that large plants were the most active in passing resolutions because of tactical and organizational considerations, one still wonders if there were other differences between the 11 percent of factories which passed resolutions and the rest who did not? Or to rephrase the question in terms of workers, who were two hundred thousand workers on record as voting for resolutions? There are several ways to measure worker participation: total number of resolutions passed (for example, by a particular industry), total number of workers involved in those resolutions, and the relative share of workers involved in those resolutions as against the total in the industry. Most resolutions—169—were passed

---

[16] *Izv. MSRD*, 20 August 1917.　　　　　　[17] See below, Chapter Eight.

by workers in machine-building plants, followed by 168 passed by ordinary metalists. It was the same group of workers, often, who passed these resolutions. Table 6-1 indicates that only two-thirds of the workers in the machine and metal industries were involved in these 337 resolutions. But each resolution-passing machine plant passed an average of 7.2 resolutions during 1917, a very high rate of activity.

TABLE 6-1. *Levels of Worker Participation in Resolutions*

Industry	Number of Workers Involved in at Least One Resolution	Percent of Total Work Force
Tram	10,950	100.0
Power and water	1,080	99.1
Leather	23,210	76.1
Railroad	32,150	75.6
Chemical	19,330	74.9
Machine building	21,470	67.6
Metal	36,810	65.1
Printing	6,270	49.8
Rare metals	730	45.5
Food	11,180	41.6
Textile	36,120	39.5
Tailoring	4,960	37.5
Wood	620	9.9
Paper	290	9.6
Mineral	200	6.1
Animal byproducts	0	0.0
Total	205,370	56.8

SOURCE: Both the total number of workers passing resolutions and the totals in the work force on which the percentages are based come from the master factory data-set (see Appendix A). The calculations are based on the assumption that all workers in a factory participated in the resolution (see note 19 below).

Merely counting resolutions then seems to indicate that the metal-workers and machine workers continued their pattern of prerevolutionary activism into the resolution process of 1917. But in terms of the extent of participation, by measuring the involvement of workers in at least one resolution, one learns that the tram, power, leather, railway, and chemical workers were all more active than metalists and machinists. The role of these industries' workers in the revolution is often ignored by historians who concentrate on the largest numerical groups of workers, especially metalists and textile workers. Perhaps the activism of 1,075 power and water workers had only a marginal effect on revolutionary politics overall, but this study is concerned not just with the workers' impact on the revolution but also with the impact of the revolution on the workers; and in the following discussion of the goals of workers, it will be important to consider why leather and chemical workers were so broadly involved in the resolution process.

A final note on the identity of the active resolution makers is that they tended to be male workers. Information on the sex ratio in individual factories is unfortunately scarce and available for only 206 plants (representing, however, one-third of all workers). Based on this limited information, factories where women made up over half the work force were significantly less involved in resolutions than factories where women numbered less than one-half of the workers.[18]

THE DYNAMICS OF POLITICAL RESOLUTIONS, MARCH TO OCTOBER

The contents of workers' political resolutions were inextricably linked with the rhythm of the revolution, and the momentum of political events in Petrograd combined with local problems to influence the concerns of Moscow workers at any given time. A pressing problem for workers in March may have either been solved or rendered irrelevant by new more important concerns later on. Moreover, the very intensity of workers' resolution activity varied with time. As Figure 6-1 indicates, the frequency of resolutions was high in March and April, fell off during the summer months, and peaked again in August, the month of both the Moscow Conference and the Kornilov mutiny, the two issues to which the largest numbers of workers addressed resolutions. (Kornilov resolutions also spilled over into September.) The relative decline in resolutions between May and July does not, of course, indicate an absolute decline in workers' political activity. During May and July, a large number of workers were involved in strikes or strike preparations; political energies in the month of June were absorbed by the municipal duma elections. Such involvement reemphasizes the point that none of the activities under discussion, including party activity, should be assumed to be the sole indicator of revolutionary participation or revolutionary activism in 1917. My goal is to assemble a composite picture of working-class revolutionary involvement.

[18] A contingency table can be constructed as follows:

	Passed at Least One Resolution	Passed None
Factories less than half women	61	48
Factories more than half women	33	64

A Chi-Square test indicates this is a significant difference at the .99 level of confidence.

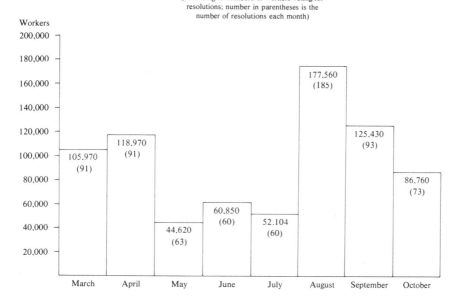

Figure 6-1

Frequency of Resolutions in Moscow

(according to numbers of workers voting for
resolutions; number in parentheses is the
number of resolutions each month)

In order to trace the change in the political attitudes expressed through resolutions, the following discussion will focus on the five most frequently mentioned points each month. These most likely reflected the most prevalent concerns of Moscow workers, although they also may have reflected the most prevalent concerns of political organizers. It is instructive to see how closely they paralleled the course of revolutionary development discussed in Chapter Three.[19]

[19] The figures on resolutions used in the present discussion are based only on those resolutions passed by representative factory meetings: general meetings, delegates' meetings, or factory committees. Of the 840 resolutions recorded from individual factories, 124 came from subgroups such as sick-fund organizations, cooperatives, and party groups, and these were excluded from the analysis. Resolutions passed by larger groups, primarily raion soviets and trade unions, were considered, but they are more difficult to compare with the characteristics of the resolution-passing body. Unless otherwise stated, the resolutions discussed below belong to the group of 716 representative factory resolutions. Every attempt was made to consider the number of workers voting for resolutions apart from the number of workers in the factory. Where attendance was reported at general factory meetings (which happened for about one-fourth the resolutions), the number of workers voting for resolutions tended to be about the same as the number of workers at the factory. (The votes on resolutions for this reason provide an estimate of factory size when none other is available.) Therefore, since the only resolutions considered here are from general factory meetings or factory committee meetings, as many votes were recorded as there were workers at the factory.

Table 6-2 indicates that just as the eight-hour workday provoked the first serious crisis for the Moscow Soviet, the issue was foremost at the local factory level in March. Slightly over 100,000 workers voted for political resolutions in this month, and about half of these demanded this symbolic fruit of the revolutionary movement. Proposed tactics for achieving the eight-hour workday varied; the largest number of workers, about 13,000 in twelve plants, stipulated that the Provisional Government decree the new workday; but an almost equal number, 12,150 in ten plants, simply resolved that the eight-hour workday be implemented in their own factories, by spontaneous action (iavochnym poriadkom) if necessary. Another 6,000 workers resolved that the Soviet should decree the shortened workday, regardless of Provisional Government action. These three points of view typified the crisis of authority which continued to plague

TABLE 6-2. *March Resolutions*

Subject	Number of Workers Voting	Number of Resolutions
Eight-hour workday	52,670	46
War aims	26,220	14
Support for Provisional Government	25,330	12
Constituent Assembly	16,740	12
Opposition to the war	15,230	7

the revolutionary movement—was the central provisional power, the local soviet, or the individual factory the legitimate locus of power? When the Moscow Soviet, as already seen, took action on this issue on March 19, the problem of the eight-hour workday disappeared from the agenda of Moscow workers' concerns. In later months, only another 12,000 or so workers passed resolutions on the subject, usually defending the eight-hour workday against attacks for unpatriotic behavior. But the underlying problem of authority implicit in these resolutions continued to dominate political life in Moscow.

Judging by the enormous pressure that local workers exerted on the Moscow Soviet to deal with the eight-hour workday issue, one can assume that the demand must have been endorsed by the vast majority of Moscow workers. But among those workers who passed resolutions on the subject, workers in two important military industries appeared especially concerned. Sixty percent of all chemical workers and 45 percent of machine-building workers expressed their support of the shortened workday. Such workers had a strong personal interest in an eight-hour workday since military plants operated longer-than-average shifts; with the eight-hour workday as the norm, such workers would now at least receive overtime bonuses for working the standard nine or ten hours each day. But these two industries, because of their vital role in the Russian war machine, were also especially aware of the dangers of a negative reaction from soldiers toward the demand, and their resolutions spoke to this point. Three thousand workers at the Dinamo plant proclaimed that any charges that their "laziness" hurt the war effort were no more than counterrevolutionary propaganda. Workers at the Vtorov explosives plant invited soldiers' representatives to examine the factory's books to demonstrate that productivity had actually increased under the new regimen.[20]

Indeed, worker concerns about the conduct of the war did not lag far behind their demands for the eight-hour workday in terms of popular support. Over 40,000 workers in March passed resolutions concerning Russia's miltary commitment. Most of these were not in outright opposition to the war; the dominant concern was to clarify the goals for which Russia was fighting. These resolutions, grouped under the classification "war aims," called for the new government to renounce any goals of annexation or indemnities and to specify conditions for peace talks. Such resolutions corresponded to the position of "revolutionary defensism" then emerging in the socialist parties' leadership as well as on the factory floor.

However, a substantial number of workers were more explicit about their opposition to the war, calling either for the soonest possible end to the fighting, for the Provisional Government to initiate peace negotiations, or simply for an outright end to the war. There were very few (published) resolutions in support of the war, despite the opinions expressed by soldiers in the Moscow Soviet debates on the war question. Six factories (with 4,200 workers) called for continuing the war to defend the revolution, a position that did not in March seem inconsistent with the policy of the Provisional Government and which was even initially endorsed by the Moscow Committee of the Bolshevik party.[21] Another 1,000 workers at the municipal workhouse resolved that Russia should continue to fight the war, at the same time pledging support to the "Social Democratic Workers' Party."[22] There were no resolutions that endorsed the Kadet party slogan of "War To the Victorious Conclusion." If there were workers in factories who shared this view, they were certainly in the minority and their voice was not heard.

A third major concern of workers in March was the problem of political power. About 21,000 workers adopted the Petrograd Soviet's cautious

[20] *Proletarii*, 2 May 1917.

[21] *Sots.-Dem.*, 21 March 1917; *Letopis' geroicheskikh dnei*, p. 43. A recent Soviet monograph on Petrograd workers shows that "revolutionary defensism" existed even among the stalwart workers of the Putilov plant (Sobolev, p. 183).

[22] *Sots.-Dem.*, 9 March 1917.

position of support for the Provisional Government "insofar as" (*poskol'ku, postol'ku*) it carried out the goals of the revolution, and another 4,000 expressed more general support of the new government.[23] The true revolutionary authority was expected to be the Constituent Assembly, which would formulate the constitutional basis of a new Russia. Such an assembly had been the goal of revolutionaries since the 1870s, and all parties now unanimously supported the idea.[24] In Moscow, 16,200 workers called for the rapid convocation of the Constituent Assembly, another 11,000 further stipulated that the new constitution create a democratic republic. With continued rumblings from Petrograd that the ruling Kadet party preferred a constitutional monarchy, Moscow's workers hastened to declare their conception of the future order.

The Constituent Assembly disappeared as a major concern of workers after March, but there is evidence that it never entirely vanished as a source of revolutionary legitimacy. As will be seen below, in October soviet power was seen by many supporters as a transitional stage until the Constituent Assembly could meet. An important source of worker mistrust of the Provisional Government throughout 1917 was the government's continual postponement of elections to the assembly, which elections would obviously place the Kadet party in a minority. But abstract ideas such as the democratic republic tended to disappear as the problems of Russia's future became obscured by the present struggle for power and authority among the elements of Russian society.

The resolutions of March reflected an early concern with abstract issues and revolutionary symbols, and they reflected the concerns of the revolutionary leadership that was instrumental at this time in setting the revolutionary agenda. Although the eight-hour workday was in fact implemented by pressure from local factory workers, it was a symbol of the spirit of Revolution as much as an economic benefit. The issues of war and political power were shared concerns of all of political Russia, and the resolutions indicating their importance for workers were largely initiated from outside the factories. In the feverish activity of March, or-

[23] Although the "insofar as" resolution represents a compromise between support of and lack of confidence in the Provisional Government, I have grouped these resolutions with other resolutions of support. This produces results for the Moscow case which do not conform to Marc Ferro's analysis of a sample of Russian workers' resolutions in March: he reports three resolutions of support of the Provisional Government and eleven of lack of confidence. My findings for Moscow reflect the opposite: twelve resolutions of support and four of no support. However, eight of these are resolutions expressing conditional support, and if one were to interpret these (incorrectly, in my view) as implying lack of confidence, my results for Moscow and Ferro's for Russia would correspond almost exactly. (See Ferro, "Aspirations of Russian Society," p. 197.)

[24] See O. N. Znamenskii, "Stanovlenie sovetov i vopros ob uchreditel'nom sobranie," pp. 3-19.

ganizers traveled from factory to factory to inform the workers; they brought with them these resolutions, which workers readily endorsed. These opinions were certainly shared by the workers who voted for the resolutions; but they were not born out of conflict, and too much weight should not be given to the degree of urgency they expressed. The nature of the March resolutions and their wide support do suggest that a large number of workers were being brought into the political arena, however, and were becoming informed about the issues of the day.

The March resolutions also reflected the obsession for unity on the part of revolutionary leaders and led. The revolutionary defensist position on the war, the wary support for the Provisional Government, and support for the all-class Constituent Assembly represented moderate political positions, a desire for compromise and conciliation. Even the supporters of the eight-hour workday, an issue that more clearly benefited the working class alone, defended their demands in terms that would not alienate the working class from other elements in society, especially the army. Thus the spirit of unity which dominated the Moscow Soviet's outlook and overshadowed partisan friction found a home on the factory floor as well.

In April, when clashes emerged among socialist parties on the war and the coalition government, revolutionary unanimity began to break down, and workers' resolutions reflected this new element of discord (look at Table 6-3).

TABLE 6-3. *April Resolutions*

Subject	Number of Workers Voting	Number of Resolutions
War aims	32,260	27
Support for Soviet	30,110	13
Opposition to the war	23,130	33
Support for Provisional Government	14,620	7
Economic measures	14,370	9

The eight-hour workday, now settled as a political issue, was replaced as the most urgent concern by the category of war aims. But whereas in March these resolutions called largely for the general slogan of peace without annexations, in April the largest single war-aims demand was for the publication of secret treaties (voted by 13,080 workers in ten factories). Such resolutions accompanied workers' hostility toward the Miliukov note in mid-April; if Moscow avoided the major demonstrations the note provoked in Petrograd, these resolutions suggest that Moscow's workers were nonetheless aroused over this betrayal of their peace goals. Indeed, although the few Moscow demonstrations against the Miliukov note centered in Zamoskvorech'e, that district produced only two protest reso-

lutions, both from small food-stuffs factories. Most resolutions calling for
the publication of treaties came from usually less active districts: Rogozhskii, Sushchevsko-Mar'inskii, and Sokol'niki. The large bulk of the 13,000
workers voting for this resolution—65 percent—were metalists; only 220
machine workers passed such a resolution. This distribution indicates that
such resolutions were not merely provoked by workers' proximity to other
more radical comrades; the desire for an honest peace was widespread
among the Moscow working population.

A new test of workers' attitudes toward the war emerged with the
Provisional Government's announcement on April 6 of a campaign to
solicit subscriptions to a Liberty Loan.[25] Banner headlines in *Izvestiia*,
Vpered, and *Trud* urged workers to buy Liberty Bonds; the Bolsheviks
opposed the loan in the Soviet, and their newspaper countered the Soviet
majority with a campaign to have workers denounce the loan. In April,
11,900 workers passed such resolutions. These were the bulk of the antiwar resolutions; others demanded the immediate commencement of
peace talks or generally condemned the war. Most vociferous in their
opposition to the loan were chemical workers and tram workers: over
one-fourth of them passed resolutions in protest on this issue.

On the other side of the question, 2,500 workers (in five factories)
supported the Liberty Loan; another 1,600 (in three factories) declared
their support, conditional on the publication of secret treaties. Most of
these supporters of the loan were printers; 2,600 of them—almost 20
percent of all printers—adopted resolutions in support of the loan, most
echoing the resolution of conditional support passed by the Moscow Soviet. This action shows how decisively the printers had shifted from revolutionary opposition before 1917 to solidarity with the new revolutionary
government; they were extraordinarily active in supporting the positions
taken by the Menshevik and SR leaders in the Moscow Soviet and in the
Provisional Government. These socialists were their own leaders, printers
recognized; and they realized also that they must demonstrate their confidence in this leadership.

If other sizable groups of workers shared the position taken by the
Moscow Soviet on the Liberty Loan, they did not bother to put their
opinions in writing. Even less did Moscow's workers support the loan by
actually subscribing. According to the information available, only two
Moscow factories purchased bonds throughout 1917.[26] The Provisional
Government's official *Vestnik* confirmed the workers' lack of response.
Two Petrograd factories, it reported, had purchased bonds, but "none-

[25] Volobuev, *Ekonomicheskaia politika*, pp. 338-349; and above, Chapter Three.

[26] The two factories buying bonds were a war plant, Natanson and Shtein, who bought
a three hundred ruble bond and donated it to the local soviet, and Reostat, an electrical-
equipment factory (*Trud*, 15 June 1917; *Russkie vedomosti*, 11 April 1917).

theless, workers, in the main, do not take their proper part in the subscription to the Liberty Loan."[27]

Possibly the most serious consequence of the Liberty Loan controversy for further revolutionary harmony was the drive, initiated by the Bolshevik party, to replace those Soviet deputies who had supported the Liberty Loan. In the aftermath of the Soviet vote on April 15 and the uproar over the Miliukov note one week later, eighteen factories, with 5,280 workers, recalled their deputies and replaced them with representatives more in line with factory opinion on the issue. It was the first time that Soviet deputies had been held accountable for their actions, and the action marked a growing political sophistication among Moscow workers. Henceforth, policy would become more important than personality in choosing representatives.

Another new element in the April resolutions was strong support for the Soviets of Workers' Deputies, notably for the Petrograd Soviet in the aftermath of the Miliukov note but also unspecified support for the soviet in general. A third element of the soviet-support resolutions called for strict supervision (kontrol') over the Provisional Government. These resolutions indicate the degree of working-class support for the democratic pole of dual power. The Petrograd Soviet could only check the government if it had the backing of its constituents, and these resolutions seem to reflect the workers' desire to demonstrate this backing. There was little outright hostility toward the Provisional Government or toward its "ten capitalist ministers," unlike the situation in Petrograd. Only 3,300 workers (in six plants) passed resolutions opposing the existing government. Slightly more, 4,700 workers in six plants, supported the transfer of all political power to the soviets at this time. The evolution of the demand of "all power to the soviets" will be examined at some length later in this chapter; at this point, it was a minority opinion shared primarily by machine workers with strong links to Petrograd. The majority of Moscow workers expressing an opinion on the political structure continued to indicate that it was sufficient for the soviets to defend the interests of the democratic elements while allowing the Provisional Government to continue to carry out its work.

There was a certain ambiguity about all of these political resolutions in April, a lack of hard distinctions among positions. It was perfectly consistent to vote against the Liberty Loan, defined here as an antiwar position, and still to support a position of war for defense only. Revolutionary democracy hoped the war could be settled honorably by the earnest cooperation of the international socialist movement despite growing indications like the Miliukov note that the aims of the two poles of

---

[27] *Vestnik Vremennogo pravitel'stva*, 27 July 1917.

dual power might be incompatible on this point. Neither were the positions of support for the Provisional Government or the soviets entirely incompatible. But a gradual change was underway which is especially noticeable when one looks at these resolutions as opposed to other types of working-class activity. Twice as many workers now expressed support for the soviets as for the Provisional Government; they appeared to identify much more with their soviets than in March. Concurrently, workers' attitudes about the war became more cautious. If the war must continue, their resolutions implied, they certainly were not going to help pay for it.

Finally, the economic situation, which had been overshadowed by the political tumult of March, began again in April to engage workers' attention, and over 14,000 workers passed resolutions calling for a variety of economic measures, which had in common that they be financed by capitalists, not by workers. Many of these resolutions were closely linked to the Liberty Loan protest. In five factories, 5,100 workers specified that the war, since it was being fought in the interests of capital, should be financed by the capitalist class. Other resolutions, echoing the ongoing debate in the Moscow Soviet on the national economy, demanded both that the tax structure be reformed to place a heavier burden on the propertied classes and that profits be strictly limited. In the economic sphere, if not in the political, the spirit of national revolutionary unity had not overwhelmed workers' basic mistrust of the bourgeoisie and the landed classes.

By May and June, their own economic welfare had become the foremost of working-class concerns. The Soviet formally considered the economic crisis in May and called for organized discussions at the local level to inform workers of the situation and to establish local opinion with respect to these issues. The political resolutions of these months clearly reflect this preoccupation with the state of the economy (see Table 6-4).

Three of these categories, "economic measures," "public regulation," and "workers' regulation" can be interpreted as opposition to the laissez-faire capitalist system that workers saw to be harmful to their own interests as well as those of the whole nation. The most popular solution to the imbalance of economic well-being in May appeared to be regulation by the coalition Provisional Government of the major sectors of the economy; by June, the emphasis had shifted to regulation of production by workers' representatives. Both elements were contained in the economic resolutions proposed by the local Menshevik and Bolshevik parties and widely debated in soviets, factory committee conferences, and factories. These resolutions demanded that workers' representatives supervise production, that large essential industries such as metal production be nationalized, that distribution of goods be centrally planned and coordinated, and that

TABLE 6-4. *May and June Resolutions*

Subject		*Number of Workers Voting*	*Number of Resolutions*
	May		
Economic measures		12,410	22
Public regulation of economy		10,540	9
No support for Provisional Government		8,080	8
Regulation of wages and prices		6,660	5
International solidarity		6,300	9
	June		
Workers' regulation of economy		28,850	15
Economic measures		24,770	21
Electoral procedures		16,200	6
Regulation of wages and prices		11,020	8
Public regulation of economy		9,600	8

prices be fixed. This was the plan presented by Kolokol'nikov to the Moscow Soviet and adopted by the majority of that body. The Bolshevik faction, it will be recalled, accepted these proposals but argued that only a government of soviets could carry them out. The resolution frequencies above indicate that almost 30,000 workers in May and more than twice that number in June adopted some of these economic points, but only about 2,500 workers each month adopted the more controversial call for soviet power. Workers still apparently wished to work within the existing structure to wage their battle for economic security, but the new stress on economic issues was accompanied by a rise in the awareness of the class base of the economic crisis.

This picture changes somewhat when one considers the response of local workers' institutions to the economic crisis. In raion soviets and factory committee conferences, Bolshevik party workers were especially active in using the economic issue to advance their own view of the revolution and its goals. For example, the Blagusha-Lefortovo district soviet voted on May 12 for the Bolshevik position on the economic situation by a margin of 62 to 41 (although 320 delegates attended the meeting). At the same time, the soviet elected a new executive committee with a decisive Menshevik-SR majority. In other districts where Bolshevik party influence was weak, Presnia and Rogozhskii, the Bolsheviks also managed to pass their economic resolutions during June. Such discrepancies between party mood and political resolutions suggest the ongoing tension between institutions and policy. Workers expressed confidence in their central institutions, from the Provisional Government to the Moscow Soviet, by demanding one, another, or all take action; but the resolutions also instructed these institutions about the action they wished to be taken—more active participation in economic regulation. It mattered less at the time which institution could best do the job than that the job be done. Only when the coalition Provisional Government continued to fail to provide economic leadership did the issue of the economy evolve into the question of political power itself.

Other political issues in May and June paled in comparison with concern about economic regulation and continuing resentment of capitalists' economic privileges. A significant number of workers reacted negatively to the entry of socialists into the Provisional Government at the end of April; almost 5,000 of the Provisional Government opposition votes explicitly objected to the coalition. At the same time, resolutions of support of the government, a popular issue in April, were passed by only 2,480 workers in May. Not even the Menshevik leaders of the Moscow Soviet had been especially warm to the idea of a coalition, accepting it only as a fait accompli.[28] From this point, Moscow's workers appeared to be increasingly alienated from the Provisional Government as an institution and tended to regard the government only in terms of concrete policies.

The international-solidarity resolutions coincided with a Soviet-inspired demonstration on Sunday, May 14, to protest the death sentence given to the Austrian socialist Friedrich Adler for his war protest. Local processions in working-class neighborhoods were estimated to include twenty to fifty thousand participants in each district, and the accompanying rallies produced a flood of resolutions.[29] This case is a good example of the resolution introduced from outside in order to raise workers' consciousness of their role in the international labor movement. No Adler resolutions appeared after this occasion.

In June with the sharp rise in resolutions on the economy, the only noneconomic topic to receive significant attention concerned the coming municipal duma elections. Almost all these resolutions appealed to workers not to depart from the city for summer holidays until after election day in order to preserve the socialist parties' chances for a united victory. Both economic and noneconomic resolutions indicate the continued appeal of revolutionary unity, characterized now, however, by a more suspicious attitude toward the propertied classes. In July, this suspicion began to be replaced in some quarters by defensive hostility, as the July resolutions demonstrate (look at Table 6-5).

The leading reaction to the July days, in terms of resolutions, was not directed toward Bolshevik adventurism, but in fact against the Provisional Government's decision to close Bolshevik newspapers. This was a clear

[28] *Izv. MSRD*, 27 April 1917, executive committee meeting of April 26.
[29] Ibid., 13 and 16 May 1917.

TABLE 6-5. *July Resolutions*

Subject	Number of Workers Voting	Number of Resolutions
Freedom of press and assembly	21,790	25
Support for cooperatives	13,800	7
Support for Bolsheviks	12,380	13
Opposition to death penalty	10,890	8
Opposition to counterrevolution	6,720	11

breach of the revolutionary compact forged during the February days; freedom of the press was a liberal as well as a democratic socialist ideal. In all, 11,300 workers protested the shutdown of socialist newspapers, a response that surely influenced Khinchuk's refusal to allow the closing of the local *Sotsial-Demokrat*.[30] Another 7,300 workers passed resolutions against the Moscow Soviet's ban on street meetings. Freedom of the press and assembly were essential elements of the revolution; revocation of these rights could augur further attacks on the revolution's achievements.

Also in connection with the July events and the hostile reaction to them, over 12,000 workers endorsed a resolution protesting the persecution of the Bolshevik party and its leaders, a resolution in fact sponsored by the Menshevik party.[31] The Bolsheviks had threatened revolutionary unity by dividing the working class against itself; but in the face of attacks from outside the working class, revolutionary democracy must defend its own. (To be sure, some of these resolutions expressed explicit endorsement of the Bolsheviks' insistence that the soviets take power; about 4,000 workers passed resolutions calling for soviet power in specific response to the July days.) Far fewer workers, 4,400, passed resolutions critical of the Bolsheviks' July demonstrations or in open support of the Soviet's ban on meetings; but the attitudes of such workers had already been expressed by the Soviet's majority decision, and further public support of this position may not have seemed so urgent. This is one problem of using resolutions as an unbiased measure of public opinion since resolutions tended to emerge in reaction to opinion established in other ways.

If the July resolutions indicate an ambivalent attitude toward the relations between the Soviet and the Bolshevik party, they indicate a growing concern among workers about the revolution's future. The repressive actions taken by the coalition government against the Bolshevik party and the reintroduction of the death penalty at the front signaled a growing

[30] Khinchuk, pp. 178-186.

[31] *Izv. MSRD*, 15 July 1917, "The duty of every conscious worker, especially socialist, is to actively enter in against any attempts at aggression and spontaneous lawlessness of unconscious crowds towards socialists, regardless of faction."

firmness on the part of the forces in power, a rise in the confidence of the counterrevolution's partisans. At the same time as workers endorsed the principle of unity in order to protect the revolution, their resolutions against the death penalty and counterrevolution voiced fear and denunciation of the rising tide of reaction. A frequent resolution pointed out the dangers of this revolutionary backlash (accompanied by demands to dissolve the old State Duma and State Council) and called for the soviets to seize power, or at the very least to act more firmly against the counterrevolutionary threat. For example, on July 13, the Sushchevsko-Mar'inskii district soviet, not one known for its militancy, condemned the July uprising and said it was dangerous because the soviets were not strong enough to seize power. But in view of the threat of the counterrevolution, the resolution called on the soviets to strengthen their activities, presumably to be ready to take power if that should become necessary.[32]

Now it was the turn of the economic situation to pale against such serious political dangers, and the only economic issue that attracted much attention in July was the formation of cooperatives. Moreover, the timing of the issue was due more to the activities of the Central Workers' Cooperative than to changes in the economic climate. The goal of this organization was to offer workers a cooperative institution apart from the dominant Moscow Union of Consumer Societies, which included elements from all levels of society. The new association would be for workers only. By July, this workers' cooperative had finally organized itself sufficiently to send representatives to factories to educate workers on the need for and benefits of a citywide worker-controlled cooperative organization. The standard conclusion to such meetings was a resolution of support, such as was voted by 13,800 workers in seven factories in July. (By July 25, the workers' cooperative had enrolled 44,400 members.)[33] It should be noted, however, that workers were engaged in economic activity on another front in July—during this month, 74,000 workers were on strike.

The month of July was an important stage in the sharpening of political as well as economic tension between the working class and the bourgeoisie. It is important, therefore, to determine just which workers were politically active during this period, for such workers acted as opinion leaders for the rest of the Moscow work force. There is evidence, of course, that a certain number of workers had left the city at this time, among them many textile workers, so this group at least would not have furnished many resolutions. Indeed, Table 6-6 shows that only 6 percent of textile workers in two plants passed any resolutions in July. Leather

[32] Ibid., 13 July 1917.
[33] *Vpered*, 27 July 1917; *Trud*, 6 August 1917.

TABLE 6-6. *Worker Participation in July Resolutions*

Industry	Number of Workers Voting	Number of Resolutions	Percent of Industry's Workers
Machine	13,280	17	41.8
Tram	3,200	2	29.2
Power	300	1	27.6
Chemical	6,500	3	25.2
Metal	13,710	21	24.3
Rare metals	320	1	20.1
Food	4,080	3	15.2
Printing	1,030	2	7.7
Railway	3,000	2	7.7
Textile	5,650	2	6.2
Leather	870	5	2.8
Clothing	170	1	1.3
Mineral	0	0	0
Wood	0	0	0
Animal byproducts	0	0	0
Paper	0	0	0

workers, another group that employed large numbers of rural migrants, participated even less. Machine-building workers in July led the Moscow work force in political resolutions, once again demonstrating the extremely high level of political awareness of this group and its involvement in opposition to the existing Soviet majority. An equal number of metalists also voted for resolutions in July, although the number represents a smaller share of all of that industry's workers.

The growing conflict between revolution and counterrevolution, sensed first by machinists in July, became obvious to many more Moscow workers in August; and the level and tone of that month's resolutions clearly reflects this rising awareness of polarization. More workers were involved in resolutions in August than in any other month, despite the concurrent apathy toward organizational activity. The Moscow Conference commanded the most attention, prompting resolutions from almost 62,000 workers as well as the more anonymous strike action of thousands of others (look at Table 6-7).

TABLE 6-7. *August Resolutions*

Subject	Number of Workers Voting	Number of Resolutions
Moscow Conference protest	61,980	65
Opposition to counterrevolution	53,980	43
Opposition to death penalty	53,360	50
Free press and assembly	43,760	40
No confidence in Soviet	19,530	28

All of the leading resolution topics in August concerned the growing threat of counterrevolution. The implication that the death penalty would be directed against the revolution symbolized the gravity of the situation, and resolutions in opposition received the support of more workers in August than any other resolution prior to that time. The defense of the democratic freedoms of press and assembly drew the support of a like number of workers. In addition, given these new threats to the revolution, workers were no longer content to pass resolutions in opposition to positions taken by the Moscow Soviet; the Soviet itself, for its refusal to sanction the Moscow Conference strike, now drew the active censure of over 19,000 workers.

Economic issues provoked little response from workers during August. The problem of food supply attracted the most attention in ten resolutions from 9,500 workers. Control over wages and prices was demanded by another 6,300 workers, and 5,000 workers in one factory passed a resolution for workers' control. But these sentiments faded against the overwhelmingly political focus of workers' attention in August. Indeed, no resolutions at all were passed in favor of economic reforms at capitalists' expense. The danger from this class was no longer in its economic power but in its political intentions, and nothing expressed those intentions more graphically than the Kornilov rebellion, which drew an immediate and massive response from Moscow workers.

In reaction to the Kornilov rebellion, a resolution demanding a series of measures to combat the counterrevolution was passed by scores of factories in late August and into September. The basic resolution, introduced by the Bolshevik party, catalogued the crimes of the counterrevolution and set an agenda for strengthening the revolution:

1. arm local workers and soldiers
2. disarm all counterrevolutionary military units
3. arrest tsarist generals
4. arrest the bourgeois eminences behind the counterrevolution: Rodzianko, Miliukov, Guchkov, Riabushinskii
5. close the State Duma, union of officers, military league, and other such bodies
6. close bourgeois newspapers and transfer their facilities to socialist parties
7. expel agents of foreign governments who aid the counterrevolution
8. requisition all automobiles and turn them over to district soviets
9. create a dictatorship of the "revolutionary proletariat and peasantry" to fight the counterrevolution, which dictatorship will:
   a. proclaim a democratic republic
   b. immediately give land to the peasants

c. decree an eight-hour workday

d. establish strict regulation of food distribution and production

Not all resolutions endorsed all of these points. Approximately 88,000 workers participated in resolutions listing one or more of these demands in August and September. (Each point was recorded separately, accounting for the larger number of workers supporting measures in opposition to the counterrevolution.)[34] But only 11,000 of these, as will be discussed below, included the demand for soviet power or "dictatorship of the proletariat." Nonetheless, it is clear that the Kornilov mutiny, as a vivid symbol of the class enemies' hostility to the revolution, received the greatest concern of any political issue in Moscow in 1917.

The September resolutions (see Table 6-8) continued to reflect workers' antipathy toward the Kornilov mutiny and the counterrevolution in general. With the loyalty of the military staff ever more suspect, workers no longer could trust that their brother soldiers would act to defend the revolution, and they now began to endorse the idea of a Red Guard composed of armed factory workers.

TABLE 6-8. *September Resolutions*

Subject	Number of Workers Voting	Number of Resolutions
Opposition to counterrevolution	103,440	85
Concern about fuel and materials	24,170	6
Red Guard	13,790	15
Concern about food supply	13,730	5
Opposition to the war	13,350	5

Economic problems, overshadowed since July by the succession of political crises, again became important to workers. The bread ration had dropped to a meager half-funt per day; in addition, workers who had weathered the summer food shortage in the countryside were now returning to Moscow eager to work and to earn a living. Textile workers,

[34] An example of the anti-Kornilov resolution, passed by the Gorodskoi raion soviet and joint factory committees, can be found in *Sots.-Dem.*, 1 September 1917. The totals given for classes of resolutions, given by month, tend to be swollen because each point is credited with the number of workers voting for the resolution. Thus, a resolution with four anti-Kornilov points, passed by a factory of 250 workers, counts as 1,000 anti-Kornilov workers. This distortion is due to the mechanical problems involved in regrouping resolution items and could be corrected only with very great difficulty and with a loss of analytical value. In most cases, the effect is not too serious. Where the distortion is great, as in this case, corrected totals have been calculated: 88,000 workers thus voted for one or more of the points classified as anti-Kornilov, or as opposition to counterrevolution.

who had been subject to an industrywide summer layoff, made up the largest group passing resolutions about food supply and fuel. Workers in this industry, typically less politicized than others with higher skill levels, wages, and urban experience, responded most readily to immediate threats to their basic existence; and the experience of six months of relative democracy had taught them that they too could express their grievances.

But even the food-supply resolutions reflected a new class consciousness in September. Workers did not just demand bread or fuel; they demanded that luxury restaurants and cinemas be closed to save fuel for their factories, and they demanded that speculators in food supply be punished for their manipulation of the market.[35] Such resolutions did not come from high party or soviet councils. They originated in local factories and soviets, and they demonstrated how deeply felt was the gulf now between the workers and the privileged classes of society.

Finally, the war reemerged in September as an issue of major concern. As the Bolsheviks embarked on their drive to marshal support for soviet power, a major point was that the soviets, when in power, would take the drastic steps needed to end the war and establish a general democratic peace.[36] At the same time, the Provisional Government, with the all-Russian Soviet's Central Executive Committee's support, had launched a campaign for a second Liberty Loan subscription, which only aggravated the differences between the defensists and internationalists in the Moscow Soviet and the Moscow work force.

By October, as Table 6-9 shows, substantive issues coalesced once again around the question of power and authority, as they had in March. The Democratic Conference had illustrated there was no future for further coalitions, and the Bolshevik call for soviet power, endorsed by the Moscow Soviet on September 5, received ever more support. Power was now the major concern of Moscow's politically active workers—power in government and power in the work place. In both cases, the workers were aligned against their class enemy, the bourgeoisie, and the perceived

TABLE 6-9. *October Resolutions*

Subject	Number of Workers Voting	Number of Resolutions
Support for soviet power	51,560	34
No support for Provisional Government	16,970	6
Support for Soviet	15,520	8
Strike settlements	10,800	3
Solidarity with workers	8,080	12

[35] *Sots.-Dem.*, 6 October 1917.

[36] Resolution proposed to the Soviet's executive committee on September 1 (*Izv. MSRD*, 2 September 1917).

polarization of society on both political and economic levels was now nearly complete.

Resolutions calling for soviet power were particularly frequent in the second half of October, contributing to the climate of expectant tension that was finally broken when the Petrograd Military Revolutionary Committee authorized the assault on the citadels of government. But the rationale behind many of these resolutions is important: soviet power was necessary in order to solve the economic crisis, not as an end in itself. (This issue will be further discussed below.) The economic situation received attention in other ways also: 10,000 workers advocated that the Moscow Soviet use its power to end all strikes in progress in favor of the workers; another 8,100 declared their solidarity with workers in the two-month-old leather strike.

The resolutions of October contrast sharply with those of March and April when workers endorsed issues of abstract principle, like democratic peace goals and the democratic republic. The experience of eight months of the revolutionary power struggle had resulted in a much more limited focus; political power for economic survival obscured any other more abstract issue. And it was on these basic issues that the disparate elements of the Moscow work force—both the advanced, politically knowledgeable and the less-experienced workers—were able to find common ground in their demands for a change in the nature of political authority. Those industries that demonstrated low overall participation in the political resolution process were most active in the months of September and October. While 27 percent of all workers passed resolutions in these months, 37 percent of food workers, 44 percent of leather workers, 32 percent of textile workers, and 52 percent of clothing workers passed political resolutions in September and October. Two factors were at work; both the cumulative experience of revolutionary participation and the gravity of these basic issues had finally brought these reluctant workers into the political arena.

POLITICAL RESOLUTIONS AS AN INDICATOR OF THE REVOLUTIONARY PROCESS

So far, this study has considered the content of these resolutions in order to illustrate the political views of workers in Moscow in 1917. Examining what the resolutions do not say, as well as further considering the details of workers' participation, will provide additional information on the political attitudes of Moscow's working class.

First of all, the lack of partisanship in the resolutions is striking. True, over 12,000 workers passed resolutions in support of the Bolshevik party in July, and a total of 47,150 expressed similar support during the whole period; but these resolutions were primarily directed against harassment of the party and did not necessarily represent partisan support.[37] After all, Trotsky had defended Chernov from the crowd in the July days, and the Menshevik Khinchuk supported the Bolsheviks' right to publish their views in the aftermath; workers did not use resolutions to breach the public unity of their class. Overall, only 34 of the 716 resolutions (from 33,100 workers) mentioned partisan political support (distributed about two to one for Bolsheviks over United Social-Democrats). Moreover, 15 resolutions from 11,800 workers called for an end to political factionalism and for the formation of a single workers' party.

A second related feature of workers' resolutions was that the sentiment for fair play for all socialist parties outweighed partisan political support. In a hundred of the resolutions, some 87,000 workers expressed the wish that socialist parties and press be allowed to carry on political activity free of outside harassment. This figure includes 1,600 printers' protests of the Military Revolutionary Committee's seizure of the liberal press during the October fighting, but most of these resolutions indirectly supported the Bolsheviks since theirs were the most harassed party and press in 1917.

Such resolutions confirm the picture presented in Chapter Five that party choice was subordinate to policy. It may therefore be inappropriate to describe the change in workers' political views by October as "Bolshevization." But when workers wished to preserve revolutionary unity while at the same time supporting a program endorsed by only one party, tensions were bound to arise. These conflicting goals, made clear in the resolution process, were not to be easily reconciled.

A point that is notably absent from the lists of most frequent resolutions is the demand for a solution to the land problem, even though many Moscow workers retained ties with their native villages. Only seventeen resolutions from 33,300 workers spoke at all to the land question, and these resolutions were distributed quite evenly over the eight-month period. The relative unimportance of this issue can be largely explained by remembering who it was who submitted the resolutions—skilled machinists and metalists, primarily, and also chemical workers, tram workers, and power and water workers. Machinists were even more urbanized than metalists; and although large numbers of chemical workers were in fact of rural origin, the industry included a large group of evacuated urban rubber workers, Latvians and Poles, who had little interest in the land

---

[37] These resolutions also tended to be from less representative groups of workers. Of the total of 840 individual factory-identified resolutions, 77 supported the Bolsheviks, but only 51 of these were from the general or factory committee meetings included in the sample of 716 resolutions. The remainder came from groups calling themselves "party cells," or meetings held on factory premises but not called by factory leaders.

question. Those who did demand land were primarily textile workers (12,000) followed by chemical workers (8,200), machinists (4,600), and metalists (4,400). Only three trade unions passed resolutions about land in 1917—the municipal employees, textile workers, and railway workers. (Municipal employees, their urban employer notwithstanding, included many coachmen, carters, porters, and odd-job men who tended to be peasant in origin.)

As was noted above, the preponderance of resolutions was passed by machine workers and metalists, who also composed the largest occupational groups in Moscow. But in terms of the share of all workers in the industry passing resolutions, the machinists and metalists fell behind several other industries—tram, power, leather, railroad, and chemical. The high degree of mobilization (participators per industry) in some cases can be explained by the peculiar structure of the industry; the power and water workers actually comprised only a small number of workers in a very few enterprises, and it would be simple for an organizer to reach them all. Likewise for the tram workers—the 11,000 drivers, conductors, and mechanics were concentrated in only seven tramway parks and were easily assembled. But tram employees also tended to be more politically aware than many Moscow workers; they had staged an effective political strike in the week before the February revolution and with the metalists were most active in opposing the war on the eve of February.

That the leather workers were politically active was demonstrated by the character of their two-month-long industrywide strike (discussed in Chapter Eight): this was a very carefully organized and well-implemented mass action, and the regular meetings held to discuss strike matters also provided a forum at which to discuss current political events. It is no surprise then that the peak month for resolutions from leather workers was September, the first full month of the strike. Many of these resolutions protested the death penalty, an issue totally unrelated to the strike, but one which peaked in intensity at the same time. Also important to the leather workers was the Kornilov rebellion; 58 percent of all leather workers passed resolutions of protest against the death penalty, 41 percent against the counterrevolution. In contrast, only 600 of 30,500 leather workers expressed support for the eight-hour workday, an issue which was of greatest concern in March.

Railway workers were a special case. Most of them were employed in the big workshops located near the rail stations, and by trade many of them were metalists; but they belonged to the railway union and even had their own railway district soviet. They were organized not so much by geographic area as by railroad line, so that the workers all along one line, for example the Moscow-Kursk line, had closer ties than the line's workers living in Moscow had with other local workers. They were united

by the line's newspaper, *Volia i dumy zheleznodorozhnika*, just as all
Moscow workers were united by the Soviet's *Izvestiia*. Railway workers
participated in the political life of the city, but they had a dual allegiance
and dual sources of information. Because the early railway unions united
all workers on a line, the leadership tended to come from the line's white-
collar departments, and the two railroad workers' newspapers tended to
represent the more moderate political views of the leadership. Thus,
much of the political information received by the railway workers was
filtered through very progovernment sources. The result can be seen in
the nature of railway workers' resolutions: those in support of the Provisional Government received the greatest attention (from 37 percent of
all workers), although the eight-hour workday, power to soviets, death-
penalty protest, and counterrevolution received substantial interest as
well. Isolation from the rest of working-class Moscow made the railway
workers a difficult group to compare with other workers. Their political
allegiance seemed to shift mercurially; for example, the Bolsheviks were
more seriously hurt among railroad workers after July than among any
other group, an observation that may be explained by the combination
of middle-class rumors about German spies in the party and the lack of
contact with other workers who knew and worked with Bolsheviks and
did not fear them. As partial corroboration of the railway workers' isolation
from the prevailing mood in Moscow, only five hundred of them passed
a resolution opposing the harassment of socialist parties.[38] As isolated as
they were from the more diverse Moscow working class, railway workers
may not have felt the same commitment to revolutionary unity that characterized most of the other worker groups in Moscow.

The greatest surprise among the workers passing resolutions is provided
by the chemical workers. As an industry, this group was not particularly
active in prerevolutionary political activity. The chemical workers were
not even unionized across the industry; instead, there were unions of
chemical workers, rubber workers, and perfume workers. The chemical
workers' strongest month for resolutions was August; and their most frequent resolution, like that of thousands of other Moscow workers, concerned the protest of the counterrevolution. What stands out most about
chemical workers, however, is that they were the group most interested
in the war issue. In fact, 62 percent of all chemical workers voted for
antiwar resolutions, and another 75 percent voted for the various war-
aims resolutions, primarily for peace without conquest. No other industry
even approached this level of involvement on the war issue; metalists had

[38] On railway workers in the revolution, see Metel'kov; I. M. Pushkareva, *Zheleznodorozhniki Rossii v burzhuazno-demokraticheskikh revoliutsiiakh*; Pethybridge, chap. 1; William G. Rosenberg, "Workers' Control on the Railroads."

the next highest level of participation in antiwar resolutions, with 31 percent of that industry's work force voting. Chemical workers were also the leading proponents of the eight-hour workday, followed by machine workers. All three of these kinds of resolutions were most frequent in the first two months of the revolution, which fact indicates that the chemical workers were able to organize much faster after February than most other industries. A look at the rate of participation of industries in March and April confirms this (see Table 6-10): in each month, 75 percent of chemical workers passed resolutions. Over 100 percent of machinists participated in March, but this figure fell to 50 percent in April.

TABLE 6-10. *Selected Resolution Participation Rates for Industries, March-April 1917*
(IN PERCENTAGE OF THE INDUSTRIES' WORK FORCE)

Industry	March	April
Metal	25	67
Machine	114	49
Chemical	76	74
Food	6	17
Leather	7	40
Textile	22	19

NOTE: The percentages may exceed 100 because workers may have passed more than one resolution each month.

The September voting results suggested that chemical workers continued their high rate of participation throughout 1917. One explanation is the influence of the urbanized Baltic workers on their less active native comrades. Such advanced workers may have provided the same catalytic effect for others in the industry that machinists demonstrated for neighboring textile workers.

What about the three largest groups of workers—machinists, metalists, and textilists? The machine workers, as is clear from Table 6-10, quickly began to express their political demands and, indeed, were among the most active group of workers even before the February revolution; 63 percent of machine workers participated in at least one strike or walkout between January 1916 and February 28, 1917; metalists were far less active, with only 39 percent involved in these incidents.[39] A comparison of factories that participated in prerevolutionary incidents with those passing resolutions in 1917 shows a high number of plants that did both. In other words, plants that were politically mobilized before the revolution

[39] See Chapter Three.

were likely to have been active in resolutions after February.[40] Machine workers, who were highly skilled and predominantly literate, played a role disproportionate to their numbers throughout 1917. In their resolutions, they differed from most of the other industries in that the most popular issue for them was wage and price controls. In addition, they were the leaders (in terms of percentage of the work force participating) on the issue of Provisional-Government control of the economy and on free press and assembly. With strong opinions on both economic and complex political questions, the machine workers were able to provide leadership for all segments of the working class.

Metalworkers behaved very much like machine workers throughout 1917, but almost always to a lesser degree. Their most frequently passed resolutions were protests of the counterrevolution and demands for power to the soviets; on economic issues they were much less active than machine workers and on the war issue, much less involved than chemical workers.

Of the major industrial groups, textile workers show themselves among the less active in passing resolutions (see Table 6-1). There are many reasons for the political lethargy of this industry. It was an industry dominated by women, who tended to be politically inactive. It was an economically depressed industry: 38 percent of textile workers were employed in plants that stopped production at least temporarily in 1917, compared to the machine workers' 26 percent, 17 percent of metalists, and 0.3 percent of chemical workers.[41] Even so, 42 percent of textilists protested the Kornilov mutiny, and there was also significant support for resolutions on the food crisis and on fuel and supply issues (18 percent on food, 22 percent on fuel). By October, textile workers had become important partisans of the demand for soviet power.

The substantial participation of workers from different industries and with different interests contributed to the complex political situation in Moscow and helped to moderate the kind of extremism present in less diverse centers such as Petrograd. The countervailing political views of workers with such disparate backgrounds and experience as those in Moscow naturally encouraged compromise; the Moscow Soviet retained

[40] A contingency table looks like this (factories with no reported incidents or resolutions were assumed to have participated in none):

	Resolution	No Resolution
Pre-February incident	100	85
No Pre-February incident	308	2,066

Thus, of 185 factories that participated in political activity before February, 100 also passed resolutions. A Chi-Square test of this relationship ($X^2 = 310.806$) is significant.

[41] These figures are probably underestimated; a factory is counted as having stopped only if some notice of this appears in the sources. There were obviously many shutdowns never reported in the press or in subsequently published documents.

significant authority among the workers because it was able to serve as a mediator among these many groups. In areas dominated by one industry, such as Petrograd or the textile towns of the Central Industrial Region, there were no countervailing forces to neutralize one another, and political extremism was more likely to emerge.

Although some industries responded more to certain issues than others—such as the chemical workers on the war—all tended to support the most popular issues: the Kornilov protest, death-penalty opposition, opposition to the war. A notable exception was the printing industry, whose workers' social and economic backgrounds were very similar to those of machine-building workers. The printers' most popular resolution was a protest against the soviet seizure of power in October, an act either supported or ignored by most workers. The printers were the only industry to show more support for defensist resolutions than for antiwar positions, and by a factor of ten to one! In general, the political position of printers was very close to that of the ruling Provisional Government: 22 percent of printers passed resolutions in support of the government and none opposed it, although 28 percent of printers expressed support for the Soviet of Workers' Deputies. They favored economic measures at the capitalists' expense and the eight-hour workday, but they were, at the same time, one of the few industries to support overtime work until the war's end, further evidence of their defensist mood.

On almost all issues, in fact, Moscow printers followed positions adopted by the Menshevik party, but it was the printers' own revolutionary history and current situation that made Menshevism seem so attractive. The printers had been the first group to organize a trade union, which they had done even before 1905. In the 1905 revolution, they strongly supported the positions of the Marxist Social-Democratic party. But in 1905, much more than in 1917, the Russian working class must have seemed small and isolated compared to the vast peasantry outside the cities. As a group reaching political maturity at this time, the printers perhaps retained this sense of isolation, and thus for them a consistent position of unity was far more important than any given political question. Their support for the Provisional Government and for the war was based on this same sense of isolation and the necessity not to alienate other classes of society. In addition, the printers' position in contemporary society reinforced this sense of the priority of unity. Far more than any other industrial group, printers lived and worked amidst other social classes. The isolation of the working class, preached by the Menshevik leaders in the Moscow Soviet, was for printers a reality. The Mensheviks argued that the workers were too weak to run the country and that democracy was too newly rooted to be able to function without the bourgeoisie.[42]

---

[42] *Izv. MSRD*, 12 September 1917.

Printers had living proof of this weakness. It was noted in Chapter Five that districts in which printers lived showed significantly lower voter participation in municipal elections. If one assumes that the politically literate printers did vote, the apathy of their neighbors must surely have sown doubts about the Moscow citizenry's readiness for socialist self-rule. And because printers were isolated from the rest of the industrial work force, they perhaps could not appreciate the political development of workers who had not been active in the years of the underground revolutionary movement. From the printers' perspective, the Bolshevik gamble for power seemed an obvious case of demagogic adventurism; and as politically conscious workers, they ardently protested.

Soviet-Power Resolutions: A Case Study of the Revolutionary Process

The preceding discussion of political resolutions has focused in a general way on some of the characteristics of those workers who participated in the process. Because of the wide range of resolutions, it has been impossible to examine all the ramifications of this process. However, taking one particular resolution, the demand for soviet power, and tracing its history between March and October provide a useful counterweight to the more general discussion above. The evolution of workers' attitudes in favor of soviet power is of course of crucial importance in understanding the entire revolutionary process. Not until October did the resolution emerge as one of paramount concern for Moscow workers, and it emerged simultaneously with the emergence of the Bolshevik party as the leading working-class party. The evidence presented here will help to make this outcome a little more understandable.

The genesis of the idea of soviet power is a long story in the history of the Russian Revolution and will not be told here. Certain members of the Bolshevik party had supported an interim government of soviets from the outset of the February revolution, and the idea was also espoused by Lenin in his April Theses.[43] The general sense of the demand was to give power to the soviets or to other "people's" institutions, either permanently or as a temporary caretaker instead of the Kadet-party-dominated Provisional Government. From the very beginning of the 1917 revolution, the call for soviet power was a minority view, but it was made in Moscow by a very important minority, the highly politicized machine-building workers.

Resolutions calling for soviet power almost always appeared in tandem with some other issue; the lesson of the Miliukov note or of the economic

---

[43] Longley, "Divisions in the Bolshevik Party," pp. 61-76.

crisis was that only a government of soviets could properly direct the course of the revolution. Such resolutions rarely represented ultimatums, as can be seen in the earliest recorded soviet-power resolution in Moscow. On March 2, a general meeting of workers at the Triumf confections factory demanded the soviets assume power until the start of the Constituent Assembly, which would be selected on the basis of secret, universal, direct, and equal suffrage.[44] This was not a maximalist demand; soviet power was advocated only as a temporary measure. It is somewhat surprising that food workers, not ordinarily known either for Bolshevik sympathies or for political activism, passed the earliest of these resolutions, but the Triumf enterprise was a special case. It was owned by the Moscow Union of Consumer Societies, and many Social-Democratic intellectuals, Bolsheviks included, had found employment in its offices, which served also as the center of the cooperative movement.

In April, a significant number of calls for soviet power (see Table 6-11) appeared in connection with the crisis over the Miliukov note and the Provisional Government's foreign policy. In a sense, the entry of soviet

TABLE 6-11. *Soviet Power Resolutions*

Month	Number of Workers Voting	Number of Resolutions
March	130	1
April	4,660	7
May	2,660	6
June	2,440	2
July	5,740	22
August	12,220	8
September	12,620	10
October	51,560	34

representatives into the government in the aftermath of the crisis represented a concession to this demand for more power to democratic institutions. Most of the May and June calls for soviet power appeared together with resolutions on the economy. In early June, workers in factories and some local soviets disagreed with the Moscow Soviet's position on government control of the economy, calling for the transfer of all power to the soviets; but the small numbers passing such resolutions suggest that this disagreement was not widespread.

The salient characteristic of these scattered soviet-power resolutions before July was the nature of the workers who passed them. Of the ten thousand or so workers who passed soviet-power resolutions, half worked

[44] "Iz istorii rabochego dvizheniia v moskovskoi gubernii v 1917 g.," p. 82.

in the metal industry: 21 percent were metalists and 32 percent were machine-building workers. Leather workers and tram workers produced one resolution each, which accounted for much of the rest of the support for soviet power during this period.

The July days changed the tone of the soviet-power resolutions since the purpose of the Petrograd rising had been precisely to compel the Soviet there to take power. In Moscow, sixteen resolutions were passed by 4,300 workers in immediate response to the uprising; 63 percent of these were machine builders, 16 percent were metalists. Most of these workers were clustered in one city district, Butyrki, which was not one of the larger industrial districts. Significantly, the Butyrki district soviet was not among the three that passed soviet-power resolutions at this time, nor was the Bolshevik party particularly strongly entrenched here. So the strong outpouring of sentiment for soviet power from Butyrki machine builders represents real grass-roots support among a skilled segment of the working-class population for a change in the structure of power. This illustrates the slow but significant diffusion of the idea that became nearly universal by October.

One additional feature of the March-July soviet-power resolutions deserves mention. It is already clear that machine-building workers predominated in expressing this demand. In particular, one Zamoskvorech'e plant accounted for three of these resolutions, including one connected with the declaration of autonomy by the Kronstadt Soviet in the Gulf of Finland, an act ignored by the rest of Moscow's workers. This plant, the Moscow telephone works, was a new enterprise engaged in military production. Many of its workers, perhaps the plant itself, had been transferred from Petrograd. In fact, the Moscow telephone works acted like a little outpost of Petrograd's Vyborg district right on the banks of the Moscow river. Bolshevik influence was certainly strong here, but the telephone workers' radicalism must have owed much to the outlook they had developed among Petrograd's militant metal and machine-building cadres. This militancy was soon tempered by the telephone workers' contact with the realities of Moscow's political life. Workers here had clashed with the Moscow Soviet once during the April days; after raiding the local commissariat for arms, the factory's leaders promised not to disobey the Soviet again. This centrally located nucleus of politicized, militant machine workers became committed to revolutionary unity as well as to radical political views; and like advanced machine workers elsewhere in Moscow, they surely exerted a catalytic effect on less knowledgeable workers in the months to come.[45]

[45] The Moscow telephone works' pre-July soviet-power resolutions are reported in *Sots.-Dem.*, 16 May, 1 and 4 June 1917. On other aspects of this plant's activities, see *Russkie vedomosti*, 26 April 1917; *Trud*, 22 April 1917; and *Oktiabr' v Zamoskvorech'e*, p. 47.

The ideal of soviet power lost some popularity in the ensuing weeks as the Petrograd Soviet appeared to cave in to the Kadets in the Provisional Government and the Moscow Soviet disappointed its constituents with its refusal to endorse the Moscow Conference strike. This study has noted the rise of resolutions of no confidence in the Moscow Soviet at this time, but the lack of confidence was grounded in the Soviet's refusal to act decisively and to assume power. During this period, interest in working-class organizations generally declined, but no institution emerged to rival the great potential authority of the soviets; and when the Kornilov mutiny placed the revolution in jeopardy, workers returned to the Moscow Soviet as their natural leader.

Once again a new wave of resolutions demanding all power to the soviets appeared in the Moscow press. Between August 27 and September 6, 11,000 workers in nine resolutions linked their opposition to Kornilov with a demand that the soviets take power. This time, metalworkers accounted for 64 percent of the soviet-power resolutions, machine workers none. (Indeed, from this moment, the machine-building workers stopped demanding soviet power, for reasons which will be considered below.) These eleven thousand workers represented only 12 percent of all workers passing resolutions against the Kornilov rebellion; but again they represented the traditional opinion leaders, and their example was soon followed by a great number of other types of workers.

On September 5, the most important soviet-power resolution of all was passed, this one by the Moscow Soviet. And now that the Soviet itself had agreed to the idea, thousands of workers expressed their own support, in marked contrast to previous occasions when Soviet decisions received little additional local affirmation. By October 25, 54,000 workers in thirty-eight plants adopted resolutions calling for power to the soviets. (Post-October 25 resolutions were not included in this analysis since their purpose was different—to ratify a new situation rather than advocate its implementation.) This study has already shown that such resolutions were the most frequently passed in the month of October. But it is the context of these resolutions, their phrasing, that is particularly important here.

Many of these resolutions cited the economic situation as the reason for soviets to take power. This was a period of renewed assault on the standard of living—bread was short, strikes protracted. On October 1, textile workers in a Zamoskvorech'e factory resolved that under current political circumstances, wages could never keep up with inflation, and that the Zamoskvorech'e district soviet should convey to the Central Executive Committee in Petrograd their demand for a transfer of power to the soviets.[46] (The Moscow Soviet may have been bypassed since it

[46] *Sots.-Dem.*, 13 October 1917.

had already accepted the notion.) Workers at the Kuchkin metal plant expressed similar views; decisive economic measures could only be implemented by soviet power. However, they added that in the meantime, under bourgeois power, workers should continue to fight for higher wages.[47] Even in mid-October, the demand for soviet power was not an ultimatum but continued to be an expression of political preference.

Many other soviet-power resolutions spoke of such a change as an interim solution until the Constituent Assembly could decide the question of political authority. On October 19, for example, workers at the Zolotorozh tram park in the Rogozhskii district resolved that only soviet power could secure the convocation of the Constituent Assembly and carry out a policy to avoid economic chaos.[48] Such a resolution spoke to workers' current needs—surviving the next few weeks and saving the Constituent Assembly whose election was only weeks away. Their desire for soviet power did not yet necessarily reflect their views about the postassembly constitutional structure.

The October soviet-power resolutions represent, in this sense, a less radical political view than that represented by the same resolutions passed in the first half of 1917. Soviet power appealed to these workers not on the basis of principle but out of a sense of desperation—there was no other remaining alternative. The changed composition of supporters of these resolutions reflects this difference. In October, only 27 percent of the workers passing these resolutions were metalists, and only 1 percent were machine-building workers. On the other hand, 25 percent of them were textile workers, a group hitherto silent on soviet power and indeed on almost all political issues.

Textile workers' interest can be explained in part by the focus on economic necessity; these were the bread-and-butter issues to which politically inexperienced workers most readily responded. But the textilists' surprising participation can also be explained by the effect of interaction between workers from different industries. A vastly disproportionate number of textile workers passing soviet-power resolutions lived in Zamoskvorech'e district. This region, the biggest industrial district in Moscow, was home to many thousands of machine-building workers and metalworkers and accounted for a disproportionate share of soviet-power resolutions throughout 1917. Zamoskvorech'e precincts also accounted for much of the interaction effect between textilists and machine workers on the Bolshevik vote in June. This same effect in October provided such workers with the link between their sorely felt economic difficulties and

[47] Ibid.

[48] *Revoliutsionnoe dvizhenie v Rossii nakanune oktiabr'skogo vooruzhennogo vosstaniia*, pp. 314-315.

the need for political change, a link not so obvious to textilists in districts with fewer politically active workers. For example, factories in the large Blagusha-Lefortovo district, which employed nearly as many textilists as Zamoskvorech'e, passed few soviet-power resolutions, and none of these came from textile plants.

But can one speak of interaction when the machine-building workers were so strikingly inactive on this issue in October? No hard evidence of contact exists, but the fact of interaction seems hypothetically plausible. Such workers had already been converted to the idea of soviet power long before October; they had no need to hold meetings and pass resolutions in order to mobilize themselves on this issue. Therefore, they may have devoted their political energies, some of them as Bolshevik agitators, to other kinds of activities. One activity would have been to convert other workers to the idea of soviet power; if one could know for certain that machine workers spoke at the meetings that passed these resolutions, the argument would be proved. At the same time, it is known from workers' memoirs that some machine-building workers and metalworkers at least were actively preparing for an expected armed confrontation in support or defense of soviet power; at the Gustav List and Mikhel'son plants, workers used the plants' tools to manufacture grenades for the use of the newly formed Red Guards.[49] Such workers may have felt the time for resolutions was past.

The soviet-power resolutions reflect the broader process of mobilizing the Moscow working class. Different segments became active in different ways and at different rates. But by October, the political views of politically active metalists meshed with the economic views of active textilists in the form of the demand that all power go to the soviets. These two groups represented the two poles of the diverse working class, and their support for soviet power indicates the broad base of this attitude. Nowhere is the situation better illustrated than at the Danilovskaia manufacture, a large textile combine that had long been a Menshevik party stronghold. On the very eve of the October insurrection, workers here passed a Bolshevik resolution of support for soviet power which even the Mensheviks endorsed "to preserve the unity of the revolutionary front."[50]

This example raises the problem of the relationship between support for soviet power and Bolshevik party influence. Clearly the idea of all power to the soviets was a central tenet of the Bolshevik party position in 1917, and the Bolsheviks were the only party to advocate this policy. Was workers' support of soviet power an automatic indication of sympathy

[49] *Ot fevralia k oktiabriu (v Moskve)*, p. 192; *Oktiabr' v Zamoskvorech'e*, p. 325; *Velikaia oktiabr'skaia sotsialisticheskaia revoliutsiia (vospominaniia)*, p. 388.

[50] *Sots.-Dem.*, 27 October 1917.

for the Bolshevik party? Examining evidence collected on party affiliation of factories who passed such resolutions reveals an important aspect of the political process in 1917.

In March and April, in the factories with known party affiliation, 19 percent of the workers were Bolshevik-inclined, 27 percent favored Menshevism. Of the factories passing soviet-power resolutions in this period, 60 percent reported a Bolshevik mood, 31 percent a Menshevik mood. Clearly there was a close correspondence between support for the Bolshevik party and for the Bolshevik position on soviet power. Likewise in September and October when 68 percent of workers with known preferences were Bolsheviks and 16 percent were Mensheviks, 90 percent of workers passing the soviet-power resolution worked in factories with a known Bolshevik mood. Only 7 percent of the supporters of this resolution came from a Menshevik factory, in this case the Bogatyr rubber plant that remained solidly Menshevik well into the civil-war period.[51] Once again one can observe a close relationship between party and policy.

However, in the crucial June-August period, the picture changes. During this time, 80 percent of workers passing soviet-power resolutions worked in factories whose known party mood favored the Socialist Revolutionary or Menshevik parties. Such workers supported the Bolshevik party position on power while endorsing Mensheviks or SRs on other issues or electing delegates from these parties. Clearly the program of soviet power was not inextricably linked with the Bolshevik party. But as long as the Bolsheviks remained the only party to advocate this increasingly popular position, they were bound to gain support.

One final note confirms the complexity of the political process that coalesced around the soviet acquisition of power in late October. The printing industry, which had shared with machine builders the leadership of the pre-February revolutionary movement, produced only one resolution in favor of soviet power. But the rationale behind this resolution confirms the place of printers as highly politically sophisticated participants in the events of 1917. On October 19, cossacks had dispersed the Kaluga Soviet, and this action was interpreted as a direct assault by the Provisional Government on the idea of soviets altogether. Printers in one Moscow printshop responded by resolving that only soviet power could preserve the soviets as an institution at all.[52] Most printers still believed in coexistence with the bourgeoisie, but their class loyalties remained strong. This resolution indicated that, if forced to choose, even the printers would side with the soviets. They differed from most of the other workers in 1917 only in that they feared the outcome of a situation in

---

[51] *Izv. MSRD*, 22 October 1917; *Desiat' let*, p. 60.
[52] *Sots.-Dem.*, 25 October 1917.

which they would have to choose, and so they sought to support compromise and conciliation as long as possible.

For many different reasons, then, workers with different backgrounds, interests, and levels of political development supported the idea of soviet power by late October. Such support was not the same thing as advocating a seizure of power by violent means; resolutions throughout 1917 cannot be assumed to be anything more than expressions of attitude, not commitments to action. But the idea of soviet power seemed to solve many problems—the class struggle perceived most acutely by skilled metalists, the economic crisis felt even by textile workers, and the problem of constitutional legitimacy shared by a wide spectrum of the work force. And just as the Bolshevik party plus soviets offered a centralized institutional structure to replace other institutions that had lost their credibility, so the Bolsheviks' sole endorsement of soviet power provided another reason for workers to lend their support when the party claimed power in the name of those soviets.

These political resolutions, despite certain drawbacks, provide a wealth of information about the political attitudes of Moscow's workers at specific times between February and October. They show that the problems of political authority and economic control remained constant concerns, with only the specific recommendations changing to fit the evolving situation. But other issues—the war, fear of counterrevolution, and specific economic problems—also provoked great concern at different times.

These resolutions tell also about which workers were active in the political process and which workers shared different political attitudes. Machine-building workers were extremely active as they were in Petrograd in 1917 and before the revolution in Moscow. They exerted an important catalytic effect on workers with less well-developed political ideologies. But other kinds of workers as well were involved in the political resolution process, contributing to the diversity of political opinion and to the general moderation of political views so characteristic of Moscow in 1917.

Above all, these resolutions depict a certain revolutionary style in Moscow. In Petrograd, street demonstrations were a far more frequent occurrence than in Moscow, where for reasons discussed previously, workers' responses to political crises were muted and moderate. Moscow workers used resolutions rather than demonstrations to express their political views; and what resolutions lack in commitment to revolutionary action, they make up for in the detail of the attitudes they express.

In considering the detail of these attitudes, one is struck not by the blind revolutionary ardor or rabid maximalism that is often attributed to the "gray masses" who made the revolution, but the sensibility and rationality of the opinions expressed. The demand for soviet power, endorsed by over fifty thousand workers in October, is usually equated with the Bolshevization of the working class. But note how complex the reasons were for making this demand—soviet power was called for to deal with the economy or to expedite the Constituent Assembly, actions that the current government had been unable or unwilling to perform. Despite a strong underpinning of class consciousness, workers in their resolutions did not respond blindly to all revolutionary events in terms of this consciousness. For example, although the lesson of the July days was further to discredit the ruling classes in the eyes of the workers, the most common reaction was to protest the infringement of the free press, not to demand the abolition of the ruling classes. Workers' early attitudes toward the Provisional Government reflected the same sensibility. Their resolutions were perhaps suspicious of the Provisional Government, its war policies, and its commitment to revolution, but the workers still indicated a great degree of faith that their message would be heard and the government would respond. Only with the continued failure of the government and its economic policies, with the inability of the Petrograd Soviet to exert meaningful pressure, did workers begin to connect hostile economic actions with the politics of counterrevolution. This study of resolutions shows very clearly how gradually Moscow's politically articulate workers came to support the extreme measure of the transfer of power to the soviets.

This process was not accompanied by an acute sense of partisan conflict. If the soviet-power position was identical to that proposed by the Bolshevik party, one can be sure from these resolutions that workers did not necessarily equate soviet rule with Bolshevik party rule. Soviet power was simply but consciously perceived as the only way out of a rapidly deteriorating situation.

The resolutions—the variety of their subjects and supporters, the patterns they formed over time—thus indicate the true complexity of the revolutionary situation in Moscow. If the revolution by October had devolved to the choice of "kto kogo" or "who will defeat whom," the ultimate escalation of class enmity and social polarization in Moscow could trace its source to the whole gamut of political issues faced by workers during 1917. The same process of gradual and logical radicalization will be examined in the next chapter from a different perspective—that offered by workers' political contributions.

SEVEN. *Dimensions of Political Attitudes:*
WORKERS' CONTRIBUTIONS TO POLITICAL CAUSES

RESOLUTIONS passed in factories, however valuable as indicators of political attitudes, are less satisfactory in measuring the degree of political commitment. Not only did the resolutions examined in Chapter Six emanate from a bare majority of the factory population, but the resolutions themselves were essentially voted in a passive way; they indicated opinions that provide much insight into the political mood of the Moscow work force, but they did not require subsequent action or commitment on the part of workers who voted for them.

Workers' contributions to political causes, on the other hand, required greater sacrifice, greater commitment. In a time when the struggle to maintain living standards became increasingly more difficult, workers reached into their pockets and voluntarily donated portions of their wages to a number of political causes. Surely such donations came far less automatically than votes for resolutions. Consequently, the nature of political contributions provides a different, in many ways deeper, insight into the political attitudes of Moscow's workers in 1917.

What they add in degree of commitment, however, political contributions lack in precision of purpose, as will become apparent. One can assume that the purchase of a Liberty Bond signified a more serious commitment than a factory's vote for a pro-Liberty Loan resolution, but the purposes of most donations were never so specific as the demands expressed in resolutions (or as those made by strikers, as shall be seen). Particularly vexing, for example, is the meaning of the "Red Gift" to soldiers, collected largely from the earnings of workers on the Sunday preceding International Workers' Day. Was this evidence of prowar sentiment, or at least progovernment sentiment, or perhaps only an expression of solidarity with the oppressed foot soldiers? Even contributions to political parties leave room for doubt. Much of the Bolsheviks' fund consisted of contributions for the purchase of a printing press for *Sotsial-Demokrat*. Did this represent partisan support for the Bolshevik party, or was it another example of workers' support for freedom of the press, for all parties to be heard?

Clearly there is a problem of interpreting the significance of the purposes of the contributions. But there can be no question that, as with the resolutions, the making of a political contribution was a significant political act. By donating money to whatever cause, workers were participating in the political life of the revolution, helping to finance institutions that carried out important political functions, sacrificing their own earnings for nonimmediate goals that they considered to be important.

Moreover, in terms of sheer participation, according to available sources, the political donation was one of the single most widespread political activities of Moscow workers. Two-thirds of all workers in almost one-half of all plants donated money to a political cause. Thus workers' political donations provide students of the revolution with unique insight into the political mood of a great many workers whose voices were not heard through any other medium. It may be recalled that only 57 percent of workers in 11 percent of the factories passed resolutions. (Voting in city elections may have involved more workers, but the nature of electoral returns precludes more exact comparison.) With these donations, historians have a sort of political statement from 239,000 workers who contributed in about four thousand separate donations a total of 1.8 million rubles. These donations constitute the basis of the discussion to follow.

THE SCOPE OF WORKERS' POLITICAL CONTRIBUTIONS

Information about contributions comes exclusively from the published newspapers and journals of 1917, primarily from the Moscow Soviet's *Izvestiia*. Beginning on March 15, *Izvestiia* printed accounts of contributions received from factories, trade unions, and individuals, for a variety of causes; most significant over the course of the year were contributions for the upkeep of the Soviet, for gifts to soldiers, and for the families of political prisoners, the victims of the revolutionary movement, and those killed at the start of the revolution in February.

Other organs were involved in this public disclosure of political contributions, although not to the same extent as *Izvestiia*. Socialist party newspapers published lists of contributors, and as with resolutions, the Bolsheviks seemed most active in publishing their sources of support. Trade union journals, which began to publish in July and later, also printed lists of their contributors, primarily for strike funds.[1]

[1] Reports of political contributions were gathered from the following newspapers—*Izv. MSRD, Sots.-Dem., Vpered, Trud, Proletarii, Zemlia i volia, Utro Rossii, Vechernii kur'er, Volia i dumy zheleznodorozhnika, Vremia, Soldat-Grazhdanin*—and from the following trade union periodicals—*Pechatnik* and *Moskovskii metallist*. The lists in *Izv. MSRD* appear to be as complete as was possible at the time, although the obvious proofreading lapses in the lists provide room for error. It is not clear that the socialist newspapers published all their contributors' names. N. I. Vostrikov, p. 134, cites Menshevik party financial records located in the Communist party archive (Tsentral'nyi partiinyi arkhiv instituta Marksa-Lenina, fond 275, opis' 1, ed. khr. 32), but whether the party archives contain records of financial contributions not reported in the newspapers is impossible to tell. Trade union

In all these publications, the typical entry listed the name of the factory, group, or individual making the donation, and the amount given, down to the last kopeck. To simplify calculations, these extra kopecks were ignored, and the ruble amount was recorded, along with the date, source, and the purpose of the donation. These were then matched with the data collected for each factory so that for almost all the contributions, there is corresponding information on the groups of workers who made them. Rarely did the donation report list the number of workers participating, so it has been assumed, as with the resolutions, that all workers in a factory participated in the contribution.

Political contributions, no less than resolutions, were solicited rather than offered spontaneously by whichever group involved. Beginning in late March, *Izvestiia* published on its front page a daily notice—"Call for Contributions"—which explained that money was needed for funding new revolutionary institutions and to help past sufferers of the revolutionary movement. Later this notice was revised to ask for aid specifically for the Soviet, and workers were urged to give a regular portion of their wages to the Soviet. In such cases, workers did not have to reach into their pockets to help out the Soviet; the factory committees saw that the proper percentage was deducted from the workers' pay. This method was used also for many other contributions—for gifts to soldiers, for trade union dues, and for strike funds. At the Volk harness factory, 1 percent was deducted as monthly dues, with half of this going to the factory library, one-fourth to the factory committee, and one-sixteenth each to the Moscow Soviet, the local soviet, *Sotsial-Demokrat* and *Soldat-Grazhdanin*.[2] Even political parties could arrange to be funded in this way; a Bolshevik recalled how the SRs in his factory first passed a resolution at a general meeting endorsing the idea of a contribution to the party and then arranged with the factory management for the amount to be deducted from workers' wages.[3]

The effect of this kind of arrangement was to give an institutional bias to the political donations of workers. It was far easier for the Moscow Soviet to collect its monthly 1 percent of wages than for an ad hoc group that might oppose certain policies of the Soviet to raise funds in this way. Consequently, the direction of the contributions tells somewhat more about the workers' mood toward institutions than toward political issues.

---

contribution records are much less complete: unions without their own organs did not report contributions (with the exception of the tea packers), and the missing issues of at least one trade union journal, *Pechatnik*, are known to have carried lists of contributors. Other trade union journals that may have contained donation records, but which could not be located during my stay in the Soviet Union, were the tailors' *Zhizn' portnykh i portnikh* and the textilists' *Tekstil'nyi rabochii*.

[2] *Sots.-Dem.*, 20 April 1917.   [3] Tumanov, p. 105.

But in the building of the revolution, the institutions created by the workers and their representatives had to play the central role, and support or lack of it for institutions was a clear measure of their legitimacy in workers' eyes. Therefore, even within the institutional framework of workers' political donations, it is possible to discern changes in support for institutions representing various aspects of the revolutionary experience. Workers' loss of faith in the military policy of the government, their strong support for the soviet as an institution, their identification of the economic crisis with class antagonisms, all these features of the revolution are reiterated through these political contributions.

As with resolutions, the nature of the participants constitutes a major feature of these donations. The 4,006 individual contributions for which data are available were made by 762 separate factories, representing 239,600 workers. This is a much higher rate of participation than for resolutions. Especially striking is the rate of participation of smaller factories: 401 out of 1,141 factories with fewer than one hundred workers made political contributions, compared to only 59 factories of this size which published resolutions. If there had been any systematic bias in reporting contributions, it would have weighed against these small factories (small sums are more easily lost; obscure factory names are more likely to be garbled and their donations misattributed), a fact that makes the strong showing of small enterprises even more impressive. Political donations thus brought out the most widespread revolutionary support among workers. This fact is of major importance in evaluating the attitudes represented by these donations.

Which industries were most involved in this kind of political support? The list of participants reads almost exactly like that for resolutions, except on a larger scale (see Table 7-1): all of the tram workers and 99 percent of power and water workers gave some money to at least one cause, followed by chemical workers, leather workers, and then metalists and machinists. Woodworkers, animal-byproducts workers, rare metalists, and paper workers were relatively less involved in contributions. In addition to participation, there were also differences in the degree of support from various industries. The average size of a total contribution per worker varied from fifty-six kopecks from railway workers to five rubles, sixty-five kopecks from printers. More important, different causes were relatively more important for different workers, an observation that will be discussed below.

THE DYNAMICS OF CONTRIBUTIONS

The direction and timing of workers' political donations were affected, as with resolutions, by the political climate, but also, because of the insti-

TABLE 7-1. *Worker Participation in Contributions by Industry*

Industry	Number of Workers Involved in Contributions	Number of Workers in Industry	Percent of Contributors
Tram	10,950	10,950	100.0
Power and water	1,075	1,085	99.1
Chemical	24,116	25,822	93.4
Leather	28,000	30,513	91.8
Machine	25,779	31,755	81.2
Metal	45,838	56,516	81.1
Textile	53,067	66,871	79.4
Food	20,987	26,890	78.0
Printing	10,496	13,498	77.8
Clothing	9,905	13,235	74.8
Mineral	2,087	3,240	64.4
Rare metals	889	1,601	55.5
Wood	3,177	6,261	50.7
Cinema	76	156	48.7
Animal byproducts	504	1,319	38.2
Paper	1,061	2,992	35.5
Railway	1,500	42,503	3.5

tutional bias of this form of political support, by factors stemming from organizational problems and characteristics. These factors will be discussed below, but first one should consider political donations as a type of political support. One obvious difference between resolutions and contributions is the relatively small number of causes toward which workers directed their monetary support.

Table 7-2 shows the purposes of contributions, total amount given, and the number of individual contributions. Four causes stand out as receiving far greater support than the rest: the Red Gift for soldiers, strike funds, the municipal election fund, and the Soviet of Workers' Deputies' fund. These four received 85 percent of all the money contributed by Moscow's factory workers.

Three of these beneficiaries clearly represented working-class interests; the strike fund, of course, was used to finance strikes against employers and was a traditional manifestation of working-class solidarity. (The distinction here between "own strike fund"—funds contributed to workers' own factory or trade union treasuries—and "others' strike fund" is that ones' own strike fund was financed presumably out of economic self-interest, while contributions to others' strike funds—almost all of them to leather workers—represented a more abstract sense of class solidarity.) The municipal election fund was solicited by the Moscow Soviet explicitly to aid in the electoral campaign for the three socialist parties endorsed by the Soviet—Socialist Revolutionary, Menshevik, and Bolshevik. The

TABLE 7-2. *Political Contributions of Moscow Workers*

Purpose	Total Rubles	Number of Contributions	Peak Month
Red Gift to soldiers	700,325	984	May
Own strike fund	400,515	740	September
Municipal election fund	234,844	343	July
Soviet of Workers' Deputies	210,093	825	June
Others' strike fund	65,723	82	September
Bolshevik party	65,138	465	August
Political victims	64,296	253	March
Social-democrats (unspecified)	18,115	80	May
Literature for soldiers	12,065	43	April
Prisoners of war, orphans	7,104	23	July
Socialist Revolutionary party	5,107	46	August
Mensheviks and United Social-Democrats	4,102	53	June
Red Guard	3,476	8	October
Education/propaganda	2,802	17	May
Workers' revolution	2,162	23	April
Constituent Assembly	1,817	5	October
Provisional Government	1,333	6	May
Socialists (unspecified)	1,096	3	May
Education/not propaganda	550	2	May
Nationalist parties	249	4	September
Unemployed workers	103	1	May
Total	1,801,015	4,006	May

goal was to return a city duma with a working-class majority, and workers were exhorted to donate half a day's pay to the fund.[4] Finally, the Soviet itself solicited funds for its ongoing operations:

> The revolutionary proletariat ought as far as possible to support, not only morally but materially, the Soviet of Workers' Deputies which stands guard over its interests. The Executive Committee of the Soviet therefore asks you, comrade workers, periodically to assign deductions from your wages for the needs of the Soviet of Workers' Deputies.[5]

The single largest recipient of contributions, the Red Gift, is not so easy to classify as the three class-oriented funds. It is certainly an important indicator of working-class attitudes about the war, an issue of crucial importance to Russian workers. It also indicates how workers tried

[4] *Izv. MSRD*, 4 June 1917, contains the first front-page announcement to this effect. A joint workers' and soldiers' soviet plenum approved the plan to collect a fund of two hundred thousand rubles on May 30 (ibid., 31 May 1917).

[5] Ibid., 14 May 1917, is the first issue in which this appeal appeared; it was published daily for much of the rest of the year.

to reach across class lines to join forces with nonproletarian elements in society. The gift itself was financed by deductions of one day's pay from the wages of cooperating workers, primarily by earnings from April 16, a Sunday. In order to celebrate International Workers' Day on April 18 (May 1 in the West) with the rest of the world proletariat and yet not deprive Russian soldiers of needed war supplies, Moscow's workers voted to work the Sunday preceding May 1 and additionally to donate all their earnings for that day for the purchase of gifts to soldiers: cigarettes, candy, shaving equipment, and reading materials. Such an act at once symbolized several political attitudes; one was support of the war, either "to the victorious conclusion" or to defend the gains of the revolution from German militarism. It also signified solidarity with brother soldiers. Workers in Moscow knew that the support of the Petrograd garrison had been essential in carrying out the February revolution.

The nature of workers' resolutions on the war helps to clarify the sentiment behind the Red Gift. Outright prowar sentiment, as already seen, was virtually absent from workers' resolutions, and it is unlikely that the Red Gift for soldiers was made out of a desire to fight the war until its triumphant conclusion. Even revolutionary defensism—fighting the war to defend the revolution from reactionary Germany—was an attitude infrequently expressed in resolutions. Far more common were resolutions of solidarity with soldiers. Working-class demands for an eight-hour workday were criticized in the bourgeois press for being harmful to the war effort, for leaving soldiers without arms. To counter this impression, workers passed resolutions or wrote letters claiming that productivity improved with the shorter day and promising not to abandon their comrades in the trenches. Early in April, a municipally owned metal-processing plant was visited by a delegation from the front concerned about defending the revolution against the kaiser; the workers assured the soldiers that the eight-hour workday would not harm production. Two days later, a general meeting of the plant voted to work April 16 and to give their earnings to the Red Gift fund.[6] War workers at the Olovianishnikov gas-mask plant, who had recalled their Soviet deputy for voting for the Liberty Loan, later ended a strike in order not to harm military production.[7] Such behavior indicates that workers' support for the war was largely support for the poor soldiers who had to fight it. But the outpouring of money for soldiers indicated also a certain ambivalence about how best to oppose the war; by sending support to the soldiers in the trenches, workers seemed to suggest that higher authority, not the rank and file, should take the steps necessary to end the fighting.

[6] *Trud*, 12 April 1917; *Izv. MSRD*, 12 April 1917; *Sots.-Dem.*, 13 April 1917; *Trud*, 14 April 1917.

[7] *Sots.-Dem.*, 2 May 1917; *Izv. MSRD*, 13 May 1917.

Workers' tacit acceptance of the war, despite the importance of solidarity with the soldiers, did not last. The prevailing attitude symbolized by the Red Gift changed because (in no small part) of the so-called Kerensky offensive of June, which ended the Russian army's holding action against Germany. Now Olovianishnikov's workers joined a citywide strike of gas-mask workers and explained their actions this way to an infantry regiment that had written to request newspapers:

> We workers, in common with all of labor, know the 300 years of oppression which has destroyed our strength, will, and being. The bourgeoisie hastens to overcome our revolutionary unity, to establish every possible obstacle to infringe upon our rights and our freedom. But raw labor and open struggle will not give the bourgeoisie a way.
> . . . Our struggle is a pledge to future generations, we ought to stand up for whatever decisive measures are demanded, and your [soldiers'] duty is to support us.[8]

The tables had turned; soldiers were called upon to support the more urgent class war instead of receiving workers' aid to wage their revolutionary war.

Furthermore, contributions to the Red Gift slowed markedly after the June offensive (look at Table 7-3). Naturally, the May Day gift meant

TABLE 7-3. *Monthly Contributions to Red Gift*

Month	Sum Donated
March	21,397
April	253,043
May	345,947
June	71,059
July	5,976
August	1,905
September	0
October	1,028

that most of the contributions would have been made around April 18, but even so, gifts to soldiers dropped very sharply. March contributions were not made in response to a special appeal, yet they totaled over 21,000 rubles. After June, workers gave very little to the army even though their brothers were still in the trenches. This would imply that the Red Gift had indeed represented a posture of defensism among workers; as the war to defend the revolution became less credible, support, even for the blameless soldiers at the front, declined.

Further complicating this assessment of the meaning of the Red Gift,

[8] *Soldat-Grazhdanin*, 23 June 1917.

however, the pattern of contributions to soldiers by industry indicates that attitudes about the war, pro or con, may not have strongly influenced support for the gift. Some of the most vocally antiwar industries (according to their resolutions) were also the largest contributors to the Red Gift: these were the metalists, machine builders, and chemical workers. In order to compare industry contributions, an average contribution has been computed for each worker in an industry.[9] Using these averages, presented in Table 7-4, power and water workers, machinists, rare metalists, and chemical workers emerge as the strongest supporters of the Red Gift. Paper, animal-byproducts, textile, and clothing workers were the least generous. But there is a problem in using these figures for comparison—the Red Gift came from one day's wage of participating workers, and machinists earned more in a day than did textile workers. Indeed, there is a strong correlation between the per-worker amount contributed from each industry and the average wage for that industry.[10] Therefore, before it is possible to examine the differences among industry contributions to the Red Gift, it is necessary to allow for the disparity in wages. In order to do this, the rubles-per-worker figure for each industry was divided by the industry's average wage. These results are presented in the last column of Table 7-4. Thus the leather workers' apparently large Red Gift contribution is more than offset by that industry's high wage,

TABLE 7-4. *Political Contributions to Red Gift by Industry*
(UNWEIGHTED AND WEIGHTED BY WAGES)

Industry	Average Contribution Per Worker	Average Contribution, Weighted by Wage
Mineral	2.10	1.43
Rare metals	3.18	1.33
Metal	2.64	1.57
Machine	4.16	1.75
Wood	1.52	1.09
Chemical	3.14	1.85
Food	1.49	.82
Animal byproducts	.94	.56
Leather	2.86	.81
Textile	1.31	.76
Clothing	1.37	.61
Paper	.60	.42
Printing	2.49	1.26
Power and water	7.20	3.71
Tram	1.34	1.40

[9] The industry totals are based on information in the master data-set on factories. Some contributions are recorded from factories whose size is unknown, but the assumption is that this effect is randomly distributed across industries and across contribution purposes.

[10] Tables showing the average wage are presented in Appendix J.

while the chemical workers' contribution becomes even more significant when this industry's relatively low wage is taken into account.

After the effects of wages are considered, the highest per-worker contribution to the Red Gift came from power workers, chemical workers, machine workers, and metalworkers. And yet, the last three industries were also among the most vociferous supporters of antiwar resolutions. Why would they be so supportive of this apparently defensist gift for soldiers? The answer lies in who within the industries contributed money. It may be recalled that only a small fraction of factories voted resolutions at all; and if the contributions of these plants are calculated separately, it appears that workers in these plants contributed less, on the average, to the Red Gift than did workers who did not pass antiwar resolutions. The average (unweighted) contributions for factories passing antiwar resolutions and those passing none are shown in Table 7-5. The machine

TABLE 7-5. *Contributions to Red Gift by Type of War Resolutions*

Industry	Average Contribution from Antiwar Plants	Average Contribution from Others
Chemical	3.07 rubles	3.17 rubles
Metal	2.40	2.74
Machine	5.50	3.61

industry does not conform to the pattern. The same plant workers who voted for antiwar resolutions were also extraordinarily responsive to the Red Gift appeal. The magnitude of this industry's contribution was really due to the workers of just three plants—Bromlei, Dinamo, and the War Industry plant—who together averaged 7.41 rubles per worker to the Red Gift. Even closer examination of the resolutions of these three plants does not adequately explain their support of the Red Gift; although in the cases of Dinamo and the War Industry plant, their antiwar resolutions came early in March, possibly before most workers became aware of the complexity of the war issue. (The War Industry plant's antiwar resolution was published together with a declaration of "insofar as" support for the Provisional Government.) It is of course possible that the resolutions may have been passed by a small majority at the general meeting. Unfortunately, any resolution could probably be discounted for some reason or other, but the fact remains that these plants were both vocally opposed to the war and yet supportive of the Red Gift sponsored by the Soviet.

Once again, this seeming contradiction indicates the complexity of the war issue. In principle, the machine-building workers opposed the war, but they were also shrewd enough to realize the importance for the revolution of close ties between the workers and the soldiers. Nonetheless, in most industries there was a clear division between factories supporting the Red Gift and those passing antiwar resolutions. This pattern is further confirmed by its reverse in the case of the printing industry, which had been the most strongly defensist in its resolutions. Printshops that passed prowar or defensist resolutions gave an average of 3.04 rubles to the Red Gift; the rest averaged only 2.33 rubles per worker.

Even more striking is the difference in contributions between small and large factories in each industry. It has already been shown that resolutions, whether for or against the war, were made by the largest plants. But it was the workers in the smaller plants, who rarely passed resolutions either way, who contributed most heavily to the Red Gift. Chemical workers in plants smaller than a hundred workers averaged 8.76 rubles per worker to the Red Gift; those in plants employing over five hundred gave only 3.43 per worker. For metal plants the ratio was 6.56 to 3.61; in machine-building plants it was 8.24 to 6.09. This pattern holds true for all Moscow workers, as Table 7-6 shows.[11] Factories with fewer than

TABLE 7-6. *Contributions to Red Gift by Factory Size*

Size of Factory	Average Rubles Per Worker
Under 100	5.52
101-300	3.60
301-500	4.26
501-1,000	2.73
Over 1,000	3.05

one hundred workers were significantly more generous toward the Red Gift than larger factories. There are several reasons for this generosity. Smaller factories were less frequently visited by outside organizers who led antiwar agitation, and they would be more likely to go along with whatever was decided by their representative body, the Moscow Soviet. This latent support for the war policy of the Soviet did not appear in resolutions because workers in small plants were rarely approached to express an opinion. There is also the influence of small-group cohesion: peer-group pressure might influence workers in a small factory to contribute, whereas in a large plant, workers hostile to the idea of the Red Gift could more easily escape such pressure to conform.[12] Finally, small

[11] Using analysis of variance, a statistical procedure that tests to see that the variation between classes is greater than the variation within each class (i.e., that the 5.52 average for the smallest class does not represent one factory with a 1,457-ruble-per-worker donation and 245 with none) yields an F-ratio (with 4 and 515 degrees of freedom) of 4.271, which is significant at the .01 level of confidence. That is, these means are not derived from wildly fluctuating figures.

[12] Olson, *Logic of Collective Action*, presents a very persuasive argument for the greater cohesion of smaller groups.

shops probably had closer relations with their employers, who may have
added company funds to the Red Gift contributions of workers, swelling
the per-worker average.[13] In addition, workers in these shops with close
employer-employee relations were probably more likely to support other
cross-class causes. They did not experience the same isolation as workers
in large industrial enterprises and were more amenable to support views
shared by nonproletarian elements of society.

Other than the Red Gift for the army, however, Moscow workers did
not strongly support causes that bridged the diverse elements of Russian
society. The Provisional Government accepted donations to such causes
as "the Provisional Committee of the Duma" and prisoners of war, but
no Moscow factories appeared in the Provisional Government *Vestnik*'s
list of contributors. In the main, workers sacrificed their earnings to causes
closer to their own interests. The only governing institution to receive
strong support was the workers' own, the Soviet.

Early in its history, the Moscow Soviet had rejected the possibility of
petitioning the government for subsidies for its operations, which included
staff salaries, publications, cultural work, and the miscellaneous expenses
associated with running a large institution.[14] In doing so, the Moscow
Soviet placed its financial well-being squarely in the hands of its constituents, and therefore workers' donations to the Soviet can measure how
they related to their most central revolutionary and class institution.

The city soviet did not enjoy the unstinting confidence of Moscow's
factory workers, as the resolutions have indicated. Especially after the
failure of the Soviet to endorse the Moscow Conference protest strike,
workers' resolutions showed strong disapproval and demanded new Soviet
elections in all factories. Nonetheless, workers returned to support the
Soviet after the Kornilov mutiny; there continued to be strong support
for the soviet as an institution, and this is confirmed by the nature of
political donations both to the Soviet itself and to its electoral campaign
fund, or Municipal Fund.

To these funds combined, Moscow workers donated over 445,000 rubles
(still nowhere near the amount given for the Red Gift). The Municipal
Fund received almost all of its contributions in July (money which must
have been at least pledged prior to the June 25 elections) and a small
amount in October, probably collected for the September local duma

[13] Some contributions were recorded as "from the workers and owners" of such-and-such
plant, but there was no way to determine the workers' share. About 5 percent of all
contributions were made by workers together with other groups—mainly white-collar workers, but also management; 11 percent of all Red Gift contributions were made jointly. The
Red Gift therefore had more nonworker support than other causes, but the answer to
whether the Red Gift in the smallest factories had more nonworker support has not been
determined.

[14] See Chapter Three.

elections. Soviet contributions were received evenly throughout the year, with a single exception, as Table 7-7 indicates. In September, contributions sharply declined. Since it is clear from the timing of the Municipal Fund contributions that there was as much as a one-month lag between the time a contribution was offered at the local level and the time it was recorded in the press, it may be assumed that the low September level represents contributions made in August.[15]

TABLE 7-7. *Monthly Contributions to the Soviet of Workers'
Deputies*

Month	Amount of Rubles	Number of Factories
March	11,436	49
April	16,410	69
May	25,549	156
June	49,650	191
July	31,193	117
August	35,800	114
September	6,657	26
October	33,698	103

In August, of course, the popularity of the Soviet fell dramatically as a result of the Moscow Conference strike. Resolutions, the strike itself, and the drop shown here in workers' donations all show how strongly Moscow's workers felt about this issue. When the Soviet in September began to take a more active role as an opponent of the looming counterrevolution, support in resolutions increased, and the flow of cash donations returned to its previous level.[16] It would be of great interest to know if financial support for district soviets increased at this time since these institutions had correctly expressed their workers' attitudes toward the Moscow Conference strike in August. Unfortunately, the institutional bias of the donations as a political measure prevents an answer—the working-class press did not report on donations to these local institutions.

Support for the Soviet seemed to be highest in the June-reported contributions, that is, those probably made in May. And indeed, the

[15] The newspaper lists of contributions usually reported money received during a two- or four-week interval. In these cases, the last date of the period was used to date the donation. If no dates were given, the date of the newspaper report was used; but in both cases, it can be seen how the dating of the contribution would lag considerably behind the time it presumably was made.

[16] *Izv. MSRD* stopped printing lists of donations after October 24, so there is no published evidence of the pattern of donations in the last month before the soviet assumption of power, donations that otherwise might have been reported in November.

notice in *Izvestiia* specifically soliciting contributions for the Soviet first appeared on May 14. The increase in support might also be interpreted as a sign of approval for the Petrograd Soviet's involvement in the coalition government as well as for its new initiatives in dealing with the economy. Workers seemed, both in May and in September, to respond to forceful leadership. On the other hand, the June peak may reflect most of all the overall economic situation; after that month, workers simply had less cash to spare as the cost of necessities soared and the future seemed increasingly uncertain.

The 825 contributions to the Moscow Soviet came from 298 individual plants. Beginning in July, the Soviet contributions became regularized, with workers in each factory contributing some percentage of their wages each month. Again controlling for wage differences, the power, chemical, and mineral workers appear to be the most generous supporters of the Soviet. The least supportive once again were animal-byproducts, wood, and paper workers. In terms of size, it was again the smallest plants whose workers gave most generously: one-third of all plants contributing to the Soviet employed fewer than one hundred workers, and their average contribution (2.82 rubles per worker) was almost twice as high as that of any other size group. Since it is less likely that management, which may have contributed to the Red Gift, would contribute to the workers' institution, this large figure must represent the greater unanimity of workers in small plants. Workers in the largest plants, those employing over a thousand, gave the least to the Soviet—just about one ruble per worker, on the average.[17]

The participation of workers in small factories once again illustrates the revolutionary involvement of workers who were not heard from in the more issue-oriented form of resolutions. These workers supported the Soviet as their representative body and accepted its political decisions with little public question.

Somewhat fewer factories (247) contributed to the Soviet's municipal election fund than to the Soviet's operations fund, but a larger sum was given (see Table 7-2). For this fund, workers were explicitly asked to contribute one-half day's pay for the purpose of electing worker representatives to the city duma, and the average contribution per worker was eleven kopecks. In contrast to the Soviet, the Municipal Fund was supported for a specific purpose—for workers to gain a political advantage over their class opponents, the industrial bourgeoisie represented by the Kadet party. The June election was very important for Moscow workers because the city duma was expected to make a number of decisions

[17] These means tested by analysis of variance yield $F_{(4, 295)} = 3.607$, and are significant at .01 level of confidence.

affecting workers' welfare—on food supply, housing, and essential services. In addition, the city was a major employer. Many factories had been taken over by the municipal government during the course of the war, and some of the most articulate working-class groups, like the tram and power workers, were municipal employees.

The June elections were an important test of political strength for the socialist parties, as was discussed in detail in Chapter Five, but no party received anywhere near the financial support that the Municipal Fund, representing all working-class parties, was given by Moscow workers. It is the nonpartisan aspect of the fund that is most significant here.[18] Workers could have chosen to donate money to specific parties, as indeed some did. But instead most chose to support this all-socialist fund, allowing the parties to share equally in their donations. This widespread support for the nonpartisan Municipal Fund paralleled the support for nonpartisanship reflected in many resolutions passed around this time in 1917 and once again underscores the tremendous appeal of revolutionary and working-class unity.

The leading contributors to the Municipal Fund in terms of weighted rubles per worker were metal, machine, and tram workers.[19] The strong support from metalists and machinists found a corollary in their "fair play" attitude in resolutions calling for freedoms of press and assembly; such experienced workers were especially conscious of the importance of showing solidarity in this test of relative strengths of competing elements in society. Tram workers, of course, were city employees; they led the strike movement among municipal workers later in the year. Negotiations leading to this strike had already begun in June, so these workers were certainly aware of the advantages of negotiating with a working-class government. (In fact, although the Soviet-endorsed Socialist Revolutionary party won the duma majority, this did not ultimately solve the conflict with city workers, who were on the verge of a general strike throughout October.)

Pecuniary self-interest clearly played a part in the Municipal Fund campaign. In general, municipally owned factories tended to support the Municipal Fund more than others; the ten municipally owned enterprises who gave to the fund composed 3 percent of the plants contributing to the Municipal Fund, but their total ruble contribution accounted for 8.7 percent of the Municipal Fund's total. Or, to look at this relationship another way: 20 percent of all municipally owned plants gave something to the Municipal Fund, and only 14 percent of all Moscow plants con-

---

[18] Actual allocations were to be made to individual parties by representatives of all parties (*Sots.-Dem.*, 20 June 1917).

[19] Appendix H gives the weighted contributions for each cause from each industry.

tributed.[20] Like contributors to the other funds discussed, Municipal Fund contributors also gave more per worker in the smallest factories: 3.85 rubles per worker in plants with under one hundred workers and 1.60 rubles per worker in plants larger than one thousand workers.

A second major working-class institution, after the soviets, was the trade union. The unions themselves were financed by membership dues, but records of these are not generally available. Support for strike funds is thus as close as one can come to determining support for the trade unions. In any case, there were large differences among industries in support given for strike funds, and the contributors to them tended to belong to the best-organized industries. Printers, metalists and machinists (who contributed to the metal union's fund), and food workers all averaged over a ruble per worker to their strike funds; almost all the other industries contributed fewer than twenty-five kopecks for each worker. Unlike the other funds, there were no significant differences among strike-fund contributors from different-sized factories, so it would appear that factory size made no difference in strike-fund support.[21]

What does appear to make a difference is the level of organization of the various industries. The printers, for example, had been unionized since before 1905 and were experienced in union affairs; and this experience must surely have taught the value of a strong strike fund. Even though not all printers' strike-fund donations have been recorded (some of them were reported in now-missing issues of their journal, *Pechatnik*), printers still had the highest average strike-fund contribution—3.81 rubles per worker.

Second in strike-fund support were the metalists and machine builders, averaging 2.63 and 3.41 rubles respectively. As with the printers, it was the strength of the union organization that was probably responsible for such high participation. The union had staged a successful one-day strike for higher wages in July, but the tariff agreed upon was to expire on October 1. In preparation for the renegotiation of the contract, the metalist union began to solicit one day's pay for a strike fund;[22] and by the end of October, the union reported it had received 279,024 rubles.[23]

[20] The usual measure involving rubles per worker is not feasible since too little is known about the size of municipal plants. Such enterprises were not included in factory lists, and sizes that are known have been taken from such sources as resolution reports that give the number of workers participating. Size is known for two-thirds of all the factories in Moscow but for only one-third of these municipally owned enterprises.

[21] Analysis of variance gives $F\ (4,\ 288) = 1.34$, which is not significant.

[22] *Moskovskii metallist*, no. 1, 12-25 August 1917, p. 5. The first mention of the strike fund was at a delegates' meeting July 16 (*Izv. MSRD*, 19 July 1917), but a report the following day, also in *Izv. MSRD*, 20 July 1917, says this meeting did not occur because of the lack of a quorum.

[23] Records of metalist contributions from factories give a total of 257,320 rubles.

The size of the food industry's strike-fund contribution is surprising, for the industry as a whole was not well organized. In fact, workers in this industry were grouped in five separate unions in 1917: the largest was the confectioners' union, but there were also unions of bakers, tobacco workers, tea packers, and sausage makers.[24] The oldest unions were those of the tea packers and tobacco workers, both established in 1905. But the tobacco industry had been particularly affected by recent mechanization and the resulting influx of women; by 1917, 18 percent of tobacco workers were men—they had composed 35 percent of the industry in 1905.[25] Indeed, it was the tea packers, rather than the tobacco workers, who were responsible for food workers' large strike-fund contributions—eighteen of the twenty contributions for strike funds came from this group of workers. The average contribution for the 4,730 workers in this branch of the food industry was 9.24 rubles, and only two of the twenty tea-packing houses in Moscow did not contribute.

Except for the metalists, these industries were involved in very little strike activity. None of the twelve strikes in the food-processing industry involved tea-packing factories; printers had very few strikes, and most of these were unsanctioned by the union. The metalists did have a large number of workers involved in strikes, but this involvement was due partly to the massive one-day strike on July 6; the threatened general strike over the next round of tariff talks in October never materialized. It would seem, therefore, that unions with widespread participation in strike funds were able to bargain more effectively because employers knew the workers had the resources to withstand a strike. The tea packers, bargaining on a national scale, spent eight months negotiating a new contract and meanwhile accumulated their strike fund. When the union finally threatened a strike, the industry representatives gave in.[26] The most protracted strikes occurred in the leather, wood, and rare-metals industries, and these workers had given very little to their strike funds— an average of twenty-five kopecks per worker in leather and rare metals, and three kopecks in the wood industry.

The leather workers were fortunate, however, in attracting the support of a large number of workers in other industries; they were the major recipients of money directed to "others' strike funds." The classwide support for the leather strike is discussed in detail in Chapter Eight; what is of interest here is the nature of contributions from workers given for somebody else's struggle. Workers might see personal advantage in contributing to their own strike fund because the benefits would return to them in case of a strike. But the return would be less tangible in the case of others' strike-fund contributions, and these must have been motivated

[24] *Moskovskie pishcheviki*, p. 7.   [25] Ibid., p. 70   [26] Ibid., p. 90.

by a sense of class solidarity, by an appreciation that unity was as important as personal security. Power and water workers, tram workers, and one chemical plant gave most generously to other workers' strike funds. (The chemical industry average was ninety-two kopecks for each worker in the industry, but this was almost entirely due to the forty thousand rubles—one day's pay—given by 6,500 workers at the Vtorov explosives plant.)[27] The only other contributors of significance were the metalworkers and machine workers. All these industries were fairly active in other political activities (resolutions and pre-February strikes); once again, this activity indicates that workers with the most political experience best understood the abstract principle of class solidarity.

Contributions to victims of the revolution—to liberated political prisoners and families of persons killed in the February revolution—also represented this sort of higher awareness of the need for revolutionary solidarity at the expense of personal gain; and again, it was the power, tram, metal, and machine workers who donated the most to this cause.

A final category of political contributions were those made to individual political parties. All parties solicited funds for their activities, especially at election time, but the Bolsheviks were the most active and the most successful. Their pitch was to raise enough money to buy their own printing press so as not to have to be dependent upon the good will or profit motive of the owners of the printshop where *Sotsial-Demokrat* was published.[28] It is plausible, therefore, that some workers contributed to this purpose for the same reasons they voted for free-press resolutions—to give the Bolsheviks their chance to compete, not because they preferred that party. Messages accompanying donations were infrequent, but there is evidence that non-Bolshevik supporters gave money for the Bolshevik press, as was the case of a group of nonparty compositors at the Kursk railroad's printshop. However, other donations for this purpose arrived with messages of strong support for the Bolshevik newspaper and for the

[27] This would mean that the daily wage at Vtorov was 6.15 rubles, but on May 2, a Vtorov worker reported that wages there averaged 2.85 rubles (*Proletarii*, 2 May 1917); these were negotiated upward to 4.80 rubles for men and 3.70 for women in late May (*Proletarii*, 26 May 1917). It is possible that the average wage could have risen to 6.15 rubles by September, when the contribution was made, but there are other indications that the size of the work force at Vtorov was shrinking, implying that the 40,000 rubles should be divided by an even smaller number, producing a larger average wage (*Vpered*, 22 August 1917). However, N. A. Vtorov (an eccentric Moscow industrialist whose mansion now serves as the residence of the American ambassador in Moscow) owned several plants in the Moscow region. The most plausible explanation of this large contribution, and thus of the chemical workers' strong showing in "others' strike fund" donations, is that it was the combined offering of all of Vtorov's plants.

[28] The printshop's owner was the liberal public organization, the Union of Cities. *Sotsial-Demokrat* was in fact printed on the same machines as the reactionary daily, *Moskovskie vedomosti* (I. V. Kuznetsov and A. V. Shumakov, *Bol'shevistskaia pechat' Moskvy*, p. 327).

party's championship of the working class.[29] In any case, the Bolshevik party received over 65,000 rubles from 465 factories, far more than any other party. Approximately 90 percent of this total was earmarked for *Sotsial-Demokrat* or the press to print it on; the balance was directed toward the party itself, either for election expenses or as unrestricted gifts.

The magnitude of these contributions for the Bolshevik party press, although not so large as nonpartisan contributions, certainly further discredits the hypothesis that only German money could have financed such a large publishing operation. In his history of the Communist party, Leonard Schapiro writes: "The probability that funds for propaganda purposes at any rate came from the Germans is further strengthened by the fact that no other source for what must have been substantial sums has come to light."[30] The source is clearly there: the columns upon columns of factory-level contributions reported in the back pages of the Bolshevik newspapers in Moscow and elsewhere.

It is not certain who was the beneficiary of eighty contributions to the "social-democrats." Most of these were reported in the Bolsheviks' newspaper and may have been intended for the Bolshevik party, in which case their fund would be even larger. But contributions to "social-democrats" may also have been either made out of ignorance of any difference between the two Social-Democratic factions or intended for the unity faction of the party (although this is less likely because the Ob"edinenie organization solicited its own funds). The leading contributors to "social-democrats" were woodworkers, an industry that had not shown much consciousness in other areas of political life. Another clue that indicates that the "social-democratic" contributions may have resulted from genuine confusion about party distinctions is that they peaked in May and declined to almost nothing after July when political differences were much more publicized.

Mensheviks and SRs received very little support from workers, as far as published reports reveal. The SRs collected slightly more than the Mensheviks, but in no industry did the average contribution outweigh that for the Bolsheviks. Tram workers gave the most money to the SRs—1,670 rubles, or an average of fifteen kopecks per worker—but they also contributed 3,162 rubles to the Bolsheviks. The Mensheviks' leading

---

[29] *Sots.-Dem.*, 27 July, 6 August 1917.

[30] *The Communist Party of the Soviet Union*, pp. 176-178. See also the sharp exchange on the subject between Joel Carmichael and Boris Souvarine in *Dissent*, Winter 1978, pp. 111-116. There Souvarine explains Schapiro's conclusion as cultural naiveté; Lenin once marveled how little French workers gave to their papers, while Russian workers regularly contributed a day's pay every week or month for their press (such a large weekly sum seems unlikely). On Russian contributions in an earlier period, see N. A. Kurashova and S. A. Livshits, "Gruppovye denezhnye sbory rabochikh na 'Pravdu' i gazety drugikh politicheskikh napravlenii."

benefactor in total rubles was the metal industry, which gave 1,671 rubles, but again the Bolsheviks received far more from the same industry— 19,160 rubles. Indeed, as one might expect from their history throughout 1917, metalists and machine-building workers were the Bolsheviks' most generous supporters, donating an average of thirty-four kopecks from metalists and fifty-four kopecks from machine-building workers. Even the printers, whose politics tended to favor the Menshevik party throughout 1917 and later, gave only 76 rubles in total to the Mensheviks and 1,116 rubles to the Bolshevik party (which did place them at the bottom of the list of Bolshevik supporters).

The overall trend in contributions to parties, as Chapter Five suggested, gives ample indication of the growing popularity of the Bolshevik party. What is most striking is the increase in all parties' contributions in the month of August. Although the reporting of party contributions was not delayed so much as Soviet and Municipal Fund contributions, it is likely that the August reports represent a large number of July donations. In the aftermath of the July days in Petrograd, Moscow Bolsheviks were particularly active in soliciting funds for their printing press; the other parties may have benefited financially by the reaction of their supporters to the Bolsheviks' increasing strength. Skvortsov-Stepanov recalled that in July the SRs began to campaign for money "for the party of Kerensky,"[31] and perhaps they were successful because of the premature grab for power of the party so basically hostile to Kerensky.

The contributions to parties in August definitely reflect an increase in party polarization after the July days. On the other hand, contributions to all parties declined sharply after August, during the period leading up to the October revolution. In part, workers were now giving their contributions to the Soviet (with its Bolshevik majority) and to strike funds. Also, most workers who wished to contribute to the printing-press fund may have already done so, although the appeals for the press continued. By September 1, the fund had received 90,641 rubles, and only about 28,000 more collected by October 11.[32]

THE SIGNIFICANCE OF WORKERS' CONTRIBUTIONS

In terms of working-class contributions, party organizations received far less financial support than institutions representing the class as a whole,

[31] In *Slovo starykh bol'shevikov*, p. 219.

[32] *Sots.-Dem.*, 2 September, 17 October 1917. The amount given to the press fund is substantially higher than the Bolsheviks' total given in Table 7-2. This is because many non-Moscow factories and nonworker individuals also contributed money. And not all contributions were made in cash—at a "discussion meeting" (surely not of workers!) in late July, contributions consisting of 234 rubles and a diamond ring were given to the Bolshevik cause (*Sots.-Dem.*, 27 July 1917).

regardless of whether an institution was dominated by one party (such as the Soviet after September). Figure 7-1 indicates the relationship of three major categories of contributions to one another and over time. "Above class" contributions were those supporting institutions that crossed class barriers, primarily the Red Gift, but also including the Constituent Assembly, the Provisional Government, prisoners of war, and war orphans. These contributions peaked in May with the Red Gift of April 16 and declined sharply after that. There was virtually no working-class support for these nonclass institutions after August. The slight increase in October was due to the Constituent Assembly, for which the election campaign was under way.

"Class, nonparty" contributions included the Soviet fund, Municipal Fund, strike funds, support for political prisoners, propaganda, and the

Figure 7-1

Total Contributions to Three Groups
of Purposes over Time

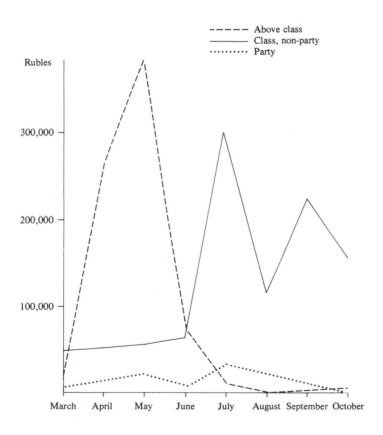

Red Guard. Support for these institutions peaked in July because of the Municipal Fund campaign but continued to be strong; the decline in August was only relative, the result of the end of campaign contributions. In September, it is true, workers' support for the Soviet fell off, but strike-fund contributions more than compensated. Workers contributed almost 209,000 rubles to their own and to others' strike funds in September.

As with resolutions and party affiliation, the overall picture portrayed by these political donations strongly suggests that a class orientation on the part of Moscow's workers became much more pronounced after June. Several factors can explain this phenomenon. First, it took just about that long for the class institutions to become organized. As will be shown for strikes, their peak in July may not have been due to external economic conditions so much as the "lead time" required to formulate demands and to organize workers in support of strikes. So the working-class-oriented contributions—to the strike funds and Soviet—also required time for organizers to explain the purpose of the funds and to prepare for the regular contributions that began to arrive at the Soviet after July. But also important in this rise of class-oriented contributions was the general political situation. The Red Gift no longer appeared as a legitimate target of working-class giving once the Kerensky offensive had given way to increasingly repressive measures in front-line and rear echelons. The July days and their aftermath signaled the weakness of the workers' Soviet, which appeared unwilling to take power and unable to resist the Provisional Government's shift toward the Right. The response of workers in Moscow was twofold. First, donations to the Soviet increased, which would help to strengthen that institution to be able to confront its political rival, the coalition government. And at the same time, donations to strike funds, the economic analogue to the Soviet, also increased. Neither cause stood necessarily for one-class rule; it was simply that, when circumstances pressed, workers devoted their scarce resources to the institutions that most closely represented their interests; and as all of Russia broke down along class lines, these institutions were those that best represented the working class.

The third category of political donations—purely partisan causes—received much less support than all-class causes, and this again demonstrates the relative lack of importance of party differences. The perceptible increase in donations in May for separate parties could well be due to the phenomenon discussed in connection with strike funds: it took that long for workers to mobilize themselves to contribute to parties. At the same time, parties were beginning to mobilize themselves for the municipal duma elections. The July peak probably represents the concerted effort by all parties to raise funds for the electoral campaign. Most significant, however, is the decline between August and September, at the same time that class contributions were increasing. Even though almost all partisan donations were directed to the Bolshevik party at this time, contributions to political parties took a distant second place to the total contributed to nonpartisan class-based institutions.

Political contributions, although a new kind of political indicator, reveal the same processes at work as did other measures examined here: a growing sense of class separateness and the continuing need for solidarity within that class. But political contributions also add a new dimension to this study of the participation of Moscow's workers in the 1917 revolution. By looking at these records, I have uncovered evidence of political activity of a group of workers whose voice was not heard through other forms of working-class expression, workers in small factories. One cannot compare the record of political contributions in Moscow to that of other cities since such work has not been done, so one cannot know if Petrograd, Baku, or Ivanovo workers might also have included a sizable share of silent donors. However, it has been possible to compare the attitudes expressed by these previously unheard-from workers with those expressed in the more public resolutions. Workers in small factories donated disproportionately to most of the causes under discussion; they were thus especially active in support of existing institutions and to some degree in support of the policies of these institutions, policies that more vocal workers often attacked in their published resolutions. Thus, despite the overriding sense of class separateness and solidarity manifested by both forms of political expressions, donations and resolutions indicate as well a fundamental difference of attitude among workers toward institutions and toward the pace of the revolution. These donations reveal that when asked to put their own hard-won earnings on the line, not all workers opposed the line taken by their leadership; most workers did not abandon their class institutions in favor of one political party, however closely identified that party was with the working class.

The conjunction of the belief in class unity and these differing attitudes toward working-class institutions helped give the Moscow revolutionary experience its special character. The most politically active workers, such as machine-building workers, tended to support the Bolshevik party, tended to perceive the revolution in class terms from the start, and tended to be more critical of their foot-dragging institutions. But such workers, thanks to their high degree of political experience, also appreciated the necessity of unity and the fact that not all their comrades shared their political views. These workers in Moscow, as their resolutions have shown, were sensible and rational; and in the light of what they observed among their comrades, they tempered their extremist views. As with the radical Petrograd transplants at the Moscow telephone works, they often submitted to the more cautious wishes of the institutions supported by the majority of their comrades. The evidence of these political contributions thus helps to explain why Moscow acted more moderately and cautiously than other centers in 1917: attitudes among workers, not just between leaders and led, differed; but since all workers shared the belief in unity, this goal took on that much more importance for Moscow's workers in 1917.

EIGHT. *Workers and the Strike Movement in 1917*

WITH the democratic era ushered in by the February revolution, the role of strikes in Russian society changed dramatically. Prior to the revolution, the strike had functioned as an important outlet for the mass of grievances endured by Russian working men and women. Given the repressive nature of the tsarist regime, a strike that was ostensibly directed against the factory management rather than against the government served as the safest way for unhappy workers to express their discontent toward the system as well as the local situation.

After the February revolution, however, the political context changed. Workers no longer needed to strike in order to express their political views, for other outlets such as public meetings, political parties, and working-class press were available. Thus the leading strikers of the pre-revolutionary period, the metal and machine workers, in 1917 led the way in adopting these new democratic forms of political participation.

The strikes that occurred in 1917 consequently reflected only one aspect, but a very important one, of working-class life—relations between workers and management, with particular emphasis on the workers' specific economic situations. The overwhelming majority of strikes in Moscow in 1917 centered on economic issues. At first wages dominated strikers' demands; then as prices soared and the value of wages fell, and as the employers as a class became increasingly hostile to the workers' revolutionary victories, workers' rights in the factory emerged as the issue most fiercely contested through the process of labor negotiations and strikes. Once again, in quite a different context from other political processes, the economic situation contributed to a tendency on the part of workers and capitalists alike to view each other with suspicion and hostility. The end result of local economic conflicts was to shape workers' attitudes about society at large and to intensify the sense of class antagonism and polarization that this study has already observed in other aspects of life in Moscow in 1917.

This chapter will examine the deterioration of labor-management relations during 1917, but the strike movement as a whole also offers, apart from its economic implications, another perspective from which to explore the rich texture of the revolutionary experience of workers. The form and structure of strikes, their timing and substance, provide valuable insight into working-class organizational maturity, workers' expectations for the revolution, as well as the evolution of class relations and the impact of the economy on working-class revolutionary activity.

In viewing the strike movement as a distinct form of working-class activity, however, one cannot ignore the relationship of strikes to the larger political context. Strikes remained an important symbol of the revolutionary movement, and they continued to epitomize the relationship between social classes in Russia. Strikes also served an important educative function. Strike participants gained first-hand organizational experience in mobilizing for and carrying out their strikes. And since strikes were extensively reported in the working-class press, nonparticipants also vicariously experienced these conflicts between labor and management; strikers and nonstrikers alike could evolve a political ideology based on the specific experience of strikers alone.

Before proceeding with an examination of the strike movement, however, the limitations of my view must be stressed. The concern here is with the working-class experience in 1917, and I shall approach the strike movement from the workers' point of view. This perspective naturally cannot reflect all the parameters inherent in any given strike. Following negotations, perhaps the workers had the final choice to strike or not, but many of the factors leading to strikes were out of the workers' hands. Some strikes were provoked by owners seeking excuses to close their plants; satisfied workers in one plant might be forced to join a strike by the encouragement or even threats from strikers in neighboring plants. In a situation in which two sets of workers made identical demands that one owner satisfied and another did not, one should realize that it was really the intransigent owner and not the workers who determined that a strike would take place. But the secrets of the board room lie beyond the scope of this study, which will confine itself to examining what the working-class side of the strike movement has to tell about the workers' revolutionary experience.[1]

The remainder of this chapter will deal with the strike movement in 1917 in both its structural and dynamic context. First will be considered the scope of the strike movement and the composition of its participants. Then follows an examination of the characteristics of strikes themselves—their goals, tactics, and particularly the changes in these characteristics over time. The final section deals with the organizational aspect of strikes and the importance of this aspect for other areas of revolutionary life.

[1] P. V. Volobuev, in *Proletariat i burzhuaziia*, offers a valuable treatment of the capitalists' side of labor conflict in 1917, but in his focus on both sides of labor disputes he understandably neglects the internal dynamics of the working class in the revolution, which forces are the concern here.

THE STRIKE MOVEMENT: GENERAL PATTERNS

There were 269 strikes in Moscow between March and October, according to contemporary newspaper reports and other sources.[2] These 269 strikes—defined simply as work stoppages with common goals—included at least 257,000 workers; some of these were the same workers striking more than once, but on the other hand, the number of striking workers is known for only two-thirds of these 269 strikes.

The number of strikes included here is substantially larger than any given in previous studies of strikes for 1917. The Russian Factory Inspectorate provided comprehensive data on prerevolutionary strikes, but its data for 1917, the source for the few Soviet historical studies on strikes in the revolution, are incomplete. According to these data, there were 576 strikes in all of Russia during the March-October period. Strike statistics gathered in 1917 by the new department of the militia are also incomplete: these indicate 467 strikes in all of Russia and only 199 for the entire Central Industrial Region.[3]

[2] The information about Moscow strikes here and throughout this chapter comes from a file constructed primarily from newspaper reports and supplemented by published archival materials, memoirs, and monographs. The amount of information on each strike varies considerably; for inclusion in the strike file, however, only knowledge of the industry on strike and the month it began was required. Other variables that turned up often enough to be useful were these: numbers of workers on strike and in the industry or factory involved, starting date and length of strike, outcome, and finally (and most important), the demands made by strikers. Unless otherwise indicated, information on strikes given in the chapter is based on this strike file. (A complete list of strike variables is given in Appendix A.)

The file is constructed from the following sources: *Gazeta-kopeika, Izv. MSRD, Proletarii, Trud, Russkie vedomosti, Russkoe slovo, Sots -Dem., Trudovaia kopeika, Utro Rossii, Vpered, Zemlia i volia; Spisok fabrik, Podgotovka i pobeda oktiabr'skoi revoliutsii v Moskve, Revoliutsionnoe dvizhenie v Rossii nakanune oktiabr'skogo vooruzhennogo vosstaniia, Revoliutsionnoe dvizhenie v Rossii posle sverzheniia samoderzhaviia, Revoliutsionnoe dvizhenie v Rossii v aprele 1917 g., Revoliutsionnoe dvizhenie v Rossii v avguste 1917 g., Revoliutsionnoe dvizhenie v Rossii v iiule 1917 g., Revoliutsionnoe dvizhenie v Rossii v mae-iiune 1917 g., Revoliutsionnoe dvizhenie v Rossii v sentiabre 1917 g.,* I. Kolychevskii, "Zabastovochnoe dvizhenie v Moskve s fevralia po oktiabria 1917 g."; Akhun and Petrov; *Letopis' geroicheskikh dnei;* GAMO, ff. 186, 2443, 633.

The major missing sources are the records of the labor section of the Moscow Soviet (presumably in GAMO, f. 66), the archives of the militia (TsGAOR, f. 406), and various trade union archives. However, only the last have been used for Moscow by Soviet scholars with freer access to such materials. See, for example, Gaponenko, *Rabochii klass Rossii,* and Trukan.

[3] Iakovleva, "Zabastovochnoe dvizhenie v Rossii za 1895-1917 gg.," cites the figure 576. Using the same Factory Inspectorate data, A. M. Lisetskii gives a total of 586 strikes (but using other sources he finds 491 for this period in the Ukraine alone) ("K voprosu o statistike zabastovok v Rossii v period podgotovki velikoi oktiabr'skoi sotsialisticheskoi revoliutsii"). Statistics gathered by the Provisional Government's department of militia are reported in M. Fleer, "K istorii rabochego dvizheniia 1917 g."

Although more complete than the previously compiled data, however, even the sample here is unquestionably only part of the whole. Based primarily on newspaper sources, it includes only those strikes important enough to merit newspaper space or whose strikers were organized enough to send in a report. It is, therefore, almost surely biased against more spontaneous, unorganized strikes that went unsanctioned or unnoticed even by the trade unions.[4] It is clear, too, that there were many more strikes known only to the unions involved. The board of directors of the tailors' union reported 119 striking shops with 1,706 workers from February to mid-May whereas the sample here shows only 17 strikes in this industry for the entire year and only 742 workers on strike in the first three months.[5]

Nonetheless, although even these data are incomplete, they are certainly sufficient to paint the broad outlines of the movement of strikes in 1917. The 269 strikes during the March-October period, as indicated, involved more than 250,000 strikers in all sectors of the work force, and at least 88,000 separate individuals among the 361,000 factory workers in the city.

Figure 8-1 depicts a general outline of the dynamics of strikes in Moscow, indicating two important facets of the strike movement. The first deals with the rhythm of strikes. In terms of strikes, the movement peaked in May with sixty-two strikes, and it declined steadily thereafter. In terms of strikers, the movement developed more slowly, peaking only in July. Both sets of figures indicate that strikes declined in number and size after July, and the July turning point corresponds quite closely to turning points in other areas of revolutionary life: the rise of counterrevolutionary sentiment outside the working class as a result of the July days, the subsequent polarization of social classes, and the concomitant rise in Bolshevik prestige. Here is an anomaly: polarization along political lines was growing after July as workers and capitalists increasingly viewed each other as class enemies. But strikes, which were one manifestation of class conflict, were decreasing at the same time. This anomaly reflects the limited role played by strikes as an indicator of the political moment. The lessons learned by strikers were adapted by October to fit other forms of political activity, as strikes lost their efficacy in the face of economic breakdown. (This point will be taken up again later.)

---

[4] Such strikes receive passing mention in some of the memoirs of the period. Workers at the Postavshchik and Gakental' plants allude to a series of short wildcat strikes which do not appear in the sources used here (*Na barrikadakh za vlast' sovetov*, p. 27; *Ot fevralia k oktiabriu* [*v Moskve*], p. 176). Furthermore, very limited access to the archival records of the tailors' trade union (GAMO, f. 633, op. 1, dd. 4, 6) turned up other strikes not recorded in newspapers or monographs. Presumably there were many more of these.

[5] *Moskovskii soiuz rabotnikh-portnykh*, p. 27.

Figure 8-1

Strikes and Strikers by Month

(Numbers in the boxes represent numbers of strikes each month.)

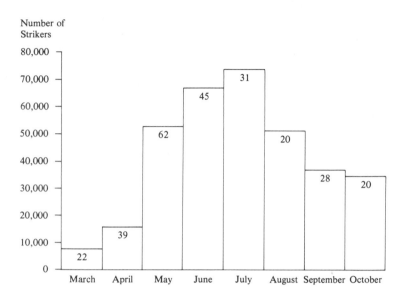

A second facet of strikes suggested by Figure 8-1 is the change in the relationship between the number of strikes and the number of strikers. The sixty-two strikes in May involved almost 54,000 workers, for an average of 866 workers in each strike. By July, however, there were almost 75,000 workers involved in only thirty-one strikes, for an average of about 2,400 workers per strike; and in August the average size was almost 2,500. This increase in the size of strikes suggests that there were significant structural changes occurring in the strike movement: larger strikes reflected improved organization and organizability on the part of the strikers. Individual factory-level strikes were giving way to industrywide strikes as workers learned how to cooperate with one another and how to combine their resources. The significance of this change will also be considered below.

Striking workers were of course drawn from the same pool as those who participated in other areas of public life, but as with resolutions, contributions, and voting, certain groups of workers engaged more fully in strike activity than others. What factors contributed to strike participation? Once again using the industry as a basic denominator of worker participation, one should consider the relationship between economic position, social background, and strike propensities. The social and economic composition of the strike force can tell the historian much about the role of the strike in the revolutionary process.

Table 8-1 presents a summary of Moscow strikes by industry for the entire period March to October. Industries have been ranked in order of their strike propensity, an index based on the ratio of the industry's share of strikers to its share in the total work force.[6] Thus, although woodworkers composed only 2.5 percent of the Moscow labor force, they accounted for almost 10 percent of all strikers in 1917, and their strike propensity is 3.13, the highest of any group.[7] Cotton workers, on the other hand, who made up 6.3 percent of the work force, accounted for less than 1 percent of all strikers, giving them a strike propensity of .02.

TABLE 8-1. *Strike Propensities of Moscow Industries in 1917*

Industry	Strike Propensity
Wood	3.13
Metal	2.64
Leather	2.35
Silk	2.00
Rare metals	1.93
Mineral	1.79
Clothing	1.60
Tram	1.57
Paper	1.25
Construction	1.07
Food	.84
Services	.56
Textile	.46
Chemical	.43
Wool	.29
Power and gas	.25
Printing	.22
Warehouse and freight	.16
Mixed fiber	.15
Cotton	.02
Animal byproducts	.00

SOURCE: See Appendix I.

[6] The total work force is given in Appendix I. This total differs from that used elsewhere in this study since it includes nonfactory workers who constituted an important segment of the Moscow strike force.

[7] If all industries had the same strike rates, the propensity to strike for each would be one; the share of an industry's strikers to the total strike force would be the same as its share of workers in the total work force. An alternate way of ranking the industries would be by total number of strikers, in which case the metalists would rank highest, followed by service workers, leather workers, and clothing workers. After all, to an outsider, the Moscow strike movement appeared to be dominated by the metalworkers, not the woodworkers. But the concern here is with internal characteristics: what was it about the woodworking

The table indicates that in 1917 in Moscow, wood, metal and leather were the most strike-prone industries, and printing, warehousing, mixed fibers, and cotton were the least active. The two leaders of the prerevolutionary strike movement, metalists and printers, once again emerge at opposite ends of this spectrum of revolutionary activity. Metalists, as has been argued, demonstrated a strong sense of class separateness, whereas printers, because of their unique position in society, tended to be less adamantly opposed to cooperation with the bourgeoisie; the respective strike patterns of these two industries reflect these differences. But with the exception of printers, there is also a strong relationship between the economic position of an industry and its propensity to strike.

Correlating strike propensity with the average wage in an industry in 1916 indicates that the industries that struck most were among the highest paid in Moscow. Table 8-2 gives the three most strike-prone industries with their 1916 ruble wage and the change in real wages between 1913 and 1916. All three had higher-than-average annual wages in 1916, and only the wages of the woodworkers declined during the war years. When all twenty-two industries are considered, this pattern changes slightly. There is a positive relationship between 1916 wages and strike propensity; the relationship becomes even stronger if the printers and gas workers, who had high wages but few strikes, are omitted from the calculation. (Gas workers demonstrated many of the same conciliationist characteristics as printers; they were a small group of highly skilled workers and tended throughout 1917 to support Menshevik positions.) On the other hand, controlling for the 1916 wage, there is a slightly weaker negative relationship between the change in wage and strike propensity: industries that struck most tended to have declining real wages over the period 1913-1916. Thus, recent and relative impoverishment also contributed

TABLE 8-2. *Wages for Industries with High Strike Propensities*

Industry	Strike Propensity	1916 Annual Wage (Rubles)	Change in Real Wage 1913–1916 (Percent of 1913 Wage)
Wood	3.13	628	80
Metal	2.64	981	114
Leather	2.35	811	121
Average for 22 industries	1.00	620	101

SOURCES: TsSU, *Trudy*, vol. 26, table 15; *Ezhemesiachnyi statisticheskii biulleten'*, 1913-1916; F. D. Markuzon, *Zarabotnaia plata fabrichno-zavodskikh rabochikh g. Moskvy.*

industry that produced almost twice as many strikers as there were workers? The woodworkers may have had little impact on the strike movement as a whole, but clearly, strikes had a big impact on woodworkers.

to the propensity to strike; but the first result indicates that even given two industries with the same rate of decline, the one with a higher 1916 wage was more prone to strike.[8]

The fact that it was the highly paid industries that tended to strike most suggests a great deal about the nature of the strike movement. Clearly, it was not relative impoverishment that drove these workers to strike. In fact, poorly paid workers could probably not afford to strike. Workers had to be prepared to risk a temporary loss of income during a strike and so would take that step only if they possessed financial reserves with which to endure a long strike. Workers in well-paid industries tended to have greater reserves than the lowest-paid workers, reserves that could sustain workers either individually or in the form of a pooled strike fund. Additionally, workers with high wages were more valuable to their employers; and if these hard-to-replace workers struck, a manufacturer might be eager to settle. Workers in such industries might well have struck more often because they expected speedy success. This phenomenon indicates that a strike action was far more than a simple response to economic deprivation; in many cases it may have been a carefully chosen weapon in the conflict between labor and capital, selected after due consideration of the entire economic and political situation.

The assumption that decisions to strike were made in a fundamentally rational way lies at the heart of my argument about the strike movement in Moscow, for it provides an expectation against which to evaluate individual strike phenomena. This rationality is clear when one considers what economic factors other than wages also affected an industry's strike propensity. Surely the overall economic position of an industry had an important effect on strikes. Workers in an ailing industry, as measured perhaps by high unemployment, would be less likely to strike since there would be a large reserve of unemployed workers willing to work for any wage or under any conditions. Unfortunately, there is little systematic information on unemployment (or productivity, another indicator of eco-

---

[8] This discussion is based on the following regression equation estimated from data appearing in Appendix J on strike propensities, wage levels, and rates of wage change in fifteen industries (excluding printing and power):

$$\text{strike propensity} = 1.414 + 0.156 \text{ wage} - .022 \text{ wage change}$$
$$(1.04) \quad (2.04) \quad (-1.57)$$

Thus an increase of one ruble per week in an industry's wage level is seen to *increase* its expected strike propensity by 0.156, while an increase of 1 percent in an industry's rate of wage change *decreases* its expected strike propensity by .022. The numbers in parentheses are "Student" t-statistics indicating the strength (statistical significance) of these effects. The hypotheses that wage level and rate of wage change exert no effect on strike propensity can be rejected at the 95 percent and 90 percent confidence levels respectively (on one-tailed tests).

nomic health) for 1917.[9] But the three industries with the highest strike propensities—wood, metal, and leather—were all heavily engaged in military production, where employment and the value of production tended to be high.

Economic factors alone only partly influenced workers' strike propensity. In many other areas of working-class life, social factors also influenced the level of political activity, and this is true for strikes as well. As shown throughout this study, urban-born workers tended to participate more in such activities as trade unions and resolutions. The same is true for strikes: industries with the highest levels of urban-born workers had the highest strike propensities.[10] Urban birth stands as a proxy for a collection of social factors; urban workers tended to have more experience both with labor-management relations and with strikes. Long-time urban residents had built up a network of contacts, so that organizing a strike was easier for them than for migrants fresh from the countryside. Finally, even if some of these workers had never personally experienced a strike before 1917, their long residence in the urban working-class milieu and their presumed contact with the working-class press before and during 1917 provided them with a better awareness of the strike tool.

The size of the work place was another factor that affected workers' propensity to strike. Table 8-3 indicates the disproportionate share of large factories in Moscow strikes. Factories employing more than three hundred workers accounted for 74 percent of all workers, but 82 percent of all strikers. Large factories could well have had the same effect on workers' experience as the urban milieu: workers learned from one an-

TABLE 8-3. *Size Distribution of Striking Plants*

Size Plant	Percent of All Workers	Percent of All Strikers
1-100	12.2	5.4
101-300	14.2	12.9
301-500	9.6	11.0
501-1,000	14.1	14.8
1,000 and more	49.8	56.0

SOURCE: Data for this table are derived from the file on factories described in Appendix A.

[9] Figures on value of production and productivity (output per worker) by industry on an all-Russian scale for 1913 to 1918 are reported in TsSU, *Trudy*, vol. 26, vyp. 1, table 19. But there is no correlation between the change in the value of production between 1913 and 1916 and the strike propensities of the ten Moscow industries which could be matched with the production data.

[10] This relationship is based on 1912 data on place of birth for Moscow residents (*Stat. ezhegodnik*, pp. 68-73). The printers, a highly urbanized group, were omitted from the calculations for the same reasons given above. The correlation coefficient for strike propensity and proportion of urban-born workers for the remaining thirteen industries was .39. (Data are given in Appendix J.)

other the value of the strike weapon and how to use it. Large factories were also easier to organize. And such plants had the advantage of greater protection for strikers; workers in these plants might have had less fear of reprisal than those more closely under the watch of management.[11] There is, to be sure, a probable bias in the reporting of strikes, so that strikes in small factories were underrepresented in press reports; but without new sources, it is impossible to estimate the extent of this bias. And in any case, this relationship between strikes and factory size corresponds to similar relationships in other areas of working-class public life in 1917, particularly with respect to resolutions and the formation of factory committees.[12]

These characteristics of Moscow strikers—high wage levels, high rates of urban-born workers, and concentration in large factories—suggest that strikes in 1917 were waged by the more experienced Moscow workers. Hence they were probably the result of some deliberation and rational choice rather than the spontaneous irrational outbursts decried by the bourgeois press and even by some labor organizers. It will be seen below how the Menshevik press in particular complained that these strikes demonstrated the immaturity of the labor movement; but as with other Menshevik views of working-class life in 1917, such a view did not entirely conform to reality. One can learn more about the basic rationality of the strike process by examining this process in greater detail.

THE STRIKE PROCESS: GOALS, TACTICS, DYNAMICS

On June 21, the workers of the Ustritsev metal plant in the Butyrki district gathered to discuss their grievances. A list of demands was drawn up, and the workers' representatives presented them to the director of the plant, together with a three-day deadline for a reply. The demands included a minimum wage, two-week paid annual vacation, and compensation for disabling injuries. Seven days later the owners refused to meet the demands, and another workers' meeting voted to strike, effective immediately.[13]

This was a fairly typical strike: it focused on worker-management issues,

---

[11] Size did not automatically guarantee immunity, of course. In 1916, six thousand strikers at the Naval shipyard in Nikolaev were sent to the army en masse (Kir'ianov, *Rabochie Iuga Rossii*, p. 241).

[12] The relationship between plant size and strikes is examined for France by Edward Shorter and Charles Tilly, who find indeed that strike rates increase in larger plants. But the authors go on to show that the organizational level of strikes decreases in larger plants, that large-scale mechanization has in fact an atomizing effect on striking workers. That is, concentration does not necessarily breed organization. They claim smaller plants have greater unanimity—and longer and more successful strikes (*Strikes in France 1830-1968*).

[13] *Vpered*, 6 July 1917; *Izv. MSRD*, 6 July 1917.

it was called only after a period of negotiation, and the workers' chief goals were a secure wage and a guaranteed vacation. It also illustrates a number of specific problems connected with the strike movement as a whole. For example, while the workers explicitly demanded economic improvement, their wants were undoubtedly more complex. By demanding compensation for injuries, workers were seeking economic security; but they were also demanding a change in worker-employer relations—workers insisted that the owners were liable for on-the-job injuries and that plant safety was their responsibility as much as the workers'.

In other strikes, the distinction between purely economic and other kinds of demands was similarly blurred. The Factory Inspectorate in 1917 made tidy distinctions between "economic" and "political" strikes, but such a division obscures the more complex wants and demands of the working class. As has already been seen, the demand for an eight-hour workday symbolized an entire range of revolutionary goals. But with the exception of this demand and the demand for back pay for the time spent on strike (both a wage and an amnesty demand), most strike demands fell naturally into one of five general categories: wages, work conditions, job control, amnesty, and non-plant-related (or political). These five areas represented quite different aspects of factory life, and certain kinds of demands were more common in some industries than in others.

Demands for higher pay, the most direct response to the deteriorating economic situation, dominated the strike movement. Nine-tenths of all strikers demanded increased wages in one form or another—increases in piece rates, daily pay, or annual salary. Sometimes workers would not press for maximum increases but would seek to equalize the differences among groups of workers. Thus, the metalworkers' union first insisted upon (and won without a strike) increases for its lowest-paid workers, the chernorabochie. Only in July did the union stage a one-day strike for across-the-board increases. The workers in the box-making workshop of a tea-packaging firm demanded only to be paid on a par with workers in the weighing section. And throughout the year, municipal workers—those in municipally owned defense factories as well as in city services—demanded parity with their comrades in private industry.[14]

Other workers demanded cost-of-living increases, "inflation bonuses," or "the living minimum" as the textile union called it in its negotiations.[15] And increasingly, as owners threatened to close down plants for certain periods of time, workers demanded guarantees of continued pay for the duration of the shutdown. As Table 8-4 shows, 92 percent of all strikers

[14] *Sots.-Dem.*, 4 July, 4 May 1917; *Izv. MSRD*, 19 May 1917.
[15] *Vpered*, 11 October 1917.

TABLE 8-4. *Frequency of Strikers' Demands*
(BY NUMBER OF STRIKERS AND STRIKES)

Demand	Number of Strikers	Percent of Total Strikers (N = 238,772)	Number of Strikes	Percent of Total Strikes (N = 269)
Higher wages	220,478	92.3	185	68.8
Vacation	80,428	33.7	33	12.3
Hiring and firing	74,238	31.1	47	17.5
Pay during shutdowns	52,760	21.9	15	5.6
Amnesty	43,536	18.2	40	14.9
Eight-hour workday	39,792	16.7	27	10.0
Other rights	30,000	12.6	2	0.7
Sick pay, care	24,152	10.1	12	4.5
Dignity (no tipping)	20,000	8.4	1	0.4
Change in job description	17,582	7.4	10	3.7
Protests about administrators	10,690	5.7	15	5.6
Other economic	10,070	4.2	3	1.1
Change in pay system	6,893	2.9	15	5.6
Work conditions (unspecified)	6,390	2.7	6	2.2
Holding prices	6,000	2.5	2	0.7
Recognition of worker organization	5,950	2.5	13	4.8
Solidarity	3,901	1.6	5	1.9
Arbitration	2,989	1.3	3	1.1
Other nonplant	2,613	1.1	1	0.4
Worker control	1,500	0.6	2	0.7
Political (unspecified)	1,050	0.4	1	0.4
Open factory	735	0.3	5	1.9
Equal pay	550	0.2	2	0.7
Other conditions	437	0.2	3	1.1
Rights (unspecified)	412	0.1	6	2.2
Amenities	230	0.1	2	0.7
Food supply	196	0.1	3	1.1

demanded higher wages; other wage-related demands were made by an additional 22 percent of strikers. It can be assumed, in addition, that an even greater number of wage conflicts were settled peacefully, either within the plant or through the mediation of the trade union conflict commissions, the Soviet's labor section, or the quasi-governmental arbitration boards (primiritel'nye kamery).[16]

[16] There were a variety of such mediating bodies. The Central Arbitration Board was formally constituted in late May and was composed of representatives from both industry and labor, with an elected chairman. In addition, many trade unions had their own parallel boards, and sometimes even individual factories had them. (The Soviet passed a law allowing arbitration boards in all enterprises with over fifty workers on April 11.) An appeals board,

This overwhelming focus by strikers on material improvement indicates the major role of strikes in 1917: at the factory level, they represented very localized conflicts between workers and their employers. Only when viewed in the aggregate did the strike movement reveal the scope of economic dislocation that threatened the existence of the Moscow work force.

A second category of plant-related demands dealt with improved working conditions. Most frequent was the demand for an annual, usually paid, vacation as with the Ustritsev workers above.[17] Another common demand was medical aid, including sick pay, compensation for injury, and improved medical service. Other working-conditions demands included changes in hours—starting times, dinner breaks, and so forth—and such amenities as boiling water to be available for tea in the factory and in factory-owned barracks, and heat to be turned on well before the start of a shift.

With the third group of demands—worker-organization or "rights" (*pravovye*) demands—workers insisted on some measure of control over their own situations. Such demands transcended basic material concerns and bordered on the political; demanding control over aspects of their lives in the work place, workers claimed for themselves a share in the decisions made about their lives. Demands for job control in local situations paralleled similar concerns about control over their livelihoods expressed in workers' resolutions in May and June on the economy, as well as the job-security activities undertaken by the nascent labor organizations.

Concern about economic control increased over the year on both the national and local levels. In the strike movement, it was over job-control issues, especially the question of workers' participation in hiring and firing

---

the *treteiskii sud*, intended to adjudicate existing agreements, was also composed of equal representatives with a neutral chairman (I. Rubin, *Primiritel'nye kamery i treteiskii sud*). The Central Arbitration Board had a long backlog of cases, and so there were also many ad hoc mediating bodies. For example, the Soviet's labor section worked to settle disputes without formal arbitration; in extreme cases (such as the arrest of management personnel by workers), labor section officials would be sent to the scene to try to ease the conflict. As has already been noted, district soviets, trade unions, and many large factories also had conflict commissions that dealt with disputes. The array of mediatory bodies is ample evidence that labor-management conflict extended far beyond the strike activity under study here.

[17] The fact that this was such a prominent issue indicates that the Moscow working class was a full-time labor force in 1917. In the nineteenth century, workers were commonly dismissed at Easter and then rehired in the autumn after a summer of agricultural work (Johnson, "Nature," pp. 70-71; Romashova, pp. 153-154; S. Lapitskaia, *Byt rabochikh Trekhgornoi manufaktury*, p. 40). But by 1917, even if many workers did retain some ties with the land, they worked full time in the city and sought the two-week vacation as much to rest as to help out their families in the fields.

decisions, that labor-management conflicts intensified by late summer and early autumn. The demand for control over hiring and firing was made by almost a third of all strikers and became the main issue in the long and bitter strike of over 22,000 leather workers from August to October.

In addition to institutional control over hiring, which meant hiring only from union lists or allowing factory committees to veto firing decisions, workers sometimes would strike over the unjust, usually politically motivated, dismissal of fellow workers. There were also occasional demands for the removal of particularly offensive administrative personnel—foremen, office workers, plant directors, or engineers.[18] These demands were sometimes accompanied by the traditional and humiliating practice of forcefully ejecting the offender by carting him out of the factory grounds in a wheelbarrow. A leather worker at the Postavshchik military-supply plant recalled such an occasion:

> A meeting was called in the mechanical shop, at which the workers demanded the presence of the engineer Graevskii, but he refused to appear. Then the aroused workers wheeled a barrow up to the shop office, dragged out Graevskii, planted him in the barrow, and rolled him away from the grounds of the plant. After this the workers' demands were satisfied.[19]

The hiring and firing issue was the most bitterly contested of the job-control demands, but in a few cases workers had to strike for an even more basic right: the recognition by the owner of the workers' committee or trade union. Such strikes occurred mainly in smaller plants (it was mentioned in 4.8 percent of strikes, but by only 2.5 percent of strikers), where owners were more accustomed to direct control over workers. In most plants, factory committees functioned freely, with disputes arising over specific rights such as hiring. Another general demand was "worker

[18] Employers' family members also appeared as objects of protest. Workers at the Lazarev metal plant in Rogozhskii struck long and with much support from other workers against the interference in factory affairs by the owner's draft-evading son (*Vpered*, 6 May 1917). Workers at the Matiukhin metal plant struck against the rude behavior toward workers by the manager's wife (*Izv. MSRD*, 25 April 1917). Such examples illustrate the importance for workers of preserving their dignity. Using rare archival sources, Mandel ("The Development of Revolutionary Consciousness") and Devlin ("Petrograd Workers in 1917") have shown how important this issue was for the skilled workers of Petrograd in 1917.

[19] *Oktiabr' v Zamoskvorech'e*, p. 90. The Sergei Eisenshtein film, *Stachka* (1925), depicts one such episode for the period before 1917. In at least one case the workers went further than this equivalent of tar-and-feathering. Workers at the Sautam leather factory attempted to drown their employer in the river, but the hapless capitalist was rescued by the intervention of the militia (*Torgovo-promyshlennaia gazeta*, 4 May 1917. The bourgeois press is invaluable for its coverage of such so-called worker excesses, which the socialist press tended to deny).

control" per se, that is, for supervision of the overall running of the plant, but this demand was not a significant strike issue. Worker control was more appropriate as a national political issue, and the strike did not appear to be the proper context for attaining this aim.

Another right claimed by striking workers can be called the "right to work." In the case of some lockouts, workers would refuse to accept their final pay and work papers (*rasschet*) and would strike until the factory was reopened. This was the case at the Rus footwear factory (which was ultimately seized by its workers in a subsequent strike). Workers demanded that the administration withdraw its announcement of a wholesale firing; and when the owners refused, a strike was declared.[20] The right to work was also the basis of the demand for owners to submit to arbitration; having reached a stalemate over what constituted a living wage, workers at the Belov wool manufacture struck in order to force their employers to participate in a board of mediation.[21]

One of the most complex of these rights demands concerned equal pay for men and women. On the surface, the equal-pay demand dealt simply with higher wages, as with the metalists' campaign to raise wages for chernorabochie. It could also be interpreted as a symbol of solidarity between the sexes, but there is reason to believe that it was intended rather to create more jobs for men by driving women out of the work force. Male workers complained that they were forced out of the labor market by cheap, unskilled female labor (a complaint registered against other outsiders as well, including prisoners of war, and Chinese and Persian laborers). By demanding that women and men receive equal pay, perhaps the men hoped to ensure that employers would hire more productive male workers in order to receive more output for their money. The evidence on this point is contradictory. One male Bolshevik organizer recalled leading the fight for higher wages for women, among other issues, presumably not in order to drive his male constituents out of the factories. But a woman Bolshevik organizer at the Dinamo machine-building plant described a different experience. Party organizers had hard work organizing women, she recalled, because the men opposed it—they saw women as competitors. And a representative of the furriers' union reported similar male hostility toward low-paid women workers in his profession.[22] The one clear case of this demand in the strike sample came as one of a number of issues raised by striking leather workers at the workshop of the Officers' Economic Society. No sex breakdown is available for this specific shop,

[20] *Trudovaia kopeika*, 25 March 1917; *Gazeta-kopeika*, 25 March 1917. A similar situation occurred at the Borisov-Beliaev tarpaulin factory (*Izv. MSRD*, 12 April 1917).

[21] *Izv. MSRD*, 23 May 1917.

[22] Batyshev, p. 185; *Dinamo: 25 let*, p. 65; *Moskovskii sovet professional'nykh soiuzov*, p. 21.

but the industry as a whole was 96 percent male in 1912 and 87 percent male in 1918, indicating that women were making possibly threatening inroads.[23] This equal-pay issue illustrates the clash between socialist theory and economic reality. Equal rights for women were fine in principle, especially to veteran workers schooled in socialist ethics; but the realization of this principle meant economic hardship for men, the major breadwinners of working-class families and the major participants in most areas of revolutionary life. It is not surprising that only a few far-seeing organizers would defend economic equality for the sexes.

The fourth group of demands, amnesty for strikers, was superficially a wage demand but cannot be considered only as such. It occurred most frequently in the form of a demand for wages to be paid for the duration of a strike and was most frequently made after the settlement of other issues. In effect workers were saying, "And we want the administration to recognize the validity of our grievances by reimbursing us for the time on strike." Back pay for strike time was considered to be just compensation for a strike provoked by the management. In some cases, strikes that were apparently settled would continue over this issue alone, as in the strike of one hundred confection workers at the Kade factory in May, who won a wage increase and vacation only to continue their strike over the amnesty issue.[24]

A final group of demands was over non-plant-related issues. After February, explicitly political strikes were infrequent.[25] There were only scattered individual non-plant-related strikes and threats of strikes in 1917, mainly over the issue of bread supplies and in solidarity with striking workers in other factories and other cities. For example, in an attempt to break a two-month-old strike, administrators at the shoe factory of the Officers' Economic Society sent its orders to other workshops; shoemakers at the Shavykin shop refused to take on this work and called a strike instead.[26]

As already seen here, wage issues dominated the overall strike movement in 1917, and clearly the strike was used primarily to gain economic benefits. But the relative importance of wages and other demands changed over the eight months from March to October. By late summer, rampant inflation wiped out wage increases even as they were being negotiated. Workers responded to this situation by striking less and looking to broader

[23] *Stat. ezhegodnik*, pp. 69, 47.

[24] *Vpered*, 3 June 1917.

[25] The Moscow Conference protest strike was in some ways a throwback to the pre-February days when workers, fearing government reprisal, expressed their political grievances indirectly, with their employers as the immediate target. Lisetskii, *Bol'sheviki vo glave*, offers an extensive survey of strikes in response to the conference across all of Russia.

[26] *Sots.-Dem.*, 22 June 1917.

change in society. Within the diminishing strike movement, demands for wages gave way to an increasing concern over job control.

Figure 8-2 depicts the evolution in the nature of demands over the eight-month period. Levels of demands are represented by the segment of the distance from zero to one hundred; thus in March political demands accounted for 13 percent, control demands 13 percent, and economic demands (wages plus conditions) the remainder—74 percent of all strikers

Figure 8-2

Change in Relative Shares of Types of Strike Demands

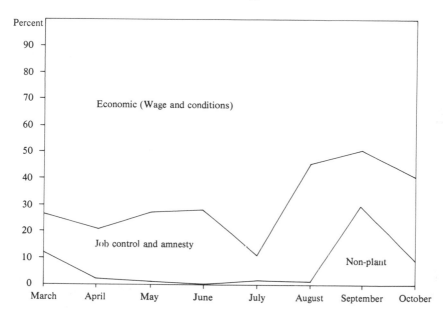

in that month. The share of economic strikes peaked in July and declined thereafter, at the expense first of job control and then of non-plant strikes. Control strikes peaked in August, but their share remained relatively constant throughout the year. Strikers with non-plant-related demands rose to 27 percent of total strikers in September, but this proportion is inflated by the general decline in all kinds of strikes in the month of September, as was shown in Figure 8-1. Only 4,500 workers, 1 percent of the labor force, made non-plant-related demands in September; all were demands for a freeze on prices.

The turning points for kinds of strikes are significant. The number of strikers making economic demands reached its peak on July 6, the day of the industrywide strike by metalworkers. Thereafter, the focus of the strikers' demands shifted more toward job control. July was a critical month in the political and economic life of Moscow, as has been seen. The municipal elections and the failed Bolshevik rising in Petrograd had intensified the focus on political matters, and new echelons of striking workers might have become more conscious of the political underpinnings of strikes. This increase in the level of political awareness was compounded by a decay of the economic situation, which affected the entire work force directly or indirectly. Once again, the symbiosis between economic and political life can be seen. The tightening of the screws in the economic arena, so well illustrated by the shift in the focus of strike demands, itself influenced the political climate and contributed to the growing sense of polarization between classes.

Nonetheless it is important to remember that even in the intensely political atmosphere after July, striking Moscow workers still primarily demanded material gains. But political life now more emphatically focused on the distribution of power between the laboring and the propertied classes, the very same two participants in the strike process. Thus even within the limited strike arena, wage demands took on both a practical and a symbolic significance. While seeking to win maximum compensation for their labor, workers may also have used wage demands to articulate a wide range of grievances against the bourgeoisie as a class, as a proxy for deeper discontents that could not be as easily expressed.[27]

Indeed, a concern for wage gains at the local level was not incompatible with active involvement in politics on other fronts, as one can see by examining the patterns of economic strikes by industry. Table 8-5 shows that the metalists, who were in the vanguard of most political activities, struck overwhelmingly for economic reasons.

On the other hand, the relative importance of wage demands for different industries also depended on the timing of strikes in each industry. Workers who struck often early in the year were responding to a different economic situation than those striking later in the year. The dominant proportion of wage strikes among metalists in fact reflects the high degree of the industry's organization: the bulk of the wage strikers (50,000) were participants in a one-day industrywide walkout in early July. With these demands won, further strikes, which in other industries included more job-control issues, were unnecessary. This description gives a picture, not entirely true, of an industry primarily concerned with bread-and-butter demands. In fact, the metalists gave considerable material support to the leather workers, who were striking for job-control issues.

Textile workers also struck predominantly for wage demands, which strike issue more accurately than metalists' strikes reflects the economic

[27] The subconscious of Moscow workers cannot be probed for corroboration of this point, but the recent study of French strikes by Shorter and Tilly discusses the ways in which wage demands were not always what they seemed (p. 68).

TABLE 8-5. *Goals of Strikes by Industry; Number of Strikers for Each Demand*

Industry	Higher Wages	Job Conditions	Worker Control	Amnesty	Political Issues	Total[a]
Power and gas	300	0	0	0	0	300
	(100.0)[b]	(0)	(0)	(0)	(0)	(100.0)
Animal byproducts	48	0	0	0	0	48
	(100.0)	(0)	(0)	(0)	(0)	(100.0)
Textile	16,680	360	2,634	1,780	0	21,454
	(77.7)	(1.7)	(12.3)	(8.3)	(0)	(100.0)
Metal	64,041	4,860	3,743	1,426	12,037	86,107
	(74.4)	(5.6)	(4.3)	(1.7)	(14.0)	(100.0)
Rare metals	1,297	388	448	180	160	2,473
	(52.4)	(15.7)	(18.1)	(7.3)	(6.4)	(100.0)
Mineral	2,454	1,161	774	387	0	4,776
	(51.4)	(24.3)	(16.2)	(8.1)	(0)	(100.0)
Printing	1,779	996	518	206	0	3,499
	(50.8)	(28.5)	(14.8)	(5.9)	(0)	(100.0)
Clothing	60,748	30,260	30,369	0	0	121,377
	(50.0)	(24.9)	(25.1)	(0)	(0)	(100.0)
Chemical	2,700	1,423	318	1,000	0	5,441
	(49.6)	(26.2)	(5.8)	(18.4)	(0)	(100.0)
Warehouse	2,180	2,077	700	0	0	4,957
	(44.0)	(41.9)	(14.1)	(0)	(0)	(100.0)
Services	63,450	39,950	42,475	500	0	146,375
	(43.3)	(27.3)	(29.0)	(0.3)	(0)	(100.0)
Construction	23,118	2,700	21,618	10,836	0	58,272
	(39.7)	(4.6)	(37.1)	(18.6)	(0)	(100.0)
Paper	4,800	4,400	2,491	2,400	0	14,091
	(34.1)	(31.2)	(17.7)	(17.1)	(0)	(100.0)
Leather	30,864	47,398	24,485	22,589	1,563	126,899
	(24.3)	(37.4)	(19.3)	(17.8)	(1.2)	(100.0)
Wood	5,652	9,938	6,443	2,132	0	24,165
	(23.4)	(41.1)	(26.7)	(8.8)	(0)	(100.0)
Food	10,090	23,100	10,048	100	0	43,338
	(23.3)	(53.3)	(23.2)	(0.2)	(0)	(100.0)
Total	290,201	169,011	147,064	43,536	13,760	663,572
	(43.7)	(25.5)	(22.2)	(6.6)	(2.1)	(100.0)

a. The totals given here do not correspond to the total number of strikers given in Appendix I because each demand struck for is added separately. That is, one strike for both wages and control by 2,000 workers would produce 4,000 "demand-strikers."

b. Numbers in parentheses represent the percentage of total strikers for each industry

position of the industry in 1917; most large textile mills closed for two months during the summer, and many others closed down altogether at some point. One might expect that given the resulting high unemployment, textile workers might better have struck for job-control and job-security issues. But as Table 8-6 shows, the bulk of the textile strikes occurred in May, before the summer closings. The dismal economic po-

TABLE 8-6. *Strikers by Month and Industry*

Industry	March	April	May	June	July	August	September	October
Printing	0	613	257	526	469	20	0	19
	(0)	(5.8)	(2.4)	(5.0)	(4.4)	(0.2)	(0)	(0.2)
Cinema	0	40	0	0	0	0	0	0
	(0)	(24.1)	(0)	(0)	(0)	(0)	(0)	(0)
Services	0	0	30,975	18,500	0	0	0	4,000
	(0)	(0)	(28.2)	(16.9)	(0)	(0)	(0)	(3.6)
Textile	180	318	10,315	4,600	2,545	2,365	3,427	700
	(0.3)	(0.5)	(17.3)	(7.7)	(4.3)	(4.0)	(5.7)	(1.2)
Animal byproducts	0	0	0	48	0	0	0	0
	(0)	(0)	(0)	(3.1)	(0)	(0)	(0)	(0)
Clothing	700	42	0	30,060	0	260	369	0
	(2.2)	(0.1)	(0)	(93.4)	(0)	(0.8)	(1.1)	(0)
Rare metals	0	174	678	920	1,055	450	0	0
	(0)	(14.2)	(55.3)	(75.1)	(86.1)	(36.7)	(0)	(0)
Metal	3,042	2,447	1,652	7,727	60,962	855	4,741	40
	(6.5)	(5.2)	(3.5)	(16.6)	(130.6)	(1.8)	(10.2)	(0.1)
Food	48	248	100	490	5,100	9,600	0	0
	(0.2)	(1.2)	(0.5)	(2.5)	(25.5)	(48.1)	(0)	(0)
Construction	0	300	800	0	0	10,400	0	0
	(0)	(1.7)	(4.6)	(0)	(0)	(59.6)	(0)	(0)
Chemical	0	0	423	1,020	967	1,310	0	0
	(0)	(0)	(3.9)	(9.3)	(8.8)	(12.0)	(0)	(0)
Leather	1,238	2,163	4,363	565	953	23,919	22,989	23,589
	(5.6)	(9.8)	(19.8)	(2.6)	(4.3)	(108.3)	(104.1)	(106.8)
Mineral	0	0	387	35	35	0	996	0
	(0)	(0)	(23.5)	(2.1)	(2.1)	(0)	(60.5)	(0)
Paper	0	41	441	450	50	0	2,000	2,000
	(0)	(1.2)	(13.3)	(17.1)	(1.5)	(0)	(60.4)	(60.4)
Wood	240	0	2,505	246	200	0	1,248	2,572
	(7.2)	(0)	(75.7)	(7.4)	(6.0)	(0)	(37.7)	(77.7)

NOTE: Numbers in parentheses indicate the percentage of the industry's work force on strike in the given month.

sition of the industry in general is reflected in the textile workers' overall low strike propensity.

At the other end of the scale, it was the builders, leather workers, and woodworkers who had the lowest percentage of economic strikers. Again this corresponds to the rhythm of strikes over time. Most of these workers' strike activities occurred in August, September, and October, when the problems of inflation and scarcity were so acute that purely wage demands could not help the workers' position. The builders and leather workers in August, and the woodworkers in September, all launched well-organized industrywide strikes, with job control as a major issue.

Subsumed in this relationship between timing and strike demands is an organizational factor. The dynamics of organization will be examined more fully below, but the above examples suggest that industries that organized late, such as the builders, could not mobilize to strike until the deteriorating economic situation made a wage strike impractical.

Finally, in addition to timing and organization, there also appears a relationship between the economic position of an industry and its economic strikes. Comparing the percentage of an industry's economic strikers with its change in real wage from 1913 to 1916 reveals that the greater the improvement, the less an industry struck for economic reasons. Conversely, those industries that had fared worst during the war struck most for economic goals in 1917. The construction workers, whose 1916 real wage had exceeded 1913's by 36 percent, struck less than half the time for economic improvements. Printers' real wages, on the other hand, dropped by almost 20 percent during this period, and 80 percent of their strikers made economic demands.[28]

Nonetheless, those industries with the highest 1916 nominal wages also tended to strike most for economic goals in 1917. The metalists and the gas workers received the highest wages of any industry, and yet 80 percent and 100 percent, respectively, of these workers demanded further wage improvement.[29] Timing here provides a clue. These were the industries that struck early because their relative affluence gave them sufficient resources; early strikes tended to be economic strikes. By the time less prosperous industries organized themselves to strike, the futility of wage demands had become apparent.

Now it is appropriate to examine the question of timing and tactics more closely. So far, this study has looked at strikes by industry, by types of demands, and over time. But it has yet to examine the internal character of the strike process, and the difference between a well-coordinated in-

---

[28] The correlation coefficient between change in real wage and economic strikes is −.644, very good for this sample. (Data are presented in Appendix K.)

[29] The correlation coefficient between nominal wage and economic strikes is somewhat weaker than in the previous correlation, +.33. (Data are given in Appendix K.)

dustrywide strike and a small unsanctioned walkout of one disgruntled shop section suggests basic differences in the organization and perceptions of the groups involved.

The strike itself took on a wide variety of forms. A strike has earlier been defined as a work stoppage with common goals; thus a strike might include one factory, even one section within a factory, several hundred factories, or, as also happened, any number of privately employed workers, especially in the service sector. Industrywide strikes required some form of coordination, usually through the trade union; but at the local factory level, there were several routes to strike action. Unsanctioned wildcat strikes seemed infrequent, although it is difficult to determine just how much so. Most unions labored to prevent premature, isolated strikes; but if these were called anyway by local workers, the unions tended to sanction them in order not to reveal their lack of authority among workers. Therefore most reported strikes appear to have had union blessings. Another infrequently reported local form was the so-called "Italian strike," or sit-down,[30] which was sometimes prompted by the employers' giving notice that he was laying off all hands in order to hire a new batch of hungrier workers.[31] Most commonly, however, workers would meet among themselves and submit their demands through the factory committee; then after waiting for an answer, they would walk off the job, declaring the place to be under boycott. There was never any mention that picket lines were formed to ward off strikebreakers, but sometimes the factory committee would appoint a guard of workers, or druzhina, to keep watch over the plant in order to prevent the owner from removing goods or raw materials.

Usually, the workers themselves would choose the moment to strike in order to maximize their opportunities for success, but strikes were frequently touched off by events outside their control: reduction of wages, layoffs, harassment or firing of worker representatives. Workers at the Serpinskii metal factory in Butyrki were negotiating for boiling water for tea to be supplied to all shifts when the owner fired the members of the factory committee. At this point, the workers called a strike, demanding water, the firing of a shop foreman, and a guarantee that factory committee representatives would not be fired.[32] Provocation by owners was some-

---

[30] The term is confusing, for an *italianskaia zabastovka* used about employers signified a lockout; the employer was described as the striker.

[31] This occurred at the Men'shikov machine-building factory in March (*Sots.-Dem.*, 25 March 1917).

[32] *Vpered*, 15 April 1917; such were also the causes of strikes at Merkurii shoe factory and Kellert Brothers' auto works (*Vpered*, 18 March 1917; *Sots.-Dem.*, 10 June 1917), and at Borisov-Beliaev leather factory and Rus shoe factory (*Izv. MSRD*, 12 April 1917; *Gazeta-kopeika*, 25 March 1917); harassment touched off strikes at Men'shikov's metal plant, the Grachev ribbon manufacture, and the Chizbro perfume factory (*Sots.-Dem.*, 25 March 1917; *Izv. MSRD*, 2 May, 10 June 1917).

times charged and was probably true often enough. An owner wishing to close an unprofitable business without arousing the ire of the government and the Soviet might find a strike to be a convenient excuse.[33]

The duration of a strike, too, depended on a number of factors, most of them also outside the workers' control. In some cases, an employer would be ready to settle, but his fellow industrialists would prevent him.[34] The October woodworkers' strike was cut short by the October revolution; with the change in power, the union voted, there was no further need to strike.[35] Thus the available figures on length of strikes (which figures exist in any case for only 39 percent of the sample) are not particularly informative.[36]

Once on strike, what were the chances of success for the workers? The result of a strike, like its duration, depended on many of the same exogenous factors, and historians' knowledge is further limited by the infrequency with which strikes' outcomes were reported.[37] Few strikes, in any case, were won outright; most were settled by compromise or with an agreement to abide by the decision of an arbitration board or other

[33] The plausibility of this hypothesis, if not its proof, is marvelously illustrated in the Satyajit Ray film released in the United States as *Company Limited* (1974). In the film the protagonist, a rising young executive, discovers that a large order is defective and cannot be delivered on time, so he arranges to provoke a strike, which will extricate his company from its contract obligations. Volobuev, *Ekonomicheskaia politika*, p. 281, presents data to indicate that the stock prices of closed firms in 1917 were higher than those for firms still operating.

[34] This was the case at the Mikhailov pouch factory in May (*Sots.-Dem.*, 25 May 1917).

[35] *Trud*, 10 November 1917.

[36] According to the sample used here, the median length of strike was sixteen days or just over two weeks. But since it can be reasonably assumed that strike reporting was biased against shorter strikes, this figure is probably exaggerated. A more complete sample from the tailors' union for February 28 to May 11 shows that 69 percent of its strikes lasted one week or less (*Moskovskii sovet professional'nykh soiuzov*, p. 28).

[37] Studies of long-term strike movements have found a relationship between the duration of strikes and their outcome: the average length of strikes was shorter in periods when success rates were high (Iakovleva, p. 33) because success usually occurred when the plant was making high profits; then the management settled quickly in order not to jeopardize its earnings. Given the weakness of Moscow information on duration, can one assume that such a relationship existed in 1917? Although the average length of strikes won outright or partially is 21.6 days, and the average length of those lost is 26.5 days (see table below), the variance within each group is so large that the difference is not significant.

Outcome	Number of Strikes	Average Length in Days
Win	28	17.5
Compromise	28	25.8
Lose	5	14.0
Plant closes	7	35.4
Win or compromise	56	21.6
Lose or close	12	26.5

outside mediator. In the Moscow sample, for which outcome is known for only one-third of all strikes, most were reported to be successful, regardless of the type of demands. But the statement "And we won all our demands" may well have included some negotiated adjustments; these would become new demands, which could then be won. Few strikes were reported lost (and strikes that ended in the closing of the plant are considered to have been lost), but again there was a bias in the reporting. Workers tended to report only their successes to the newspapers; even those who reported defeat tried to disguise it somehow. On August 17, the union of tobacco workers voted to end its members' three-week-old strike on the grounds that the industry's products were needed for defense; and the union asked the employers, also in the name of defense, not to exploit their workers in the meantime.[38] In fact, the workers had lost; the directors of the union admitted they were forced to end the strike because of low morale. The workers were beginning to return to work anyway, and the union had to go along or suffer a loss of authority among its membership.[39]

According to strike reports, all industries won (or compromised on) more strikes than they lost; although only the paper workers won more than half of all their strikes, including those with outcome unknown. The tailors fared worst of all, winning or compromising on five strikes, losing four. If better information were available on outcome, one might expect a relationship between outcome and the degree of organization—poorly organized strikes would be less likely to succeed. Certainly the clothing industry was one of the most decentralized and thus more difficult to organize.

Toward the end of October, reflecting the increasing class-based bitterness throughout society, a new kind of strike "settlement" appeared: the seizure of the factory by striking workers. At Iurasov's furniture factory, management and workers threatened each other with arrest: the employer charged that workers had illegally seized property while the workers in turn accused the management of violating labor laws. Workers at the Rus shoe factory arrested their factory manager and locked him in his office; at Dinamo, aroused workers shot at (but missed) their plant manager.[40] In mid-October, some of the leather workers and woodworkers, who had been striking for over a month, would wait no longer for a settlement. The leather union voted October 19 for the Soviet to seize all factories that had not yet settled. That same day, the strike committee at the large defense plant of M. Dement occupied all entrances to the

[38] *Vpered*, 23 August 1917; *Russkoe slovo*, 23 August 1917; *Izv. MSRD*, 23 August 1917.

[39] *Moskovskie pishcheviki*, p. 81.

[40] *Russkie vedomosti*, 21 October 1917; *Utro Rossii*, 22 October 1917; *Dinamo: 25 let*, p. 86.

plant and forcibly seized the keys and books from the director. The factory management appealed to the Provisional Government for help, but one week later that government had fallen, and the plant remained under the workers' control.[41] Workers at the wood factory Ganzen, who had occupied their factory pending the outcome of their industrywide strike, finally began to operate the plant under their own supervision on November 1.[42]

Underlying these episodes, whose reports are too scattered to permit more systematic analysis, is the issue of organization. If strikes were largely individual ad hoc affairs, as indicated by the variety of tactics and experiences above, they were too widespread a phenomenon to be ignored by the leaders of the working class. The strike movement as a whole provided observers with an indicator of the degree of workers' economic discontent, and for participants, strikes helped to educate, to teach the importance of organization and planning. But the strike movement also illustrated to labor leaders the basic tension between localism and central organization which was considered generally in Chapter Four. Drawing on the strike experience of the Moscow working class, this study will examine this issue now in more detail.

THE ROLE OF ORGANIZATION

In 1917 as before, the strike phenomenon offered the labor movement a valuable tool to use in interpreting and mobilizing the attitudes of Moscow workers, and the strike therefore provided special opportunities for labor leaders. By harnessing the workers' deep economic frustration with the institutions of organized labor, these leaders could exert powerful pressure on the centers of power in Russia. Trade union and soviet activists therefore hastened to utilize these local conflicts over local issues to achieve more fundamental gains for workers; clearly this utilization necessitated better and stronger organization.

But as seen in Chapter Four, progress toward organization, toward class solidarity, was not inexorable, and at times it must have seemed to workers and organizers alike that their goals were not in harmony. The strike movement surely indicated to more seasoned political organizers the great gulf between the workers' perceptions of their goals (and how to achieve them), and the professional activists' vision of a well-organized labor movement. If workers' memoirs can be trusted (and on this point I think they can), most strikes were spontaneous, and workers resisted subordination to institutional controls.

Time and again, one reads of workers defying their factory committee

[41] "Zabastovka rabochikh-kozhevnikov Moskvy v avguste-oktiabre 1917 g.," p. 80; *Russkie vedomosti*, 21 October 1917; *Russkoe slovo*, 21 October 1917; *Sots.-Dem.*, 27 October 1917.
[42] *Russkie vedomosti*, 21 October 1917; GAMO, f. 66, op. 13, d. 3, ll. 2-3.

or union by striking without permission. The workers in the mechanical shop at the Postavshchik plant were the first to strike after February, demanding higher pay, but the Menshevik-led factory committee refused to support them. Against the counsel of the factory committee a mass meeting in the workshop convinced the plant administration to grant the mechanics' demands.[43] Later in the year, a metal union organizer summarized his views of such experiences.

> Having worked only several days in our union's conflict commission, I had to confront the grievous fact of the lack of discipline of our comrades. Representatives of individual factories, coming with complaints about entrepreneurs, reported that they had already presented ultimatums with the threat of a strike. Such a phenomenon is utterly abnormal and undesirable—it serves as an indicator of our lack of organization.[44]

Trade union leaders felt that they could best represent their constituents, with respect to strikes, by maximizing the chances of success while minimizing the cost. That meant formulating realistic demands that could be won, backed with both the threat of an effective labor stoppage and adequate strike funds to discourage strikebreaking.[45] But for most unions this was a long-term goal. In the interim, union leaders had to stabilize what appeared to them to be the chaotic development of local strikes. The unions' first concerns were to establish channels for the assuaging of conflict in order to gain the time to gather resources and to organize workers for a unified push for a slate of demands with which to confront the already-organized employers' groups. Continual local strike activity disrupted this process, drew union officials (of which there were few enough as it was) away from organizational activity in order to settle immediate disputes, drained existing strike funds, and diminished the wage base for further collections. There was also the ever-present danger of owners provoking strikes to justify plant shutdowns. These factors provided ample reason for the unions to try to prevent premature strikes. To serve their members, unions developed bureaucratic instruments to deal with conflicts and worried instead about permanent organizations, union dues, office space, and journals.

For workers, however, the unions' suggestion to forego immediate demands in favor of greater gains in some indefinite future required something of a leap of faith. Workers could quickly lose confidence in the

[43] *Na barrikadakh za vlast' sovetov*, p. 90. A similar incident occurred at the Military Artillery plant (Batyshev, p. 185).

[44] G. Mel'nichanskii, in *Moskovskii metallist*, no. 1, 12-25 August 1917.

[45] See P. A. Garvi's version of this "trade union calculus of strikes" in *Tret'ia vserossiiskaia konferentsiia professional'nykh soiuzov*, p. 269.

efficacy of a trade union organization when they were urged to live a little longer with existing abuses, or worse, when they won strikes the union cautioned them to avoid. A worker at the Gakental' arms plant boasted that his comrades had won strikes without the "interference" of the union; at the Postavshchik plant, workers in one shop bypassed even the local factory committee and won their demands by threatening the owner with violence.[46] Even as experienced as the printers were, their leaders had to exhort them to refrain from separate strikes.[47] The textile union distributed an appeal to workers to refrain from individual acts (*vystuplenie*) and threats against administrative personnel; such outbursts not only took up the valuable time of union representatives who were forced to mediate but also diminished the authority of the union in the eyes of the owners, making further negotiations more difficult.[48] And if individual factories bowed to the leadership and waited for a negotiated settlement, mass unrest exerted a steadily increasing pressure on union bargainers. After two months of talks, the tailors' union reported it could "no longer restrain" its members and announced a strike of thirty thousand military-uniform makers for two days hence.[49] The moral authority of the woodworkers' union could not stop a growing number of wildcat strikes in September and October, and the union was forced to call an industrywide strike in order to take "orderly control" of the movement.[50]

In the face of this tension, union leaders sought ways to control the spontaneous strike energy of their members and at the same time to strengthen their own authority. For the leadership, the logical alternative to scattered individual strikes was to combine industrywide negotiations with an accompanying strike threat, but this could not work without adequate preparation. The metalworkers' union illustrates one successful effort. Having achieved by negotiation a minimum pay level for its unskilled laborers, the union proceeded to negotiate an industrywide wage schedule or tariff. During May and June, union representatives investigated conditions in the factories and prepared demands; in mid-June, talks with industry representatives began. The metalists demanded only wage increases (which accounts for their high proportion of economic strikes) and sent the matter to a labor court for arbitration. Progress was slow and a strike was called for June 26, but a delegates' meeting decided to give the court another try. The pressure from below continued to build, however, and another delegates' meeting on July 3, after hearing reports

[46] *Ot fevralia k oktiabriu (v Moskve)*, p. 176; *Oktiabr' v Zamoskvorech'e*, p. 91.

[47] *Vpered*, 19 May 1917; *Sots.-Dem.*, 4 July 1917.

[48] GAMO, f. 627, op. 2, d. 14, l. 12, hectographed notice from the textilists' central board of directors.

[49] *Izv. MSRD*, 2 July 1917.

[50] *Trud*, 21 September, 7 October 1917; *Izv. MSRD*, 7 October 1917.

of local unrest, voted to begin the strike at 8:30 a.m. on July 6. All plants (50,000 workers) pledged to participate. The strike began that Thursday morning as scheduled, with public meetings at the Vvedenskii People's House in the heart of the Lefortovo factory district and elsewhere, but it ended before the day was out. The labor court had agreed to expedite the negotiations, and the union in turn agreed to await its decision. A week later, the union had won its wage demands, the industrialists were appeased with a productivity guarantee, and the conflict was over.[51]

Between March 1 and October 25, twenty-nine other industries carried out large-scale strikes. None was so immediately successful as the metalists', but one strike stood out as the model of planning and organization: this was the leather workers' strike that began on August 16. The dynamics of this strike tell students of the revolution much about the interplay between workers and their leaders, about the evolution of tactics, and about the intersection of strikes with the broader political issues of the revolution.

Preparation for a new industrywide labor agreement had formally begun at a joint conference of Moscow and Petrograd regional leather workers on June 5 and 6, held in Petrograd. The Moscow union representatives returned with a two-part set of demands. The chief point was a carefully specified wage scale ranging from 5.50 to 13 rubles a day (average daily pay was then about 2.50).[52] The second part consisted of a series of general demands: eight-hour workday, ten-minute grace period for tardiness, hiring and firing with the agreement of the trade union via the factory committee, and hiring of youths under sixteen years only in special circumstances. Further, the proposal specified an annual two-week paid vacation for all workers with at least three months' tenure, pay for factory committee members for time spent on committee work, and provision of clothing for workers in wet sections of production.[53] These demands were endorsed at a meeting of Moscow delegates and factory committee members on June 17,[54] and negotiations with the leather-industry owners' association began June 27.

According to the union secretary's history of the strike, the industrialists countered with their own slightly lower wage proposals but refused to grant any of the other demands except for the ten-minute grace period. The reply was couched in terms of defense: the Fatherland (literally *Otchestvo*) was in danger, and vacations were unjust while soldiers spent twenty-four hours a day in trenches.[55] To accent their counterproposal,

---

[51] *Sots.-Dem.*, 23 June 1917; *Vpered*, 5 July 1917; *Trudovaia kopeika*, 7 July 1917; *Izv. MSRD*, 12 July 1917.

[52] I. S. Iuzefovich, *Iz klassovykh boev 1917 g.*, p. 4.

[53] *Vpered*, 25 June 1917.   [54] *Sots.-Dem.*, 24 June 1917.

[55] Iuzefovich, pp. 56-57, 61.

the factory owners began to talk about closing down production because of shortages of needed materials.[56] Three days later on June 30, the union leaders presented a delegates' meeting with a summary of the situation. The mood in the factories, replied the delegates, was militant; the leather workers' locals wanted to strike. The meeting concluded with a resolution to collect a strike fund (one day's pay, collectible July 6, plus 1 percent of future wages) and, in the meantime, to await the owners' next move.[57]

Shortly after that, the union leaders reported via the press that the owners promised a new answer by July 11, and union members were urged to await the outcome. Although the owners' reply is not recorded, it must have been given, for the union held another delegates' meeting on July 13. The mood was still militant (*bodroe nastroenie*) and the workers were ready to strike, but once again the representatives voted to try for a peaceful resolution. By a vote of 250 to 50, they agreed to give the arbitration board two weeks to reach a settlement, and only after that time to strike.[58] By July 15, the union had collected a strike fund of 19,440 rubles even though public appeals indicated that factories were responding slowly to the call for the fund.[59]

On the twenty-fourth of July, the delegates gathered once more. The owners had agreed to participate again in an arbitration chamber, but with a different composition. It was difficult to restrain the workers this time. Once again the leadership urged patience and self-control, but the rank and file was adamant; they could no longer go hungry, factory delegates claimed, while the owners were making huge profits. But no strike vote was taken, apparently, until a delegates' meeting on August 9. At this time, only thirteen delegates opposed the strike; the real issue was whether to strike immediately or to wait five more days. Supporters of delay won, but the vote was closer than before, 196 to 125.[60] At this meeting, a strike committee was chosen and began to act.

This committee was quite different in composition from the union's board of directors, or pravlenie, which had directed negotiations to this point. As far as can be determined, the strike committee was more politically active; its eleven members included five Moscow Soviet representatives, four veterans of pre-1917 trade unions, and one municipal duma candidate. The committee also appeared more politically radical: three committeemen had publicly accused the directors of incompetence earlier in the spring;[61] six were known to be members of the Bolshevik party (compared to three of nine pravlenie members). The strike com-

---

[56] *Sots.-Dem.*, 6 July 1917. [57] Ibid.; *Izv. MSRD*, 2 July 1917.
[58] *Trud*, 18 July 1917; *Sots.-Dem.*, 18 July 1917; *Izv. MSRD*, 16 July 1917.
[59] *Sots.-Dem.*, 21 July 1917; *Trud*, 21 July 1917; *Izv. MSRD*, 20 July 1917.
[60] Trukan, p. 204, citing material from the union's archive in TsGAOR.
[61] *Proletarii*, 2 May 1917; *Vpered*, 3 May 1917.

mittee's chairman, the lawyer G. I. Libin, was a moderate, a veteran of the Bund and the old union of boot makers; but the only holdover from the *pravlenie* was its lone Bolshevik, Novikov, who was additionally a Soviet deputy, factory committee member, and the one (unsuccessful) candidate for the city duma.[62]

The new committee immediately drafted and posted a long set of rules for the strike. It would begin at 11:00 a.m. on August 16; workers would leave their jobs without noise or incidents. The factory committees were to provide protection for the plant and goods inside. Above all, the committee established a very tight system of control over the strike: "Workers, on all questions concerning the strike, should immediately address the factory committee, which in its turn will contact the district strike committee, and this committee shall report to the Central Strike Committee." (There were six of these district strike committees corresponding to existing sections of the union.) With this apparatus, the central strike committee expected to keep in close touch with the masses. Factory meetings were to be held every other day, district committee meetings once a week, and all communications would be published in the working-class press.[63]

The strike began well. Meetings throughout the city explained the goals of the strike; contributions from all over Russia flowed into the strike fund. By late September, the union was able to spend 10,000 rubles a day in strike benefits:[64] each worker received 1.10 rubles a day (up to 3.30 for families). Workers whose factories had settled would return to work and donate 25 percent of their wages to the fund. By October 6 the union was able to pay out 1.70 a day to single workers.[65]

The leather workers' solidarity worried the government, if not the industrialists. Three days after the strike began, Menshevik Minister of Labor Skobelev journeyed to Moscow to try to effect a compromise. He offered the union an immediate vacation, hiring and firing only by the administration but with safeguards against arbitrariness, and the rest to be negotiated. The workers agreed, and on orders of the strike committee, were all at their places, ready to work, on August 21. But at eleven o'clock the word came—the owners would not accept the compromise—and the strike continued.[66]

It continued for nine more weeks. Employers in the forage-cap branch of the industry capitulated early, and by mid-September the number of

---

[62] The list of committee members comes from Iuzefovich; other information is from my file of data on individuals active in Moscow in 1917.

[63] "Zabastovka rabochikh-kozhevnikov," pp. 64-65.

[64] *Moskovskii sovet professional'nykh soiuzov*, p. 92.

[65] *Vpered*, 10 October 1917.

[66] *Golos kozhevnika*, no. 4-5, 1 December 1917.

strikers in the Moscow industrial region had been reduced from 110,000 to 80,000.[67] But by then both sides had hardened their positions; the chief point at issue became the question of who could hire and fire workers or, in other words, job security and control. And it was this point that other workers stressed in their support of the striking leather workers. Typical was the resolution of the workers at Dinamo: the leather workers were fighting for the rights of all workers, and their firmness was applauded. "Your cause is our cause," the Dinamovtsy concluded and sent their comrades five thousand rubles.[68] In the same spirit came contributions from all over Moscow, from factories, trade unions, and district soviets.[69]

But the industrialists seemed in no hurry to resume production. Strike Committee Chairman Libin assessed the situation at a meeting of the Central Bureau of Trade Unions on September 25; the small owners (such as the cap makers) were prepared for concessions, he reported, but not the big ones because every day of the work stoppage increased the value of the goods in their warehouses.[70]

By mid-October, with threatened strikes in several other large industries, the union of leather workers faced new internal problems. Although a delegates' meeting had endorsed the strike committee's tactics on October 6, a radical faction demanded a general strike of all Moscow workers plus sequestration of plants not yet settled. Other "anarchically minded" members demanded terror and the arrest of owners.[71] A delegation sent to Petrograd produced a fragile agreement with the aid of the ministers of trade and labor, but the accord collapsed over the wording of the hiring-and-firing provision.[72] On the sixteenth of October, the delegates instructed the strike committee to ask the Moscow Soviet to prepare for the sequestration of struck plants.[73] The next day, the seventeenth, a group of shoe-factory owners agreed to a settlement;[74] on the nineteenth, against the counsel of the strike committee, the delegates voted for immediate sequestration by the city soviet (which did not accept this mandate).[75] At the Dement factory, the local strike committee forcibly seized control of the plant, and similar action was taken at the Rus factory.[76]

---

[67] These are figures given by the sources, but they include plants all over the Moscow region. By my estimate, there were 22,089 leather workers in Moscow, and this number has been used in calculating the number of leather-industry strikers used in this chapter.

[68] *Izv. MSRD*, 5 October 1917.

[69] *Golos kozhevnika*, no. 2-3, 7 October 1917, gives a partial list of contributors. See Chapter Seven for a discussion of these contributions in another context.

[70] *Moskovskii sovet professional'nykh soiuzov*, p. 88.   [71] Iuzefovich, p. 88.

[72] *Sots.-Dem.*, 17 October 1917.   [73] *Vpered*, 18 October 1917.

[74] Ibid., 19 October 1917.   [75] *Sots.-Dem.*, 21 October 1917.

[76] See above. Excesses such as these were publicly denied by the union (*Sots.-Dem.*, 24 October 1917), but the take-over was reported to police as well as in the bourgeois press (see "Zabastovka rabochikh-kozhevnikov," p. 80).

Three days later, amidst rumors of general strike, counterrevolution, and armed insurrection, the leather workers' strike ended. Workers would receive 50 percent of their wages for the time on strike, and all other issues would be resolved by a new arbitration panel, except for the right of hiring and firing. "The right to fire workers belongs exclusively to the administration of the enterprise."[77] But there followed guidelines and grievance procedures, which somewhat limited this right. The settlement was virtually the same as the agreement offered by Skobelev in August, and on that basis, the union claimed victory.[78]

How is this "victory" to be interpreted? It was not the union's solidarity that finally secured a settlement so much as the possibility that this labor dispute would be replaced by a political situation much more damaging to the capitalists' interests than curbs on firing procedures. As will be seen in the final chapter, all of Moscow expected some kind of imminent resolution of the growing political tension. In view of the rumored Bolshevik rising, perhaps leather-factory owners settled the strike as an inducement to their workers not to support such a radical political move.

The leather workers' case exemplifies the complexity of the strike phenomenon. Labor, management, and government all had the power to affect the outcome of these disputes, but no single party had complete control over the course of events. The leather workers' strike was a model of organization, but the union could not win its demands without the exogenous threat of the Bolshevik insurrection. Why had the metalists, whose strike was no better organized, won their demands so quickly in July? Part of the reason was the timing—the economy was healthier in July than in August and September. The metal industry itself was healthier than the leather industry. The lure of profits through production could not have been great enough to convince leather manufacturers to compromise on their rights as employers, especially when they could make money through inflation just by holding onto their leather goods. Finally, the chief issue in the leather workers' strike was not money, as with the metalists, but the rights of factory owners; and in the era of inflation and the hardened atmosphere of mutual distrust that characterized the autumn of 1917, such rights were much dearer to owners than a few paltry rubles added to workers' pay packets.

The leather strike symbolized the shift, apparent in all facets of revolutionary life, away from seeking economic solutions to a demand for political answers. The leather workers' strike was the best they could do, given the situation. They were equipped with solidarity, money, and leadership, but they were hampered by factors outside their control; and in the traditional arena of labor-management conflict—the strike—they

---

[77] "Zabastovka rabochikh-kozhevnikov," p. 81.

[78] *Golos kozhevnika*, no. 4-5, 1 December 1917.

could not defeat the owners. Through the medium of this long and bitter strike, the leather workers (and other workers who paid attention) began to realize that in the current situation, strikes had outlived their usefulness. Political solutions were called for, and by sanctioning a soviet sequestration of plants on October 19, this very visible segment of the working class was in effect voting for soviet power a full week before the Military Revolutionary Committee embarked on the same course. The leather workers' strike was an important milestone on the road from traditional class conflict fought in the context of "bourgeois" society to out and out class war, in which victory would mean the elimination of that society.

The strike of Moscow leather workers also illustrates the evolution of relationships within the working class. This strike suggests very strongly that rank-and-file workers exerted a continual pressure on the leadership for action. Union leaders saw the early strike movement as spontaneous and ineffectual and managed by midsummer to enforce "union discipline."[79] But their tactics of patience yielded no results, and members of the pravlenie were replaced by their critics, who responded to mass pressure by calling the general strike. Again, in two months pressure from below forced the new tactic of sequestration, against the strike committee's advice. Throughout, the mass response was characterized as "spontaneous" and "undisciplined," but by October it was at any rate a more articulate spontaneity, and it was this growing articulation that forced the leadership to respond. The lesson for political leaders was clear: if workers learned to demand accountability from their strike leaders, they could learn to demand the same from their political representatives as well.[80]

In this discussion of strike organization and tactics, the influence of party politics on the strike movement has been neglected. This neglect is largely due to the fact that partisan politics had a far smaller impact on the course of individual strikes than the strike movement as a whole had on the development of party policies. For example, the leaders in the leather workers' strike did not claim to speak for particular parties (the party affiliations of individual leaders could be determined only with

[79] An achievement reported in ibid., no. 1, 1-15 August 1917.

[80] It is as possible, perhaps, to exaggerate the spread of political awareness among the leather workers as among other groups. The active segment of the Moscow working class may have been growing smaller as it grew more militant, so perhaps the absolute number of militant workers was not increasing. To be sure, many leather workers left the city after August 29, as the strike committee no doubt permitted in order to save on strike benefits ("Zabastovka rabochikh-kozhevnikov," p. 69). Perhaps the constituents of those delegates who voted for sequestration on October 19 were different from those who had endorsed the union's policies before September 1, but the moderates everywhere in Russian political life were fast disappearing.

difficulty), and party rhetoric played no role in strike reporting.[81] Soviet historians have lately ascribed an important leadership role to the Bolshevik party for the entire period of the strike movement in 1917,[82] but the research done here shows little evidence of party participation in strikes as a calculated policy.

The strike movement in general, however, could not be ignored by party leaders of any political persuasion. It is hardly coincidental that the rash of resolutions on the economic crisis began during May, the month of the greatest number of strikes. Both strikes and resolutions were responses to deteriorating economic conditions. Significantly, the response of both Mensheviks and Bolsheviks to the growing crisis was not to acclaim workers' willingness to stand up to capital, but rather to argue that the solution to the crisis was not strikes, but centralized economic planning.

The Menshevik newspaper, *Vpered*, was explicit on the inefficacy of strikes: even if workers won wage demands, the high costs of production were ultimately passed on to the workers as consumers. And wage gains would soon be wiped out by the resulting inflation. "Is there a way out?" editorialized the paper on May 25. "There can be only one way out, and that is government involvement in industrial life and resolute measures in the area of fiscal policy." The ultimate result of the kinds of excessive demands that led to strikes was the disruption of production, which was harmful to the workers as well as to the country. Menshevik Labor Minister Skobelev told workers on June 28, "At the present time, spontaneous actions are taking precedence over organization. . . . You sometimes win such high wages that industry is disrupted and the treasury [to whom industrialists turned for more subsidies] is exhausted."[83]

Bolshevik leaders were also wary of excessive strikes, but for different reasons: they feared that industrialists would use the strike movement as an excuse to stop production entirely. Then workers' demands would be for nought and the revolutionary situation would dissipate, leaving the bourgeoisie in firm control of society. In their May resolution on the economic crisis, Bolsheviks had not explicitly discouraged strikes but emphasized that the only solution to the crisis was central planning carried out by a working-class government, a government of soviets. Throughout

---

[81] A large number of strikes were identically reported in all the major socialist newspapers. Overall, *Izvestiia MSRD*, the nonparty Soviet organ, carried the largest number of individual strike reports. The Bolshevik *Sotsial-Demokrat*, which had reported the most resolutions, was second.

[82] See, for example, B. M. Freidlin, *Ocherki istorii rabochego dvizheniia v Rossii v 1917 g.*, p. 204; and A. M. Lisetskii: "Under the direction of the Bolsheviks, every strike was transformed into a genuinely political action [vystuplenie]" ("Predvaritel'nye itogi geograficheskogo i otraslevogo raspredeleniia stachek v Rossii, ikh dlitel'nosti i rezul'tatochnosti," p. 375).

[83] Quoted in Ruban, p. 169.

the summer, there were many instances of Bolshevik attempts to hold back potential strikes.[84] In late July, the party's Sixth Congress adopted a resolution that urged workers not to be provoked into strikes: "The proletariat should not succumb to the provocations of the bourgeoisie, who very much desire at the present time to incite workers to a premature fight."[85]

The Bolshevik fear of a premature struggle continued to dominate the party's policy on strikes in October. The party endorsed the leather workers' strike because it was politically inexpedient to do otherwise, but Moscow party leaders feared that a spread of the strike movement would lead to a premature general strike, which they would not be able to control. Such a strike would certainly jeopardize the chances for success of the armed insurrection then being planned. The secretary of the textile union, a longtime Bolshevik, reported his views to the Moscow Soviet executive committee:

> To stop the workers' movement will be impossible, because their patience and organization have limits. When hunger is at your very throat, then no kind of organization, no kind of discipline can restrain the workers, and we understand that in the present critical time, such an action can threaten fearful consequences.[86]

The strike movement was only one aspect of a wide spectrum of working-class activity in Moscow, but its development illustrates how closely related were all aspects of working-class life. Economics, politics, and social conflict all influenced one another in the turmoil of 1917, and the strike process exemplified this relationship. Workers' strike opponents emerged as political opponents, strike leaders were also political leaders, and strikes that began as reactions to economic dislocation became contributors to further dislocation, fueling the spiral of economic and political tension.

Workers who began in March by striking for wage increases had turned their energies by October to achieving more direct control over their lives in the factory, but control was now seen to be achieved best by political rather than economic means. Within this transformation, one can see the essential rationality of striking workers, already demonstrated by the substance and character of their strikes. What may have appeared to observers, from Bolsheviks to factory owners, as anarchy and "indiscipline"

---

[84] A. M. Lisetskii, "O nekotorykh osobennostiakh zabastovochnoi taktike bol'shevikov v period podgotovki velikoi oktiabr'skoi sotsialisticheskoi revoliutsii," p. 93; and Stepanov, pp. 77-93.

[85] *Shestoi s"ezd RSDRP (bol'shevikov)*, p. 255.

[86] A. M. Lisetskii, "Iz istorii stachechnoi bor'by proletariev Moskvy nakanune i v khode vooruzhennogo vosstaniia," p. 10.

was actually a logical response to the prevailing situation. Strikes for incremental gains no longer made sense by autumn; and as political tensions rose, the overall level of strikes declined, however well publicized were the few that occurred.

But this study of the strike process has also illustrated one of the major problems of the labor movement in 1917—its inexperience. Leaders who could effectively coordinate the demands of individuals with their own institutional interests and needs were simply in too short supply, and too often the lesson of a strike for its participants was the loss of faith in the institution that tried to lead it. Even in the leather workers' strike, despite the election of successively more responsive and militant leaders, workers in some individual factories flouted the authority of the strike committee and seized their plants on their own initiative. Their need to reach a solution overcame whatever faith in solidarity such workers had gained over the course of 1917. And so one sees once again the critical dilemma of October 1917: Moscow's workers may have collectively realized the need for decisive political measures, but their institutional framework had not really matured enough to lead them toward their goal. This dilemma was to shape the course of the actual seizure of power by the Moscow Soviet, as the final chapter will reveal.

NINE. *Moscow's October*

We are for those who know how to make life cheaper.

ZAMOSKVORECH'E VOTER IN NOVEMBER [1]

THE "OCTOBER DAYS"

THE month of October in Moscow offered little hope that the twin economic and political crises could be peacefully resolved. With winter closing in, shortages of food and fuel became even more threatening. Grain shipments continued to dwindle; the daily bread allowance was to fall to a meager half-funt (about eight ounces) again on October 24. The causes of such shortages were complex, but many workers felt that the government and its supporters deliberately sabotaged the economy in order to consolidate their own political and economic positions. This deep sense of suspicion and hostility underlay the development of the strike movement in October; it was further fueled by the shrill attacks of the liberal press on the Bolshevik-led soviets and by the sudden onset of an apparent currency shortage in mid-October; this latter meant that workers and employees could not receive their wages. [2]

Elsewhere in Russia newspapers reported ongoing confrontations between the bourgeoisie and the proletariat; the true complexity of class relations and the political situation was disguised by the now-habitual application of the categories and the rhetoric of class struggle. In Ivanovo-Voznesensk on October 21, "a worker-host is raising its fighting banner" against the "enemy—capital." This is how the local strike committee announced the start of a strike by 300,000 textile workers in the Ivanovo-Voznesensk region. [3] In the Donbass coal-producing area, continuing conflicts between workers and managers had nearly halted production altogether. At the end of September at the request of the mine owners the government had dispatched cossacks to the area to help preserve order. [4] On October 19, as noted above, cossacks routed the Soviets of Soldiers' and Workers' Deputies in Kaluga. The refusal of garrison units to obey their marching orders had been the primary reason for the punitive expedition of cossacks, but as in Moscow, mutual hostility between the

---

[1] *Russkie vedomosti*, 21 November 1917.   [2] Yarkovsky, p. 187.
[3] *Izv. MSRD*, 24 October 1917.
[4] Volobuev, *Proletariat i burzhuaziia*, pp. 256-260.

soviets and the local bourgeoisie had exaggerated the level of tension. Both the Bolshevik-dominated soldiers' soviet and the Menshevik-led workers' soviet fell victim to the cossacks' force, sowing the seeds of panic in the Moscow population. On October 21, the following terse communication from Tula appeared in *Izvestiia*:

> Kaluga is in the hands of Cossacks. The Soviets are dispersed, arrested; there have been casualties. We are defenseless. Punitive units are moving on Tula, Briansk, Novozybkov. Strength: one armored car, rapid-fire machine guns, and a regiment of dragoons.

The Bolsheviks' *Sotsial-Demokrat* screamed, "Today Kaluga, tomorrow Moscow!" On the same day, the front page of *Izvestiia* carried a report of the formation of a "black guard" organized and armed by the bourgeoisie.[5]

In Petrograd, the situation also appeared to be drawing to a confrontation between classes. Writing on October 18 in Maxim Gorky's paper *Novaia zhizn'*, the Bolshevik Kamenev openly dissented from the party's decision to stage an uprising; this was the first time that the rumored coup had received public confirmation.[6] Meanwhile, Kerensky had laid plans to send to the front the revolutionary units of the Petrograd garrison, and in response the Petrograd Soviet had authorized the formation of a committee to coordinate the city's defense against an anticipated counterrevolutionary assault. This Military Revolutionary Committee, composed primarily but not exclusively of Bolsheviks, began to function on October 20; its task was to assume control of the city's military forces, that is, to keep the Kerensky government powerless in its own capital. Alexander Rabinowitch has argued that the Bolshevik Central Committee, knowing that the Petrograd working population would support a soviet seizure of power only in self-defense, intended to provoke Kerensky into an attack on the Military Revolutionary Committee, the Bolsheviks, and the Soviet.[7] The Kerensky cabinet indeed responded to the challenge by ordering the arrest of Bolshevik leaders free on bail from imprisonment for their July-days activities, forcibly closing the Bolshevik party newspapers on October 24, and calling up loyal troops to report for duty at the Winter Palace. The Military Revolutionary Committee began to act— twenty-four hours later its representative Trotsky announced to the Petrograd Soviet that the Provisional Government had been overthrown.

Moscow, as elsewhere, had been expecting some sort of resolution to the crisis of power. Central authority was collapsing; banditry continued

---

[5] *Sots.-Dem.*, 22 October 1917; *Izv. MSRD*, 21 October 1917.

[6] Rabinowitch, *Bolsheviks Come to Power*, p. 222.

[7] Ibid., p. 224; see also Mandel, chap. 5.

to prevail in the suburbs; and in the central residential districts, home-owners were forming their own vigilante squads. The presence of thirty thousand garrison troops was no guarantee of order; on the contrary, the regional military commander had ordered the troops' weapons to be locked up to prevent their uncontrolled use.[8]

Everyone expected that the Second All-Russian Congress of Soviets would respond to the growing grass-roots demand for the soviets to take power. Already on October 15, textile union leader Rykunov tried to placate restive union delegates: "It may be that in the near future we will have to take power into our hands, and we cannot shirk from this, since it is a question of existence."[9] The Moscow Soviet on October 19 had asserted its authority over the economic sphere by "decreeing" an end to economic strikes. And as seen in Chapter Six, a wide spectrum of Moscow workers was now endorsing the demand for soviet power.

Nonetheless, the news from Petrograd was met with great trepidation both outside and inside the halls of the Moscow Soviet headquarters. A self-styled Plekhanovite socialist recalled the news that circulated throughout privileged Moscow on the day after the coup: "Before noon of that day, Moscow knew for a certainty that Petrograd was in the grasp of a reign of terror. A marauding mob was plundering the city, and killing anyone who opposed it."[10] The Moscow Soviet's chairman Viktor Nogin brought the first accurate report to the October 26 meeting of the Soviet executive committee. Nogin, a member of the Bolshevik Central Committee, had opposed the insurrection and now stressed the defensive nature of the seizure of power, lamenting that all socialist parties would not rally behind the presidium of the Congress of Soviets.

> Individual representatives of the Mensheviks and SRs told me that they would not separate from us in this responsible and difficult moment of the Russian Revolution. I was certain that during the October revolution, as happened in February, all socialists would be in one camp, that other parties would not break with us, would not betray us, leaving us alone to walk into the fire. I was certain that at the Congress of Soviets all parties would try to unite and find a common language.[11]

[8] Grunt, *Moskva 1917-i*, p. 295.

[9] *Revoliutsionnoe dvizhenie v Rossii nakanune oktiabr'skogo vooruzhennogo vosstaniia*, p. 298.

[10] Yarkovsky, p. 194. He and his friends soon learned the "true" nature of the soviet victory in Petrograd, which "was accomplished by the Bolsheviks with the help of illiterate blundering workers and ignorant soldiers who did not understand the real meaning of the slogans that they loudly repeated" (p. 199).

[11] *Sovety v oktiabre. Sbornik dokumentov*, p. 33.

But the Mensheviks and some SRs had demonstratively walked out of the congress, leaving moderate Bolsheviks like Nogin indeed alone to walk into the fire.

This isolation contributed to the embattled mentality of the leaders of Moscow's October. Convinced that the Bolshevik party alone could not rule, but that the seizure of power, once begun, must be played out to the end, Moscow Bolsheviks reluctantly made preparations to support the rising in the capital city. Their reluctance, the sense of betrayal by the old comrades with whom they had amicably quarreled through the summer, their exaggerated fear of the forces of the opposition all contributed to the indecision that prolonged the struggle for power in Moscow.

For ten days, starting on October 25, local power hung in the balance. The sequence of events of those days, elements of which are so exhaustively recalled by every contemporary memoirist, are not easily reconstructed. The parties of the class struggle soon lined up behind two "fighting centers." The Moscow Soviet elected its own Military Revolutionary Committee on October 25, primarily for defensive purposes, while the opponents of soviet power rallied behind a Committee of Public Safety, which drew its members from the city duma. Significantly, there were no representatives of the Provisional Government on the committee formed presumably to defend that government. Neither group appeared to want to take action; both claimed their purposes were defensive only. Indeed, the goal of both sides was to ensure the convocation of the Constituent Assembly, still seen by all parties as the ultimate arbiter of the fate of the revolution. The banner headline of the Bolsheviks' *Sotsial-Demokrat* announcing the soviet victory in Petrograd in fact proclaimed, "The Convocation of the Constituent Assembly Is Guaranteed: Power has been Transferred to the Soviets."[12]

Since neither side wished to begin offensive operations, military action began in Moscow only on October 27 after two days of unsuccessful negotiations between representatives of the Military Revolutionary Committee and the Committee of Public Safety. Street skirmishing between progovernment military cadets (*junkers*) and revolutionary soldiers began on the night of October 27 with an exchange of fire in Red Square. The Kremlin, at first in the hands of troops loyal to the Soviet, was surrendered (some said by deception) to the Committee of Public Safety. During the next two days, the military position of the Soviet side deteriorated, and defenders of soviet power feared imminent annihilation. On October 28, Nogin bravely set out from Soviet headquarters on Tverskaia street to the nearby duma building in order to negotiate. On the way he was arrested,

---

[12] *Sots.-Dem.*, 26 October 1917.

taken to the military barracks opposite the Kremlin, insulted, and threatened with bayonets before being released. His chauffeur later reported overhearing plans of these same troops to blow up the Kremlin.[13] In the Soviet headquarters that night, secretaries were busy destroying papers; the Military Revolutionary Committee prepared to go down fighting.[14] In the cramped one-room office of the Central Bureau of Trade Unions, union activists decided to issue a call for a general strike. They had no typewriter but would not have used it if they had for fear the sound of typing would reveal their presence to the armed students who had laid seige to the area.[15]

Also on the twenty-eighth, neutral elements led by the all-Russian railway union executive committee (Vikzhel) attempted to negotiate an end to the fighting. Both protagonists in Moscow agreed to a twenty-four-hour cease-fire; Vikzhel, members of the Menshevik and SR parties, the Orthodox church's Metropolitan of Moscow all tried to reach some compromise that would avert the feared civil war. Moderate socialists continued to insist on an interim government formed from all socialist parties—from the Popular Socialists to the Bolsheviks. (This position was not unacceptable to many Bolsheviks; Nogin, Zinov'ev, Kamenev, Rykov, and Miliutin even resigned from the Central Committee in part because party leaders refused to accept a broad-based coalition of socialists, albeit under the structure of the soviets.) But the Moscow Military Revolutionary Committee said it would only agree to a compromise in which the Committee of Public Safety acknowledged the fact of soviet power and of the decrees on land and peace voted by the Congress of Soviets after the seizure in Petrograd. By this time, it was clear that the preponderance of military force was on the side of the Military Revolutionary Committee, and there was less need for them to compromise. They rejected another attempt of Mensheviks and SRs to negotiate a cease-fire on November 1. Early on November 3, the Kremlin was retaken by soviet forces; at four o'clock that afternoon the last bastion of the Committee of Public Safety's strength, the Alexander military school in Lefortovo, also surrendered. Military victory in Moscow belonged to the soviets.[16]

Political victory was not so certain. Despite the decisions taken by the Congress of Soviets in Petrograd to enact the Bolshevik program of land, peace, and workers' control, the Bolshevik party assured fellow socialists that the Constituent Assembly would proceed as scheduled. The Moscow

---

[13] *Sovety v oktiabre*, p. 65.

[14] Ibid., p. 57; Grunt, *Moskva 1917-i*, pp. 285, 324.

[15] Marshev, p. 55.

[16] *Sovety v oktiabre*, pp. 31-86; S. Mel'gunov, *Kak bol'sheviki zakhvatili vlast'*, pp. 277-382; *Moskovskii voenno-revoliutsionnyi komitet; Triumfal'noe shestvie sovetskoi vlasti; Letopis' geroicheskikh dnei*; Grunt, *Moskva 1917-i*, chap. 6.

8. Damage from October fighting in central Moscow. Most of this damage and
that in the Kremlin was inflicted by long-range artillery shelling from the Sparrow
Hills.

Military Revolutionary Committee continued to function as the city political center until November 9, when the first plenary session of the
Moscow Soviet since October 25 was held.

The discussion at the session reflected the degree of confusion about
both the actual events of the Moscow fighting and the immediate consequences of soviet power as well. Each political party had been internally
sundered by the bloody events just ended. Moderate Bolsheviks such as
Nogin were countered by hard-line party members who shared the sense
of extreme class isolation and hostility that had been building within the
Moscow work force. Responding to Menshevik denunciations of Bolshevik
political terror at this meeting, V. A. Avanesov exclaimed to loud applause,

> We do not have a policy of terror, but we do have a policy of carrying
> out the will of the people, and this policy we will not disavow. If this
> policy means that we will have to send ten or twenty factory owners
> to prison, then so we will send them.[17]

[17] *Sovety v oktiabre*, p. 81.

Another voice from the assembly, replying to a Menshevik query about who gave the Military Revolutionary Committee the right to dissolve the democratically elected city duma, cried out, "We elected it, and we will chuck it out!"[18]

At the same session, the regular Menshevik organization quarreled with the internationalist Menshevik-Unityists about the legitimacy of the October revolution. Boris Kibrik repeated the Menshevik refrain that this was a bourgeois-democratic revolution; and even though the Bolsheviks had triumphed in the streets, this did not mean that the objective social and economic conditions were ripe for the demise of the capitalist system.[19] The United Social-Democrats, on the other hand, had actively worked within the Military Revolutionary Committee until the revolution seemed secure. They realized that victory by the forces of the Committee of Public Safety would have doomed not only the Bolsheviks, "whose tactics we do not endorse," but the whole proletariat as well; it would sound the death knell for the revolution.[20]

The same reasoning split the Socialist Revolutionary party. Right SRs rallied around the Committee of Public Safety, but the newly consolidated left wing of the party, opposing the idea of an insurrection, nonetheless joined the struggle once it began. A Left SR spokesman, the soldier Sablin, explained he participated in order to secure the future of the Russian republic. He fought not for the ideals of Lenin and Trotsky—"I fought, rather, like all my comrade Left SRs in the ranks of soldiers and Red Guards, for a single-structured socialist government."[21]

It is clear from the debate at this acrimonious session of the Moscow Soviet that the October fighting in Moscow and the subsequent political organization based on it were two separate phenomena that did not necessarily share common supporters. Most participants joined the fighting out of a conviction that the very revolution depended on it. Victory for the Committee of Public Safety meant a victory for Kaledin, Kornilov, and Kerensky and would certainly destroy any chance for a democratic government of soviets or anything else that the Constituent Assembly might create. What was to be done with the victory won in the streets was something else entirely, and many participants believed this question was for the Constituent Assembly to decide.

It is from this perspective that one must consider the activity of Moscow's workers in the October fighting. Moscow did not rise in order to seize power for the soviets, but to defend the soviets from the counterrevolution. Despite the crescendo of sentiment for soviet power among Moscow workers in the last weeks before October 25, there were few

---

[18] Ibid., p. 69.
[20] Ibid., p. 55.
[19] Ibid., p. 74.
[21] Ibid., p. 57.

9. Funeral procession for working-class casualties during the October fighting. The victims of the October days were buried ceremoniously next to the Kremlin wall.

among these workers who advocated or even expected that this power would be seized by force. Consequently, when the Military Revolutionary Committee began its operations under a veil of great confusion about the stakes involved, Moscow workers were not ready to mobilize. By and large, throughout the October days they stayed near their factories, watching and waiting.

THE WORKERS IN OCTOBER

The level of working-class participation is open to dispute, of course, and so is the significance of this participation. Did those workers who remained out of the fighting do so out of indifference to the soviet cause or because there was no need for mass participation given the nature of the contest? Unfortunately, the plethora of participants' memoirs devoted to these

10. Red Guards posing for camera in November 1917. Even before the October days began, clothing workers had been sewing special Red Guard uniforms for workers such as these.

crucial days almost all stress very personal, adventuristic aspects of the fighting; they provide little evidence of the level of activity of Moscow's workers from October 25 to November 3.[22] But one can still try to assess this activity using the evidence at hand.

First, there were the Red Guards, those workers commanded by the Military Revolutionary Committee who actively fought in the streets of Moscow, many of whom lost their lives. Throughout the summer, individual factories had organized armed or semiarmed units of young men, usually for the defense of their own factories. After the Kornilov mutiny, these units were augmented by fighting squads, formally Red Guards, organized under the aegis of factory committees, raion soviets, or Bolshevik party committees. Most were poorly armed; the dominant theme of Red Guard memoirs about October is not the use of weapons but rather

---

[22] The major sources of these memoirs are *Desiat' let*; *Dinamo: 25 let*; *God bor'by, Khamovniki v oktiabre 1917 g.*; *Krasnaia Presnia v 1905-1917 gg.*; *Moskva v oktiabre 1917 g.*; *Moskva v trekh revoliutsii*; *Na barrikadakh za vlast' sovetov*; *Oktiabr' na krasnoi Presne*, 1922; *Oktiabr' na krasnoi Presne*, 1927; *Oktiabr' v Khamovnikakh*; *Oktiabr' v Zamoskvorech'e*; *Moskovskie bol'sheviki v ogne revoliutsionnykh boev*; *Oktiabr'skie dni v Moskve i raionakh*; *Oktiabr'skie dni v Sokol'nicheskom raione*; *Ot fevralia k oktiabriu*; *Ot fevralia k oktiabriu (v Moskve)*; *Slovo starykh bol'shevikov*; *Staraia i novaia Danilovka*; *Velikaia oktiabr'skaia sotsialisticheskaia revoliutsiia (vospominaniia)*, vol. 1; *Za vlast' sovetov*; *Zheleznodorozhniki i revoliutsiia*.

the search for them. By October 25, when the Red Guard had become a formal adjunct of the Moscow Soviet, there were probably about 6,000 guards in the entire city.[23] They were predominantly young, for married workers were discouraged from joining.[24] Probably about half were Bolsheviks of mostly recent vintage; the non-Bolsheviks tended to be members of no party.[25] Of seventy-two factories known to have furnished Red Guard units, about half were metal and machine producers. (All of the units reported to have formed before July were from such plants.)[26]

The overwhelming impression offered by their memoirs is that these Red Guards were very young, undisciplined, and radical but not doctrinaire; for them the October revolution was the great adventure in their lives, as going to war in 1914 had been for a generation in Western Europe. Some older Bolsheviks recognized and feared this adventurism. The Sokol'niki party secretary refused to allow local youth-group members to join the Red Guard and remained seated on a box of rifles to emphasize her point. But the youths dislodged her from her seat and set off anyway to join the action.[27] Eduard Dune, sent to Moscow as part of the Tushino Red Guard, was amazed to find his co-worker Evel' in the thick of the fighting. Evel', who was currently scandalizing his mates by courting a nonproletarian office employee, had been rejected by the Tushino Red Guard because of his "hooliganism." Now, free of any chain of command, Evel' was fighting where he pleased—more "hooliganism," recalled Dune, not without a touch of envy.[28]

Most Red Guards did not participate in any action. Memoirs suggest the main activities of these combatants were searching for arms and patrolling factories and other vulnerable points in the outlying working-class districts. Closer to the action, women served mostly as messengers between raion and central headquarters and as nurses. Most of the fighting took place in the city center and in the adjacent neighborhoods of Zamoskvorech'e. This raion boasted the city's largest Red Guard contingent of perhaps 1,500, but the most important military units here were in fact soldiers from several reserve infantry regiments and from a detachment of about 850 veterans of the front only just released from imprisonment for revolutionary behavior. (These were the soldiers marching through Red Square to the aid of the Military Revolutionary Committee on October 27 who became the first targets of the Committee of Public Safety's military cadets.)

The military objectives of the Red Guard in Moscow (as in Petrograd)

---

[23] Tsypkin, *Krasnaia gvardiia*, p. 105.   [24] Dune, p. 47.

[25] Tsypkin, *Krasnaia gvardiia*, p. 107.

[26] These figures come from my factory file. Tsypkin does not analyze his sample of Red Guards by occupation or industry.

[27] *Desiat' let*, p. 85.   [28] Dune, pp. 52-53.

were first, the main centers of communication—bridges, newspaper offices, telegraph and telephone stations—and second, stores of arms. Since neither side fielded large military detachments, there were no seiges, pitched battles, or assaults on barricaded enclaves. Late in the fray, the Military Revolutionary Committee gained control of some artillery and used it to shell the Kremlin from the vantage point of the Sparrow Hills several miles away. At the same time, outlying units of Red Guards uncovered reserves of arms in the railway yards near Sokol'niki; these they provided to Red Guards now arriving from provincial towns and factory settlements to aid in the struggle. It is possible that by the end of the fighting, the Military Revolutionary Committee could count on up to 30,000 armed supporters,[29] but by then they were not really needed.

More difficult to uncover is the situation in the factory districts surrounding the center. With the heaviest concentration of the fighting directed at central focuses of local power, there was nothing really for the workers in the outskirts to do. Workers in the southernmost Danilovskii district feared those cossacks last reported on the march from Kaluga and set up barricades to prevent their entry into the city.[30] But most Red Guards mustered their units in their factory courtyards and waited for something to happen. On the critical October 28, the Military Revolutionary Committee finally called for a general strike to obstruct the forces of the Committee of Public Safety, but there had been little industrial activity in any case; traffic was hindered by the dangerous situation in the city center, and who could work when the sound of gunfire could be heard rattling through the old city? A bizarre sense of holiday prevailed. Some workers gathered at their plants in order to hear the latest political news; others arrived to drink with their fellows. A Red Guard courier recalled arriving wounded at a plant whose workers were drinking and playing cards. They laughed at first at her appeal for help; but when they saw she was bleeding, they volunteered to form a squad and fight the opposition.[31]

The prevailing climate of nonparticipation in the factory districts can be read two ways. There were those workers, like Eduard Dune's father, a Menshevik, who did not himself volunteer but who sympathized with the cause his son had gone to defend.[32] The card players and the defenders of Danilovka might also be included in this category, and there were surely many more. But the prevalent passivity was read another way by the Menshevik and SR press: in Zamoskvorech'e, reported the SRs' *Trud*, the Military Revolutionary Committee's cause was unpopular, and Bolshevik leaders could not rouse the workers to active participation. The

[29] Tsypkin, *Krasnaia gvardiia*, p. 106.
[30] *Na barrikadakh za vlast' sovetov*, p. 52.
[31] Karpova, p. 35.   [32] Dune, p. 47.

Mensheviks' *Vpered* (both of these parties were of course officially extremely hostile to the insurrection) charged that Bolsheviks had to threaten repressive measures in order to enlist Zamoskvorech'e workers in the fighting brigades.[33]

I believe that the passivity of most Moscow factory workers during October can indeed be seen as a commentary on their attitudes about soviet power and its forcible seizure. I have argued above that resolutions were easily passed when no more serious commitment was called for. Politically, the majority of the city's working population probably favored soviet power, but not so strongly that they were willing to risk civil war or to die for it. Those workers and soldiers who joined the fighting, like the SR Sablin above, did so out of a belief that they were now defending the very survival of the soviets as legal institutions. By the time this fact had filtered into the working-class districts, victory was nearly in hand, and potential defenders did not need to make a decision about going to the aid of the soviet.

There was, to be sure, as little willingness to die for the old order. The Committee of Public Safety was estimated to have only 6,000 or so troops at its disposal; A. Ia. Grunt cites archival call-up notices of garrison officers who were "not at home" when ordered to report.[34] After the soviet victory, local bank and municipal employees, and some teachers and hospital workers joined the growing backlash against soviet power and refused to work. The Bolsheviks called this sabotage, but again, one must separate attitudes toward the seizure of power and toward the subsequent exercise of that power.

The distinction between political support for soviet power and participation in the October fighting can perhaps best be made with the help of Table 9-1. The range of attitudes with respect both to armed combat and to the subsequent arrangement of power can be grouped under four separate positions. Both participants and nonparticipants in the street fighting could each support immediate soviet power or oppose soviet power at least before the Constituent Assembly. It seems clear from the wording of October soviet-power resolutions, from studies of working-class and Bolshevik activist attitudes in Petrograd, that many politically active workers fought for soviet power only as a defensive reaction to the perceived attack on the soviets by the Kerensky government.[35] I would guess, in fact, that most of the Red Guards in Moscow, especially the older, urbanized, experienced ones, fought primarily for defensive reasons. The SR Sablin, whose statement to the Moscow Soviet was quoted

[33] *Trud*, 28 October 1917; *Vpered*, 30 October 1917; *Izv. MSRD* reported on the other hand that Zamoskvorech'e workers were "quiet and ready" (27 October 1917).

[34] Grunt, *Moskva 1917-i*, p. 297.

[35] See above, Chapter Six; Rabinowitch, *Bolsheviks Come to Power*; Mandel, chap. 5.

TABLE 9-1. *A Model of Working-Class Participation in the October Days in Moscow*

	Workers Against Soviet Power Prior to the Constituent Assembly	Workers for Immediate Soviet Power
Combatants	Red Guards moderate Bolsheviks Left SRs United Social-Democrats urban workers	Red Guards Left Bolsheviks urban workers
Noncombatants	Mensheviks SRs printers (urban workers)	non-Red Guard resolution-passers moderate Bolsheviks (Nogin) rural migrants

above, is clearly one of these defensists, and so were the leaders of the United Social-Democratic faction, who realized that once fighting had begun, victory for the Committee of Public Safety would be "the worst possible outcome."[36]

Donat Cherepanov, a veteran SR now siding with the newly formed left SR wing, echoed this view. His faction opposed the soviet take-over before fighting began and hoped to end the bloodshed by compromise once it had started. But their "neutrality" had limits:

> When comrades phoned us from the raions and asked what they should do when the junkers attacked them, we said that raion soviets should defend themselves by all possible measures, and besides that, our [party] bureau specifically resolved that if the Committee of Public Safety raised the bony hand [!] of counterrevolution, then our neutral position would be immediately transformed into a fighting position.[37]

It is also clear, however, that other Red Guards shared the Left Bolshevik conviction that soviet power must and could be won by an armed insurrection. This was the culmination of the politics of class confrontation, of "kto kogo." The Menshevik metalist Grigor'ev, cited in Chapter Five, perhaps belongs to this group of insurrectionists who fought for immediate soviet power; it was a matter of defeating the capitalists. The divisions between the positions are of course not absolute. Even the hard-line Bolshevik Avanesov said that a forcible seizure of power would not have been necessary if Kerensky had not first taken hostile action in Petrograd.

---

[36] *Sovety v oktiabre*, p. 55.   [37] Ibid., p. 59.

But once battle had begun, it must be carried out to the end; this meant terror, confiscation of food, and martial law in the cities.[38]

Among the nonparticipants who nonetheless supported immediate soviet power, I would include all those workers who supported resolutions for soviet power but who did not enlist in the ranks of the Red Guard. Many of these workers had come from textile plants, and I would argue that they constituted the least urbanized stratum of the Moscow work force. The struggle for Moscow was not their struggle. The variation within this group is of course substantial: some workers did not fight because the battle seemed well in hand by the time they were ready, others did not fight because of the risks involved. Clearly these two positions reflect different degrees and kinds of commitment to soviet power.

I would also include here the moderate members of the Bolshevik party, typified by Viktor Nogin, the peacemaker who did all he could to avoid an armed confrontation. The Moscow party committee in fact had opposed an armed insurrection all along. In adopting the Central Committee's October 10 resolution on the insurrection, the Moscow Committee omitted the clause about insurrection, calling instead for the "liquidation" of the Kerensky government, not its "overthrow" (*sverzhenie*). As A. Ia. Grunt points out, this resolution was not intended for publication, so the omission of the call for insurrection cannot be seen as a propaganda ploy to mollify the defensists among their supporters.[39]

I would assert that this position of nonparticipatory support for immediate soviet power was the dominant one among Moscow workers. The events of 1917 had created a climate, as already seen, in which power to the soviets, the working-class representative, appeared as the only solution to the multiple crises of power, food, production, and war. But this belief was not so strongly held as to motivate many workers to volunteer for the barricades. I have argued above that nonurban workers were the least politicized of the Moscow factory work force, and it must surely have been these apolitical workers who, although accepting the basic concepts of the class-struggle view of society, stood aside when the time came to test their beliefs. Many workers at the Trekhgornaia textile manufacture (and surely elsewhere) actually left the city during the October fighting. The Trekhgornaia factory committee on November 7 gave the absent workers one week to return without jeopardizing their jobs, but the textile workers returned slowly because the deadline was extended

[38] Ibid., p. 81.

[39] The resolution is in *Podgotovka*, p. 350. Grunt's contention (*Moskva 1917-i*, p. 246) is an important admission from a Soviet scholar and reinforces the argument made by Rabinowitch in *Bolsheviks Come to Power*.

by ten more days on December 1.[40] Here is one concrete example of the passive role played in October by those apolitical, little-urbanized workers who remained aloof from the revolution throughout 1917.

The final position belonged to those workers, soldiers, and socialists who opposed soviet power and refused to fight even to defend the soviets from counterrevolution. The most noteworthy exponents of this position, the regular Menshevik organization, went even further: they were ideologically opposed to the very concept of soviet power. The Mensheviks agreed to enter the Military Revolutionary Committee on October 25 only in order to convert that body to an all-democratic organ, to preserve order, and to forestall civil war; having failed, their representatives walked out.[41] Still insisting that the workers' cause remained a minority cause, the Mensheviks opposed the soviet seizure both ideologically—because capitalism in Russia had not yet reached its logical development—and on purely pragmatic grounds—because the seizure would surely lead to civil war.[42] Washing their hands of any share in what they viewed as illegitimate power, the Mensheviks' representative declared on November 9:

> We considered this [leaving the Military Revolutionary Committee] our sacred duty to the proletariat; you may not agree with us, but this was our point of view; we are not novices in revolutionary struggle, and in defense of the interests of the working class we considered it obligatory to follow our point of view to the end.[43]

Among the workers, printers were the only organized group to oppose and not just to ignore both the fighting and the transfer of power to the soviets. As was seen in Chapter Six, the only published resolutions protesting the October insurrection came from the printshops. Few printers—mostly the very young—were known to have joined the Red Guard. In Presnia, where printers had actively joined the 1905 rising, one printshop was reported to have furnished a Red Guard unit, but it consisted of only five men.[44] This same shop, despite electing a Bolshevik as its Soviet deputy on September 23, voted overwhelmingly (293 to 7) during the October days for the Menshevik resolution calling for the creation of an all-socialist democratic power.[45]

Exacerbating the printers' already well-known antipathy toward the Bolsheviks was the decision made by the party's "fighting center" (not

[40] "Protokoly fabrichno-zavodskogo komiteta Trekhgornoi manufaktury (okonchanie)," *Istoriia proletariata SSSR*, no. 9, 1932, pp. 165, 171.

[41] *Sovety v oktiabre*, p. 37.

[42] Ibid.   [43] Ibid., p. 53.

[44] *Oktiabr' na krasnoi Presne*, 1927, p. 145.

[45] *Sots.-Dem.*, 23 September 1917; *Vpered*, 3 November 1917.

the Military Revolutionary Committee, which had not yet been elected) on October 25 to close down the city's bourgeois press.[46] Troops were apparently dispatched to the presses of the four major bourgeois dailies, which action prompted angry meetings by the printers thus prevented from working: not even Tsar Nicholas had so seized printing presses, declared a resolution from the workers of the large Levenson shop.[47] It was only a short time before the new soviet government felt compelled to enact a more general decree on censorship which enraged not only the printers but also provoked the resignation from the Central Committee and government by Nogin and others.[48]

It is easy to see the spark of self-interest which motivated the printers to oppose the Moscow Soviet's infringement on freedom of the press. But one must remember that the printers, by the nature of their work, shared the Menshevik party's sense of working-class isolation. Soviet power, held by a minority, would inevitably lead to civil war and dictatorship, argued the Menshevik leaders in the Soviet.[49] Workers at the big Sytin printing plant in Zamoskvorech'e echoed this fear, resolving by a vote of 980 to 20 on October 30 that they did not want to criticize the workers' and soldiers' movement but that they could not actively support a movement that would lead to the ruin of the working class.[50]

Thus working-class support for the soviet seizure of power in Moscow was by no means unanimous, but neither was there significant opposition. Workers in two machine-building plants in addition to the printers passed resolutions critical of the Bolsheviks' actions, but the majority of workers simply stood aside while power hung in the balance and then resumed their day-to-day tasks of working, finding food, and keeping warm.

One characteristic stood out among the vocal minority of the Moscow

[46] *Oktiabr' v Moskve*, p. 319. The document authorizing the press seizure is reproduced in *Letopis' geroicheskikh dnei*, between pp. 496-497. The reasons prompting the seizure do not appear in the sources, but it was decided only in the middle of "great friction" (*Triumfal'noe shestvie*, p. 312). The Bolsheviks subsequently justified their action by claiming that the papers were tending to "corrupt" the workers' and soldiers' mass—they were printing "genuine slander" (*Sovety v oktiabre*, pp. 36, 44).

[47] *Vpered*, 4 November 1917. See also *Trud*, 29 October 1917, and *Vpered*, 28 October 1917.

[48] *Izv. MSRD*, 8 December 1917. At least one other press was seized during the October days, this one by "armed anarchists." The printers' response in this case was to appeal to the Military Revolutionary Committee to retake the shop and approve everything printed there (A. Iakovlev, "Moi vospominaniia"; *Dokumenty velikoi proletarskoi revoliutsii*, p. 220).

[49] *Sovety v oktiabre*, pp. 37, 39.

[50] *Vpered*, 31 October 1917. A slightly different version was reported in *Pechatnik*, 28 November 1917. Here the resolution says the workers would go into the streets, but not for the support of the Bolsheviks. This would put them in the upper left-hand box of Table 9-1.

work force. This was the strong desire, despite the sharp rise in class hatred, for a compromise solution to the fighting and to the struggle for power. Most of the moderate socialists indeed worked hard for a peaceful outcome, one that would not necessarily give power to the Bolshevik party alone. That the conflict had led to bloodshed was blamed by all on the intransigence of the "other side," the Committee of Public Safety.[51] The railway union and the union of post and telegraph workers (not considered heretofore because, as employees, they were not represented in the Moscow Soviet) actively worked for a negotiated settlement. This sentiment was much stronger in Moscow—thanks to its mixed class composition—than elsewhere.

Even in victory, the soviet partisans voiced little hostility toward the vanquished. True, left-wing Bolsheviks like Avanesov thought nothing of imprisoning their foes; and Nikolai Bukharin, when asked what would happen to the millions of middle-class Russian peasants who did not realize their interests corresponded to the workers', was said to have replied, "We will arrest them."[52] But the dominant mood among Moscow Bolsheviks, both party leaders and rank and file, was more conciliatory. Aleksei Rykov, a moderate like Nogin (and who much later allied with Bukharin in the "Right Opposition" to Stalin's leadership) declared himself to be an enemy of repression and terror and guaranteed full freedom of elections to the Constituent Assembly. "As soon as the Constituent Assembly convenes, power will be transferred to it."[53]

Rykov and Nogin both resigned from the party's Central Committee in protest over the introduction of press censorship. A subsequent Moscow Committee meeting discussed the impropriety of Nogin's now remaining chairman of the Moscow Soviet, but many Bolshevik leaders felt that Nogin's position was widely shared by the Soviet deputies and that he should remain as chairman. Eventually the historian M. N. Pokrovskii, although seriously ill at the time, was tapped as the compromise chairman over Nogin and the radicals' candidate G. Lomov, but even this solution illustrates the continued preference of many Moscow workers and Bolsheviks for compromise and conciliation.[54]

---

[51] *Sovety v oktiabre*, p. 53.

[52] Ibid., p. 85. The charge was made by the Menshevik Kibrik.

[53] Ibid., p. 44.

[54] *Triumfal'noe shestvie*, pp. 326-330, Moscow Committee meeting of November 13. Of course, those who warned that Nogin's removal would antagonize Bolshevik supporters themselves shared the moderate position on the Moscow Committee, men such as Ratekhin, Ignatov, Burovtsev, and the printer Borshchevskii. These were party workers active primarily in central organs and trade unions, but three of the four were of working-class origin. Other committee members, long-time Bolshevik intelligenty rather than workers (Kostelovskaia, Zemliachka, Belenkii, and Vladimirskii) spoke from personal involvement in raion organizations; they argued that the local mood was hostile to Nogin. The raions represented

A Red Guard officer, describing the final surrender of the Alexander military school, boasted that the soviet forces gave the junkers their freedom, something the junkers would not on their part have done if they had won. And a representative of wounded Red Guards, thanking the Moscow Soviet for the wine sent to them in the hospital, explained they had shared it with wounded junkers. "In the hospital we say that different parties cannot exist, we decided among ourselves to distribute the wine and show the junkers that Bolsheviks are not so fearsome."[55]

Such incidents suggest that party members from the working-class and soldiers' rank and file strongly favored conciliation. Indeed, their position was not far removed from that of the other socialist parties, except that the Bolsheviks were prepared to fight if necessary to defend the soviet. Thus it would appear that there was significant grass-roots support in Moscow for a moderate solution to the problem of power. Class hatred was more pronounced in October than in February, but it was by no means so decisive a feature as it may have been in industrial centers like Petrograd and the textile towns in the Central Industrial Region.

This being the case, the spirit of compromise nonetheless seemed to disappear in Moscow during the course of the next few months. The Council of People's Commissars' decree on press censorship remained in force; on December 8 Moscow was declared to be under a state of emergency, with bans on street meetings and new curbs on the press, all enforced by a new military revolutionary tribunal.[56] An acute sense of incipient civil war gripped the Bolshevik leaders of the Moscow Soviet, and the moderating influence of the city's work force had to compete with a growing hostility by those in power toward all who opposed the new regime. This hostility and the accompanying civil-war mentality surely shaped the development of soviet power over the next few months and years in ways that this study cannot pursue. But if one follows the trends already established a little way beyond October, some factors that shaped the development of Soviet society may come into focus.

THE END OF 1917

The transfer of local and state power did not instantly solve the chronic problems of the economy. Those supporting soviet power may have shared the anonymous Soviet deputy's confidence that "there would" be bread three days after the fall of the Provisional Government (see Chapter

---

by these activists, however, were those without strong Bolshevik organizations and support. In any case, the choice of the ailing Pokrovskii as chairman indicates how strongly both sides valued unity. An assistant could carry out all of Pokrovskii's duties, it was argued, but it was important that someone of Pokrovskii's stature be the nominal chairman at least.

[55] *Sovety v oktiabre*, pp. 58, 48.   [56] *Izv. MSRD*, 8 December 1917.

Three), but in fact the answer to Boris Kibrik's question was, there was not. Grain reserves continued low after October. Promised shipments of grain mysteriously vanished en route. On November 18, the food-supply agency reported that 935 grain-filled railway cars were on the way from Siberia, but by December 1 only 665 of these could be accounted for. At that point, the prevailing daily bread ration of one-half funt meant that the city's food supplies would last only until December 11. By December 21, the scarcity was so critical that the ration was reduced to one-eighth funt, the equivalent of about three slices of bread.[57]

Such distress had never occurred under tsarism, and in the Moscow Soviet on December 21 the Unityist Galperin warned the new rulers that hunger had overturned first Nicholas, then the government of Mensheviks and SRs, and it would soon turn out the Bolsheviks.[58] But whereas under the tsar and the Provisional Government it was government ineptitude that had aggravated the food crisis, the situation now was different, as Galperin, perhaps unwittingly, claimed: "The [Ukrainian] Rada is not ours, Siberia has separated itself, Kaledin [in the Kuban grain belt] wages war."[59] Now blame for the crisis could be pinned on external causes— counterrevolutionary war and separatism. Such a situation contributed to the growing seige mentality on the part of leaders of the Soviet.

The city's industrial economy fared no better in the first weeks of soviet power. Old strikes between workers and private owners continued, but the economic situation was so dismal that new ones were discouraged. The leather workers, it will be recalled, had agreed to return to work October 24 with many strike issues still unresolved. Now the union agreed to drop some of its demands because of the new political context. The demand for a six-hour working day before Sundays and holidays, made when "the bourgeoisie was in power," was inappropriate in a workers' state. In order to ensure maximum productivity for the workers' revolution, the union directed its members to follow the forty-eight hour workweek decreed by the new Council of People's Commissars.[60]

But other factors countered these attempts to raise productivity. Military plants, long dependent on government subsidies for their viability, were now denied these subsidies as the creaky tsarist war machine ground to a halt. The victims of demobilization, however, included workers as well as capitalists. Workers at Mikhelson's Russkaia mashina plant implored the soviet government to assume ownership of the factory: one thousand workers and their families remained "without shelter, without a crust of bread" so long as the plant received no subsidies to meet its

---

[57] *Russkie vedomosti*, 1 and 22 December 1917.
[58] *Izv. MSRD*, 21 December 1917.
[59] Ibid.   [60] Ibid., 6 December 1917.

wage bill.[61] Even in factories where the government's decree of control had been implemented, there were chronic shortages of cash to pay wages and often no fuel with which to power the plants.[62]

Unemployment, which had apparently only threatened in July and August, now assumed massive proportions. The precise degree of joblessness is impossible to measure; but according to one statistical source, the number of factory workers in Moscow dropped by 25 percent from 1917 to 1918 (the exact dates of these counts are not given, but the 1918 figure is probably for August). The metal industry was hardest hit, losing over twenty-five thousand jobs in this year, down 44 percent. (The textile industry, not dependent on military orders, was less affected—down only 6.5 percent in Moscow—and textile employment actually rose in Moscow province.)[63]

No one knows for certain how much of this decline began in the last months of 1917 or what happened to the estimated minimum of fifty thousand factory workers without work. The city population also declined after October 1917 but nowhere near so precipitously as the factory work force, suggesting that many unemployed workers remained in the city, hoping to find work or to eke out some kind of living and thereby placing added pressure on the city's resources.[64]

The continuing economic collapse, as suggested above, provided volatile fuel for the dominant feature of this immediate post-October period— an escalation of polarization by class. Jan Yarkovsky, a prisoner of war released in order to work in the office of a military plant, wryly recalled that the post-October food crisis had made no dent in the habits of his circle. The old whirl of engagement parties and birthday celebrations continued as before. "In spite of the shortage of food, abundant refreshments were available for everyone."[65] This inequality of consumption had earlier provoked demands by workers that bakeries be prohibited from baking sweet pastries; with the basic bread ration approaching one-eighth of a pound, such patterns of consumption depicted by Yarkovsky must surely have contributed to mass anger toward the possessing classes.

This class-based anger now more than ever operated in both directions. Since July the middle and upper classes had indeed become more arrogant about their privileged place in society; and this arrogance, manifested by venomous attacks on the Bolshevik party as the symbol of the working class, intensified after October.

---

[61] *Uprochenie sovetskoi vlasti v Moskve i moskovskoi gubernii*, pp. 215-216.

[62] Ibid., p. 196.

[63] *Fabrichno-zavodskaia promyshlennost' g. Moskvy*, p. 1.

[64] The adult population declined by 42,000 or 3.7 percent. The biggest decline came among children (*Stat. ezhegodnik*, p. 15).

[65] Yarkovsky, p. 283.

Bank officials and employees went on strike immediately after the October revolution, and the new government was unable to withdraw money to finance its operations. On December 2, to protest the dissolution of the city duma, the higher municipal employees began a strike whose plan almost exactly paralleled the strike of lower city employees a month and a half earlier. Nonessential employees struck first, followed day by day by strikes in successively more crucial areas of public welfare. The entire operation was coordinated by a central strike committee. On December 5, school teachers joined the strike.[66]

Over the same weekend, on Sunday, December 3, the Moscow Union in Defense of the Constituent Assembly organized a grandiose demonstration to protest the postponement of the Constituent Assembly from November 28 to January 5. Sponsoring groups included the union of engineers, the joint bureau of SRs and Mensheviks, students' organizations, trade and industrial employees' groups, and many others. Rallies of separate groups were held in the morning all over the city, and then the entire mass assembled in Red Square at noon. *Russkie vedomosti* exulted that a hundred and fifty thousand people had gathered in support of the Assembly.[67]

The Soviet's *Izvestiia* on December 3 took up the challenge and attacked the demonstration in sharp terms of class war. "Comrade SOLDIERS and WORKERS," screamed a banner on December 3:

The enemies of the people—kadets and right socialist-revolutionaries summon you to a demonstration against the Government of Soviets of Workers', Soldiers', and Peasants' Deputies.

Not one soldier and not one worker should take part in a demonstration of our enemies. (Emphasis in the original.)

It was immediately after these days that the city soviet declared a public emergency, banning all public meetings and prohibiting publication of the nonsocialist press.

In preparation for the Constituent Assembly elections scheduled for November 18-20, the solemn organ of the bourgeoisie, *Russkie vedomosti*, had constantly intoned warnings about the evils of Bolshevism. Its leading article on November 19, the second day of voting in the assembly, employed terms like "Bolshevik anarchy" and "Bolshevik usurpation" and warned against adopting even the compromise position of the moderate socialists.

[66] *Russkie vedomosti*, 3 December 1917; *Moskovskie bol'sheviki v ogne*, pp. 68-69.
[67] *Russkie vedomosti*, 2, 3, and 5 December 1917.

There are two paths before the country: The path of deepening class struggle and destruction of the state on one side, and the path of the consolidation of Russia and the establishment of firm state power on the other.

For Kadet as well as Bolshevik partisans, there was no middle choice.

The results of the Constituent Assembly elections again clearly revealed this polarization. The Bolsheviks received approximately 353,000 votes (including 90 percent of the garrison), or 47.9 percent of the total. The Kadet party won 35.7 percent of the vote, about 260,000 ballots, which represented a substantial increase over September when the party had won 102,000 votes and 26 percent of the total. Such an increase appeared to be a moral victory for the party of "firm state power," and *Russkie vedomosti* inferred from the returns that "the growth of bolshevism in the last two months has virtually stopped."[68] Such a conclusion ignored the plain fact that after the soviet seizure of power, the Bolshevik party surpassed its September vote by 153,000 votes, or 75 percent!

Voting was heavy during these elections, a phenomenon that belies the evidence of apathy revealed by the election campaign. *Izvestiia* devoted little attention either to the elections or to the assembly itself, scheduled at that point for November 28. The liberal *Russkoe slovo* reported that the elections were proceeding quietly, without agitational meetings or queues at the polls. The working-class vote was said to be down; the Moscow Soviet had given workers three days off to vote, but most workers, said the paper, instead took a three-day holiday and went home to their villages.[69]

Constituent Assembly electoral returns were never reported for all districts in the city, so direct comparisons with the June and September votes are impossible. By the last day of the voting, however, 70 percent of Moscow's eligible voters had cast their ballots, a participation rate higher than ever before. Even judging by incomplete returns, one can see that turnout continued to be higher in factory districts than in central residential districts: 75 percent voted in industrial Piatnitskii, for example, and only 60 percent voted in Arbat.[70]

The most significant feature of the election was of course the division of votes between Kadets and Bolsheviks. In percentage of total vote, the remaining parties did even more poorly than in September, as Table 9-2 indicates. The Socialist Revolutionaries, who emerged as the largest

[68] Ibid., 24 November 1917.

[69] *Russkoe slovo*, 21 November 1917. The liberal and Menshevik press persistently overplayed the rural connection of Moscow workers. They never seemed to grasp what has been demonstrated in this study, that the most active workers were those with the fewest ties to the countryside.

[70] Ibid.

TABLE 9-2. *Electoral Results by Party in Three 1917 Elections*

Party	June	Percent	September	Percent	November	Percent
Kadet	108,781	18	101,846	26	260,279	35
Socialist Revolutionary	374,885	61	54,410	14	61,394	8
Menshevik	76,407	12	15,787	4	19,790	3
Bolshevik	75,409	12	199,337	51	353,282	47
Democratic-Socialist bloc (Plekhanovites)	. . .	. .	413	. .	33,366	4
Total	615,393	100	387,280	100	746,809	100

party in the overall Russian vote with 40 percent, played no role at all in the urban elections. In all provincial capital cities together, the SRs won just 14 percent of the vote, the Bolsheviks 36 percent, the Kadets 23 percent.[71] The cities were the center of class antagonisms, and the Moscow elections confirmed this. Roving reporters captured a sense of the motivations of voters which sounded strikingly similar to comments in September. "Citizens, vote for the Bolshevik list!" appealed an agitator in Zamoskvorech'e. "The Bolsheviks will give you everything. The Kadets will give you tsar and police."[72]

It was an effective appeal. The Mensheviks and SRs had given nothing. "We tried number three, let's try number five. Perhaps we'll receive something," said another Zamoskvorech'e voter.[73]

If the Bolsheviks had lost ground relative to the Kadets in November, it was only because both sides were consolidating their positions. One need only to look at the size of the Bolsheviks' numerical vote to disprove the Kadets' assertion that the momentum had shifted their way. The polarization reflected by this outcome, however, further tied the hands of the moderate elements in the city. What leverage could moderates like Galperin, Nogin, and Rykov exert when the Bolshevik party had no rivals for the allegiance of the city's working class?

The triumph of the seige mentality on the part of Bolshevik leaders, grounded in the hostility of the Kadet-led forces, was bolstered by the many weaknesses within the camp of "democracy." This study has touched on one of these weaknesses before: the growing breakdown, or rather atomization, of public life. The September duma elections revealed some of this breakdown, with the proliferation of tiny interest-group parties such as the "union of apartment renters," "society of renters of rooms, corners, and cots," "union of householders," even the "Khamovniki raion residents' group." In the wake of the raion duma elections, local insti-

[71] L. M. Spirin, *Klassy i partii v grazhdanskoi voine v Rossii*, pp. 416-423.
[72] *Russkoe slovo*, 21 November 1917.
[73] *Russkie vedomosti*, 21 November 1917.

tutions increasingly took charge of local affairs and ignored the wider political world. For example, the response of householders to the escalation of crime in the city was to form local committees to defend their specific neighborhoods, "defending their domestic hearths from thieves with oven forks and pokers, and turning their backs on all that happened."[74]

This fragmentation of urban life was repeated in the October fighting. The socialists claimed at least three "fighting centers": the Military Revolutionary Committee, the Bolshevik party's separate "fighting center," and the Central Trade Union Bureau's "revolutionary center." Individual raions became virtually autonomous during the ten days of fighting, not always because of lack of communications with the center. Many districts were simply frustrated with the inactivity of the central Military Revolutionary Committee.[75] And shortly after October, the Danilovskii subraion petitioned the Soviet to become a full-fledged raion, a move opposed by the parent Zamoskvorech'e district leaders.[76]

In addition to increasing localism, the trend toward overlapping institutions continued. The raion dumas had formed a "soviet of raion dumas" even before the October revolution to coordinate the activities of these new organs of local self-government; this soviet challenged the authority of the city duma elected in June. After October, with the city duma dispersed, the soviet of raion dumas assumed administrative control of municipal institutions.[77] But was this not now a function of the Soviet of Workers' Deputies? The parallel structure continued until March 1918, when the noncooperation of at least one raion duma compelled the Soviet to reorganize the dumas as sections of the Soviet apparatus.[78]

The October revolution saw an increase in the amount of reported crime as central authority continued to weaken. News of cat burglaries, armed robberies, and murders appeared daily in the liberal and socialist presses. One Red Guard veteran recalled "The October fighting came and went—we were victorious. Again the lathes started up, again the chimneys smoked. But we could not lay down our rifles, for banditry arose." It even happened that elements "hostile to the revolution" wormed their way into the Red Guard and by their criminal acts discredited the workers' militia.[79]

---

[74] A. Voznesenskii, "Moskva v oktiabre 1917 g.," p. 167.

[75] Al'tman, p. 268.   [76] *Izv. MSRD*, 23 and 26 November 1917.

[77] *Russkie vedomosti*, 21 November 1917. The paper called the body "a handful of imposters." On December 6, the scheduled elections to the duma were canceled on the grounds that the soviet of raion dumas was sufficiently representative (ibid., 5 December 1917).

[78] M. F. Vladimirskii, "Moskovskie raionnye dumy i sovet raionnykh dum v 1917-1918 gg.," p. 94; G. S. Ignat'ev, *Moskva v pervyi god proletarskoi diktatury*, pp. 46-48.

[79] *Desiat' let*, p. 90.

Most of this rise in crime had no direct political implications, but one incident does illustrate the problems of breakdown of authority and the proliferation of parallel, competing authorities. According to *Russkie vedomosti*, a group of armed sailors descended on the Gabai tobacco factory on the Petersburg *chaussée* on November 17; they demanded and received, with the threat of force, four cases of cigarettes. The band next showed up at the Dukat tobacco plant some blocks away with the same demand. The Dukat factory committee protested, and the chairman, Evgen'ev, who was also chairman of the tobacco workers' trade union, suggested they all go to the Military Revolutionary Committee to verify the sailors' authorization. On the way, the sailors tried to force the factory committee to go instead to their own "headquarters," but the workers convinced the sailors to go to the Military Revolutionary Committee. Once at the center, the committee told the sailors they were wrong to seize cigarettes in this way; the sailors menacingly threatened to appeal to Petrograd for authority. Finally, the two sides "compromised"—the Revolutionary Committee would authorize the sailors to requisition ten cases of cigarettes.[80] Here one has the usual clash of authority on several levels. Sailors confronted workers, both victors of October. The organizational experience of Evgen'ev, chairman of both his factory committee and his trade union, barely overcame the armed threats of the sailors. Even the currently ruling Military Revolutionary Committee had to compete with the specter of its Petrograd counterpart. And the net result was that the sailors, by agreeing to work within the soviet framework (but really by dint of their arms), received what they started out to get.

Compounding the inherent weakness of the new institutional order, at all levels of working-class activity there was "colossal work to do." Because of the load, recalled one of the professionalisty, "the old trade union methods went to the archives."[81] There was no time now for the old routine of investigation and negotiation. Unions now demanded and then threatened force. The sensitivity of the new rulers to the differing views of their constituents was no doubt dulled by the enormous pressure of work. Consequently, the thinly spread soviet activists had little time or patience for the old pleasures of debate. As work increased, tempers flared; within the Soviet executive committee, factional differences became much sharper. The Bolshevik majority was struggling with the many problems of overcoming the opposition of white-collar employees, of the Kadets, of the institutional anomie: there was no time to deal politely with the constant criticism of the Mensheviks. The latter, for example, refused to join the presidium of the Soviet after October because the Soviet was an instrument of power, and the Mensheviks did not believe

[80] *Russkie vedomosti*, 29 November 1917. [81] Kozelev, p. 25.

in soviet power. "This is not firm power," proclaimed Kipen, "but a disintegration of all power."[82] Such principled abstention did not help carry the workload. The Mensheviks, however, continued to sit in the executive committee, regularly protesting the increasing curbs on free press and on meetings, protesting the arrests by raion soviets of veteran friends of the working class.[83]

Such fractionalism spilled over into other areas of public life, contributing to the sense of Bolshevik embattlement. For example, on November 18, a large meeting of "press workers" (from pressmen to proofreaders) assembled at the Salamon circus. The purpose of the meeting was to defend freedom of the press. The organizers appeared to be Kadets, but the Menshevik chairman of the printers' union, Chistov, gave an official address. As he read the union directors' resolution protesting Bolshevik infringement of press freedom, a group of Bolshevik printers began to shout from the floor that the resolution was not representative. At this point, the argument nearly "transformed itself into a more expressive form" as representatives of each faction tried to gain the speakers' platform. The dispute was symptomatic of the polarization not only between classes but of the divisions within the working class as well. In the case of the printers' union, the Menshevik moderates held a majority—this resolution had in fact received the votes of 224 union delegates, and 31 Bolsheviks had walked out in protest.[84]

But across the wide spectrum of the working class, the Mensheviks' refusal to participate in the new soviet government rendered them politically bankrupt. The workers still valued the Mensheviks' treasured concept of unity even while demanding soviet power. By refusing to participate in that power, the Mensheviks destroyed their last argument for working-class support. They also did worse; by refusing to participate in soviet power on the grounds that such power would threaten civil war, they so weakened the government as to allow the extremists to dominate policy, thereby making a civil war that much more certain.

With the Menshevik leaders' self-destruction, the prevailing feeling of class unity that exerted strong influence as late as October was eventually undermined by the continuing political crisis. On the one hand, the polarization between classes contributed to the consolidation of power on the working-class side by the soviets. But it also raised the real trauma of civil war, an emergency that could only be dealt with by military dictatorial methods. On the other hand, the continuing parallelism of institutions and the sharp fractionalism within them weakened these in-

---

[82] *Izv. MSRD*, 15 and 16 November 1917.

[83] Ibid., 9 December 1917. The arrest victim was E. O. Kabo, a Menshevik intelligent who survived to publish her admirable study of Moscow workers in 1928.

[84] *Russkie vedomosti*, 21 November 1917.

stitutions as all-democratic organs and permitted the Bolsheviks to fill the vacuum left by the institutional anomie. And all the while the scarcity of food and the uncertainty about jobs surely prevented the rank-and-file workers, who had always been most enthusiastic about all-class unity, from taking active steps to defend that unity. The result was the triumph of one-party rule, the victory of the politics of the perpetual emergency.

Conclusion

A revolution teaches, and teaches fast.

LEON TROTSKY[1]

THE role of the Russian working class has hardly been minimized in existing studies of the 1917 revolution. Standard works on the subject agree that workers helped to spark the February revolution, that workers underwent a significant radicalization during the course of 1917, and that this radicalization contributed to the success of the soviet seizure of power in October. The assessment of the workers' role has varied according to the perspective of the historian; "radicalized" workers have been heroes or unwitting villains, but none of the conventional histories has adequately explored or explained this process of radicalization.

Consider three excellent histories of the Russian Revolution. Leon Trotsky's *History of the Russian Revolution* appeared in English in 1932. Trotsky's emphasis on the workers in 1917 derives from his Marxist principles, and he treats workers as revolutionary heroes. Trotsky admits that the Russian working class was not steadfastly revolutionary from the beginning of 1917, primarily because of the influx of nonproletarian elements during the war. But the events of 1917, together with Bolshevik leadership, combined to radicalize the Russian workers. Reviewing the April demonstrations, the July days, the Kornilov mutiny, and October, Trotsky writes, "under these events, so striking in their rhythm, molecular changes were taking place, welding the heterogeneous parts of the working class into one political whole."[2] The strike takes on special importance in Trotsky's view: the "increasing" number of strikes both indicated workers' increasing radicalism and served to initiate the more backward workers into the realities of class conflict. Trotsky's working class, however, remains more or less monolithic. He writes of "molecular processes in the mind of the mass"[3] which led to soviet power in October, but his chosen metaphor suggests that the processes were too minute and too obscure to be analyzed; all that can be seen are the results (a conscious revolutionary class in October) and some of the forces that produced them (strikes, capitalist offensives, and the Bolshevik party). The workers are

[1] *History of the Russian Revolution*, vol. 1, p. 390.
[2] Ibid.   [3] Ibid., vol. 2, p. 243.

crucial in Trotsky's history, but they remain obscure "masses" with the merest hints of heterogeneity and of internal, "molecular" dynamics.[4]

William Chamberlin offers the Russian Revolution without Marxism and without Trotsky's self-justification. He too finds a radicalization of the mass in 1917. Like Trotsky, he sees the strike as an important indicator of the radicalization of workers since strikers proceeded first from peaceful conflicts over wages and hours, then to local implementation of workers' control, and finally to support for the Bolshevik program of soviet power.[5] In Chamberlin's study, which deals with other aspects of 1917 besides the workers' movement, this radicalization is uniform across the entire working class. The radical outcome is then explained by the composite characteristics of a peculiarly Russian model proletarian:

> The predestined standardbearer of the social revolution according to Marx proved to be . . . the Petrograd metal worker or the Donetz miner, sufficiently literate to grasp elementary socialist ideas, sufficiently wretched to welcome the first opportunity to pull down the temple of private property.[6]

Finally and quite recently, John Keep has offered a history of the revolution from a social perspective.[7] Keep focuses on workers and peasants and their emerging revolutionary institutions, but his view of the working class seems shaped by the Menshevik historical bias predominant in the West: the Russian working class was so recently formed from the peasantry that workers' political responses in 1917 were insufficiently mature.[8] Cultural activities could not possibly be carried on by workers such as these, for example, so Keep asserts that " 'education and culture' was often a euphemism for political propaganda."[9] Such workers' political activity, in Keep's interpretation, was determined almost exclusively by economic need—the lower the wage and bread ration, the more radical the political response. Moreover, Keep, like Chamberlin, stresses the radicalism of the unskilled: untutored peasant-workers were quick to respond to radical solutions like factory seizures.[10] Finally, Keep describes the radicalized working class in October: "Driven to near-despair by the

---

[4] Ibid., vol. 1, p. 403, and vol. 2, p. 243.

[5] *Russian Revolution*, vol. 1, p. 266.   [6] Ibid., vol. 1, p. 275.

[7] *Russian Revolution: A Study in Mass Mobilization.*

[8] Keep's view can be traced in part to his use of sources. He treats Soviet sources with due skepticism, but seems to accept the reliability of the bourgeois press in 1917. He reserves his greatest skepticism, however, for sources generated by the workers themselves. For example, he rejects the value of using workers' resolutions as historical evidence (ibid., p. 115).

[9] Ibid., p. 81.

[10] Ibid., p. 25, on radicalism in 1914; pp. 68-69; p. 82.

economic crisis, their nerves kept on edge by incessant propaganda, they responded uncritically to the appeals of a party that promised untold blessings once 'soviet power' had been achieved."[11] Keep devotes more attention to the activities of workers than previous historians, and he has assembled much information on the scope of the labor movement. But his workers seem to proceed toward their reflex radicalism in one great wave, and the complexities within the working class which might tend to soften his view are ignored.

Such are some conventional views of workers when they are treated as part of the more general social and political history of 1917. How has this more specialized study of Moscow workers added to or altered this view?

First of all, the view that the workers are one uniform mass must be rejected. Urbanized workers possessed different values from those of workers recently migrated from the countryside; workers in small shops faced organizational constraints different from those confronted by workers in large plants; workers living in purely working-class neighborhoods formed different attitudes from those of workers living in socially mixed neighborhoods. Metalworkers, because of these and other characteristics, behaved differently in 1917 from textile workers; former Petrograd metalworkers even behaved differently from Muscovite metalists. Printers, despite a similar urban background, generally rejected the metalists' positions on political issues.

The range of diversities and antagonisms among workers themselves has been demonstrated over and over in the preceding pages. The workers in artisanal trades were the ones who most quickly organized trade unions after February. Urbanized metalworkers were the earliest to advocate soviet power; textile workers who lived near metalworkers later on endorsed soviet power but for primarily economic reasons. Metalworkers least of all cast their votes for the hugely popular peasant-oriented Socialist Revolutionary party in the June city duma election. Workers in small plants tended to be more generous toward soldiers than were workers in large plants. Workers with relatively high wages tended to strike more often and more easily than poorly paid workers.

Nonetheless, having analyzed the molecular structure of the working class in more detail than previous studies, does not this study arrive at the familiar conclusion that there was by October a radicalized, unified working class? The workers were radical, yes, in the sense that many of them supported soviet power in one way or another. They were unified, too, in the sense of common class identity. But such adjectives oversimplify the important political and social processes of 1917; and by examining

[11] *Ibid.*, p. 95.

these processes, this study can add to the prevailing views of the revolution.

This study has emphasized revolutionary dynamics as well as the revolution's October result. The workers who took to the streets in February were the very same individuals who had supported soviet power in the autumn, but they had changed in many ways. Eight months of relative political freedom may not be long compared to the evolution of Anglo-American civic traditions, but they permitted a modicum of intensive political education for the Moscow working class. The experience of electing deputies, debating resolutions, discussing contributions, and choosing political parties all helped to educate workers and to develop their political as well as class consciousness. Workers learned how to differentiate among political parties. They learned how to conduct meetings, how to express themselves. They learned how to evaluate the opinions and behavior of their own colleagues and of those outside their class.

Not all workers learned at the same rate; they certainly did not all arrive at the same political conclusions. The militant metalworkers at the Moscow telephone works soon adjusted their extremist positions to mesh with the more moderate Moscow social and political climate. But metalworkers and machine workers continued to act as opinion leaders; and when they lived and worked near other workers with less political experience, like the textile workers, the two groups together combined to act in very forceful ways. These are examples of the internal dynamics that the monolithic view of the working class tends to ignore.

Once the dynamics of the revolutionary process receives careful attention, other new aspects of 1917 emerge. One of the most important here is the overwhelming evidence not of workers' notoriously irrational militancy but in fact of its opposite. The behavior of Moscow's workers in 1917 suggests a working class that was both highly rational in its responses to the political and economic pressures of 1917 and extremely patient as well. The leather workers' strike of August and September provides a good example. The best-known episodes of this protracted strike were the workers' espousal of soviet power on October 19 and the seizure of two factories by striking workers when the leather workers, in Chamberlin's analysis, demonstrated the widespread desire to "pull down the temple of private property."[12] In fact, the majority of workers did not seize their plants; rather, they took the more moderate, disciplined step of asking the Soviet, as a legitimate organ, to sequester leather plants in order to force a settlement. The history of the strike helps explain some of the frustrations that finally provoked 1,000 out of 22,000 strikers to seize their factories. The workers had been ready to accept in August the

[12] See Chamberlin, vol. 1, p. 269.

settlement that the owners finally acceded to in October; the union throughout the strike had been more willing to compromise than the intransigent owners. Finally, the behavior of the leather workers during the strike indicates some of the lessons learned during revolutionary 1917. Leather workers were relatively nonurbanized, prime candidates for "irrational" and "undisciplined" behavior, yet their strike was a model of organization. Such a strike would have been improbable six months earlier.

The basic rationality and patience of Moscow workers can be seen in the resolution and contribution processes as well as in many aspects of the strike movement. Workers' resolutions, as Chapter Six has shown, were remarkable for their sensibility rather than their maximalism. Workers' contributions, many from factories not otherwise politically active in 1917, indicated a sizable social base for restraint; these workers supported their institutions and supported their leaders, often in opposition to the more vocal minority who sponsored political resolutions. This was not just political inertia; this support for institutions represented support for the cause of working-class unity, a cause that almost all politicized workers in Moscow endorsed. Finally, the logic of working-class behavior can also be seen in two aspects of the strike movement. Chapter Eight has indicated first that workers who tended to strike most were those with the highest wages. These workers had the reserves to withstand a strike; they knew they were valuable enough to an employer to expect a speedy victory. Secondly, strikes in general and wage strikes in particular diminished over the course of 1917. As inflation increased and output declined, Moscow workers did not struggle hopelessly for higher wage demands, but instead they chose both to strike for control over their jobs and to seek broader political solutions for their problems.

One must therefore reject the image of the Russian working class as uniformly irrational, poorly educated, and incapable of independent participation in the political process. One must reject in particular the myth that the revolution in the cities was carried out by dark semipeasant masses "who did not understand the real meaning of the slogans they loudly repeated."[13] Yes, of course, many Moscow workers were more rural than urban; but when one looks at the participation levels of different segments of the urban labor force, the fact that skilled urban cadres, not the unskilled peasant mass, were the leading political actors can be seen over and over again. These workers possessed experience, political connections, and the degree of economic security which enabled them to function freely and easily in the political life of 1917. Thus metalists and printers participated most frequently in the prerevolutionary strike move-

[13] The phrase is Yarkovsky's in *It Happened in Moscow*, p. 199.

ment. Metalists led the labor force in the frequency of political resolutions, and they catalyzed their neighboring nonurban textile workers to vote Bolshevik in the June duma elections. Urban workers also led the strike movement, further evidence that strikes in 1917 were much more than spontaneous reactions to immediate threats.

The revolutionary working class takes on new complexity in this context. The existence, demonstrated here, of a leading, politically experienced segment of the working class uniting over time with other varying but less mature segments, plus the existence of a dynamic revolutionary process suggest new approaches to the familiar and important problems of radicalization, Bolshevization, class consciousness, and organization.

What was the nature of the radicalization process that occurred within the working class in 1917? Chamberlin describes the increasing radicalism of workers' demands from higher wages to workers' control during the strikes, and from dual power to soviet power in the political arena.[14] Trotsky clouds the issue by claiming that the radicalism of the masses ("a hundred times to the left of the Bolshevik party," in Lenin's famous phrase) was for the most part an unconscious radicalism.[15] Radicalism becomes almost an innate characteristic of workers by virtue of their working-class position.

This study examines how and why the radicalization process occurred. Radicalization was an incremental process, which took place in response to specific economic and political pressures, and it reflected the political maturation of an increasing number of workers. Factory take-overs and independent declarations of workers' control are commonly cited as evidence of radicalization. "The activity of factory committees . . . thoroughly destroyed in the minds of the workers any respect for the rights of private ownership," writes Chamberlin.[16] Keep asserts that delegates favoring workers' control at the Petrograd factory committee conference "took this slogan in its literal sense, as meaning a real transfer of power to the men's chosen representatives. . . ."[17] But the workers of the Trekhgornaia manufacture did not become radicalized because they now gathered once a week to make decisions about hot water in the dormitories and about personality conflicts on the shop floor. Rather, radicalization took place when the factory management announced a long-term suspension of work for lack of fuel and the factory committee found ample reserves in a neighboring district.[18] Radicalization took place when other workers read about these incidents or heard about them in the factory or in the neighborhood tavern. The radicalization of October, when even the Bolsheviks

---

[14] Chamberlin, vol. 1, p. 142.
[15] Trotsky, vol. 1, pp. 381-382.
[16] Chamberlin, vol. 1, p. 273.
[17] Keep, *Russian Revolution*, p. 89.
[18] "Protokoly fabrichno-zavodskogo komiteta Prokhorovskoi Trekhgornoi manufaktury," no. 8.

admitted they were hard pressed to restrain workers from independent acts of violence, was the culmination of the months of revolutionary experience, not the sudden blossoming of maximalist desires and class hatred that workers had secretly harbored all along. "Radical" metalworkers and Bolshevik activists were now at odds with "radical" textile and leather workers because organizational maturation had not kept pace with political developments. The newly politicized workers did not have the capability to express their outrage in the same disciplined way as the radical urban cadres of March and April.

The partisan analogue of radicalization in 1917 was Bolshevization. Here too the study of Moscow workers suggests the complexity of the Bolshevik rise to power. "Bolshevization" is too often used in a purely formulaic way; a district soviet passes a Bolshevik-sponsored resolution on the economic crisis—presto, they are Bolshevized. The Bolshevization of Moscow workers, and presumably elsewhere in Russia, was rather more complex. The process by which the majority of workers identified their interests with the Bolshevik party program was a product of rational, logical choices that corresponded to the changing political and economic nexus.

This process has been seen here in a dozen different ways. In resolutions, workers often endorsed Bolshevik positions without committing themselves to the party on all political questions. The May economic resolutions, the Liberty Loan opposition campaign, the death-penalty issue were all Bolshevik political positions that won support—but for the positions, not for the party. The Moscow Conference strike illustrates the important division between party and policies: even though the majority of workers shared the party's view of the State Conference, the Bolsheviks could not call out workers simply on their own authority but had to rely on that of district soviets and the trade union leadership. Finally, the evolution of the demand for soviet power exemplifies the Bolshevization process. Soviet power was supported by Moscow workers for the practical results they expected it to bring: economic management the workers could trust, honest attempts to make peace, and a guaranteed convocation of the Constituent Assembly. By October, a wide spectrum of workers favored soviet power; but since only the Bolshevik party advocated this power as part of their political program, support for soviet power inevitably translated into support for the Bolshevik party.

These reconsiderations of the meaning of radicalization and of Bolshevization in turn lead to a new consideration of the meaning of class consciousness in the Russian revolution. How closely bound were the political processes of 1917 with the formation of working-class consciousness? Had the Moscow working class by October become a class "for itself" as well as a class "in itself"?

E. P. Thompson concludes his magisterial *Making of the English Work-*

ing Class with a discussion of the elements that contributed to the English workers' very specific sense of class consciousness. These elements, such as the Radical party's political culture of the early 1800s, William Cobbett's rhetoric about social justice, and the Owenites' vision that the people themselves could change their social and economic positions, gained concreteness in the struggle to enact political reform in the 1830s. In the process, workers gained a collective self-consciousness based on their political traditions as well as their economic position in society; the result—English class consciousness.[19]

This process was not and could not have been the same for Russian workers in 1917; Thompson's brief is that class "happened" in England in a fashion peculiar to England. This study of Moscow workers in 1917, however, indicates some elements that contributed to Moscow working-class consciousness by October.

Russian working-class political culture was overwhelmingly a socialist political culture. This was the legacy both of a socialist revolutionary movement that predated the rise of a working class and of the influence of Marxist analysis on that emerging working class. Furthermore, a democratic socialist political and economic order seemed the logical next step for Russia, where the state had always been closely involved in economic activity and where the activity of public organizations during the war had legitimized popular participation in economic administration. The workers' economic-control resolutions of May and June, and the June duma elections, demonstrated this socialist consciousness; the resolutions stipulated active state and public intervention in the economy, and in the elections workers voted almost exclusively for the three parties bearing the socialist label.

This socialist consciousness was not yet class consciousness, consciousness of class struggle. The prevailing sentiment of Moscow workers during the first few months of the revolution was for national unity in the defense of the revolution, exemplified in workers' appeals for solidarity with the army. Of the three socialist parties, the Bolsheviks offered the most class-oriented position, and they were relatively less popular during this period than the Socialist Revolutionaries and Mensheviks, who stood for compromise and solidarity with all elements of revolutionary Russia. Strikes during the period almost all were called to demand wage increases, an indication that workers were willing to function within a multiclass framework.

The events of the summer of 1917 combined with growing class antagonism to change this socialist consciousness into class consciousness. Economic strikes became less successful, and capitalists seemed less will-

---

[19] Thompson, *Making of the English Working Class*, pp. 711-832.

ing to treat workers as equal partners in labor-management relations. The coalition government failed to enact the minimal socialist demands of workers, and the onus fell first on the capitalists, who were seen to be sabotaging the revolution as well as the factories. That the revolutionary unity of March fell apart along class lines can be attributed to economic conditions in Russia but also to the fact that the class framework was after all implicit in socialist consciousness. Capitalists began to behave as Marx said they would: no concessions to the workers, no compromise on the rights of factory owners. Mensheviks and SRs tried to straddle both sides of the class split; this appeal can be seen in the mixed social composition of their supporters. The Bolsheviks, however, had offered the most consistent class interpretation of the revolution, and by late summer their interpretation appeared more and more to correspond to reality. The language of class struggle provided workers who had no theoretical understanding of Marx with a familiar conceptual tool with which to understand the actions of the Provisional Government; the continued failure of the government to solve the problems of the war and the economy, translated into class terms became deliberate sabotage by the workers' natural class enemy. By October, the soviets of workers' deputies, as the workers' only class organ, seemed to class-conscious workers to be the only government they could trust to represent their interests. The combination of theory and experience had produced Moscow's class consciousness.

The class consciousness of October, however, by the same logic as it developed, represented that particular historical moment. Once the theoretically articulate workers left the city with the Red Army, once the dictatorship of the proletariat had eliminated the sense of struggle against the ruling capitalist class, the set of circumstances which had produced class consciousness in 1917 would change. If the class-pure Bolsheviks, once in power, were also to fail to provide political responsiveness and economic security, if nonclass ties such as regional, ethnic, or occupational bonds were to assert more appeal than class solidarity, perhaps the consolidation of the Moscow workers around their class representative, the Bolshevik party, might eventually have weakened. More research is needed on the working class during the civil war and the early years of soviet power; it should be carried out with an eye toward the complexities of the revolutionary process which have been demonstrated here.

Finally, by looking beyond one-dimensional notions of radicalization and by examining the roots of the October revolution, another significant aspect of the revolution has emerged which deserves far more study than it has received: the failure of organizational development to keep pace with political development. Chapter Four has documented the growth and failings of working-class organizations in 1917. Lenin, Trotsky, and Chamberlin appear to attribute organizational weakness to the organizations themselves, to the organizations' insufficient radicalism, to their failure to respond to grass-roots political changes. In fact, the organizational history of 1917 reveals the legacy of the relatively rapid formation of the Russian working class and the years of repression by the tsarist political system. Perhaps a revolution teaches political and class consciousness in eight months, but organizational success took not just consciousness, but practice as well. Such practice had been limited to the urban cultural institutions that had attracted Moscow's workers before 1917; only after February did organizational practice finally become available at all levels of working-class life. A newspaper report in June from the suburb of Tushino announced that even the children were organizing. In 1914, children there played war games, but now they played at democracy. Tushino children constructed red banners with such slogans as "Long live free children," they conducted singing processions through the Provodnik factory, and they held "formal meetings, elected chairmen and committees."[20]

The urbanized segment of the labor force provided the critical element in whatever organizational stability existed in 1917; when the Tushino children grew up, they would add to that element. But ironically, the success of soviet power and then the demands of the civil-war emergency took just these experienced cadres out of the factories and the city, and in the 1920s the slow process would have to begin again, under new conditions. The further implications of the workers' organizational immaturity will not be explored here, but many questions arise. Hannah Arendt has suggested that the collapse of independent workers' institutions after October (very well documented by John Keep) contributed to an atomization of society which weakened resistance to Stalin's consolidation of power.[21] Did the failure of these working-class institutions in fact facilitate the rise of Stalin or someone like him to centralized, absolute rule? Clearly the questions raised by this approach to the Russian Revolution suggest new items for the agenda of study of postrevolutionary Soviet society.

The primary focus of this study has been the workers of Moscow in order to understand the role of workers in 1917 and to explain the complex processes that culminated in the October revolution. But an equally important goal has been to examine the revolution outside the capital city

[20] *Sots.-Dem.*, 28 June 1917.
[21] Hannah Arendt, *The Origins of Totalitarianism*, pp. 319-321; Keep, *Russian Revolution*. See also Marshall S. Shatz on the later implications of this postulated atomization: "Soviet Society and the Purge of the Thirties in the Mirror of Memoir Literature."

of Petrograd; and while this study has not explored the revolutionary experience of Moscow in its entirety, some new insights nonetheless emerge.

Both 1917 revolutions in Moscow are usually viewed as slow-motion instant replays of the Petrograd revolutions. "The overturn in Moscow was only an echo of the insurrection in Petrograd," writes Trotsky of February. In October Moscow's workers continued to be more backward than Petrograd's; they lacked fighting experience, and therefore the insurrection in the second capital was not so quickly successful.[22] The social, economic, and political analyses of the preceding chapters, however, indicate not that Moscow's working class was more backward, but that it was more socially complex than Petrograd's. Skilled metalworkers played an important role in the revolution wherever they were, but these workers were not the only ones involved in the revolution, and the degree of a city's revolutionary zeal cannot be linked only with the numerical or proportional size of its skilled metalist work force. Moscow's workers, as has been seen, interacted with one another and with members of other social classes, producing more muted and less impulsive responses to such events as the April crisis and the July insurrection.

The experience of Moscow suggests that there was more than one model of the revolutionary process in 1917 rather than time-lagged variants of the Petrograd model. Further work on other Russian cities and regions in 1917 might well produce a new reassessment of the significance of Petrograd and of the process of the revolution. If Petrograd, as the center of government, had had Moscow's mixed social composition, would the capital city have been polarized along class lines so early? Was there an alternative to the sharp class antagonisms that Petrograd transmitted to less-polarized provinces? Did this example of polarization affect the development of class consciousness in Moscow and elsewhere? Or was Petrograd's radicalism, and Moscow's moderation, due as much to the attraction of the capital's factories for underground socialist revolutionaries as to its social composition? At any rate, like different strata of workers, Moscow and Petrograd interacted in 1917; it is important to remember that one did not merely follow the other.

A final goal of this study has been to demonstrate the value and feasibility of social history in its application to the Russian Revolution. The results of this approach have modified common perceptions of the role and significance of workers in 1917; they have indicated the complexity of the revolutionary process. There is more work to be done, however, in order to understand the revolution and its consequences. Further studies of this and other revolutions must continue to look at processes,

[22] Trotsky, vol. 1, p. 141, and vol. 3, p. 279.

at complexities, at contradictions. The example of Moscow in 1917 can supply some building blocks for future work and future comparisons: the categories of peasant versus worker, socialist versus class consciousness, artisanal versus factory work can be applied to other contexts. In time, historians and readers will have a new synthesis and a deeper understanding of the Russian Revolution and the process of social change.

APPENDIX A. *Processing Information on Moscow Workers*

FACED with masses of potentially informative tidbits on factory life—here a memoirist's observation that Bolshevik influence declined after July in a railway shop, there a newspaper report of violence toward a factory owner—the best way to organize the material was to accumulate all the information about individual factories and consolidate this information by factory. The resulting factory file has provided an enormously rich fund of information on Moscow working-class activity in 1917.

Several stages were required to create the factory file that has been referred to in the text. First, a list of factories was accumulated using existing lists (*Spisok fabrik*, Sovet s"ezdov) and supplemented with factories named in contemporary reports. (The records of contributions turned up a number of factories—especially state or municipally owned—which were not found in other lists.) A master card for each factory was prepared containing name, address, type of output, and size of work force. Then information specific to each factory—newspaper and documentary reports on strikes, resolutions, contributions, etc.—was filed with the corresponding factory master card. Finally, all other observations about specific factories were culled from memoirs, documents, and statistical collections and recorded on the master card. The resulting boxes of cards constitute the factory file.

For ease in dealing with all this information, much of it was categorized, coded, and punched onto computer cards. The basic categories of information are given in Table A-1, along with the relevant sources (where a specific source has furnished all the information for a particular category) or types of sources. The forty-two categories, or variables, in Table A-1 constitute the master factory data-set referred to in the text.

For the analyses of resolutions and contributions, separate data-sets were constructed using variables specifically relating to these materials. The variables in these data-sets are listed in Tables A-2 and A-3. The information about contributions and resolutions was then matched with the corresponding factory data, providing complete descriptive information about factories involved in these activities.

For the analysis of strikes, I did not use the factory data-set but constructed a separate strike data-set from information filed by individual factories and also collected from trade union materials, chronicles, and other sources. In many cases of industrywide strikes, names of individual factories involved were not given, so the data on individual factories was not usable. Table A-4 gives the variables employed in the strike data-set.

TABLE A-1. *Variables Employed in Factory File*

1. Factory identification number
2. Factory qualifier: evaluation of whether the factory really operated in 1917, according to source and date of information
3. Location by precinct
    Sources: *Spisok fabrik* and Sovet s"ezdov for addresses; maps in *Statisticheskii atlas g. Moskvy i moskovskoi gubernii, Istoriia Moskvy,* and Baedeker, *Russia,* and *Sovremennoe khoziaistvo g. Moskvy; Ulitsy Moskvy* for locations.
4. Location by local soviet district
5. Location by local duma district
    Source: *Soldat-Grazhdanin,* 30 August 1917.
6. Primary industry
    Sources: *Spisok fabrik;* Sovet s"ezdov.
7. Secondary industry, if any
8. Factory size, in number of workers
    Sources: *Spisok fabrik;* press reports.
9. Approximate share of women in the factory work force
10. Percentage of women in the factory work force
    Sources: Sick-fund membership report in *Ezhemesiachnyi statisticheskii biulleten' g. Moskvy,* December 1916; deferment commission reports throughout the year in *Soldat-Grazhdanin* and *Trudovaia kopeika.*
11. Mechanized or hand-operated factory
    Source: *Spisok fabrik.*
12. Evacuation from western provinces
    Source: *Spisok fabrik.*
13. Approximate share of workers living in factory barracks
    Source: I. M. Koz'minykh-Lanin, *Vrachebnaia pomoshch' fabrichno-zavodskim rabochim g. Moskvy.*
14. Private or public ownership
    Source: Inferred from the name of the factory, or from press reports.
15. Operating status: temporary or permanent shutdowns
    Source: Press reports.
16. Productivity during the March-October period
    Source: *Ekonomicheskoe polozhenie Rossii nakanune velikoi oktiabr'skoi sotsialisticheskoi revoliutsii,* vol. 2.
17. Unemployment: jobs available or workers fired
    Source: *Moskovskii metallist* for jobs available.
18. Deferments lost, in percentage of total work force
    Sources: Reports of deferment-verifying commissions given in *Soldat-Grazhdanin, Trudovaia kopeika.*
19. Representative on War Industry Committee?
    Source: I. Menitskii, *Revoliutsionnoe dvizhenie voennykh godov* (Moscow, 1924), vol. 2, pp. 121-122.
20. Sick fund active in factory?
    Source: *Ezhemesiachnyi statisticheskii biulleten' g. Moskvy,* December 1916.

21. Number of prerevolutionary incidents: strikes, walkouts, protests
    Sources: Police reports in TsGAOR, fonds 63, D.O. (102).
22. Representative at first meeting of the Moscow Soviet?
    Source: *Organizatsiia i stroitel'stvo sovetov rabochikh deputatov v 1917 g.*
23. Representation in Soviet of Workers' Deputies in May-June?
    Source: List in *Izv. MSRD*, supplemented by individual reports.
24. Representative on any other public body?
    Source: Press reports.
25. Union affiliation of factory, if any
    Source: Press reports.
26. Participation in strike of February 28
    Source: Police reports in TsGAOR, fond 63.
27. Date of formation of factory committee
    Source: Press reports.
28. Date of formation of Red Guard unit
    Sources: G. A. Tsypkin, *Krasnaia gvardiia*, press reports, memoirs.
29. Size of Red Guard unit
    Source: Same as above.
30. Reliability of information on party affiliation
31. Party affiliation—March
32. Party affiliation—July
33. Party affiliation—October
    Sources: Press reports, memoirs, documents (see Chapter Five for fuller discussion).
34. Number of strikes March-October
    Source: Press reports (see Chapter Eight).
35. Number of resolutions published
    Source: Press reports (see Chapter Six).
36. Eight-hour-workday response
    Source: Press reports.
37. Liberty Loan response
    Source: Press reports.
38. April-crisis response
    Sources: Press reports, memoirs.
39. July-days response
    Sources: Press reports, memoirs.
40. Moscow Conference response
    Sources: Press reports, memoirs.
41. Number of participants in Moscow Conference protest strike
    Source: Press reports.
42. Kornilov-mutiny response
    Source: Press reports.

TABLE A-2. *Variables Employed in File of Resolutions*

1. Factory identification number
2. Resolution identification number
3. Month of resolution
4. Day of month of resolution
5. Type of meeting passing the resolution
6. Attendance at meeting, in percentage of workers in the factory
7. Was meeting held during factory hours?

8. Presence of outside speakers
9. Disruptions during the meeting
10. Alternative resolutions offered
11. Vote on resolution: percentage of those present voting yes
12. Source of resolution report (up to five for each resolution)
13. Points in the resolution (up to ten for each resolution)

TABLE A-3. *Variables Employed in File of Contributions*

1. Factory identification number
2. Contribution identification number
3. Month of contribution
4. Day of month of contribution
5. Source of contribution report
6. Purpose of contribution
7. Participation of employees in contribution
8. Contribution represents full- or half-day's wage, if known
9. Amount of contribution, rounded off to lower ruble

TABLE A-4. *Variables Employed in File on Strikes*

1. Strike identification number
2. Real or threatened strike
3. Industry
4. Does industry do defense work?
5. Number of workers involved in strike
6. Number of workers employed in factory or industry
7. Date strike began
8. Number of days in strike
9. Presence of organization
10. Outcome
11. Factory (industry) mechanized?
12. Strike demands (up to ten for each strike)

APPENDIX B. *A Note on Statistical Sources*

THE lack of comprehensive statistical information for Moscow for 1917 necessitates the use of material that is not entirely appropriate but which, with the proper caveats, can nevertheless be used to advantage. In brief, four major censuses, taken in 1897, 1902, 1912, and 1918, provide detailed information on Moscow and its inhabitants. The first, *Pervaia vseobshchaia perepis' naseleniia Rossiiskoi Imperii*, provides in admirable detail information about the workers in various occupations by chast', age, sex, and place of birth. The obvious disadvantage of this material is that it is dated and that the twenty years between the data collection and the period under study saw significant changes in the complexion of Moscow's working class. But it is the only source that distributes occupation by district, and this is especially useful for those areas within the Sadovoe, which was already built up in 1897 and whose social composition probably did not change much in this time.

The 1902 census suffers from the same defects, but it is useful also for its detailed occupational listing by age group and by soslovie.

The 1912 census has been reported only partially—in occasional appendices to the city's monthly statistical bulletin, in preliminary form in the *Trudy* of the city statistical department, and in the statistical yearbook published in 1927 (*Ezhemesiachnyi statisticheskii biulleten' g. Moskvy; Trudy stat. otdela MGU*, vyp. 1; *Stat. ezhegodnik*). The 1912 material on sex and place of birth by occupation is of great value.

The 1918 census of industry and occupation, published in TsSU, *Trudy*, vol. 26, vyp. 1, provides the greatest frustration—for two reasons. First, unlike the 1897 census, it has not yet been published in detail for each province and major city. Thus, information is available on literacy by occupation for all of Russia and on literacy for each province, but not on literacy by occupation for each province. Thus, one is forced to approximate for Moscow from the results for Russia as a whole. More serious is the great change in the composition of the labor force, which change took place between February 1917 and August 1918 when the census information was collected. The working population of Moscow shrank by one-half during this time, but not, unfortunately, uniformly. Workers closely connected with village life probably returned during this period of land reallocation and urban famine, so the information reported for 1918 on workers' attachment to their villages is underestimated; those workers with such ties were not likely to be in the cities to be counted.

In addition, politicized cadre workers also left the city to serve in the Red Army. This can be seen clearly in the age profile for almost every occupation: there is a sharp decline in the number of twenty- to twenty-five-year-old males. Thus the 1918 census, closest to the period under study, provides in many ways the most distorted information.

APPENDIX C. *Moscow Trade Unions in 1917*

Union	Date Formed	Membership at Peak
Confectioners	March 3	13,000 (October)
Municipal employees	March 4	40,000 (May)
Plumbers	March 6	2,200 (August)
Bakers	March 8	12,000 (August)
House porters	March 8	2,500 (July)
Leather workers	March 8	18,000 (June)
Chauffeurs	March 9	1,500 (July)
Cooks	March 14	4,000 (August)
Electrical repairmen	March 14	—
Electrical workers	March 14	1,500 (July)
Gold-silver workers	March 14	4,000 (April)
Tailors	March 14	36,000 (August)
Domestic servants	March 16	1,500 (August)
Button makers	March 19	—
Carters	March 19	—
Chemical workers	March 19?[a]	3,000 (June)
Perfume workers	March 19	5,000 (July)
Sausage makers	March 19	800 (June)
Textile workers	March 19	111,000 (August)
Waiters	March 21	9,000 (May)
Watchmakers	March 21?	—
Construction workers	March 22	13,000 (September)
Laundry workers	March 23	2,418 (October)
Tobacco workers	March 23	4,146 (July)
Printers	March 25[b]	16,500 (August)
Woodworkers	March 25	7,000 (May)
Cardboard workers	March 26	2,000 (October)
Newspaper workers	March 26?	—
Freight handlers	March 27	1,300 (July)
Metalists	March 29	65,000 (August)
Brick makers	April 4	3,500 (July)
Inn employees	April 9?	—
Yard keepers	April 9	10,000 (May)
Unskilled laborers (chernorabochie)	April 11?	—
Rubber workers	April 12	7,000 (June)
Bath employees	April 16?	—
Hospital employees	April 16?	2,000 (May)
Hairdressers	April 21	600 (August)
Sewage workers	April 23	—
Tea packers	April 23	3,601 (August)
House painters	April 24	400 (May)
Glassworkers	April 26	40,000 (October)

APPENDIX C.—*continued*

Union	Date Formed	Membership at Peak
Exchange artel employees	April 27	7,000 (June)
Cooperative employees	April 30	700 (June)
Couriers	April 30	800 (May)
Technicians	May 1	400 (May)
Technicians and draftsmen	May 1	—
Concrete workers	May 7?	—
Ribbon weavers	May 7?	—
Hat makers	c	900 (June)
Photographers' assistants	May 15	—
Engravers	May 18	—
Carriage builders	May 28	—
Stove setters	May 28	768
Pharmacy employees	May 29	—
Sausage-casing workers	May	90 (May)
Cinema workers	June 28	—
Railway workers	July 10	20,000 (October)
Jewelers	July 13	—
Cement workers	September 15	—
Brush makers	?	—
Cemetery workers	?	—
Furriers	?	—

SOURCES: *Moskovskii sovet professional'nykh soiuzov*, contemporary newspapers, trade union journals, memoirs, and monographs on individual unions.

NOTE: In many cases, exact date of formation and size of membership cannot be determined from available sources.

a. Definitely by May 20.

b. Formally chartered on this date.

c. May 9.

APPENDIX D. Precinct-Level Voting Results: June 25 City Duma Elections

Precinct	Kadet	Popular Socialist	SR	S-D(M)	S-D(B)	Edinstvo	Liberal Democrat	Total Votes	Total Eligible
Alekseev	704	38	5,311	934	918	4	9	7,918	10,605
I Arbat	3,447	256	4,186	716	194	52	35	8,886	16,695
II Arbat	3,957	310	4,711	994	306	103	43	10,424	20,356
I Basmannyi	2,929	217	5,963	1,234	925	38	41	11,347	18,268
II Basmannyi	1,260	72	4,937	1,011	1,468	8	25	8,781	13,020
Blagushinsk	845	30	7,758	2,353	2,606	7	15	13,614	17,487
Bogorodsk	560	56	2,400	2,081	719	2	12	5,830	7,561
Butyrki	1,431	62	5,922	1,374	1,603	24	25	10,441	15,076
Gorodskoi	1,146	81	3,392	340	259	13	17	5,248	8,458
Dorogomilovo	1,090	49	9,045	1,174	539	12	24	11,933	17,612
I Lefortov	2,552	151	9,290	2,496	5,302	12	38	19,841	26,947
II Lefortov	1,419	59	6,441	2,199	3,554	7	32	13,711	15,870
III Lefortov	981	37	5,910	1,053	1,521	1	8	9,511	10,491
Mar'ino-roshch	633	39	8,122	2,279	1,705	9	52	12,839	21,744
I Meshchanskii	2,714	214	8,202	1,512	1,161	24	19	13,846	22,357
II Meshchanskii	930	62	5,326	1,098	770	12	23	8,221	13,134
III Meshchanskii	4,036	260	13,719	2,992	1,863	69	25	22,964	37,771
IV Meshchanskii	2,924	248	9,880	3,266	2,014	44	29	18,405	26,338
I Miasnitskii	1,965	201	2,911	480	170	34	12	5,773	12,357
II Miasnitskii	1,607	197	2,855	443	155	19	16	5,292	9,378
III Miasnitskii	1,101	102	4,030	518	204	16	16	5,987	10,094
Novo-Andron evsk	816	27	9,539	2,383	1,652	14	36	14,467	22,360
Petr-Razumovsk	635	109	4,108	432	347	15	7	5,653	8,198
Petrovskii	4,379	127	7,605	1,073	1,108	10	12	14,314	18,181
I Prechistenskii	3,940	263	4,380	1,310	391	58	34	10,376	18,370

II Prechistenskii	3,746	315	4,289	1,215	344	39	26	9,974	18,443
I Presnia	2,070	123	11,049	441	1,318	44	56	15,101	22,504
II Presnia	2,413	151	7,575	1,790	583	43	24	12,579	20,625
III Presnia	1,853	141	11,206	1,703	977	10	36	15,926	24,293
I Piatnitskii	2,879	226	8,826	1,304	1,003	47	20	14,309	22,698
II Piatnitskii	2,667	200	11,381	2,163	2,241	28	30	18,710	25,776
I Rogozhskii	1,573	788	4,098	2,074	540	23	12	9,108	15,603
II Rogozhskii	1,498	131	7,447	1,413	557	19	11	11,076	17,430
III Rogozhskii	1,963	173	9,539	1,530	1,928	10	10	15,153	22,919
I Serpukhov	1,134	71	6,937	1,831	4,720	8	23	14,724	20,400
II Serpukhov	1,709	166	8,853	1,903	5,123	9	14	17,777	26,367
I Simonovka	202	19	3,485	368	1,290	0	19	5,383	7,445
II Simonovka	495	30	6,407	766	651	14	22	8,385	11,372
I Sretenskii	1,936	99	5,668	689	575	28	19	9,014	16,031
II Sretenskii	2,890	283	6,772	1,112	769	43	19	11,888	20,643
I Sushchevskii	3,892	261	10,754	2,214	1,513	66	65	18,765	37,070
II Sushchevskii	2,027	143	9,747	1,738	1,622	23	36	15,336	24,621
III Sushchevskii	3,144	242	8,397	2,978	1,921	71	39	16,792	26,761
I Tver	2,496	197	3,367	600	264	46	20	6,990	11,403
II Tver	3,011	247	4,735	695	333	44	21	9,086	18,117
III Tver	1,623	130	3,006	363	296	17	14	5,449	10,182
I Khamovniki	2,531	180	11,726	2,903	2,674	22	33	20,069	39,653
II Khamovniki	2,274	228	4,401	993	404	41	24	8,365	14,836
Cherkizovo	1,356	33	8,544	1,204	1,516	8	24	12,685	16,129
I Iakimanskii	2,295	163	6,290	1,578	643	26	77	11,072	16,833
II Iakimanskii	2,384	141	8,060	1,505	1,459	39	40	13,628	21,711
I Iauzskii	2,029	235	3,556	473	320	45	6	6,662	16,129
II Iauzskii	2,593	245	4,890	964	822	35	38	9,587	16,106
Total	107,980	8,588	355,237	73,321	67,442	1,451	1,374	615,393	980,828

SOURCES: *Izv. MSRD*, 27-29 June 1917; *Russkoe slovo*, 2 July 1917.

APPENDIX E. *Statistical Procedures for Voting Analysis*

SOME of the statistical materials presented in Chapter Five have been examined using two statistical measures of correlation, the Spearman rank correlation and multivariate regression by ordinary least squares.

The rank-correlation coefficient is the "sturdier" of the two methods—it does not use the numerical value of the variables but correlates the ranks of each variable. This is especially useful when the value of a variable (such as the level of SR support from different industries) is not very reliable but when the relative values (the ranks) can be accepted. In the example in the chapter, each industry's SR "mood" and the share of its workers born outside Moscow were correlated. If the correlation between SR mood and peasantness were perfect, the strongest SR industry would also be the strongest peasant industry, the second strongest would be the same, and all the way to the end—the least SR-oriented industry would also be the least peasant in origin. In this case, the correlation coefficient would be $+1$. If the opposite were perfectly true, if SR-supporting industries were the least rural in origin, the strongest SR industry would be last in terms of rural workers; the correlation coefficient (r) would then be -1. If there were no relationship between the two variables, the coefficient would be zero. The test of the relationship, then, is to see if the coefficient is significantly greater or smaller than zero.[1]

The multivariate regression permits a more complex analysis of the relationship among variables: regression analysis can be used to investigate the dependence of a single variable on several others. This is the procedure used in the analysis of the June and September elections. The goal was to find out the relationship between each pair selected from five dependent variables (variables to be explained)—participation, Kadet vote, SR vote, Menshevik vote, and Bolshevik vote—and a set of independent (explanatory) variables—those characteristics that, it was hypothesized, might affect voting behavior. These were share of working-class residents, literacy, share of females, share of refugees, and the share of each of eighteen industries. (Most industries were too small for their effect to be measured and were not included in the actual analysis.) While

---

[1] Blalock, *Social Statistics*, p. 18; Frederick Mosteller and Robert E. K. Rourke, *Sturdy Statistics*, chap. 6; Richard A. Comfort, *Revolutionary Hamburg*, pp. 175-178.

the rank-correlation method is limited to bivariate relationships among variables, the least-squares method permits a study of the effect of several variates on a single variable of interest. If one could not measure the effects of several variates on the dependent variable, that is, if one could not allow for working-class residents, for example, and found high separate correlations between voter participation on one side and working-class districts and big metalist districts on the other, that person would not know whether or not it was only the metalists who were responsible for the big turnout. Therefore, each regression equation (one for each of the five dependent variables) was estimated with several independent variables. For example, I calculated the relationship between Kadet vote and four so-called demographic characteristics: working-class precincts, literacy, sex, and refugees. The question is, how much of the variation in Kadet vote in different precincts can be explained by these factors? If one seeks the relationship between Kadet vote and working-class precincts, the procedure calculates how much is explained by the other three variables and then determines how much of the remaining variation can be attributed to the share of working-class residents. In other words, suppose there are two precincts with different percentages of the vote for the Kadets, but each has the same share of literate, female, and refugee voters. Does the difference in the size of working-class populations in the two precincts explain a significant amount of the Kadet-vote difference? In this analysis, the answer is yes: in both June and September, when the other demographic variables are allowed for, there is a significant (one can be at least 95 percent certain it is not accidental) negative relationship between working-class districts and Kadet votes.

The following table gives an example of the results from such a multivariate analysis: four independent variables—proletarian district, metalists, textilists, and chemical workers—were used to try to explain each of the five dependent variables. The pluses and minuses indicate positive or negative relationships: one of either means the relationship is statistically insignificant (less than 95 percent level of confidence), two indicates a confidence level of 95 percent, and three indicates 99 percent confidence—a very solid relationship.

	Partici-pation	Kadet Vote	SR Vote	Menshe-vik Vote	Bolshe-vik Vote
Working-class population	+ + +	− − −	−	+	+ + +
Metalists	+	− − −	+	−	+ +
Textilists	−	−	−	+	−
Chemical workers	+ + +	− − −	−	−	+ + +

A final word of warning: procedures such as this are subject to the so-called "ecological fallacy," the assumption that if there is a relationship between two variables in a given precinct (where other factors are also present), such as printers and Kadets, it is the printers who were actually voting for Kadets. It has been pointed out in the text that this is not necessarily true, and so conclusions based on this procedure must always be tempered by consideration of the fact that a problem does exist here.

APPENDIX F. *Most Frequent Points in Resolutions in 1917: Before Grouping* (25 OF 393 POSSIBLE POINTS)

Resolution	Number of Workers Voting	Peak Month
Oppose death penalty	76,040	August
Support power to soviet	75,300	October
Fight counterrevolution	53,790	September
Protest Moscow Conference	42,070	August
Support peace without annexation	31,500	March
Support Soviet	31,450	April
End war (generally)	30,810	September
Free political prisoners (e.g., Trotsky)	30,630	September
Control prices	28,950	June
Support worker kontrol'	28,670	June
Protest high property and income tax	28,210	June
Reelect Soviet	27,150	August
Arrest capitalists and counterrevolutionaries	26,930	September
Support Provisional Government conditionally	25,050	March
Control production	23,640	September
Oppose shutdown of socialist press	23,380	August
Close bourgeois press	23,120	September
Arm workers	22,560	August
Protest Liberty Loan	21,410	April
Oppose harassment of Bolsheviks	21,290	July
Oppose coalition	21,140	October
Support Provisional Government decree eight-hour workday	20,730	March
Call Constituent Assembly quickly	20,580	March
Dissolve State Duma, State Council	20,510	August
Limit profits	19,410	May

APPENDIX G. *Most Frequent Points in Resolutions in 1917: After Grouping* (20 POINTS OF 54 GROUPS)

Resolution	Numbers of Workers Voting	Peak Month
Oppose counterrevolution	173,770	September
Support soviet power	91,900	October
Support free press and assembly	79,980	August
Oppose the war	76,110	April
Oppose death penalty	76,040	August
Support economic measures at capitalists' expense	73,330	April
Support Soviet	72,040	April
State specific war aims	70,270	April
Support eight-hour workday	64,790	March
Oppose Moscow Conference	61,980	August
Support Provisional Government	48,510	March
Support wage-price controls	48,130	September
Support Bolsheviks	47,150	August
Support worker kontrol'	43,870	June
Support Provisional Government kontrol' of economy	41,880	May
Show no support for Provisional Government	40,610	October
State concern about fuel, materiel, supply	38,280	September
Call for land	33,310	April
Show no support for Moscow Soviet	33,230	August
State concern about food supply	30,900	September

APPENDIX H. Contributions by Industry: Rubles Per Worker
(AVERAGED; WEIGHTED BY WAGES)

Industry	Red Gift	Municipal Fund	Soviet	Own Strike Fund	Others' Strike Fund	Political Victims	Bol-sheviks	Men-sheviks	S-Ds	SRs
Mineral	1.43	.18	.75	.01	0	.09	.10	0	0	.003
Rare metals	1.33	.36	.18	.25	0	.16	.11	0	0	.009
Metal	1.57	.69	.41	1.56	.07	.17	.20	.018	.02	.012
Machine	1.75	.70	.37	1.43	.10	.27	.23	.012	.06	.016
Wood	1.09	.12	.16	.03	.03	.07	.13	.005	.06	0
Chemical	1.85	.43	.84	.01	.92	.09	.14	.004	.11	.014
Food	.82	.39	.24	1.03	.02	.04	.06	.003	.02	.001
Animal byproducts	.56	.06	.01	0	0	0	0	0	0	0
Leather	.81	.12	.30	.25	0	.02	.06	.004	.02	.001
Textile	.76	.31	.19	.05	.01	.04	.02	.001	0	0
Clothing	.61	.18	.27	.02	0	0	.07	.002	.05	0
Paper	.42	.47	.03	.01	0	.03	.12	0	0	0
Printing	1.26	.19	.42	1.93	0	.07	.04	0	.003	.003
Power	3.71	.35	2.25	.79	.50	.55	.54	.05	0	.04
Tram	1.40	.81	.58	.05	.44	.40	.30	0	0	.16

APPENDIX 1. Strikes and Strikers in Moscow in 1917

Industry	Number of Strikes	Percent Total Strikes	Number of Strikers	Percent Total Strikers	Total in Industry	Percent Moscow Work Force	Strike Propensity
Wood	26	9.7	6,059	2.5	3,311	0.8	3.13
Metal	69	25.7	75,620	31.7	46,682	12.0	2.64
Leather	38	14.2	32,107	13.4	22,089	5.7	2.35
Silk[a]	3	1.1	13,000	5.4	10,631	2.7	2.00
Rare metals	15	5.6	1,399	0.58	1,225	0.3	1.93
Mineral	4	1.5	1,715	0.72	1,646	0.4	1.79
Clothing	17	6.3	31,171	13.1	32,180	8.2	1.60
Tram	1	.4	5,314	2.2	5,314	1.4	1.57
Paper	4	1.5	2,491	1.0	3,309	0.8	1.25
Construction	9	3.4	11,518	4.8	17,447	4.5	1.07
Food	12	4.5	10,386	4.3	19,973	5.1	.84
Services	15	5.6	37,661	15.8	109,677	28.1	.56
Textile	17	6.3	16,655	7.0	59,690	15.3	.46
Chemical	10	3.7	2,801	1.2	10,931	2.8	.43
Wool[a]	7	2.6	2,354	1.0	13,419	3.4	.29
Power and gas	1	.4	300	0.1	1,406	0.4	.25
Printing	15	5.6	1,378	0.6	10,624	2.7	.22
Warehouse and freight	10	3.7	2,157	0.9	21,858	5.6	.16
Mixed fiber[a]	6	2.2	1,063	0.4	10,413	2.7	.15
Cotton[a]	1	0.4	238	0.1	24,741	6.3	.02
Animal byproducts	3	1.1	0[b]	0[b]	1,555	0.4	.00[b]
Total	268	99.9	257,772	99.9	390,587	100.0	1.00

SOURCES: *Stat. ezhegodnik*, p. 47; *Spisok fabrik*; Grunt, "Moskovskii proletariat"; Gaponenko, *Rabochii klass Rossii*, p. 443.
a. Silk, wool, mixed fiber, and cotton are subgroups of the textile industry and are not included in total figures.
b. The number of strikers is unknown for the strikes of animal-byproducts workers.

APPENDIX J. *Economic and Social Characteristics of Striking Moscow Industries*

Industry	Strike Propensity	1916 Wage	Change in Wage 1913-1916	Percent Born in Moscow
Wood	3.13	628	.80	6
Metal	2.64	981	1.14	14
Leather	2.35	811	1.21	6
Silk	2.00	337	.67	—
Rare metals	1.93	—	—	9
Mineral	1.79	521	.91	7
Clothing	1.60	502	.97	17
Tram	1.57	—	—	4
Paper	1.25	501	1.00	15
Construction	1.07	500	1.36	3
Food	.84	566	1.00	11
Services	.56	—	—	4
Textile	.46	554	1.03	4
Chemical	.43	553	1.06	14
Wool	.29	486	1.13	—
Power	.25	917	.90	—
Printing	.22	757	.81	27
Warehouse	.16	—	—	—
Mixed fiber	.15	691	1.25	—
Cotton	.02	563	.92	—
Animal byproducts	.00	555	.81	—

SOURCES: Wages and changes in wages from TsSU, *Trudy*, vol. 26, table 15; also for changes in wages, *Ezhemesiachnyi statisticheskii biulleten'*, 1913-1916, and Markuzon, *Zarabotnaia plata*; percentages from *Stat. ezhegodnik*, pp. 68-73.

APPENDIX K. *Economic Strikes and Industry Wage Levels*

Industry	Percent of All Strikers in Strikes for Wages or Better Conditions	1916 Wage	Change in Wage 1913-1916
Construction	44.3	500	1.36
Leather	61.7	811	1.21
Wood	64.5	628	.80
Paper	65.3	501	1.00
Rare metals	68.1	—	—
Services	70.6	—	—
Clothing	75.0	502	.97
Mineral	75.7	521	.91
Chemical	75.8	553	1.06
Food	76.6	566	1.00
Printing	79.3	757	.81
Textile	79.4	554	1.03
Metal	80.0	981	1.14
Warehouse	85.9	—	—
Power	100.0	917	.90
Animal byproducts	100.0	555	.81

SOURCES: TsSU, *Trudy*, vol. 26, table 15; *Ezhemesiachnyi statisticheskii biulleten'*, 1913-1916; Markuzon, *Zarabotnaia plata*.

Selected Bibliography

SOME sources with only one citation in the notes have not been included in the Bibliography, but are referred to in the Index. Individual memoirs included in collections have not, with a few exceptions, been listed separately here. The authors of such memoirs, when cited in the notes, are likewise included in the Index.

The Bibliography has been arranged under four headings: archives; contemporary newspapers and journals; primary sources, such as memoirs, documents, and statistical materials; and secondary and other works, both Western and Soviet, including reference works.

ARCHIVAL SOURCES

Gosudarstvennyi arkhiv moskovskoi oblasti (GAMO)
    fond 66, Moskovskii sovet rabochikh deputatov
    fond 186, Professional'nyi soiuz metallistov
    fond 627, Professional'nyi soiuz tekstil'shchikov
    fond 633, Professional'nyi soiuz portnykh
    fond 2443, Zavod Dinamo
    fond 3872, Trekhgornaia manufaktura
    fond 4569, Moskovskii sovet rabochikh deputatov
Tsentral'nyi gosudarstvennyi arkhiv oktiabr'skoi revoliutsii (TsGAOR)
    fond 63, Moskovskoe okhrannoe otdelenie
    fond D.O. (102), Departament politsii

NEWSPAPERS AND JOURNALS

Delo naroda. Petrograd, 1917. Daily. Socialist Revolutionary.
Ezhemesiachnyi statisticheskii biulleten' goroda Moskvy. Moscow, 1912-1917.
    Monthly bulletin. (Abbreviated as *Ezhemesiachnyi statisticheskii biulleten'*.)
Gazeta-kopeika. Moscow, 1917. Daily.
Golos kozhevnika. Moscow, 1917. Leather workers' union.
Golos rabochei kooperatsiia. Moscow, 1917. Moscow Union (of Cooperatives)
    Society.
Golos zheleznodorozhnika. Moscow, 1917. Daily. Moscow junction railway organization.
Izvestiia Moskovskogo soveta rabochikh deputatov. Moscow, 1917. Daily. (Abbreviated as *Izv. MSRD.*)
Izvestiia Moskovskogo voenno-promyshlennogo komiteta. Moscow, 1917.
Izvestiia Moskovskoi gorodskoi dumy. Otdel obshchee. Moscow, 1917.

Izvestiia Vremennogo ispolnitel'nogo komiteta moskovskikh obshchestvennykh organizatsii. Moscow, 2 March 1917.
Moskovskie vedomosti. Moscow, 1917. Daily.
Moskovskii metallist. Moscow, 1917. Metalists' union.
Pechatnik. Moscow, 1917. Printers' union.
Proletarii. Moscow, 1917. Daily. United Social-Democratic.
Rabochaia zhizn'. Moscow, 1917. Municipal workers' union.
Russkie vedomosti. Moscow, 1917. Daily.
Russkoe slovo. Moscow, 1917. Daily.
Soldat-Grazhdanin. Moscow, 1917. Daily. Moscow Soviet of Soldiers' Deputies.
Sotsial-Demokrat. Moscow, 1917. Daily. Bolshevik. (Abbreviated as *Sots.-Dem.*)
Torgovo-promyshlennaia gazeta. Petrograd, 1917. Daily.
Trud. Moscow, 1917. Daily. Socialist Revolutionary.
Trudovaia kopeika. Moscow, 1917. Daily.
Utro Rossii. Moscow, 1917. Daily.
Vecherniaia pochta. Moscow, March 1917.
Vechernii kur'er. Moscow, 1917. Daily.
Vedomosti komissariata moskovskogo gradonachal'stva. Moscow, 1917. Daily.
Vestnik Vremennogo pravitel'stva. Petrograd, 1917. Daily.
Volia i dumy zheleznodorozhnika. Moscow, 1917. Daily. Moscow-Kursk railroad.
Vpered. Moscow, 1917. Daily. Menshevik.
Vrachebnaia zhizn'. Moscow, 1917. Russian medical association.
Vremia. Moscow, 1917. Daily.
Zemlia i volia. Moscow, 1917. Daily. Socialist Revolutionary.

Memoirs, Documents, and Statistical Materials

Akhun, M. and V. Petrov, eds. *1917 god v Moskve. Khronika revoliutsii.* Moscow, 1934.
Armi. "Sredi prachek." *Kommunal'nyi rabotnik,* 1927, no. 20, p. 21.
Arosev, A. Ia. *Kak eto proizoshlo (oktiabr'skie dni v Moskve).* Moscow, 1923.
――――. *Moskovskii sovet v 1917 godu.* Moscow, 1927.
Astakhov, P. "Moskovskii rafinadnii zavod." *Golos sakharnika,* 1922, no. 8, p. 30.
Atsarkin, A., and A. Zverev, eds. *Nashe rozhdenie.* Moscow, 1931.
Avdeev, N., ed. *Revoliutsiia 1917 goda. Khronika sobytii.* 6 vols. Moscow-Leningrad, 1923-1930.
Batyshev, I. G. "O rabote sushchevsko-mar'inskoi raionnoi dumy v Moskve v 1917 godu." *Istoricheskii arkhiv,* 1957, no. 4, pp. 184-192.
Belousov, Ivan. *Ushedshaia Moskva: Zapiski po lichnym vospominaniiam s nachala 1870 godov.* Moscow, [1927].
Bel'skii, A. "V goriachie dni (moskovskaia telefonnaia stantsiia)." *Proletarii sviazi,* 1927, no. 21, pp. 26-27.
Bobrov, A. "Vospominaniia (1917-1919 gody)." *Kommunal'nyi rabotnik,* 1924, nos. 9-10, p. 28.
Bondarev, A. "V nashem raione (vospominaniia)." *Kommunal'nyi rabotnik,* 1927, no. 21 (189).
Borshchevskii, A. "Moskovskie pechatniki v dni oktiabria." *Pechatnik,* 1923, no. 12, p. 20.

Burachenko, O. "Dumy i vospominaniia." *K piatiletnemu iiubileiu sushchestvo-vaniia vserossiiskogo ob"edineniia shveinikov*. Khar'kov, 1922.

Buryshkin, P. A. *Moskva kupecheskaia*. New York: Chekhov, 1954.

Desiat' let. *Sbornik materialov Iu. O. K. Sokol'nicheskogo raiona k 10-letniiu oktiabr'skoi revoliutsii*. Moscow, 1927.

Dinamo: 25 let revoliutsionnoi bor'by. Moscow, 1923.

Dokumenty velikoi proletarskoi revoliutsii. Vol. 2. Moscow, 1948.

Dune, Eduard. "Zapiski krasnogvardeitsa." MS. Nicolaevsky archive, Hoover Institution on War, Revolution, and Peace. Stanford, California, n.d.

Dvinov, Boris L. *Moskovskii sovet rabochikh deputatov, 1917-1922 gody. Vospominaniia*. New York, 1961.

Dvintsy. Sbornik vospominanii. Moscow, 1957.

Dvorianchikov. "Krasno-Presnenskii zavod." *Golos sakharnika*, 1922, no. 8, pp. 29-30.

Ehrenburg, Ilya. *People and Life*. New York: Alfred A. Knopf, 1962.

Ekonomicheskoe polozhenie Rossii nakanune velikoi oktiabr'skoi sotsialisticheskoi revoliutsii. Dokumenty i materialy. 3 vols. Moscow, 1957-1967.

Fabrichno-zavodskaia promyshlennost' goroda Moskvy i moskovskoi gubernii 1917-1927 godov. Moscow, 1928.

Filipenko, M. K. "Moia zhizn'." *Delegatka*, 1924, nos. 2-3, p. 18.

Filippov. "Proidennyi put'." *Kommunal'nyi rabotnik*, 1929, nos. 9-10, pp. 22-24.

Gavrilov, V. "Moe uchastie v oktiabr'skoi revoliutsii 1917 goda." *Moskovskii pechatnik*, 1921, no. 11, p. 11.

God bor'by. Sbornik. Moscow-Leningrad, 1927.

God raboty moskovskogo gorodskogo prodovol'stvennogo komiteta (mart 1917-mart 1918 gody). Moscow, 1918.

Gorshkov, I. V. *Moi vospominaniia o fevral'skoi i oktiabr'skoi revoliutsii 1917 goda v Rogozhsko-Simonovskom raione*. Moscow, 1924.

Grunt, Ian. "Stranitsy proshlogo." In *Put' k oktiabriu*, vol. 3, pp. 88-89. Moscow, 1923.

Iakovlev, A. "Moi vospominaniia." *Moskovskii pechatnik*, 1921, no. 11, p. 9.

Iashnov, E. E. *Dostatachno-li khleba v Rossii?* Petrograd, 1917.

Iasnetsov, O. "Moskva." *Proletarii sviazi*, 1920, nos. 15-16, pp. 16-21.

———. "Pervye dni na moskovskoi telefonnoi seti." *Proletarskaia revoliutsiia*, 1927, no. 20, p. 29.

Ibragimov, Sh. N. "O Lefortovskom raione (s 1915 goda do nachala 1917 goda)." In *Put' k oktiabriu*, vol. 5, pp. 139-165. Moscow, 1925.

Ignatov, E. N. "Iz istorii moskovskogo tsentral'nogo biuro professional'nykh soiuzov. (Pervye shagi vo vremia fevral'skoi revoliutsii.)" In *Materialy po istorii professional'nogo dvizheniia*, vol. 4, pp. 109-140. Moscow, 1925.

———. "Mobilizatsiia kontr-revoliutsionnykh sil k moskovskomu gosudarstvennomu soveshchaniiu i vseobshchaia zabastovka rabochikh." In *God bor'by*, pp. 55-64. Moscow, 1927.

Il'in. "Spravilis' sami." *Kommunal'nyi rabotnik*, 1927, no. 20, p. 21.

"Iz istorii rabochego dvizheniia v moskovskoi gubernii v 1917 godu (mart-aprel')." *Istoricheskii arkhiv*, 1957, no. 1, pp. 79-106.

"Iz vospominanii o moskovskom oktiabre. (Rechi uchastnikov vechera vospominanii 1921 goda.)" *Proletarskaia revoliutsiia*, 1922, no. 7 (10), pp. 214-224.

"K voprosu o chislennosti promyshlennogo proletariata v Rossii nakanune oktiabria." *Istoricheskii arkhiv*, 1961, no. 5, pp. 158-165.

Karandasov, A. "Golos rabochei Moskvy." *Novyi mir*, 1957, no. 9, pp. 145-148.

Karpova, M. "Moskovskaia rabotnitsa v oktiabr'skoi vosstanii." *Kommunistka*, 1927, no. 10, p. 29.

Kh., R. "Profsoiuzy gorodskikh rabochikh i sluzhashchikh v 1917-1918 godakh." *Kommunal'nyi rabotnik*, 1927, no. 20, p. 12.

Khain, A. "Soiuz masterovykh i rabochikh i kommunisticheskaia partiia." *Zheleznodorozhnik*, 1927, no. 17, pp. 19-20.

Khamovniki v oktiabre 1917 goda. Moscow, 1922.

Khinchuk, L. M. "Iz vospominanii o fevral'skoi revoliutsii v Moskve." *Proletarskaia revoliutsiia*, 1923, no. 1(13), pp. 178-186.

Kolokol'nikov, P. [K. Dmitriev]. *Professional'noe dvizhenie v Rossii*. Vol. 1, *Organizatsiia soiuzov*. Petrograd, 1917.

Konovalova, A. "Pervye lastochki oktiabr'skoi revoliutsii." *Delegatka*, 1924, no. 10, p. 5.

Kotomka, L. "Rozhdennye revoliutsiei." *Molodoi kommunist*, 1957, no. 8, pp. 108-113.

Kozelev, B. "Oktiabr' i soiuzy." *Vestnik truda*, 1921, nos. 10-11, p. 16.

Krasnaia Presnia v 1905-1917 godakh. Sbornik vospominanii druzhinnikov krasnoi Presni 1905 goda i krasnogvardeitsev 1917 goda. Moscow, 1930.

Lebedev, Ia. "Moskva protestuet." *Novyi mir*, 1957, no. 8, pp. 159-162.

Lenin, V. I. *Polnoe sobranie socheneniia*. 5th ed. 55 vols. Moscow, 1958- .

Letopis' geroicheskikh dnei. Khronika vazhneishikh istoriko-partiinykh revoliutsionnykh sobytii v Moskve i moskovskoi gubernii. Moscow, 1973.

Litveiko, Anna. "V semnadtsatom." *Iunost'*, 1957, no. 3, pp. 3-18.

Liudvinskaia, T. F. "Butyrskii raion Moskvy v bor'be za vlast' sovetov." *Istoricheskii arkhiv*, 1957, no. 5, pp. 224-236.

Makevtsev, N. "Piat' let tomu nazad." *Kommunal'nyi rabotnik*, 1922, no. 5(82), pp. 6-7.

Mamontov, M. "Dvizhenie rabochikh po obrabotke blagorodnykh metallov v Moskve (po lichnym vospominaniiam)." In *Materialy po istorii professional'nogo dvizheniia*, vol. 5, pp. 185-190. Moscow, 1927.

Marshev, M. *Moskovskie profsoiuzy v oktiabr'skie dni. Vospominaniia uchastnika*. Moscow, 1927.

Materialy k istorii Prokhorovskoi Trekhgornoi manufaktury: Torgovo-promyshlennoi deiatel'nosti sem'i Prokhorovykh gody 1799-1915. Moscow, 1915.

Menitskii, I. "Zavod 'Dinamo' v 1915 godu." *Proletarskaia revoliutsiia*, 1923, no. 1(13), pp. 243-246.

Milonov, Iu., ed. *Moskovskoe professional'noe dvizhenie v gody pervoi revoliutsii*. Moscow, 1926.

Monakhov, A. "Pered oktiabrem (moskovskie vospominaniia)." *Kommunal'nyi rabotnik*, 1924, nos. 9-10, p. 26.

―――. "V puti k sotnemu nomeru." *Kommunal'nyi rabotnik*, 1924, no. 4(100), pp. 7-8.

Morozov, N. K. *Sem' dnei revoliutsii. Sobytiia v Moskve. Dnevnik ochevidtsa*. Moscow, 1917.

Morozov, P. "Podraion pechatnikov-bol'shevikov (vospominaniia)." *Pechatnik*, 1927, nos. 7-8, p. 12.

"Moskovskaia obshchegorodskaia konferentsiia RSDRP(b), Moskva, 1917." *Proletarskaia revoliutsiia*, 1922, no. 10, pp. 481-485.

Moskovskie bol'sheviki v ogne revoliutsionnykh boev. Sbornik vospominanii. Moscow, 1976.

Moskovskie pishcheviki do ob"edineniia (1917-1921 gody). Moscow, 1928.

Moskovskii oblast'noi s"ezd rabochikh-stekol'no-farforovago proizvodstva, 2-i, 1917. Protokol. Moscow, 1917.

Moskovskii sovet professional'nykh soiuzov v 1917 godu (protokoly). Moscow, 1927.

Moskovskii sovet rabochikh i soldatskikh deputatov. Otdel truda. *Kak organizovat' zavodskii (fabrichnyi) rabochii komitet.* Moscow, 1917.

Moskovskii voenno-revoliutsionnyi komitet. Dokumenty oktiabria-noiabria 1917 goda. Moscow, 1968.

Moskovskoe vooruzhennoe vosstanie po dannym obvinitel'nykh aktov i sudebnykh protokolov. Vyp. 1. Moscow, 1906.

Moskva v oktiabre. Moscow, 1919.

Moskva v oktiabre 1917 goda. Vospominaniia krasnogvardeitsev, uchastnikov oktiabr'skikh boev. Moscow, 1934.

Moskva v trekh revoliutsii. Vospominaniia, ocherki, rasskazy. Moscow, 1959.

Na barrikadakh za vlast' sovetov. Vospominaniia uchastnikov oktiabr'skikh boev 1917 goda v Zamoskvorech'e. Moscow. 1934.

Nachal'nyia uchilishcha vedomstva ministerstva narodnogo prosveshcheniia v 1914 godu. Petrograd, 1916.

"Nezabyvaemye dni. Vecher uchastnits oktiabr'skogo perevorota." *Delegatka*, 1927, no. 20, pp. 4-5, 10.

Nosov, S. "Oktiabr'skii molodniak." *Kommunal'nyi rabotnik*, 1927, no. 20, p. 22.

"O chislennosti i kontsentratsii rabochego klassa Rossii nakanune velikoi oktiabr'skoi sotsialisticheskoi revoliutsii." *Istoricheskii arkhiv*, 1960, no. 1, pp. 76-116.

Obzor deiatel'nosti moskovskogo soiuza rabochikh pechatnogo truda (s 28 fevralia 1916 goda po 1 ianvaria 1918 goda). Moscow, 1918.

"Odin iz epizodov." *Kommunal'nyi rabotnik*, 1927, no. 20, p. 23.

Oglodkova, A. "Vospominaniia ob oktiabr'skikh dniakh." *Pravda*, 7 November 1920, p. 3.

Oktiabr' na krasnoi Presne. Vospominaniia. Moscow, 1922.

Oktiabr' na krasnoi Presne. Vospominaniia k x godovshchine. Moscow, 1927.

Oktiabr' 1917 goda v Moskve i moskovskoi gubernii. Obzor dokumentov. Moscow, 1957.

Oktiabr' v Khamovnikakh 1917 godu. Sbornik statei i vospominanii. Moscow, 1927.

Oktiabr' v Moskve. Materialy i dokumenty. Moscow-Leningrad, 1932.

Oktiabr' v Zamoskvorech'e. Moscow-Leningrad, 1957.

Oktiabr'skaia revoliutsiia i fabzavkomy. Materialy po istorii fabrichno-zavodskikh komitetov. Moscow, 1927.

Oktiabr'skie dni v Moskve i raionakh. Moscow, 1922.

Oktiabr'skie dni v Sokol'nicheskom raione, po vospominaniiam uchastnikov. Moscow, 1922.

Organizatsiia i stroitel'stvo sovetov rabochikh deputatov v 1917 godu. Sbornik dokumentov. Moscow, 1928.

Ot fevralia k oktiabriu. (Iz anket uchastnikov velikoi oktiabr'skoi sotsialisticheskoi revoliutsii.) Moscow, 1958.

Ot fevralia k oktiabriu (v Moskve). Sbornik statei, vospominanii, dokumentov. Moscow, 1923.

Pares, Bernard. *My Russian Memoirs.* London: Jonathan Cape, 1931.

Paretskaia. "Predoktiabr'skie dni (vospominaniia)." *Kommunal'nyi rabotnik,* 1927, nos. 18-19, pp. 20-21.

Paustovsky, Konstantin. *The Story of a Life.* Translated by Joseph Barnes. New York: Vintage Books, 1967.

Perepis' Moskvy 1882 goda. Vyp. 1-3. Moscow, 1884-1886.

Perepis' Moskvy 1902 goda. Moscow, 1904.

Perepiska sekretariata TsK RSDRP(b) s mestnymi partiinymi organizatsiiami (mart-oktiabr' 1917 goda). Sbornik dokumentov. Moscow, 1957.

Pervaia vseobshchaia perepis' naseleniia Rossiiskoi Imperii, 1897 goda. Vol. 24, *Moskva.* St. Petersburg, 1904.

Pervyi obshchezemskii s"ezd po narodnomu obrazovaniiu 1911 goda. Moscow, 1912.

Petrov, P. "Oktiabr'skie dni v Moskve. Podgotovka k oktiabriu (zavod 'Serp i molot')." *Metallist,* 1927, no. 41, p. 40.

"Piat' let"—iiubileinyi sbornik TsK soiuza rabochikh-kozhevnikov. Moscow, [1922].

Piatyi oktiabr'. Sbornik, posviashchennyi 5-oi godovshchiny velikoi oktiabr'skoi revoliutsii. Moscow, 1922.

Podgotovka i pobeda oktiabr'skoi revoliutsii v Moskve. Dokumenty i materialy. Moscow, 1957.

Popov, M. "Moskovskie pechatniki v dni fevral'skoi revoliutsii (vospominaniia)." *Pechatnik,* 1927, nos. 7-8, pp. 13-14.

Pozharnyi. "Odno vospominanie." *Kommunal'nyi rabotnik,* 1925, no. 20, pp. 3-4.

Prechistenskie rabochie kursy. Sbornik statei i vospominanii k 50-letiiu kursov (1897-1947 gody). Moscow, 1948.

"Prodovol'stvennoe polozhenie v Moskve v marte-iiune 1917 goda." *Krasnyi arkhiv,* 1937, no. 2(81), pp. 128-146.

Professional'noe dvizhenie rabochikh khimikov i stekol'shchikov 1905-1918 gody. Materialy po istorii soiuza. Moscow, 1928.

"Protokoly fabrichno-zavodskogo komiteta Prokhorovskoi Trekhgornoi manufaktury." *Istoriia proletariata SSSR,* 1931, no. 8, pp. 105-171; 1932, no. 9, pp. 154-178.

Pupko, S. L. "Iz kur'ezov revoliutsionnoi bor'by. (Nasha stachka 17-go goda)." *Kommunal'nyi rabotnik,* 1924, nos. 9-10, p. 25.

Pustova. "Rabotnitsa v oktiabre." *Pravda,* 7 November 1920, p. 3.

Put' k oktiabriu. Sbornik statei, vospominanii i dokumentov. 5 vols. Moscow, 1923-1925.

"Rabochee dvizhenie v Moskve v 1914-1917 godakh. (Neizdannye arkhivnye materialy, so vstupitel'noi statei K. Voinovoi)." *Proletarskaia revoliutsiia*, 1923, no. 2(14), pp. 469-551.

Rabochee dvizhenie v 1917 godu. Moscow, 1926.

Reed, John. *Ten Days That Shook the World.* New York: Vintage Books, 1960.

Revoliutsionnoe dvizhenie v Rossii nakanune oktiabr'skogo vooruzhennogo vosstaniia (1-24 oktiabria 1917 goda). Moscow, 1962.

Revoliutsionnoe dvizhenie v Rossii posle sverzheniia samoderzhaviia. Moscow, 1957.

Revoliutsionnoe dvizhenie v Rossii v aprele 1917 goda. Aprel'skii krizis. Moscow, 1958.

Revoliutsionnoe dvizhenie v Rossii v avguste 1917 goda. Razgrom kornilovskogo miatezha. Moscow, 1959.

Revoliutsionnoe dvizhenie v Rossii v iiule 1917 goda. Iiul'skii krizis. Moscow, 1959.

Revoliutsionnoe dvizhenie v Rossii v mae-iiune 1917 goda. Iiun'skaia demonstratsiia. Moscow, 1959.

Revoliutsionnoe dvizhenie v Rossii v sentiabre 1917 goda. Obshchenatsional'nyi krizis. Moscow, 1961.

Rigosik, S. "Pervye komsomol'tsy (vospominaniia)." *Molodaia gvardiia*, 1933, no. 5, pp. 119-131.

Rodinov, S. "Odna desiataia veka." *Kommunal'nyi rabotnik*, 1927, no. 21, p. 20.

Rossiia v mirovoi voine 1914-1918 (v tsifrakh). Moscow, 1925.

Rozanov, N. "Revoliutsionnaia rabota." *Moskovskii pechatnik*, 7 November 1923, pp. 11-12.

Rubin, I. *Primiritel'nye kamery i treteiskii sud.* Moscow, 1917.

S., K. "V nashem raione." *Kommunal'nyi rabotnik*, 1927, no. 21, pp. 20-21.

Sapronov, T. V., ed. *Iubileinyi sbornik po istorii dvizheniia stroitel'nykh rabochikh Moskvy.* Moscow, 1924.

———. *Iz istorii rabochego dvizheniia (po lichnym vospominaniiam).* Moscow-Leningrad, 1925.

Savin, S. "Nakanune reshitel'nogo boia (vospominaniia)." *Kommunal'nyi rabotnik*, 1927, no. 19, pp. 21-22.

———. "Zashchita Khamovnikov." *Kommunal'nyi rabotnik*, 1927, no. 20, p. 13.

Sbornik materialov moskovskogo komiteta obshchestvennykh organizatsii. Moscow, 1917.

Sed'maia (aprel'skaia) vserossiiskaia konferentsiia RSDRP (bol'shevikov). Protokoly. Moscow, 1958.

Shelaev. "V masterskikh Moskovsko-Kazanskoi zheleznoi dorogi." In *Put' k oktiabriu*, vol. 3, pp. 181-186. Moscow, 1923.

Shest' let na revoliutsionnom postu. Moscow, 1923.

Shestoi s"ezd RSDRP (bol'shevikov). Avgust 1917 goda. Protokoly. Moscow, 1958.

Sigma. "Simonovtsy v boiu (zavody 'AMO' i 'Dinamo')." *Metallist*, 1927, no. 41, pp. 42-44.

Sirota, V. "Oktiabr'skie boi v Gorodskom raione Moskvy." *Proletarskaia revoliutsiia*, 1929, no. 11(94), pp. 91-99.

Skvortsov-Stepanov, I. I. "Pered oktiabrem." *Novyi mir*, 1970, no. 11, pp. 218-236.

Slavnye traditsii. K 100-letiiu zavoda 'Krasnyi proletarii' imeni A. I. Efremova. Moscow, 1957.

Slovo starykh bol'shevikov. Iz revoliutsionnogo proshlogo. Moscow, 1965.

"Sobranie rabochikh Trekhgornoi manufaktury-aktivnykh uchastnikov revoliutsii 1917 goda." *Istoriia proletariaia SSSR*, 1931, no. 7, pp. 280-284.

Sokol, V. "Chto ia pomniu." *Proletarskaia revoliutsiia*, 1921, no. 2, pp. 139-147.

Sovet s"ezdov predstavitelei promyshlennosti i torgovlia, Peterburg. *Fabrichno-zavodskaia predpriiatiia Rossiiskoi Imperii.* St. Petersburg, 1914.

Sovety v oktiabre. Sbornik dokumentov. Moscow, 1928.

Spisok fabrichno-zavodskikh predpriiatii moskovskogo raiona, zaniatykh ispolneniem rabot na gosudarstvennuiu oboronu. Moscow, 1915.

Spisok fabrik i zavodov Moskvy i moskovskoi gubernii. Moscow, 1916.

Staraia i novaia Danilovka. Rasskazy rabochikh fabriki imeni Frunze. Moscow, 1940.

Statisticheskii atlas goroda Moskvy i moskovskoi gubernii. Moscow, 1924.

Statisticheskii ezhegodnik gorod Moskvy i moskovskoi gubernii. Vyp. 2. Moscow, 1927. [Abbreviated as *Stat. ezhegodnik.*]

Strelkov, N. V. *Avtobiograficheskii ocherk bol'shevika-podpol'shchika zavoda imeni Vladimir Il'icha.* Moscow, 1935.

Sukhanov, N. N. *The Russian Revolution 1917.* Translated by Joel Carmichael. 2 vols. New York: Harper and Row, 1962.

Sukhodeev, I. *Svobodnye chasy rabochego (gimnastika i igry na svezhem vozdukhe, kniga, isskustvo, sel'skoe khoziaistvo, ekskursii, semeinyi krug).* Moscow, 1917.

Teleshev, A. "Iz kalendaria proshlogo (o rabote v tsentral'nom soiuze)." *Kommunal'nyi rabotnik*, 1924, nos. 9-10, pp. 19-21.

Tret'ia vserossiiskaia konferentsiia professional'nykh soiuzov, 3-11 iiulia (20-28 iiunia st. st.) 1917 goda. Stenograficheskii otchet. Moscow, 1927.

Triumfal'noe shestvie sovetskoi vlasti. Vol. 1. Moscow, 1963.

Trudy statisticheskogo otdela moskovskoi gorodskoi upravy [abbreviated *Trudy Stat. otdela MGU*]. Vyp. 1, *Glavneishiia predvaritel'niia danniia perepisi goroda Moskvy 6 marta 1912 goda.* Moscow, 1913.

Tsentral'noe statisticheskoe upravlenie [abbreviated TsSU]. *Trudy.* 35 vols. Moscow, 1917-1926.

Tsentral'nyi Voenno-promyshlennyi komitet, otdel po obezpecheniiu promyshlennykh predpriiatii rabochim sostavom. *Materialy k uchetu rabochago sostava i rabochago rynka.* 3 vols. Petrograd, 1916.

Tsereteli, I. G. *Vospominaniia o fevral'skoi revoliutsii.* Paris: Mouton, 1958.

Tumanov, E. D. "Vospominaniia." *Bor'ba klassov*, 1931, nos. 6-7, p. 104.

Uprochenie sovetskoi vlasti v Moskve i moskovskoi gubernii. Dokumenty i materialy. Moscow, 1958.

V odnom stroiu. Vospominaniia aktivnykh-uchastnikov revoliutsii v Moskve. Moscow, 1967.

V oktiabr'skie dni. Iz vospominaniiakh uchastnikov oktiabr'skoi revoliutsii v Shcherbakovskom raione Moskvy. Moscow, 1957.

V oktiabr'skie dni. Vospominaniia uchastnikov velikogo oktiabria v Oktiabr'skoi raione. Moscow, 1957.

Vasil'ev, P. V. "Vospominaniia o 1917 godu." *Bor'ba klassov*, 1931, nos. 6-7, pp. 114-120.

Veger, I. [Senior]. "K istorii moskovskogo soveta rabochikh deputatov." *Proletarskaia revoliutsiia*, 1926, no. 1(48), pp. 217-232.

Vek nyneshnii i vek minuvshii. Rasskazy rabochikh sukonnoi fabriki imeni Petra Alekseeva. Moscow, 1937.

Velikaia oktiabr'skaia sotsialisticheskaia revoliutsiia. Khronika sobytii. 4 vols. Moscow, 1957-1962.

Velikaia oktiabr'skaia sotsialisticheskaia revoliutsiia. Vol. 1, *Sbornik vospominanii uchastnikov revoliutsii v Petrograde i Moskve*. Moscow, 1967. [Abbreviated as *Velikaia oktiabr'skaia sotsialisticheskaia revoliutsiia (vospominaniia)*.]

Verkhovskii, A. I. *Na trudnom perevale.* Moscow, 1959.

————. *Rossiia na golgofe (iz pokhodnogo dnevnika 1914-1918 godov).* Petrograd, 1918.

Vladimirskii, M. F. *Oktiabr'skie dni v Moskve.* Moscow, 1927.

————. "Moskovskie raionnye dumy i sovet raionnykh dum v 1917-1918 godakh." *Proletarskaia revoliutsiia*, 1923, no. 8(20), pp. 79-94.

Volodina. "Oktiabr' na 'Krasnoi Roze' (vospominaniia)." *Rabotnitsa*, 1923, no. 11, p. 18.

"Vospominaniia rabotnits." *Delegatka*, 1925, no. 11, p. 4.

Voznesenskii, A. N. "Moskva v oktiabre 1917 goda (vospominaniia)." *Byloe*, 1926, no. 1(35), pp. 157-186.

————. *Moskva v 1917 godu.* Moscow, 1928.

Vyskrebentsev, I. "Stachka." *Kommunal'nyi rabotnik*, 1927, no. 20, p. 14.

Yarkovsky, Jan M. *It Happened in Moscow.* New York: Vantage Press, 1961.

Za vlast' sovetov. Sbornik. Moscow, 1957.

"Zabastovka rabochikh-kozhevnikov Moskvy v avguste-oktiabre 1917 goda." *Istoricheskii arkhiv*, 1957, no. 6, pp. 61-81.

Zabrodin, V. "U gazovshchikov." *Kommunal'nyi rabotnik*, 1927, no. 20, p. 15.

Zheleznodorozhniki i revoliutsiia. Sbornik vospominanii. Moscow, 1923.

SECONDARY AND OTHER WORKS

A.M. Gor'kii i sozdanie istorii fabrik i zavodov. Sbornik dokumentov i materialov. Moscow, 1959.

Al'tman, S. G. "Bol'shevizatsiia raionnykh sovetov Moskvy i ikh deiatel'nost' v marte-oktiabre 1917 goda." Candidate's dissertation, Moskovskii oblast'noi pedagogicheskii institut imeni N. K. Krupskoi, 1963.

Andreev, A. M. *Sovety rabochikh i soldatskikh deputatov nakanune oktiabria.* Moscow, 1970.

Angarskii, N. *Moskovskii sovet v dvukh revoliutsii.* Moscow-Leningrad, 1928.

————. "1917 goda v izdaniiakh moskovskogo Istparta." *Proletarskaia revoliutsiia*, 1928, no. 1(72), pp. 268-279.

Antipin, G. G. *Zariad'e.* Moscow, 1973.

Antonova, S. I. *Vliianie stolypinskoi agrarnoi reformy na izmeneniia v sostave rabochego klassa (po materialam moskovskoi gubernii 1906-1913 godov)*. Moscow, 1951.

Antoshkin, D. V. *Fabrika na barrikadakh: Trekhgornaia manufaktura v 1905 godu*. Moscow, 1930.

———. *Professional'noe dvizhenie sluzhashchikh 1917-1924 godov*. Moscow, 1927.

———. "Rabochie Trekhgornoi manufaktury v 1917 godu." *Istoriia proletariata SSSR*, 1931, no. 8, pp. 46-79; 1932, no. 9, pp. 49-76.

Arapova, L. I. "Bol'shevizatsiia munitsipal'nykh organov (raionnykh dum) Moskvy nakanune velikoi oktiabr'skoi sotsialisticheskoi revoliutsii." *Trudy Moskovskogo gosudarstvennogo istoriko-arkhivnogo instituta*, vol. 26, 1968, pp. 143-147.

Arendt, Hannah. *The Origins of Totalitarianism*. Cleveland: World Publishing, 1958.

Arutiunov, G. A. *Rabochie dvizhenie v Rossii v period novogo revoliutsionnogo pod'ema 1910-1914 godov*. Moscow, 1975.

Astrakhan, Kh. M. *Bol'sheviki i ikh politicheskie protivniki v 1917 godu*. Leningrad, 1973.

Avrich, Paul H. "The Bolshevik Revolution and Workers' Control in Russian Industry." *American Slavic and East European Review*, 1963, no. 1, pp. 47-63.

———. *The Russian Anarchists*. Princeton: Princeton University Press, 1967.

———. "Russian Factory Committees in 1917." *Jahrbücher für Geschichte Osteuropas*, vol. 11, no. 2, 1963, pp. 161-182.

Baedeker, Karl. *Russia: A Handbook for Travellers*. Facsimile reprint of 1914 Leipzig edition. New York: Arno Press, 1971.

Balashova, L. I. "Rabochii kontrol' nad raspredeleniiam v period podgotovki sotsialisticheskoi revoliutsii." *Voprosy istorii*, 1973, no. 5, pp. 47-58.

Bater, James H. "The Journey to Work in St. Petersburg, 1860-1914." *Journal of Transport History*, n.s. 2, 1974, no. 4, pp. 214-233.

Benet, Sula, ed. *The Village of Viriatino*. Garden City, N.Y.: Anchor Books, 1970.

Bibliograficheskii ukazatel' po istorii fabrik i zavodov. Moscow, 1932.

Blalock, Hubert M. *Social Statistics*. 2nd ed. New York: McGraw-Hill, 1972.

Blumer, Herbert. "Early Industrialization and the Laboring Class." *Sociological Quarterly*, vol. 1, 1960, pp. 5-14.

Bogoslovskii, S. M. *Boleznost' fabrichno-zavodskikh rabochikh moskovskoi gubernii*. Moscow, 1923.

Bonnell, Victoria E. "The Politics of Labor in Pre-Revolutionary Russia: Moscow Workers' Organizations 1905-1914." Ph.D. dissertation, Harvard University, 1975.

———. "Radical Politics and Organized Labor in Pre-Revolutionary Moscow 1905-1914," *Journal of Social History*, 1978, no. 2, pp. 282-300.

Bratskaia mogila. 2 vols. Moscow, 1923.

Briggs, Asa. "The Language of 'Class' in Early Nineteenth-Century England." In *Essays in Labour History*, edited by Asa Briggs and John Saville, pp. 43-73. London: Macmillan, 1960.

Brinton, M. "Factory Committees and the Dictatorship of the Proletariat." *Critique*, 1975, no. 4, pp. 78-86.

Bron, Jean. *Le Droit à l'existence du début du XIXe siècle à 1884.* Vol. 1 of *Histoire du mouvement ouvrier français.* Paris: Les Editions ouvriers, 1968.

Brooks, Jeffrey. "Readers and Reading at the End of the Tsarist Era." In *Literature and Society in Imperial Russia,* edited by William Mills Todd III, pp. 97-150. Stanford: Stanford University Press, 1978.

Burdzhalov, E. N. "O taktike bol'shevikov v marte-aprele 1917 goda." *Voprosy istorii,* 1956, no. 4, pp. 38-56.

———. *Vtoraia russkaia revoliutsiia. Moskva, front, periferiia.* Moscow, 1971.

Chaadaeva, O. N. "Vooruzhenie proletariata v 1917 godu." *Istoriia proletariata SSSR,* 1932, no. 11, pp. 15-58; 1933, no. 3(15), pp. 3-44.

Chamberlin, William Henry. *The Russian Revolution.* 2 vols. New York: Macmillan, 1935.

Cohen, Stephen F. *Bukharin and the Bolshevik Revolution.* New York: Alfred A. Knopf, 1973.

Cohen, Theodore. "Wartime Profits of Russian Industry 1914-1916." *Political Science Quarterly,* vol. 58, 1943, pp. 217-238.

Cole, G.D.H. *Studies in Class Structure.* London: Routledge and Kegan Paul, 1955.

Comfort, Richard A. *Revolutionary Hamburg: Labor Politics in the Early Weimar Republic.* Stanford: Stanford University Press, 1966.

Cornelius, Wayne. "Urbanization as an Agent in Latin American Political Instability: the Case of Mexico." *American Political Science Review,* vol. 63, 1969, pp. 833-857.

Dahrendorf, Ralf. *Class and Class Conflict in Industrial Society.* Stanford: Stanford University Press, 1959.

———. *Conflict after Class: New Perspectives on the Theory of Social and Political Conflict.* Noel Buxton Lecture, University of Essex. London: Longman, Green and Co., 1967.

Daniels, Robert V. *Red October: The Bolshevik Revolution of 1917.* New York: Charles Scribner's Sons, 1967.

Davydovich, M. "Khoziaistvennoe znachenie zhenshchiny v rabochei sem'e." *Poznanie Rossii,* vol. 3, 1909, pp. 119-131.

Demidov, V. A. "Zemliacheskie organizatsii i ikh rol' v bor'be bol'shevistskoi partii za soiuz rabochego klassa s trudiashchim krest'ianstvom v period podgotovki oktiabria." *Uchenye zapiski Leningradskogo gosudarstvennogo pedagogicheskogo instituta imeni A. I. Gertsena,* 1958, no. 175, pp. 79-108.

Deutscher, Isaac. *The Prophet Armed 1879-1921.* Oxford: Oxford University Press, 1954.

Devlin, Robert. "Petrograd Workers in 1917: Rational, Self-Disciplined, and Autonomous." Paper presented to the New England Slavic Conference, April 1977.

Downs, Anthony. *An Economic Theory of Democracy.* New York: Harper and Row, 1957.

Duveau, Georges. *La Vie ouvrière en France sous le second empire.* 3rd ed. Paris: Gallimard, 1946.

Dvinov, Boris L. *Pervaia mirovaia voina i rossiiskaia sotsial demokratiia.* Inter-

University Project on the History of the Menshevik Movement, paper no. 10. New York, 1962.

Engelstein, Laura. "Moscow in the 1905 Revolution: A Study in Class Conflict and Political Organization." Ph.D. dissertation, Stanford University, 1976.

Entsiklopedicheskii slovar'. St. Petersburg: F. A. Brokgauz and I. A. Efron, 1895.

Entsiklopedicheskii slovar'. 7th ed. St. Petersburg: Bros. A. and I. Granat, 1913.

Ermokhin, N. D. "Iz istorii revoliutsionnoi bor'by bol'shevikov Moskvy i moskovskoi gubernii v gody pervoi mirovoi voiny." *Uchenye zapiski Moskovskogo oblast'nogo pedagogicheskogo instituta imeni N. K. Krupskoi*, vol. 249, vyp. 12, 1969, pp. 19-45.

Evsenin, Ivan. *Ot fabrikanta k krasnomu oktiabriu: Iz istorii odnoi fabriki*. Moscow, 1927.

Ezergailis, Andrew. *The 1917 Revolution in Latvia*. Boulder, Colo.: The East European Quarterly, 1974.

Falkova, Zh. Z. "Strakhovanie rabochikh nakanune i v gody pervoi mirovoi voiny (do fevralia 1917 goda)." In *Pervaia mirovaia voina*, edited by A. L. Sidorov, pp. 349-366. Moscow, 1968.

Ferro, Marc. "The Aspirations of Russian Society." In *Revolutionary Russia: A Symposium*, edited by Richard Pipes, pp. 183-199. New York: Anchor Books, 1969.

―――. "La Naissance du système bureaucratique en U.R.S.S." *Annales Economies, Sociétés, Civilisations*, 1976, pp. 243-265.

―――. *La Révolution de 1917*. Vol. 1, *La chute du tsarisme et les origines d'octobre*. Paris: Aubier, 1967. Vol. 2, *Octobre, naissance d'une société*. Paris: Aubier-Montaigne, 1976.

―――. "The Russian Soldier in 1917: Undisciplined, Patriotic, and Revolutionary." *Slavic Review*, 1971, no. 3, pp. 483-512.

Flanigan, William H. *Political Behavior of the American Electorate*. 2nd ed. Boston: Allyn and Bacon, 1972.

Fleer, M. "K istorii rabochego dvizheniia 1917 goda." *Krasnaia letopis'*, 1925, no. 2(13), pp. 239-243.

Florinsky, Michael T. *The End of the Russian Empire*. New York: Collier Books, 1961.

Fourastié, Jean. *Machinisme et bien-être: Niveau de vie et genre de vie en France de 1700 à nos jours*. Paris: Editions de minuit, 1962.

Freidlin, B. M. *Ocherki istorii rabochego dvizheniia v Rossii v 1917 godu*. Moscow, 1967.

Galili y Garcia, Ziva. "The Menshevik Revolutionary Defensists and the Workers in the Russian Revolution of 1917." Ph.D. dissertation draft, Columbia University, 1979.

Gaponenko, L. S. *Rabochii klass Rossii v 1917 godu*. Moscow, 1970.

Garvi, P. *Rabochaia kooperatsiia v pervye gody russkoi revoliutsii, 1917-1921*. MS. Hoover Institution on War, Revolution, and Peace. Stanford, California, 1935.

Geroi oktiabria. Kniga ob uchastnikakh velikoi oktiabr'skoi sotsialisticheskoi revoliutsii v Moskve. Moscow, 1967.

Gindin, I. F. "Russkaia burzhuaziia v period kapitalizma. Ee razvitie i osobennosti." *Istoriia SSSR*, 1963, nos. 2-3, pp. 57-80, 37-60.

Gitelman, Zvi Y. *Jewish Nationality and Soviet Politics: The Jewish Sections of the CPSU, 1917-1930*. Princeton: Princeton University Press, 1972.

Gleason, William. "The All-Russian Union of Towns and the All-Russian Union of Zemstvos in World War I: 1914-1917." Ph.D. dissertation, Indiana University, 1972.

Glickman, Rose. "The Russian Factory Woman, 1880-1914." In *Women in Russia*, edited by Dorothy A. Atkinson, Alexander Dallin, and Gail W. Lapidus, pp. 63-84. Stanford: Stanford University Press, 1977.

Gliksman, Jerzy. "The Russian Urban Worker: From Serf to Proletarian." In *The Transformation of Russian Society*, edited by Cyril E. Black, pp. 311-323. Cambridge: Harvard University Press, 1960.

Goodey, Chris. "Factory Committees and the Dictatorship of the Proletariat (1918)." *Critique*, 1974, no. 3, pp. 27-47.

Gorelik, Anatolii [Grigorii Gorelik]. *Anarkhisty v rossiiskoi revoliutsii*. Argentina, 1922.

Gorozhankina, N. P. "Partiinaia organizatsiia Trekhgornoi manufaktury." *Istoriia proletariata SSSR*, 1931, no. 5, pp. 159-168.

Goubert, Pierre. "Historical Demography and the Reinterpretation of Early Modern French History: A Research Review." In *The Family in History*, edited by Theodore K. Rabb and Robert I. Rotberg, pp. 16-27. Cambridge: M.I.T. Press, 1971.

Groman, V. V. *Obzor stroitel'noi deiatel'nosti v Rossii*. St. Petersburg, 1912.

Grunt, A. Ia. "Istoricheskie zametki o 'Moskovskom oktiabre.' " *Istoriia SSSR*, 1972, no. 5, pp. 69-89.

———. "Iz istorii vozniknoveniia dvoevlastii v Moskve (komitet obshchestvennykh organizatsii)." In *Sverzhenie samoderzhaviia*, edited by I. I. Mints, pp. 151-165. Moscow, 1970.

———. "Mogla li Moskva 'nachat' '?" *Istoriia SSSR*, 1969, no. 2, pp. 5-28.

———. "Moskovskii proletariat v 1917 godu. K voprosu o chislennosti, sostave i territorial'nom razmeshchenii." *Istoricheskie zapiski*, vol. 85, 1970, pp. 67-111.

———. *Moskva 1917-i. Revoliutsiia i kontrrevoliutsiia*. Moscow, 1976.

———. "Munitsipal'naia kampaniia v Moskve letom 1917 goda." *Istoriia SSSR*, 1973, no. 5, pp. 112-127.

———. "Opyt analiza statisticheskikh svedenii o sostave moskovskogo soveta rabochikh deputatov v 1917 godu." In *Istochnikovedenie, teoreticheskie i metodicheskie problemy*, pp. 450-465. Moscow, 1969.

———. *Pobeda oktiabr'skoi revoliutsii v Moskve*. Moscow, 1961.

———. "V podderzhku predlozhenii I. F. Gindina i L. E. Shepeleva." *Istoriia SSSR*, 1965, no. 1, pp. 229-232.

———. "Vozniknovenie moskovskogo soveta rabochikh deputatov v 1917 godu." *Istoriia SSSR*, 1967, no. 2, pp. 11-28.

Guseinov, F. A. "O bol'shevistskikh fraktsiiakh v sovetakh v 1917 godu." *Voprosy istorii KPSS*, 1968, no. 10, pp. 111-122.

Haimson, Leopold. "The Problem of Social Stability in Urban Russia, 1905-1917."
Slavic Review, 1964, no. 4, pp. 619-642; 1965, no. 1, pp. 1-22.

Hamerow, Theodore S. *Restoration, Revolution, Reaction: Economics and Politics in Germany 1815-1871*. Princeton: Princeton University Press, 1958.

Hartwell, R. M. "The Standard of Living during the Industrial Revolution."
Economic History Review, vol. 16, 1963, pp. 135-146.

Hasegawa, Tsuyoshi. "The Formation of the Militia in the February Revolution: An Aspect of the Origins of Dual Power." *Slavic Review*, 1973, no. 2, pp. 303-322.

Heer, Nancy Whittier. *Politics and History in the Soviet Union*. Cambridge: M.I.T. Press, 1971.

Hobsbawm, E. J. "From Social History to the History of Society." *Daedalus*, 1971, no. 1, pp. 20-45.

———. "The Labour Aristocracy in Nineteenth-Century Britain." In *Labouring Men*, pp. 321-370. New York: Doubleday, 1964.

———. "Peasants and Rural Migrants in Politics." In *The Politics of Conformity in Latin America*, edited by Claudio Veliz, pp. 43-65. London: Oxford University Press, 1967.

Ia—ii, V. "Tseny na produkty i zarabotnaia plata moskovskogo rabochego." *Statistika truda*, 1918, no. 1, pp. 8-11.

Iakovleva, K. N. "Zabastovochnoe dvizhenie v Rossii za 1895-1917 gody." In *Materialy po statistike truda*, edited by S. G. Strumilin, vyp. 8, pp. 3-60. Moscow, 1920.

Ignatenko, T. A. *Sovetskaia istoriografiia rabochego kontrolia i natsionalizatsii promyshlennosti v SSSR (1917-1967 gody)*. Moscow, 1971.

Ignat'ev, G. S. *Moskva v pervyi god proletarskoi diktatury*. Moscow, 1975.

Ignatov, E. N. "Moskovskii sovet ot fevralia do oktiabr'skikh dnei." *Vlast' sovetov*, 1923, nos. 11-12, pp. 51-66.

———. *Moskovskii sovet rabochikh deputatov v 1917 godu*. Moscow, 1925.

Istoriia Moskvy. 6 vols. Moscow, 1952-1959.

Istoriia rabochikh Leningrada. 2 vols. Leningrad, 1972.

Istoriia sovetskogo obshchestva v vospominaniiakh sovremennikov. Annotirovannyi ukazatel' memuarnoi literatury. 3 vols. Moscow, 1961.

Istoriia zavoda "Dinamo." Moscow, 1961.

Iuzefovich, I. S. *Iz klassovykh boev 1917 goda (stachka moskovskikh kozhevnikov)*. Moscow, 1928.

Ivanov, L. M. "O soslovno-klassovoi strukture gorodov kapitalisticheskoi Rossii." In *Problemy sotsial'no-ekonomicheskoi istorii Rossii*, edited by L. M. Ivanov, pp. 312-340. Moscow, 1971.

———. "Preemstvennost' fabrichno-zavodskogo truda i formirovanie proletariata v Rossii." In *Rabochii klass i rabochee dvizhenie v Rossii (1861-1917)*, edited by L. M. Ivanov, pp. 58-40. Moscow, 1966.

———, ed. *Rabochii klass i rabochee dvizhenie v Rossii (1861-1917)*. Moscow, 1966.

———, ed. *Rossiiskii proletariat: Oblik, bor'ba, gegemoniia*. Moscow, 1970.

Johnson, Kenneth. "Causal Factors in Latin American Political Instability." *Western Political Quarterly*, vol. 17, 1964, pp. 432-446.

Johnson, Robert E. "The Nature of the Russian Working Class: Social Characteristics of the Moscow Industrial Region 1880-1900." Ph.D. dissertation, Cornell University, 1975.

———. *Peasant and Proletarian: The Working Class of Moscow in the Late Nineteenth Century.* New Brunswick: Rutgers University Press, 1979.

———. "Peasant Migration and the Russian Working Class: Moscow at the End of the Nineteenth Century." *Slavic Review*, no. 4, 1976, pp. 652-664.

Kabanov, V. V. *Oktiabr'skaia revoliutsiia i kooperatsiia (1917 god-mart 1919 goda).* Moscow, 1973.

Kabo, E. O. *Ocherki rabochego byta. Opyt monograficheskogo issledovaniia domashnego rabochego byta.* Vol. 1. Moscow, 1928.

Kaplan, Frederick, I. *Bolshevik Ideology and the Ethics of Soviet Labor.* New York: Philosophical Library, 1968.

Kasarov, G. G. "Bor'ba moskovskogo proletariata protiv 'rabochei gruppy' moskovskogo oblast'nogo voenno-promyshlennogo komiteta." *Vestnik Moskovskogo gosudarstvennogo universiteta*, 1974, no. 3, pp. 34-45.

Kasitskaia, D. L., and E. P. Popova. "Polozhenie i byt rabochikh Prokhorovskoi Trekhgornoi manufaktury." *Istoriko-bytovye ekspeditsii, 1949-1950.* Vyp. 23, *Trudy Gosudarstvennogo istoricheskogo muzeia*, pp. 172-183. Moscow, 1953.

Katsenelenbaum, Z. S. *Uchenie o den'gakh i kredite.* 2 vols. Moscow, 1926.

Keep, John H. L. " 'The Great October Socialist Revolution.' " In *Windows on the Russian Past*, edited by Samuel H. Baron and Nancy W. Heer, pp. 139-156. Columbus: American Association for the Advancement of Slavic Studies, 1977.

———. *The Russian Revolution: A Study in Mass Mobilization.* New York: W. W. Norton and Co., 1976.

Kin, D. "Bor'ba protiv ob"edinitel'nogo udara." *Proletarskaia revoliutsiia*, 1927, no. 6(65), pp. 3-71.

Kir'ianov, Iu. I. "Ob oblike rabochego klassa Rossii." In *Rossiiskii proletariat: Oblik, bor'ba, gegemoniia*, edited by L. M. Ivanov, pp. 100-140. Moscow, 1970.

———. *Rabochie Iuga Rossii, 1914-fevral' 1917 goda.* Moscow, 1971.

Koenker, Diane. "Urban Families, Working-Class Youth Groups, and the 1917 Revolution in Moscow." In *The Family in Imperial Russia: New Lines of Historical Research*, edited by David L. Ransel, pp. 280-304. Urbana: University of Illinois Press, 1978.

Koenker, Roger. "Was Bread Giffen?" *Review of Economics and Statistics*, 1977, no. 2, pp. 225-229.

Kokhn, M. P. *Russkie indektsy tsen.* Moscow, 1926.

Kol-ev, S. "Nekotorye predvaritel'nye dannye o perepisi goroda Moskvy." *Statistika truda*, 1919, nos. 11-12, pp. 16-22.

Kolychevskii, I. "Obzor literatury po istorii 1917 goda v raionakh Moskvy." *Proletarskaia revoliutsiia*, 1928, no. 5(76), pp. 184-187.

———. "Zabastovochnoe dvizhenie v Moskve s fevralia po oktiabria 1917 goda." *Proletarskaia revoliutsiia*, 1926, no. 8(55), pp. 55-117.

Kor, I., ed. *Kak my zhili pri tsare i kak zhivem teper'.* Moscow, 1934.

Koz'minykh-Lanin, I. M. *Artel'noe kharchevanie fabrichno-zavodskikh rabochikh moskovskoi gubernii*. Moscow, 1915.

————. *Artel'noe kharchevanie rabochikh odnoi shelkokrutil'noi fabriki v Moskve*. Moscow, 1914.

————. *Grammotnost' i zarabotki fabrichno-zavodskikh rabochikh moskovskoi gubernii*. Moscow, 1912.

————. *Ukhod na polevye raboty fabrichno-zavodskikh rabochikh moskovskoi gubernii*. Moscow, 1912.

————. *Vrachebnaia pomoshch' fabrichno-zavodskim rabochim goroda Moskvy*. Moscow, 1912.

Krupianskaia, V. Iu. "Evoliutsiia semeino-bytovogo uklada rabochikh." In *Rossiiskii proletariat: Oblik, bor'ba, gegemoniia*, edited by L. M. Ivanov, pp. 271-289. Moscow, 1970.

————, and N. S. Polishchuk. *Kul'tura i byt rabochikh gornozavodskogo urala (konets XIX-nachalo XX veka)*. Moscow, 1971.

Kruze, E. E. *Polozhenie rabochego klassa Rossii v 1900-1914 godakh*. Leningrad, 1976.

Kukushkin, S. *Moskovskii sovet v 1917 godu*. Moscow, 1957.

Kurashova, N. A., and S. A. Livshits. "Gruppovye denezhnye sbory rabochikh na 'Pravdu' i gazety drugikh politicheskikh napravlenii (1912-1914 gody)." In *Rossiiskii proletariat: Oblik, bor'ba, gegemoniia*, edited by L. M. Ivanov, pp. 209-239. Moscow, 1970.

Kurlat, F. L. "Nekotorye voprosy istorii oktiabr'skoi revoliutsii v Moskve." *Vestnik Moskovskogo gosudarstvennogo universiteta*, 1963, no. 6, pp. 31-43.

Kuznetsov, I. V., and A. V. Shumakov. *Bol'shevistskaia pechat' Moskvy*. Moscow, 1968.

Labrousse, E. *Le Mouvement ouvrier et les théories sociales en France de 1815 à 1848*. Paris, Centre de Documentation Universitaire, n.d.

Lande, Leo. "The Mensheviks in 1917." In *The Mensheviks*, edited by Leopold H. Haimson, pp. 1-91. Chicago: University of Chicago Press, 1974.

Lapitskaia, S. *Byt rabochikh Trekhgornoi manufaktury*. Moscow, 1935.

Laslett, Peter. "Age at Menarche in Europe since the Eighteenth Century." In *The Family in History*, edited by Theodore K. Rabb and Robert I. Rotberg, pp. 28-47. Cambridge: M.I.T. Press, 1971.

Laverychev, V. Ia. *Po tu storonu barrikad (iz istorii bor'by moskovskoi burzhuazii s revoliutsiei)*. Moscow, 1967.

————. *Tsarizm i rabochii vopros (1861-1917 gody)*. Moscow, 1972.

Leiberov, I. P., and O. I. Shkaratan. "K voprosu o sostave petrogradskikh promyshlennykh rabochikh v 1917 godu." *Voprosy istorii*, 1961, no. 1, pp. 42-58.

Leninskii zakaz. Sto let tipografii 'Krasnyi proletarii'. Moscow, 1969.

Levi, E. "Moskovskaia organizatsiia bol'shevikov v iiule 1917 goda." *Proletarskaia revolutsiia*, 1929, nos. 2-3(85-86), pp. 123-151.

Levin, I. D. "Rabochie kluby v Peterburge (1907-1914 gody)." In *Materialy po istorii professional'nogo dvizheniia v Rossii*, pp. 89-111. Moscow, 1925.

Liashchenko, P. I. *Istoriia narodnogo khoziaistva SSSR*. 4th ed. Vol. 2. Moscow, 1956.

Liebman, Marcel. *The Russian Revolution*. Translated by Arnold J. Pomerans. New York: Vintage Books, 1970.

Lisetskii, A. M. *Bol'sheviki vo glave massovykh stachek*. Kishenev, 1974.

————. "Iz istorii stachechnoi bor'by proletariev Moskvy nakanune i v khode vooruzhennogo vosstaniia (oktiabr'-noiabr' 1917 goda)." *Uchenye zapiski Kishenevskogo gosudarstvennogo universiteta*, 1964, no. 72, pp. 3-19.

————. "K voprosu o statistike zabastovok v Rossii v period podgotovki velikoi oktiabr'skoi sotsialisticheskoi revoliutsii." *Trudy kafedry istorii KPSS, Khar'kovskogo gosudarstvennogo universiteta imeni A. M. Gor'kogo*, vol. 7, 1959, pp. 271-283.

————. "O nekotorykh osobennostiakh zabastovochnoi taktiki bol'shevikov v period podgotovki velikoi oktiabr'skoi sotsialisticheskoi revoliutsii (po materialam Ukrainy)." *Uchenye zapiski Khar'kovskogo gosudarstvennogo universiteta imeni A. M. Gor'kogo*, 1959, no. 103, pp. 93-106.

————. "O nekotorykh voprosakh kolichestvennoi kharakteristiki zabastovochnogo dvizheniia v Rossii v period podgotovki oktiabria (mart-oktiabr' 1917 goda)." *Uchenye zapiski Kishenevskogo gosudarstvennogo universiteta*, 1963, no. 65, pp. 3-15.

————. "Predvaritel'nye itogi geograficheskogo i otraslevogo raspredeleniia stachek v Rossii, ikh dlitel'nosti i rezul'tatochnosti (mart-oktiabr' 1917 goda)." *Uchenye zapiski Kishenevskogo gosudarstvennogo universiteta*, 1969, no. 112, pp. 365-385.

Livshits, A. "Raspredelenie moskovskikh rabochikh po vozrastnym gruppam." *Statistika truda*, 1919, nos. 11-12, pp. 22-23.

Logunova, T. A. *Moskovskaia krasnaia gvardiia v 1917 godu*. Moscow, 1960.

Longley, D. A. "The Divisions in the Bolshevik Party in March 1917." *Soviet Studies*, 1972, no. 1, pp. 61-76.

————. "Some Historiographical Problems of Bolshevik Party History (The Kronstadt Bolsheviks in March 1917)." *Jahrbücher für Geschichte Osteuropas*, vol. 22, no. 4, 1975, pp. 494-514.

Lukashev, A. V. "Bor'ba bol'shevikov za revoliutsionnuiu politiku moskovskogo soveta rabochikh deputatov v period dvoevlastii." *Voprosy istorii KPSS*, 1967, no. 8, pp. 59-72.

————. "Po sledam odnoi oshibochnoi publikatsii." *Voprosy istorii KPSS*, 1969, no. 11, pp. 103-107.

Mandel, Mark David. "The Development of Revolutionary Consciousness among the Industrial Workers of Petrograd between February and November 1917." Ph.D. dissertation, Columbia University, 1977.

Markuzon, F. D. *Zarabotnaia plata fabrichno-zavodskikh rabochikh goroda Moskvy v 1913-1920 godakh*. Moscow, 1922.

Marshall, T. H. *Citizenship and Social Class*. Cambridge: Cambridge University Press, 1950.

Matossian, Mary. "The Peasant Way of Life." In *The Peasant in Nineteenth-Century Russia*, edited by Wayne S. Vucinich, pp. 1-40. Stanford: Stanford University Press, 1968.

McKay, John P. *Pioneers for Profit: Foreign Entrepreneurship and Russian Industrialization 1885-1913.* Chicago: University of Chicago Press, 1970.

Melgunov, S. *Kak bol'sheviki zakhvatili vlast'. Oktiabr'skii perevorot 1917 goda.* Paris: Editions la Renaissance, 1953.

Mendel, Arthur P. *Dilemmas of Progress in Tsarist Russia: Legal Marxism and Legal Populism.* Cambridge: Harvard University Press, 1961.

Mendelsohn, Ezra. *Class Struggle in the Pale: The Formative Years of the Jewish Workers' Movement in Tsarist Russia.* Cambridge: Cambridge University Press, 1970.

Menitskii, I. *Russkoe rabochee dvizhenie i sotsial-demokraticheskoe podpol'e Moskvy v voennykh godakh.* 2 vols. Moscow, 1923.

Metel'kov, P. F. *Zheleznodorozhniki v revoliutsii.* Leningrad, 1970.

Mindlin, E. "Izmeneniia chisla, sostava i oplaty truda rabochikh moskovskogo okruga za 1911-1916 gody." *Statistika truda,* 1919, nos. 5-7, pp. 10-13.

———. "Rabochee vremia i zarabotnaia plata na predpriiatiiakh moskovskoi oblasti za 1914-1918 gody." *Statistika truda,* 1919, nos. 8-10, pp. 8-14.

Mints, I. I. *Istoriia velikogo oktiabria.* 3 vols. Moscow, 1967-1973.

———, ed. *Sverzhenie samoderzhaviia.* Moscow, 1970.

———. "Velikii oktiabr'—povorotnyi punkt v istorii chelovechestva (nekotorye itogi i zadachi izucheniia problemy)." *Istoriia SSSR,* 1975, no. 6, pp. 3-21.

Moscou et ses environs. Geneva: Les Editions Nagel, 1968.

Moskovskaia provintsiia v 1917 godu. Moscow-Leningrad, 1927.

Moskovskii soiuz rabotnikh-portnykh v 1917 godu. Moscow, 1927.

Moskva v dvukh revoliutsiiakh, fevral'-oktiabr' 1917 goda. Moscow, 1958.

Mosteller, Frederick, and Robert E. K. Rourke. *Sturdy Statistics: Nonparametrics and Order Statistics.* Reading, Mass.: Addison-Wesley, 1973.

Muzyleva, L. V. "Novye dannye o vyborakh v raionnye dumy Moskvy v 1917 godu." *Voprosy istorii KPSS,* 1971, no. 8, pp. 113-117.

Na presnenskom valu. Moscow, 1961.

Nelson, Joan. "The Urban Poor: Disruption or Political Integration in Third World Cities?" *World Politics,* vol. 22, 1970, pp. 393-414.

Netesin, Iu. N. "K voprosu o sotsial'no-ekonomicheskikh korniakh i osobennostiakh 'rabochei aristokratii' v Rossii." In *Bol'shevistskaia pechat' i rabochii klass Rossii v gody revoliutsionnogo pod'ema (1910-1914 gody),* edited by L. M. Ivanov, pp. 192-211. Moscow, 1965.

Noyes, P. H. *Organization and Revolution: Working-Class Associations in the German Revolutions of 1848-1849.* Princeton: Princeton University Press, 1966.

Ocherki istorii moskovskoi organizatsii KPSS: 1883-1965 gody. Moscow, 1966.

Ocherki po istorii oktiabr'skoi revoliutsii v Moskve. Moscow, 1927.

Ocherki po istorii revoliutsionnogo dvizheniia i bol'shevistskoi organizatsii Baumanskogo raiona. Moscow-Leningrad, 1928.

Oktiabr' v Moskve. Moscow, 1967.

Olson, Mancur, Jr. *The Logic of Collective Action: Public Goods and the Theory of Groups.* Cambridge: Harvard University Press, 1965.

———. "Rapid Economic Growth as a Destabilizing Force." *Journal of Economic History,* vol. 23, 1963, pp. 529-552.

Orlov, V. P. *Poligraficheskaia promyshlennost' Moskvy.* Moscow, 1953.

Pankratova, A. M. "Proletarizatsiia krest'ianstva i ee rol' v formirovanii promysh-lennogo proletariata Rossii (60-90e gody XIX veka)." *Istoricheskie zapiski*, vol. 54, 1955, pp. 194-220.

Pares, Bernard. *Russia between Reform and Revolution.* New York: Schocken Books, 1962.

Pazhitnov, K. A. *Polozhenie rabochego klassa v Rossii.* Vol. 3. Leningrad, 1924.

Pervushin, S. A. "Dvizhenie vol'nykh tsen v gody revoliutsii (1917-1921 gody)." *Vestnik statistiki*, 1921, nos. 1-4, pp. 180-230.

Pethybridge, Roger. *The Spread of the Russian Revolution: Essays on 1917.* London: St. Martin's Press, 1972.

Pipes, Richard. *Social Democracy and the St. Petersburg Labor Movement 1885-1897.* Cambridge: Harvard University Press, 1963.

Pushkareva, I. M. *Zheleznodorozhniki Rossii v burzhuazno-demokraticheskikh revoliutsiiakh.* Moscow, 1975.

Rabb, Theodore K., and Robert I. Rotberg, eds. *The Family in History.* Cambridge: M.I.T. Press, 1971.

Rabinowitch, Alexander. *The Bolsheviks Come to Power: The Revolution of 1917 in Petrograd.* New York: W. W. Norton and Co., 1976.

————. *Prelude to Revolution: The Petrograd Bolsheviks and the July 1917 Uprising.* Bloomington: Indiana University Press, 1968.

Radkey, Oliver H. *The Agrarian Foes of Bolshevism: Promise and Default of the Russian Socialist Revolutionaries February to October 1917.* New York: Columbia University Press, 1958.

————. *The Election to the Russian Constituent Assembly in 1917.* Cambridge: Harvard University Press, 1950.

————. *The Sickle under the Hammer: The Russian Socialist Revolutionaries in the Early Months of Soviet Rule.* New York: Columbia University Press, 1963.

Ransel, David L. "Abandonment and Fosterage of Unwanted Children: The Women of the Foundling System." In *The Family in Imperial Russia: New Lines of Historical Research*, edited by David L. Ransel, pp. 189-217. Urbana: University of Illinois Press, 1978.

————, ed. *The Family in Imperial Russia: New Lines of Historical Research.* Urbana: University of Illinois Press, 1978.

Rashin, A. G. *Formirovanie rabochego klassa Rossii.* 2nd ed. Moscow, 1958.

Remeslenniki i remeslennoe upravlenie v Rossii. Petrograd, 1916.

Rieber, Alfred J. "The Moscow Entrepreneurial Group: The Emergence of a New Form in Autocratic Politics." *Jahrbücher für Geschichte Osteuropas*, vol. 25, nos. 1-2, 1977, pp. 3-20, 174-199.

Romanov, M. "Rabochii sostav i ego dvizhenie v promyshlennykh predpriiatiiakh goroda Moskvy v period voiny." *Statistika truda*, 1918, nos. 6-7, pp. 1-8.

Romashova, V. I. "Obrazovanie postoiannykh kadrov rabochikh v poreformennoi promyshlennosti Moskvy." In *Rabochii klass i rabochee dvizhenie Rossii (1861-1917)*, edited by L. M. Ivanov, pp. 152-162. Moscow, 1966.

Rosenberg, William G. *Liberals in the Russian Revolution: The Constitutional Democratic Party, 1917-1921.* Princeton: Princeton University Press, 1974.

————. "The Russian Municipal Duma Elections of 1917: A Preliminary Computation of Returns." *Soviet Studies*, 1969, no. 2, pp. 131-163.

Rosenberg, William G. "Workers and Workers' Control in the Russian Revolution." Review essay. *History Workshop*, 1977, no. 5, pp. 89-97.

———. "Workers' Control on the Railroads and Some Suggestions Concerning Social Aspects of Labor Politics in the Russian Revolution." *Journal of Modern History*, vol. 49, no. 2, 1977, p. iii.

Roth, Guenther. *The Social Democrats in Imperial Germany: A Study in Working-Class Isolation and National Integration*. Totowa, N.J.: Bedminster Press, 1963.

Rougerie, Jacques. *Procès des Communards*. Paris: René Julliard, 1964.

Rozhkova, M. K. *Formirovanie kadrov promyshlennykh rabochikh v 60-nachale 80-kh godov XIX veka*. Moscow, 1974.

———. "Sostav rabochikh Trekhgornoi manufaktury nakanune imperialisticheskoi voiny." *Istoriia proletariata SSSR*, 1931, no. 5, pp. 169-187.

———. "Sostav rabochikh Trekhgornoi manufaktury v 1917 godu." *Istoriia proletariata SSSR*, 1931, no. 8, pp. 100-104.

Ruban, N. V. *Okiiabr'skaia revoliutsiia i krakh men'shevizma*. Moscow, 1968.

Salisbury, Harrison E. *Black Night, White Snow: Russia's Revolutions 1905-1917*. New York: Doubleday, 1978.

Saul, Norman E. *Sailors in Revolt: The Russian Baltic Fleet in 1917*. Lawrence: Regents' Press of Kansas, 1978.

Schapiro, Leonard. *The Communist Party of the Soviet Union*. 2nd ed. rev. New York: Random House, 1971.

Schneiderman, Jeremiah. *Sergei Zubatov and Revolutionary Marxism: The Struggle for the Working Class in Tsarist Russia*. Ithaca: Cornell University Press, 1976.

Schorske, Carl E. *German Social Democracy 1905-1917*. Cambridge: Harvard University Press, 1955.

Schwartz, S. *Fabrichno-zavodskie komitety i profsoiuzy v pervye gody revoliutsii*. MS. Hoover Institution on War, Revolution and Peace. Stanford, California, 1935.

———. *The Russian Revolution of 1905: The Workers' Movement and the Formation of Bolshevism and Menshevism*. Translated by Gertrude Vakar. Chicago: University of Chicago Press, 1967.

Selitskii, V. Ia. *Massy v bor'be za rabochii kontrol' (mart-iiul' 1917 goda)*. Moscow, 1971.

Shatz, Marshall S. "Soviet Society and the Purges of the Thirties in the Mirror of Memoir Literature." Review essay. *Canadian-American Slavic Studies*, vol. 7, no. 2, 1973, pp. 250-261.

Sher, V. V. *Istoriia professional'nogo dvizheniia rabochikh pechatnogo dela v Moskve*. Moscow, 1911.

Shikheev, N. "Istoriia zavoda AMO." *Bor'ba klassov*, 1931, nos. 3-4, pp. 57-73.

Shorter, Edward, and Charles Tilly. *Strikes in France 1830-1968*. Cambridge: Cambridge University Press, 1974.

Sidorov, A. L. *Ekonomicheskoe polozhenie Rossii v gody pervoi mirovoi voiny*. Moscow, 1973.

Sindeev, I. *Professional'noe dvizhenie rabochikh-stroitelei v 1917 godu*. Moscow, 1927.

Smirnov, A. E. "Bor'ba za rabochii kontrol' nad proizvodstvom i sovety v period dvoevlastiia (po materialam tsentral'noi Rossii)." *Vestnik Moskovskogo gosudarstvennogo universiteta*, 1968, no. 2, pp. 19-33.

Smirnov, A. S. "Zemliacheskie organizatsii rabochikh i soldat v 1917 godu." *Istoricheskie zapiski*, vol. 60, 1957, pp. 86-123.

Smirnov, Aleksei. "Zemledelie i zemledelets tsentral'noi promyshlennoi gubernii." *Russkaia mysl'*, vol. 7, 1901, pp. 173-186.

Sobolev, G. L. *Revoliutsionnoe soznanie rabochikh i soldat Petrograda v 1917 godu. Period dvoevlastiia.* Leningrad, 1973.

Sovremennoe khoziaistvo goroda Moskvy. Moscow, 1913.

Spirin, L. M. *Klassy i partii v grazhdanskoi voine v Rossii.* Moscow, 1968.

St., A. "Biudzhet moskovskogo rabochego." *Statistika truda*, 1919, nos. 1-4, pp. 1-5.

Stepanov, Z. V. *Rabochie Petrograda v period podgotovki i provedeniia oktiabr'skogo vooruzhennogo vosstaniia.* Moscow-Leningrad, 1965.

Strumilin, S. G. *Zarabotnaia plata i proizvoditel'nosti truda v russkoi promyshlennosti za 1913-1922 gody.* Moscow, 1923.

Suny, Ronald G. *The Baku Commune, 1917-1918: Class and Nationality in the Russian Revolution.* Princeton: Princeton University Press, 1972.

Svavitskii, N. A. "Pitanie moskovskikh rabochikh vo vremia voiny." *Vestnik statistiki*, 1920, nos. 9-12, pp. 70-100; 1921, nos. 1-4, pp. 154-179.

Swayze, Harold R. *Political Control of Literature in the USSR, 1946-1959.* Cambridge: Harvard University Press, 1962.

Taniaev, A. *Ocherki dvizheniia zheleznodorozhnikov v revoliutsii 1917 goda.* Moscow-Leningrad, 1925.

Thompson, E. P. *The Making of the English Working Class.* New York: Vintage Books, 1963.

———. "Time, Work-Discipline, and Industrial Capitalism." *Past and Present*, 1967, no. 38, pp. 56-97.

Tiutiukin, S. V. *Voina, mir, revoliutsiia. Ideinaia bor'ba v rabochem dvizhenii Rossii 1914-1917 godov.* Moscow, 1972.

Trotsky, Leon. *History of the Russian Revolution.* Translated by Max Eastman. 3 vols. London: Sphere Books, 1967.

Trukan, G. A. *Oktiabr' v tsentral'noi Rossii.* Moscow, 1967.

Tsypkin, G. A. "Ankety krasnogvardeitsev kak istoricheskii istochnik." *Voprosy istorii*, 1966, no. 5, pp. 199-202.

———. *Krasnaia gvardiia v bor'be za vlast' sovetov.* Moscow, 1967.

Tucker, Robert C. *Stalin As Revolutionary, 1879-1929.* New York: W.W. Norton and Co., 1973.

Tugan-Baranovsky, M. I. *The Russian Factory in the Nineteenth Century.* Translated from the 3rd Russian edition (1907) by Arthur and Claora S. Levin. Homewood, Ill.: Richard D. Irwin, 1970.

Ul'ianov, A. N. *Pervye demokraticheskie vybory v moskovskuiu gorodskuiu dumu.* Moscow, 1917.

Ulitsy Moskvy. Spravochnik. Moscow, 1972.

Usloviia byta rabochikh v dorevoliutsionnoi Rossii (po dannym biudzhetnykh obsledovanii). Moscow, 1958.

Utkin, A. I. "Ekonomicheskaia polozhenie moskovskikh rabochikh posle pervoi russkoi revoliutsii." *Vestnik Moskovskogo gosudarstvennogo universiteta,* 1974, no. 1, pp. 41-53.

Vasil'ev, B. N. "Sotsial'naia kharakteristika fabrichnykh rabochikh." In *Rabochii klass i rabochee dvizhenie Rossii (1861-1917),* edited by L. M. Ivanov, pp. 141-151. Moscow, 1966.

Velikaia oktiabr'skaia sotsialisticheskaia revoliutsiia. Bibliograficheskii ukazatel'. Moscow, 1961.

Volobuev, P. V. *Ekonomicheskaia politika vremennogo pravitel'stva.* Moscow, 1962.

———. "Leninskaia ideia rabochego kontrolia i dvizhenie za rabochii kontrol' v marte-oktiabre 1917 goda." *Voprosy istorii KPSS,* 1962, no. 6, pp. 39-55.

———. "Nereshennye voprosy istorii rabochego klassa nakanune velikoi oktiabr'skoi sotsialisticheskoi revoliutsii." In *Voprosy istoriografii rabochego klassa SSSR,* edited by M. P. Kim, pp. 69-73. Moscow, 1970.

———. "Proletariat—gegemon sotsialisticheskoi revoliutsii." In *Rossiiskii proletariat: Oblik, bor'ba, gegemoniia,* edited by L. M. Ivanov, pp. 51-66. Moscow, 1970.

———. *Proletariat i burzhuaziia v Rossii v 1917 godu.* Moscow, 1964.

Von Laue, Theodore H. "Russian Labor between Field and Factory, 1892-1903." *California Slavic Studies,* vol. 3, 1964, pp. 33-65.

———. "Russian Peasants in the Factory, 1892-1904." *Journal of Economic History,* vol. 21, 1961, pp. 61-80.

Voronkova, S. V. "Stroitel'stvo avtomobil'nikh zavodov v Rossii v gody pervoi mirovoi voiny (1914-1917 gody)." *Istoricheskie zapiski,* vol. 75, 1965, pp. 147-169.

Vostrikov, N. I. *Bor'ba za massy: Gorodskie srednie sloi nakanune oktiabria.* Moscow, 1970.

Vucinich, Wayne S., ed. *The Peasant in Nineteenth-Century Russia.* Stanford: Stanford University Press, 1968.

Wade, Rex. *The Russian Search for Peace, February-October 1917.* Stanford: Stanford University Press, 1969.

———. "Spontaneity in the Formation of the Workers' Militia and Red Guards, 1917." In *Reconsiderations on the Russian Revolution,* edited by Ralph Carter Elwood, pp. 20-41. Cambridge: Slavica Publishers, 1976.

Weiner, Myron. "Urbanization and Political Protest." *Civilisations,* vol. 17, 1967, pp. 44-50.

Wildman, Allan K. *The Making of a Workers' Revolution: Russian Social Democracy 1891-1903.* Chicago: University of Chicago Press, 1967.

Wolfe, Bertram. *Three Who Made a Revolution.* Boston: Beacon, 1948.

Wrigley, E. A. *Population and History.* New York: McGraw-Hill, 1969.

Zaitsev, V. "Zabolevaemost' i smertnost' rabochikh v Rossii v 1913-1916 godakh." *Vestnik truda,* 1921, no. 9(12), pp. 45-110.

Zelnik, Reginald E. *Labor and Society in Tsarist Russia: The Factory Workers of St. Petersburg 1855-1870.* Stanford: Stanford University Press, 1971.

———. "The Peasant and the Factory." In *The Peasant in Nineteenth-Century Russia,* edited by Wayne S. Vucinich, pp. 158-190. Stanford: Stanford University Press, 1968.

———. "Russian Bebels: An Introduction to the Memoirs of Semen Kanatchikov and Matvei Fisher." *Russian Review*, vol. 35, nos. 3, 4, 1976, pp. 249-289, 417-447.

Zhirnova, G. V. "Russkii gorodskoi svadebnyi obriad kontsa XIX-nachala XX vekakh." *Sovetskaia etnografiia*, 1969, no. 1, pp. 48-58.

Znamenskii, O. N. "Stanovlenie sovetov i vopros ob uchreditel'nom sobranie (mart-oktiabr' 1917 goda)." *Istoriia SSSR*, 1977, no. 4, pp. 3-19.

Zubekhin, I. P., and M. S. Koloditskii. "Moskovskii sovet rabochikh deputatov nakanune oktiabria." *Istoriia SSSR*, 1967, no. 5, pp. 28-39.

Index

Abrikosov factory, 22, 33, 64, 192, 227
Adler, Friedrich, 246
alcohol consumption, 62-63, 161
Alekseev-Rostokinskii raion, 163
Alekseevskoe precinct, 19
amnesty, as strike issue, 308
AMO plant, 40, 133; factory committee, 146
anarchists, 188n, 208, 220
Andreeva, M. T. (worker), 64
animal-byproducts workers, 35, 272, 277, 282
April demonstrations, 112-113
Arbat district, 17
Arendt, Hannah, 365
army, 100, 138, 330; demobilization of, 140-141; Moscow garrison, 98-99, 101-102, 122, 135, 331, 350. See also soldiers
artels, 39; boarding, 55-56, 159
artisans, 22, 24, 26, 37, 39, 175, 182; apprentices, 66; residential patterns of, 16, 19-20; and trade unions, 148, 154-155, 164; in West, 10
Astakhov, Illarion Tikhonovich, 98
Avanesov, Varlaam Aleksandrovich (1884-1930), 334, 341, 345

bakers, 157, 164, 172
Basmannyi raion, 19, 169
Belenkii, Grigorii Iakovlevich, 345n
Belorussov, Semen Sergeevich (1870-1940), 101n
Belousov, Ivan, 51
Belov manufacture, 307
Benno-Rontaller factory, 152n
Blagusha-Lefortovskii raion, 19, 125, 245, 265; soviet, 163, 182, 233. See also Lefortovskii raion
Bogatyr plant, 32, 266
Bogorodsk uezd, 49
Bogorodskoe precinct, 20
Bolshevik party, 181, 188, 191, 208, 224, 231-232, 338; attitudes toward workers, 45, 53; composition of, 198-200, 222-223; and economic issues, 120, 162, 219, 245; in elections, 116, 137, 197, 201-202, 206, 210-212, 350-351; and factory committee conference, 165; fear of counterrevolution, 128; harassment of, 122-123, 208, 247; after July, 124; and June demonstration, 115; and Liberty Loan, 111-112; Moscow committee, 123, 145, 239, 332; 342; in Moscow Soviet, 104-105, 136, 191; and Moscow State Conference, 124; before 1917, 89; in October, 342, 345; organization, 14, 196, 286; and power, 114, 136, 142, 265; and Preparliament, 137; and raion soviets, 166; Sixth Congress, 327; and strikes, 326; and trade unions, 148, 167-168, 185, 199; views of revolution, 225; and war, 110, 239; worker support for, 182, 186, 196, 198, 200, 204-206, 208-210, 214-216, 218-220, 223, 225-227, 253, 256
Bolshevization, 254, 268, 362
Bonnell, Victoria E., 168n
Borisov-Beliaev factory, 307n, 314n
Borshchevskii, Aleksandr Stepanovich (1886-1938), 345n
Botkin tea firm, 22
Briansk railway station, 20
brick makers, 164
Brokar factory, 32
Bromlei plant, 18, 30, 33, 278
Bronnitsy uezd, 49
Bublikov, Aleksandr Aleksandrovich, 133
building workers, 39-40, 313; trade union, 157, 164
Bukharin, Nikolai Ivanovich (1888-1938), 120, 137, 345
Burovtsev, Mikhail Vasil'evich, 345n
Buryshkin, Pavel A., 98
Bushurin, 129
Butyrki raion, 19, 262; soviet, 20, 153, 162

Studies of the Russian Institute

ABRAM BERGSON, *Soviet National Income in 1937* (1953).

ERNEST J. SIMMONS, JR., ed., *Through the Glass of Soviet Literature: Views of Russian Society* (1953).

THAD PAUL ALTON, *Polish Postwar Economy* (1954).

DAVID GRANICK, *Management of the Industrial Firm in the USSR: A Study in Soviet Economic Planning* (1954).

ALLEN S. WHITING, *Soviet Policies in China, 1917-1924* (1954).

GEORGE S. N. LUCKYJ, *Literary Politics in the Soviet Ukraine, 1917-1934* (1956).

MICHAEL BORO PETROVICH, *The Emergence of Russian Panslavism, 1856-1870* (1956).

THOMAS TAYLOR HAMMOND, *Lenin on Trade Unions and Revolution, 1893-1917* (1956).

DAVID MARSHALL LANG, *The Last Years of the Georgian Monarchy, 1658-1832* (1957).

JAMES WILLIAM MORLEY, *The Japanese Thrust into Siberia, 1918* (1957).

ALEXANDER G. PARK, *Bolshevism in Turkestan, 1917-1927* (1957).

HERBERT MARCUSE, *Soviet Marxism: A Critical Analysis* (1958).

CHARLES B. MCLANE, *Soviet Policy and the Chinese Communists, 1931-1946* (1958).

OLIVER H. RADKEY, *The Agrarian Foes of Bolshevism: Promise and Default of the Russian Socialist Revolutionaries, February to October, 1917* (1958).

RALPH TALCOTT FISHER, JR., *Pattern for Soviet Youth: A Study of the Congresses of the Komsomol, 1918-1954* (1959).

ALFRED ERICH SENN, *The Emergence of Modern Lithuania* (1959).

ELLIOT R. GOODMAN, *The Soviet Design for a World State* (1960).

JOHN N. HAZARD, *Settling Disputes in Soviet Society: The Formative Years of Legal Institutions* (1960).

DAVID JORAVSKY, *Soviet Marxism and Natural Science, 1917-1932* (1961).

MAURICE FRIEDBERG, *Russian Classics in Soviet Jackets* (1962).

ALFRED J. RIEBER, *Stalin and the French Communist Party, 1941-1947* (1962).

THEODORE K. VON LAUE, *Sergei Witte and the Industrialization of Russia* (1962).

JOHN A. ARMSTRONG, *Ukrainian Nationalism* (1963).

OLIVER H. RADKEY, *The Sickle under the Hammer: The Russian Socialist Revolutionaries in the Early Months of Soviet Rule* (1963).

KERMIT E. MCKENZIE, *Comintern and World Revolution, 1928-1943: The Shaping of Doctrine* (1964).

HARVEY L. DYCK, *Weimar Germany and Soviet Russia, 1926-1933: A Study in Diplomatic Instability* (1966).

(*Above titles published by Columbia University Press.*)

HAROLD J. NOAH, *Financing Soviet Schools* (Teachers College, 1966).

JOHN M. THOMPSON, *Russia, Bolshevism, and the Versailles Peace* (Princeton, 1966).

PAUL AVRICH, *The Russian Anarchists* (Princeton, 1967).

LOREN R. GRAHAM, *The Soviet Academy of Sciences and the Communist Party, 1927-1932* (Princeton, 1967).

ROBERT A. MAGUIRE, *Red Virgin Soil: Soviet Literature in the 1920's* (Princeton, 1968).

T. H. RIGBY, *Communist Party Membership in the U.S.S.R., 1917-1967* (Princeton, 1968).

RICHARD T. DE GEORGE, *Soviet Ethics and Morality* (University of Michigan, 1969).

JONATHAN FRANKEL, *Vladimir Akimov on the Dilemmas of Russian Marxism, 1895-1903* (Cambridge, 1969).

WILLIAM ZIMMERMAN, *Soviet Perspectives on International Relations, 1956-1967* (Princeton, 1969).

PAUL AVRICH, *Kronstadt, 1921* (Princeton, 1970).

EZRA MENDELSOHN, *Class Struggle in the Pale: The Formative Years of the Jewish Workers' Movement in Tsarist Russia* (Cambridge, 1970).

EDWARD J. BROWN, *The Proletarian Episode in Russian Literature* (Columbia, 1971).

PATRICIA K. GRIMSTED, *Archives and Manuscript Repositories in the USSR: Moscow and Leningrad* (Princeton, 1972).

RONALD G. SUNY, *The Baku Commune, 1917-1918* (Princeton, 1972).

EDWARD J. BROWN, *Mayakovsky: A Poet in the Revolution* (Princeton, 1973).

MILTON EHRE, *Oblomov and his Creator: The Life and Art of Ivan Goncharov* (Princeton, 1973).

HENRY KRISCH, *German Politics under Soviet Occupation* (Columbia, 1974).

HENRY W. MORTON AND RUDOLF L. TÖKÉS, eds., *Soviet Politics and Society in the 1970's* (Free Press, 1974).

WILLIAM G. ROSENBERG, *Liberals in the Russian Revolution* (Princeton, 1974).

RICHARD G. ROBBINS, JR., *Famine in Russia, 1891-1892* (Columbia, 1975).

VERA DUNHAM, *In Stalin's Time: Middleclass Values in Soviet Fiction* (Cambridge, 1976).

WALTER SABLINSKY, *The Road to Bloody Sunday* (Princeton, 1976).

WILLIAM MILLS TODD III, *The Familiar Letter as a Literary Genre in the Age of Pushkin* (Princeton, 1976).

ELIZABETH VALKENIER, *Russian Realist Art. The State and Society: The Peredvizhniki and Their Tradition* (Ardis, 1977).

SUSAN SOLOMON, *The Soviet Agrarian Debate* (Westview, 1978).

SHEILA FITZPATRICK, ed., *Cultural Revolution in Russia, 1928-1931* (Indiana, 1978).

PETER SOLOMON, *Soviet Criminologists and Criminal Policy: Specialists in Policy-Making* (Columbia, 1978).

KENDALL E. BAILES, *Technology and Society under Lenin and Stalin: Origins of the Soviet Technical Intelligentsia, 1917-1941* (Princeton, 1978).

LEOPOLD H. HAIMSON, ed., *The Politics of Rural Russia, 1905-1914* (Indiana, 1979).

THEODORE H. FRIEDGUT, *Political Participation in the USSR* (Princeton, 1979).

SHEILA FITZPATRICK, *Education and Social Mobility in the Soviet Union, 1921-1934* (Cambridge, 1979).

WESLEY ANDREW FISHER, *The Soviet Marriage Market: Mate-Selection in Russia and the USSR* (Praeger, 1980).

Library of Congress Cataloging in Publication Data

Koenker, Diane, 1947-
Moscow workers and the 1917 Revolution.

(Studies of the Russian Institute, Columbia University)
Bibliography: p.
Includes index.
1. Labor and laboring classes—Russian Republic—Moscow—
Political activity—History.
2.   Russia—History—Revolution, 1917-1921.
3.   Moscow—Social conditions.
I.   Title.   II.   Series: Columbia University.
Russian Institute. Studies.
HD8528.K63   305.5′6   80-8557
ISBN 0-691-05323-5

*Diane Koenker is Assistant Professor of History
at Temple University.*